CAN AMERICA SAVE ITSELF from DECLINE?

Volume II

BY THE SAME AUTHOR

Nonfiction
Manufacturing Hope: Post-9/11 Notes on Politics, Culture, Torture, and the American Character

Can America Save Itself from Decline?: Politics, Culture, Morality Volume I (2009-2015)

Drama
Two Plays of Life and Death: Who Cares?: The Washington-Sarajevo Talks and *Kate and Kafka*

CAN AMERICA
SAVE ITSELF
from DECLINE?

POLITICS, CULTURE, MORALITY

Volume II

CARLA SEAQUIST

Copyright © Carla Seaquist, 2021

All rights reserved.
Contact Author via website: www.carlaseaquist.com

ISBN: 978-0-578-85914-9

Cover image: Johannes Vermeer, "The Geographer" (c. 1668-69),
Städelsches Kunstinstitut, Frankfurt, Germany

Publication sources:
All the contents of this book were originally published in *HuffPost* and *Medium*, except for the following which, for thematic or space reasons, were not included. All these titles can be found on the internet or at www.carlaseaquist.com.

For *HuffPost*:
"To Ensure No Harm, Shouldn't a Psychologist Be in the Interrogation Room?: The APA Ban on Torture" (8/13/2015); "Is American Capitalism Becoming More Human?" (4/18/2016); "Elizabeth Warren for Secretary of the Treasury" (6/29/2016); "Hillary's Vow to the 99%: 'Our Economy Should Work for Everyone, Not Just Those at the Top'" (10/19/2016); "For a New Day, Give Hillary and the Democrats a Massive Mandate" (11/1/2016); "Mourning a Friend Who Saved My Life" (3/27/2017); "Of Love, Recommitment, and 'Dover Beach'": Letter to my husband on our 40th wedding anniversary (7/24/2017); "Dear PBS: Keep 'The Charlie Rose Show,' But Put a Woman in His Place" (11/30/2017)

For *Medium*:
"Put the Brakes on Trump's Anti-Democracy Chaos. Vote Nov. 6" (11/4/2018); "Three Takeaways for Democrats from U.K.'s Conservative 'Landslide' Victory" (12/16/2019)

Morgan-Guidinger Press
Gorham Printing, Centralia, WA
Cover design: Kathy Campbell

DEDICATION

—

DR. JOSEPH G. BELL
Worldly philosopher, acerbic wit, dear friend

and

LARRY SEAQUIST
Humane leader, brilliant strategist, dear husband

CONTENTS

Foreword..xv

Free Speech vs. Responsible Speech: We Need to Talk, Again...........1
Racist Police, Courts, Fraternities: Who Says We Don't Need
Affirmative Action Anymore?...8
Fifty Shades of Shame: Playing at Torture..........................13
Books for Our Times: *Losing Our Way*, by Bob Herbert...............16
Post-Charleston, Ferguson, Newtown: How "Advanced" Is America?...23
Books for Our Times: *Winner-Take-All Politics*, by Jacob S. Hacker
and Paul Pierson...29
Atticus Finch as Racist Bigot: "More Human"?.......................37
The Speech Hillary Clinton Should Give to the 1% on Capitalism
and Income Inequality..43
Corporate "Talent" Must Imagine Worst-Case Scenario,
i.e., Ruination..49
Writing for Our Post-9/11 Times....................................54
Refugees Are Not the Problem, My Fellow Americans. Fear Is........64
Whatever Happened to the Famous American Ability to Say
"Nuts" to Charlatans, Crazies, and Fear-Mongers?...................69
The Anger Election of 2016: How Will We Handle Our Anger?.........74
Trump's Crudeness: A Crude American Culture Is Shocked, Shocked....79
Pop Culture Captures Campaign Politics.............................81

Classic Political Films for This Historic Presidential Campaign........84

London Rejects Fear and Elects Its First Muslim Mayor...............91

Making History, Our First Woman Presidential Nominee
"Remembers the Ladies"...95

Beware the Disrupter With No Follow-Up Plan (A Post-Brexit Lesson)...99

Support the Police *and* Address Police Violence:
The True "Law and Order"...102

Books for Our Times: *Listen, Liberal,* by Thomas Frank..............106

Bernie Sanders, Moral Hero 114

If Republicans Repudiate Donald Trump on Moral Grounds,
They Could Truly Reform Their Party................................117

"Make Government Work Better": What Every Democratic
Politician Should Promise in This Election..........................120

Clinton's "Deplorables" Gaffe Lets Trump Seize the High Ground....123

Books for Our Times: *It Can't Happen Here,*
by Sinclair Lewis (a Novel)...127

Hillary the Lion-Hearted Does Battle with the Trumpasaurus........134

Atoning for Slavery: An Institution Grapples With Its
Original Business Model...138

Hillary Clinton Polled "World's Most Admired Woman"
a Record 20 Times. Why the Hatred Now?............................142

Trump Is Not the Solution to Your Anger............................144

The "Normalization" of Donald J. Trump? Not!......................147

Why My Young Nephew Resolves to Become More Political..........151

Classic Films of Human Drama: Rx for Our Fraught Times..........156

How to Fight the Forthcoming Ethics Scandals? Make a Phone Call..163

Barack Obama, President of Character and Integrity.................166

There's a Whole Lot of Anti-Trump Resistance Going On............171

For Effective Resistance, Keep It Nonviolent, Respectful, and Clean..177

The (Rich) Dog Not Barking: "No More Tax Cuts for Me,
Thanks, I'm Good" 181

France Votes for Rationality Over Fear 184

Plays for Our Times: *Oslo*, by J.T. Rogers 187

Julius Caesar with Trump Assassinated: Not Helpful to
Anti-Trump Resistance 192

Not Merely "Anti-Trump," the Resistance Seeks to Re-normalize
America 197

Donald Trump, Defender of Western Civilization? Not! 200

A "Breaking Bad" Culture Got Its President 204

Books for Our Times: *The Retreat of Western Liberalism*,
by Edward Luce 210

The Conscientious "Peacenik": An Underrepresented Voice in
The Vietnam War 217

How to Deter Sexual Predators Like Harvey Weinstein?
Career Ruination and "Good Guys" Speaking Up 222

A Historic Reckoning on Sexual Harassment: In Low Times,
a Good Sign 226

Republican "Values Voters" Revealed as Serious Hypocrites 232

Democrats Need a New Message: How About "Economic
Justice for All"? 237

Plays for Our Times: *The Humans*, by Stephen Karam 242

Alabama Votes for Sanity and Decency—and Inspires the Country ... 247

Films for Our Times: *Darkest Hour* 251

Donald Trump, Ugliest American Ever? 257

Counter-Forces to the Chaos: We're Becoming Constitutionalists,
Ethicists, Candidates for Office, and Other Good Things 262

Democrats: Stop Running Against Nancy Pelosi 268

Marching for Their Lives, the Kids Get Serious—
More Serious Than the "Adults" 271

Once a Champion of Human Rights, America Now
Inhumanly Separates Migrant Children from Their Parents 275

Surrendering America's Most Precious Mantle,
"Leader of the Free World" 279

First Reformed: Dangerous Heresies of a Man of the Cloth............284

World Cup 2018: An Equal-Opportunity Tonic for an Angry
and Divided World...288

Can a Narcissist Comprehend the Meaning of Treason?...............291

How to Keep a Good Marriage During Bad (Trumpian) Times.......295

The Republicans and Donald Trump: A Faustian Bargain
(Annotated) 298

Classic Foreign Films of Human Drama: Rx for Our Fraught Times 307

Is America Having a Breakdown or a Reckoning?
7 Arguments for Reckoning 317

Defending Democracy, Democrats Go High, Republicans
Go Ever Lower 324

Inaction on the Ghastly Jamal Khashoggi Killing Gives
Autocrats What They Crave: Impunity............................328

Books for Our Times: *The Jungle Grows Back: America and
Our Imperiled World,* by Robert Kagan 331

Plays for Our Times: *A Doll's House, Part 2,* by Lucas Hnath 337

Book: *Honorable Exit: How a Few Brave Americans Risked All to Save
Our Vietnamese Allies at the End of the War,* by Thurston Clarke 342

Impeaching Trump Would Be Right in Principle,
But Disastrous Politically...346

D-Day at 75: Rededicating Ourselves to the Mission.................349

Model for the New Man, Right Here in River City....................352

"Let's Take Back Our Democracy—and Improve
It While We're At It": Democrats' Winning Strategy in 2020.........356

My Fellow White Americans: Are We About Blood Identity—
or America's Ideals? 361

A Moderate and a Progressive Mix It Up—and Find Consensus 364

Capitalists Rethink Capitalism—Maybe 372

The Hong Kong and Moscow Protests: In Authoritarian Places,
a Yearning for Democracy...376

Censure, Not Impeachment: Make a Moral, Not a Political Statement...381

Abandoning an Ally on the Battlefield: America the Treacherous?....385

In Reckoning, America Recovers Its Moral Compass.................389

TV for Our Times: "Our Boys" and "Press" 393

Trump the Corrupt as Champion of Anti-Corruption? 398

Republicans Stand by a President Who Pardons Accused
War Criminals 402

Classic Screwball Comedies: Rx for Our Fraught Times..............406

"A Low Dishonest Decade": The Poet Points the Way Upward.........415

American Colossus, Get Thee to Rehab: Learn to
Exercise Power Wisely..421

Films for Our Times: Syria's Tragedy Reflected in *The Cave*
and *For Sama* 425

"Lawlessness Normalized": What Acquitting Donald Trump Means ..430

Films for Our Times: *Parasite*......................................434

Memo to All Women: Best Way to Protect #MeToo
Is to Think #UsToo 438

Democrats Default to Normalcy: Joe Biden's Super-Tuesday Miracle ...443

Biden-Warren 2020?.. 446

In a Plague-Time, We Need Truth and Experts......................450

In a Plague-Time, Reaching Out to Friends While Self-Isolating......456

In a Plague-Time, the Heroic (in Hospitals) and Not-Heroic
(in the White House) 463

In a Plague-Time, Redefining the "Essential" Worker 468

In a Plague-Time, Seeking Beauty, Truth, Lightness.................473

In a Plague-Time, Can-Do Nation Is Unmasked as Can't Do 481

In a Plague-Time, Fat Cats Fatten and Little Guys Help Out 486

White America Must Stand with Black America for Equal Justice 491

With Racial and Sexual Reckoning, a Moral Awakening
in America? 495

In a Plague-Time, Doubly Plagued by Our Mask-Defying
Independence 500

Trump's Storm-Troopers: An Ominous Signal for November 503

What Joe Biden Should Promise #BlackLivesMatter Protesters—
Now—As They Face Trump's Storm-Troopers 508

John Lewis: Good Trouble: Stirring Documentary of a Hero for
Our Times 513

In a Plague-Time, Classic Films of Character and Courage 517

How to Foil Trump's Mail-Tampering? Vote Early! 529

94 Million Eligible Voters Did Not Vote in 2016.
Democrats: Get Out THAT Vote! 532

With Categorical Denunciation of Violence, Biden Can Now
Prosecute the Case Against Trump 534

This Pandemic Could Be Over By Now—IF Our President
Believed in Government 538

"The Moral Obligation to Be Intelligent"—Now More Than Ever 541

In a Plague-Time, Rereading Albert Camus' *The Plague* 545

Trump Becoming COVID Patient #1 Restores the Pandemic
as Campaign Issue #1 557

No, America Is Not "Irredeemably Evil." Democrats: Show
Our Love of Country 560

Books for Our Times: *Twilight of Democracy: The Seductive Lure
of Authoritarianism,* by Anne Applebaum 564

For Republicans, 2020 Election is Political. Democrats
Understand It is Existential. 568

Are We Producing More History Than We Can Consume....?.........572

Nothing Works—and Everything Matters Profoundly 576

"Shut Up, Hamlet, and Drive": Appeal for an Essential Art 579

Build Back Better with Biden—for a Fairer, Smarter,
Greener, Deeper America..591

In a Plague-Time, Running for Elective Office: Personal Insights 595

The American People Save American Democracy—Just Barely.......599

End-Essay: Can America Save Itself from Decline?...................603

Images: Select Listing..611
More About the Author..612

FOREWORD

HISTORY SURPRISES—AND HOW.

What I thought was a one-off has become a series. When I published *Can America Save Itself from Decline?* in early 2015, I had no idea there would—very soon—be good cause to think of that book as Volume I of a series.

But when Donald Trump announced in June 2015 his campaign for President of the United States, proudly touting his racist and xenophobic program in service of his mission to "Make America great again"—and when public response to his anti-democratic message became passionate, massive, and ultimately victorious—I knew America's decline was not only not arrested, it accelerated. Thus, Volume II's size.

In Volume I, I traced how the notion of American decline took root and persisted, even during the comparatively sunny years of Barack Obama's presidency: the polls showing increasing majorities of Americans believed America to be on "the wrong track" and the future to be less bright for their children than it was for themselves; the disillusion with the country in its "comeback" from the terrorist attacks of September 11, 2001, when supposedly "everything changed"—but little did; and the disillusion increasing after the financial crash of 2008, a crash caused by Wall Street, which soon enough was back to its old risky ways. Volume I began with that marker, with a pro-Main Street commentary titled "Recovery Without a Reckoning."

Now, with Donald Trump in the White House almost four harrowing years, we can itemize the ruin. In addition to the racism and xenophobia made explicit, we see a Justice Department become Trump's personal legal team; we see America, the former champion of human rights, now separating migrant children from their parents; we see America, once "Leader of the Free World," cozying up to strongmen autocrats; we see this proto-autocrat's assault on fact and truth ("fake news"). And now, just defeated for a second term by Democrat Joe Biden, Trump is knocking off every last institutional guardrail to deny the election result. Stunningly, this four-year performance—and a criminal lack of performance in managing the federal response to the coronavirus pandemic—earned Trump in 2020 the vote of *nearly half the electorate*. If anyone still questions the notion of America's decline, this marker should give them pause.

As a commentator, I had no choice but to track Trump in his—what?—"disruption": Trump—anti-democratic, crude, amoral—hit the trifecta of my beat: politics, culture, and ethical-moral issues. I love America—the *idea* of it—and I write in defense of that beautiful idea: rule of law, equality, fair play, second chances. As a deep reader and playwright, I have tracked the degradation of American culture—the "anything-goes" ethos of its literature, film, TV, theatre—and I see how little it instructs or comforts us in this chaos-cum-pandemic. To recur to the disrupter archetype: America has long been fascinated with it (see: Facebook's motto "Move fast and break things"), yet despite all the chaos, half of America cannot see this disrupter has no follow-up plan. Even with Trump gone from the White House, he, and anti-democratic Trumpism, will remain a force. Thus the need for this series' Volume III. I will remain on duty: Just how low does this descent go? With Joe Biden in the White House, can we head for what the Roman poet Virgil called "the upper air"? I will keep writing, hoping this Dark Age can be transformed into a Renaissance.

As harrowing as Trump's four-year Reign of Error has been, however, History had another surprise: the emergence of a formidable counterforce—the conscientious American public.

If we did not understand how precious is our democratic form of government—of, by, and for the people—we do now, having watched Donald Trump, and the Party of Trump (once known as the Republicans), attack taken-for-granted rights, like voter enfranchisement. If we did not appreciate the beautiful idea of America, we do now, seeing those migrant children pulled from their parent's arms. If we did not understand the historic problem of racism and a Trump-driven resurgence of white supremacy, we do now, seeing the agonizing video of George Floyd, a Black American, asphyxiated under the knee of a white police officer, whose hand was propped nonchalantly on his hip. In protest, conscientious America, Black and white, poured into the streets, in numbers that were the largest in American history. To protest Trump's record of sexual assault, the Women's March the day after his inauguration set another record in turnout. As to turnout, voter turnout in this 2020 presidential election was also the biggest in a century, with voters braving the coronavirus, standing hours to ensure their vote. The protest, the vote, a recovered Americanism = tools for action, unity. And, bless them: Historic numbers of conscientious Americans are running for office, from local school boards to Congress.

Will this counter-force be enough to save American Democracy, reverse our decline? That is the question compelling conscientious America, also much of the world, as it struggles with the forces of anti-democracy/strongman rule everywhere.

In this journey, I thank especially my late mother, Mildred Lofberg, who died during the course of this volume. While Mom and I had our issues—she was Republican, I am Democrat—we were united in our concern for the moral health of the country. It is those close conversations that I miss most, but the memory of them informs my work.

And notably, Joe—Dr. Joseph G. Bell. Volume I was dedicated to Joe, because of our years of yeasty exchanges over the American idea—Joe emphasizing America as a capitalist entity, me emphasizing it as a democracy. Joe gets the dedicatory nod again in this volume, because: Not long after Trump's surprise election, Joe said, "You know, I think Donald Trump may be just the stinker to get John Q. Public off the sofa." As ever, Joe was right: Trump got America off the sofa! And as ever, eternal thanks to my husband Larry Seaquist, former Navy captain, former state legislator, now also a writer. Larry is my *compagno di vita*, first reader, best friend, and co-dedicatee.

CARLA SEAQUIST
November 19, 2020
Gig Harbor, Washington

Free Speech vs. Responsible Speech: We Need to Talk, Again

WE NEED TO talk—again—about how we exercise our basic, elemental, Constitutional right to free speech.

Up front, let's make clear we are *not* talking about censorship of that most precious of rights, the right to express ourselves freely without punishment. But we *are* talking about a more responsible exercise of that right, one that considers consequences and motives, one that will ensure we continue enjoying that right.

Forcing the free-speech debate back to the forefront are two related events happening in close succession.

In December, news of a movie comedy (*The Interview*) about two American doofuses tasked by the CIA to assassinate the leader of North Korea—a high point shows the Dear Leader's head exploding—so incited the ire of the North Korean government that it hacked the computer system of the movie's producer, Sony Pictures, whether to destroy the movie or interfere with distribution, it's not clear. What is clear is that North Korea is a nation with nuclear weapons and a wildly erratic leader. The Obama administration had to respond to North Korea's hacking as a cyber-security breach, by threatening "proportional" payback "at a place and time and manner that we choose."

Really? All this unfunny saber-rattling over a dumber-than-dumb comedy? Trying to defuse the situation, Mr. Obama added, "I think it says something about North Korea that they decided to have the state mount an all-out assault on a movie studio because of a satirical movie." Maybe so, but then, what does this contretemps say about American notions of comedy, of culture?

More recently, and more lethally, in Paris in January two radicalized French Muslims stormed the offices of Charlie Hebdo, a satirical newspaper that makes a point of skewering Mohammed the Prophet, and killed five of the paper's cartoonists, along with others. Perceived by the French public as an attack on one of its foundational pillars—the French Enlightenment's achievement of free speech—the public days later filled the streets by the millions with a march reasserting this right, with signs proclaiming "*Je suis Charlie*"—"I am Charlie." Joining them were Muslims bearing signs proclaiming "*Je suis juif,*" showing solidarity with the four Jewish customers killed in a kosher supermarket in a coordinated attack by another radicalized French Muslim.

One week later, Charlie Hebdo, instead of a "*Merci*" to the Muslims who came out in solidarity, put out its first post-attack edition with a cover again showing the Prophet Mohammed, albeit with an ostensibly more benign message, "*Tous est pardonne*"—"All is forgiven"—though who's doing the forgiving is left ambiguous. Given that many Muslims take any depiction of the Prophet as blasphemous at the most or insulting at the least, Muslims across the world are roiled again, with some out in the streets, protesting and threatening death to the Infidels.

Similarly, almost ten years ago, there was the furor over the Danish newspaper *Jyllands-Posten* and its publication of caricatures of Mohammed—most notably, showing a bomb embedded in the Prophet's turban—which led to worldwide riots, and some 250 deaths. Unmoved, the late contrarian Christopher Hitchens scoffed at "the babyish tantrums" of the Islamic world and "this sickly babble about 'respect.'"

Do we see a pattern here? Inciting all three incidents is the blunt instrument of satire, with the same follow-up: free-speech absolutists' insistence on the right to offend.

While satire can be brilliantly and uniquely apt, it can also be the middle-schooler in the house of humor, glorying in its goal to be wicked, to insult and humiliate. As various commentators have noted, when satire "punches up"—at royalty and heads of state, politicians, the aristocracy, and the professions—it can act as a powerful corrective to those in authority when they abuse their power over the citizenry. France produced possibly the greatest such artist, Honoré Daumier, who portrayed the king as Gargantua inhaling the nation's assets (Daumier was jailed six months for his insolence); he also skewered the stupidities of politicians as well as the pretensions of the bourgeoisie and the practitioners of law and medicine.

But serious ethical-moral questions arise when satire "punches down"—at the poor and the oppressed. Insulting and humiliating the helpless is a bully's game, an abuse of responsibility and power ("Can't take a joke, huh?").

In the case of *Charlie Hebdo*, the insult and humiliation are aimed at a once-great civilization, Islam, now on the downside from the West, with millions of its adherents living in misery in *banlieues* encircling Paris and other cities. Daumier, with his empathy for the poor and the worker, would not likely join in the "fun." Far from amusing, *Charlie Hebdo's* humor is pornographic and profane, especially regarding Mohammed (Google for particulars). Moreover, this pornographic and profane attack, aimed ostensibly at Islamic terrorists, is also, given satire's blunt edge, felt by ordinary Muslims who hold the Prophet sacred and dear. Also, it has to be asked: How does the paper's depiction of Mohammed with an outsize hooked nose not compare with the vilest caricatures of Jews of the past, now broadly condemned? It must also be asked: How can the French, a thinking people, not think of their not-so-distant past, and present responsibility, to peoples they once dominated as colonial masters?

The paper is quite correct about the grave dangers of radical Islam, but is it not responsible in some part for that radicalization, with its insulting, humiliating "humor"? *Charlie Hebdo* cannot duck its responsibility by touting itself as a *"journal irresponsable."* Nothing, of course, justifies their murder.

And, finally, there's this contradiction: *Charlie Hebdo*, reasserts a surviving staffer, is against all religious extremism—"Everyone can be religious, but extremist thoughts and acts we cannot accept." With moderate Muslims now asked to speak out more against Islamist extremism, how can the paper continue to get a free pass with its own extremism? At the same time, it must be noted the Arab press can be equally extremist in its caricatures of the Jews and Israel. Offense is given all around. But again, offenders do not deserve murder.

The right to offend: Stepping back and considered more generally, the insistence on the right to offend, to insult and humiliate, has ramifications and repercussions that reach deep and cost dearly. Here are three:

One: It exacerbates conflict among nations. International Relations 101 teaches that conflict among nations, as the bloody historical record shows, very often stems from one nation perceiving it has been "dissed" by another—that "sickly babble about 'respect'" is universal and profound—and taking revenge. See: Germany after World War I, whose humiliation enabled an opportunistic Hitler to seek world domination and start World War II. In this sense, one might regard the international system as one big sandbox, filled with children giving and taking offense. To extend the metaphor, it's a dereliction of responsibility when the big kids—America, France—throw their comparatively bigger buckets of sand in the eyes of the little guys, then insist on their right to do so, rather than their responsibility to maintain peace in the sandbox.

Two: It diverts us from our responsibilities. Insult and humiliation— and our increasingly shrill insistence on our free-speech rights to indulge in other low forms of discourse—create a distraction from our very real, very serious responsibilities. In fact, indulgence can *prevent* acknowledgment of responsibility.

Case in point: America acknowledging responsibility for torture during the Bush years. Just before the Sony Picture brouhaha, the Senate Select Intelligence Committee released a report of its six-year study that presented, in more gruesome detail than previously reported, the heinous practices used to break detainees suspected of terrorism, practices that became U.S. Government policy. Finally, some of us thought: a reckoning on torture. But then, a "comedy" about two clownish Yanks offing North Korea's leader swamped the airwaves and—*poof*—momentum gone. One might argue truly weighty issues eventually weigh in, but do they? Neil Postman's book of some decades ago, *Amusing Ourselves to Death*, seems prophetic. One might also ask: Where were America's artists, putative humanists, when America was torturing other human beings? Answer: exercising their free-speech rights to say irrelevant, neurotic, profane, anti-human things, "breaking bad," defining humanity downward—"What torture?" *Are we serious?* No.

Three: It leaves us with a depleted culture. Free-speech absolutists' insistence on the right to offend, to say and write offensive and profane things, along with the right to blaspheme, has created an environment, a culture-scape, in which little is held dear or beautiful and almost nothing is sacred. And we, the instigators, are the losers for it, depleted spiritually. Rather than a Golden Age, ours is one of brass, and getting brassier. Moreover, it might be said, fighting for the right to offend can be seen as the frantic overreaction of a culture in trouble, in decline even, as America and France show evidence of being.

To reverse our downward course, we need to get a grip, get responsible. Assert our rights, yes, but also tend to our responsibilities, and in so doing, protect those rights. Would that we emphasized our responsibilities as fervently and energetically as our rights! It's the path not only to maturity but security.

Encouragingly, in the realm of political cartooning, some are rethinking their approach in the aftermath of the *Charlie Hebdo* attacks. *The New York Times* writes:

> "...[A]mid all the 'I am Charlie' marches and declarations on social media, some in the cartooning world are also debating a delicate question: Were the victims free-speech martyrs, full stop, or provocateurs whose aggressive mockery of Islam sometimes amounted to xenophobia and racism?"

Noting this question unfolds differently in different countries, the *Times* continues:

"...[T]he conversation could be especially acute in the United States, where sensitivities to racially tinged caricatures may run higher than in places like France, where historically tighter restrictions on speech have given rise to a strong desire to flout the rules."

The *Times* cites American cartoonists reconsidering "what privilege means, and a feeling that you don't need to insult people, especially downtrodden people, to make your points." Others question *Charlie Hebdo*'s "ugly, racist" covers as "simply cruelty hiding behind the idea of free speech." Joe Sacco, author of graphic novels (*Footnotes in Gaza*), states that while he decries the murders, "I also come from the position of trying to understand why people are affected by images, and not just say 'Why can't you take a joke?' An image of Muhammad in some compromising position isn't meant as just a joke." Sacco takes aim "at people in power, rather than attacking...people who might feel themselves marginalized or persecuted."

For the rest of us, we already accept curbs on a vast array of rights, enforced by the state, in the name of responsibility to the general welfare. The right to drive a vehicle does not mean we can abuse that right and endanger others by speeding or playing bumper-cars. The right to marry does not mean we can abuse our spouse physically or emotionally. Absolutists, including those for free speech, by definition don't like curbs, but how else can society not only function, but survive? In the area of gun rights, absolutists insist on their untrammeled right to all manner of firearms, without restriction, heedless of the carnage caused.

As to speech, there already stands a long-accepted sanction against yelling "Fire" in a crowded theater. As *USA Today* writes:

"In 1919, the Supreme Court ruled speech that presents a 'clear and present danger' is not protected by the First Amendment. Crying 'fire' *in a quiet, uninhabited place is one thing, the court said. But 'the most stringent protection of free speech would not protect a man in falsely shouting fire in a theater and causing a panic.'*

Can it not be said that, given today's dense and volatile world, we do indeed live in a crowded theater? And that there is a "clear and present danger" in heaping verbal fire on the tinder?

Again, none of this is to call for censorship, by the state or any other body. But it is to call for taking personal responsibility for minding our mouths. And it's to argue with free-speech absolutists this point: That those of us taking a more moderate stance would of course, as Voltaire would, fight to the death to defend free speech, including the right to offend—a "regrettable necessity" as *Vox's* Matt Yglesias puts it. But it *is* valid to note that defending the right of free speech doesn't mean one cannot object to that right's application or abuse, that embracing a broad strategy doesn't rule out objecting to an operational tactic.

This is also to note that responsible speech is not the appeaser's way out, or the Victorian way, as free-speech absolutists like to accuse. The slain *Charlie Hebdo* editor's defense of his right to offend—that he'd rather "die standing than live on my knees"—is, no disrespect to the dead intended, absurd. Being responsible is hard, hard work. The reptilian exists in all of us, in responsible people too, but it's our responsibility to subdue that beast—the struggle of civilization and its discontents—and speak and act in ways that, for the greater good, enhance human dignity.

C.J. Jung, the Swiss psychologist, once wrote that in pondering the end of the world, he could not speculate how it would come: through evil or stupidity? Unhappily, at this chaotic moment in history, we have both destructive forces hard at work—the evil of radical extremism *and* stupid expression unbridled—and not much in the way of counter-forces of equal power pushing back. Calling all grown-ups, calling all grown-ups....

—*HuffPost*, February 3, 2015

Racist Police, Courts, Fraternities: Who Says We Don't Need Affirmative Action Anymore?

AMERICA IS NOW so sufficiently "post-racial" that affirmative action is no longer needed as corrective action. So ruleth the U.S. Supreme Court.

In a series of recent cases filed by police and fire departments, school districts and colleges, the Court, in closely-contested rulings, has weakened or even wiped out affirmative action's race-conscious policies designed to overcome and rebalance our history of discrimination in employment and admissions. Reflecting the new conventional "wisdom" that affirmative action is itself discriminatory, Chief Justice John Roberts wrote in a 2007 decision, "The way to stop discriminating on the basis of race is to stop discriminating on the basis of race."

As if! Clearly, not everybody read the ruling, because an awful lot of discriminating—white against black, mainly—is still going on. Similarly, the Court has attacked the 1965 Voting Rights Act on grounds that its protections are no longer required in our post-racial society.

Proof that racism still operates, and operates to a virulent and institutionalized degree, is provided in the U.S. Department of Justice's recent report on the police practices and—astonishingly—the court system of Ferguson, Missouri, prepared after its investigations into the police killing last summer of black teenager Michael Brown.

In essence, the DOJ report describes a shakedown operation whereby a mainly white police department, upheld by a mainly white judiciary, treats its mainly black population as a source of municipal revenue, extracted via arbitrary fines, arrests and jailings for traffic violations, jaywalking and other concocted infractions of the law. One example: A black man cited for pedophilia because he was napping in a car near a park full of children, and because he gave his name to the arresting officer as "Mike" instead of "Michael." (This man subsequently lost his job as a federal contractor.) This incident is by no means isolated; the report makes clear many blacks in Ferguson have had similar experiences. Nor is Ferguson's racism an isolated case, as President Barack Obama noted in commenting on the report; it afflicts many other jurisdictions around the country.

And now comes news of racial retrenchment in another venue: At the University of Oklahoma, a fraternity, Sigma Alpha Epsilon, clarifies its racist policy—chanted by members in party mode on a bus, caught on video that went viral—to wit, that no black man (the n-word is used) will ever be allowed into their hallowed cohort, with the kicker added that lynching is permitted to prevent such contamination.

Wasn't racism—*if* it existed at all in post-racial America—supposedly subtle? Not only is there nothing subtle about the jaw-dropping examples cited above, there is something in them of the antediluvian—the slave-master exerting his "rights" over his property, up to and including the right to lynch.

What's saddening is this: There was apparently no one in either setting—in all of Ferguson or the fraternity—who, either from a position of authority or as a peer, tried to call a halt to the racist practices as they took place. No one questioned the rightness or wrongness of the outrageousness of what they were doing—least of all Ferguson's judges, who after all rule on right and wrong. Again, astonishing.

Granted, in the case of the shameful fraternity action, kudos go to the University's president David Boren for expressing heartbroken disgust and shutting down the campus' SAE house. And it is cheering—very—to see the vast public outrage and revulsion expressed at both the Ferguson and fraternity cases: What a lot of race-conscious people we have. But one wonders about these same people: If a racist act were performed in their midst, how many would have—*in that moment*—resisted peer pressure or bucked their superior's orders and actually stuck a stick in the proceedings? I'm just saying: A race-conscious counterforce is needed to battle racism as wrong, immoral, unethical—on the ground, in its face, all the time.

Which is why we still need affirmative action: Inasmuch as the infection of racism still exists, then affirmative action and its antibiotic of race-consciousness is needed as long as that infection persists, which is to say: probably forever. (The infection of sexism also persists, witness the increased rates of rape and sexual harassment.)

After all, it is the role and responsibility of an affirmative action officer to delineate the problematic environment, outline steps to reform it, and then go out and enact those steps. For example, regarding Ferguson's police department, any affirmative action officer worth his/her mandate would have noted the department's almost all-white ranks (of 54 officers, only four were African-American), juxtaposed against the 67 percent black community it serves, and called out, *"Whoa!"*

I speak as a former practitioner. To achieve parity between a department—police or other—and the community is serves, you'd review job qualifications and tests for bias, set hiring goals (goals, not quotas), get sign-on from city leadership, and personally guarantee community groups that the city is a fair employer. With new hires in place, conferring a better race and gender balance, you'd then give The Commandments to all: Thou shalt not express racist or sexist epithets, thou shalt not harass each other, etc. Rinse and repeat, many times.

If a new hire doesn't perform, you back the department's decision to terminate; if any employee meets with discrimination, you fix the problem, invoking federal or state procedure or, as I had to, create it (with a no-harassment policy.) In this way, peace—and parity—reign.

But it seems nothing of the kind operated in Ferguson, because, once again, we were in post-racial times.

And it seems the SAE fraternity operates completely oblivious to the advances achieved by the civil rights movement this last half-century. (That SAE was founded in the South just after the Civil War may be relevant.) *Washington Post* columnist Eugene Robinson, who is African-American, after calling the frat brothers "soft, pampered, privileged, ridiculous," indirectly makes an excellent case for affirmative action:

"Let's imagine the video never surfaced. With halfway decent grades, degrees from Oklahoma's flagship university and the connections that Sigma Alpha Epsilon's old-boy network could provide, the boys on that bus could be expected to end up in executive positions with the power to hire and fire. What chance would an African-American job applicant have of getting fair consideration?"

As expected, free-speech absolutists are raising the point about the frat boys' free-speech rights, but that point is not having impact: The public remains disgusted with their racist hijinks.

This contrasts with the recent terrorist killings in Paris of cartoonists at the newspaper *Charlie Hebdo* for racist depictions of the Prophet Mohammed, which triggered a massive public response—*"Je suis Charlie"* ("I am Charlie")—upholding the freedom to offend. As *The New York Times* speculated about national differences, the debate about free speech "could be especially acute in the United States, where sensitivities to racially tinged caricatures may run higher than in places like France, where historically tighter restrictions on speech have given rise to a strong desire to flout the rules." In other words, "I am SAE" is not happening here.

Of course, it must be said that affirmative action in its latter incarnation was a fairly easy target for the Supreme Court to attack, because its practitioners did not maintain control of their narrative. Redefined by its opponents, affirmative action came to be decried for championing "preferential treatment" of "unqualified" minorities, for pushing hard-and-fast "quotas" instead of the more aspirational "goals," toward which a "good-faith effort" is made. Semantically, I was grateful my job title was equal opportunity officer: Equal opportunity is readily accepted as an all-American value, while affirmative action triggers resistance against perceived favoritism.

If affirmative action—or, better, equal opportunity—is to be reinstated, we need to "build it better," as the new mantra goes. And its practitioners need to keep control of their instrument. We can take heart from President Obama's speech at the 50th anniversary of the Selma march, that "we are strong enough to be self-critical."

And of course the Supreme Court needs to reverse itself on its recent decisions weakening affirmative action—which is not likely to happen. Yet the Court left an opening, a remedy: Many of those same decisions, while doing away with affirmative action *as a requirement*, nevertheless leave it *as an option*. Let's press for that option to be exercised on all sides, in the spirit of self-criticism and self-correction.

Supreme Court Justice Sonia Sotomayor points the way. In one of those decisions—*Schuette v. Coalition to Defend Affirmative Action* (2014)—she took aim at Chief Justice Roberts' above-cited line of 2007, "The way to stop discriminating on the basis of race is to stop discriminating on the basis of race."

Taking exception, Justice Sotomayor wrote last year:

"The way to stop discrimination on the basis of race is to speak openly and candidly on the subject of race, and to apply the Constitution with eyes open to the unfortunate effects of centuries of racial discrimination."

Which is to say: The Justice points to affirmative action, equal opportunity—and justice.

—*HuffsPost*, February 25, 2015

Fifty Shades of Shame:
Playing at Torture

I DON'T USUALLY COMMENT on trash—life is too short—but when a piece of trash makes a cultural statement, I brake.

Fifty Shades of Grey, a tale of sexual bondage that began life as a novel breaking all sales records and print runs, has now taken on extended life by becoming a blockbuster movie, very likely playing at a theatre near you. All sorts of subsidiary spin of this phenomenon are being exploited, including hotels offering special *Fifty Shades of Grey* weekends (the ads are unclear what the special add-ons are). Two sequels to the book are out, forming a trilogy of trash.

All of which noise has made its creator, E.L. James, the world's richest author, eclipsing even J.K. Rowling of *Harry Potter* fame, thanks to a heretofore untapped taste in the general public for sex of a kinky kind.

And "trash" is the appropriate term to apply to *Fifty Shades*. Critics, not always diligent in executing their responsibilities as cultural gatekeepers, in this instance have met their duty and pretty universally savaged both the book and the movie as poorly conceived, plotted, written. Anecdotally, readers and viewers who partake admit they do so as, tee-hee, a "guilty pleasure."

So how is all this a cultural statement? Why isn't it just an anomaly of publishing or a new low in pop culture?

Because—dare I say it?—a moral point is involved. Or rather, it was missed entirely. The public ignored a moral crime—more specifically, a war crime—and instead, via a vehicle of trash, turned this crime into a fun thing. We are talking about torture and the varying reactions to it.

When news of Abu Ghraib broke in mid-2004, exposing the

atrocities of torture inflicted by the U.S. military based in Iraq on detainees suspected of terrorism, some of us doubled over in shame at how this great nation, once upon a time a moral beacon to the world, could trash the Geneva Conventions and descend to torturing those in our custody. The searing images from Abu Ghraib and other "black sites"—showing, among other methods, men shackled to walls or ceilings, hanging in extreme pain or unconscious—propelled some of us to protest in the streets, in public forums, and in print.

Our numbers in protest were never huge, though. The broader public seemed not to share in our revulsion at the obscenity of Abu Ghraib, but reacted with a shrug ("Meh").

So it came as no surprise, sad but no surprise, that the image of a shackled human being—in a tale cunningly titled *Fifty Shades of Grey*—rather than generating pity and protest, instead was broadly seen and embraced as a massive turn-on.

In other words: *Playing at torture is now fine, while actual torture is disregarded.*

Moreover, while the masses were turning on to play-torture, they missed their chance at a reckoning and redemption for the real thing: Last December, the U.S. Senate Select Intelligence Committee released its report describing in more gruesome detail than previously reported the methods and extent of the torture the U.S. used against foreign detainees during the Bush administration. Given the massive media spotlight, some of us hoped for an accounting and moral repair—at long last!—for the war crime of torture committed in our name.

But, alas, that outcry soon faded. Moral protest was smothered by the general public's indifference and the masses went back to their cheap thrills, like a cheesy bondage novel-turned-movie. To paraphrase what Noel Coward said of some popular music, "Extraordinary how potent cheap literature is."

Of course, I will be thought as uptight, unsophisticated about contemporary sexual practices, and confused about the line between the private realm and the outer world. Still, one's private realm should not prevent one—nor blind one—from rising to a test of national character, taking necessary action in the outer world, most especially moral action.

What all this *Fifty Shades*-generated noise says about the American character and culture is sad, even tragic. What a falling-off there has been from the moral clarity and fire of the civil rights movement of recent decades, and before that, the role America played after World War II in establishing the Universal Declaration of Human Rights, and our staunch support over a century's time of the various Geneva Conventions governing the rules of war and war crimes.

Now we play at torture—and giggle about it—and let the real crime of torture go?

For shame, people. Fifty shades of shame.

—*HuffPost*, April 22, 2015

Books for Our Times:
Losing Our Way, by Bob Herbert

Fifth in an ongoing series, Books for Our Times

LOSING OUR WAY is a book that will resonate with many thoughtful Americans who feel, like the author, that America has lost her way in this last half-century. That would be most Americans, actually: Two-thirds of the American public tell pollsters they feel the country is on "the wrong track."

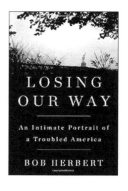

With this book, Bob Herbert, a former *New York Times* opinion columnist and now a senior fellow at Demos, a public policy think tank, seeks to answer the question put directly to him by a World War II veteran: "What happened to us?" He begins by looking back to a more hopeful and vibrant time in America—the author's growing-up years in the 1950s and early '60s in Montclair, New Jersey—then moves forward, tracing our falling-off in chapters devoted to key macro measures: our crumbling infrastructure, unnecessary wars, failing schools, vanishing jobs, and the "ruinous" disparity of income and wealth.

In particular Herbert focuses on the years since the financial crash of 2008, when "for much of the population, the very notion of economic security evaporated":

> "Spirits sank along with bank balances. The Great Recession and its dismal aftermath showed unmistakably that a great change had come over the country. The years that had been unkind to the middle class were positively brutal to the working class and the poor. The United States was no longer a place of widely shared prosperity and limitless optimism. It was a country that had lost its way."

Keeping it human, and avoiding a dry recitation of data, Herbert tells his tale through the stories of ordinary Americans personally bearing the brunt of those falling measures. Thus his subtitle, *An Intimate Portrait of a Troubled America*.

The first chapter, for example, one of several on our crumbling infrastructure, opens with a figure literally falling through the air: a woman, Mercedes Gorden, trapped in her car as it fell 80 feet into the river when the Interstate 35 bridge in Minneapolis collapsed during drive-home rush hour, in 2007—and who survived, enduring many surgeries and emotional battles, supported by a fiancé who stood by her throughout.

Likewise, Herbert traces our recent wars, too many and not necessary, in the story of Dan Berschinski, who lost both legs while leading his unit in Afghanistan and who undergoes a grueling rehabilitation, finally to stand and walk on his own two new legs. Our failing education system is traced through both a remarkable principal in an elementary school in a tough neighborhood in Pittsburgh, who doles out more love than many of her charges get in their fractured homes, and two other women in Pennsylvania who organize a successful protest to the draconian $1 billion in cuts to education ordered by the new Tea Party-backed governor, bent on slashing government spending on public services.

To illustrate the vanishing jobs market, Herbert cites multiple individuals—for example, representing the middle class, an out-of-work architect who can't find work in a collapsed housing market; a former marketing executive who tearfully says, "I'm an embarrassment to my family"; another former middle-management executive forced to sell his blood. Representing the next generation are the newly-minted college graduates who can't find work in their major, live at home, and put off marriage and forming a family. Like Herbert, the architect recalls his youth in post-World War II America when the country seemed a secure, stable place. (Herbert, it should be noted, is African-American.)

Laced through these portraits are an abundance of facts. In the chapters on infrastructure, we learn that 600,000 bridges in the U.S. have been designated "structurally deficient"; that "fracture critical" means a system without fail-safe mechanisms; that President Dwight Eisenhower's grand project of building the interstate highway system made us a modern economy. Throughout the book Herbert cites the findings of hundreds of studies, but wisely leaves their details to a 25-page section of end notes, the better to make his people-centered points, here about infrastructure:

> *"Study after study has shown that rebuilding the infrastructure is the quickest way to put large numbers of people to work and that the return for each dollar invested in infrastructure renewal is significantly greater than all other investments in the nation's economy. With the nation's physical plant in such sad shape at a time when millions of Americans are in dire need of full-time work, it's criminal to neglect this biggest of all bangs for the national buck."*

He extols previous Presidents who, even in hard times, tended to America's physical structure: Abraham Lincoln during the Civil War built the transcontinental railroad; Franklin Roosevelt during the Great Depression established the Tennessee Valley Authority and built bridges, roads, schools, hospitals, housing. "Of course we spent money," said FDR, "it went to put needy men and women without jobs to work." The author faults the Obama administration for the "willful refusal to acknowledge the screaming need for a massive, long-term rebuild America campaign."

As to the vanishing jobs market, Herbert cites "the sorrowful truth... that the era of limitless job growth that built the American middle class was gone." A sorrowful statistic: In the five years since the Great Recession's onset, "more than half of the American workforce endured the loss of a job, a cut in pay, or an involuntary reduction to part-time employment." And the stress is killing: As an expert testified to Congress, "The lower people's income... the earlier they die and the sicker they live." Damningly, Herbert notes, "while the jobs crisis was the single most critical issue facing the country, there was no concerted effort on the part of the government to deal with it in any sustained way."

"Welcome to the new world of employment in America, where job insecurity is the norm, wages are depressed, benefits are few, and anyone can be thrown onto the jobless rolls at any moment and stay there for months or years at a time. The most terrible of all of America's wounds is its chronic, insidious unemployment. It's a wound that is vast, deep, festering, and tragically resistant to healing. And it's changing the very character of the nation."

As for our endless wars, Herbert cites President George W. Bush for waging war on the cheap, by breaking with a tradition extending from Madison through Reagan to call for national sacrifice, raise taxes in wartime, provide properly for the wounded. He cites the public's indifference to these wars, fought by the few: "That indifference ... is what makes it so easy to go to war again and again and again." He excoriates the prevailing view "that the only way to make American power credible was to use it." He has one word for our self-destructive wars since Vietnam: "Madness." Recurring to double amputee Dan Berschinski, "It bothered me that there seemed to be no collective sense that it was insane to allow the maiming of men like Dan."

What comes through in all these portraits, taken from various angles, is—to use a term neither Herbert nor his subjects use—the suffering of the middle and working classes, "existential" stress borne for the most part stoically. Some might call these people victims, but the author doesn't. As I read on, I kept thinking of Samuel Beckett's character in his novel *The Unnamable* who says, "I can't go on. I'll go on."

Which is why the reader grows all the angrier, as Herbert does, when he dispenses with the documentary tone he uses in most of the book to let fly at the fact that all this vast damage was unnecessary, that "the devastating wounds that have caused Americans such pain were self-inflicted." He does not let the public, the people where his heart clearly lies, off the hook:

"...[A]s a society we ... behaved irresponsibly, self-destructively, for decades. We lost sight of the effort and sacrifice required to build *and maintain a great nation. We refused to fend off the destructive excess of free-market zealots and casino capitalists. Greed was not only tolerated but encouraged, and that led to catastrophic imbalances in wealth, income, and political power. Over time the great American ideals of fairness and justice for all, and the great American values of thrift and civic engagement, began to lose their hold on us. We embraced shopping."*

He goes on: "We fought wars that should never have been fought. We allowed giant banks and predatory corporations to plunder the nation's wealth and resources without regard for the damage done to the economy, the environment, or the people."

For this plunder of the nation, Herbert reserves his most forceful fire for "the powerful moneyed interests—the 'malefactors of great wealth,' as Teddy Roosevelt so memorably called them—who have been the ones most responsible for driving the nation into such a wretched state of affairs." He describes a "toxic alliance" of government, mega-corporations, and giant banks, an alliance "fueled by limitless greed and a near-pathological quest for power," that "reshaped the rules and regulations" to heavily favor the interests of those who were already well-to-do. "In the process they trampled the best interests of ordinary Americans."

"Job creation was never a priority of the nation's corporate, banking, and political elite. They argued, with nonstop vehemence, that everyone would benefit from industrial and financial deregulation, from the erosion of safety-net support and the weakening of labor unions, from unchecked globalization and the wholesale replacement of live workers by machines, and from the rampant privatization of services originally designed to meet public needs. It was a philosophy that allowed the fortunate few to amass greater riches than anyone on the planet had ever previously dreamed of."

Elsewhere, the author goes on:

"America was trapped in a Catch-22...: There was no way for the middle class to prosper (or even survive) in the absence of well-paying jobs. But a high-tech, globalized economy shaped according to the dictates of shortsighted, profit-obsessed Wall Street financiers and corporate CEOs would never create enough good jobs for the middle class to retrieve its past glory. Corporate profits rebounded to record levels after the Great Recession in large part because of the savings that management realized by savaging payrolls. The very idea of paying a decent and secure wage for ordinary workers had become anathema in the business world."

Lambasting further the heartlessness of today's capitalists, Herbert cites "the unconscionable mistreatment of workers by corporate executives," whose salaries are now on average three hundred times more than their workers' salaries, with many pulling down millions more.

The subsequent impoverishment of American workers accounts, Herbert asserts, for failing education performance: Poor students, given their resources and stress levels, generally do poorly academically. And in a chapter titled "Cashing in on Schools," the author goes after the "profiteers"—those in the "corporate stampede to cash in on the public education system"—who seek to privatize a historic and core public institution, with charter schools, dubious online programs, and various "reforms" enriching their investors, not the students. "Backtracking on education," he says, "is the societal equivalent of mainlining heroin."

So: Having lost our way, how do we find it again? "The United States," says Herbert in his epilogue, "needs to be reimagined," away from "the unabashedly selfish, terminally competitive, winner-take-all philosophy that has steered U.S. policy for most of the past forty years" and into a "monumental ditch."

Fittingly, in a book long on the personal and short on policy, Herbert looks not to Washington but to direct action from Main Street—for a mass movement to come into being, demanding a return to the American ideals of fairness and opportunity. Why direct action? Because the changes required to set the country on a more equitable direction "will never be initiated by the banking and corporate elite or the politicians in their thrall. The uncomfortable and mostly unspoken reality of power politics in the United States is that the interests of the very wealthy and those of the middle class and the poor are not the same."

A demoralized public might feel Herbert's proposal of a mass movement is a cop-out, that it is up to our political leaders to right the train. But he urges us on:

"The odds against a new citizens' movement emerging and ultimately changing America's cultural and economic landscape are no more unrealistic than the original odds against the civil rights movement or the women's movement or the labor movement of old. None of those movements were taken seriously in the beginning. And yet they endured and ultimately prevailed. If our nation is to be changed for the better, ordinary citizens will have to intervene aggressively in their own fate. The tremendous power in the hands of the moneyed interests will not be relinquished voluntarily."

I hope Main Street will read *Losing Our Way*, because, while it churns repetitively in parts, this one's for and about you. I hope it will inspire the conscientious citizens, the life blood of any polity but exhausted by all the calamities described in the book, to find the juice to mount the next great citizens' movement, to get this great nation back on track. And I hope the myriad Presidential candidates, Republican and Democrat alike, now declaring for 2016 and assiduously lining up their big-money donors, will study this book and reconnect to the humanity on exhibit there.

Bob Herbert, reporter and humanist, has rendered us all a signal public service.

—*HuffPost*, May 28, 2015

Post-Charleston, Ferguson, Newtown: How "Advanced" Is America?

IN THE EARLY aftermath of the massacre of nine African-American parishioners, including their pastor, gunned down by a white male shooter in their house of worship, Charleston's Emanuel A.M.E. Church, a sorrowful President Barack Obama posed this challenge in his White House press conference:

> *"At some point, we as a country will have to reckon with the fact that this type of mass violence does not happen in other advanced countries. It doesn't happen in other places with this kind of frequency. And it is in our power to do something about it."*

What marks a country as advanced? More than the technological achievements of working lights and running faucets, the mark of an advanced society is reflected in its adherence to high principles, its moral character, its striving for excellence, and its commitment to the general welfare. At the least, every one of its citizens should feel safe in his home, in the streets, and certainly in his place of worship.

We Americans think of ourselves as advanced, at least technologically. The images of the first man on the moon, put there by American ingenuity and organization less than 200 years after the country's founding, can still thrill.

But many of us are keenly aware that vital threads in the social fabric have come unstrung, and, unstrung, threaten to unravel the whole. Place names evoke atrocity. Ferguson and Baltimore: the killing of unarmed black men by white police. Newtown: the massacre of small schoolchildren by a deranged shooter. Virginia Tech, Fort Hood,

Aurora: more massacre by the deranged. Along with place names, we remember the names of the dead: Trayvon Martin, Michael Brown, Eric Garner.

After each of these atrocities, the call goes out for a reckoning—but little comes of it.

Perhaps the massacre in Charleston, with its trifecta of lethal elements—guns, race hatred, and, new to the mix, white supremacy—will spur the public, heartbroken and weary over this cavalcade of death, to press for action.

Gun control. Really, action on this matter should be compelling by now. How much carnage must we bear? As the President put it post-Charleston, "Once again, innocent people were killed in part because someone who wanted to inflict harm had no trouble getting their hands on a gun."

While there's now a rush to gun stores to arm up, as occurred after other massacres, and while support for gun rights has steadily increased in recent years, there is nevertheless strong public support for various safety measures to control those rights. A recent Pew poll shows 85% of those polled approve of background checks for gun sales and 80% feel people with mental illness should not be able to buy guns (though why both figures aren't 100% is a mystery). And it's nonsense to hold, as Republicans do, that mental illness is more the problem than guns. It's not either-or, but both-and: We can attend to both—gun control *and* mental illness.

Other countries view America as barbaric, hardly advanced, in the carnage we permit—and they are right: The carnage *is* barbaric. As *The Washington Post* wrote post-Charleston in support of the President:

> "It isn't an accident that massacres like this one are extremely rare in other advanced countries that don't fetishize gun ownership the way we do. Believe it or not, there are violent people in England or Romania or Japan, but without our ready access to guns, the damage they do is limited."

While the President's challenge about advanced nations referred specifically to gun violence, the following two elements of the Charleston massacre certainly factor into a consideration of whether a nation is advanced or not.

Race hatred. While it is the case—a proud case—that as a nation America has made great progress in civil rights, most notably when a majority of voters elected an African-American to the White House but also, significantly, re-elected him to a second term, it also appears to be the case that certain segments of our society take vicious exception to this progress, and have become more blatant in the Obama era.

Obama-hatred, breathtaking in its virulence, has not been sufficiently combatted by Democrats; they should reform altogether. Some want Mr. Obama to be more "out there" on race, and since Charleston he has, notably in his eulogy for the murdered pastor, Clementa Pinckney. But to become perceived as "the angry black man" in the White House could risk making the race issue all about him, rather than the *collective* problem it properly is.

Republicans were hesitant to attribute the Charleston massacre to race hatred. But when a white man walks into a black church and murders black people, what other interpretation is there? Masters of subtle race-baiting, Republicans must, as *The New York Times* delicately puts it, "carefully calibrate" their words both to "appeal to minorities while also energizing white conservatives." As *The New Yorker* writes, Republicans, who

> "rely heavily on the votes of white southerners ... have sometimes been driven to cultivate support among gun groups, anti-immigrant groups, 'patriot' groups, and other inflammatory organizations that cluster around the right fringes of their party and beyond. And even when they aren't actively courting these entities, many prominent Republicans have been reluctant to say anything that could incur their wrath."

White supremacy. This is the new element in the mix—white supremacy: the ugliest face of race hatred—thrust to the fore by the Charleston shooter who, before killing the black parishioners, recited the white supremacist cant, "You are raping our women and taking over the country. You have to go." Photos of the shooter with the Confederate battle flag and the emblems of apartheid South Africa and Rhodesia confirm the connection. Bubbling under the surface for decades and growing increasingly rancid, white supremacist "thinking" now posits that a "white genocide" is underway, waged by inferior races, not just in the U.S. but world-wide.

Dealing with this phenomenon will be difficult, as white Americans continue to lose demographic ground to faster-growing minority groups. But at the least we need to unpack the historical fact that, no matter how vigorously whites may have worked for blacks' civil rights, it is the case that, in the beginning, the white race brought the black race to this country—in chains—and thus have the duty to see those chains in all their manifestations—social, political, economic—completely broken.

Removing the Confederate flag, a symbol of white supremacy, from public places and putting it in a museum is a first step. Republican South Carolina governor Nikki Haley is to be commended for recognizing that a symbol of heritage embraced by many Southerners has been hijacked as an emblem of race hatred. (Of the "heritage, not hate" formulation, however, African-American writer Jelani Cobb notes, "The great sleight of hand is the notion that these things were mutually exclusive.") Notable also is Republican state representative Norman Brannon's candor in supporting the flag's removal. A friend of Pastor Clementa Pinckney, who also served in the legislature as a senator, he stated: "It took my buddy's death to get me to do this. I should feel ashamed of myself." Encouragingly, other Southern states are following suit and select retailers are removing the flag from stock.

But much more reckoning must be done, beyond a flag, and it will take more candor, more courageous leadership, and more effort from We the People. At a time when the public is retreating in disgust from gridlock politics and voter participation is dropping, all citizens must stay engaged. Weary as we are, consider how weary blacks are in insisting their lives matter. (Whites joining in solidarity with blacks at post-Charleston memorials is a stirring sight.) President Obama by himself can't get us to that vaunted place, the "post-racial society"; it is up to us. How to go about it?

One major way is to push back—emphatically—at any racist or white supremacist expression, starting with the forthcoming Fourth of July family picnic. This will be difficult—Americans prize free speech, everyone's speech, as an elemental right—but the Charleston massacre makes a powerful case: Two friends of the shooter now express regret that, hearing the shooter's wild fantasies earlier, they did not stop him. One friend, reported by *The New York Times*, now feels guilt: "I feel we could have done something and prevented this whole thing."

Another friend says of the shooter, "He was a racist; but I don't judge people." Americans, especially of recent generations, pride themselves on being non-judgmental. But there is a vast difference between tolerance of personal opinion and tolerance of criminal plans. Nine people are dead because judgment was suspended. This friend also said the shooter spoke of wanting "to start a civil war," but the friend didn't take him seriously. We must take white supremacy seriously.

At the national level, leaders in all walks—political, religious, business—need to work forward from this historic moment in Charleston, when guns, race hatred, and white supremacy came together in a fatal but also revealing combination. Leaders must understand the power of their words to ignite or construct, and take care.

In our cultural fare, creative minds must rethink the hip trend of "breaking bad" and pursue the much harder (and more dramatic) task of showing characters pushing back against the bad to break good. Spare us the dramatic investigation into the heart of the Charleston shooter and his ilk. Give us tales of the likes of parishioner Tywanza Sanders, the young man who during the massacre tried to dissuade the shooter and who died trying to protect his aunt. Where does such moral character come from?

Advanced nations, in the tales they tell themselves, don't fetishize violence, dysfunction, or pathology, as we do at present. Instead, a nation truly advanced has a capacity and relish for moral drama: tales of characters examining the rightness and wrongness of things and taking action, as ancient Greece did at its height. Granted, many Greek dramas were tragic, but the real tragedy for America is if we continue to glorify the amoral and mock the moral. American culture offers little to stay the hand of a shooter, to connect him to the humanity of his soon-to-be victims, even as he looks into their faces, and offers too much that negates that shared humanity.

Meanwhile, other advanced countries might temper their criticism of America for its race hatred, especially if these other advanced countries are mono-ethnic or are guilty of ostracizing members of their own societies as lesser. How one's country maintains its mono-ethnicity might bear investigation, and reform. America is a multi-ethnic melting pot working out, for all the world to see, the problems afflicting all peoples of all nations throughout History.

To point our way, we have the memory of Martin Luther King, Jr. It was Dr. King's genius as a strategist—to hold America accountable in its stated profession to love both the Bible and the Constitution—that got us to this comparatively advanced stage in race relations and that can guide us through this reactionary time. To do unto others as we would have done unto us, and to treat each other as equal before the law: This is the formula for racial comity—and a truly advanced nation.

—*HuffPost*, June 30, 2015

Books for Our Times: *Winner-Take-All Politics*, by Jacob S. Hacker and Paul Pierson

Sixth in an ongoing series, Books for Our Times

To ENSURE A book's long life, authors should pick a big problem that remains unsolved and big. Money in politics, for one. This time, not the money in political campaigns, but the money that secures and exerts power in Washington.

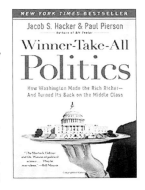

Winner-Take-All Politics, published in 2011 and surveying the ruin of the 2008 financial crash, can serve as a useful diagnosis, if not a roadmap, to the debates in the upcoming 2016 presidential election. With income inequality and the struggles of the middle and working classes cited by Democratic and Republican candidates alike as central to their campaigns (more so to Democrats than to Republicans), this book explains how moneyed interests came to reign supreme and how everything else—the country and the people therein—comes in a distant second. The subtitle is *How Washington Made the Rich Richer—and Turned Its Back on the Middle Class*.

Authored by two professors of political science—Jacob S. Hacker at Yale and Paul Pierson at Berkeley—this book details the "thirty-year war" beginning in the 1970s when moneyed interests mounted an organized campaign—with the cooperation of politicians from *both* parties—to secure the policies that ensure that their interests prevail, while also "structuring the economy to shift the risks of their new economic playground

[29]

downward." It is an odyssey taking us from "Broadland," a place of broadly-shared prosperity in the early post-World War II years, to a place political thinker Robert Frank calls "Richistan," where only the richest prosper.

How is this possible, the authors ask in their introduction: How can a Richistan develop in a democracy? How did we move from a "mixed economy, where fast growth was widely shared," toward a winner-take-all "capitalist oligarchy"?

> *"If government has played a central part, how could this happen? In a country where public officials must regularly face the judgment of citizens at the polls, how could their efforts come to so persistently favor the very few?"*

Hacker and Pierson take the rest of the book to answer this question, casting their tale in the context of "a long struggle rooted in the interplay of American democracy and American capitalism." Through this lens, they focus on the legislation and regulation-writing that lock in advantage and—equally important—the legislative "drift" that does little to reduce that advantage and spread prosperity around.

Enroute, the authors in Part One, "The Winner-Take-All Economy," present the data, showing the stratospheric increase in incomes of the 1%, the "have-it-alls," contrasted with stagnating incomes for everybody else. Graphs usually make my eyes glaze over, but they popped open at the one showing the increase in average household after-tax income 1979-2006, with only an 11% rise for the poorest fifth—and a 256% rise for the top 1%. Likewise the graph showing the plunging tax rates of the rich, thanks to tax cuts, loopholes, evasion. Tax audits on the rich have also plummeted, while—astonishingly—"about the only area where audits have gone up is among poorer taxpayers."

With the middle and working classes suffering stagnating social mobility, vanishing retirement benefits, debt accumulation, also tax audits, the metaphor of a rising tide lifting all boats no longer pertains; instead,

"What if the modern economy looks...more like a system of locks, where those who don't get through the gates are left behind? Yachts are rising, but dinghies are largely staying put....Indeed, there is reason to suspect that the dinghies are staying put in part because the yachts are rising—that the rich are closing the locks behind them to capture resources that would otherwise have enhanced the living standards of everyone else."

Who are our era's super-rich? Executives and managers in business and finance mainly, notably those in finance, about whom, the authors have little good to say, in light of the '08 crash they largely were responsible for: The financial "innovations" they concocted "proved to be just fancier (and riskier) ways of gambling with other people's money." Moreover—importantly—"most of these 'innovations' could occur only because of the failure to update financial rules to protect against the resulting risk"—drift in action (or inaction). Bailing out this "talent" was the furious taxpayer.

A brief history of the American story is given, from our blessed starting point—land in abundance—to rising industrialism and the Gilded Age, to Progressive reform and Teddy Roosevelt's trust-busting to restrain "unfair money-getting," to the Great Depression and FDR's New Deal, establishing "a new economic order—built on the conviction that the federal government had a responsibility to stabilize the economy, provide economic security and ensure at least a modicum of redistribution from rich to poor."

A brief survey of thought on the perils wealth poses to governance is also given, from Plutarch ("An imbalance between rich and poor is the oldest and most fatal ailment of all republics"), to Hume ("Where the riches are in a few hands, these must enjoy all the power and will readily conspire to lay the whole burden on the poor"), to Montesquieu ("To men of overgrown estates, everything which does not contribute to advance their power and honor is considered by them as an injury"). In the new American republic, Madison feared "the mischief of faction," believing the most common source of faction to be the "unequal distribution of property."

Favorite philosopher of America's economic "winners" is Adam Smith. Their skyrocketing gains are "simply the impersonal beneficence of Smith's 'invisible hand,' the natural outcome of free-market forces," with government having no role at all in wealth-creation. Which, the authors say, is all myth:

> "The truth is that most people have missed the visible hand of government.... They have talked about the minimum wage, the Earned Income Tax Credit, Medicaid...in short, programs that help those at the bottom. The real story, however, is what our national political elites have done for those at the top, both through their actions and through their deliberate failures to act."

This story is told in Parts Two and Three: How *did* money-power acquire the politics it needs? Cautioning against looking only at elections and their spectacle, as today's media tend to do, the authors examine the policy-making machinery itself, the unspectacular but vital through-line of lobbying and legislation—*"what the government was actually doing"* (their italics)—that has resulted in today's "managerist" system, in which managerial elites are in position to extract resources.

Getting granular, the authors propose that this transformation began in the fall of 1972, when the National Association of Manufacturers moved its main offices from New York to Washington. As its head officer observed:

> "We have been in New York since before the turn of the century, because we regarded this city as the center of business and industry. But the thing that affects business most today is government. The interrelationship of business with business is no longer so important as the interrelationship of business with government."

Business had experienced setback after setback in the years prior, not only during Lyndon Johnson's Great Society but also Republican Richard Nixon's tenure, when "Washington undertook a vast expansion of its regulatory power, introducing tough and extensive restrictions and requirements on business in areas from the environment to occupational safety to consumer protection."

Getting even more granular, the authors (who characterize themselves as sleuths) trace the galvanizing call to action to a 1971 memo from future Supreme Court justice Lewis Powell, written when he chaired the education committee of the U.S. Chamber of Commerce. In it Powell declared the "American economic system is under broad attack," against which mobilization for political combat was required:

> "Business must learn the lesson ... that political power is necessary; that such power must be assiduously cultivated; and that when necessary, it must be used aggressively and with determination—without embarrassment and without the reluctance which has been so characteristic of American business.... Strength lies in organization, in careful long-range planning and implementation, in consistency of action over an indefinite period of years, in the scale of financing available only through joint effort, and in the political power available only through united action and national organizations."

This battle plan has been carried out brilliantly, "a domestic version of Shock and Awe." The metrics impress: In just a decade's time, corporate public affairs offices in Washington grew from 100 to over 500; registered corporate lobbyists grew from 175 to 2,500; corporate PACs increased from 300 in 1976 to over 1,200 by the mid-'80s. The Chamber doubled its membership in that period and tripled its budget. Corporate coalitions formed (Business Roundtable for one); corporate-funded think tanks arose (American Enterprise Institute); corporate PAC giving increased "massively." And growth on all these fronts has been runaway ever since.

Equally impressive are the legislative "products" achieved by corporate lobbying, launching the rich into the stratosphere. The authors go into great detail, naming names and organizational sponsors, to describe tax cut after tax cut after tax cut; the adoption of the capital gains tax (allowing payment at the comparatively low rate of 15%, used especially by those in finance) and the "carried interest" provision "that allows this sweetheart deal"; the gutting of the progressive tax rate; the back-dating of stock-option values, "reset retroactively to provide big gains for executives":

> "When the Financial Accounting Standards Board, which oversees accounting practices, tried to make firms report the costs of stock options like other compensation...it was beaten back by a bipartisan coalition in the Senate galvanized by industry opposition. This is a textbook example of drift."

While Republicans are the principal promoters of these products, Democrats have participated too, feeling forced by the onslaught of corporate money in Washington to "show the love" toward business. Former senator Phil Gramm is cited as a Republican who was a particularly ardent champion of the rich. Calling Wall Street a "holy place," Gramm was key to repeal of the Glass-Steagall Act and the creation of legislation prohibiting regulation of derivatives, both of which enabled much greater risk-taking and much bigger paydays for Wall Street.

But Democrats have been co-enablers of the winner-take-all economy. The savings-and-loan debacle of the '80s was a "thoroughly bipartisan affair," with Democrats joining in to free up the industry of regulation. One of those Democrats, Senator Chuck Schumer, has proved a special friend of Wall Street (which, granted, lies in his district). Schumer was key to passage of the capital gains/carried interest package, supported Gramm's bill to repeal Glass-Steagall, and led bipartisan efforts to sharply reduce the fees Wall Street pays the federal government and to reduce SEC oversight of credit-ratings agencies. While Gramm "was more often the battering ram" for the economic elites, "Schumer, by contrast, was more often the master of drift":

"[Schumer] was the one who made sure that his party—the one most likely to push for serious oversight of Wall Street—remains as friendly as possible to the interest of the captains of finance."

Sadly, Democratic politicians, in tending more to corporate interests, have become less diligent in championing the middle and working classes. The legislative drift allowed by Democrats and by increased use of the filibuster—"the No Deal rather than the New Deal"—has meant billions of dollars of lost revenue for programs to aid Middle America. Middle America has also suffered from the decline of unions and the civic organizations that once were its stalwart defenders, like the American Legion, which successfully mounted a nationwide campaign after World War II to secure the G.I. Bill. Now these organizations focus more on social issues (EMILY's List on pro-choice candidates) than the pocketbook issues so crucial to those struggling in a damaged economy. Little wonder people tell pollsters they do not feel politicians feel their plight; they're right, the authors say.

Meanwhile, the economic elites get all the representation they need, and as the authors claim, it matters little who or what party occupy the White House; what's key are whose hands work the levers of government. Contrary to partisan expectation, it was the Republican Richard Nixon who accelerated financial regulation, while continuing LBJ's social program. It was under Democrat Jimmy Carter that the first major tax cuts were passed and the first steps toward financial deregulation were taken. And it was the Democrat Bill Clinton who took financial deregulation to its height, with repeal of Glass-Steagall. Republican Ronald Reagan stands out less for his legislation and more for his anti-union (firing the federal air traffic controllers) and anti-statist stances—"Government is not the solution, government is the problem"—masking the fact that government very much *is* a capitalist's solution.

What's the solution for Middle America? Organization, organization, organization, urge the authors. To counter the organization of the moneyed interests, Middle America needs to grow the reform organizations that can call on their membership to press for reform in a comprehensive and sustained way. The present winner-take-all economy is not "economic destiny," the authors assert, but a product of politics; thus, the solution is through politics. A very tall order, yes, but the authors harken to the Progressive era of the early 20th century as proof America has reformed itself before.

As for the authors' claim about the irrelevance of who sits in the White House: I take issue, to this extent. Inasmuch as a George Washington visionary has not emerged from Wall Street or the corporate sector since the '08 crash, one who combines business savvy with a humanitarian feeling for Middle America and who could reset the balance more equitably, we *could* look to a President to craft that rebalance. Even if Middle America attained more degree-certified education, as Hacker and Pierson note, it still would be on the downside from the managerist state; the balance needs resetting. The great experiment of American capitalism and democracy has always borne internal tension; the problem is, there's not tension enough now, all the power lies with the moneyed elites. Who among the presidential candidates could reintroduce that tension, for better equilibrium? Who could persuade Wall Street to preserve, if not the common good, then the American "brand"?

So far, only the Democratic candidates qualify. Bernie Sanders' rapid rise in the polls is due to his full-throated attack on "the billionaires." Hillary Clinton is being pulled left by Sanders, but while she's stomping for Middle America, Clinton's economic policy prescriptions fall short of root-and-branch reform. The Republican candidates still recite the elites' playbook, businessman Donald Trump most bombastically.

For insights helpful to Middle America, *Winner-Take-All Politics* takes the prize. While the book could benefit from crisper organization (there's some authorial drift; thank heavens for the index), it nevertheless presents all the factual ammunition and clarifying diagnosis of our predicament that any reformer and motivated citizen could need. To a New Day.

—*HuffPost*, July 30, 2015

Atticus Finch as Racist Bigot: "More Human"?

IT'S BEEN A tough season of late for heroes. They are shattering all around. Lance Armstrong, who beat cancer to win the Tour de France a record seven times, is revealed to be a doper who bullied other cyclists into silence. Greg Mortenson, who claimed to build hundreds of schools in Afghanistan, a humanitarian project described in his book *Three Cups of Tea*, is revealed to be a fraud. Bill Cosby, who used his fame as a comedian to lecture his fellow African-Americans on how to live, is now alleged to be a major lecher, drugging women to have sex with them.

Possibly toughest of all—no less so because he is fictional and not a real person—is the loss of Atticus Finch, the lawyer and father of the narrator in Harper Lee's beloved novel *To Kill a Mockingbird*, who risked his reputation and his family's safety to go against the white establishment of the 1930s South to represent and defend in court a black man, Tom Robinson, falsely accused of raping a white woman.

As all the world knows by now, that characterization of Atticus has been damaged, if not destroyed, by the revelation in Ms. Lee's newly published novel—*Go Set a Watchman*, which picks up the action of *Mockingbird* twenty years later—that Atticus Finch in his older years became a racist bigot.

Atticus Finch: racist bigot? Much of the media coverage of this stunning revelation can be filed under the heading "To kill an icon." Why does this loss feel so acute? Because the Atticus Finch of *Mockingbird* was something we do not have in this reduced, amoral age: a moral hero. To do what he did—defending a black man—in a region of the country that only generations earlier held black people as slaves, and doing the defending alone—at a time preceding an organized civil rights movement—qualified him as a true moral hero, one who, weighing the rightness and wrongness of things, steps up and does the right thing.

It was this Atticus Finch, the moral icon, for whom parents named their sons; in fact, the name has grown in popularity with the years. Countless lawyers went into the law because of this Atticus. Countless people who endured a cold childhood wished they'd had Atticus as a father. *Mockingbird* is a curriculum staple in the nation's schools. The film adaptation, winning its star Gregory Peck an Oscar for best actor, has become a classic. The American Film Institute voted Atticus Finch the №1 movie hero of all time. He inspired, profoundly, this cultural icon.

Now, in *Watchman*—it's painful to relate the following—we have an Atticus who, as discovered by his now-grown daughter, has a pamphlet lying around titled "The Black Plague" and who attends the local council dedicated to preserving the second-class stature of blacks and opposing "mongrelization." Who asks his daughter: "Do you want Negroes by the carload in our schools and churches and theaters? Do you want them in our world?" Who admonishes his daughter for her idealistic view of racial equality: "The Negroes down here are still in their childhood as a people." Who denounces the U.S. Supreme Court (the novel is set in the 1950s in the era of the *Brown v. Board of Education* school desegregation decision) and wants his home state of Alabama "to be left alone to keep house without advice from the N.A.A.C.P."

As described further by a reviewer:

> *"Atticus ... isn't a vicious white supremacist bent on hurting black people. But he's committed to states' rights and Southern tradition, and sees only catastrophe in an integrated society. In essence, a man who's used*

the courts in search of racial justice seeks to keep blacks in their place with the help of the law. Under a mask of dedication to American-style self-reliance—he's said to have 'a constitutional distrust of paternalism and government in large doses'—Atticus supports racism."

Unsettling as these revelations are, also unsettling is the commentary attesting that such revelations make Atticus "more human." Not so.

To be sure, in attesting to a racist Atticus as "more human," commentators, to the extent they make it clear, claim this development adds complexity and complication to an idealized portrait of Atticus in *Mockingbird*, one painted by an innocent and idolizing young daughter. O.K., true: Atticus *is* now more complex, more complicated.

But if you hold what it means to be human to a high standard, if you define humanity upward and not downward toward pathology, then someone who categorically denies the humanity of an entire class of people, based on whatever grounds, and reserves all authority for his own class, as the racist does, then that person cannot be said to be fully human himself. He is *less* human, not more. This includes the Atticus of *Watchman*, who condescends to blacks as a people still in their childhood.

This tendency to redefine humanity downward is increasingly evident in our new cultural icons. See: Chemistry teacher Walter White of the wildly popular TV series "Breaking Bad"—this title itself illustrates the downward tendency—who, terminally ill, cooks meth to provide for his family, an objective presumably making this criminal "more human." See: Mob boss Tony Soprano, of the wildly popular TV series "The Sopranos," who "whacks" his rivals and becomes "more human" by sharing the stresses of his criminal life with a psychotherapist. The power of these icons is seen in the example of Gordon Gekko, amoral financier of the 1987 film *Wall Street*, whose credo "Greed is good" filtered into the culture and became the norm. See: Countless Wall Street types who cite this credo as their mantra. Cultural degradation comes about step by downward step; it then becomes "only human" to engage in these reduced norms, permitting everything from cooking meth to whacking rivals to taking risks that blow up the financial system.

(Parenthetically, regarding Armstrong, Mortenson, and Cosby cited earlier, I don't detect any explaining away of their sins—doping and bullying, fraud, and lechery, respectively—as making them "more human.")

With the revelation in *Watchman* of Atticus Finch as racist, this Atticus does indeed become "more human" in this respect: If he did harbor the racist leanings in *Mockingbird* that are made manifest in *Watchman*, then in defending Tom Robinson as vigorously as he did in *Mockingbird*, he achieved, precisely because of his own profound internal struggle, something even greater than was recognized at the time. Atticus did a great and good thing—for Tom, for society—*despite* his true racist self.

I would like to think that the Atticus Finch so universally loved as a moral icon would himself ultimately recognize his own internal contradictions, the hideous flaw in his own humanity, and take himself to account. The path might be via his lawyerly training and faith in the law. In *Mockingbird* he calls the courts "the great leveler"; he might pull himself level, finally, with the Tom Robinsons of the world.

Or Atticus might have a catharsis—fully recognizing late what he did not know earlier—and fully recognize the great human wisdom he mouthed in *Mockingbird*, that: "You never really understand a person until you consider things from his point of view, until you climb into his skin and walk around in it." When I as a questing teen first heard that line, I knew it was Truth. For Atticus the white supremacist to climb into the skin of Tom Robinson and truly recognize Tom's humanity, and Tom's moral heroism, would redeem Atticus and make him truly "more human." More than that, it would make Atticus and Tom "more human" to each other.

I also hope against hope Harper Lee has a third novel in store, that takes the events of *Mockingbird* and *Watchman* and weighs them at the end of the day. In *Watchman*, when Atticus' racism fully penetrates, the daughter lashes out: "I'll never believe a word you say to me again. I despise you and everything you stand for." While Atticus deserves this outburst and the daughter is entitled to her fury at the loss of her idol, nonetheless she comes across as self-righteous. (In our twenties we can be awfully self-righteous, especially when we are right.) Adding complexity and complication, the father she now attacks is the same father who planted the fundamentals of racial justice she embraces. It would be fascinating to see the daughter, fully matured, seek to understand the forces that shaped her father, and to see Atticus seek to resolve his contradictions, or be forced to. Squaring their circle—in microcosm, America's Original Sin—would yield the "more human" tale as well as history.

In all the media play about *Watchman*, I couldn't help wondering how the film incarnation of Atticus, Gregory Peck, would react to the revelation his character was deep down a bigot. Peck was a life-long champion of civil rights, who chose his roles carefully. In *Gentleman's Agreement*, he played a reporter investigating anti-Semitism in '40s America. When it came to Atticus, Peck personally identified with him: "I never had a part that came close to being the real me until Atticus Finch." It would be fascinating to see Peck furrow the brow and grapple with Atticus' racism.

Some of the media play took down *Mockingbird* itself, noting the latent racism in that Atticus. An essay titled "Mockingbird, Inc." not only questions (rightly) the circumstances behind the publication of *Watchman*, citing an over-eager publisher, but also takes down the Atticus Finch of *Mockingbird*, snidely reducing him to "a walking soapbox for moralistic bromides." Such takedown, however, begs the question: *How did that "moralistic" Atticus Finch become so beloved?* In an amoral time such are ours, we want—no, we *need*—the moral hero. Mob bosses who whack rivals can never fill that yearning, no matter how "human" they're made out to be.

In all this it should be noted that black people generally do not regard *Mockingbird* as highly as white people do. Nobel laureate Toni Morrison calls it a "white savior" narrative that reduces blacks to mere spectators in their own struggle for equality.

How timely this discussion, this moral drama is. In this post-Charleston, post-Ferguson moment, when black people are claiming ever more insistently that black lives matter, it is becoming ever more clear that white supremacy and white privilege must be unpacked and resolved—by white people. As historian Taylor Branch says, "Things are starting to shake loose." Isabel Wilkerson, African-American writer, asks, "Could we now be at the start of a true and more meaningful reconstruction?" To get us there, we will need all sorts of heroes.

To kill a racist bigot (metaphorically)—and gain true humanity.

—*HuffPost*, August 31, 2015

The Speech Hillary Clinton Should Give to the 1% on Capitalism and Income Inequality

FAT CATS, MEMBERS of the 1 Percent, the Filthy Rich: Just kidding....

I come in peace and I come with a proposal—an investment proposal and a course-correction—to restore and secure this great country going forward. You, America's wealthy class, are key to the American Renaissance.

At the moment, you and your kind—and this is no kidding—are not held in high esteem by the general public. Rightly or wrongly—rightly, I would submit—the public holds your class, those members operating and speculating on Wall Street, responsible for crashing the economy in 2008, which led to the worst economic upheaval since the Great Depression of the 1930s. The public's anger exploded—understandably, I would also submit—when their hard-earned tax dollars were used to bail out those irresponsible institutions responsible for the crash.

Acting on that low estimation of your class, my Democratic opponent for the White House, Senator Bernie Sanders, vows once in office to make war—a "political revolution"—on the millionaires and billionaires. His combative stance is garnering a huge and energetic following, reflecting the public's deep anger and discontent with the state of things generally and, specifically, with the income inequality now rising to historic heights.

Meanwhile Donald Trump, billionaire and leading Republican contender, is giving your class heartburn—and picking up populist points—by talking about raising taxes on "the hedge fund guys" and ending the practice of corporations avoiding U.S. taxes by setting up shell corporations abroad. While I agree with these proposals in general, there are other aspects of Mr. Trump's bombastic approach—call him "the ugly capitalist"—that give Capitalism a bad name and strike exactly the wrong chord at this hinge moment in American history.

So: Between a President Sanders and his pitchfork and a President Trump and his turbo-capitalism, you have me: Hillary Clinton, Broker. Rather than mindlessly engage in class warfare or mindlessly pursue more dog-eat-dog Capitalism, can we not sit on our oars a moment and redefine the kind of Capitalism that best serves America and, doing so, make a course-correction? We are talking historic here.

Theories and their systems become caricatures of their original objective if not handled wisely and recalibrated. Communism is one example; perhaps Capitalism is another. Certainly the human costs, if not the utility, of dog-eat-dog Capitalism have become too dear. Adam Smith's *theory* of "the invisible hand" of individual self-interest driving the free market has become, today, the harsh *reality* of a hand of gargantuan size extracting the lion's share of our nation's profits and assets. History shows that nations dominated by extractive elites, while they may thrive for a while—think Rome or Spain—in the long run cannot prevail, either as a nation or an elite.

Now, you may think the term "extractive" too harsh, but how is it not factually correct? How is the fact that the top 1% control 40% of the nation's wealth, with their incomes rising 18% in just the last decade—how is this not extractive? You may call it a talent for optimizing opportunity, but others call it extractive.

So, the question becomes: Can the wealthy elite in America become less extractive? Can America find its way to a more equitable place and make this crucial course-correction? To quote a winning campaign slogan, "Yes, we can."

America has always represented the Land of Opportunity. Unique in the history of humankind, a history replete with autocratic rule and faceless masses, America's grand project has been to take two systems—Capitalism and Democracy—and create a working construct powered by and in turn empowering both the citizen and the capitalist. Equilibrium is required, or the project breaks down. If the capitalist extracts too much reward and the citizen too little, or if the capitalist dominates the political sphere leaving the citizen powerless, the system is in disequilibrium. On both counts, America is at present in disequilibrium.

So, my proposal and my appeal to you: Rather than extract, reinvest. Reinvest in this grand project—America's historic Capitalism-and-Democracy machine—and restore equilibrium.

This machine works best when it works for all, citizen and capitalist alike. Perhaps this machine reached peak performance in the decades after World War II. Granted, it helped that we won the war and could build from an intact industrial base. But it also helped that workers could earn a living wage, could afford to buy a house, could afford to send their children to college, could afford to take the occasional vacation.

That ideal state does not exist anymore. Today CEOs make 300 times what their workers take home, compared to only 20 times as much in the 1960s—while workers' wages have remained stagnant for decades. Now people on Main Street may work two jobs just to make ends meet, they go into debt to finance a house or send their children to college, they live in nerve-racking anxiety. To maintain this unbalanced system, the wealthy elite has secured the politics it needs, with fleets of Washington lobbyists and, thanks to a compliant Supreme Court, unlimited campaign donations.

How did this breakdown happen? The reasons are various—some say greed, others say corruption, too much of a muchness. The culture changed, too: In the immediate post-World War II period, Gordon Gekko would have been just a Disney-cute reptile, not the espouser of the "Greed is good" mentality dominant today.

But whatever the reasons for the breakdown, can we not organize ourselves better? In his essay titled "Politics," the great American philosopher Ralph Waldo Emerson in 1844 posed a test applying to all nations at all times when he asked: "Are our methods now so excellent that all competition is hopeless? Could not a nation...devise better ways?"

We need to devise a better Capitalism, one with a human face.

Now, a first reaction from your quarter is to cry "Redistributionist!"—to fear the loss of one's assets through confiscatory taxation. But, honestly and to put it plainly: *Hasn't a kind of redistribution already taken place, with the wealthy elite's leaps in wealth and assets*, especially since the 2008 financial crash?

Another notion I hear among the wealthy is that Americans don't work hard enough. But how does that square with the demonstrable fact that, despite their stagnant wages, American workers are more productive than ever? And the notion that Main Street is resentful of wealth, heard in Mitt Romney's 2012 presidential run, is off the mark. Americans don't resent wealth; they just want their fair crack at it. We're all capitalists here; nobody is arguing for a barter economy or a command economy run by the state; we all salute the market economy. But I will argue, we can argue, for a market economy that's more equitable, for Capitalism with a human face.

Capitalism with a human face: What is that? What does it mean for you, the wealthy elite? I am no economist, but I am a politician, and being among the people of Main Street, I hear the anger, the anxiety, the sorrow. Imagine living with no financial security, none. This state of things cannot be maintained without reaching a flashpoint, with who knows what consequences. How to prevent that flashpoint?

For one thing, by paying your fair share of taxes. Enough with CEOs paying at a lower rate than their secretaries. Main Street has heard this *ad nauseam* and, frankly, they're sick of it. Those CEOs should do the equitable thing and fix it. And no more shell corporations set up abroad to avoid taxes at home. That lost revenue means our roads and bridges and railways and airports—the very infrastructure on which the American economy moves—fall into disrepair and collapse, sometimes with fatal results. Flying into U.S. airports today, as I hear many of you say, is like flying into a third-world country. Well, let's fix that. And stand for financial regulation—smart regulation—not block it. Systems cannot function without rules.

Other reforms, to be specified, would follow from the course-correction I propose; my focus here is on the general. None of this is rocket science, it is simple equity. Generally, it means giving up gains that, to put it plainly, are ill-gotten, and remitting those gains to the American people. At the least, it means reinvesting in Brand America—and why wouldn't you reinvest in the very foundation of your wealth? At most, it means renewal of America's grand project.

All this may strike you as bold, outrageous, even radical. As Emerson said, "Nothing so astonishes as common sense and plain dealing." But I say it because it needs to be said *and* done and because—more plain dealing—no such voice has been heard from your class saying these things *and* doing something about it, no voice who could ask the ultimate question: "How much is enough? How many homes, how many yachts, how many *tchotchkes* do we need?"

Imagine if Mitt Romney, wealthy financier, had campaigned in this mode. If he had addressed, say, income inequality and declared: "It's simply not right that my class gets to enjoy all the fruits of this great system of ours, while people not so fortunate suffer in poverty, untreated illness, the terrible anxiety of not knowing what the next day will bring. I grieve over that, it's simply not right. And if you elect me, I'll endeavor to redress that balance." And if Romney had said to his Wall Street peers: "As stewards of America's great financial system, we must take responsibility for the recent crash, not duck it. For in campaigning I have met the good souls of Main Street and, I tell you, it is simply wrong that they be injured further by forces within our control. We must see our mission as one that maximizes returns not just to our companies, but to this great country."

That Romney, business-savvy and humane, echoing Teddy Roosevelt, might very well have been elected President (and might have prevented Donald Trump). That Romney might also have been the savior of American Capitalism.

So, I say what Mitt Romney did not say, nor has any Republican candidate said in this campaign so far, and I ask that you work with me for a course-correction. While Democrat Bernie Sanders advocates a similar course-correction, it is, again, as a declaration of war—on you.

Finally, I have to ask: As investors, *why* would you re-invest in the same Republican policies that broke the economy in the first place and, moreover, could do and did little to repair it? *Why would you do that?* Just asking. And, since Democrats believe in government, if elected I vow to make government work better. Your tax dollars remitted to the U.S. Government should work much, much better.

The idea that we are all in the same boat is a cliché, an old one, but it is profoundly true: We really are all of us—the 1% and the 99%—in the same boat. We must all take care not to capsize the boat in which we are all passengers, we must all do our part to repair our leaking craft. On the horizon lies a New Day for America. All hands on deck!

—*HuffPost*, September 21, 2015

Corporate "Talent" Must Imagine
Worst-Case Scenario, i.e., Ruination

YOU WOULD THINK a corporation with high-priced "talent" in its executive suite could imagine the risks—to the corporation if not to consumers or their own employees—if it crossed the legal line. Of course, you'd hope those executives wouldn't even think of crossing that line. But if they did, you'd think they could imagine the worst-case scenario—corporate ruination—if their illegal risk-taking blew up on them.

Ruination, as in: Plummeting stock price. Screaming headlines. Recalls and fixes. Hearings and investigations. Lawsuits and damages. Employees thrown out of work. Consumer trust destroyed. Possible liquidation of the corporation itself and extinction of the brand. Prison. Ruination of a graphic and no-kidding kind.

Most corporations, through continuous mission review, operate with a sound sense of corporate self-survival. But in several outstanding cases of late—Volkswagen, General Motors, Peanut Corporation of America—apparently not. The consumer is left to wonder: What *were* they thinking? And if a corporation's product could kill them—such as a car or food—the consumer understandably becomes livid.

Take Peanut Corporation of America: Astoundingly, it knowingly shipped salmonella-tainted peanut butter paste to companies that then, unknowingly, used it to manufacture products such as cookies, crackers, and airline snacks, ultimately killing nine people and sickening as many as 20,000 others. Even though lab tests showed salmonella in their product, the bottom line trumped lethal implications: Emails from the CEO ordered employees to "Just ship it" and "Turn them loose" and complained that delay "is costing us huge $$$$$."

That CEO was recently sentenced to 28 years in prison, longest sentence in U.S. history for a food contamination case. Also doing time are his brother, the company's food broker, and (sick joke) the company's quality-control manager. Apparently, at no time did the brothers game out the downside of their criminal machinations, but doubled-down on them over the two-year period of the outbreak (2008-09). Meanwhile, their quality control was a joke: Despite lab reports showing otherwise, the company created fake certificates affirming salmonella-free product. So much for public safety.

General Motors, likewise astoundingly, continued manufacturing—for more than a decade—certain models whose ignition switch could automatically shut off the engine when the car was in motion, as attested to by upset customers and dealers. Exacerbating the problem: When the engine shut off, the air-bag could not deploy, which in a crash could be life-saving. The crash statistics: 124 dead and 275 injured, 17 of whom included brain damage, paralysis, or amputation. Yet only recently, in 2014—despite knowing of this problem as early as 2001—did GM issue recalls of the questionable models.

Why didn't the red light go on at GM, signaling an imminent P.R. disaster for the company, not to mention a human one? Corporate culture may be the problem, according to an internal investigation: It cited a "resistance to raising issues" and "information silos" that block information-sharing. It also noted employees and managers were urged to report "smart," not use words like "defect" but neutral ones like "issue." Cost concerns also leach the human from the equation: A GM manager closed down an investigation into the ignition defect, saying the "lead time for all solutions is too long," "the tooling cost and piece price are too high," and none of the proposed fixes "represents an acceptable business case." Clearly, "business case" needs rethinking.

Perhaps GM's new CEO, Mary Barra, can rescue the company. Certainly she came in asking the right question: What took the recalls so long? She is also endeavoring to put the customer first and foremost in the company culture. But it remains to be seen if GM can recapture its storied name, given the raft of lawsuits, hearings, and even more recalls. (The regulatory agency overseeing GM, the National Highway Traffic Safety Administration, also needs to step up its game: It repeatedly held there was insufficient evidence to merit an investigation of the ignition problem.)

And now, the scandal commanding headlines is Volkswagen. Astoundingly—pardon the repetition, but it's the best word describing all these scandals—for seven years, since 2008, Volkswagen has been installing a "cheat device" in their diesel models that turns off the emissions system when undergoing an emissions test, but out on the road spews 40 times the legal levels permitted. The hypocrisy: proudly touting "clean diesel" while pumping ungodly amounts of toxics into the atmosphere!

VW stock has fallen 30% and market value 43% since the scandal broke; VW owners trying to resell are finding few buyers for their car, diesel or standard. But this is not only a corporate and consumer scandal, it is a national scandal for Germany: Vaunted "German engineering" and the country's post-World War II rehabilitation as honest and trustworthy have taken hits, while the government expresses grave concern for the economy if its biggest manufacturer and biggest exporter falters. In Wolfsburg, the one-company town where VW is headquartered, a local newspaper reports workers and residents gripped by tension and fear.

Why didn't the red light go on at Volkswagen? The CEO during this era was famously ambitious, determined to grow market share in the U.S., where there's room for growth in diesel sales; he was also famously a bully of subordinates in the pursuit of those ambitions (he resigned when scandal broke). But VW managers are likewise famously known for their engineering prowess: Did they not engineer a worst-case scenario, mapping out the ruination to come if they proceeded with the cheat device, and present it to the bullying CEO? As to the cheat device, with so many engineers in the mix, it beggars belief for them to claim ignorance.

And it beggars belief that no one—no one?—in the executive suites of these three corporations saw catastrophe coming. Thus it is—through self-inflicted wounds, blindly delivered—the world's largest carmaker (VW) and second-largest (GM) are brought low and the Peanut Corporation of America is done and liquidated.

We all know of course about company loyalty and peer pressure and competitive career tracks getting in the way of reform, but they all count for nothing if the company is damaged or disappears. Why is it such a rare thing to see company loyalty translate into constructive self-criticism and course-correction? Why should peer pressure keep one from raising the alarm about practices that could destroy the company the peers all serve?

Why is it almost unheard of for a corporate figure to make the moral case, that pushing bad product—salmonella-tainted food, a faulty ignition switch, a cheat emissions device—is simply *wrong*?

And how is it possible that a CEO who brings disgrace to the company, as in VW's case, gets a $66.9 million farewell package?

What would it take to make a corporation reform, apart from management growing a conscience? Perhaps a consumer advisory board, to convey the consumer's point of view, but only if it reported directly to the CEO. A staff ethicist might instruct the corporation on its compact of trust with the consumer and the public. A staff filmmaker might make a *The Day After*-type film, to make graphic the human and corporate toll when risk-taking goes bad or fatal (the lawsuits, the hearings, the coffins, etc.).

Even better at painting a worst-case scenario: a staff eschatologist, to map out the end-times of the corporation, complete with liquidation and extinction of brand, if redemption and reformation don't occur.

It also might focus a corporation's attention if its executives were brought up on murder charges. Unbelievably, legal action against Peanut Corporation and General Motors for fatalities caused by their products has been, of necessity, prosecuted as *fraud* cases, not manslaughter. As the federal prosecutor who negotiated a settlement with GM said in his press briefing, it is not a crime "to put into the stream of commerce a defective automobile that might kill people." The law on this point would need changing, but if murder charges were added to the worst-case scenario of corporate risk-taking, we might see greater corporate responsibility.

Whatever the means, corporations need to imagine—fully imagine—their ruination if a company practice has bad results. It means taking full responsibility, maturing as a corporation. It could also mean—imagine this—lives saved and trust restored.

—*HuffPost*, October 27, 2015

Writing for Our Post-9/11 Times

I.

THERE IS A scene in a little-known but fine film from 1947 called *Odd Man Out* that, ever since I first saw it a few years ago, has stayed with me for its metaphoric power.

The film is about a leader of the Irish Republican Army, the I.R.A., played by a young James Mason, who is shot during a robbery shortly after the opening credits and who spends the rest of the film seeking refuge, all the while losing blood and growing weaker and weaker. No one gives him aid, not even sympathizers, some of whom consider the reward they'd get for turning him over to the occupying English police, who are hard on his trail.

Finally, in a noisy pub, the dying man encounters an artist, a portrait painter, who instead of giving comfort or getting a doctor, as you'd expect a humanist to do, hauls him off to his studio—*to sit for a portrait*. Played with maniacal energy by a young Robert Newton (who'd later scare the wits out of little kids playing the pirate Long John Silver), the artist daubs away at his easel, babbling about painting "the truth of life and death," something to be captured "in the eyes"—while his subject, a specimen of life, is literally dying in front of him, sagging in his chair, delirious.

I have a horror of being that kind of artist.

The film's director, Sir Carol Reed, clearly thought likewise. This was after all an Englishman telling a tale about the Irish "troubles," critical of the English abuse of power and intent on portraying the humanity of the occupied Irish—as a true artist must.

The basic question is: *As writers, what is our relationship to our times?*

Is it like that portrait artist, oblivious to his dying subject? Because, I submit, America in this post-9/11 era exhibits many signs of dying and decline: the wars; the extreme political polarization; the extreme income inequality; the fear, the anger, the bombast; the coarsening of the culture; the absence of reason and the prevalence of crazy. Polls show a big majority of Americans feel America is in decline. So: *In these wild and crazy times, do you feed the wild and crazy—or do you fight it?*

I will get to these questions later, but first I'd like to relate my own journey to my own position. What follows is what has worked for me as the framework through which I approach my writing. It may work for you too—or not. You choose.

It was the early 1990s, I was living in Washington, D.C. and working on a play, my second. It was a comic drama, in which the Life Force embodied by the actress and force of nature Katharine Hepburn contends with the Death Force, embodied by the death-loving Modernist author Franz Kafka, played out in an end-of-the-world setting, the Sanatorium Ultime. I was having great fun, working out—in the abstract—how the Life Force would push the Death Force to discover his own will to live.

Meanwhile, in real life, there were regular reports in the news of the city of Sarajevo, "the Paris of the Balkans," besieged by snipers shooting from the hills surrounding the city. U.N. peacekeepers were in place but did nothing to keep peace. Instead, while the world watched on TV, Sarajevans were forced to run through Sniper's Alley, in peril for their lives, to cross the city. This slow-burning atrocity had been going on almost two years and would extend to four, the longest siege of the 20th century.

I am sorry to say it took the second-anniversary marker and a particular set of photos of ordinary Sarajevans running through Sniper's Alley to finally cause the penny to drop for me: The comedy about Life and Death I was working on in the abstract was unfolding in real life, as tragedy, in Sarajevo. I realized then—anticipating the portrait painter of *Odd Man Out* I'd see years later—that I needed to quit with the abstract and deal with the real. The world impinged—finally.

Through a Sarajevo journalist in D.C., I was put in touch with the man running one of Sarajevo's last independent radio stations. Most other stations had gone ethnic, spewing hate-talk. Vlado was, as he told me, determined to stay normal and civilized, do interviews, give out survival tips (like how to detect a landmine), and, with schools shut down, broadcast schooling on-air. But before I made that first I call, I dithered: Of what possible use could Tailored Lady be in a war zone?

Finally, one Sunday afternoon in December 1994 I placed the call and reached him, as he sat in complete darkness (no electricity), teeth chattering from the cold (no heat)—and it changed my life and (he said) saved his. In the Hell of war, Vlado needed a lifeline, while I had been looking all my life for a test of my character.

"The first thing I want to say to you, Sir, is: I think a great crime is happening to Sarajevo." "So," Vlado replied, "do you have some troops with you?" I offered for broadcast my first play, about how people find reasons to let a crime go forward, as the world was doing with Sarajevo. Vlado said fine, he'd be my translator. Days later, after a man in desperation committed suicide on the station's steps, Vlado called me: "I *need* to talk to you." "Vlado, I am not a psychiatrist." "Don't worry, all the psychiatrists have abandoned us"; he said I sounded normal, strong. "I don't know, Vlado, people say I'm intense." "Please," he said, "be intense with me." Deal! Bond sealed. From the depths of the siege—the sniping soon escalated to shelling—through his escape and struggle as a refugee desperately looking for work, we protected our bond, now sacred. Finally, after he landed a job at Radio Free Europe, in Prague, we met. It was a reunion of old friends, comrades.

Now, the writer's challenge: The challenge was not in writing a play about our bond, nor even calling into a war zone. With Vlado's permission, I typed up our dialogues—easily done: every word was incised on my brain—and faxed them to him: He said they made him see his situation more clearly, also confirmed for him his humanity. When I landed the first theatrical reading, he hoped it would wake a sleeping world.

But, on the road to production, in a dozen readings around the U.S., there was resistance, even derision from producers at the idea of a sacred bond. "This is Mother Teresa meets Saint Francis of Assisi, can't they flirt with each other?" "No," I said, "you don't flirt with a traumatized person, besides I am married." Reference was often made to the "hot" novel of the time, *Vox*, about phone sex. Aging woman, no children: Clearly I was looking for excitement, not a test of character, a "noble deed." And clearly my husband had to be jealous, not the trusting husband who was proud his wife had met her test. Vlado as hero was readily accepted, but my character needed to be needier, "so an American audience can relate." When I told Vlado that, he said, "*Why* would I talk to a noodle?" He expressed condolences for my culture.

The three productions I did secure were with theatres who, bless them, accepted my pitch of the play as a tale of the saving power of normalcy and the human connection amid chaos. With these theatres— Chicago's Victory Gardens Theater, Washington's Studio Theatre, and Indianapolis' Phoenix Theatre—and with a workshop in New York, I worked to move the play from docudrama to universal drama.

These checks with Vlado—"Guess what Mr. Producer wants now?"— led me to see that Sarajevo wasn't the only place under siege; so was America, with its culture degrading and growing vulgar, narcissistic, neurotic, pathological. These checks with Vlado also led me subsequently, after five rough years of "development" with other producers, to make a major fix: I inserted into the script the offstage character of "Mr. Producer," who reflects this vulgarized American culture and whose lines are delivered by my character, replayed to Vlado for his reaction. "Mr. Producer" made his debut at the third production, in Indianapolis. I prize the audience's explosive laughter at Mr. Producer's insistence the American character be needier.

To step back a bit for historical context: When the Cold War between America and the Soviet Union ended in 1989, with the fall of the Berlin Wall, Americans declared themselves the winners—and thereafter, with no existential competition to keep us sober and serious, we held ourselves to few standards, high or otherwise. In the go-go '90s, anything went—and anything did. What might have become a Golden

Age instead became increasingly brassy, "smash-mouth." In my field, American theatre hit a low with Eve Ensler's *The Vagina Monologues*; audiences went along, giggling.

What's a serious writer to do?

II.

What *is* a serious writer to do in a culture going off the rails, decadent, un-serious?

Sometimes it's not your own volition that decides the way forward, but external events, History. The terrorist attacks of 9/11—the shock, the deaths, the tragedy—decided it for me. From our apartment high on Connecticut Avenue in the nation's capital, we could see the Pentagon on fire, filling the sky with black smoke. In that moment of truth I knew: I did not want merely to *react*, to respond to that historic day as a playwright, dramatizing how fearful we all felt. No, I wanted to *act*, help make sense of whatever was coming at us next, be a voice of reason in what I felt would be a time of fear and confusion. Turning points can turn you around, totally.

I wrote an essay titled "Reinventing Normalcy," submitted it to *The Christian Science Monitor*—and spent the next eight years contributing commentary there. Over time my editors and I scoped out my beat, a capacious one—politics, culture, and ethical-moral issues—written in a style they called "big-think in a personal voice." The *Monitor's* editorial guidelines stress a "bias for hope": I could paint an issue as bleak as it needed to be, but, please, leave the reader with an action step or a constructive thought. That approach suited me fine, as artist and as American: Tragedy had struck America, but we need not succumb to it. I apply the same guidelines with the same beat writing now for *The Huffington Post*.

Torture is something I never imagined America, a moral beacon in the post–World War II world, could sanction. When the scandal at Iraq's Abu Ghraib prison broke in May 2004, revealing the torture our military engaged in, I felt such overwhelming shame for our nation that I fired off a letter to the editor of *The New York Times* that day (it was published); continued writing for the *Monitor* on the subject, protesting the Bush administration's practice of torture; and now write on it for *The Huffington Post*, protesting the Obama administration's decision not to pursue an accounting.

A sensitive point I must raise: I was disappointed that more writers—putative humanists—did not protest the human depredation of torture. How could this be? To make a long disquisition short: Some writers pride themselves on pushing "the edge," discovering new depths in human awfulness. Those of us who pursue "the core" would say: No wonder artists peddling edgy anti-human product were silent on torture. One can't create pathology *and* protest it.

And a note about obsession: I'd like to say that writers, if lucky, have a subject that grabs them and won't let go. But I'm not sure obsession is a lucky thing. Torture was not a subject I ever would have chosen, but it grabbed me and did not let go. As a serious artist, and the moral artist I'd come to see myself, I felt I had to respond. But I also could see, in my anguish, I could make myself sick, give myself a Messiah complex. I *had* to stop the keening in my heart and convert it to something more abstract in my head—and I did. After all, we need to live another day to do our work.

Which brings us back to our theme: writing for our post-9/11 times. That historic day, when America was attacked, called forth our most serious, honorable selves. Though the culture had already turned brassy, as discussed, some of us hoped for an American Renaissance, the shock of being attacked forcing us into Truth and Beauty. For a while, a New Day seemed upon us: Irony was declared dead, acts of kindness were reported by the media, Hollywood producers held off releasing racy or violent films, saying it was "too soon." But, alas, soon enough, that unity of serious purpose faded and "smash-mouth" was back with us, and then some.

Distressingly, "smash-mouth" has become permanent. Fourteen years is time enough to recover our senses and build toward a New Day.

Instead we have two American-led wars sowing chaos; cowboy capitalism going unreformed; polarization so profound it permits government shutdown; and a public so turned off that voter rates are plummeting and political candidates tout their outsider status and lack of governing experience. And there's the stupid-making fear. This is a nation reaching stall speed.

"But—but—but," you might say, "I just want to write about my garden." Fine, all power to you, even though I myself am drawn to the disturbance outside the garden, threatening the garden's very existence. My problem is not with writers writing about their gardens, the beauty and solace to be found there, though I'd suggest that occasional reference to the chaos and noise outside the garden would make the beauty and solace derived all the more beautiful and consoling. No, my problem is with writers, the "transgressive" artists, who feed the chaos and noise, the wild and crazy, who fly their freak flag when coherence is desperately needed.

For example, the creators of the wildly popular TV series "Breaking Bad," about a high-school chemistry teacher who, learning he has terminal cancer, seeks to provide for his family "after" by cooking and selling high-grade meth. Seen soberly: In these wild and crazy times, to push stories of characters breaking bad is, frankly, to *push at an open door*. And this door is held wide open by critics, our cultural gatekeepers, who, not understanding the rise and fall of nations, accelerate our fall by lauding "Breaking Bad" as "raw" and "daring." I'll grant you "raw," but what is "daring" about an anti-hero pursuing his nefarious ends *without serious moral pushback?*

Same goes for Tony Soprano, mob boss of the wildly popular TV series "The Sopranos," "whacking" his rivals—to little serious moral pushback.

Notice how seldom today's anti-heroes have an equally weighted antagonist? Recall that Gordon Gekko, mighty financier in the film *Wall Street* whose motto was "Greed is good," was ultimately brought down not by a heroic type but by an underling even greedier than he who squealed to the feds. Believe it: Some people *do* want to live heroic and noble lives, and if not that, a morally good life; your characters might, too.

Another example of wild and crazy "art": the bondage novel, *Fifty Shades of Grey*. I am aware the author is English, but sales of the book in the U.S. have been off the charts. Which is especially troubling because, while the book's characters play at torture, America—again, no fiction—engaged in the real thing abroad, to little public protest, certainly little compared to the enormous interest in the book (making its author the world's richest). Naturally I had to write about this moral disconnect in a commentary titled "Playing at Torture: Fifty Shades of Shame."

Culture is key. If a culture signals it's O.K. to, say, play at torture, cook meth to stoke the family coffers, or whack your rivals, then culture becomes very important, as important as politics. And we who create the content of culture are thus elemental.

Of course, if you're a narcissist, as too many of today's artists are, oblivious to our post-9/11 times with its unreason and anxiety and fear—the opposite of Camus' artist *engagé*—you are freed up to imagine whatever you want, following it down, down, down whatever path. I doubt the creators of "Breaking Bad" or "The Sopranos" even noticed the downward tilt of the ship of state. But there is the verdict of History and such "artists," I believe, will be found on the wrong side of it. It is good to look inward, as narcissists do, but not at the expense of missing what's going on in the outer world. Recall the root of the word "narcissism" is *narke*, which means stupor.

Wrong side of History, right side of History: This all bears on the moral point and artists courageous enough to make it. Curiously, at a time when so much is wrong in America, writers are regularly warned against "getting moral," rendering judgment, and critics uphold this injunction. I ran into this injunction in an early workshop: When I proposed my first play, the one about people finding reasons to let a crime go forward, the workshop leader wrinkled his nose, "Ooh, sounds moral." But Shakespeare would no doubt say that moral questions are not only the most dramatic but the most important: See: *Hamlet, Macbeth,*

King Lear. Writers regularly hear another injunction, attributed to Chekhov, that a writer's only responsibility is to raise questions, not provide answers. All these injunctions against making the moral point leach our work of meaning and profundity and account for cultural drift.

Here's an injunction *for* the moral point: At a time when stupidity seems on the rise, literary critic Lionel Trilling reminds us of "the moral obligation to be intelligent." That bears repeating: "the moral obligation to be intelligent."

A final consideration for the American writer and bearing on the moral point: As the global superpower, even in decline, we have outsized power *vis-à-vis* other countries; English is the world's *lingua franca*, along with American culture, both pop and high. But a superpower also has a moral responsibility to handle its power appropriately. Similarly, its artists have a responsibility to consider the "can" and the "should": Do I write on Subject X simply because my culture is on top and because I can (again, Eve Ensler in monologue with her vagina) or should I, considering the world's sorry state and America's decline, not? A superpower *and* its artists must be self-critical.

Of course, we must make the moral point with finesse—subtly, imaginatively, maybe with humor as George Bernard Shaw advises— but make it. One way is to reintroduce the hero or a character on a moral quest, or give the anti-hero a proper antagonist. Enough with "breaking bad," the wild and crazy, the transgressive; let's break good, sane, moral. Enough with pushing the edge; let's push core. And let's redefine humanity upward: Countless times I have heard writers explain that, to make their central character "more human," they added a kink, like self-mutilation. Enough with defining humanity downward. At this post-9/11 moment, Americans are already down. Rather than give our audience what we think it wants, spectacle and shock, let's give it what it *needs* but is not getting of late—substance, moral meaning, reasons to hope and believe.

For, like that heedless portrait painter in *Odd Man Out*, do we daub away while our subject lies dying? Or do we recognize the stakes and write to them? Your choice.

Your choice will reflect your definition of the purpose of art. I subscribe to Samuel Johnson's definition: The purpose of art is to help us enjoy life or endure it better.

And a final word about joy: There's a bias in American culture that to be serious and moral is to be grim and unexciting. But hinge historical moments—which is where we are now—are inherently dramatic, thus exciting. And there is such joy in contending with questions that matter and pushing yourself, as the late playwright August Wilson urged, to the "limits of your instrument."

With America at a hinge historical moment, the stakes could not be higher. The pattern of great nations throughout History has been one of rise and rise, then decline and fall. America, in decline, can still reverse course and rise again—uniquely, we believe in reinvention, and we are not fatalists, not yet—but only if our citizens sober up, get serious, and act. The same goes, doubly so, for our artists.

In sum, American artists must do something both historically and artistically new: Rewrite our unfolding Tragedy and create a New Day. Will we? Can we?

This commentary is condensed from a speech given at a writers' conference organized by Tacoma Community College and held at its Gig Harbor (WA) branch, Nov. 6-7.

—*HuffPost*, November 12, 2015

Refugees Are Not the Problem,
My Fellow Americans. Fear Is.

IT'S SAD HOW quickly the world's pre-eminent refuge from war and persecution—the United States of America—can forget its roots: Except for Native Americans, we all of us descend from refugee or immigrant origins.

But fear can obliterate that common heritage instantly. Republicans especially seem quick to forget and to succumb to fear of the outsider, also to play the fear card.

Days after the ISIS-engineered attacks in Paris on Nov. 13, which killed 130 and wounded hundreds more, and in opposition to President Obama's proposal to resettle 10,000 Syrian refugees in the U.S. in the coming year, 26 Republican governors—half the governors in the nation—declared they would not allow any Syrian refugees to settle in their states, even though they lack the authority to countermand federal action. Another four GOP governors (and one Democratic governor), while not barring these refugees, would impose increased screening.

And now, the Republican-controlled U.S. House of Representatives has passed a bill to "pause" the entry of Syrian and Iraqi refugees into the U.S. Its sponsors claim the bill—with an Orwellian title conceived in fear but promising safety: the American Security Against Foreign Enemies (SAFE) Act of 2015—would "put in place the most robust national-security vetting process in history." *Which we already have* (about which, more later).

If we need proof that fear hardens the heart and makes one illogical, consider:

The refugees who are the target of these pusillanimous GOP reactions are the same refugees whose desperate trek from their failing states in the Middle East toward the refuge of Europe, often ending in drowning at sea, has broken the world's heart in images dominating the news for months. Rather than rushing *to* ISIS, as Republicans fear, they are fleeing for their lives *from* ISIS, seeking refuge from terror on all sides. Especially the Syrian refugees: These benighted souls are truly caught between a rock (a vicious president, Bashar al-Assad, who's killed more than 200,000 of his citizens) and a hard place (a vicious ISIS, or Islamic State).

Of course, terrorists mingling among the tides of refugees are a real possibility. But it is crucial—*crucial*—to distinguish the enemy from the innocent in the field. (The Syrian passport found on one of the dead ISIS killers in Paris, which ignited GOP opposition to Syrian refugees, has been confirmed by French authorities to be fake—an instance of ISIS disinformation. The killers appear to be French nationals.)

Unable at all to distinguish enemy from refugee are the Republican presidential candidates, who are playing the fear card to a dangerous, unconstitutional, un-American, even vile degree—with frontrunners Donald Trump and Ben Carson the most outrageous.

Trump is agreeable to creating a national registry to track Muslims in the U.S., completely blind to the sad lessons of World War II and similar stigmatization of the Jews in Europe. Assailed for the proposal, Trump has yet to reject the idea, asserting, "We're going to have to do things that we never did before"—an open-ended statement fraught with danger, like former Vice President Dick Cheney's assertion after 9/11 that we needed to go to the "dark side" and torture. Trump also asserts, "It's all about management." No, Mr. Trump, it's about values, ethics, and remaining true to our immigrant and refugee origins.

Carson, not to be outdone in vilifying Muslims, compared them—astonishingly—to "rabid dogs" roaming the neighborhood, claiming it's simply a matter of intellect to do so. (Carson later claimed he was not speaking of Muslims generally, only of terrorists, but a video shows otherwise.)

Other GOP candidates covered themselves in ignominy. While Jeb Bush called out Trump for the Muslim registry—properly connecting the dots between registry and internment camps—he also proposed allowing only Christian Syrians into the U.S., not Muslims. Ted Cruz also advocates for Christian Syrians. Both men go against the American tenet forbidding religious tests. And now, Marco Rubio proposes closing not only mosques in the U.S., but any centers where Muslims get "inspired." These appeals go over with the GOP's white, angry, older, less-educated base.

Advantage: ISIS. For "leaders" committed to fortifying our national security, with this venom they supply ISIS with a potent recruitment tool: Via the social media it manipulates so well, ISIS can point to myriad examples of America's "war on Islam."

President Obama rightly condemns the Republican fear-mongering and Muslim-bashing. To be sure, leading conservative commentators have expressed dismay: David Brooks writes that Republicans have "stained themselves with refugee xenophobia" and Kathleen Parker describes GOP actions as "morally reprehensible."

Morally reprehensible or not, a majority of Americans agree with the Republican stand that Syrian refugees should be kept out of the U.S., according to two new polls: a bare majority—53% (Bloomberg) and 56% (NBC).

Of course this is not to suggest opening the entry gate to all, no questions asked. The vetting process for refugees into the U.S. must be rigorous—and it is. Commenting on the present system while decrying the House's so-called SAFE Act, *The New York Times* in an editorial pointedly titled "Refugees from war aren't the enemy" states:

> *"The bill disregards the complicated current process, which already requires that applicants' histories, family origins, and law enforcement and past travel and immigration records be vetted by national security, intelligence, law enforcement and consular officials."*

This current vetting process is arduous, taking 18 to 24 months or more. And, it works: Of the 745,000 refugees resettled in the U.S. since

9/11, only two (2) have been arrested on terrorism-related charges. The newly-enacted SAFE Act would make an already arduous system "untenable," says the White House, by requiring personal sign-off from the heads of the FBI, Homeland Security, and National Intelligence for each and every Syrian and Iraqi refugee.

(Parenthetically, all the anti-refugee venom is much ado about not very much: The U.S. has resettled only 1,854 Syrian refugees since 2012. Of more concern than refugees is the much less rigorously-vetted visa waiver program, for visitors and tourists, which last year allowed 20 million people from 38 countries into the U.S.)

Happily, to counter all the anti-refugee venom, Democrats have stepped forward. Democratic mayors of major cities—including New York, Chicago, Los Angeles, Boston, Pittsburgh, Baltimore—have issued a welcome to Syrian and Iraqi refugees who make it through the vetting processes. This list includes cities in conservative states: Houston, Dallas, Phoenix, Santa Fe. Also, 16 Democratic governors have put out the welcome sign for Syrians and Iraqis. (Two GOP governors have joined them.)

And all the Democratic presidential candidates —Hillary Clinton, Bernie Sanders, Martin O'Malley—have taken strong and humane stands welcoming Syrian and Iraqi refugees. Given the present firestorm, it's clear refugees, immigration, and how to counter ISIS will be a top issue in 2016—and a crucial test for Commander-in-Chief.

Not all Democrats struck a humane note, though: The mayor of Roanoke, Virginia, proposed internment camps for Syrian refugees, invoking the camps President Franklin Roosevelt, also a Democrat, established for Japanese-Americans during World War II—a decision now universally deplored, for which the U.S. Government in 1988, under Republican Ronald Reagan, apologized and made reparations. Unlike today's Republicans, Roanoke's mayor apologized for giving offense to Muslims.

One can't dispute Republicans' concerns about terrorism's threat to national security, concerns which Democrats fully share, but one can argue how best to proceed—and impugning Muslim refugees, again, plays into Islamic terrorism's hand. Impugning Muslims also prevents Republicans from facing up to their calamitous war in Iraq, one consequence of which is Syria's dissolution, all of which produced ... the Syrian and Iraqi refugees.

It is to be hoped that Muslims, American and foreign, can hear the positive message amid all the slurs. But already Muslim-Americans report feeling a backlash and are girding for worse. As the national spokesman for the Council on American-Islamic Relations (CAIR), Ibrahim Hooper, says of the avalanche of anti-Muslim venom, which he feels is worse than after 9/11: "What else can you compare this to except to prewar Nazi Germany?" Solidarity marches would be in order.

Finally, for perspective, two points: 1) In the aftermath of the Nov. 13 terrorist attacks in Paris—France's 9/11 as some in France are calling it— France has committed to resettling 30,000 Syrian refugees over the next two years, to honor its "humanitarian duty." 2) It must be said about the U.S.: More dangerous than refugees, or even terrorists for that matter, is the gun mayhem in this country, which carnage has produced, at an average of over 30,000 deaths per year, over 406,000(!) deaths from guns since 2001. If only Republicans saw the peril within.

In the military, a first rule of engagement is called IFF—Identify: friend or foe. In the mortal fear generated by the heinous terrorist attacks in Paris, too many Americans have misidentified the foe (ISIS) for the friend: the refugee. In doing so, we also misidentify ourselves and our origins: Once upon a time, we all were one of "them."

—*HuffPost*, December 2, 2015

Whatever Happened to the Famous American Ability to Say "Nuts" to Charlatans, Crazies, and Fear-Mongers?

SHORTLY AFTER THE onset of the Battle of the Bulge, one of World War II's hardest-fought campaigns, with the Americans surrounded by German troops, when the American commander General Anthony McAuliffe was given the enemy's ultimatum to surrender or face annihilation, he famously replied: "NUTS!" The general put that in writing—a one-word message, all capital letters, with exclamation point.

Why famous? Not only because it remains one of history's most succinct utterances in battle, but also because "Nuts!" seems—or seemed at the time—to convey a quintessential American capacity, burnished as a cherished aspect of our self-image, to call a spade a spade, dispense with nonsense and niceties, get to the meat of things, and, especially vital before going into battle, forcefully draw the brightest of red lines, push back at the malign use of power, and rally courage.

Two postwar films reflect that capacity. In *Battleground*, an American officer further down the line is asked by a German envoy to clarify the meaning of Gen. McAuliffe's reply: Is it affirmative or negative? "'Nuts!' is strictly negative," the American says, concluding with a verbal shove, "On your way, bud." Contrasted with European sophistication, a bracing expression of American directness.

And in *The Best Years of Our Lives*, a veteran who lost both hands in the war, now come home, confronts a man peddling a revisionist view that the wrong enemy was fought. To whom the vet, after asking if 400 of his buddies who died when their ship was sunk were fighting the wrong enemy, finally says "Nuts!" in another way, with equally bracing clarity: "Look here, mister, what are you selling anyway?"

Since forever, the American character in both life and art has prided itself on its down-to-earth vantage point and, from there, calling out "Nuts!"—or words to that challenging effect—on all phonies, charlatans, confidence men, snake-oil salesmen, flim-flam artists, anyone trying to "pull a fast one" or put over something "slick." In sum: Gen. McAuliffe's "Nuts!" was a response that would resonate instantly with his troops and the American public alike.

Where oh where is that famous ability these days?

Of the cavalcade of bilge meriting a collective and full-throated "Nuts!" in recent years, where to start? There's the "birther" *faux*-controversy. There's the extreme anti-government ranting. There's the never-ending effort by a Republican-held Congress to repeal Obamacare. There is the gun mania—and carnage—that belies our claim to civilization. Readers will no doubt have their own nominations.

Because there was a dearth of "Nuts!" cast at these noxious trends at their outset, they have become entrenched and churn more noxiousness. The attempts to repeal Obamacare now number 62, despite the Supreme Court twice upholding the Affordable Care Act (ACA) as the law of the land. Anti-government ranting, accelerated by the Tea Party to the proposed ACA, now infects the entire GOP, with all the Republican presidential candidates railing against Big Bad Government. The recent takeover of a federal wildlife installation in Oregon by renegade ranchers is only the latest manifestation of this anti-government hatred. It's just nuts, however, to think the American behemoth can be run without central control.

As to the "birther" claims, which persist despite Mr. Obama providing his birth certificate confirming his Hawaiian birthplace and American mother: Among all Republicans, 44% still falsely believe Mr. Obama is foreign-born, while 54% believe he is Muslim (he is Christian). Among those supporting Donald Trump, the current Republican presidential front-runner, those numbers jump to 61% and 66%, respectively, thanks in big part to the misinformation campaign spearheaded by Trump himself for years now. Yet where are the Democrats, or even the Republican statesman, putting it to Mr. Trump: "Nuts to you, mister, what are you selling?"

Of course, with today's extreme partisan polarization, when it comes to the "Nuts!" challenge, one person's pecan is another's macadamia.

Even so, the Republican presidential candidates as a lot are especially deserving of the "Nuts!" challenge that, once upon a time, Americans hurled at charlatans, crazies, and fear-mongers. All of them—Trump, Cruz, Rubio, Carson, Bush, Christie, Fiorina, Paul, Huckabee (Kasich excepted)—take standard GOP positions and crank them up to the extreme, whether on immigration (Deport the 11 million undocumented!), refugees (Keep out the ISIS-loving Syrians!), Obamacare (Repeal first day in office!), guns (Hands off our Second Amendment!).

And what was that craziness from Ben Carson about ancient Egyptians using their pyramids as granaries? In normal times, eyes would roll and the candidate would get the net.

To date, the GOP presidential debates have served as springboard for candidates to outdo each other in the hyperbole of fear. But hyperbole, absent a moderating temperament, becomes dangerous, volatile. Ted Cruz' vow to "carpet bomb" parts of the Middle East so thoroughly that we'll see "if sand can glow in the dark" should, in its bald threat both to use nuclear weapons and to kill civilians, disqualify him as a potential Commander-in-Chief. Trump's remark to an Alabama crowd, that a protester in their midst (who happened to be African-American) maybe "should have been roughed up," should—along with his zeal for internment camps, group registries, and deportation, combined with an apparent lack of moral compass—raise the fear, the well-founded fear this time, of Trump's jack-boot tendencies.

And all around, we hear Trump supporters gush that the main reason they support their man is because "He tells it like it is." Really? What Trump tells is, well, nuts, from his opening announcement that Mexico sends us "rapists" and "murderers" to every crude remark onward. People confuse the audacity to say "politically incorrect" things with the audacity of the entertainer who'll do anything to keep the spotlight.

By contrast, the Democratic candidates come off so sane they risk seeming boring—which only reflects the corrosive effect Republican charlatanry, craziness, and fear-mongering have had on our political discourse.

Extreme political polarization notwithstanding, one still hopes that the more egregious cases meriting a collective and full-throated "Nuts!" would pierce through, especially those cases calling on "the well known American humanity" which the above-cited German ultimatum at the Battle of the Bulge appealed to.

Guns, for one. If the horror of—the following is not a typo—over 406,000 gun deaths in the U.S. since 2001 cannot pierce American humanity and provoke not just "Nuts!" but "For the love of God, this must stop," what can? At the moment, with the ISIS-fomented massacres in Paris and San Bernardino, we have near-mass hysteria over refugees-who-might-be-terrorists coming into the country, yet there is nothing at all like hysteria over *almost half-a-million* gun deaths here since 2001.

How can this be? How can the National Rifle Association, contorting itself into ever more bizarre defenses against even elementary gun safety measures, not be called out as the supreme flim-flam artists they are? *If* domestic terrorism is now such a threat, then how can the NRA, and Congressional Republicans in its thrall, not even support blocking gun sales to *terrorist* suspects on the federal watch-list? Truly nuts. Instead, conservatives mocked the tears President Obama shed when he recently announced his (modest) executive actions on gun safety, tears that fell when he touched on the children cut down by guns. "Nuts!" doesn't suffice, "For shame" does.

It is possible we are now so deep in charlatanry, craziness, and fear-mongering that we are past the point where a simple "Nuts!" can even penetrate, much less signify. Complicating the picture is the public's rising anger: A recent "rage survey" shows Americans all along the political spectrum—three-quarters of Republicans and two-thirds of Democrats—are, as a *New York Times* editorial puts it, "spitting mad" that "they're living in a less-powerful America, that life hasn't turned out the way they had hoped, and that for them, the American dream has died." Beware, my fellow Americans: Angry people are manipulable by demagogues.

Meanwhile, sadly, our culture's creative artists don't help much, being in thrall with "breaking bad" and defining humanity downward to pathology.

None other than Abraham Lincoln may point the way forward. Speaking of the need to abolish slavery, he said, with profound wisdom: *"We must disenthrall our selves, and then we shall save our country."* One way to disenthrall starts by recapturing our once-famous ability—air-clearing, humanity-restoring, nation-saving—to say "Nuts!"

—*HuffPost*, January 14, 2016

The Anger Election of 2016: How Will We Handle Our Anger?

WITH THE OUTSIZED victories of outliers Donald Trump and Bernie Sanders in the New Hampshire primary, the essence of 2016 becomes clear: This election is about anger. Trump is riding a dangerous xenophobic anger among Republicans, while Sanders is riding a righteous anger among Democrats at a "rigged economy."

Both kinds of anger—the xenophobic kind against outsiders, the righteous kind against money-power—are broad-based, as New Hampshire confirms: Those supporting Trump and Sanders span from young to old; from working-class to middle-class to the wealthy; men and women. That anger is white-hot (*The New York Times* uses the word "fury"). And that fury is anti-establishment: Burning at the far ends of the political spectrum, this fury scorns the Republican and Democratic powers-that-be perceived to be responsible for the present chaos.

The bombshell news of the death of Supreme Court justice Antonin Scalia last Saturday raises the stakes of this election even further, along with the thermostat, if that evening's Republican presidential debate is any sign: After bowing their heads in silence for Scalia, the candidates lit into each other with new levels of viciousness. Senate majority leader Mitch McConnell demands President Obama hold off naming Scalia's replacement; Mr. Obama pledges to proceed per his Constitutional duty. We now have an electoral *and* a Constitutional battle; the anger will scale even higher.

An angry public is a volatile one. Historically, anger has fuelled revolutions; it is the "change agent" without peer. Prime example: our own American Revolution. But, mishandled, anger can also blind and end in more chaos, even civil war.

We can manage the volatility, as historically Americans have shown. But a happy outcome depends on wise handling of the anger and on the understanding—on the part of the presidential candidates *and* the electorate—that we are playing with fire. This isn't just another "watershed" election; this one involves the fire brigade.

More than the usual partisan tug-of-war for the White House, this election coalesces around forces building for a long time and now bubbling to the fore.

Trump's campaign theme—"Make America Great Again"—reflects the anger of those who see America in decline in recent decades, both in the world and at home ("We don't win anymore"). The caricature of a capitalist, he observes the workings of the marketplace, democracy, and international relations and sees winners and losers. This message is a siren call especially to white middle- and working-class Americans who are angry at losing their jobs to globalization, seeing their demographic role shrinking, and whose mortality rates are accelerating *vis-à-vis* other groups.

But rather than honestly addressing our myriad problems and seeking to repair them ourselves, Trump points the finger at others: immigrants, refugees, Muslims, ISIS, China, Japan, Mexico. Forget self-examination, flex muscle. In his New Hampshire victory speech, Trump promised to "rebuild our military" ("It's going to be so big, so strong, so powerful, nobody will mess with us"), "build the wall" (between the U.S. and Mexico), and "start winning again" ("We're going to win so much, you are going to be so happy, we are going to make America so great again, maybe greater than ever before"). Trump also promises to "bomb the [expletive deleted] out of ISIS."

It's the mentality of a profoundly insecure individual. But it also appeals to a profoundly insecure country at present. Trump proposes to make America great again by doubling down on a bully's tactics—insults, scorched-earth policy, playing by his own rules, employing tactics like "roughing up" and waterboarding "or worse" (torture).

It must be noted that Trump is capitalizing on an angry brew stoked by the GOP for some time now, as traced by a number of observers, including E.J. Dionne in his new book, *Why the Right Went Wrong*. As the *Times* columnist Nicholas Kristof writes:

> "Over the decades [the Republicans] pried open a Pandora's box, a toxic politics of fear and resentment, sometimes brewed with a tinge of racial animus, and they could never satisfy the unrealistic expectations that they nurtured among supporters."

Sanders' theory of the case—a moral theory—that the economy is rigged in favor of the millionaires and billionaires, who buy the politics they need through unlimited campaign contributions, is having an equally profound impact, especially among those Americans struggling since the 2008 Wall Street-generated financial crash. Seeing the 1% reap almost all the rewards in the so-called "recovery," while their own wages remain stagnant, makes Sanders supporters see red.

And justifiably so: As Sanders often declares, a founding principle of the American project is the principle of fairness. And basic economic and financial fairness by no means applies at this moment. Americans are singular in world history in their insistence on fairness (even while acknowledging that life itself is not always fair).

But in their anger, neither Sanders nor his supporters have mapped out a viable path to that New Day of fairness, income equity, universal healthcare, free public college. Raising the minimum wage to $15 goes only so far; the tax system must be addressed, with major tax hikes required, but Sanders is vague on specifics, other than calling for a "political revolution." The Republican response, should Sanders become the nominee, is predictable: "Seventy-four-year old socialist revolutionary wants to raise your taxes sky-high."

Hillary Clinton, who lost resoundingly to Sanders in New Hampshire (38% to 60%) would be well-advised to address this underlying anger of Sanders supporters—about fairness—and then *provide the map to that New Day*. If she instead attacks Sanders himself, as she occasionally does, rather than addressing the very American demand for fairness, she will alienate his supporters and, should she become the nominee, in their anger they could sit out the election.

Making America great again by invoking first principles like fairness, rather than stoking populist anger: It's the way to go, I believe, but will we?

Worryingly, on the Republican side, Trump's successes have pushed the rest of the field further to the right, with all of them fanning the populist anger, each trying to be tougher than the other. Even the more moderate John Kasich, who placed second in New Hampshire, advocates building a U.S.-Mexico wall. At least Kasich tries to modulate the anger, by asking Americans to listen to each other more.

On the Democratic side, it all depends on Sanders getting more specific, Clinton getting statesmanlike, and both managing, not stoking, liberal anger. It was encouraging to see in the first post-New Hampshire Democratic debate, two days after her loss, Clinton attacking the issues while also mapping out specifics; Sanders, though, remains unspecific. Both would do well to address the angry helplessness that supporters of the GOP candidates feel at America appearing to lose its place in the world.

As to the anger in the body politic, various commentators warn against making too much of it, arguing such anger is "self-indulgent" and that, compared with the rest of the world, America is doing quite well economically. Maintaining this comparative perspective as the presidential campaign heats up further will be a test. It remains the case, however, that, in absolute terms, many Americans are suffering, thus the appeal of the messages of Sanders and Trump and the anger they variously invoke. Will the general election sort all this out?

As to anger in a President: Temperament is not often cited as a quality voters consider in a President, but an angry Donald Trump in the White House would be catastrophic and only accelerate America's decline, especially in the capacity of Commander-in-Chief, brandishing the sword in a tinderbox world. The way to an American Renaissance is through a new Enlightenment, not anger and bombast.

Here I salute President Obama, who has been the model of temperance in office on all fronts. Perhaps the Republican fury at him stems from their not being able to knock him off his even keel? That his hair has turned grey in office may bespeak what it takes to hang on to one's keel. That temperance will be tested in the nomination fight over Justice Scalia's seat. History will judge Mr. Obama highly.

Back to the angry present: We can take heart at the record turnout in Iowa and New Hampshire, also at the record turnout of young people at a time when their anger at a scanty jobs market and crushing college debt might have muted them.

Anger: While it can be a propellant endlessly regenerating itself, anger can blind us and, as Shakespeare tells us, make us deaf—to compromise, nuance, specificity; we now disparage the motivation and character of our political opposites. Homer tells of Achilles, whose anger ultimately led to his downfall, anger being his Achilles' heel.

With the establishments of both parties sidelined, the onus for handling our anger—at a declining America, at the abrogation of the American principle of fairness—is on the presidential candidates and on us, We the People. If we mind and manage our anger, we could mature as a people and reverse our decline.

—*HuffPost*, February 15, 2016

Trump's Crudeness: A Crude American Culture Is Shocked, Shocked

ARE WE THERE yet? Are we at the nadir?

Donald Trump's boast at last week's Republican "presidential" debate, that his (shall we say?) "equipment" was more than adequate, marks a new low in a long and storied history of campaigning for the White House, which explains the scare-quotes around "presidential." One thinks of Abraham Lincoln and weeps; Republicans, as they frequently remind us, are the party of Lincoln. Crude is the only way to describe the Republican front-runner's pathetic and tasteless strutting.

While the partisan crowd inside that debate hall enjoyed it, outside and across the land, the reaction to Trump's crude boast has been a big and resounding "Yech!" The "grey lady" of American journalism and our newspaper of record, *The New York Times*, ran on its front page a critical piece with the once-upon-a-time unbelievable title, "A national descent into Trump's pants." To be fair, conscientious Republicans recoiled as much as Democrats.

However, this general development—trafficking in the crude and raunchy—is hardly new to American culture itself, not at all. Our popular culture—"popular" because it's embraced by the general public—has grown increasingly raw in these last decades. The evidence is everywhere. To be fair again, this decadence has to be laid at the feet of liberals (Hollywood among other venues) rather than conservatives.

As one who continually exhorts us to seek what the poet calls "the upper air," I will not get specific and itemize the various exhibits emanating from the sludge now surrounding us. But scan the pop culture landscape—the comedy scene, TV sit-coms, movies (even the "family-friendly" fare), "edgy" literature and theatre, pop music, "bold" advertising, all aided and abetted by critics who extol the "bent" and "twisted"—and you will readily find "the rank weed," as English poet Alexander Pope characterized it:

> *"In the fat Age of Pleasure, Wealth, and Ease,*
> *Sprung the rank Weed, and thriv'd with large Increase."*

The only good thing, then, in that big and resounding "Yech!" to Trump's crude boasting is this: A crude America woke up, recognized its fallen state, and, in a response more visceral than conscious, recoiled in disgust. *Finally!* That recoil is a sign of health: We are not too far gone for recovery. It also shows we still have certain expectations of presidential conduct.

This presidential election of 2016 promises not only a political reckoning—of a disintegrating Republican party. It promises also, perhaps, a cultural reawakening, even recovery of the American soul. From nadir to a New Day, from "Yech!" to the Renaissance: The hour is late, but it's not impossible. Yes!

—*HuffPost*, March 9, 2016

Pop Culture Captures
Campaign Politics

WHEN A NUDE picture of a potential First Lady of the United States is used in a presidential campaign, and when that news, with photo, makes the public airwaves as it did on the venerable *PBS NewsHour*, we know that pop culture has met head-on with the campaign process and captured it. And it's not a pretty picture.

By now most of news-tracking America knows that a photo of the wife of Republican front-runner Donald Trump, who in her past life as a "top model" posed nude for *British GQ*, was featured by an anti-Trump super-PAC in ads to promote support for Texas senator Ted Cruz, running in second place.

A media storm erupted (so many storms this campaign season!), this one over both the issue of women—both men defended their wives, Trump's misogyny and need for "arm candy" became more pathetically apparent—and over the validity of political action committees. Almost lost in all the noise is this astonishing fact: A potential First Lady posed nude for publication?

But then, pop culture has become distressingly crude and low. Nudity by now is old hat, as is profanity and violence (diplomacy is for wusses). Additionally, survey today's pop culture—movies, television, pop music—and note the snark and meanness of it; the crazy and dysfunctional of it; the cynicism; the grossness; the testosterone. It's a landscape grown, to no small degree, dystopian and hopeless.

All these characteristics fairly describe Election 2016, at least on the Republican side.

Once upon a time, popular culture provided sustenance to the masses. During the Great Depression of the 1930s, popular culture served as a lifebelt, to lighten spirits, assuage suffering, even inspire. There was the popular music of the big bands. There were the movies, taken in weekly as a double feature. Screwball comedies combined style with a human take on life, including hardship, and produced reasons to carry on. William Powell's hobo in *My Man Godfrey* reminds his hobo friend that "prosperity is just around the corner," to which the friend says, "I wish I knew which corner." You felt they'd keep looking for that corner, with good result, in solidarity.

And now? Pop culture is a crude joke, a poke in the eye, not really very entertaining or inspiring. And with this cycle, in 2016, it has entered presidential politics.

Of course, pop culture began to encroach on campaigns in earlier cycles, with celebrities throwing campaign fundraisers, rock music replacing Sousa marches at campaign rallies, candidates in debates citing lines from the popular lexicon ("Where's the beef?" and "Read my lips: no new taxes"). But by and large, prior to this cycle, the presidential campaign retained a properly presidential tone, if one can use the term "proper" anymore. After all, who could be said to be more ill at ease with pop culture than the GOP's last standard-bearer, Mitt Romney?

It's no accident that the chief importer of this crudeness into presidential politics is Trump himself. Apart from his business career, where he might have remained unknown to the general public forever, he achieved breakout fame with his "reality TV" show, "The Apprentice," in which applicants for jobs got the verdict—"You're fired" "You're hired"—from The Boss himself. This show is such a cartoon of a real-world workplace, with its darkened interview room, dramatic tension, and Wizard of Oz-like atmosphere, that the term "reality show" should be, well, fired, let go.

Interestingly, this merging of pop culture and politics is occurring in a campaign cycle when populism, the *vox populi*, is exerting itself more forcefully against the establishments of both parties than at any other time in recent memory. In theory, pop culture's meet-up with populism might make a perfect marriage, but how differently it's playing out in practice.

On the Democratic side, populist Bernie Sanders is running a campaign right out of a Frank Capra movie, giving voice to the plight of the ordinary guy, railing against the wealthy elites about income inequality and money-power in politics, things Sanders has been railing against for decades, thus earning his supporters' trust, even love.

On the GOP side, Trump likewise evokes a powerful populism, one that has some causes in common with Sanders' base, like wage stagnation and jobs lost overseas. Not to deny the racism and xenophobia of Trump's base, but as Nicholas Confessore of *The New York Times* reports, this base has defensible reasons to oppose hurtful trade agreements and immigrants perceived as taking their jobs. Too bad this base's tribune is a joker, not serious, continually disrupting his own "program" with another verbal lulu (the latest, saying women should be "punished" for abortions).

In a way, with populism so prominently in the picture now, we are seeing the screwball comedies of the '30s playing out again. Often in those scenarios, the masses—in the form of an intrepid young man: Clark Gable, Cary Grant, William Powell—met the wealthy elite—in the form of a lovely and game young woman: Claudette Colbert, Katharine Hepburn, Carole Lombard—and, after the masses taught the wealthy elite a few necessary lessons, marriage ensued.

Is there a happy ending for us today? Can the masses, in this wild presidential campaign, teach the wealthy elite (and their politicians) the necessary lessons that will ensure the American project can proceed for all in the 21st century? If Bernie Sanders is elected, or Hillary Clinton now that Sanders has nudged her to the left, the odds of a positive outcome are good. But not so with the hustler Trump.

In the idiom of pop culture, Trump needs to be voted "off the island." In Trump's own idiom, this "loser" needs to hear "You're fired"—and dumped into the dustbin of History.

—*HuffPost*, April 4, 2016

Classic Political Films for This Historic Presidential Campaign

A SURREAL REALITY-TV HOST emerging as the GOP's front-runner, a democratic socialist making serious impact in an America traditionally allergic to the s-word, a woman making the strongest case to date for the White House, the fervor of populist anger and turnout, and the volatility of the whole mix—this 2016 presidential campaign is not a normal campaign. This one feels truly historic, seismically consequential, even dangerous, if the violence Donald Trump stokes at his rallies escalates to the real bloody thing.

In the world's oldest democracy, America's artists, including those in film, have long grappled with the drama inherent in a system of government by and for The People—the drama of individuals, well-meaning or not, taking The People's pulse and throwing their hat into the ring; the methods, straight or slick, used to sway The People's vote; the tactics, fair or not, used against equally ambitious opponents; the negotiation, conscious or not, with the money-power of politics; and, once in office, with one's hands on power, the potential for corruption. Power, the Holy Grail of political struggle, has fascinated artists from the ancient Greeks onward.

Film, being a popular art form, is a natural medium to portray the struggle for power in a setting where The People play a central role. While American cinema generally focuses on the personal and not the political,

[84]

we nonetheless have many classic titles about campaign politics in the vault. Some of those films are discussed below. Each addresses some aspect of our present situation, though not the totality of it (about which, more later). Because this presidential election is so consequential and no laughing matter, the films cited are dramas; thus a film like *The Great McGinty*, the Preston Sturges comedy in which a tramp is elected mayor, is not included. Readers will have their own nominations.

All the King's Men (1949)

This film, with its chilling transformation of Willie Stark from good-guy small-town politician to despotic governor, manipulator of the law and The People, perhaps best represents the dangers of a Donald Trump presidency—not the good-guy part (it never existed), but the despotic and manipulative part. Interestingly, the first half of the film, when good-guy Willie runs for county treasurer and then governor, he sounds like a Bernie Sanders: "Free medicine for all people, not as a charity but as a right," "My study is the heart of the people." But after losing twice, he "learns how to win": by amping up the populist pitch ("I'm going to soak the fat boys and I'm gonna spread it out thin") while financing his campaign with big-money deals (banks, oil companies)—and he wins the governor's seat. The ensuing corruption is not readily apparent: Willie "builds and builds"—roads, hospitals, colleges—which pleases The People, but the building is done with dirty hands, enforced by Willie's private army.

The tragedy of the film, and of Robert Penn Warren's Pulitzer-winning novel on which it is based, is that plenty of good guys hold their noses and go along, including the narrator Jack Burden (John Ireland), who starts out as a reporter covering Willie's first campaign and ends up the keeper of Willie's list of political favors. Burden's entire hometown circle—his girlfriend, his best friend who's a doctor, that friend's uncle who's a judge who becomes Willie's attorney general—all succumb to Willie, with tragic results (suicide, ruin). The film climaxes (spoiler alert) when Willie is assassinated by the doctor friend.

With Trump bragging about his "yuge" numbers, when I viewed the film this time, I noticed especially the surging crowds, beginning with the opening credits, with Willie seen from behind, working the crowd. After the assassination, Burden sees his redemption as telling that crowd, belatedly, what the real Willie Stark was like. That would be a difficult book to write: As Willie said (echoing Trump!), "Just make it up as you go along." This film, directed by Robert Rossen, won Oscars for Best Picture and Best Actor, for Broderick Crawford (pictured at top) as Willie.

Meet John Doe (1941)

The film most closely portraying the likes of Bernie Sanders has to be *Meet John Doe*, the Frank Capra classic about an Everyman spokesman for "the little man" set in the Great Depression. Played by

Gary Cooper, "John Doe" begins as an accidental Everyman, the brainchild of a columnist (Barbara Stanwyck) who, desperate to keep her own job, fakes a letter from "A Disgusted American Citizen." This fictitious John Doe lost his job four years earlier, can't find work, thought it was all due to "slimy politics" but has come to feel "the whole world is going to pot," so in protest he threatens to jump off City Hall on Christmas Eve. Cooper, an out-of-work baseball player, agrees to the impersonation at first, enjoying warm food and new clothes, despite his pal Walter Brennan's warnings about the evils of having a bank account and owning things.

But in the movie's second half, John Doe becomes a more intentional Everyman—and more like Bernie Sanders. When John Doe gives a speech on national radio pitched to the John Does of America—"We've been in there dodging left hooks since before history began to walk"—and urges all John Does to reach out to each other—"You can't be a stranger to a guy who's on your own team"—John Doe clubs begin popping up all over, becoming a national movement. When he learns ambitious oilman D.B. Norton (Edward Arnold) is bankrolling the clubs as his own path to the White House, declaring there's to be "a new order of things" and what America needs is "an iron hand, discipline," John Doe connects the dots between a corrupt capitalism and the political process and revolts—making a moral argument sounding much like the one Sanders has delivered on the campaign trail for months.

Some critics deride Capra for sentimentalism ("Capra-corn"), but his human touch with The People and faith in democracy elevates. As Stanwyck's jaded editor says, "I'm a sucker for this country. I like what we got here."

The Best Man (1964)

While the odds of a contested convention in either party diminish with each passing primary, it still could happen. Sanders, trailing Hillary Clinton in delegates, vows to stay in til the end. Trump, presumptive GOP nominee now that his last opponents have dropped out, could commit one outrage too many, say, play "the woman card" in a way repulsing even his anti-everybody base, and it's convention on.

If so, *The Best Man* is the best film dramatizing the raw power struggle of an open convention—the dynamics of candidates and staffs, playing defense and offense to action both actual and conjectured, hatching dirty tricks in desperation. In a smart screenplay by Gore Vidal, based on his stage play, power is the point or the subtext of every line. Henry Fonda plays Secretary of State William Russell, an intellectual who's diffident in his quest for the presidency, not really comfortable with ambition; his wife (Margaret Leighton), estranged because of his infidelities, makes a "treaty" and shows up for him. His major opponent is Communist-hating Senator Joe Cantwell (Cliff Robertson): "We gotta get tough," echoing today's GOP contenders.

The prize endorsement to be landed is that of ex-President Art Hockstader (Lee Tracy), a pure politician comfortable with infighting and compromise. In scenes that crackle, Hockstader grills both Russell (whom he favors, except for the diffidence) and Cantwell on the uses of presidential power. Hockstader's sudden death hours later, before his endorsement is announced, forces the launching of dirty tricks by both Russell, reluctantly, and Cantwell, energetically. (Spoiler alert): It doesn't work out for either of them—and a dark horse wins the nomination.

The Last Hurrah (1958) and *The Candidate* (1972)

New media, or more specifically social media, features in the current presidential campaign, with Twitter blasts from the candidates themselves driving much of their own media operation. In the previous era, a new medium—television—begins to feature in the John Ford film, *The Last Hurrah*, and a dozen or so years later, in *The Candidate*, assumes the form and force that we know today.

In *The Last Hurrah*, Frank Skeffington, played by Spencer Tracy, announces he will run for a fifth term as mayor of an unnamed New England city (Boston?). As he tells his sports-writer nephew (Jeffrey Hunter), whom he invites on the campaign trail for "historical" reasons, Skeffington knows his kind of campaigning—gathering together any crowd that will listen to him—is "on its way out, just as I am." Henceforth, "It'll all be TV and radio—streamlined, nice and easy." The anti-Skeffington coalition supports the telegenic but simpering Kevin McCloskey, who will undergo a pioneering at-home TV interview, with family involved. At this point the film drops its examination of the impact of TV on political campaigns to focus more on the anti-Skeffington coalition: They are of the old Yankee stock who still resent the Irish newcomers "crowding in." This time (spoiler alert) they win: Skeffington loses. (The director, John Ford, was Irish-American.)

The Candidate, on the other hand, is largely played out before the TV camera, with image coming to dominate over content. In this context, messaging trumps policy proposals, as the hyper-telegenic and smart senatorial candidate Bill McKay, played by Robert Redford, soon finds out. A leftist lawyer, McKay fights on two fronts: with his campaign manager (Peter Boyle) who pushes him to shift to the center, as well as with his Republican opponent, a popular incumbent.

The stress of it all—on mush-speak, on image—causes McKay to have several comic breakdowns. Perhaps most famous is the final scene, in which, victorious but far adrift from his starting point, McKay turns to his campaign manager and asks: "What do we do now?" (Redford was the film's executive producer.)

Mr. Smith Goes to Washington (1939)

If the present unpleasantness becomes too much—and we haven't even gotten to the general election yet, which likely will pit Donald Trump against Hillary Clinton and which many commentators predict will be historically brutal—there is always the classic *Mr. Smith Goes to*

Washington, to remind us of the possibilities of politics and the idealism that (spoiler alert) motivates more office-seekers than today's cynicism can acknowledge. The director once again is Frank Capra.

The storyline is well-known: Jefferson Smith, leader of the Boy Rangers organization and played by Jimmy Stewart, is appointed to fill the seat of a senator who's died. Mr. Smith arrives in Washington in full naïveté. When he learns of the corruption of Senator Joseph Paine (Claude Rains), his home-state mentor and friend of his late beloved father—Paine is in league with the political machine run by "Big Jim" Taylor (Edward Arnold again) and they have plans for the land Jeff proposes for a national boys' camp—Jeff, disillusioned, packs up and leaves, making a last stop at the Lincoln Memorial. There, his once-cynical but now adoring aide Saunders (Jean Arthur) finds him and begs him to continue the fight. He does, and mounts one of cinema's most famous sequences: his filibuster on the Senate floor.

This "Capra-corn" invokes the American ideal of "looking out for the other guy," an ideal we've lost sight of today. It also satisfies in this regard: The corrupt Sen. Paine tries to shoot himself and, failing, rushes to the Senate floor to exonerate the exhausted Mr. Smith. Cured of his naïveté but not his decency, Mr. Smith will go on.

Another positive reminder of what politics can achieve is HBO's upcoming *All the Way*, about President Lyndon Johnson's battles to pass the historic Civil Rights Act of 1964. Starring Bryan Cranston, it is based on the first part of Robert Schenkkan's superb two-part play *All the Way*.

Finally: Unless I am blanking, there is no American film that captures the totality—and danger—of our present campaign mix: a populist anger so great on the Trump side that it's ready to wreck our governmental institutions, and on the Sanders side, that urges "political revolution" without much of a roadmap; a dangerous demagogue (Trump) who destroyed his primary opponents with Pinocchio-level lies and insult, who prizes unpredictability in foreign relations, and who's fine with torture; and a growing anxiety in the conscientious public that the fabric of American democracy—and decency—is giving way.

Part of the present totality is Hillary Clinton's campaign for the White House, for which Hollywood has no story, thus we have not discussed it here. Shamefully, Hollywood has never treated a serious woman's quest for political power seriously.

Can Mr. Smith—and now, of course, Ms. Smith too—still get to Washington? If they can, can they resurrect the mechanisms of our democracy? Once upon a time, movies gave us possibility, but movies today, and the arts in general, are more about destruction and decay (tragedy), not rebuilding and reform (renaissance).

Analyze *that*, Hollywood—all of it, seriously. *Can* Mr. or Ms. Smith get to a New Day?

—*HuffPost*, May 9, 2016

London Rejects Fear and Elects Its First Muslim Mayor

WITH 50% OF Americans agreeing with fear-mongering Donald Trump that Muslims must be barred from entering this country, the fact that London, one of the world's most important cities and capital of the country with whom we have a "special relationship," just elected the first Muslim mayor in its long and storied history must seem incomprehensible to half the U.S.

The fact that Sadiq Khan won with 57% of the vote and his closest opponent, who played the terrorist card against him, got only 43% of the vote—giving this son of a bus driver from Pakistan, who grew up to become a human rights lawyer, Labour member of Parliament, and cabinet minister, *the biggest personal mandate of any politician in British history*, in an election drawing the biggest turnout ever—must seem equally incomprehensible to many here in the U.S.

But those are the remarkable facts. What a difference fear makes.

Here in America, amid a fear-driven and apocalyptic Republican presidential campaign—with each primary victory Trumps renews his promise, "We're gonna build a wall, folks!"—the question we Americans must ask ourselves is this: *When did we become so afraid*—of Muslims, of "the other"?

Demographically, London provides more potential tinder than the U.S.: Fully one-eighth of London residents are Muslim and, overall, one-quarter are foreign-born, making London a cosmopolitan magnet. London also has had its catastrophic 9/11 event: the terrorist attacks by radical Islamists on the city's transportation system—the underground and a bus—on July 7, 2005, now known as 7/7, that left 52 dead.

In this combustible context, when Islamophobia is on the rise—in London, here, and throughout the West in general—almost everything depends on political leadership.

Unlike the race-baiting and divisive Trump, Sadiq Khan ran an inclusive campaign, with the slogan, "A mayor for all Londoners." Likewise, on the campaign trail and in the media, Khan presented himself as all-inclusive, containing multitudes: "I'm a Londoner, I'm European, I'm British, I'm English, I'm of Islamic faith, of Asian origin, of Pakistani heritage, a dad, a husband."

While Khan made clear he is not a "spokesman for Islam," stressing, again, he'd be a mayor for all Londoners, at the same time he fronted the threat of radical Islam and pointed to himself as someone uniquely able to counter Islamist terrorism:

"Clearly, being someone who is a Muslim brings with it experiences that I can use in relation to dealing with extremists and those who want to blow us up.... What better antidote to the hatred they spew than someone like me being in this position?"

After the Paris terrorist attacks last November, in a speech Khan said that Muslims have a "special role" to play in countering terrorism

"not because we are more responsible [for terrorism] than others, as some have wrongly claimed, but because we can be more effective at tackling extremism than anyone else."

On the subject of countering extremism, in his mayoral campaign Khan said:

"My experience in... taking on the preachers of hate was saying to them it's compatible being British, being Western, being Muslim. I've experienced the receiving end of this extremism, whether it's the extremists campaigning against me when I stood for Parliament in 2005 and 2010 and 2015, saying somehow it was haram—sinful—to vote, let alone to stand for Parliament. I've been on the receiving end of a fatwa [death sentence] when fighting for equality in relation to same sex marriage..., so I understand what that's like."

Upon his victory, achieved with an inclusive campaign, Khan exulted in the record turnout and his record mandate:

"That shows what a wonderful city we are. We're not simply tolerating each other—you tolerate a toothache. I don't want to be tolerated. We respect, we embrace, and we celebrate, which is fantastic."

Contrast that positive outlook with the preacher of hate Donald Trump, who spews against nearly everybody—Muslims, Mexicans, Chinese, Japanese, women.

To be sure, there was hateful spewing in the London mayoral race. Khan's closest opponent and a conservative, Zac Goldsmith, tried to smear Khan with the terrorist tag, accusing Khan in his lawyer role of representing terrorists and charging Khan of giving "oxygen and cover" to them. (Khan's response: A lawyer sometimes represents clients he does not agree with.) Goldsmith also charged that Khan shared a speaker's platform nine times with an imam whom he accused, falsely, of supporting radical Islam. Both charges were fanned by the conservative press and repeated by conservative Prime Minister David Cameron in Parliament (on video). (The P.M. has since apologized "for any misunderstanding.")

Impressively, Khan shows no fear in pushing back at fear-mongers, as he did in his own campaign. Already Khan is calling out Trump on his fear-mongering, saying Trump is "ignorant" about Islam, "alienates" mainstream Muslims, and "plays into the hands" of the extremists" (on video). He adds he hopes Trump "loses badly" and offers to help Hillary Clinton in that task. (Presumably his offer extends to Bernie Sanders too, should Sanders become the Democratic nominee.) As Khan says, "I think what we've shown—and I hope it's a lesson that Hillary and others in America take on board—hope does trump fear, forgive the pun."

Also impressively, Khan would reject a President Trump's offer to make an "exception" to his ban on Muslims and invite him to Washington. Khan's reason? "This isn't just about me. It's about my friends, my family, and everyone who comes from a background similar to mine." (Cleverly, Khan now invites Trump to London to visit his Muslim family and get educated about Islam. Stupidly and hypocritically, Trump calls Khan "very rude"—this from Donald the Rude—and challenges him to an I.Q. test!) Of course Trump now weasels on his Muslim ban, claiming it was just a "suggestion," not a real vow. Point: Sadiq Khan for moral leadership.

Now, back to the question: Why are Americans so susceptible at this point in our history to a fear-monger, such that he is now the presumptive nominee of one of our two major political parties? When did we become so afraid of Muslims, of "the other"?

It would take a book to unpack the reasons. Understandably, the recent terrorist attack in San Bernardino by radical Islamists would be cited as one, but does that truly justify all the fear and hysteria? Certainly, the signs of that fear and hysteria are everywhere: a citizenry armed to the teeth; gun sales setting records; states passing "concealed carry" laws permitting citizens to carry guns onto college campuses and even into churches; and the above-mentioned major political party stoking the fear and hysteria with over-the-top demagogy and a near-treasonous scorn of President Obama for not saying the words "radical Islamic terrorism."

Perhaps it comes down to national culture. The English have a reputation for "the stiff upper lip," while Americans don't. (We used to have a similar rep, for grinning and bearing it, also for being cool.) Perhaps we Americans might take a cue from our transatlantic "special relationship." As a wag writing for *The Economist* put it, invoking England's famous World War II slogan "Keep calm and carry on": Sadiq Khan won the London mayor's race by defying fear and conveying civility—with a campaign whose slogan might have been (wrote the wag) "Keep Khan and carry on"—a campaign which, admirably, Londoners embraced, building a bridge to their multi-ethnic future.

So, my dear fellow Americans: Keep calm and carry on—with much less fear, O.K.?

—*HuffPost*, May 19, 2016

Making History, Our First Woman Presidential Nominee "Remembers the Ladies"

EARLY IN THE creation of our Constitution, Abigail Adams in March 1776 wrote to her husband John Adams, a leading Founding Father, and famously appealed to him: to "Remember the Ladies, and be more generous and favourable to them than your ancestors." John Adams, otherwise a wise man who would become a wise President, in this instance was dismissive and mocking in reply: "As to your extraordinary Code of Laws, I cannot but laugh."

Two hundred and forty years later, Hillary Rodham Clinton, in securing the requisite number of delegates to win the Democratic presidential nomination and become the first woman of any party to do so in American history, took to the stage last Tuesday night and, in her opening remarks, paid silent homage to Abigail Adams and remembered the ladies.

Specifically, Clinton remembered the women, and men, who worked on behalf of the rights of women, who climbed into the arena to do political and cultural battle:

"Tonight's victory is not about one person. It belongs to generations of women and men who struggled and sacrificed and made this moment possible."

Continuing in a historical vein, Clinton noted:

"In our country, it started right here in New York, a place called Seneca Falls, in 1848, when a small but determined group of women and men

came together with the idea that women deserved equal rights, and they set it forth in something called the Declaration of Sentiments, and it was the first time in human history that that kind of declaration occurred. So we all owe so much to those who came before, and tonight belongs to all of you."

In including men among those honored in the struggle for women's rights, Clinton showed more magnanimity than John Adams did in his role as Constitution-shaper. In his defense, John would plead the exigencies of rebellion against the British, with "the bands of Government" loosened all about. In his response to Abigail, he cited children and apprentices grown "disobedient." He complained—fatefully for the country's future—that "Indians slighted their Guardians and Negroes grew insolent to their Masters." And now his wife brings "the first intimation that another Tribe more numerous and powerfull than all the rest were grown discontented."

It is the height of counter-factual history, and yet imperative to consider: If the conceptual framework of the U.S. Constitution had been less "tribal" (that is, white) and more focused on power-*sharing*, think of the lives not lost and not deformed because of tyranny. Abigail herself pointed to the problem: "Remember all Men would be tyrants if they could."

In a way, it is apt that it took another woman to deliver on Abigail's demand to remember the ladies, even if it took 240 years: Abigail threatened rebellion from the ladies if their interests were not included in the Constitution. In that famous letter to John, she wrote (these spellings are hers):

> "If perticullar care and attention is not paid to the Laidies we are determined to foment a Rebelion, and will not hold ourselves bound by any Laws in which we have no voice, or Representation."

Thus it is altogether fitting and proper that Hillary Clinton, in achieving the highest peak in national life a woman has scaled to date, saluted those who struggled and sacrificed for women's rights, those of us who made the long-running "Rebelion."

Some of us recognized that, if things went better for us collectively, things would go better for us individually. We looked around us, in our workplaces and public spaces, and where we saw imbalance, we sought balance. We got nervy and organized; we made speeches when we might have preferred listening; we called ourselves feminists and never forsook the term. We endured the shrugged shoulders and rolled eyes of friends and coworkers, including other women, who thought we were fools. We suffered the scorn of more traditional women who thought we were radicals. We abided stern lectures from our elders, and from other "Guardians" and "Masters," on the sacrilege of upending the natural order.

For we knew "the natural order" was not right, not natural. The full rights and dignity of women had yet to be affirmed, there was more organizing and lobbying and legislating to do. We climbed into the arena to make History by altering History.

Which is why Hillary's historic win of the presidential nomination last week, while not treated in the media as a particularly big deal, was a big deal to some of us, and so moving. It felt like History-making hard work was rewarded at last, while also reminding us of all the female talent that was held back or thwarted throughout the ages because of "tribal" stereotyping.

Of course, winning the nomination does not mean winning the White House. The general election coming up, pitting Hillary Clinton against Donald Trump—misogynist, xenophobe, tyrant—promises to be brutal. While I am not convinced Hillary playing the "woman card" is sound strategy (just as Barack Obama did not play the black card in his campaign), rest assured Mr. Trump will employ his entire arsenal of insults and smears, much of it aimed at womanhood while simultaneously reinforcing his own (white) manhood.

Complicating the ascent of this particular woman is the fact that many women reportedly do not like Hillary. To whom I would say:

Remember, Ladies, your sisters in political life have to leap many more hurdles than their male cohorts do. A little sympathy, please? And to the media: Why isn't the likeability standard applied to male politicians? Of course, if we are truly grown up, why is likeability even a standard?

Meanwhile, the world wonders at our struggle: Currently, eighteen (18) countries are led by women. Examples in the recent past include Golda Meir, Indira Gandhi, Margaret Thatcher. The world's oldest democracy hasn't produced one yet?

Back into the arena, Troops! Our "Rebelion" is not done.

—*HuffPost*, June 13, 2016

Beware the Disrupter With
No Follow-Up Plan
(A Post-Brexit Lesson)

WHAT DO YOU call leaders who lead their nation off a cliff, then, surveying the wreckage, they cut and run? How about "unconscionable"?

Such is the case with the two lead instigators of the movement to get Britain out of the European Union, the so-called Brexit—Boris Johnson, the conservative former mayor of London and Nigel Farage, leader of the far-right, anti-immigration U.K. Independence Party, UKIP.

First, Johnson and Farage pushed their electorate with scare tactics and misrepresentations to vote for exit. Then, when they succeeded, causing a political and economic earthquake—the British pound immediately fell to a 31-year low (almost 15%), London may lose its primacy as a world financial center, who knows what lies ahead for the ordinary bloke?—both Johnson and Farage abandoned the field.

What kind of responsible leadership is that? These disrupters cause the earthquake, then vanish at the clean-up and recovery? Unconscionable.

Adding ignominy to irresponsibility, before bowing out, both walked back their prior claims of what Brexit would achieve for Britain: that monies the government sent to the E.U. would be rerouted to the National Health Service (Farage, on video), that the scurrilously anti-immigrant Brexit campaign wasn't about immigration at all, not really (Johnson, in a column).

Clearly, these disrupters had no follow-up plan to victory. One wonders, then, how serious they were. Johnson in particular—brilliant, witty, host of a very successful summer Olympics in London—was known to have ambitions to become Prime Minister. Apparently, though, he's more wit than wisdom, or even political know-how: Just days after the

Brexit vote, Johnson announced he would not stand for P.M. and guide the nation out of the upheaval he spearheaded.

(Johnson's conservative rival, Prime Minister David Cameron, resigned immediately upon the Brexit vote, but Cameron's resignation is understandable: Advocating that Britain remain in the E.U., he has no wish to oversee a divorce he did not want.)

Days later Farage resigned as head of UKIP. In his announcement (video), it's clear he too had no follow-up plan to victory: He simply wanted Britain out of the E.U., full stop. Once he achieved that, not wanting to be a "career politician," what more could he want? (How about continuity?) Also, as his parting shot, Farage made a singularly ungracious and disruptive speech to the European Parliament (video).

The lesson for America, of course, is this: We have a major disrupter in our midst—Donald Trump, presumptive GOP presidential nominee. Learning from our British friends, we must ask: Should he win, how serious would Trump be about governing? Trump's whole campaign—from destroying his Republican presidential rivals with insults and smears, to his notions of what he'd do once in the White House—is based on disruption.

But Trump's disruption is for spectacle, not reform or coherence. Indeed, the burden to disprove this claim would lie with Trump's supporters: Where is the rationale for any of his proposals? Trump states flatly that, in foreign relations, he would prize "unpredictability," i.e., disruption. In an unsettled world, such behavior from the superpower would be... unconscionable. Don't think Trump wouldn't be disruptively unpredictable in domestic affairs, too.

Disrupters and disruption are all the vogue now, especially in technology and business. For sure, disrupting the business-as-usual, establishment model is sometimes the only way forward, as Bill Gates and others demonstrated with their computer revolution. The history of capitalism is replete with other instances of "creative destruction."

But disrupters come with various intentions, good or ill; they come more or less equipped with follow-up plans post-disruption; and they come more or less serious and responsible. In an article titled "The Disruption Machine," Jill Lepore of *The New Yorker* discusses disruption's downside, "what the gospel of innovation gets wrong." An important distinction: The stakes in technological disruption bear on profits, while the stakes in the public realm—politics—are mediated, as Lepore writes, by "obligations, your conscience, loyalty, a sense of the commonweal" (or should be).

Lord knows, the political establishment throughout much of the world invites—begs for—disruption. In the Brexit case, the European Union, originally established to prevent another European war like World War I and II, has shown itself ineffective in managing the recent Eurozone debt and refugee crises, while encumbering member states with sometimes silly regulations. Can the E.U. reform itself? With Britain's exit, will other members follow suit? Or could disruption lead to renewal?

Here in the U.S., the political establishment likewise begs for disruption, after years of partisan dysfunction, decades of American jobs shipped overseas, decades of stagnant wages squeezing the middle and working classes in real suffering, and more—all leaving Americans wondering if America the Great is in decline. No wonder this presidential campaign features two disrupters: Trump and, on the Democratic side, Bernie Sanders. (Hillary Clinton is more steward than disrupter.) People desperately want change.

But Bernie Sanders is a constructive disrupter: A deeply committed man of the people, he's railed for years against income inequality and money-power in politics, while advocating for free public college tuition and universal healthcare. Though he too was rather light on a follow-up plan if he won—he did not map out the trillions in new taxes required to pay for it all—one could trust this disrupter. But Trump?

We who love Britain pray that the Brits will recover, but in this post-Brexit moment, there is considerable buyer's remorse there. We who love America should note that remorse: My fellow Americans, beware the disrupter with no follow-up plan.

—*HuffPost*, July 8, 2016

Support the Police *and* Address Police Violence: The True "Law and Order"

BEWARE THE DEMAGOGUE taking advantage of a crisis.

With Donald Trump declaring himself "the law and order candidate" in the wake of recent racial tragedy—the killings of two black men by white police officers in Baton Rouge and St. Paul and the massacre in Dallas of five police officers at a #BlackLivesMatter protest by a black madman out to "kill white people" in revenge—Trump takes a hard line and only one side of a very big problem.

And now, with the tragic killing of three police officers in Baton Rouge by a black man, Trump doubles down on his call: "We demand law and order." Law and order is featuring heavily as a theme at the Republican national convention, underway this week. Indeed, the convention's theme of the first day was "Make America Safe Again," echoing Trump's campaign slogan, "Make America Great Again."

"Law and order": Harking back to the racial manipulations of Richard Nixon and George Wallace in the 1960s, the call for "law and order" is commonly understood as a racially-coded call for maximum force from the police, forget community relations. Indeed, Trump now enthusiastically embraces Nixon and his nefarious strategy.

Downplaying the mounting evidence of black men dying at the hands of the police, Trump after Dallas demanded unquestioning allegiance to law enforcement:

> *"It's time for our hostility against our police and against all members of law enforcement to end and end immediately, right now."*

To keep the discussion honest and constructive—and to avoid a repeat of 1968: Nixon's racial politics won over "the silent majority" and left America's structural racism intact—it is vital that, rather than be silent, We the Conscientious People put our hand on the tiller of fast-moving events and declare:

"No, we can do both: We can support the police and address police violence."

For this is not an either-or question, it is both-and: We can both support our police, who—*in the vast main*—render valiant service by putting their lives on the line day and night to protect us. And at the very same time we can address the brutality of those lesser officers, far fewer in number, who too readily take a black life, as we have seen in too many horrific instances filmed by bystanders.

Trump is being joined by other law-and-order hard-liners; together, they are framing the debate in hot rhetoric and targeting #BlackLives Matter. A false argument over priorities—blue lives vs. black lives—is shaping up. One police chief called #BlackLivesMatter protesters "criminals"; another police chief called #BLM a "radical hate group." Yet another called #BLM "a terrorist group" (this chief has been ousted). Rudy Giuliani, New York's "9/11 mayor" who's evolved into an unprincipled fear-monger, on *Face the Nation* called #BLM "inherently racist." Likewise Trump calls #BLM "inherently racist."

But by demonizing a movement, law-and-order hard-liners ignore both the human tragedy of black lives lost, as well as the operational problem of police violence. Conscientious people must prevent the movement's stigmatization. As a #BLM leader, DeRay Mckesson, said after the Baton Rouge police killings: "The movement began as a call to end violence. That call remains."

It should be noted Trump's law-and-order call occurs in a period of major decline in crime rates. That bears repeating: We currently enjoy a decline in crime rates. One wonders, then, how Trump's motivation in calling himself the "law and order candidate" is anything other than political or his point anything other than racial. Demonizing a movement is a classic political tactic. (#BlackLivesMatter came into existence in 2012 *in response to* the Trayvon Martin murder.)

To be sure, some #BLM protesters use anti-cop language—and to keep the moral high ground, they should stop it, as President Obama urges. But it is also the case that some police officers have taken black lives in a manner conveying that, indeed, those lives did not matter. Can these points not be conceded, so real debate can take place? (Memo to #BLM: Since police reform is your objective, using anti-cop language only forces the police into a defensive crouch, *not* open to reform.)

It is to be hoped that where a police department can weed out its racist cops, it will. Good cops suffer deeply the taint that a few bad cops give the department and the entire profession. Especially since the Michael Brown killing two years ago by a police officer in Ferguson, Missouri, law enforcement has been under pressure to reform. Under review is the warrior versus guardian mindset; the President's Task Force on 21st Century Policing recommends adopting the guardian mindset.

As it happens, the Dallas P.D., now suffering the grievous loss of five officers, might serve as a model. A practitioner of community policing and de-escalation training, the Dallas P.D. boasts a reduced crime rate and a reduced rate of excessive-force complaints: In the past five years there were 150 to 200 per year, in 2015 just fourteen (14). Its chief, David O. Brown, has earned universal kudos for his handling of the massacre and its aftermath.

Still, bad cops exist, as the president of the Black Police Officers Association of Greater Dallas acknowledges on the *PBS NewsHour*. He calls on President Obama and Congress to pass laws that would purge bad cops across the country.

For his part, President Obama urges "mutual respect" on all sides to resolve this most obdurate of American problems, race. Presumptive Democratic presidential nominee, Hillary Clinton, has spoken of "white privilege": Privileged as we are, we might acknowledge that, in any encounter with the police, a white American's first reaction is not likely fear, while a black American's first reaction is.

In passing, this positive note: At the march in Dallas that ended in massacre, before the mayhem started, #BlackLivesMatter protesters were taking selfies with the Dallas cops who were protecting them—a fleeting image of police-community solidarity. (Hold that picture.) The double irony is that the cops were protecting a march that was protesting police brutality.

And, bearing on law and order: Since Texas law allows guns to be openly carried, guns were openly carried by some #BlackLivesMatter protesters (and who knows how many guns were concealed), making the job—once the sniper's bullets were flying—of identifying friend from foe exceedingly difficult for the cops. Ohio, site of the Republican convention, also has open-carry laws, which Governor John Kasich declines to revoke—despite the urging of the Cleveland police. People: *Should we not rethink these gun laws?* (Memo to protesters: Leave the guns at home.)

Finally, conscientious people need to insist on another both-and: Both black lives *and* blue lives matter. Everybody wants justice.

Public discourse in America has become simplistic and binary: Either you're for X or against it, no nuance allowed. In political campaigns, with the power to govern at stake, this binary tendency becomes sharper, even more so in a time of fear. And fear defines the present moment. Ominously, Trump predicts more protest violence this summer. Prominent black writer Jelani Cobb writes that, taken together, these new calamities—Baton Rouge, St. Paul, Dallas—"have the feel of a national turning point."

Donald Trump, breaking all taboos on race to appeal to beleaguered whites, has weaponized the divisive rhetoric and now claims the mantle of law and order. Conscientious Americans must jam Trump's one-note law-and-order hard line, by insisting we can do both: We can support the police *and* address police violence.

—*HuffPost*, July 20, 2016

Books for Our Times:
Listen, Liberal, by Thomas Frank

Seventh in an ongoing series, Books for Our Times

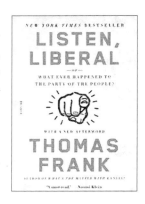

MUCH ANALYSIS THIS presidential season has focused on how far adrift the Republican party has moved from its base and its principles, this drift allowing for a take-over by an outsider (Donald Trump). But the same drift—from base and principles—has occurred in the Democratic party as well, as Thomas Frank describes in his broad and blistering survey, *Listen, Liberal: Or, What Ever Happened to the Party of the People?*

Frank, author of the influential *What's the Matter with Kansas?* and other books, is unsparing in his brief against the Democratic party. After all, the modern-day GOP never held itself out as anything other than the party of the plutocrats, with a bank vault for a heart. But the Democrats: It was "the party of the people," or supposed to be, until it too suffered a take-over by money, money, money and betrayed its historic dedication to the working and middle class. Frank writes as a broken-hearted liberal. This book might be titled *What Ever Happened to Liberals?*

Happily for the reader, Frank is a broken-hearted liberal with a sense of humor, as seen in his opening:

> "*There are consequences to excessive hope, just as there are to other forms of intemperance. One of these is disillusionment, another is anger, and a third is this book.*"

The "excessive hope" he refers to, of course, was raised with President Barack Obama's signature campaign slogan of "hope and change." In a pattern repeated throughout the book—raised hopes, dashed dreams—the author, a self-described "person of vivid pink sentiments," had his liberal heart broken when Obama, once inaugurated, spoke of striking "a grand bargain" on his pet deficit and tax deal with the obstructionist Republicans. "In a split second I understood the whole thing: that big compromises like this were real to the president, but 'change' was not."

What infuriates Frank even more: Mr. Obama early on had "the perfect opportunity for transformation"—an Ivy League "brain trust," a Democratically-controlled Congress, a public yearning for far-reaching reform. But: It didn't happen. Instead, Obama "saved a bankrupt system that by all rights should have met its end." Obama whiffed. But so did an earlier Democratic president, Bill Clinton. "This is a book," the author declares, "about the failure of the Democratic Party—about how they failed when the conditions for success were perfect."

Not only that, but since the 1970s Democrats have even turned on "the people" and tried to undo Franklin Roosevelt's nation-saving New Deal! *How could this happen?*

To explain how, Frank introduces the subject of inequality. Our "bankrupt system" desperately needs transformation because it allows gross and growing inequality—of income, well-being, spirit. But the dry term "inequality" doesn't begin to convey Frank's meaning. With heart and fire, he writes:

> *"'Inequality' is shorthand for all the things that have gone to make the lives of the rich so measurably more delicious, year on year for three decades—and also for the things that have made the lives of working people so wretched and so precarious. It is visible in the ever-rising cost of health care and college; in the coronation of Wall Street and the slow blighting of wherever it is you live; in the dot-com bubble, in the housing bubble, in whatever bubble is jazzing the business pages as you read this."*

Frank nails the problem thus: "'Inequality' is a euphemism for *the Appalachification of our world*" [my italics]. Inequality is why "some people find such significance in... the hop content of a beer while *others will never believe in anything again*" [my italics again]. In a word: Appalachification crushes. To ameliorate the crushed, Frank accuses Democrats of doing "vanishingly little." He further cites them for "snoozing through the liberal hour": Rather than take action, they're merely waiting for demographic shifts in the future to give them the Congressional majorities they need.

Stepping back further, the author says that, properly understood, inequality is not just an "issue," but "the eternal conflict of management and labor"—"with one side pinned to the ground and the other leisurely pounding away at its adversary's face." Frank harks back to the nineteenth century, when inequality was understood as "the social question": For once, he says, "their polite Victorian euphemism beats ours." In properly grand fashion, Frank states the central question: *"This is nothing less than the whole vast mystery of how we are going to live together"* (my italics again).

By now, the reader will say: "This is what Bernie Sanders has been shouting about." Apparently Frank's book went to press before Sanders launched his presidential campaign in May 2015—and went on to catch fire with progressive Democrats in the primaries—for Sanders is mentioned nowhere in the book. (Lopsidedly, Hillary Clinton, Sanders's opponent, comes in for extended examination.)

Frank charts a brief history of "the party of the people"—perhaps too briefly: He devotes one sentence to the ignominious period when "the Party of the People was also, once, the Party of Slavery and the Party of the Klan." Taken in the overall, though, the noble lineage stretches from James Madison, who identified "unequal distribution of property" as the main cause of "faction," to Sen. Thomas Hart Benton, who in 1835 distinguished the two parties as "founded on the radical question, whether PEOPLE, or PROPERTY, shall govern." Skipping over the slavery period, Frank picks up with William Jennings Bryan's Cross of Gold speech in 1896 and Franklin Roosevelt in 1936 deploring "economic royalists." And of course there was FDR's New Deal, which saved a nation brought low by the Great Depression. Frank quotes Harry Truman for a 1948 speech explicitly identifying the Democrats with the common folk. "The Democratic Party represents the people," Truman said:

> "It is pledged to work for agriculture. It is pledged to work for labor. It is pledged to work for the small businessman and the white-collar worker. The Democratic Party puts human rights and human welfare first. But the attitude of the Republican gluttons of privilege is very different. The bigmoney [sic] Republican looks on agriculture and labor merely as expense items in a business venture. He tries to push their share of the national income down as low as possible and increase his own profits. And he looks upon the Government as a tool to accomplish this purpose."

This brief history is only a prelude for Frank to level his most damning accusation: that—starting in the 1970s and '80s with "futurist" liberals, whose thinking was acted on with special vigor in the administration of Bill Clinton but also in that of Mr. Obama—the Democratic party betrayed this sacred pledge to the people by shifting its focus to the professional class.

Among these "futurist" Democrats (Frank names names), the "thinking" went thus: Industrial society has gone into eclipse, the future belongs to "change" and "high-tech," the workers—the core of the New Deal coalition—are the principal group arrayed against these forces of change, labor unions are an economic drag on this change, let's welcome the technical expert! (One sees the moral vacuity of the term "change.") By the early '90s the Democratic Leadership Council (DNC) declared that to "do business" in a "post-industrial, global economy," we (these are Frank's words) "needed to reform 'entitlements' (i.e., Social Security), privatize government operations, open charter schools, get tough on crime, and all the rest of it."

This "grubby dialectic" of the DNC, led by Bill Clinton, infused his administration when he took power in 1992. Frank is acid on his legacy of betrayal to the people:

"[I]t was Bill Clinton's administration that deregulated derivatives, deregulated telecom, and put our country's only strong banking laws in the grave. He's the one who rammed the North American Free Trade Agreement (NAFTA) through Congress and who taught the world that the way you respond to a recession is by paying off the federal deficit. Mass incarceration and the repeal of welfare, two of Clinton's other major achievements, are the pillars of the disciplinary state that has made life so miserable for Americans in the lower reaches of society. He would have put a huge dent in Social Security, too, had the Monica Lewinsky sex scandal not stopped him. If we take inequality as our measure, the Clinton administration looks not heroic but odious."

And for whom were the people betrayed? The professionals, the "well-graduated":

"an enormous and prosperous group, the people with the jobs every parent wants their child to grow up and get. In addition to doctors, lawyers, the clergy, architects, and engineers—the core professional groups—the category includes economists, experts in international development, political scientists, managers, financial planners, computer programmers, aerospace designers, and even people who write books like this one."

Wrenching liberalism even further away from a philosophy exalting the sons of toil is the new "knowledge economy"—"specifically, the knowledge economy's winners: the Silicon Valley chieftains, the big university systems, and the Wall Street titans."

Warming to his theme—radiating actually—Frank excoriates the "well-graduated" for their betrayal. What gives this class its status is learning and expertise, which a complicated world requires; thus we grant them elevated status—in exchange for a tacit promise of public service: "The professions are supposed to be disinterested occupations or even 'social trustees.'" But—and this is Frank's key question:

> "What happens when an entire category of experts stops thinking of itself as 'social trustees'? What happens when they abuse their monopoly power? What happens when they start looking mainly after their own interests, which is to say, start acting as a class?"

But it did happen: The well-graduated betrayed "the people." Of course there are many exceptions—individuals who are educated *and* conscientious—but, *as a class*, Frank has a point about professionals. While the Gilded Age reformers known as "progressives" saw professionalization as a positive thing—an enlightened managerial class would "bring about an industrial peace that would be impossible under the profit motive alone"—today, "that system of professionalism was long ago subverted and transformed into something different and more rapacious":

> "Today we live in a world of predatory bankers, predatory educators, even predatory health care providers, all of them out for themselves."

The turn toward predatory behavior Frank traces to the modern-day liberal's unquestioning respect for expertise: their "blindness to predatory behavior *if it comes cloaked in the signifiers of professionalism*" [my italics again]. Exhibit A: the "complex" financial instruments that drove the 2008 financial crisis:

> "For old-school regulators ... undue financial complexity was an indicator of likely fraud. But for the liberal class, it is the opposite: an indicator of sophistication. Complexity is admirable in its own right."

About inequality, Frank cites professionals for a "profound complacency." Indeed, he contends, inequality is essential to professionals' class identity. Frank traces this complacency to the "pathologies of professionalism": the need for status, the tendency toward orthodoxy, the fact that professionals don't listen to anybody but other professionals, certainly not to the people. It's this complacency that allows liberals now to prioritize social issues over the economic reforms the people so desperately need. Finally, in advocating that blue-collar workers become better educated, liberals take the pressure off themselves to reform base economic conditions:

> "While this interpretation might have made... narcissistic sense to the well-graduated, it allowed Democrats to ignore what was happening in the real economy—from monopoly power to financialization to labor-management relations—in favor of a moral fantasy that required them to confront no one."

Sadly, organized labor, a traditional Democratic constituency, has lost its primacy of place, largely because it "signifies lowliness, not status." "Solidarity, the core value of unions, stands in stark contradiction to the doctrine of individual excellence."

In sum: Frank's indictment of liberals is stinging and comprehensive. Note there's not much here about Republican obstructionism. According to Frank, Democrats betrayed the people all by themselves.

The bulk of the book is Frank's detailed defense of his argument. He documents liberals' hopeful junctures and wrong turns from the Seventies to the present. On occasion he wields too broad a brush; for one thing, he shorts education for its humanistic value. Also, Frank is short on prescription. Probably he would agree: Liberals need to grow a heart as well as a spine again.

For me, the value-added element is Frank's revelations of the "well-graduated," set out in the first 50 pages. Suddenly, Republican gibes about Democrats as "limousine liberals" computed—the condescension of today's liberals of "fly-over country," of "red-necks," of organized labor. Not that the Republicans themselves got out of their limousines to help "the people." But between the contempt of both Republicans *and* Democrats, no wonder some working- and middle-class Democrats will vote for Donald Trump, the outsider who promises better trade deals and jobs, jobs, jobs.

Thomas Frank has written a book as original and compelling as George Packer's *The Unwinding*. In its broad-gauge tracing of the shifting contours of our modern landscape, it resembles C.P. Snow's 1959 book, *Two Cultures*, about the growing chasm between the arts and the sciences. I hope delegates to the Democratic national convention, underway this week, have copies of Frank's book on them. A convention would be a good place to throw the metaphoric grenade, pull out the drawing board, and demand of the like-minded: *Listen, liberals! We need a reset!*

—*HuffPost*, July 25, 2016

Bernie Sanders, Moral Hero

AT A TIME when so much in this world is wrong, a leader who "does the right thing"—the moral thing—is triply important: He advances the cause of rightness in a world of wrongness; he heals that hurting world; and, because his quest is moral, he provides his followers with the tools and the banner to carry on.

Bernie Sanders, in raising the moral question of inequality of income, has performed an act of incomparable value and one long overdue in our skewed capitalist system.

To hear Bernie state explicitly, over and over and over until he was hoarse, that it is not right—*it simply is not right*—that so few Americans enjoy economic security while the vast majority do not: How elevating, how tonic, how necessary! That millions and millions of Americans responded demonstrates that his quest to address the rightness and wrongness of things has struck us in our deepest and best selves.

And now, at the Democratic national convention, when Bernie had to concede the race for President to his opponent Hillary Clinton: To urge his delegates to support Hillary, as he did in his speech, then, during the roll call, to urge that Hillary be selected by acclamation—what grace, what magnanimity. And, when booed by his own supporters when he urged party unity, Bernie continued to make the moral argument—"It is easy to boo, but it is harder to look your kids in the face who would have to live under a Donald Trump presidency": More grace and magnanimity, in what must have been a heart-breaking turn.

Of course, income inequality isn't Bernie's only issue. There's also his call for free public college and universal healthcare, among others. But all these issues relate to the vast and growing imbalance of income—and all are now included, thanks to Bernie, in the 2016 Democratic party platform.

It takes a special kind of courage to undertake a moral quest—knowing the overwhelming forces arrayed against you, knowing the sheer inertia of a system long in place. But Bernie was no hapless Don Quixote, tilting at windmills. He is bigger and better than that: Our capitalist system simply has to change and Bernie simply—simply?—got into the arena to declare that simple truth. That's what moral heroes do: They do the right thing, no matter the obstacles and no matter how long the endurance test.

Moreover, it takes a special courage for someone in, shall we say, the later chapters of life to press and prosecute a moral campaign, all-consuming as such campaigns are. Hopefully the very rightness of his campaign against income inequality will give special meaning to his "last hurrah" as a presidential candidate.

Moral leadership is rare. How rare? History presents some few examples: Jesus, Joan of Arc, Abraham Lincoln, Dietrich Bonhoeffer (German theologian who defied Hitler), Martin Luther King, Jr. It should be noted all these historical figures died for their moral cause. Moral heroes, touching on core things, arouse strong reaction.

Sadly for our world, amoral behavior is far more prevalent than the moral kind. Breaking example: Donald Trump saying he hopes the alleged Russian hackers of the Democratic national committee's emails will find Hillary Clinton's missing State Department emails. If that isn't treason—literally inviting foreign espionage—it's in the zone, and done merely for political gain and/or moral-free whim. It's simply *unimaginable* Bernie would say or do anything so odious.

Like the big majority of Democrats, I would have been happy with either Bernie or Hillary as our presidential nominee. My admiration for the Senator grew and grew as he showed himself more and more a *Mensch*. I did want him to specify how he would achieve his costly program, but apparently he felt it was politically unwise to do so. He did succeed, however, in making his case: There is considerable public support for a "political revolution" on the inequality question.

Now, Democrats have to win big in November, not only to keep the

White House, but also take back the Senate—where Bernie, by rights, should have his pick of committee chairmanships. And where Bernie can lend support to President Hillary Clinton as she tries to "do the right thing."

Bernie Sanders will of course fight on, because moral leaders have to. Given the inexorableness of their mission, they can't give up. (Vacations are allowed, though.) Equally important, and promising, Bernie's cause—income inequality—will live on, because it is propelled not by "special interests," but by its moral rightness.

Bernie Sanders, moral hero: A grateful nation thanks you. Who will step up next?

—*HuffPost*, July 28, 2016

If Republicans Repudiate Donald Trump on Moral Grounds, They Could Truly Reform Their Party

WITH DONALD TRUMP's latest moral outrage—denigrating the Muslim-American parents of a dead war hero and claiming his "sacrifice" as a businessman equates to a hero's ultimate sacrifice—Republicans up and down the line, from elected leaders to the party's grass roots, have to be pondering their presidential pick.

Republicans are famously loyal. They also have long claimed the mantle of moral rectitude, which high claim has suffered badly of late—with a war of choice (Iraq), a descent into torture, a preference for the 1% over the 99%, a dedication to an unregulated free market, no matter the destruction it wreaks, among other moral failings. And these failings compound: Out of the failed state of Iraq arose ISIS, which Republicans out of moral guilt try to put on President Obama.

But, starting right now, today, Republicans could mount a moral reawakening of their party—by repudiating their moral catastrophe of a presidential nominee.

Let them count the ways in which Donald Trump fails the moral test—denigrating the Muslim-American parents and their heroic son, denigrating the judge of Mexican-American heritage, denigrating women as "fat pigs," threatening nuclear warfare, advocating torture, inviting foreign espionage to find Hillary Clinton's missing State Department emails, the list is long and various—and then, let them declare a New Day for the Grand Old Party.

Yes, it may mean losing the election in November, but the Republicans are going to lose anyway (I predict). Besides, basic political calculus dictates: The bigger Trump's loss and the more it is attributed to his moral failings, thanks in part to the case made by Republican reformers (with lots of help from the Democrats, of course), the stronger the hand of those GOP reformers post-election and the cleaner the slate from which to proceed.

Otherwise, if no moral reform is mounted, after Trump's loss in November the GOP establishment, or whatever desperate members remain of it, will try to reinstate the old—discredited—Republican brand. Not good. Or, might moral reform be the way the GOP establishment recovers its best self?

At the moment, it is painful to watch GOP "leaders" like House speaker Paul Ryan, Senate majority leader Mitch McConnell, and Senator John McCain all denounce Trump, but then fail to withdraw their endorsement. President Obama now calls on Republicans to do exactly that: repudiate Trump. As Mr. Obama puts it, "The question they have to ask themselves is: If you are repeatedly having to say in very strong terms that what he has said is unacceptable, why are you still endorsing him?"

Indeed. Of course, given Republicans' loathing of Mr. Obama, his advice won't likely be taken. But this doesn't mean the advice isn't sound or is a Trojan horse. This Democrat believes our democracy functions better with a strong two-party system.

Moreover, were Republicans to mount and succeed with their party's moral reawakening, they'd be better able to recognize the moral standing of the opposing party. Democrats are beyond tired at being tagged as amoral or pagan by the errant Republicans. True moral rectitude recognizes the validity of all humans.

Moral reform is the most profound and most powerful kind of reform. It provides a "firm foundation," as Martin Luther, the first Protestant, demonstrated in his argument against an errant Catholic Church in the 16th century. Moral reform is possible in all human endeavors, including politics.

So, Republicans: Be a "profile in courage." Be a Martin Luther, who in protest said, "Here I stand, I can do no other." Or, less grandly, as the

Nike ad urges, "Just do it"—because you know sooner or later it *must* be done. Repudiate Donald Trump and proceed with your party's moral reform. History, country, conscience—and party—require it.

—*HuffPost*, August 4, 2016

"Make Government Work Better": What Every Democratic Politician Should Promise in This Election

WITH GRASSROOTS ANGER driving this presidential election—anger at government, anger at Congress, anger at Wall Street, anger at the elites and the establishment, heck, anger at everything—Democrats could make electoral headway by addressing one of those objects with this do-able promise: "Make government work better."

And Democrats are the ones to make such promise, because, unlike Republicans who have ranted against all things government for generations now, Democrats still believe government can work for the benefit of the people.

Government touches our lives in many ways—at the federal, state, and local level. But those ways in recent years have not been altogether good, even including, sorry to say, during the Democratic administration of Barack Obama.

The stories of governmental ineptitude and waste of the Obama years are legion: The Department of Veterans Affairs forcing veterans into unconscionably long wait times for appointments, with vets dying without proper attention. The Internal Revenue Service improperly auditing conservative groups. The General Services Administration's lavish departmental conference in Las Vegas. The Secret Service's various scandals, too many to cite, jeopardizing its mission to protect the President.

And who can forget the totally bollixed rollout of Obamacare, which ate the news for a good year and which still taints the program, despite its ultimately smoother—and successful—operation. Readers will have other examples.

Sometimes it's the nearby snafu, at the state or local level, that rankles the worst. Here in Washington state, the Department of Corrections mistakenly released 3,300 prisoners before their terms were up, due to computer error. *Wait: Aren't humans in charge of the cell keys?* This failure of central mission drives citizens nuts and, in this case, fear for their safety. Sadly, this happened on a Democratic governor's watch.

Mission review in the agencies should be conducted constantly, to ensure that the central mission is being met—and to ensure, at the very least, that no more prisoners are released prematurely due to computer glitches. (Washington is not the only state guilty in this regard; so are Michigan, California, and Nebraska.)

In reaction post-snafu, it's not enough for an agency head to cite complexity or enormity of scale as the reason for an operational snafu. Presidents and governors who appoint agency heads absolutely need to ensure their appointees bring executive and managerial skills and are not just being rewarded for political favors.

Over time, the unending drip-drip-drip of government snafus in the media creates, like the halo effect, a smear effect that, in the mind of the increasingly angry citizen, goes beyond the inept agency in the headlines to smear all of government. Indeed, the question becomes for the angry citizen: Does *any* government agency work as it should—and as it did, once upon a time, in Franklin D. Roosevelt's administration during the Great Depression and World War II. Richard Nixon's Watergate scandal is marked by many observers as the advent of the public's declining trust in government.

It is the citizen, of course, who is most injured and ill-served when a government snafu occurs. But the other injured party, one not often recognized, is the highly-skilled and dedicated public servant, who, by the millions, graduate top of their class and head to Washington, D.C. or the state capitals to render service to the public. It's a noble profession, public service, but after decades of anti-government venom and innumerable snafus, one wonders how much longer the same quality will want to become the much-maligned "bureaucrat"?

Democrats: We have a repair job to do. At the Democratic national convention in July, much was said about government's role, but not much was said, either in speeches or the party platform, about making the government we have work better. In a hurting economy, government waste infuriates. In a nation unsure of its greatness, government ineptitude disheartens.

Democratic politicians can give heart and gain votes by vowing to make government work better. Especially with the visible public projects that seem never to get finished, like road or bridge repair, vow to finish them—and then, once in office, do it. A strong example: Democratic presidential nominee Hillary Clinton's vow to launch a $275-billion national infrastructure program, if she is elected.

Of course, to make government work better, we need political leaders who behave better. This is not to condemn the entire current roster, not at all; the Democrats in Congress are the members trying to make that dysfunctional institution functional; they are dedicated public servants of sound character. But, recurring to the smear effect again: All it takes in today's angry atmosphere is just one bad actor (for one, ex-Congressman Anthony Wiener), indulging in tasteless behavior or wrongdoing, to smear all of his cohorts, leading the public to conclude all politicians are perverts or crooks. This is a massive load for the conscientious politician (of whom, again, there are many).

And once in office, legislators must appropriate sufficient budget funds to the agencies, so agencies can get their legislated job done. A Congress back in the control of Democrats could end the endless Republican budget games.

To conclude: Donald Trump has stoked the anger and disillusion in the country with his slogan, "Make America Great Again," proposing authoritarian and xenophobic means to achieve a better day. Democrats recognize the perils of the present moment, but, more hopeful, believe adherence to America's foundational ideals will bring us to that better day, thus our favorite slogan, "We Can Do Better."

So, Democrats: Make the U.S. government—once a marvel in world history—work better.

—*HuffPost*, August 25, 2016

Clinton's "Deplorables" Gaffe Lets Trump Seize the High Ground

WHAT A DIFFERENCE a gaffe makes. As an unexpected gift from the gods, Donald Trump, pouncing on his opponent's verbal misstep, seizes the high ground—a place he could never, ever occupy on his own.

Following the breath-taking, totally avoidable gaffe Hillary Clinton made at a New York fundraiser, in which she loaded whole classes into a "basket of deplorables"—saying "half" of Trump's supporters were "racist, sexist, homophobic, xenophobic, Islamophobic, you name it"—Trump instantly tweeted this in their defense:

"Wow, Hillary Clinton was SO INSULTING to my supporters, millions of amazing, hard working people. I think it will cost her at the polls!"

Thus the candidate who's taken American presidential politics on a road lower than it has ever been—with his appeals that are not dog-whistle subtle but blatantly racist, sexist, homophobic, xenophobic, Islamophobic, you name it—gets to stand up as The People's Defender.

This is, after all, the man who got a running start at the presidency by promoting the racist "birther" myth, claiming our first African-American president, Barack Obama, is not American-born. And now—deplorably!—damage done and no repentance, Trump acknowledges Mr. Obama is American. The media are flatly using the term "lie." Then Trump lies again by blaming Hillary Clinton for starting the birther myth.

This is a man so sexist he says of Clinton—so insulting—"Does she look presidential, fellas? Give me a break." His xenophobia leads him to attack the Muslim parents of a son who sacrificed his life for his unit in Iraq. Trump's motto "Make America Great Again" is the siren song of white Americans angry at their loss of primacy, an appeal based on blood rather than our foundational ideals of equality and fair play. Into this dark space the white supremacist alt-right movement has risen to prominence.

Outrageously, ominously, Trump stokes violence. He signals his supporters may have to defend their Second Amendment rights if Clinton is elected and takes away their guns, and now, stunningly, he suggests her Secret Service agents should disarm ("See what happens to her"), all meaning—what?—he invites her assassination?

Truly: "Deplorable" is the word best describing the depths to which Trump has dragged America. But, thanks to his opponent's verbal gaffe, Trump now vaults to the moral upside, again a place he could never normally occupy.

Post-gaffe, Clinton next day tried to walk back her "deplorables" comment, saying she did not mean to demean "half" of Trump's supporters. But, for that news cycle at least, she was on the downside and parsing couldn't help.

Meanwhile, reinforcing his fraudulent claim to the high ground, Trump days later gave a speech in statesman mode, at the National Guard's annual convention, expanding on his defense of working-class Americans "viciously demonized" by Clinton, who "looks down on the proud citizens of our country as subjects for her rule":

> *"Hillary Clinton is an insider supported by powerful insiders attacking Americans who have absolutely no political power. Hillary Clinton spoke with hatred and derision for the people who make this country run. She spoke with contempt for the people who thanklessly follow the rules, pay their taxes and scratch out a living for their family; a hard-earned living, too."*

This from the man who viciously demonizes all opponents. Expect to hear this *faux*-statesman message non-stop until November.

Rule №1 in campaign politics is: Never attack or malign the voter. How could Clinton, a savvy politician with decades in public life—but more to the point, a dedicated humanitarian—forget this basic rule about honoring the voter's humanity? As Democrats know by now (or their campaign managers should), Republicans are quick to cudgel "limousine liberals" who mock "fly-over country."

The proper target for attack, of course, is one's opponent, especially an opponent who maligns America's foundational ideals and draws voters to his skewed view—as Trump is doing with dismaying success. Revealed in this ugly campaign are—deplorable fact—the considerable number of racists, sexists, homophobes, xenophobes, and Islamophobes who do indeed find shelter and fuel in Trump's rancid views. Some may be, as Clinton said, "irredeemable."

But another rule of campaign politics is this: Voters are redeemable. Those Trump supporters who are not racist or sexist, etc., but who are hurting in this economy *can* be reached, and it will take all the former Secretary of State's diplomacy to do it. Clinton gestured to them in the second part of her "deplorables" speech, but nobody heard it. Honoring their humanity, she described them as:

> *"people who feel that the government has let them down, the economy has let them down, nobody cares about them, nobody worries about what happens to their lives and their futures, and they're just desperate for change. It doesn't really even matter where it comes from."*

Hillary Clinton can recover from her "deplorables" comment—and retake the moral high ground, where she absolutely needs to get, no more stumbles—by doing proper penance and apologizing for appearing to slur Trump's supporters (in contrast to Trump's non-apology for his birther fraud) and by resuming her attack on Trump himself—and not his supporters—for his bigoted, deplorable campaign.

But more crucially, Clinton needs to unleash her inner humanitarian, to reconnect with voters at their deepest level. Enough with the 10-point plans, show us passion, most especially the passion to change for the better the lives of those working- and middle-class voters she cited who are "just desperate for change."

In these hard and unhappy times, Trump is touted the change agent and Clinton the status-quo candidate. But if the status-quo candidate became a crusader for change, she could rescue us from the fate—truly deplorable—of a Trump presidency.

—*HuffPost*, September 20, 2016

Books for Our Times: *It Can't Happen Here*, by Sinclair Lewis (a Novel)

Eighth in an ongoing series, Books for Our Times

THROUGHOUT THIS UGLY presidential campaign, the prospect of fascism coming to America has been raised repeatedly to describe a Donald Trump presidency. Polls at this time show Hillary Clinton and Trump uncomfortably close.

While the term "fascist" is often flung loosely, to disparage someone or something the speaker doesn't like or agree with, it's still the case that democracies, based on popular support, are vulnerable when that popular support flows to a strongman leader promising a New Day. Fascism

is generally understood to be strongman rule; after that, it gets less clear.

Since these are turbulent times and this type of leader is likely to come forward again, it's important to understand the dynamics of the mix. Best to return to the dictionary. The full definition of fascism given by the Merriam-Webster dictionary is this: "a political philosophy, movement, or regime...that exalts nation and often race above the individual and that stands for a centralized autocratic government headed by a dictatorial leader, severe economic and social regimentation, and forcible suppression of opposition."

Trump's actions in many ways meet this definition. Though he presents nothing so coherent as a political philosophy, he stokes the resentment of white America over its lost primacy—"Make America Great

Again"—by scapegoating the aliens among us (the 11 million illegal immigrants) and dangerous outsiders (Muslims, Mexicans), leading white supremacists to embrace him warmly. Invoking a collapsed America, Trump presents himself as a strongman savior: "Nobody knows the system better than me, which is why I alone can fix it" and "I am your voice." He stokes violence, from the roughing-up of protesters at his rallies, to suggesting active defense of the Second Amendment if Clinton is elected, to suggesting Clinton's Secret Service agents disarm ("See what happens to her"). And Trump is fine with torture.

Is the barbarian, the fascist, at our door?

Sinclair Lewis thought so when, in 1935, the depths of the Great Depression, he wrote his novel *It Can't Happen Here*—"it" being the fascism he saw spreading in Europe with Hitler and Mussolini and at home with the demagogue Huey Long. The common American response was, "It can't happen here," but Lewis saw the fragility of democracy, especially if faced with organized violence, and concluded, "It can." News stories filed from Europe by his wife, journalist Dorothy Thompson, on the Nazis' anti-Semitism and their establishment of concentration camps fed his anxiety. Lewis wrote his *cri de coeur* of a novel in just four months.

By then Lewis had already won the Nobel prize for literature (in 1930, the first American to do so) for his powerful novels published in the 1920s—*Main Street, Babbitt, Arrowsmith, Elmer Gantry,* and *Dodsworth.* These iconoclastic works skewered the boosterism and smugness of America's growing middle class. But with that middle class largely wiped out by the Wall Street crash of 1929, and with fascism spreading in Europe, Lewis could hardly engage in his usual skewering of character; he went after the system. *It Can't Happen Here* is satiric and heartless.

Lewis allowed himself no historical perspective, but set his novel in his own time; in fact, a bit ahead. The novel opens in the summer of 1936, just before the Democratic national convention. While fascism is often thought of as a right-wing phenomenon, Lewis shows it taking form on the left. President Franklin Roosevelt is expected to be nominated again as the party's standard-bearer. (Lewis uses historical figures throughout: FDR, Huey Long, Father Coughlin, William Randolph Hearst.) But times remain bad since the '29 crash and FDR is seen as not doing enough.

Enter the demagogue presenting himself as the people's savior—Berzelius "Buzz" Windrip. A senator and a radical redistributionist, Windrip promises a $5,000 cash payment to every family, while soaking the rich. His attacks on the enemy within—the Jews and the Negroes—are frontal and ugly. Not surprisingly, he has the ardent support of the League of Forgotten Men, a 27-million-member organization stirred to fever pitch by the Jew-hating Bishop Prang. (The language Lewis uses in these passages, and the n-word for Negroes, sickens.) Ominously, Windrip has a private army at his back, the Minute Men, an erstwhile marching organization.

Eyeing the White House, Windrip wrote the apocalyptic *Zero Hour—Over the Top*, "the Bible of his followers, part biography, part economic program, and part plain exhibitionistic boasting"; excerpts open many chapters. Launching his presidential campaign, Windrip announces the "Fifteen Points of Victory for the Forgotten Men," to include: government control of all finance and all labor unions; tax hikes on the rich, capping incomes; a commission to study a $5,000 cash payment to families; and prohibitions on Negroes voting, women working outside the home, and anyone advocating Communism, Socialism, or Anarchism, on pain of treason. Point 15 is key: Upon his inauguration, Congress shall cede emergency powers to the president, with Congress only advising and the Supreme Court stripped of its "power to negate."

Why would anybody support such a restrictive regime? To usher in "a Paradise of democracy in which... every humblest worker would be king and ruler," a paradise ensured by a strengthened executive.

Windrip wins the nomination, forcing FDR to form the Jeffersonian Party (and exit the novel). At a rally in New York's Madison Square Garden days before the election, Windrip's speech shows him in full demagogue mode:

"....it's true, it's absolutely true I do want power, great, big, imperial power—but not for myself—no—for you!—the power of your permission to smash the Jew financiers who've enslaved you, who're working you to death to pay the interest on their bonds; the grasping bankers—and not all of 'em Jews by a darn sight!—the crooked labor leaders just as much as the crooked bosses, and, most of all, the sneaking spies of Moscow that want you to lick the boots of their self-appointed tyrants that rule not by love and loyalty, like I want to, but by the horrible power of the whip, the dark cell, the automatic pistol!"

Windrip wins the White House and immediately enacts his Fifteen Points, which enactment entails—"It can't happen here!"—"the whip, the dark cell, the automatic pistol." When Congress in a joint resolution declares his action unlawful (only in fiction does Congress act), Windrip declares martial law, enforced by the Minute Men, now the armed auxiliary to the Regular Army. Unemployment is reduced to zero by placing the workless in labor camps, where they are subjected to extreme hardship. The political parties are abolished, with only one allowed: the American Corporate State and Patriotic Party (the Corpos). Concentration camps are set up to hold the resisters and traitors. Arrests, torture, and executions follow.

At this point, just a third into the book, the reader wonders at the implausibility of events and how they relate to our presidential campaign. But then the reader wonders: With Donald Trump's authoritarian grasp of the law, what *would* the deportation of 11 million illegal aliens be like? Recall Trump, regarding torture, initially said of the generals, "If I say do it, they're gonna do it." (He later recanted, sort of.) And so the reader reads on in this otherwise extremely unpleasant book.

For me, the novel's best element, the value added, is the point-of-view character: Doremus Jessup, aged 60, the editor of a small Vermont newspaper, "locally considered a 'pretty smart fella but kind of a cynic.'" It's through Doremus' eyes that we see the gathering storm embodied by Windrip, who's rarely presented close-up. As a liberal and intellectual,

Doremus knows he's seeing fascism on the hoof. But as is often true of liberals and intellectuals, he feels helpless in the face of force and violence—much like liberals feel *vis-à-vis* Trump. Tracking Doremus' intellectual fits and starts, I kept thinking of Captain Ahab's disdain for his first mate Starbuck's "soft humanity." Doremus' evolution to heroic action gives the novel its human thrill.

Back when Windrip is one among many presidential candidates, Doremus has this to say to the town's owner of the granite quarry, who favors Windrip:

> *"Yes, I agree it's a serious time. With all the discontent there is in the country to wash him into office, Senator Windrip has got an excellent chance to be elected President... and if he is, probably his gang of buzzards will get us into some war, just to grease their insane vanity and show the world that we're the huskiest nation going. And then I, the Liberal and you, the Plutocrat, the bogus Tory, will be led out and shot at 3 a.m. Serious? Huh!"*

Doremus notes, "There's no country in the world that can get more hysterical... than America. Look how Huey Long became absolute monarch over Louisiana," and says, if Windrip wins, it means "a Fascist dictatorship!" To which the quarry owner says:

> *"Why are you so afraid of the word 'Fascism,' Doremus? Just a word—just a word! And might not be so bad, with all the lazy bums we got panhandling relief nowadays, and living on my income tax and yours—not so worse to have a real Strong Man, like Hitler or Mussolini—like Napoleon or Bismarck in the good old days—and have 'em really run the country and make it efficient and prosperous again."*

So, says Doremus, "Cure the evils of Democracy by the evils of Fascism?" To which the response is: "It just can't happen here in America."

This denial Doremus encounters all around. He finds the townspeople's take-away of Windrip's Fifteen Points are three: the tax hikes on the rich; the condemnation of the Negroes, "since nothing so elevates a dispossessed farmer or a factory worker on relief as to have some race, any race, on which he can look down"; and the $5,000 payment. Argument is defenseless against a dream: "This is revolution in terms of Rotary." Nor can he get his "heedless" family to engage the fascist danger. As the Windrip juggernaut gains, Doremus sighs, "But what can I do? Oh—write another editorial viewing-with-alarm, I suppose!" His endorsement goes to the Republican nominee, Walt Trowbridge, who suffers "from the deficiency of being honest and disinclined to promise he could work miracles." Consoling himself, Doremus thinks:

> "What I've got to keep remembering is that Windrip is only the lightest cork on the whirlpool. He didn't plot all this thing. With all the justified discontent there is against the smart politicians and the Plush Horses of Plutocracy—oh, if it hadn't been one Windrip, it'd been another....We had it coming, we Respectables....But that isn't going to make us like it!"

With Windrip's election, Doremus initially pulls inward, trying to reread the classics, relearn Latin, dive deeper into his religion (Universalist), but nothing allays the guilt: "Too many years he had made a habit of social duty. He wanted to be 'in' things." But, with Minute Men making arrests and the concentration camp looming, to be "in" things now carries life-and-death risk. Doremus takes the risk.

He writes an editorial attacking the Administration, is arrested, is released to advise his replacement at the paper. As the peril rises further—his son-in-law is executed, his hired man becomes a power-mad Minute Man, his lawyer son is offered a judgeship in the Windrip administration if he, Doremus, would soften his attitude—Doremus takes radical action: *"I think it's time now for me to begin doing a little high treason"* (italics mine). Taking the leap, he's determined to "see if there's any dirty work at the crossroads I can do." He finds it, ultimately, after being tortured in a concentration camp and escaping, in the New Underground, a rebel organization run from Canada by the former Republican presidential nominee, Walt Trowbridge.

Meanwhile, Buzz Windrip, with his imperial designs on all North America—he made war on Mexico—after two years is deposed and exiled by his Secretary of State, who in turn is murdered days later by his Secretary of War. It should not surprise that, in all this calamity, no family gets their $5,000 cash payment and, with labor unions outlawed and wages remaining stagnant, the big industrialists are the only winners.

A New Day for America must rest with the New Underground. The last we see of Doremus, he is dodging a posse, riding to a cabin hidden in the Northern Woods, where, Lewis writes, "quiet men awaited news of freedom."

To conclude: *It Can't Happen Here* is a strange, strange novel, with a serious, serious message: Beware the leader in rough times promising a New Day via violence. Let's not let it happen here.

—*HuffPost*, October 1, 2016

Hillary the Lion-Hearted Does Battle with the Trumpasaurus

FINALLY! HILLARY CLINTON got off the back foot in her battle with the Trumpasaurus—the behemoth who's wrecked the political landscape and now threatens to take the White House—and, in an audacious attack, she bested him, leaving him stunned.

It was a thrilling sight at the first presidential debate: Clinton, calm, coifed, and prepared like an actor taking on the part of a lifetime, decimating the Blowhard-Who-Never-Prepares, Donald Trump. Cannily, Clinton invoked personal references and served them up in unending volley—Trump's millionaire father, her own small-businessman father, contractors who were "stiffed" by Trump, a Miss Universe whom Trump as pageant owner maligned as "Miss Piggy" and "Miss Housekeeping" (she is Latina)—to pierce through the big man's thin skin.

It worked. Trump seethed and, seething, revealed his real beliefs: that it's "smart" not to pay taxes. That he cheered the collapse of the housing market because he could snap up distressed properties ("That's called business, by the way"). That business, as he practices it, is not about serving the client's interests but his own profits. That, sure, contractors get "stiffed" if he declares himself unsatisfied with their finished work.

All these were revelations—each stunning on its own—that *none* of his sixteen Republican primary opponents were able either to elicit or make stick. Investigative reporters have unearthed many of Trump's more questionable business practices and biographical sleaze. The media now refer to his many misrepresentations as "lies." But, dismayingly, little has stuck.

Until, that is, the lady in the red pantsuit, working her sword-arm in front of an audience of 90 million—largest ever for a debate—made it stick, resoundingly and dramatically. Trump was left blithering. He was still rampaging about the "Miss Universe" jab almost a week later, tweeting responses at 3 a.m.

Such a feat took a battle plan—strategy, tactics, study, rehearsal. It also took an innate faith in the American people that the points she aimed to make about Trump would compute onstage in a way they hadn't when presented as news (they did, and how). Taking the longer view, that performance also required all the battle-scarred experience, speechifying, and time spent in the trenches that Clinton has racked up in more than four decades devoted to public service. Experience does count.

It also took—let us acknowledge it—courage. Simple but all-too-rare courage, the lion-hearted kind. The kind of courage Anonymous defined as "fear that has said its prayers." With her campaign stalled, and under withering criticism from Democrats as well as Republicans for her self-inflicted "deplorables" gaffe, she *had* to produce at that debate. And, digging deep, she did. Hillary Clinton demonstrated the mettle required for the White House.

As a feminist I'm not one for any special pleading for women in public life. Male or female, candidates must clear the bar, no handicapping allowed. But, apart from the rigors of the job interview, this presidential campaign featuring our first female nominee has been suffused in misogyny, unleashed by none other than Trump himself. When in the debate Hillary cited Trump's reference to women as "pigs, slobs, and dogs," insults now free-flowing in the public, that was pushback, long in coming, from all women sick of being demeaned. You don't think that took courage?

And to those who say both performances, Clinton's and Trump's, were farce, I say: This is the man who's taken campaign politics to a new low, starting with reference to the size of his manhood. Hillary faced the classic problem: How do you wrestle with a pig? Doing so is usually thought to be a lose-lose proposition: You both get dirty *and* the pig enjoys it. Hillary finally solved that problem, not by going abstract or platitudinous, but by raising each ugly Trumpism, parrying with personal examples, then executing by taking it to higher ground.

For this reason, Hillary's debate performance was more than great spectacle with rhetorical zingers. When she thrust home, it was to make a higher, *human* point. About Trump calling Miss Universe "Miss Piggy," this life-long humanitarian struck the human note: "Donald, she has a name." She worked the same humanizing effect on stiffed contractors and dumb taxpayers. As Michelle Obama says, "When they go low, we go high." In this low and dishonest age, going high and human is exhilarating, also possibly nation-saving.

(Message to young people: This is how you combat a bully. You unmask him, inch by inch by inch. You can start now with the class bullies who, aping Trump, taunt Latino classmates with "Build a wall." Think Hillary, and Michelle, and go to it.)

Finally, Hillary Clinton deserves a citation for courage for bearing the false burden of the media's false equivalence, of treating her candidacy on a (low) par with Trump's. Yes, she's made mistakes, notably her decision as Secretary of State to use a private email server: You only have to work one day in Washington to know any work-product instantly becomes property of the U.S. Government. But this mistake pales in comparison to Trump's myriad business frauds and serial lies. And, unlike No-Apology Trump, Hillary has apologized for her mistake. She did so again in that first debate, before going on to stun the Trumpasaurus.

That lion-hearted display has re-energized Hillary's campaign, her supporters, and Democratic candidates down-ballot. Showing new fire in attacking a rigged economy, Clinton is exploiting the revelation she forced out of Trump that it's "smart" not to pay taxes ("What does that make the rest of us?"). Her new ad exploits the revelation reported by *The New York Times* that in 1995 Trump declared a loss of almost one billion dollars and possibly avoided paying taxes for nearly two decades.

Meanwhile Trump, becoming increasingly erratic, promises to descend even lower in the next debate. Hillary will be ready.

Finding her sword-arm—finally—Clinton has come into her best self, which I predict will carry her to victory. But whatever the outcome, it's enough to have seen Hillary the Lion-Hearted do battle with the Trumpasaurus and best him. It gives one, in this wretched presidential campaign, a whiff of the mythic and a glimpse of a New Day.

—*HuffPost*, October 4, 2016

Atoning for Slavery:
An Institution Grapples With
Its Original Business Model

IT IS ALTOGETHER fitting and proper that, in this period of heightened racial tensions and resurgence of white privilege, it is a university, a seat of higher learning and a religious-based one at that, which seeks to atone for America's Original Sin—slavery.

Georgetown University, the Roman Catholic-affiliated institution in Washington, D.C., falling on straitened times, in 1838 kept its doors open with the sale of 272 slaves—men, women, and children—from its plantations in nearby Maryland to plantations in Louisiana. The sale was worth $3.3 million in today's dollars.

Doing the right thing—making recompense—Georgetown, one of America's elite universities, recently announced it will take a series of historically unprecedented steps, including granting preference in admission to the descendants of those 272 slaves who were sold, as well as to the descendants of those slaves who remained indentured to Georgetown and labored to its benefit.

Additionally, Georgetown will issue a formal apology for its part in this ugly chapter in American history, erect a monument to its slaves, rename two buildings that honor Jesuit priests who facilitated the sale of the 272, and establish an institute for the study of slavery. Last year it launched the Georgetown Memory Project, to track these descendants. While slaves elsewhere were lost in anonymity, in Georgetown's case descendants could be identified, thanks to meticulous record-keeping.

Along with doing the right thing, Georgetown is saying the right thing—things that could usefully be repeated across the nation at this moment. University president John J. DeGioia, the major force behind this reconciliation effort, has been eloquent in finding the words to face elemental truth. He speaks of the "two evils" of slavery: the enslavement of human beings itself and the rupture of slave families upon sale. He speaks of the early Georgetown Jesuits' "failure of moral imagination." Declaring that "our moral agency must be channeled to un-do this damage," Dr. DeGioia on Sept. 1 addressed a formal gathering of slave descendants along with faculty and students, saying:

> "This community participated in the institution of slavery. This original evil that shaped the early years of the Republic was present here. We have been able to hide from this truth, bury this truth, ignore and deny this truth.... As a community and as individuals, we cannot do our best work if we refuse to take ownership of such a critical part of our history. We must acknowledge it."

Indeed: How can our "best work" go forward when "this original evil" goes unaccounted for? How can conscience square with the enslavement of fellow human beings? How have we and ours benefited—unknowingly or, worse, knowingly—from slave labor, both current and in the distant past? These are the hard questions any number of universities, museums, corporations and whole industries, municipalities and states, even individual families, might ask themselves.

Pointing the way, Georgetown University last year began to examine its origins, issuing a 102-page report titled "Slavery, Memory, and Reconciliation." Especially compelling is the discussion of the university's original business model: From its Maryland plantations established in 1700 to the founding of the university in 1789 and beyond, slavery was central, built-in. As the report outlines:

> "Plantation profits and proceeds from the sale of slaves on those plantations were seen as a source of funding for the school. Bequests and other charitable gifts were also a significant part of the funding model.... Given a regional economy that was largely agricultural, this benefaction can also be in large part linked to the U.S. slave economy.

A recruitment strategy oriented to the South deepened the school's links to slavery, and the general attitude of Jesuit faculty and students favored slavery as at least a necessary evil. Into the nineteenth century, as tensions between pro- and anti-slavery opinion grew, the mood at the College was pro-slavery and ultimately pro-Confederacy."

Thus a business model based on "original evil" becomes institutionalized and is reinforced over time and by culture to become a given, a norm, not to be re-examined. How many other institutions, notably those dating from the 18th and 19th centuries, will have the courage to undertake such examination of their business model or origins story?

Still, it is astonishing that Jesuit priests, putative men of God, could ever have accepted slavery as a "necessary evil." The Vatican urged emancipation and keeping the slave families intact, but these stipulations went unfulfilled. According to the report, among Jesuits on the East Coast three factions formed around the sale of the 272: One faction, the smallest in number, opposed the sale on moral principle and favored emancipation; another, the largest, favored keeping the slaves as (curiously) a "religious obligation"; and the third, which included the most powerful figures, argued for sale. (Sadly, this disposition of priestly morality, rather than model, would match that of "the flock" at most any time in human history.)

Other elite universities with a long history—Harvard, Brown, Columbia, University of Virginia—have likewise acknowledged the ignominy of their early involvement with slavery, often, it should be noted, under pressure from student protests. But Georgetown is the first to take affirmative action on behalf of the injured parties, its slave descendants. Craig Steven Wilder of M.I.T., a scholar of universities and slavery, gives credit to Georgetown: "It's taking steps that a lot of universities have been hesitant to take." Wilder also credits Georgetown for dealing with "the humanity of the problem," not just as public relations. Much depends, though, on the thoroughness of Georgetown's outreach.

Georgetown might do even more: In addition to preferential

admissions treatment—the kind of preference given generations of children of white alumni—Georgetown might offer financial assistance to those slave descendants admitted. Going further, it might, as *The New York Times* editorializes, establish a scholarship fund "specifically for descendants who are poor and generationally disadvantaged by the legacy of slavery from which Georgetown profited." The University's endowment of $1.45 billion suggests its financial recompense could include this broader category of the "generationally disadvantaged."

Additionally, these elite universities might form a consortium—to coordinate best practices of institutional re-examination and also, importantly, guide the general population in a re-examination long overdue and now heated to the boiling point.

Which is why Georgetown's act of recompense for the "original evil" of slavery comes at a propitious time. Certainly for African-Americans and Georgetown's slave descendants, it could have come earlier—much, much earlier. But in another context, it is timely: With the racist and xenophobic "presidential" candidacy of Donald J. Trump, with the sudden rise to prominence of the white supremacist alt-right movement, and with the forceful white pushback at the #BlackLivesMatter movement ("All lives matter"), the morally weak cause of white supremacy has never been in such a loud and angry, unfettered and unapologetic voice ("Apologize? *Why* apologize?"). Nuance is gone, making calm reconsideration of white power and privilege difficult.

But perhaps Georgetown's reminder that human enslavement is America's "original evil" and racism our abiding sin will penetrate.

Martin Luther King, Jr. promised that "the arc of the moral universe is long, but it bends toward justice." Now is the time for all good people to lend their weight and bend that arc.

—*HuffPost*, October 20, 2016

Hillary Clinton Polled "World's Most Admired Woman" a Record 20 Times. Why the Hatred Now?

IT'S AMAZING TO go from "World's Most Admired Woman" to "Lesser of Two Evils" in one year. How did that happen?

As recently as last year, Hillary Clinton was polled by the Gallup organization as the world's most admired woman. That capped a record twenty (20) times Clinton has been so honored. Even Eleanor Roosevelt, the most honored woman of her day, polled fewer times (13) than Clinton. Last year's honor meant beating out such international icons as Malala ("I am Malala") Yousafzai, Queen Elizabeth, and Michelle Obama.

Of course, the reputational fall happened because of Donald Trump's vicious campaign against Clinton for the White House, in which this con artist regularly slimes her as "Crooked Hillary" and "Lying Hillary" and vows, if elected, to put her in jail. The Hillary hatred among Trump supporters, and even among some on the progressive left, is scary. Again, how'd it happen?

I know, I know: the emails. As Secretary of State, Clinton used a personal server instead of a departmental one. Which was a major mistake on Clinton's part *and* for which she has apologized many times (something Trump never ever does, but should). It's absurd—absurd— to equate emails with Trump's sleaze. And there was the too-cozy relationship between the Clinton Foundation and the State Department when Hillary Clinton was Secretary. If she wins the White House, the Clinton Foundation will stop accepting foreign donations.

But, people, these several mistakes simply do not rise to the level of Trump's malfeasance—the bankruptcies that destroyed others while allowing Trump to continue living like a billionaire, the fraudulent and now defunct Trump University, Trump's non-payment of taxes while ordinary Americans pay their fair share. If Trump wins, the killer issue will have been... Hillary's emails. Really?

Nor do Clinton's character flaws equate to anything like Trump's repugnant behavior—the denigration of Muslims, Mexicans, the disabled, the women he has allegedly assaulted sexually.

Hmmm, denigration of women. Think that has anything to do with the Hillary hatred...?

Trump has called women "pigs, slobs, and dogs." He insults Hillary as a candidate: "Does she look presidential, fellas? Give me a break." (Note his callout to "fellas.") Saddest are the women blindly babbling their anti-Hillary, anti-woman hatred.

Again, this is the woman who 20 times —*20 times*—was polled "World's Most Admired Woman," while, again, the estimable Eleanor Roosevelt managed it only 13 times.

Tellingly, Hillary Clinton's 20-time record as world's most admired woman spans the 30 years of her public life that Trump now derides and points to as abject failure: her years as First Lady, then U.S. Senator, then Secretary of State. To quote the fear-mongering Trump himself, "Something's going on, folks."

Something *is* going on, folks. Trump has manipulated the general discontent of the public and out of it created a dangerous reactionary campaign—against non-white Americans, against foreigners, against women.

Eleanor Roosevelt would weep. Wake up, America.

Note: Donald Trump in 2015 was polled by Gallup as the world's second most admired man, after Barack Obama and tying Pope Francis. The only other time Trump placed in the top 40 of this poll appears to be in 2011, with 1% of the vote.

—*HuffPost*, November 4, 2016

Trump Is Not the Solution to Your Anger

"LET ME BE perfectly clear." Usually it's the politician who says those words to the public. But in this historic presidential campaign, it's the public who's made itself perfectly clear: Americans are angry—very. This has been the anger election.

And Donald Trump's supporters have been especially loud and clear in articulating their anger. How loud and clear? Let me count the ways:

You are angry about jobs going overseas and leaving you with a low-paying, no-benefits job in the service industry. You are angry about your community being hollowed out because of those lost jobs and shuttered factories. You are angry at immigrants, illegal and legal, who compete for the remaining jobs and, in the process, change the complexion of your community from what it once was. You are angry that America, the greatest country in the history of the world, appears to be losing out in a globalized economy—with bad trade deals, mainly—and that you, too, are losing out and are being left behind. You are angry at the stupid politicians in Washington who've allowed this slow-moving catastrophe to happen and at the unfeeling Wall Street bankers who bankroll it. America has always been about winning and you want to win again. You deeply want America to be great again.

Donald Trump's solution to your anger—your suffering—is to, figuratively, blow the place up: level Washington, level Wall Street, tear up trade deals, tear up treaties, even tear up the Constitution. What release it would be simply to raze the place, to lay waste! But also: What ruin it would leave. Deep down, you know anger is crazy-making, it is not a wise counsel, not when electing a President of the United States.

In contrast, Hillary Clinton as President would approach our collective problems, not as a wrecking machine like Trump, but as the repair-person, the problem-solver.

Like it or not, government has a role in our lives; in fact, America's greatness starts with its governmental framework, as laid out by our Founding Fathers. A complex entity like America can't be run from state capitals or by the Chamber of Commerce. But government hasn't been working well of late—as you've made abundantly clear in this campaign. We need government to work better, run by smart politicians.

Whip-smart, Hillary Clinton knows government, she knows Washington, she knows where the levers of power are. (Her 30 years in public life, which Trump disparages, have given her a map and keys.) Importantly, Clinton is the diplomat who works well with others, including her opponents, as she demonstrated during two terms as a U.S. Senator working with Republicans. Can you see Trump working well with *anybody?*

As President, Clinton would serve the 99%—and of course Trump supporters are part of the 99% (a fact forgotten in this divisive campaign).

Clinton has stressed the 99% in recent speeches: "Our economy should work for everybody, not just those at the top." Her stance on Wall Street is tough: "Wall Street can never be allowed to wreck Main Street again. No bank can be too big to fail and no executive can be too powerful to jail." She turned against the Trans-Pacific Partnership in response to the anger of Bernie Sanders and his supporters over unfair trade deals—anger which you share. With her trade experience, Hillary could help solve the problem of inequitable trade deals that concerns us all.

While there's considerable overlap of issues important both to Trumpsters and Democrats—unfair trade deals, jobs going overseas, Wall Street remaining untamed—it's over solutions that Hillary differs, radically, with Trump. On jobs, her solution is more economic growth, not deporting 11 million illegal immigrants, as Trump would do. Democrats believe in inclusion, Trump advocates exclusion—barring Muslims from the U.S., imposing religious tests on immigrants, etc. Trump's exclusionary policies would wreck the best thing about America: our melting pot.

Which touches, finally, on the issue not confronted head-on in this ugly campaign, but played on none-too-subtly by Donald Trump: the decline of white America. (Trump set the groundwork for his presidential campaign with the birther movement, trying to delegitimize President Barack Obama, our first African-American president.) Much of your anger is over white America's perceived loss of primacy and power in national life, a trend that, given present demographics, will continue. If it means anything, this white American believes, with all her heart, that America does best when every citizen, not just white Americans, feels an integral part of the whole.

As we go to the polls on Tuesday, we might ask ourselves: Are we America the home of the brave—or home of the fearful? Donald Trump represents a fearful America, thus his wrecking machine of a campaign. Americans are fundamentally problem-solvers, not ones to waste ourselves in anger. Elect Hillary Clinton, problem-solver, and let us solve our way out of the present chaos to a New Day.

—HuffPost, November 8, 2016

The "Normalization" of Donald J. Trump? Not!

IT STARTS: THE "normalization" of Donald J. Trump, the man who achieved the heights in American life—the White House—by taking the low road. Specifically the low road of racism, misogyny, and xenophobia.

The normal hallmarks of the transfer of power are being rolled out and extended to the man who, as *The New York Times* editorialized, "pulped" the American dream, the dream described by Hillary Clinton in her concession speech as "big enough for everyone"—for "all races, and religions, for men and women, for immigrants."

Already the *pro forma* visits have taken place. First was the White House, where President Barack Obama graciously received the man who launched his own bid by seeking to delegitimize our first African-American president via the birther movement. Next was Capitol Hill, meeting with smiling Republicans who prior to the election were grimly staying their distance from their toxic nominee.

Already we have the "60 Minutes" interview with the President-elect and his family, conducted in the gold-leaf plushness of Trump Tower. And we have *Times* columnist Maureen Dowd chuckling on "Charlie Rose" that Trump may be more surprised than anyone at his election, that probably "he's sitting up in Trump Tower with a cheeseburger, what the heck." What's more normalizing than a cheeseburger?

And now come the appointments. Causing vehement uproar initially is the appointment of Stephen K. Bannon as Trump's chief strategist and senior counselor. Civil rights groups and Democrats fear Bannon, former head of the hard-right Breitbart News, "will bring anti-Semitic, nationalist and racist views to the West Wing." Even a Republican strategist declares, "The racist, fascist extreme right is represented footsteps from the Oval Office. Be very vigilant, America."

Now comes the astonishing appointment of Sen. Jeff Sessions as Trump's Attorney General. Sessions, before he became senator, was rejected for a federal judgeship when officials testified he made racist comments—including calling an African-American lawyer "boy." Our top job at Justice goes to a man known to be hostile to civil rights?

Rudy Giuliani, rumored for Secretary of State, last year made the outrageous charge, "I do not believe that the president loves America"—claiming Mr. Obama was not "brought up the way you were brought up and I was brought up through love of this country." This xenophobe might be chief diplomat? Before, during, and after his tenure as mayor, Giuliani has had a "fraught history with New York's black and brown residents."

And we haven't even discussed the misogyny expressed by Trump in the campaign against Hillary Clinton ("Nasty woman"). And recall the xenophobia against Muslims and Mexicans that Trump engaged in early on, igniting his defiantly "politically incorrect" campaign.

These toxins released by Trump are now being freely expressed by the public. Anti-Muslim hate crimes jumped 67% from 2014 to 2015 (Trump announced for president June 2015). Before and since the election, Trump supporters, out in public and in schools, shout "Build that wall" at Latinos and pull *hijabs* off Muslim-American women's heads. Since the election swastikas, deportation threats, and racist graffiti have proliferated. And this shocker: Two West Virginia municipal officials (both women, one the mayor) expressed pleasure on Facebook at the prospect of seeing Trump's fashion model wife in the White House, rather than the "ape in heels," Michelle Obama! Properly, both officials have resigned. Describing Michelle Obama, a First Lady *par excellence*, in such a despicable manner cannot ever become "normal." For shame.

It's not enough that—belatedly—President-elect Trump says to his supporters, "Stop it," as he did, turning to the camera, on "60 Minutes" when interviewer Lesley Stahl related various ugly incidents committed by his supporters. Poisoner-in-Chief now wants the poisoning to stop?

The word that comes to mind is "hypocrite."

Much quoted is the observation about Trump, by *The Atlantic*'s Salena Zito, that "the press takes him literally, but not seriously; his supporters take him seriously, but not literally." But if that is so, Trump supporters are naïve at best and morally compromised at worst if they do not take Trump's toxic methods literally, given their capacity to hurt and even kill. Economic suffering, while valid, cannot justify these methods.

No, it's up to Democrats to reinstate the American ideals of tolerance, equality, fair play. (And moderate Republicans, too: I note little pride among them at Trump's win, just surprise.) It needs to be heard loud and clear: Not only "No"—to racism, misogyny, xenophobia—but "Hell, no." These evils can never ever become "normal." They must be resisted, daily. This is not the stubbornness of a sore loser, but principle. We need to reinstate "political correctness," which in truth is another term for our foundational ideals.

Right now, though, Democrats are stunned and deflated by Trump's victory. Like you, I *so* wanted to advance into a New Day, and to see Trump cast into our rear-view mirror, an artifact of history. But, given the gains made by Democrats in recent decades combatting racism, misogyny, and xenophobia, not to mention electing and re-electing our first African-American president, we might look at this recent election as a massive reaction: a reactionary election. The stage is now set for a Renaissance.

To get there, the Democratic party must reform. Importantly, it must renew its original commitment to the working class, the class we forfeited in favor of moneyed interests and lost to Trump. And, importantly, Democrats must recommit to the ideals we hold dearest—tolerance and equality—as Trump, once in office, seeks to normalize their opposites. We can be grateful our nemesis is unusually clear-cut.

All this is not to say Democrats don't wish Trump success. For the good of the country, good luck to him in bringing back jobs, infrastructure repair, etc. But do it, Mr. Trump, without bias or prejudice or violence—or else you'll have the majority of the electorate, the popular majority that voted for Hillary Clinton, at your door.

Meanwhile: "Stay angry," urges liberal thinker Leon Wieseltier. It is the only way to uphold our principles. Let us "maintain our disgust at the low and malign politics that have just prevailed":

> "Trump's success vouches only for his strategy. It says nothing about his probity or decency. Those Americans who are ashamed that we have elected as our president a man bursting with prejudices and lies are right. Their shame makes America great again."

Continuing, Wieseltier writes: "Difficult times are giving way to dark times, and dark times require a special lucidity and a special vigilance and a special ferocity about principle." Providing context, he reminds us "moral progress and social progress are never linear and unimpeded and inevitable":

> "If you demand justice, prepare for instability, and for the exploitation of instability by political reactionaries who weaken the wounded with nostalgia and fantasies of exclusiveness.... There is nothing Sisyphean or cynical about this. It is the abiding condition of a democracy comprising conflicting ideals. The fight is never over."

And the immediate fight? Not to let racism, sexism, xenophobia—that is to say, Trumpism—become "normal." Nothing less than America's soul is at stake. Arise, the Resistance.

—*HuffPost*, November 18, 2016

Why My Young Nephew Resolves to Become More Political

BELOW IS AN email exchange between my nephew, Zackary Castle, and me. Zack is 28, has an M.B.A., and works in Las Vegas as a store manager for Starbucks (thus his reference to Starbucks CEO Howard Schultz). His first email came 10 days after the election of Donald J. Trump. Zack writes about resolving to become more political. By posting our exchange I am hoping other young people resolve likewise.

Zack writes (Nov. 18):

Hi Carla,

Thanks for continuing to send your posts to me. I don't always get to read them, but when I do I always enjoy what you have to say.

I've been feeling passionate as of recently about what is going on in the country and am wishing I would have been more so during the election. I have made a vow to myself that I won't stand around and just watch things around me anymore, but take a stand now when I believe we need it the most. Your words help encourage me to do more and I appreciate that.

Just wanted to share that.

As one of my idols Howard Schultz would say, "Onward."

Love, Zack

Carla writes (Nov. 20):

Dear Zackarino,

At a time when this country has just dealt itself a devastating blow in electing the demagogue and lout Donald J. Trump as President, your resolve as a young person to get more informed and more involved in the political process is THE BRIGHTEST SPOT imaginable. Truly! Good on you, Dear Nephew, and bravissimo!

[Pause for eyes tearing up....]

I think it is very interesting, and very hopeful, that a young person such as yourself recognizes something horrible just happened to America, and that we did it to ourselves. It's also very hopeful that you as a young person believe that being more informed and involved can bring us a New Day. Democracy is all about the demos, the people, and democracy only works when the people are informed and involved. Clearly you "get it," innately, about democracy's engine. We are "it"—the engine.

So, what do YOU think happened in this election? And what do you think needs to be done to get us on the upward path? I am reaching out to various "thought leaders," and you just nominated yourself— congratulations.

Meantime, congratulations on joining the ranks of the engaged. I'll share a little secret with you: Engaged people have the most fun. More than the kvetchers, or the cynics, or the nihilists, or the bored or disillusioned, the engaged not only make constructive contributions to the common good, they are more alive than the aforementioned ankle-biters. You'll know them by the sparkle in their eyes (and your own).

I take my cue about being engaged from the French philosopher and World War II Resistance fighter, Albert Camus. I was in high school when I first read Camus, insisting that in time of war writers be engagé (active, not passive) and counseling against "bad faith." He won the Nobel for literature for his novels "The Plague" and "The Stranger" and for his commentary. At first his command to be engagé had a romantic appeal to me, but I've come to see it as the absolute standard: You can never, ever quit the field, most especially when things go bad or dark. You must be the citizen engagé.

There's another plus: engaged people get to feel good about themselves, virtuous even. Critics call that righteous self-satisfaction and smugness, but it sure beats feeling guilty or misspent or negligible. And sooner or later we all come to judge our own lives: Best, in the end, to have given a damn than not even to have tried. Like Teddy Roosevelt said, all honor goes, not to the critic, but to the person who steps into the arena to do battle. Best to be the Happy Warrior.

In conclusion: I do believe we who are engaged—whose number now includes you—can turn this desperate situation around in America. But it will require, as the engaged also understand, taking "the long view." Ultimately I do believe we can save ourselves. Americans, thank Heaven, are not fatalists, not yet. And if we have young blood, such as your esteemed self, joining our ranks, how can America lose?

Much love, Dear Nephew, and yes, "Onward."

Love, (Aunt) Carla

Zack writes (Nov. 27):

Dear Carla,

As I finished reading your email for probably the 10th time over the past week, I have contemplated your question, "What do I think happened in this election?" When I first read it my thought was, heck, I have no clue. A political science degree would probably come in handy for this. I wake up with a knot in my stomach worrying about my future as a young gay man and how I could face the people in my life who didn't understand my feelings, didn't understand why I couldn't vote for Trump, or were too busy thinking about the latest Clinton email scandal to really realize what else was happening in this election.

When I look back at the last year, what did I miss that would have made me think that what happened on Nov. 8th could actually be a reality? The first time I voted, in 2008, I knew I was voting for change. The very first African-American President! I could only imagine what barriers he had to go through to get where he was on that day. And I could only imagine what he would continue to do and how hard he would have to fight to get what he wanted to accomplish. Although President Obama was challenged at every turn, that man did more than I could have ever imagined.

When I think about it, I see some similarities between President Obama's campaign and President-elect Trump's campaign. We all know that Donald Trump didn't face many barriers in his life and actually probably created more of them (barriers, I mean) for other people. But for some reason, like Obama, he was able to relate to the everyday American better than his opponents. Although Hillary Clinton is leading the popular vote by over two million, you would think she related better. But the millions of people who voted for Trump: He reached them better, that's plain and simple.

Other than reaching more people where it counted, I think this election was just very different. I have talked to other friends who have seen many more elections than I have and they all say the same. I think this country is changing on its own. I think the biggest thing is that people are tired of not being heard. And in a democracy, that's not good. Although Obama may have done a lot for some people, I think there are still a lot of people out there who just didn't want "more of the same." The next four years with Donald Trump will definitely be different than we have ever seen before. But I don't think it will be a good kind of "different."

So, I still have a knot of uncertainty in my stomach, but there is one thing that is not going to change. I'm still going to spend my life with my partner Jeremy. Because no matter what, no one is taking that away from me and I'll do whatever it takes to make sure that never happens. So, civil rights will become my mission—which I truly believe helps the common good in America, not just myself. And for courage, I will look back to President Obama.

There's only one way to go and, as we said, that is "Onward." I will become a Happy Warrior.

Love, Zack

—*HuffPost*, November 30, 2016

Classic Films of Human Drama: Rx for Our Fraught Times

THIS POLARIZED NATION does not agree on much anymore, but by universal agreement Americans are united in feeling this last presidential campaign was the worst ever. Without reciting details—we're a nation in recovery—it was a contest in which the candidate with an R after his name took us on a tour of the lower depths.

Moreover, since our presidential campaigns run so long, for a good (or bad) year and a half, our exposure to a rotting campaign process was prolonged enough to cause profound revulsion, even a kind of trauma. I know I am not the only American forced to ask during that unedifying spectacle, *How low can we go?*

Which is why I found myself yearning for movies presenting human beings in a more elevated light, where honor, integrity, courage, love, simple human connection, are on view and in play. Where humanity is defined upward, even heroically, as in the classic films of the '30s through the '60s, rather than defined downward into pathology, as so much contemporary film portrays humanity, played by anti-heroes. Where characters seem more authentic, without the quirks and "attitude" of today's film.

Here are eight such classics of human drama. They all feature a central character or an ensemble grappling with a crisis, either historic in scale (war and its aftermath, a foundering economy), or moral in nature (good versus evil), or intimately personal (love, midlife crisis). All portray humans relating with honest feeling. And, while all the films are dramas, when the humor arises, it reverberates.

High Noon (1952)

Symbolically and humanly, this is a film speaking to us now: A town marshal, alerted that a gang of bad guys is heading his way, seeks allies among the townspeople to help mount a defense. In the end, finding no allies at all, he faces the killers alone (and survives).

In his most iconic role, and at the height of his maturity, Gary Cooper (pictured at top) plays Marshal Will Kane as a man whose steely resolve must become steelier as one potential ally after another begs off with excuses, most invoking family—little understanding that, when mortal danger threatens, the family requires their own skin and resolve in defense. Grace Kelly plays Kane's new wife Amy, a Quaker who urges him to escape with her, but who, in the end, stays. After the shootout, the townspeople show themselves—finally. Before departing, Kane throws down his badge in disgust. In a way, this film throws down a challenge to us: Written during the McCarthy witch-hunt era, another dark time in America, and skillfully directed by Fred Zinneman, this film asks: Who will do battle with the forces of chaos? And who will find excuses not to?

Casablanca (1942)

I know, I know: such a chestnut. But in this moment of severe dislocation—*Quo vadis*, America?—it might be good to spend time in a mythical bar in North Africa with a group of refugees fleeing the Nazis, all desperate to get to America, which to them shines as a moral beacon (which is why this film, directed by Michael Curtiz, is my all-time favorite). If the contrast between America then and America

now is too great for you (and very likely it is), you might focus on the film's subtheme: Bar owner Rick Blaine's slow-building return to the fight. When the film opens, Rick is a burnt-out case, cynical about the world or fighting for any cause. But by film's end he's found the spark again, and his humanity, and rejoins the fight.

Of course Rick's journey to get there is well known: Of all the gin joints in all the towns in all the world, his great lost love Ilsa walks into his, the Café Américain, with her freedom-fighter husband Viktor Laszlo, all of which rekindles what Rick and Ilsa had back in Paris. As indelibly portrayed by Humphrey Bogart and Ingrid Bergman, their love story is glorious. And the supporting cast is memorable, too, notably the Vichy wit, Captain Renault (Claude Rains). But this time around, focus on Rick's return to the fight. I trust the relevance to our Trumpian present is clear...?

How Green Was My Valley (1941)

This film about the loss of a way of life—the coal-mining industry in Wales—and its impact on a large family of sons—the sons are forced to leave—is told in loving retrospect by the youngest son, the one who got an education. These themes—the still-  struggling coal industry, the volatile issue of immigration—resonate today. The film's parents, played by character actors Donald Crisp and Sara Allgood, remain stoic as their sons migrate elsewhere, including to America, a decision forced at the paymaster's window in the form of ever-reduced wages. (The sons will surely turn their mother's quips into myth wherever they settle.) The only daughter, played by Maureen O'Hara, makes a bad marriage with a wealthy scion after her true love, the pastor played by Walter Pidgeon, concludes he could never provide for her. The superb child actor Roddy McDowall, playing the point-of-view character, matures before your eyes when he retrieves his father's body after an explosion in the mine.

These events describe a tragedy, an economic one. But this beautifully-acted film, directed by John Ford, reminds us that these tragedies—some call it "change" or "disruption"—befall real human beings, real families. There may be no more real a family in all cinema than this film's Morgan family: Its heartbeat becomes your own.

The Best Years of Our Lives (1946)

This film of veterans coming home from World War II always repays viewing. *The Best Years of Our Lives* follows three men anxious about how their families will receive them and how they will fit  into a postwar America. Al, a banker played by Fredric March, comes home to wife Milly (Myrna Loy) and grown children (daughter played by Teresa Wright), only to find it tense going and turning to drink. Fred, played by Dana Andrews, suspects his wife (Virginia Mayo) has been less than faithful and is drawn to Al's daughter, Peggy. Homer, who lost both hands in the war, has the tensest homecoming. Homer is played by non-actor Harold Russell, who lost both hands in a wartime accident; he won the Oscar for Best Supporting Actor.

Rather than replayed in flashback, the war reverberates in the characters' faces and voices and, most starkly, in Homer's hooks. His anxiety about reconnecting with his fiancée Wilma provides the film's most moving drama, especially when, to make clear what she's in for if she marries him, he shows her how he gets into and out of his prosthetic harness. Fred's war comes back to him when, after being fired from his job as a soda jerk and waiting for a flight out of town, he wanders onto an airfield of decommissioned bombers, finds himself inside one of them, and breaks into an existential sweat. The film ends on a hopeful note, with a wedding. Director William Wyler may be the best director ever of real human beings relating.

The Third Man (1949)

It might seem odd to select this noir film set in postwar Vienna as an exemplar of human drama. But, ultimately, it's about a man who belatedly comes to see the criminal soul in his old pal and, in the end,
stops him. Also the film's climax takes place in the city's sewers—a rather fit metaphor for the present era.

Holly Martins, a writer of Westerns engagingly played by Joseph Cotten, is lured to the city by a job offer from old friend Harry Lime, only to learn upon arrival Lime has died. But Lime is not dead; he's on the lam for peddling bad penicillin on the black market; his victims include little children. It takes the full movie for Martins to work out who his friend really is, aided by evidence provided by an impatient Major Calloway (Trevor Howard at his sardonic best). Meanwhile Martins falls in love with Lime's grieving girlfriend Anna (Alida Valli). Lime himself finally appears in the film's second half, to menace Martins. Played by Orson Welles in a sleek phase, Lime is chilling. The film is directed by Englishman Carol Reed, written by Graham Greene, and scored with memorable zither music. In its examination of the truth and consequences of a friendship, how good to see that, in the end, Martins' decency vanquishes his friend's evil. Still, he doesn't get the girl. Life.

Dodsworth (1936)

Turning to more personal themes, this film is a story about a couple going through a midlife crisis, though in the '30s it might not have been called that. Sam Dodsworth, a successful car manu-
facturer, has retired and takes his wife Fran on a long sojourn in Europe—where the marriage falls apart. Fran, insecure about aging, allows

every swain to court her, from a young David Niven on the boat over to an aging playboy in Paris (Paul Lukas). Sam fights for the marriage, reminding Fran of their history together. (And he's crafty: Note the scene in which he wonders aloud what Fran's swains would think if they knew she's become a grandmother.) Happily for Sam, his future also sails on the aforementioned boat: a beautiful American expatriate, whose path he crosses again in Italy, where she lives on the cheap.

Playing Sam with American robustness is the great actor Walter Huston. Ruth Chatterton plays his shallow wife, whose devastation at finally losing Sam is moving. The expatriate is played by Mary Astor, for once cast as kind and wise, not snarky or sly. William Wyler directs again, from a novel by Sinclair Lewis. For all its wrenching sorrow at midlife, *Dodsworth* portrays a good man ultimately getting his due: not only a new and more suitable mate, but a glimpse of new and exciting work to come.

The Bicycle Thief (1948)

The tenuous existence of the working class in bad times is brilliantly reflected in the postwar Italian film *The Bicycle Thief*, in which the worst thing that can happen to a worker is signaled in the title: His bicycle, crucial to his new-found work as a poster-hanger, is stolen. While the film tracks the man's increasingly desperate search around the infinitude of Rome, his little son, Bruno, is at his side throughout, sharing the panic and, wise beyond his years, offering solace. Sadly, he witnesses his father's final desperate act: stealing a bicycle himself—and getting caught. The utter humiliation of father and son is hard to watch—and should be seen by those who feel the poor have only themselves to blame for their suffering. Astonishingly, the leads are played by non-actors; the boy, Enzo Staiola, has an especially expressive face. This film, directed by Vittorio De Sica, is often cited as one of the best films of all time.

Guess Who's Coming to Dinner? (1967)

At a time when race relations have soured, and with the recent election described as a "whitelash" against minorities, it is useful to revisit this film about a white woman falling in love with an African-American man and coming home to announce the wedding to her parents. Even though the parents are liberals—her father Matt (Spencer Tracy) is a newspaper publisher, her mother Christina (Katharine Hepburn) owns an art gallery—they have misgivings about a marriage between Joey (played by Hepburn's real-life niece Katharine Houghton) and John (Sidney Poitier in a strong performance). Not my favorite Hepburn-Tracy vehicle (*Woman of the Year* is), this film earns points in showing everyone, including John's parents who arrive for the momentous decision, listening to each other so intently. Hard to argue with that.

I hope these gems will hearten the reader downcast about this dismal presidential election and the turbulence to come. While some of the films are tragic, somehow the characters' humanity never is. It remains to be seen—it is the drama we have yet to write—if America can avert tragedy and achieve higher ground. These films, in their humanity, point the way upward.

—*HuffPost*, December 12, 2016

How to Fight the Forthcoming Ethics Scandals? Make a Phone Call

First in a series, Annals of Resistance

ETHICAL QUESTIONS ARE bound to loom over the forthcoming Trump administration. Indeed, ethical violations—questions of right and wrong—will likely be a theme.

With a cabinet full of extremely wealthy people whose confirmation hearings are going forward without the traditional ethics reviews completed; with Trump's global business empire going undivested and his taxes going undisclosed, at his insistence, thus exposing him to all sorts of future ethical liability; and with Trump constantly misrepresenting the truth, misrepresentations that news organizations like *The New York Times* now simply call "lies," we are heading into murky waters.

Which makes saying goodbye to the Obama administration—which was, ethically speaking, remarkably clean—all the harder.

But we are here and must deal with reality: How can the conscientious public fight back against the forthcoming ethics scandals?

By making a phone call. More to the point, lots of phone calls over the coming four years.

In happy fact, an ethical victory has *already* been scored—the Congressional ethics office was saved from gutting—and the method of rescue was none other than the phone call, an overwhelming barrage of them from conscientious citizens. This victory risks being forgotten in the non-stop media circus that is Donald J. Trump.

In a benighted move by House Republicans to gut the independent watchdog Office of Congressional Ethics as their very first act in the new session, public outrage was so massive and blistering when this news broke that the phone lines on Capitol Hill lit up, forcing a GOP rethink and a complete reversal.

How massive and blistering was the barrage? As Rep. Walter B. Jones, Republican from North Carolina, "surprised" at the number of calls to both his district and Washington offices, put it: "People are just sick and tired. People are just losing confidence in the lack of ethics and honesty in Washington."

Clearly, the public has a keener bead on Trump's campaign promise to "drain the swamp" in Washington than Congressional Republicans, who had to be reminded. It is universally understood that this particular swamp is an ethical one, rife with ethical violations, thus to drain it requires, well, ethics—the stringent application of stringent ethics. A full-strength Congressional ethics office is crucial to that task.

Trump himself weighed in on the attempted gutting of this ethics watchdog—*after* the public made known its outrage—with a tweet: "With all that Congress has to work on, do they really have to make the weakening of the Independent Ethics Watchdog, as unfair as it may be, their number one act and priority. Focus on tax reform, healthcare and so many other things of far greater importance!"

Note, please, that Trump does not object to gutting the ethics watchdog, "unfair as it may be," but only to the *timing* of the gutting. Also, some news organizations wrongly credited the ethically-challenged Trump with championing the rescue of the Congressional watchdog. Here Trump was no actor, certainly no ethical actor, but a reactor—to outrage already registered by the public.

Score one for the public, the Conscientious Public.

And stand by to make more calls: While the Office of Congressional Ethics has been saved, the House GOP nevertheless changed a rule allowing members to claim sole control of their records, notably expenditures, even if the OCE wants to investigate—which semi-guts the OCE again. This ethical fakery begs to be called out, so: Call it out.

That which was saved once by the phone can be saved again by a redial. Of the various means of communicating with leaders in Washington—including the phone call, the letter, the email, messages posted on Facebook and Twitter—the phone call is particularly powerful. As *Times* columnist David Leonhardt explains:

> "Congressional staff members privately admit that they ignore many of the emails and letters they get. They also admit that phone calls are different. They have to answer them. Other people in the office hear the phone ringing and see their colleagues on the line. Phone calls are a tangible sign of public opinion, which is why they have been effective before."

This still may seem small-bore to some, like bringing a knife to a gunfight, or worse, a tin can like kids used to use for backyard communication before the digital revolution. But, again, recall the showdown already won by the public over the Congressional Ethics Office. The phone call, especially if mounted in organized fashion, registers.

For now, about Trump nominees' Senate confirmation hearings going forward without a full ethics review (at Democrats' insistence, the hearings process has been slowed): Check the schedule, find out which Senate committee conducts which hearing, and call the member Senators to insist on a full ethics review for each nominee. Conducting these reviews is the Office of Government Ethics. Decrying the incoming administration for "sheer recklessness" in trying the ram the confirmations through without ethical review, *The New Yorker*'s Evan Osnos describes such review "a controlled explosion" that can protect against a problem appointee. "Will Americans swamp the switchboards again to demand better? Republicans are betting that the answer is no." Prove them wrong.

Finally, with the ethically-challenged Donald Trump taking power January 20, here's the phone number of the White House switchboard: 202-456-1414. Put that number on speed-dial.

—*HuffPost*, January 16, 2017

Barack Obama, President of Character and Integrity

IN THESE FIERCELY contentious times, it is a remarkable thing, if you are President, to see your approval rating *go up* as your term of office ends. Often the public cannot wait for the occupant of the White House to vacate the premises.

With his numbers rising steadily for months, Barack Obama left the White House with an approval rating of 59%, according to a number of polls. Given the ferocity of this last election, with victory going to the opposing party, an ascending trajectory is rather miraculous.

By contrast, while newly-inaugurated Donald Trump saw his popularity soar immediately after his election, it plummeted during his two-month transition: Trump entered the White House with a 40% approval rating—lowest in the modern presidency. Usually a President enters office with highest ratings and then, after the hurly-burly of political combat and public disillusion, those ratings fall (as happened to Mr. Obama's predecessor, George W. Bush, whose rating on departure was 34%).

Can it be accident that Obama's rating ascends while Trump's descends? These crisscrossing ratings reflect, I believe, our nostalgia-in-advance for the departing Mr. Obama and rise in direct proportion to our dread-in-advance of a Trump presidency. (Of course Trump complains his low rating is due to "rigged" polling.)

No doubt the public observed Mr. Trump's behavior during his transition, notably his attacks on the intelligence community and the media for raising questions about his close ties with Russia's Vladimir Putin, a leader who bears the U.S. no good will, as well as his attacks via retaliatory tweet against any and all critics, be it union leader, film actress, or civil rights icon—things it is simply inconceivable Mr. Obama would do—and the public had to wonder: Can this man control his hot temper and become presidential?

On this point of personal control, our nostalgia-in-advance for Mr. Obama relates directly, I also believe, to that ultimate thing—character—or Character, as capitalized by early American philosopher Ralph Waldo Emerson because of its moral component. Presidential approval ratings reflect not only agreement with policy and a liking for personality; they reflect—the thing hardest to command and the most important to secure—respect. Respect is the salute we give to Character.

In short: Barack Obama has it—Character—while Donald Trump *is* one, a character, a cartoonish one.

It takes Character, as Mr. Obama demonstrated over and over, to execute the world's most difficult job. Recall when Mr. Obama entered office, we were on the brink of a repeat of The Great Depression, threatening America and the world with its ravages. But Mr. Obama did not quake (not publicly), nor did he waste time excoriating his predecessor. Nor did Mr. Obama lash out in attacks on Congressional Republicans who infamously conspired on the very day of his first Inauguration to oppose him in all things. With the nation on the brink of economic collapse, such opposition must have struck Mr. Obama as akin to treason, but we didn't hear it. Nor did the GOP's continuing obstruction throughout his eight years in office get a rise out of him.

And it takes Character of a special kind to forebear when large swaths of the public rise up to voice objection to the legitimacy of your presidency and indeed to your very being, with declarations to "take back our country"—a message it doesn't take a linguist to translate is Dog Whistle for "Get that black man out of our White House." How revolting now to see enter the White House, and how remarkable Mr.

Obama's grace in welcoming him, the man who promoted the scurrilous birther movement questioning Mr. Obama's legitimacy, the man who, finally conceding birtherism has no basis—is in fact a lie—could not bring himself to apologize to the man he injured. Unlike his predecessor, Mr. Trump is completely devoid of Character.

This may be why there is little pride displayed among Republicans at Mr. Trump's ascension—there's the thrill of victory, yes, but little pride—nothing like the pride Democrats felt that historic night in 2008 when we, at long last, elevated an African-American to the White House and began to exonerate ourselves for the nation's sin of slavery. Instead of pride, Republicans must finesse the fact that Mr. Trump enters office with the blot of racism on his character, as birther-promoter, among other blots (sexual predator, xenophobe, etc).

I often wondered about Mr. Obama's inner weather, what it was like for him inside his head and his soul when the going got rough, especially when his very being was questioned, when he actually had to produce the long form of his birth certificate to placate the birthers. Surely, like every last one of us, the Furies arose in him and had to be quelled, which Mr. Obama always succeeded in doing, while we manage it far less often (and Mr. Trump not at all). We have to admire Mr. Obama's self-control, the only exertions of which can be seen in his hair grown grey. That's called integrity: the hanging on to Character and never sullying it or letting it go.

Appropriately, there were some few times when he loosened his self-control and openly grieved—for the little children massacred in Newtown, for the young African-American men killed by police, for the members of an African-American church gunned down by a white supremacist in Charleston, for our war dead.

This is not to say Mr. Obama never put a foot wrong. I still question his use of military drones to kill terrorists, as drones are a cheap and easy-to-assemble weapon for terrorists to use against us. I wish he'd done more for infrastructure, not only to bolster our buckling bridges and roads, but to give jobs to the working class that, disillusioned, eventually went for Trump. I wonder, given the public's appetite for wholesale change as seen in Trump's victory, if Mr. Obama might have gone for a wholesale reform of Wall Street, rather than the half-measure that is Dodd-Frank. And I wish Mr. Obama had spearheaded an international coalition to save Syria.

And, long an opponent of torture, I still believe Mr. Obama erred when he decided against prosecuting the administration of his predecessor, George W. Bush, for descending to the practice of torture (in Iraq). I can understand Mr. Obama's resistance to "relitigating" the past; perhaps an investigation rather than prosecution might have served. But not even to examine this moral blot, this ugly mark on America's shield, was, I believe, a grave error, one that will cause History to wonder about this highly moral President and his otherwise laudable record.

But Mr. Obama put his foot right innumerable times. Character without achievement would mean he was little more than an estimable guy. In Mr. Obama, character came with achievement: again, saving the economy—for which he is not given enough credit (but about which he does not grouse, another sign of Character); saving the auto industry, an iconic American industry; claiming healthcare as a right, not a privilege, and enacting landmark legislation, a mountain Democrats since FDR have wanted to summit; extricating us from war in Iraq and stabilizing Afghanistan; spearheading a historic international agreement on climate change, the first step toward saving the planet for future generations.

As for failing to deliver on a "post-racial" America, which absurdly some fault him for: In truth, Mr. Obama did his part, by modeling racial tolerance and pointing the way, but he alone can't effect social change. *That* is on us, the society: Society must want to change. Mr. Obama is himself post-racial, but, sadly, America is not. Same goes for "post-partisan": Again, it was Republicans who refused to work with him from Day One, despite his extended hand, thus he resorted to executive action and we remain more divided than ever.

Mr. Obama is a student of History; he understands its ebbs and flows. I imagine he has the wit to think History has a very strange sense of irony to replace him with his diametric opposite. Mr. Obama may see this diametric recalibration as a sign of his having made a mark: the bigger the action, the bigger the re-action. With Mr. Trump vowing to undo everything Mr. Obama achieved, the historian in Mr. Obama may reasonably hope for—and in his post-presidency he will actively work toward—restoration of his programs in future election cycles; at the least, during his presidency he set the template. As archetype Mr. Obama may be seen as a tragic optimist, as I wrote earlier: He does the right thing, like healthcare or climate change—*even knowing that all his hard work may come to nothing.* Doing the right thing *is* the thing. Again, this is Character.

Emerson defined Character as "the moral order seen through the medium of an individual nature." About moral character, he wrote, "Rectitude is a perpetual victory, celebrated not by cries of joy, but by serenity," adding, "It is disgraceful to fly to events for confirmation of our truth and worth" (something Mr. Trump does perpetually). Emerson also wrote of Americans in the main: "Our frank countrymen... have a taste for character, and like to know whether the New Englander is a substantial man, or whether the hand can pass through him." But Emerson also said of the world, "History has been mean; our nations have been mobs."

This past election, our frank countrymen let anger get the better of them, yielding a President who is mean and low. It remains to be seen if the American people have the Character—Mr. Obama's Character—to right the balance and save the Republic.

—*HuffPost*, January 26, 2017

There's a Whole Lot of Anti-Trump Resistance Going On

Second in a series, Annals of Resistance

NOVEMBER'S POLITICAL EARTHQUAKE—THE election of the demagogue Donald Trump—sent liberals into shock, even trauma. Heartfelt keening of shame and revulsion was heard throughout the land. Thanksgiving gatherings saw little thanks given; "No politics" was the rule at many tables; non-attendance was the out for many liberals, to avoid Trump-voting relatives. Same for the Christmas holidays, with perhaps more philosophical reflection reigning.

A four-year lamentation looked to be in store.

But that languor—God bless America!—is not the case in the New Year. When the new reality struck—the inauguration on Jan. 20 of *President* Donald John Trump; his controversial cabinet nominations, with some nominees vowing to take down the departments they would head; his extremist executive orders in his first weeks—it triggered, and continues to trigger, popular resistance, people-in-the-streets resistance. Citizens heretofore apolitical are getting off their sofas and heading out.

Why? Because, deep in their bones, these Americans sense the existential threat a President Trump poses—a threat not only to our public institutions, but to America's foundational ideals: rule of law, equality, separation of church and state, and more. Who knows what other treasured precept will come under attack, since Trump is an equal-opportunity offender. "Existential threat" is often used to describe a crisis, but this time the threat *is* existential: the existence of our very democracy is at stake, something many Americans did not know was so dear to them until under attack.

Let us survey the ways this resistance—multi-form—is taking shape: The day after Trump's inauguration, and planned as defiant resistance to the newly-installed Groper-in-Chief, the Women's March took place in more than 600 cities around the country, with the largest in Washington and New York. With better diversity than historically has been the case, and with men joining the ranks, the Women's March proclaimed a broad range of issues—equality and civil rights, healthcare and reproductive rights, immigration rights, among others. At an estimated 4.2 million, the Women's March of 2017 may be the largest mass protest in American history. (Interesting: It took Donald Trump to get women who once resisted the term "feminist" to cease their resistance and embrace the term.) Sister marches around the world included another 3 million.

Days later, when Sen. Elizabeth Warren persisted when closed down by majority leader Mitch McConnell in confirmation hearings of sometime-racist Jeff Sessions for Attorney General, the #ShePersisted meme went viral and will no doubt persist, both as general rallying cry and as a potential Warren for President 2020 campaign.

Likewise impressive were the spontaneous protests at the nation's airports to Trump's executive order banning Muslims traveling from seven Muslim-majority countries to the U.S. Lawyers came forward, from the ACLU and other organizations, to volunteer their services to bewildered families. The order was overturned, thanks to officials from my state (Washington), including the judge, James Robart. Altogether, a good start to Immigrant Nation's resistance. Long overdue is a solidarity march with our fellow Muslim-Americans.

Also overdue is a show of solidarity with the DACA "dreamers," children born outside the U.S. who were brought here by undocumented Hispanic parents and are thus non-citizens, if Trump rescinds their protections enacted by Mr. Obama. Trump's recent executive order calling for a crackdown on "sanctuary" jurisdictions targets not just the undocumented with criminal records, as Trump touts, but can deem an undocumented person a criminal simply by virtue of being undocumented, thus deportable. With arrests now underway, a test looms.

Meanwhile, grassroots resistance groups across a spectrum of issues are rapidly being organized by #Resist: Meetup (already 1,000 groups formed). The Indivisible Guide, formed by former Capitol Hill staffers and modeled after highly effective Tea Party principles, is targeting Republican members of Congress in their districts; to date it has over 10 million page-views and over 6,000 local groups have signed on since it came online mid-December. Protests may be multi-form: As a co-chair of the Women's March recognized, "This is the moment for us to show up for one another... versus being... stuck in our silos." Showing up in these protests are masses of young people, bless them. Says *The New York Times*, this energy is "bursting out at demonstrations and town hall meetings across the country."

As to town halls, Republicans are finding them suddenly contentious, filled with protesters. As *RealClearPolitics*, a conservative site, titled a recent commentary, "There's No Escape from the GOP's Town-Hall Hell."

Coming up: Scientists from across America and the world will march on Washington on Earth Day, April 22, in the March for Science. On that day scientists will walk out of the lab and into the streets to counter the Trump administration's claim, among others, that climate change is a hoax: "Listen to the evidence." Within a week of its announcement, 1.3 million supporters had signed up for the march.

Look also for public-school teachers to mount protests to Trump's newly-confirmed Education Secretary Betsy DeVos. With DeVos advocating that public monies be directed to private and charter schools, outraged tax-paying parents should be out in the streets, too, along with the teachers.

And with Trump rolling back the "fiduciary rule" that President Obama put in place—the rule requiring that financial managers prioritize their client's interests over their own—look for John Q. Public to protest. The Wall Street and corporate capitalists in Trump's cabinet, whose top priority likewise is not likely John Q. Public, will also present fodder for protest. The Consumer Financial Protection Bureau, whose top priority *is* John Q. Public, lies in Republican sights. Getting hit in the pocketbook may be the fastest way to turn true-believing Trumpsters into the streets.

Other issues sure to prompt resistance when the new administration acts on them include: the repeal *and* replacement of President Obama's Affordable Care Act; any exploitation of public lands; torture. Should Trump order a return to the illegal and shameful practice of torturing terrorist suspects, all humanists should rise up.

(And if white supremacist/apocalyptic visionary Stephen Bannon continues to exert his influence on Trump as senior advisor, especially if he keeps his principal's seat on the National Security Council, a place where political advisors never should be, most definitely not one with an apocalyptic bent, he may inspire his own dedicated anti-Bannon resistance.)

Resistance needn't be registered only in the streets. Staying at your bureaucrat's post and doing your job despite heat from the administration also qualifies as resistance.

While it's a fair criticism to say the press prior to the election actually abetted the showman in the race, by focusing on the campaign's horse-race aspects, it is also fair to say that, since the election, the press has been rigorous in exposing the new administration's misrepresentations—and not afraid to call them lies when needed. Solid reporting is best resistance to Trump's incessant accusations of "fake news."

The federal civil service is gearing up. *The Washington Post* quotes an anonymous Justice Department employee, vowing: "People here will resist and push back against orders they find unconscionable." Methods to resist orders considered illegal include slow-walking those orders; leaking to the press; posting vital public information via social media. Legal counsel is being sought on what to do if illegal orders are received. At the State Department a dissent cable on Trump's refugee ban drew 1,000 signatures. A former CDC immunologist created a "resistance page" to post vaccine information (Trump is famously anti-vaccine). The union representing EPA scientists may form a fundraising arm to "defend federal scientists we anticipate will be disciplined for speaking out or for defending scientific facts." Writes the *Post*, speaking generally of federal workers: "The resistance is so early, so widespread and so deeply felt that it has officials worrying about paralysis."

Resistance can also manifest across the partisan divide, theoretically.

Republicans are invited to create their own profile in courage, by resisting Trump when need be. So far most GOP leaders, including those who vowed "Never Trump," support the new President. The standout is Sen. John McCain, who vows to fight Trump on torture, opposed Trump's Muslim travel ban, and, most recently, defends the media, warning that suppressing a free press is "how dictators get started."

Congressional Democrats of course form the left's frontline resistance. Though badly outnumbered, they are fighting the good fight. Democratic-controlled states such as New York and California vow to invoke states' rights if ordered to comply with federal directives they deem unconstitutional; some cities will do likewise.

How effectively will this multi-form anti-Trump resistance manifesting itself around the country work out? Some commentators worry that, in this diffuse array, coherence will be lost, also that such resistance is less *for* something than *against*.

But it can also be argued—in fact, it's the argument being made now, organically, by the activist public—that a resistance movement made up of many moving parts is *precisely* the way to combat Trump's multi-form provocations: every resister protesting that which he or she cares most passionately about. Moreover, that resister, in defending a treasured precept—be it rule of law, equality, separation of church and state, or other—is actually engaged in a positive action, is *for* something. It just may happen that, in this resistance to save our democracy, we'll all become constitutionalists, ethicists, and small-d democrats, but that's a subject for later.

Of course the ultimate question, the decisive question, is: Will this resistance endure, will it sustain itself, to become a proper, capital-r Resistance? To do so requires—in addition to a compelling idea that compels allegiance—organization, strategy, long-term commitment, and an *esprit de guerre* combined with adherence to nonviolence. A recent example, Occupy Wall Street, was a disappointment in this regard: While Occupy had a compelling idea—that the American economy works for the 1% but not the 99%—it disdained political involvement and organization, and ultimately it fizzled out.

One bright sign of current staying power: Since the November election, and energized by the success of the Women's March, a reported 13,000 women—that's right: 13,000—plan to run for office, according to *New York Magazine*, with most running in local races. (This figure combines EMILY's List data and sign-ups at the incubator sites SheShouldRun and VoteRunLead.) It is to be hoped that, the further Trump humiliates the office of President, even more women will run, will persist.

In a sobering cover essay "How to Build an Autocracy" for *The Atlantic*, conservative David Frum writes that he fears Donald Trump could set America down the path to a "repressive kleptocracy"—if Congress remains polarized and the public listless. In this quest, a strongman leader like Trump seeks to discredit the media, "nurturing the idea everybody lies and nothing matters," and to subvert democratic institutions (Trump's claims of voter fraud and rigged system). For a manipulator like Trump, resistance can be a "resource," not a problem, with "the conservative entertainment-outrage complex" eager to assist him: "The more offensively the protesters behave, the more pleased Trump will be." Still, in "this moment of danger," says Frum, who again is a conservative, we have a "duty to resist":

> *"By all early indications, the Trump presidency will corrode public integrity and the rule of law—and also do untold damage to American global leadership, the Western alliance, and democratic norms around the world. The damage has already begun, and it will not be soon or easily undone. Yet exactly how much damage is allowed to be done is an open question—the most important near-term question in American politics. It is also an intensely personal one, for its answer will be determined by the answer to another question: What will you do? And you? And you?"*

To the Resistance.

—*HuffPost*, February 2, 2017

For Effective Resistance, Keep It Nonviolent, Respectful, and Clean

Third in a series, Annals of Resistance

WITH ANTI-TRUMP RESISTANCE "bursting out" across the country, as *The New York Times* describes it, some rules of the road—or rather, of the street—are in order. They are simple and have been historically proven successful: Keep all resistance nonviolent, respectful, and clean.

These all-purpose rules also apply to resistance conducted off the streets—in town halls, in lobbying, in campaigning for office. And they might decompress family gatherings where anti-Trump and pro-Trump supporters are likely to mix (or not).

Maintaining this discipline becomes all the more crucial as Republican lawmakers seek to introduce legislation to curb mass protests. *The Washington Post* reports such efforts by Republicans in 18 states (as of Feb. 24) since Donald Trump's inauguration:

> *"From Virginia to Washington state, legislators have introduced bills that would increase punishments for blocking highways, ban the use of masks during protests, indemnify drivers who strike protesters with their cars and in at least one case, seize the assets of people involved in protests that later turned violent."*

The majority of these anti-protest bills were defeated, but five have been passed—in North Dakota (4) and South Dakota (1)—according to The Voice Project. No doubt there will be more such attempts, including bills to indemnify those who use their cars to "accidentally on purpose" run down protesters in the streets. Thus, our resistance must be by-the-book defensible.

Remember, the right-wing outrage-amplification machine will pounce on any misstep on the part of liberals. That lone misstep will be amplified to tarnish the well-meaning effort of the entire mass. So check any impulse to do the wild-and-crazy and consider how it could be manipulated to hurt the common purpose.

Keep resistance nonviolent

The masses out in the streets on the day of Trump's inauguration, and the weeks since, are concrete evidence of the profound resistance to this administration that exists and is building around the U.S. (World: Take note, please, all is not lost here.) It is on us, the world's oldest democracy, to conduct this resistance in a nonviolent way, without bloodletting.

Unfortunately, on Inauguration Day in Washington, there were several outbreaks of violence, with six police injured (none seriously, fortunately). Reportedly those responsible for the violence were mask-wearing individuals, presumably anarchists or young toughs. To their credit, others in the crowd tried to shout these marauders down. But it can easily be seen, with the media too often following the "If it bleeds, it leads" precept, how spiraling violence at protests could dominate the news. Tactically, nonviolent resistance neutralizes and controls the opponent's aggression.

The ultimate aim of nonviolent resistance, wrote Martin Luther King, Jr., is a moral one: "to awaken a sense of shame" in the opponent. Ultimately liberals, whose mission in essence is moral—tolerance, dignity, civil and human rights, rule of law, peace, simple humanity—want to reach those Trump supporters who subverted their conscience for the economic relief and jobs that Trump promised: How else could they abide Trump the sexual predator, the racist, the proto-autocrat who's fine with torture and violence? If liberal resisters resort at any point to violence, they subvert both their own moral essence and their outreach to the opposition.

Trump supporters, as one man angrily emailed me, equate the anti-Trump resistance with rioting. Let's not prove them right. With passions running high, keep calm when resisting. And beware "protesters" in masks.

Keep resistance respectful

"Respectful" here is used in two senses: civilized behavior and respect for the law, from the Constitution down to local ordinances.

Case in point illustrating both meanings: the recent student protest at Vermont's Middlebury College to the appearance of conservative Charles Murray, co-author of *The Bell Curve*, which argues that African-Americans are intellectually inferior to whites. The student protesters not only turned their backs to Murray, which is defensible, but they shouted him down, forcing him from the stage. When he and his Middlebury host went to another location to stream his talk, protesters pulled fire alarms to drown him out. Upon leaving, both were roughed up by individuals wearing masks. (Again, beware "protesters" in masks.)

The Bible for liberals is the First Amendment of the Constitution, guaranteeing free speech. By shutting him down, the Middlebury protesters abrogated Murray's own right to the free speech that they themselves purport to cherish. As *Times* columnist Frank Bruni put it, by issuing "repressive rules about what people should be able to say and hear," students at this liberal college in fact displayed illiberalism.

Voltaire points the way here: "I disapprove of what you say, but I will defend to the death your right to say it." It's cliché, but it holds: The antidote to speech you don't like or approve of is more speech. Liberals need to learn to *argue*.

As for local ordinance and other rules of the street, the American Civil Liberties Union (ACLU), a leader in organizing against Trump's policies, provides a guide on street resistance. (Ex., you cannot block a road without a permit.)

Keep resistance clean

Again, to keep the moral high ground, resistance needs to be kept clean. Liberals can be profane and salacious (see: today's movies and TV), but, in the context of resistance, profanity and salaciousness hurt the cause.

Case in point: the pink "pussy hats" in the historic Women's March which took place the day after Trump's inauguration. Yes, these hats were intended to be a "creative and impactful" response to Trump's repugnant bragging during the campaign about grabbing women by their, um, private parts (which is, technically, sexual assault). But what was intended as a clever use of a vulgarism can be turned around to make the *wearer* a joke. As the above-cited Trump supporter emailed me: "What's with all the women wearing vaginas on their heads?"

In communication, especially in politics, avoid handing your opponent the "frame" by which to label you and your cause, counsels linguist George Lakoff, author of *Don't Think of an Elephant*. The p-word frames women and their cause as less than serious—and why ever would women, in their continuing quest for dignity and authority, do that to themselves? It also frames sexual assault, Trump's instigating offense, as less than the serious crime it is. I realize this particular train has left the station, but with more follow-on events planned for the Women's March, how about rethinking those hats? Hey, how about ball caps that say "Make America Sane Again" or "Make America Human Again"?

In this existential struggle against an administration seemingly bent on destroying so much of what liberals value, we will prevail with disciplined resistance. And, during Trump's tenure, if resistance is carried out in a manner that's nonviolent, respectful, and clean, it will pull in those who have not participated in protest but who realize that, on the other hand, they cannot passively sit by as Trump dismantles the America we love.

To the disciplined Resistance.

—*HuffPost*, March 21, 2017

The (Rich) Dog Not Barking: "No More Tax Cuts for Me, Thanks, I'm Good"

DURING THE RECENT Republican attempt to repeal and replace Obamacare, which fortunately went down in defeat, there was much talk about the 24 million people who would lose their health insurance if Trumpcare became the law of the land.

There was also talk of how the "savings" realized from removing those 24 million people from the insurance rolls would accrue to the wealthy, in the form of tax cuts.

But, unless I missed it, in all this discussion there was no talk—none —coming from the super-rich that such tax cuts were not necessary, were too much of a muchness, were in fact unseemly, given that 24 million people would have lost their insurance, only to benefit the already overflowing coffers of the rich.

Did anybody hear it from the rich: "No more tax cuts for me, thanks, I'm good"? (I didn't think so.)

Nor did President Trump, putative tribune of the little guy, raise objections that the healthcare package going forward would hurt the little guy while further enriching the rich guy ("Whoops!"). But by now we know Trump doesn't always read the documents being passed before him.

What's especially discouraging: Where was the show of heart among the super-rich—the heartsick recognition—at the prospect of 24 million *souls* being shoved off the insurance rolls? That image was the perfect prompt to show some of what we're not seeing among the rich these days: heart. Apparently for the rich, greed and the counting-house trump all else, including the suffering of their fellow Americans.

Granted, the rich are adept at "giving back" in charity drives and galas—*after* the fact of accumulating their base wealth working the system to their gross advantage.

That system—American turbo-capitalism—has produced the biggest imbalance in income between rich and poor since 1928, the year before the Great Depression hit. "Starting in the mid- to late-1970s," according to a Pew Research Center report, "the uppermost tier's income share began rising dramatically, while that of the bottom 90 perccent started to fall."

About this growing inequality, there has likewise been much talk. But, again, are we hearing cries from the rich that this inequality, and the suffering and insecurity it inflicts on so many, is intolerable, unendurable, cannot be allowed to continue, must be amended? (No.)

Sure, we occasionally hear from investor Warren Buffett, "Oracle of Omaha" and one of the world's richest people, lamenting how he pays taxes at a lower rate than his secretary. But nothing comes of this lamentation in terms of tax reform that would reduce that inequality. "Redistribution" is anathema to the rich.

There is a term for this type of grasping super-rich: "extractive elites."

In their book *Why Nations Fail*, economists Daron Acemoglu and James A. Robinson trace how, in case after tragic case throughout history, extractive elites are the principal reason why great nations decline and fall. Specifically (to quote from my review), those nations fail when, through political control, "an elite extracts the economic assets—natural or manufactured—by means of monopoly, coerced labor, expropriation of land, and exemption from taxation." Likewise Nobel economist Joseph Stiglitz warns of the catastrophic price of income inequality.

With tax reform next on the Trump legislative agenda, the rich will get a do-over—to compensate for their silence on the healthcare bill. Will one of their number step up to declare, "Enough with all the tax cuts!" and argue for a more equitable tax system? Will the rich meet this test, which at bottom is a moral test? Will the Republicans, their faithful Congressional minions?

(Per recent reports, Trump plans to revisit the healthcare bill before getting to tax reform, so once again the rich will get to reconsider the "losers" of Trumpcare. In this round Trump threatens to reduce the federal subsidies that enable poorer people to buy health insurance. Will this finally prompt the rich to say, "No way"?)

In the case of tax reform, there is time for the rich to show their heart. The last major tax reform bill, signed by President Ronald Reagan in 1986, took two years to hash out and assemble. And no doubt Trump will find the issue more complicated than he imagined. Thus the rich have time to organize and lobby for a more equitable tax system. But of course, organizing prowess is the least of it; growing a heart is.

For years, this writer has advocated for a George Washington visionary to step forth from Wall Street or the corporate sector, one who combines business acumen with a humanitarian feel for his/her fellow citizens, who'd propose the reforms that would put a human face on American capitalism, who'd rebalance America's great experiment of Capitalism and Democracy—to bolster the democracy that is faltering and temper the capitalism that is turbo-charged (and, by the way, bolster the USA brand). This visionary risks being called a traitor to his/her class, but also a savior of the nation.

Donald Trump is not that George Washington visionary, he is not a savior, but if he were pushed by his rich cohorts in a saving direction....

With America in trouble, perhaps decline, if our extractive elites stopped extracting and started shouldering their fair share of the tax burden, we might see a reversal of fortune.

—*HuffPost*, April 17, 2017

France Votes for Rationality Over Fear

AN AMERICAN LIBERAL can only envy France at this moment.

In their presidential election last Sunday, the French people—despite suffering major terrorist attacks on French soil, despite enduring a sluggish economy that's especially hurtful to the young, and despite living (sort of) with an unassimilated immigrant population—nevertheless rejected the politics of fear and isolation peddled by the far-right nationalist Marine Le Pen and threw in their lot—*emphatiquement*: 66% to 34%—with Emmanuel Macron, political independent, Europeanist, technocrat, young, positive.

And if they did not vote emphatically for Macron, they considered the prospect of the extremist leader of the National Front, with its racist, anti-Semitic, and pro-Nazi origins, moving into the Elysee Palace, and thought, *"Non, non, non, c'est impossible."*

The French people voted with intelligence for rationality, forswearing fear. Score one for civilization.

As *The New York Times* editorialized, "French voters were not seduced by nativist illusions and instead chose a youthful and optimistic president who believes that France must remain open, progressive, tolerant and European." In his victory speech, Macron acknowledged the anger and disillusion driving Le Pen's supporters, said he respected them, and vowed to give them less reason to vote for extremist remedies in future.

By contrast, the American electorate, enduring similar problems as the French but to a lesser degree, nevertheless succumbed to the barking fear-monger who blames "the other" and the fraudulent huckster promising miraculous deliverance, Donald J. Trump. And if they considered his odious baggage—his xenophobia, his racism, his misogyny, his amorality, and, crucially, his dangerous autocratic tendencies—they gave what might be called a Gallic shrug and said, "Meh, OK."

In brief, America last November betrayed its roots as Immigrant Nation and its foundational ideals of equality, fair play, rule of law, human rights. Since then, the world's Exceptional Nation has been committing a slow suicide. To be sure, a powerful resistance movement has risen up, wherein lies our salvation (if the resistance persists). But the environment in which we operate is driven by the lies, whims, and calculations of a president who doesn't read and has zero sense of history.

France, on the other hand, remains in the realm of logic, rationality, principle, possibility. With this important vote France honors its proud humanist history as a seat of the Enlightenment, which pride Macron cited in his victory speech.

Importantly, in this era of angry populism, Macron also shows us how to combat the fear-monger: head-on and all-in.

In the one and only one TV debate held prior to French presidential elections (itself a rational development, unlike the endless debates in the American system), Macron squared off against Le Pen and, to her face, called her "the high priestess of fear." Taking the offensive (and sounding quintessentially American), he accused Le Pen of "defeatism" in the face of France's various challenges; he energetically parried with fact each and every point she made—all of which allowed Le Pen little space to work her fear-mongering and reduced her to name-calling. In that performance, Macron was widely acknowledged as crushing Le Pen.

One of civilization's biggest discontents is the conventional wisdom that the forces of light, the civilized, are on the downside of any argument with the forces of dark, that, *faute de mieux*, they must be on the defensive, not the offensive. How often do we hear that Milton's Satan had all the best lines and all the energy? And French intellectuals, a notoriously pessimistic lot, for years have been publishing doom-ridden books on France's decline (*declinisme* is now part of public discourse).

But mark well Macron's muscular performance in the presidential debate: He went on the offensive, powerfully so, and vanquished the fear-monger (while seeming to enjoy himself in the process). Civilization gets a new tool.

Of course none of this is to discount the severe challenges Macron faces, nor the continuing threat of the National Front: It had its best postwar showing ever in this election, garnering one-third of the vote. In the legislative elections coming up in June, the results of which will determine how successfully Macron can govern, Macron vows to field candidates for all offices, but he established his party, En Marche! (On the Move!), only last year and lacks a deep organization. Le Pen likewise will field multiple candidates to increase her party's presence in the Parliament.

Meanwhile, the two establishment parties which traded the baton in governing the country since World War II, the Socialists and the Republicans, have been sidelined and cast into disarray by the forces represented by Macron and Le Pen.

Much will depend on how successfully Macron addresses the anger and disillusion among Le Pen's supporters, much of which focuses on France's immigrant population. France must address this seemingly intractable problem, by facing its colonial past and its responsibility for a more thorough assimilation. It must solve the problem that recent terrorist attacks in France have been perpetrated by Muslims raised in France as French citizens.

France is now in uncharted seas. But at the least, with this resoundingly affirmative vote, it sails with a compass and its wits. *Bon chance, la France.*

—*HuffPost*, May 11, 2017

Plays for Our Times: *Oslo*, by J.T. Rogers

First in a series, Plays for Our Times

WHAT DOES THE 2,500-year-old art of the Drama have to say to our tumultuous times, the early 21st century? With the weakening of the post-World War II international order—institutional bulwarks have failed to protect the individual against the ravages of a globalized economy and unending armed conflict; democracy's spread has been checked by ineffective leadership, resurgent populism and nationalism, and the threat of authoritarianism—our times as a consequence are marked by extreme polarization, loss of identity, disillusion, anger. And, sadly, culture—film, books, TV, also drama—does not offer many tools to counter the political chaos. In both politics and culture, the rational gives way to the irrational, the civil gives way to the angry.

In the belief that culture, even more than politics, could juice the recovery of our faltering democracy, this series will examine plays that reflect our age's tumultuous political and social forces and, importantly, point the way upward. Ancient drama tended toward Tragedy, even Shakespeare saw politics as corrupting, so of necessity the focus here will be on modern drama. While much modern drama is big on dysfunction and despair, this writer-playwright is not. This series features protagonists pursuing what once were described as noble ends; at the least, they try to control the chaos, not exploit it or give in to it.

* * *

Oslo, by J.T. Rogers

Oslo is a play about possibility: the possibility that enemies, if brought together and enabled to see each other as human beings, can become, if not friends, then at least incapable of shooting each other when they return home.

Here, the most intractable of enemies in modern times—the Israelis and the Palestinians—are brought together by Norwegian diplomats, a husband-and-wife team, to forge the so-called "Oslo Channel," the back-channel negotiations that ultimately led to the ground-breaking Oslo Accords, signed by Yitzhak Rabin and Yasser Arafat in the White House Rose Garden in 1993.

Playwright J.T. Rogers has taken a real-life event—with the real-life representatives of the Israeli and Palestinian sides and with the real-life Norwegian diplomats, Terje Rod-Larsen and Mona Juul, serving as our Virgils—and, with keen dramatic clarity, imagined what it was like at the negotiating table, as well as all the maneuvering required to get the parties back into the room when one or the other side walks out.

While the Oslo Accords ultimately collapsed—Rabin's assassination two years later by a Zionist extremist ushered in a right-wing government and more Israeli settlements in disputed territory; the Palestinians resumed mounting intifadas against Israel and elected the radical Hamas organization to leadership—what Oslo accomplished was historic. That is, for the first time ever the Palestinian Liberation Organization recognized the legitimacy of the state of Israel; for the first time ever Israel recognized the P.L.O., ultimately upgraded to the Palestinian Authority, as the representative of the Palestinian people; and both sides agreed to resolve their differences peacefully.

In essence, then, the Oslo process is about getting human beings to recognize each other's humanity. As such, it is the very stuff of drama, and *Oslo* takes it to high heights, while inflecting the drama with the quirks and humor that human beings display as they desperately seek their objectives. Peace accords entail lots of drama.

In dozens of short scenes, interspersed with lengthier ones, Rogers deftly knits together nine months of complex diplomatic history. Mona Juul acts as both calming influence on the talks and narrator of this complex history, often with droll humor. Showing, in the first scene, how she and Terje persuaded their foreign minister to host the talks, and noting how the foreign minister is married to a colleague of Terje's at the research institute Terje founded, she says in an aside, "In Norway we take nepotism to an entirely new level. It's a very small country and we think and behave as such." Also Norway has something the biggest player, the U.S., can never have: "the appearance of neutrality."

It is Terje's vision and method, however, that are key. At important junctures, he reminds all that in chaos comes opportunity: "The grip of history is loosening. The Berlin Wall has just fallen; the Soviet Empire, disbanded." And: "The world is cracking open. All I am saying is to think about new possibilities. Imagine what can be achieved *now!*" And when the murder of an Israeli border guard by a Palestinian threatens to disrupt the talks: "I know, it's tragic, but these are perfect conditions for progress. The desperation they are feeling, on both sides, *this* is our ally."

As to method, Terje advocates the gradualist over the totalist method, where all sides to a conflict bring all their demands to the table, the method the Americans prefer (the overbearing Americans come in for sly jabbing). With the gradualist method, adversaries focus on a single issue, resolve it, then move on to the next issue, as they build a bond of trust. (Johnny Walker whiskey also helps.) It's when Terje persuades Israel's deputy foreign minister of the validity of his method that the play's action commences. Their plan: These back-channel talks are to supplement, like "a tributary," the totalist-oriented main channel conducted by the Americans, though the Americans can't ever know about Oslo's back-channel. What could go wrong?

The bulk of the play shows how all that can go wrong, does: intransigent parties, offense taken and apology demanded, constant power plays between and among the parties, leaks to the press, the Americans finding out—at a diplomatic reception an American diplomat calls out to Terje, "How are the secret negotiations going?"—and disruptive life disrupting with its tragedies (incidents of Israeli or Palestinian deaths swallowing the headlines).

But *Oslo* makes the case that watching ice thawing can be fascinating. The parties arrive with roles already cast: the Israelis as occupiers, the Palestinians as terrorists. Both parties know that, if they fail, they become targets for the extremists on their sides, notably the Israelis for daring to deal with an organization declared by Israel (and much of the world) as a terrorist organization, the P.L.O. The stakes could not be higher, success could not be more chimerical.

The first exchange does not go well: When an Israeli mentions the weather at home, the lead Palestinian says: "I have not been home since 1967 when every man, woman, and child in my village was forced to flee our homeland before the advancing hordes of Zionism." Things go better when one of the Palestinians and one of the Israelis, getting personal, discover they both have daughters named Maya. As the two diplomats know, though, "When you unleash the personal, the Furies can come out." (The Furies can come out in totalist discussions, too, but never mind.)

Proceeding gradually, getting personal, the parties make headway on their base demands—the Palestinians' demand for dignity, the Israelis' demand for security. But of course demands for dignity and security run into endless sticking points. When, at a very late point, it seems all will founder, Mona makes her own demand of both parties, the Israelis and the Palestinians—and speaks for the entire world:

> "Listen to me. You have fought each other—killed each other—for fifty years. Your mothers and daughters and sons have died, and nothing has changed. The world has washed its hands of this conflict, because they do not believe you can change. No one else is coming to help you. So it is up to you. Stay in this room and find a way forward."

The way forward is found, again, then bogs down, again. Enter, at long last, the Israeli Foreign Minister, Shimon Peres, consummate diplomat, to remind the Israeli party: "What we must not do is allow the details to obscure the bigger picture." To the shock of his countrymen, he states that Israel *needs* the P.L.O.: "Well I don't love them either, but when I look at the alternatives, I become very romantic." Finally, when the Palestinians' demand for a presence in Jerusalem looks to collapse the talks once and for all, Peres points the way: "In the name of... constructive ambiguity... we will accept that in the *final* stage of *further* negotiations, the future of Jerusalem will be addressed." What a curtain line: "constructive ambiguity." Reaching peace—an objective neither of the parties ever expected in their lifetimes—leaves stunned joy.

With the play's action coursing ahead—the point is the process—there is scant time for deep character development or soliloquys, just short speeches. (The play is set to become a film.) A factual quibble: Mao Tse-tung is given credit for saying "It's too soon to tell" if the French Revolution was successful. It was Mao's Foreign Minister, Zhou En-lai.

Again, while the Oslo Accords ultimately did collapse—over issues that had to go unaddressed in the back-channel talks: the Palestinians' right of return, the growth of Israeli settlements, Jerusalem—it is encouraging to know that, *with the right method and the right vision, the road to peace can be trod again.* Especially in these tumultuous times, believing that chaos presents opportunity could be life-saving.

In his Foreword to the script, Rogers says he looks to tell stories "that are framed against great political rupture." Thus his choice (and mine) of protagonists: "complicated, articulate people driven to achieve something far greater than themselves." In Terje Rod-Larsen and Mona Juul, he found them.

Though they would insist the parties to the peace talks were the real protagonists, Terje and Mona meet the "but for" test: But for them, the main action—the Oslo Channel and the Oslo Accords—would not have happened. Their journey began one year before the action of the play took place, when in Gaza they encountered an Israeli soldier in face-off with a Palestinian, both no more than boys. Stung by the hatred and fear in the eyes of both, Terje and Mona decided to act: "Would you not try anything to give those two boys a different narrative?"

These protagonists give us two gifts: a different narrative—hopeful, human, non-dystopian—and the hope that peace accords can happen again.

Note: After this posting, "Oslo" won the 2017 Tony award for Best Play.

—*HuffPost*, May 31, 2017

Julius Caesar with Trump Assassinated: Not Helpful to Anti-Trump Resistance

THERE IS A whole lot of anti-Trump resistance going on at the moment, seeking to bolster American democracy in the aftermath of the election of the amoral showman Donald Trump to the White House.

Rather than sink in despair for the next four years, thousands of Americans have announced plans to run for elective office. Thousands of pop-up groups, organized by Indivisible and others, have arisen, with varying agendas—saving healthcare and climate change policy in their states, countering Trump's proposed tax cuts to the rich, etc. States and cities have joined in, by recommitting to the objectives of the Paris climate accord that Trump has recently abandoned.

The common denominator of this resistance movement? Reversing the damage—*averting the tragedy*—of Trump's bulldozer presidency, to save our badly-faltering democracy. It's a remarkable thing, if you think about it: Great nations historically, once they enter decline, always fall. But America, with this resistance, is striving to reverse her decline. Americans not being fatalists (yet), we have a fighting chance.

Which is why the New York production of *Julius Caesar*—you know the one, it was all over the news: with Donald Trump portrayed as Caesar, complete with mop of blond hair and Slovenian wife—is hurtful to the resistance's salvage operation. Not only is the play a tragedy—Shakespeare's full title is *The Tragedy of Julius Caesar*—but, as every high-school student knows, it features an assassination.

It was this element—Caesar's assassination—that Trump supporters fastened on and protested to high heaven, making it a media monster and shoving it from the arts pages to the front page of *The New York Times*. At a time of extreme polarization, Democrat versus Republican, when polls show we now impugn the worst intentions to the other side, it's a production like this that feeds conservatives' worst suspicions of the anti-Trump resistance: that not only is it anti-anti just for the sake of opposition, but seeks to foment unrest, rioting, maybe even assassination. (This production's pre-scheduled run ended June 18.)

So vehement was the reaction to the production that the theater—the storied Public Theater, founded by Joseph Papp—was forced to issue a statement, declaring its production "in no way advocates violence toward anyone." In it the Public restated both its intention—"Shakespeare's play, and our production, make the opposite point: those who attempt to defend democracy by undemocratic means pay a terrible price and destroy the very thing they are fighting to save"—and its goal as a "civically-engaged theater" to foster discourse, as the "basis of a healthy democracy."

But lofty intentions got trumped by the proxy Trump's bloodied corpse.

In his program note, director Oskar Eustis, who is also the theater's artistic director, was silent on the choice of a Trump proxy, but expressed fear for our democracy's fragility: "The institutions that we have grown up with, that we have inherited from the struggle of many generations of our ancestors, can be swept away in no time at all." Continuing, he wrote, "when the ground is slipping away from under us and all that is solid melts into air, leadership is as transitory and flawed as the times." In an interview with the *Times*, Eustis spoke of his production as "a progressive's nightmare vision" of destabilized democratic norms.

Certainly, given these beliefs, if you see Trump as a latter-day prototype of Caesar's autocrat—which many liberals do, myself included—then theoretically you are justified in casting a Trump proxy in the title role. But, given the extreme "choler" (as Shakespeare might put it) of the public since the earthquake of Trump's election, you also run a risk of losing your argument in the backfire, which indeed happened. No doubt this production was thrilling—as theater, to liberals. (Reviews were positive.) But as political event, as conversation-enabler, the backfire only reinforced the conservative's view of liberals as a sneering, elitist, anything-goes, nothing-sacred lot, so why talk to us?

(Eustis disappointed when, in the *Times* interview, he blamed the backfire on the "right-wing hate machine." No, Mr. Eustis, other liberals can have a problem with your firecracker choice of Trump as the assassinated Caesar.)

Of course, here's where the traditional liberal argument for the absolute right of free speech and artistic choice will force itself into the discussion. (Most artists being liberal, this argument comes up constantly.) But here again is where the argument for responsibility, and for greater situational awareness, also must be made.

As for the right to free speech: As a liberal I repeat Voltaire's vow to defend "to the death" anyone's right to express things of which I may disapprove. But there is a limit to free speech, enunciated by the jurist Oliver Wendell Holmes, calling for responsibility: We cannot falsely cry "Fire" in a crowded theater. In this instance, where we have both a literal theater and the larger figurative theater beyond, crowded and choleric and combustible, we have the responsibility—to the public— not to torch the place.

As for the right to artistic choice: Artists often say they can't be held responsible for how their (bold) choices are taken by the public. And many declare, as a kind of law, that there is no connection between a work of art and any criminal act committed by an individual "inspired" by said work of art. This credo of exemption is echoed by *The Washington Post* theater critic in defense of the Public's bloodied Trump: "*Seeing something enacted on a stage doesn't mean you should go out and do it yourself*" [his italics]. But, this is to say art has no effect at all. In combustible times, are we really so sure?

Holding ourselves responsible for our artistic choices, I submit, would mature our art. Comedian Kathy Griffin's "joke" of holding up a mask of Trump's severed head was instantly and universally denounced as irresponsible and out of bounds (a hopeful sign, I think). In his *Times* interview Eustis noted that Griffin's "joke" occurred while his Trump-as-Caesar production was in rehearsal, and he confessed his reaction was "Whoops." That "Whoops" says lots. (By contrast, Griffin's reaction—saying her career is over and Trump has ruined her life— also says lots: about blinding narcissism.) Another "Whoops" was likely sounded when last week a leftist known for extreme anti-Republican views opened fire on Republican members of Congress playing baseball.

Turning to the play, finally: What a shame that all the controversy has detracted from the play itself, because Shakespeare's moral wisdom would be instructive at this singular and sad juncture in America's history, when we have descended from the honorable likes of Washington, Adams, Lincoln, and Roosevelt, to the proto-autocrat Trump. Eustis is spot-on when he says *Julius Caesar* can be read "as a warning parable to those who try to fight for democracy using undemocratic means. To fight the tyrant does not mean imitating him."

How instructive, then, to compare and contrast our times with ancient Rome, understanding that Rome's fall will begin with Caesar's assassination. How useful to know that, in the eyes of some (Cassius), Rome was already at a low point: "Age, thou are shamed! / Rome, thou hast lost the breed of noble bloods!"

How instructive to see Caesar as the great man becoming a tyrant: "I rather tell thee what is to be feared / Than what I fear; for always I am Caesar." "Danger knows full well / That Caesar is more dangerous than he." As Cassius says, "Why, man, he doth bestride the narrow world / Like a Colossus, and we petty men / Walk under his huge legs and peep about." (Unlike Trump, Caesar disdains "base spaniel fawning.")

How instructive to see good men, "all honorable men," Brutus and Cassius centrally, perceive themselves increasingly oppressed by Caesar and rationalize their way to murdering him. Brutus especially, "with himself at war," suffers internal "insurrection" (imagining Caesar as a serpent's egg that must be killed in the shell), eventually to conclude he must participate in this "piece of work that will make sick men whole" and slay Caesar's ambition. And when the work is done, this good man stoops low and bathes his arms in Caesar's blood.

How instructive to watch Marc Antony, Caesar's ally, noting a mourning Rome is a dangerous Rome, brilliantly manipulate the malleable crowd in his funeral oration against the conspirators, "all honorable men." How terrible to watch Antony's prophesy come to pass, when in the name of the slain Caesar "the dogs of war" are let loose ("Cry 'Havoc!'"), with "carrion men, groaning for burial," with the play's falling action taking down all the conspirators, by suicide.

But all this instruction, and the poetry and psychological insight, are lost this time around in the media frenzy. Which is a shame, because in rereading the play I was especially struck by this line, from Brutus, which—in this moment when we are led by a heedless, amoral president—would resonate deeply: *"Th' abuse of greatness is when it disjoins / Remorse from power."*

There is another line from the play that may point our way. Early on, as Cassius plies Brutus to join the plot to kill Caesar, he says: *"Think of the world."* Granted, Cassius' purpose is nefarious, but the line can be read more expansively. I urge my fellow artists, when creating work for these disjointed times—and serious artists yearn to join the mix—think of the world and the effect your creation may have on it.

And think of the anti-Trump resistance. Will your creation help or hinder what millions of stout souls, working their sword-arms at the barricades, are trying to do to rescue America? Again, if you think about it: Great nations historically, once they enter decline, always fall. But America, with this resistance, is striving to reverse her decline. Artists are more prone to think in a tragic key, but the resistance is trying to avert tragedy, mightily.

Friends, Romans, liberals: "Think of the world." And think of the resistance.

—*HuffPost*, June 22, 2017

Not Merely "Anti-Trump," the Resistance Seeks to Re-normalize America

Fourth in a series, Annals of Resistance

SINCE THE DEMOCRATS lost the special Congressional election in Georgia last week—the fourth they've lost since Donald Trump's victory in November—a new media narrative is emerging: that Democrats need to find a theme more compelling than just being anti-Trump or echoing the anti-Trump resistance.

As *The Washington Post*'s Philip Rucker declared on "Charlie Rose," "Hashtag Resistance... is not going to be enough."

But the resistance is not merely a negative force, rising against Trump for opposition's sake only. While it starts in opposition, it has taken on a more constructive meaning.

Properly understood, the resistance stands against the normalization of the proto-autocratic, amoral Trump and his administration in their dismantling of America's institutions and foundational ideals.

And standing *against* the normalization of Trumpism means the resistance stands *for* the re-normalization of American life. We have been not-normal for a long, long time.

Trump seems not to understand how a democratic government is supposed to work, that it functions by laws and rules, not the whims of one (unbalanced) individual. The resistance, by its various actions and its ideological and intellectual firepower, is giving new life to our democracy, which has grown tired and dysfunctional. Thus the energy of the resistance, its dynamism, its passion. The sleeping giant awakens.

The Women's March, for example. Declaring, among other causes, that Trump's repellant behavior toward women—his boast of groping their private parts—cannot ever become normalized, women by the millions poured into the streets of our cities the day after Trump's inauguration, making it the biggest march in history. The follow-on? By one count, 13,000 women have announced plans to run for office.

To protest the normalization of Trump's anti-science policies, including the denial of climate change, scientists massed by the thousands in hundreds of cities across the country and the world on Earth Day, April 22, in the March for Science. As follow-up, the March for Science website announces: "We marched. Now we act." In unhinged times, score one for reason, the scientific method, and re-normalization.

Resisters are becoming constitutionalists: Protesting Trump's refusal to divest his vast business empire from the presidency, we now know about the Emoluments Clause, banning presidents from receiving payments or gifts from foreign governments. (This month the Attorneys General of Maryland and the District of Columbia filed a lawsuit against Trump for "flagrantly" violating this clause.) With Trump's several efforts to ban Muslims from entering the U.S., resisters now know about the Establishment Clause, forbidding discrimination on the basis of religion.

On myriad other fronts working for America's re-normalization, resisters are also becoming ethicists, relearning the need to make value judgments, and becoming small-d democrats, relearning the truth that democracy, based on the *demos* or the people, needs the people's active participation—getting informed, running for office, voting, resisting.

All this re-normalizing activity is the very "juice" (as they say in Washington) of the resistance movement. This juice comes from a positive, not a negative place. Kicking in instantaneously after the November election, the resistance shows America's immune system—fighting against Trumpism—is in good working order.

And if the Democratic party had one fraction of this juice right now, it would be in better shape. Running parallel to the Democratic party, the resistance is where the new blood is flowing, with young people signing on. Resisters who run for elective office will likely run as Democrats, or as Independents.

Losing a presidential election always prompts major self-examination, and since November's earthquake loss, Democratic leaders in Washington have been caught up in a debate over the party's direction: whether, in taking on Trumpism, to stay centrist or take a left turn. The party's problems, then, are not with the resistance, but are internal. The Democratic party itself needs to re-normalize and get back to representing the middle- and working-classes.

At this moment of Democratic disarray, the resistance provides the through-line for liberal thought and energy. Resisters must push back at the negative connotation now being ascribed to them, of being merely anti-Trump. Controlling the narrative—that the resistance is working *against* the normalization of Trump's anti-democratic politics and *for* re-normalization of American life—is vital. *Vive la resistance*.

—*HuffPost*, June 28, 2017

Donald Trump, Defender of Western Civilization? Not!

THIS MUST BE what's called an "irony of history." Donald J. Trump, leading *offender* of Western civilization, just tried to pass himself off as its leading *defender*?

In his recent speech in Warsaw, Poland, the president served up a bookend to his inaugural address, the one describing "American carnage." Outlining the glories of Western civilization—"We write symphonies"—he cast those glories as under siege: "The fundamental question of our time is whether the West has the will to survive." Then, in defense of that civilization, this supremely uncivilized man went full Churchillian, about which, more later.

With history coursing onward at dizzying speed—due in no small part to Trump the anarchic disrupter—the commentariat, lacking time and perspective, was relatively quiet about Trump's astonishing claim. And now we're deep into another Trumpian media frenzy, this one about the president's son, Donald, Jr., and his alleged ties to the Russian government—the same government our intelligence community says tried to disrupt our last election—so the focus again is on collusion, possible treason or impeachment, not Western civilization.

But any lover of the humanities and Western civilization cannot let the moment pass. Donald Trump cannot ever be normalized as Western civilization's defender. In his Warsaw speech, the hypocrisies, the offenses, began immediately.

Early on, Trump invoked the Polish people's joy when, after communism fell, they were free to

celebrate mass with their Polish pope, John Paul II, saying with one voice, "We want God." Casting himself as one of them, Trump declared, "As I stand here today... their message is as true today as ever. The people of Poland, the people of America, and the people of Europe still cry out, 'We want God.'" This, from the un-godliest man in Christendom.

Then, after extolling a strong Europe as a "blessing to the West and to the world" (when has our crude president used the word "blessing" before?), Trump extolled "the transatlantic bond between the United States and Europe," claiming it to be stronger than ever. This would be the bond Trump assailed in his campaign, calling NATO "obsolete," whose Article 5, the mutual defense commitment, he coyly refused to endorse in his previous visit to Europe but coyly endorsed, in passing, in this visit.

Further on, Trump cited the glories of Western civilization, its symphonies among them. We "cherish inspiring works of art that honor God": again the God reference from this un-godly man. (It must be noted Western art also honors the human being.) "We treasure the rule of law": This, from the man who welshed on business deals and now has lawyered up to counter investigations into the Russia allegations. Warming to his theme, Trump then said we in the West "treasure the right to free speech and free expression": This, from the man who's declared the press "the enemy of the American people" and assails news critical of him as "fake news."

Warming further to his themes of truth and freedom, Trump then voiced this howler: "We empower women as pillars of our society and of our success." How did our Groper-in-Chief manage not to smirk?

(Little noted by the media, after Trump spoke of women empowered, he went on to say, "We seek to know everything so that we can better know ourselves." This certainly sounds like the Western spirit of inquiry, but coming from this man who's a complete stranger to himself? Sad.)

As hypocritical, even sacrilegious, as anything Trump uttered in Warsaw was this: Trump delivered his speech in Krasinski Square, a sacred place memorializing the valiant members of the Warsaw Uprising in their doomed efforts to throw off their Nazi occupiers in World

War II. "Those heroes remind us that the West was saved with the blood of patriots; that each generation must rise up and play their part in its defense, and that every foot of ground, and every last inch of civilization, is worth defending with your life." Pretty words, and blasphemous, from a man who ducked military service and who, during his campaign, scorned a genuine war hero, Sen. John McCain, saying he likes heroes who "weren't captured."

Its glories notwithstanding, all is not well in the West. As Trump said in Warsaw, the West, especially Europe, is under siege from "dire threats to our security and to our way of life"—principally, in his view, "radical Islamic terrorism." He declared: "The fundamental question of our time is whether the West has the will to survive. Do we have the confidence in our values to defend them at any cost? Do we have enough respect for our citizens to protect our borders? Do we have the desire and the courage to preserve our civilization in the face of those who would subvert and destroy it?"

Going full Churchillian, Trump concluded: "I declare today for the world to hear that the West will never, ever be broken. Our values will prevail. Our people will thrive. And our civilization will triumph."

But: Trump's definition of civilization is narrow and dark, the antithesis of the humanist definition of Western Civilization, as it's properly understood—which Trump doesn't.

Martin Luther's Reformation created space for the practice of religions other than Roman Catholicism—but Trump would prioritize Christianity. Concluding the Thirty Years' War with the first peace conference, the Treaty of Westphalia (1648) established the system of sovereign nation states enduring to this day—which Trump seems determined to upend with his disdain for treaties and alliances, his allergy to peace, his preference for walls over bridges, his approval of torture. The Enlightenment extolled and normalized scientific inquiry and reason—but Trump disdains science, having pulled the U.S. out of the Paris climate accord because he deems climate change a "hoax" and having installed a rabidly anti-science administrator at the Environmental Protection Agency. As for reason, it is to laugh. As for the beauties of Renaissance painting, sculpture, and architecture, Trump remains untouched.

Strangely, tellingly, nowhere in his speech did Trump cite Western Civilization's crowning triumphs—democracy and human rights. Instead, Trump stresses religion, tradition, and, as we know by now from his dog-whistle appeals, white supremacy.

Of course Western Civilization has its black marks—for one, exercising dominance without proper regard for less powerful states (e.g., colonialism); in other words, it hasn't always played well with others. Western Civilization has had its breakdowns, most recently and egregiously, World War I and II. And, at present, it *is* under siege from various forces—globalization and sagging economies, weakening democratic institutions, creeping decadence and cynicism, loss of faith, and, yes, radical Islamic terrorism and the droves of refugees its depredations have disgorged into Europe.

But Western Civilization, and civilization in general, is also under siege from another force: base leaders posing as saviors, like Trump, who manipulate their public's fear and unease for their own autocratic, and ultimately uncivilized, ends. It is the habit of autocrats to wrap themselves in civilization's trappings, the better to hide their malfeasance. Purporting to be a defender of Western Civilization, as Trump did in Warsaw, is classic.

Finally, it must be said: The very notion of "civilized," whether in the West or anywhere else in the world, carries with it the universally-recognized qualities of honesty, decency, honorableness, trustworthiness, tolerance, empathy, ethical consciousness, simple kindness, and, importantly, the ability to play well with others—none of which qualities our base president possesses.

Taking heart, let us remember that the Renaissance—rebirth—arose out of the Dark Ages. Employing the qualities of character and the habits of mind gifted us by Western Civilization, let us work toward our rebirth.

—*HuffPost*, July 17, 2017

A "Breaking Bad" Culture Got Its President

IT IS THE custom in America that, after a calamity happens—whether political, social, mechanical, or act of nature—we turn immediately to investigating how and why it happened. We do so because we presume that understanding the how and why will enable us to build toward a New Day. Americans are pragmatic that way, or at least we are when at our best.

To explain the how and why of Donald Trump's ascendency as president—a seismic calamity to liberals, a surprise gift to Trumpsters—the commentariat in these ten months has produced libraries of political analysis, tracing over the last half-century an increasingly angry Republican politics, fanned by flame-throwers like Barry Goldwater and Newt Gingrich, with an assist directed at government by Ronald Reagan—anger that the huckster Trump exploited to blow up the party and take the White House.

But Trump cannot be understood only as a political phenomenon. Donald J. Trump is also a *cultural* phenomenon, a product—the exemplar—of an increasingly amoral popular culture that, over this half-century, developed parallel to our angry politics. For liberals still in a daze over Trump's election, it is useful to consider this cultural context. After all, we *choose* our political party, but we *live* immersed in a culture.

Perhaps the cultural signpost best reflecting the loss of our moral compass was the wildly popular and critically acclaimed TV series of recent years, "Breaking Bad," its break with moral norms made tauntingly explicit in its title. Actually the break with norms occurred decades earlier, with this series' story-line taking the trend to a new low: A high-school chemistry teacher, told he has terminal cancer, aims to provide for his family "after" by using his scientific know-how and becoming a producer of high-grade meth.

Lauding such degradation of character and capitalism, reflected in both "Breaking Bad" and Donald Trump, would be unthinkable to preceding generations, notably the Greatest Generation, the one that endured the Great Depression largely without a social safety net, then fought, suffered, and won World War II, securing liberty for us, their children. But such degradation *is* thinkable today: A critical mass of the electorate, hearing the cultural O.K. to "break bad," last November pulled the lever for a spectacularly amoral man, a predatory capitalist of basest character.

How could we fall so low? First, the dam broke—or rather, was broken—then came the flood. First to be sundered was the moral code, the sense of right and wrong developed over centuries of civic practice, democratic evolution, philosophy, religion. Then, after moral "deregulation," came the flood—sexual and marital norms breaking down; profanity overpowering wit and even common sense; pornography brought in from the fringe (remember the fringe?) and poured into the mainstream, to a point where today any muchness of a muchness is called "porn" (e.g., "real estate porn"?). Most damningly, children are now exposed to, and hurt by, what once upon a time was restricted to the adult sphere; meanwhile, many adults have become children pursuing their dishonorable heart's desire, which is easier now because we got rid of honor, too.

How was the moral code sundered? If you grew up in the post-World War II years, from the 1950s on, you noticed that in almost every grouping—the playground, the dorm, the work world, in society—when it came to a discussion of what should be done in that moment or, more elementally, what should be, there was always a voice in the group calling down the "should" and taunting the group's acting moral arbiter as "party-pooper" (the term "party" reflecting a general lack of seriousness). In this way, voiced incessantly and derisively, a stigma was born for my generation, the boomers. Boomers grew allergic to making any moral discrimination whatsoever, for dire fear of being called "judgmental." "Sow the wild oats and hope for crop failure" served as our moral code. Tragically, we passed this pattern on to our children.

And, tragically, in this way—by mishandling and abusing the liberty secured for us by the Greatest Generation—America lost its moral compass.

(To be sure, the Greatest Generation had its faults—notably racism, sexism, anti-Semitism—which a cohort of the boomers, myself included, sought to correct early on by allying with our African-American friends in the civil rights movement. Real milestones in debarring race and sex discrimination were achieved in employment and education. But a reaction to all this "political correctness" has set in—another fault-line Trump exploits.)

Mirroring the public's loss of moral compass, our cultural fare— films, TV, books, theater—makes it a point to "push the envelope" of whatever's left of propriety and taste, setting up a dynamic whereby artists up the ante or get sidelined. *Bonnie and Clyde* (1967), whose title characters gleefully announce "We rob banks," set the violent and nihilistic tone for succeeding filmmakers. The sexual explicitness of *Portnoy's Complaint* (1969) did likewise for succeeding novelists. In TV, "Breaking Bad" was begot by "The Sopranos," the hit series whose lead character "whacked" his rivals dead. In theater, serious examination of moral subjects got whacked by *The Vagina Monologues*. Critics, nominal gatekeepers, got hip to such "transgressive" artists and praised their "bent" and "twisted" product; weirdly, these artists earned prestige for their "courage" to push at a *wide-open* door. No wonder then, that with so much envelope-pushing over decades, there's not much envelope left anymore.

No wonder, also, that all this envelope-pushing and trashing of things moral triggered *major* pushback—from the conservative right. Conservatives in the postwar era, from Goldwater to Nixon to Reagan to the Bushes, have made political hay by pointing to the worst of liberal licentiousness and winning power. Some liberals naively think an "anything-goes" mentality is just a free-speech issue, with no moral consequence, but generations of conservatives have dominated public life in big part by claiming to be America's moral protectors. This claim allows for much hypocrisy, of course, the most egregious current example being evangelical Christians finding the amoral Trump morally acceptable and becoming his most ardent supporters.

In his recent essay "How America Lost Its Mind," Kurt Andersen in *The Atlantic* traces a related loss, also beginning in the '60s, "the beginning of the end of reason": the increasing relativism of truth and fact, when America became "untethered from reality," when the mantra became "Do your own thing, find your own reality, it's all relative." Again, conservatives benefited, by claiming to be Truth's defenders, while also railing against relativism's undercutting of "venerable and comfortable ideas—certain notions of entitlement (according to race and gender) and aesthetic beauty and metaphysical and moral clarity." Meanwhile, Andersen writes, "anything-goes relativism" enabled the far right to become more unhinged than the left, producing "gun-rights hysteria, black-helicopter conspiracism, climate-change denial, and more." And the big beneficiary of this "fantasy-industrial complex"? The faker Donald Trump.

As described here, the onus for our present dark and unhappy moment, this dramatic falling-off since the Greatest Generation, would seem to lie with liberals. And if we are truthful, we deserve much blame: Liberals disposed of the moral compass and Truth, conservatives reacted to save those invaluable things. Liberals acted—irresponsibly—and conservatives reacted, not always responsibly, but with the advantage of acting in defense.

What is to be done? How do we achieve a New Day and save America? Can we?

In a way, course-correction is already underway—seen in our grief at the damage America has wrought upon itself, in our nausea with the hair-raising daily reality of this wrecking crew of an administration, in our profound and heartfelt yearning for a return to decency and normalcy, out from under the shadow of the hideous Trump. We are flailing badly, groping in the dark. May I submit that, out of deep and profound need and not mere want, what we are groping for is... our moral compass, which we misplaced decades ago. To return to decency and normalcy, we need that compass.

It means "anything-goes" liberalism can't go anymore. Like comedian Kathy Griffin holding up a mock severed head of Trump, a prank which drew universal condemnation, not only from conservatives but from other liberals. That pushback was moral discrimination working, dimly perceived. Liberals have a problem with limits, but responsible liberalism requires consideration of consequences.

Recovering decency and normalcy also means (pardon the forthcoming explicitness) "breaking good." It means getting over the kneejerk habit of mocking virtue, honor, truthfulness, purpose, dignity. It means redefining humanity upward, from pathology and dysfunction, back to the realm of goodness and nobility. We *need* to do this, pragmatically speaking, if we are to save ourselves from the moral calamity of Donald Trump. Great nations decline because of moral decay. The only way we will arrest our present decline and prevent its becoming permanent is by recovering our moral compass.

We can do this. In fact, in Charlottesville, Virginia, in the deadly confrontation just days ago between the neo-Nazi/alt-right and a brave group of counter-protesters, we may at last have found our moral compass. The powerful pushback from the public and corporate America against Trump's equivalence of the alt-right with the alt-left, a small militant group he's contemptibly conflating with the counter-protesters, is the only heartening thing in this tragic event: The American people are taking a moral stand, declaring such equivalence is wrong. Only a president breaking spectacularly bad could ever countenance the Nazi swastika on our shores. Doing so, Trump has forever abdicated any moral authority—the ultimate authority he can never wield.

It may be that Donald Trump's sole utility as president will be forcing Americans to come to our moral senses. Lord knows, regarding the rightness and wrongness of things, he presents us with what Zorba the Greek called "the full catastrophe." In typical American fashion, we will get there circuitously: after sowing the wild oats, hoping for redemption. But this time we must replace hope with effort. We must—and we can—deliver our own redemption.

—*HuffPost*, August 28, 2017

Books for Our Times:
The Retreat of Western Liberalism, by Edward Luce

Ninth in an ongoing series, Books for Our Times

WRITTEN SINCE THE earthquake election of Donald Trump as president of the United States, this book is a head-clearing attempt to explore the underlying disorder and distemper in liberal democracy, in America and throughout the West, that produced such presidency. As this author states repeatedly, Trump is merely a symptom, not a cause, of this disorder. For readers looking for context, this primer is a good start.

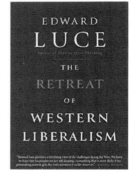

Looking back to the fall of the Berlin Wall in 1989, when liberal democracy was declared the winner in the long struggle against the Soviet communist system and, in victory, spawned democratic transformations around the world, the author charts the retreat of liberal democracy worldwide since those heady days, beaten back by the powerfully disruptive counter-forces of nationalism and populism.

The principal cause of liberalism's retreat? According to the author (and I think he is right), stagnant wages over several decades, causing existential insecurity and understandably vengeful anger in the working and middle classes.

Edward Luce, a British-born journalist, is a columnist and commentator for the well-regarded British newspaper, *The Financial Times.* Long based in the U.S., he has reported from the Philippines and India.

With a degree in Philosophy, Politics, and Economics from Oxford (the ideal major for these chaotic times), Luce has a wide-ranging c.v., including stints as speechwriter to Pres. Bill Clinton's treasury secretary and, earlier, as trainee at the European Commission, an experience that "inoculated me for life against working in a bureaucracy.... Journalism promised wind in my hair on an open road." His book, *Time to Start Thinking: America in the Age of Descent*, traced the advent of America's decline in the hollowing-out of its middle class.

This book, *The Retreat of Western Liberalism*, is heavier on diagnostics than therapeutics and is written in a churning discursive style, rather than the tidier theme-driven style of a historian. Luce is writing from the barricades, sending us bulletins. Though he says he wouldn't dare venture a manifesto so early in Trump's tenure, he does call in a few coordinates for attack.

Luce opens with a crackling, wind-in-the-hair start: Hearing East Germany had opened Checkpoint Charlie, uniting Berlin, Luce and four other students are driving at high speed to Berlin, to get their piece of the Berlin Wall. Having grown up in the Cold War's nuclear shadow, the prospects were Wordsworthian: "Bliss was it in that dawn to be alive, / But to be young was very heaven." "Democracies would take the place of the Warsaw Pact, whose regimes were falling like dominoes to peaceful demonstrators. It was not just autocracy that was dying but nationalism. Borders were opening up. Global horizons beckoned. A unipolar world was dawning." That "unipolar" world was dominated by the big winner—America—the hyper-power.

Flash forward nearly thirty years later, after Trump's election, Luce is in Moscow to attend a conference on the "polycentric world order," which, he writes, "is Russian for 'post-American world.'" "While my friends and I had danced on the rubble of the Berlin Wall, a brooding [Vladimir] Putin had watched his world crumbling from 130 miles away, at his KGB office in Dresden.... Later he would describe the dissolution of the Soviet Union as the 'greatest geopolitical tragedy of the twentieth century.'" Now America was led by a man "who admired the way politics was done in Russia."

How did this happen? How came America to be on the downside? Luce rightly cites America's hubris, our "oceanic post-Cold War triumphalism." Putin championed the idea of "multipolarity" in a bid at power-sharing, but America disdained the move. About the idea of multilaterialism: "As Madeleine Albright, the U.S. Secretary of State in the late 1990s, put it, 'It has too many syllables and ends with an 'ism.'"

But the present disarray of liberal democracy is also the result of oceanic forces, beyond America, to which Luce devotes the bulk of his book, divided in four parts.

Part One, "Fusion," tracks the radical impact of globalization on Western economies. While the rest of the world is catching up to the West in material progress, "between half to two-thirds of people in the West have been treading water—at best—for a generation." And with the coming automation, artificial intelligence, and "the rise of the rest," most notably China ("the most dramatic event in economic history"), "The downward pressure on the incomes of the West's middle classes in the coming years will be relentless." Though, relatively speaking, we still enjoy advantages, "The West's souring mood is about the psychology of dashed expectations rather than the decline in material comforts," manifested in falling rates of workforce participation, opioid addiction, rising intolerance and incivility. It is very un-American to feel shut out of society: "The West's drift to pessimism has been most radical in the land of optimism." In our newly-digital world, grievance is given a powerful voice.

Economic growth could help—if it occurred. Fast economic growth is a historical anomaly: "Between the fall of the Roman Empire and the Middle Ages there was basically none." But in America, we got used to it: "Between 1870 and 1970—the century of the West's greatest productivity growth—incomes grew far faster than ever experienced." "Within the blink of a historical eye, life went from nasty, brutish and short to pleasant, bright and relatively lengthy." But no more: "Half of Americans would be unable to pay a $400 medical emergency bill without going into debt."

Business' response has been sub-optimal: In addition to off-shoring production, "The fastest-growing units in the big Western companies are the legal and public relations departments. Big companies devote the bulk of their earnings to buying back shares and boosting dividend payments. They no longer invest anything like what they used to in research and development. The future loses out." Meanwhile, the wealthy get wealthier, exacerbating the problem of income inequality. And the "losers" are multiplying: In 2000, a third of Americans described themselves as lower class; by 2015 that number had risen to almost half.

Part Two, "Reaction," explores the degeneration of Western politics. Sadly, it was America herself who did greatest damage to democracy's "brand," with its response to the 9/11 terrorist attacks: Not only enacting the Patriot Act, "which gave the green light to multiple dilutions of constitutional liberties," but the tragic invasion of Iraq on false grounds, both of weapons of mass destruction and bringing democracy to Iraq: "It is highly questionable whether democracy can be installed from the barrel of a gun." And there was the moral degradation of Abu Ghraib, the torture chamber where the U.S. meted out humiliations on Muslim prisoners. "It is hard to overstate the damage the Iraq War did...to the credibility of the West's democratic mission." We stand accused of bad faith in our own democratic traditions.

Equally, the Wall Street-induced financial crash of 2008—whether you blamed it on "greedy investment bankers or the incompetence of financial regulation"—dealt another blow to the West's democratic reputation. Luce is insightful in noting that the "so-called global recession was primarily an Atlantic one," while "the rest of the world continued to expand." Indeed, "growth in China, the world's largest autocracy, picked up...after 2008. The contrast did wonders for China's global image. It was also a boon to its political reputation." Autocrats around the world took notice.

Thus we see the emergence of "illiberal democracy," erstwhile democracies taking on undemocratic qualities and turning autocratic, as in Hungary, Poland, Venezuela. The numbers are sobering: Around 1970, there were some 30 democracies in the world, but, inspired by Democracy winning the Cold War, by the millennium there were more than 100 worldwide. Today, however, reflecting this turn toward autocracy, we have 25 fewer democracies. "What we do not yet know is whether the world's democratic recession will turn into a global depression."

Meanwhile, liberal parties in the West took a wrong turn: When the jobs went away, instead of campaigning on strong economic platforms, they advocated identity politics. Luce cites Hillary Clinton's presidential campaign, while also noting Labour in the U.K. was blind to labour's increasing distress. "Millions who backed Trump in 2016 had voted for Barack Obama in 2008. Did they suddenly become deplorable? A better explanation is that many Americans have long felt alienated from an establishment that has routinely sidelined their economic complaints." Enter, Donald Trump: "To be clear, Trump poses a mortal threat to all America's most precious qualities. But by giving a higher priority to the politics of ethnic identity than people's common interests, the American left helped to create what it feared."

Reflecting these distressing trends, Luce notes polls showing growing numbers in the West, most concernedly the youth, who feel a slackening allegiance to democracy, even preferring the army or a strongman in charge. He notes that both China and Russia aim "to rupture the West's claim to universalism." The reader notes how this rupture is being achieved *by the West against itself.* Luce also files a cultural note: the disappearance of heroes ("Everyone has some tawdry angle") and the need to revive the humanities. "In Enlightenment terms, our democracies are switching from John Locke's social contract to the bleaker Leviathan of Thomas Hobbes. We are on a menacing trajectory brought about by ignorance of our history, indifference towards society's losers and complacency about the strength of our democracy. It has turned society into a contest of ethnic grievances, in which 'awakened whites'—as the alt-right now call them—are by far the largest minority."

Part Three, "Fallout," explores the implications of declining Western hegemony. "Though the U.S. remains the most potent military power on earth, and its most technologically innovative, Americans are losing faith in their system. Donald Trump offers a cure worse than the disease." Luce predicts that "chaos is far likelier than China to fill America's shoes."

Part Four, "Half Life," poses the question Lenin and Tolstoy posed, "What is to be done?" Understandably, Luce's recommendations are skimpy; he cites other thinkers also scrambling. And he confesses to "grave doubts about history's long arc." But enlightened policy would at the least call for a fortified social safety net, with universal healthcare, increased minimum wage, perhaps Universal Basic Income. Mainly because both business and government, of the left and right, have successfully divested themselves of the responsibility to protect their employees/citizens: "To one degree or another—most sharply in the U.S. and the U.K.—societies are creeping back to the days before social insurance. What was once underwritten by government and employers has been shifted to the individual," or what's called "privatizing risk."

Here we come to a subject worthy of attack: the elites. "Whatever your remedies to the crisis of liberal democracy, nothing much is likely to happen unless the West's elites understand the enormity of what they face. If only out of self-preservation, the rich need to emerge from their postmodern Versailles." Luce is wicked on the Davos elite, that annual gathering of "the world's wealthiest recyclers of conventional wisdom," nattering on about "disruptive thinking" and "the digital public square." For elite obtuseness, Luce cites Wall Street banker Stephen Schwarzman's over-the-top response to Pres. Obama's proposed modest tax hike: "It's like Hitler invaded Poland." "Eight years later Schwarzman was silent when Trump announced his Muslim travel ban. But he was jubilant at the news Trump was planning to scrap Obama's Wall Street reform.... I very much doubt the future of Western democracy crossed his mind." This must change. These elites' allegiance is to the international economy, whence come their profits, not the nation. Meanwhile, angry populaces are raising national flags. "The world's elites have helped to provoke what they feared: a populist uprising against the world economy."

The other subject for attack, of course, is Trump himself: a *faux*-populist who as president is pushing policies favoring the elite (tax cuts, deregulation); a channeler of rage, not knowledge; a strategist of confusion ("The war against truth is being waged from the White House"); a man totally bereft of character or conscience. Luce believes Trump ultimately will fail, causing even more destabilization: "America will not become great again under Trump. There will be a lethal mood of betrayal and frustration when he fails. Who knows where that could lead."

The reader trusts Luce will point the way with future books, hopefully with less wind-in-the-hair churn and more hands-on-the-wheel focus. As this book outlines, there is no end of subject, nor urgency. And, there is hope: The "retreat" of Luce's title suggests the possibility of a revival, a comeback. As the author writes: "Western liberal democracy is not yet dead, but it is far closer to collapse than we may wish to believe. It is facing its gravest challenge since the Second World War. This time, however, we have conjured up the enemy from within. At home and abroad, America's best liberal traditions are under assault from its own president. We have put arsonists in charge of the fire brigade. The bad news is that populists such as Donald Trump... are winning the fight. The good news is the fightback has a lot of room for improvement."

—*HuffPost*, September 25, 2017

The Conscientious "Peacenik": An Underrepresented Voice in *The Vietnam War*

THE VIETNAM WAR, the masterful 18-hour documentary by Ken Burns and Lynn Novick, will likely become—and deserves to become—the public touchstone for discussion and reference of that most contentious of our modern wars, Vietnam.

In its scope—presenting testimony from both the Vietnamese and the American sides—and in its depth—presenting, most importantly, veterans and their family members, as well as policymakers, journalists, intelligence officers, and members of the anti-war movement—*The Vietnam War* sets the gold standard in documentary. In organizing disparate materials—White House tapes, news articles, books—into a comprehensible overview, the film's writer, historian Geoffrey Ward, renders another public service, as he did in the Burns films on the Civil War and World War II.

With respect, however, as a former protester, a "peacenik," I submit that the portrait of the anti-war movement as presented in the film shortchanges the movement in its own scope and depth, especially its moral depth.

In short: We who protested saw early on that the war in Vietnam was a lie and a fraud and, being a lie and a fraud, it was morally wrong. Thus, given the war was morally wrong, the object of our anger was *not the soldier being sent to this benighted war,* but the leaders responsible for committing us to it and keeping us in it: presidents Lyndon Johnson and Richard Nixon. The film gives the impression that calling a returning vet "Baby Killer" was par for the anti-war movement; in the last episode an activist tearfully apologizes, as well she should. But the rest of us—most of us?—rather than disparaging the soldier in Vietnam, we grieved for him.

We grieved, because it meant that soldiers being sent to a lie of a war would become killers for no valid reason. Of course we understood war is all about killing, but some wars are valid and some, not. Many of us, students at the time, had fathers who fought in World War II, a valid war, a good war; we knew the difference, and Vietnam, as clearly as we could see anything in our young lives, did not qualify; in fact it was a desecration. You did not have to be a priest or a philosopher to see, down the road, that a soldier who killed for invalid reasons would sooner or later pay with his soul. Souls would be defiled, corrupted; a lifetime of moral suffering would be visited on the surviving vet. *Stop the madness!*

Proof, of the most sorrowful kind—testimony to injury of the soul—was provided late in the film as the veterans speak of their return home. Tim O'Brien recounts finding himself in a peace march—and feeling, finally, some measure of peace for the first time since he shipped out. Bill Ehrhart and John Musgrave, on seeing the soon-to-become-iconic photo of the dead student protester at Kent State shot by the National Guard, both describe breaking down sobbing—and joining the anti-war movement; Musgrave contemplated suicide. James Gillam laments the loss in Vietnam of "the civilized version of myself." One who left the U.S. for Canada, Jack Todd, despite a lifetime being called "coward," clearly grieves giving up his American citizenship. None spoke of their soul *per se* and its damage, but it was implicit in their sorrow.

Which is why this protester cried out to the television, repeatedly: "*That* was why I protested!" *Would that you all had been spared this damage to your souls.*

In the shattering coda, as Tim O'Brien reads from his brilliant short story, "The Things They Carried," and we watch the vets, American and Vietnamese, whom we have come to know intimately, listening to O'Brien's majestic words—"They carried the weight of memory": Their faces are pained, some haunted. The protester cries out again: *Would that you had been spared the memory, the pain, the haunting.*

Also haunting: the soldiers who did not come home. Who can forget Denton "Mogie" Crocker, who grew up during the Cold War hating the Reds and was so eager to join the fight against the Communists in Vietnam that he ran away from home to force his parents to sign his enlistment papers; who soon after enlistment evinced doubts about the war to his beloved sister; and who, in a letter from Vietnam to his best friend just before he was killed, revealed despair, saying he had become an atheist. What is that but the loss of a young man's soul? *Would that Mogie had been spared.*

Earlier in the film, anti-war leader Bill Zimmerman claims that, as the war widened and the draft widened in parallel, the anti-war movement became less a moral protest and more a "self-interested" one. Not so; for many of us it remained always a moral protest, which, yes, bled over into self-interest, as we did not want to see our brothers or friends called up to kill, or be killed, in an immoral war.

Throughout the film, the imagery of the anti-war movement tends to feature, shall we say, the more fun-loving of our number, with footage included of the Woodstock bacchanalia and Jane Fonda's outrageous antics in Hanoi. As the war wore on and some protesters unwisely resorted to violence, forgetting peace was the whole point, the media, always drawn to the bright shiny—and noisy and violent—object, focused on this element, rather than on the serious protesters; the film goes there, too. (Activist Zimmerman does acknowledge finally that a "strategy of violence" was wrong. Somehow he is the only protester included in the film's coda.) It should also be noted that, as the war wore on and news of troop involvement in drugs and fragging increased, more and more older adults joined the students in protest.

The film does present one serious protester, Eva Jefferson Paterson, who was a student organizer on her campus. She is shown doing respectful battle with Vice President Spiro Agnew on TV—Agnew there to argue for the righteousness of the federal crackdown on student protesters and Paterson there to push back, and winning, by making the point that young people, "your children," are being turned into things to be afraid of. Paterson, I submit, represents the majority of the protest movement.

For many of us student protesters, the Vietnam War was the first time we protested anything, the first time we argued seriously, and righteously, for anything, but we had to, because Vietnam was a matter of life or tragic death, of body *and* soul. Some arguments with family and friends caused breaks that never healed. Still, it is with no exultation that the anti-war protester is vindicated by this documentary, with nearly all participants involved on-camera agreeing that, in the final analysis, the Vietnam war was a "failure." I wonder if this film, so comprehensive in scope and depth, convinced any pro-war advocate.

Also damaged by the Vietnam war: America itself, its soul. As noted several times in the film, that damage has never healed. We still argue about who is a patriot and if protesting official policy makes one unpatriotic. We still are heedless (see: the Iraq war) of a lesson Vietnam absolutely should have taught us: that a war's premise must absolutely be so sound, morally as well as geopolitically, that it justifies the troops' suffering or death. And, tragically, loss of faith in government stems from this era. As veteran John Musgrave notes, his was the last generation to believe their leaders. As veteran Karl Marlantes notes, hardest to stomach was the lying.

All these thoughts, and the same angry sorrow I felt during the Vietnam era, were stirred up again over the two-week span this film ran. (Actually, I feel again, in this era of President Donald Trump, the same angry sorrow.) But the film also presented new information, most notably the Vietnamese point of view: Both North and South finally considered the war a tragic thing, ending, as it started, in bloody civil war for national liberation. On the American side, it is devastating to hear, on White House tapes, the lack of feeling for the troops expressed by Johnson or Nixon or their advisors: So often the war was prolonged—and the troops' suffering prolonged—because an election loomed.

Strange, too, to hear on tape that both presidents, fed junk intelligence by F.B.I. director J. Edgar Hoover, discussed us protesters as Communist-inspired. Such belief was par for Nixon, but sad coming from Johnson, who'd had the heart to enact the 1964 Civil Rights Act and the 1965 Voting Rights Act, but this misperception of the anti-war movement was another blind spot in his tragic fall into an impossible war. Both presidents could not recognize a moral crusade when they saw it.

(Several years ago I visited a childhood classmate, our class funnyman, who was dying of cancer. He had served in Vietnam and he wanted to talk about the war, finally. "It was awful," he said. A medic, he described his role: "All I did was gather body parts and put them in body bags." "I am so sorry, Bob. I was trying to bring you home, by protesting, marching." "I know you were, Carla. Thanks, really.")

To conclude: In its comprehensiveness, *The Vietnam War* should serve as stimulant to debate and education. Studied carefully, this film could help us connect the dots from one tragic era to our own, with the objective of mitigating more tragedy. The film's great asset is its talking heads, especially the men who fought and suffered.

Again, it is with respect for this masterpiece that I file this protest on behalf of the protester. Ultimately, one wants one's moral purpose understood. Many of the soldiers interviewed in this film, in going off to Vietnam, expressed a purpose that could be defined as moral: to stop the spread of Communism, to serve the nation, to replicate the valor of the World War II generation. (Tragically, it was the war itself that was morally lacking.) As the film plays out, and as the veterans speak from their deepest experience, we see and understand the moral journey they took. The conscientious protester, who also took a moral journey, asks the same consideration.

—*HuffPost*, October 2, 2017

How to Deter Sexual Predators Like Harvey Weinstein? Career Ruination and "Good Guys" Speaking Up

FINALLY, A SEXUAL predator gets seriously hammered. Are we at a reckoning point?

In the media firestorm launched two weeks ago by *The New York Times* with its major investigative article, followed by another in *The New Yorker*, both describing in nauseating detail film producer Harvey Weinstein's 30-year history of alleged sexual harassment, assault and even rape of young actresses and female employees, we have seen Weinstein's mighty career destroyed pillar by pillar.

The ruin so far:

Weinstein's own film production company, Weinstein Company, has fired him.

The Academy of Motion Picture Arts and Sciences has ousted him, by a vote "well in excess of" the two-thirds majority required of the 54-member board. Weinstein had amassed 300 Oscar nominations and won 81 times, including five times for Best Picture (*The English Patient, Shakespeare in Love, Chicago, The King's Speech,* and *The Artist*). For his role in all these wins, he was "the most-thanked man in America" at Oscar ceremonies (God was sixth). Expulsion from the Academy, per the hometown newspaper *The Los Angeles Times*, means "virtual exclusion from Hollywood itself."

There's more. The Producers Guild of America has ousted him (that vote was unanimous). Weinstein Books, an imprint of the Hachette Book Group, has been terminated. As a Hachette spokesperson said, "Given recent developments, we think a name change is in the best interests of our authors," no doubt to the relief of those authors, to whom Weinstein is now poison. France is moving to strip Weinstein of his

[222]

Legion of Honor. "[T]his behavior is in contradiction with honor," a spokeswoman for President Emmanuel Macron said.

Additionally, Weinstein's wife has left him, expressing sorrow for the women her husband has hurt. His brother, Bob, with whom he co-founded Weinstein Company and its predecessor, Miramax, has called him "sick and depraved" (though, in breaking news, Bob Weinstein too is now accused of sexual harassment). And there is a resounding lack of voices—a void—from the film community supporting Weinstein.

As downfalls go, Weinstein's is pretty thorough and dramatic. And sexual predation is the cause, not the usual trigger of financial malfeasance or personal rivalry. Does this mean that the crime of sexual assault—and it's important to remember it is a crime of *violence*, not passion—is *finally* getting serious attention?

If so, does this mean that ruination of career and reputation will serve as the magic deterrent, in ways that legal threats and moral appeals have not?

Coming to light is the ugly tale of how Weinstein used his power and money to avoid criminal prosecution to date: He would hire private investigators to dig up dirt on any woman daring to file a complaint, hire top-flight lawyers to threaten her with career ruin or even entry into the film business, then buy her silence with a relatively small sum of money and, key element, a legally-binding nondisclosure agreement. But no more: Police in New York and London have started criminal investigations. According to *The Guardian*, Weinstein could face five to 25 years in prison if the latest sexual assault charges are tried in criminal court. Meanwhile, members of his legal team are bailing out.

Hollywood has long been plagued by sexual predation. The Academy acknowledges as much, saying in a statement about Weinstein's ouster:

> "*We do so not simply to separate ourselves from someone who does not merit the respect of his colleagues but also to send a message that the era of willful ignorance and shameful complicity in sexually predatory behavior and workplace harassment in our industry is over.*"

Of course, the problem of sexual predation afflicts not just Hollywood, but other spheres—notably the military and college campuses, where rates of sexual assault in recent years have risen to historic levels. Why the increase? Conjectures are many, but my take is that it is in reaction, brutal reaction, to several decades of women advancing in the work world and acquiring some measure of political power. How reactionary is seen in the election last November of Predator-in-Chief Donald Trump to the White House (put there, sadly, by a preponderance of women voters).

To those of us who prosecuted the problem early on, present reality is discouraging. In the late 1970s, as equal opportunity officer for the City of San Diego, I drafted one of the nation's first municipal policies prohibiting sexual harassment on the job, to protect the women we were moving into nontraditional areas like police work and firefighting. (This was before the Equal Employment Opportunity Commission promulgated its guidelines in 1980.) Our policy required a complainant to keep a journal of offenses, while maintaining exemplary conduct. Resolution was reached by sitting both complainant and alleged offender down with their department head, the boss, where enlightenment invariably took place, e.g., porn festooning a workspace was quickly understood to constitute a "hostile work environment," thus not permitted; pulling a woman's hair constituted "battery," also not permitted.

But keeping a journal of offenses does not suffice when facing a boss like Harvey Weinstein and his defense team. And a sexual predator in the White House may cue a new normal in the acceptance of what is in actuality a hideous, traumatizing crime.

More is needed—much more. In a word, allies are needed. Peers, to exert on the miscreant in their midst the kind of pressure that can count the most: peer pressure.

Thus the call for "good guys" to speak up—"guys" here meaning men (women speaking out against predators get nowhere). Needed are men who are profiles in courage, like actor Brad Pitt, who confronted Weinstein on behalf of his then-girlfriend, actress Gwyneth Paltrow.

That move freed Paltrow of Weinstein's advances, but all other women remained his targets. Meanwhile, it beggars belief that so many Hollywood players now profess themselves to be "shocked, shocked" at the revelations of Weinstein's predation—it's long been an inside joke. The joke is stale, Hollywood, and is emphatically not funny.

Likewise, good guys in the military and on college campuses and elsewhere: When you hear of sexual predation, you need to step up and speak out on behalf of the women who are your fellow soldiers, sailors, pilots, and Marines, the women who are your fellow students—the women who are your fellow human beings.

So, perhaps the pincer strategy—the threat of career ruin on one hand and the peer pressure of good guys on the other—can stem the scourge of sexual predation. Predators at large, before they make another nasty move, should picture their hard-won career going down in flames, like Harvey Weinstein's, spelled out in headlines running daily for two weeks now in *The New York Times*, the paper of record.

And, calling all good guys: Enough with serving in the reserves. You are needed at the front. Speak up!

—*HuffPost*, October 18, 2017

A Historic Reckoning on Sexual Harassment: In Low Times, a Good Sign

AT LONG LAST, sexual predators across the workscape are being taken down—and the sound of careers crashing is thunderous. From the standpoint of simple justice, it's about time. Finally, behavior that's become too common is being seen for how truly ugly and damaging it is.

The question is: Why now? Why is the pushback to the stubborn problem of sexual harassment and assault in the work world reaching a tipping point now, when America itself—politically, culturally, morally—is at a historically low point, in what many call decline?

In other words: *How can you fall in already-fallen times?* At a time when our moral compass has long been lost, why isn't this scandal just another nothing-burger? And at such a cacophonously noisy time, why are women's voices *finally* being heard?

That this reckoning *is* indeed happening signals, I believe, encouraging things about America's capacity to course-correct and perhaps reverse our decline (more later).

The scandal exposing sexual predators that began with movie mogul Harvey Weinstein roars on, snaring others. As *The New York Times* notes in another front-page story, "Disaster metaphors—tsunami, hurricane, avalanche, landslide—seem to be in endless rotation to describe the moment, but the point is that a great many powerful men have seen their careers disintegrate, and with astonishing speed." (A partial listing follows; the details, which I don't care to describe, are in the hyperlinks.)

In the media, they include: Mark Halperin, influential MSNBC political analyst and co-author of the bestseller book *Game Change*; Leon Wieseltier, Brookings Institution senior fellow and former literary editor—and moral philosopher—at *The New Republic*; Michael Oreskes, head of news at National Public Radio and formerly an editor at the *Times*. These men have lost their jobs and likely their careers, too.

Careers in Hollywood continue to crash: Film director James Toback and producer Brett Ratner have been accused by numerous women of sexual misconduct—in Toback's case, by an astonishing 238 women to date. Kevin Spacey, two-time Oscar winner for Best Actor, is accused of raping a 14-year-old male over 30 years ago, triggering a series of other accusations against him, causing his ouster from the hit TV series "House of Cards." Dustin Hoffman, another two-time Oscar winner for Best Actor, is accused of sexual harassment of a 17-year-old female intern.

Politics is another arena where men wield dominant power, not always humanely. At the state level, in the legislatures—including California, Massachusetts, Florida, Illinois, Washington—women lawmakers and lobbyists, either individually or collectively, have come forward to allege sexual misconduct of their male colleagues. In California nearly 200 women signed a letter circulated by the "We Said Enough" campaign citing a toxic work environment in Sacramento. Is D.C.'s Capitol Hill next?

In the policy world, in a gathering convened by *Politico*'s Susan Glasser, women national security professionals sounded off against "an adversary closer to home: piggish men." No doubt women in other fields are convening for the same purpose.

Meanwhile, the scandal spreads abroad. The U.S.-based #MeToo social media campaign, in which millions of women have gone public with their allegations, has spawned similar campaigns in France, Italy, and Spain, also in Arab countries. In Britain, one cabinet minister has resigned and another cabinet minister is under investigation for allegations of sexual misconduct. Renowned Islamic scholar Tariq Ramadan has been placed on leave from Oxford over allegations of rape.

And there'll be more. In breaking bombshells, Republican Senate candidate Judge Roy Moore is alleged to have initiated sexual encounters with under-age girls, including a 14-year-old. And comedian Louis C.K. is alleged by five women to have—here I'll defer to the hyperlink. The comedian admits the allegations are true.

Crucially, and the reason for the tsunami force: Women are realizing once again the value of collective action. Pushback requires lots of people pushing back—a truism overlooked in the occasional cycles of "I'm-not-a-feminist" reaction. This time enough women have come forward to say "Enough" with being pawed, groped, propositioned, or worse at work—to positive and powerful result.

Also crucially, other men, the "good guys," are now more aware of what some women colleagues have endured, and vow to step up and assist with the pushback.

And men who were in a position to stop the abuse but didn't, like film director Quentin Tarantino, who started out as Harvey Weinstein's protégé and went on to establish a big Hollywood career, have admitted their complicity: "I knew enough to do more than I did." (If Tarantino, creator of ultra-violent films like *Pulp Fiction*, follows up with a redemption tale, it'll have to focus on this moral complicity, also the damage done by the violent male—in other words, it means becoming a more human artist.)

But again, Why a reckoning now? One can only speculate, as it's impossible to correlate cause and effect during a tsunami. But I'm speculating this mindset may be at work: With an admitted sexual predator in the White House, signifying a shameful low in the annals of the American presidency, with that predator ensconced in federal power, then at least the nearer predator can be addressed and taken down ("Enough"). We've also had more than enough of the drip-drip-drip over the years of allegations about Bill Cosby, Bill O'Reilly, and Roger Ailes, not to forget the miasma surrounding former president Bill Clinton.

Another reason for a reckoning now: This time the sheer accretion of sordid detail and gross force of so many alleged predators has finally registered with the public. And what it registers—finally—is this: Sexual harassment is not just sexual. It is, at bottom, about the predator's contempt for women and his need to subjugate these lesser beings to his sick self. And if he is in a position of power, as these men were, not only do they inflict personal trauma and blight their victims' careers. These men also exert outsized power to shape our culture—movies and TV, the news, the political arena. And women, sick of it all, are coming together to push back. Women now know it is not they who need to "get over it." *It is men who humiliate and abuse women who need to get over it.*

The implications of this reckoning are enormous—and encouraging. If we can recalibrate the exercise of our national power in a wiser way, if we can establish more equitable power-sharing between men and women, and if we can do this while at the bottom of the abyss (or on its slope), then there is hope for a New Day for us at higher altitude. America, so big and so powerful for so long, has at times abused its power, been predatory (e.g., engaged in torture). We, both as a nation or as individuals, don't always consider that with power comes responsibility: We *could* do X with our power, but *should* we? No such weighing occurred to the alleged predators.

Another implication: This scandal has moved us to seek our moral compass once again. Decades ago we set it aside, not wanting to be "moralistic" or "judgmental," which action permitted pornography, profanity, all manner of what used to be called sin. But at the heart of sexual harassment lies a great wrong, a sin if you will, of one human being abusing and abasing another human being. In our modern American way, with this reckoning we may be backing into moral consciousness once again. Few women are couching their harassment allegations in moral terms, but at the same time they cry out at its wrongness, judging it wrong. And the public also judges it thus.

All of which bodes well: To get to higher ground, to reverse America's decline, we need to handle power better and use a moral compass. Because of this scandal, we are doing both.

Finally, the question: Will it last, this reckoning on sexual harassment, or will it fade away, only to allow in the next set of predators? As the *Times* writes, "We've seen this movie before," but it also acknowledges, "This sequel seems to have a surprise ending, or at least a plot twist: The public outrage is deeper and more sustained, and the dominoes continue to fall."

Institutions and professions assure us they are strengthening their anti-harassment policies, but, clearly, such policies have not worked to date. I wonder if deterrence—witnessing, as we have for over a month now, one big man after another crashing and burning in a big and dramatic way—may stay the predator's hand better than any reprimand or even criminal conviction with prison time. For what is destroyed in these spectacles are not just career or "brand," but name and reputation. These men are finding out how dear one's name is, and one's reputation—reputation, said Shakespeare, is "the immortal part of myself"—both of which, once gone, can never be reclaimed. I cannot imagine any ambitious man countenancing that spectacle for himself, that loss. (In fact, predators-still-at-large must be turning to prayer right now, hoping for a miracle.) Note also the men in the news are drawing no support from their professional colleagues, none. The humiliation is total—and such total humiliation may deter. Note, too, the poetic justice: the predator humiliated, as he humiliated women.

Of course the present spectacle involves men in fields that have always drawn the spotlight. But: What protection do women elsewhere in the work world have against the predator in their midst? That predator, given the powerful reach of the media, can hardly miss the headlines tracing the destruction of, for one, comedian Louis C.K.'s career—and his message about the power he held over women and how "I wielded that power irresponsibly." Memo to predators: Listen up.

My one fear in all this is that a false allegation will be filed by one woman or several, which could be spun to cast doubt on the validity of the entire ongoing reckoning. Memo to women: Maintain exemplary conduct and solidarity with your sisters.

Ever since the 9/11 terrorist attacks, America has been in extreme churn. Some may feel this sexual harassment scandal is yet another manifestation of decay, another inch further into the abyss. But glints of salvation can be seen: the moral reckoning, the recalibration of power relations. And, importantly, in the spotlighted arenas—movies and TV, the media, politics—we have to capitalize on this moment and demand more respectful treatment and portrayal of women.

More than other scandals, this one in its sordidness is forcing a sober look in the mirror and a profound desire to get clean—as a people, as a nation. We yearn for a New Day. Who knew the rallying cry would be, not something like "Fifty-four forty or fight," but "Keep your predatory hands off me." But History can surprise.

—*HuffPost*, November 13, 2017

Republican "Values Voters" Revealed as Serious Hypocrites

IT WAS BAD enough for the nation's soul that Republican evangelicals—the self-designated "Values Voters"—supported the totally values-free candidate Donald Trump and boosted him into the presidency, becoming the most reliable bloc of his base since he took office.

Now, in the upcoming Senate race in Alabama, these same voters purporting to reflect Christian values are standing by the embattled former judge Roy S. Moore, despite the disturbing allegations from a series of women—at last count, nine (9)—that Moore had inappropriate sexual encounters with them when he was in his thirties and they were under-age.

Says a Moore supporter, "He's nothing but a godly man trying to make this country come to its senses because of liberals and the other side trying to protect their evil ways." Says a pastor supporting Moore, "I don't know how much these women are getting paid." This same pastor said he'd vote for Moore *even if* he was proved to have sexually molested the girls: "There ought to be a statute of limitations on this stuff."

Seriously? I pray you, Values Voters: Don't do this. Think of the nation's soul: Putting an alleged sexual predator in the Senate, after putting an *admitted* sexual predator in the White House, only reinforces the wrong path taken in the 2016 presidential race—elevating political gain over character—and further hurts a hurting America.

Christianity traditionally has preached the importance of moral character and action, expected both in our leaders and in ourselves. Christianity has also preached against the wickedness of hypocrisy: saying one thing—the moral thing—but doing its opposite, while maintaining a façade of rectitude. "For they preach, but do not practice," as the Bible puts it. It's a good precept, whether you are Christian or not. But in recent decades, the conservative right has "evolved" its thinking in a more politically expedient direction. While still requiring adherence to moral values in their personal lives, they've become far more lenient of the politicians they support, starting with their embrace of Ronald Reagan, a divorced Hollywood actor. Why the expediency? Because, they believe, the pursuit of their Holy Grail—to do away with abortion—requires it. For years their focus was on getting Congress to reverse *Roe v. Wade*, the Supreme Court's ruling on abortion, but more recently their focus is the composition of the Court itself. The conservative right supports candidates vowing to reshape the Court so as to overturn *Roe v. Wade*, also protect religious freedom.

This shift in stance is remarkable. As political philosopher Samuel Kimbriel writes in *The Washington Post*, citing a Public Religion Research Institute survey, "Whereas in 2011 only 30 percent of evangelicals thought that a person who commits immoral acts in their personal life could still behave ethically in their public duties, by 2016, that figure had leaped to 72 percent." Regarding the allegations against Roy Moore, Kimbriel notes that while many on the right condemn his candidacy:

> *"Still, the fact that there is even a debate on whether the allegations, if true, are disqualifying is deeply revealing. It betokens a Protestant right that is open to establishing a pattern whereby even egregious moral failure is a price worth paying for political and cultural power, and whereby one need not seek actual goodness, but rather need only not to exceed the badness of one's opponents."*

Speaking of opponents, the far right regularly brands the opposition as bad, even evil. In the 2016 presidential race, with Democratic candidate Hillary Clinton holding abortion rights as "sacrosanct," to evangelicals she became evil incarnate. But since when do the Scriptures preach hate? What about "Love thy neighbor"—and thy opponent—"as thyself"? Strange, how support for morally dicey candidates like Trump and Moore, constructed as that support is on expedient and contingent grounds, translates into hard unyielding hatred of opponents.

Moore is a queasy-making piece of work. The allegations of the women against him are hard to read but credible, describing acts with teenage girls that should disturb any conscience, most especially a Christian conscience. Moore vehemently denies the allegations, characterizing them as "political," but no less a skeptic than Senate majority leader Mitch McConnell says, "I believe the women." (Thank you, Mitch McConnell.) But Values Voters hate McConnell too, arch-representative of the Republican establishment. (Of "political" note: the Russian disinformation campaign in the U.S., which, regarding this race, cites pastors claiming that the anti-Moore allegations reflect a "war on men" and that women are the real sexual predators.)

It's hard to imagine Moore as a judge, given his questionable judgment to date girls half his age. Moore was expelled from the bench twice (as chief justice), the first time for refusing to remove a monument to the Ten Commandments he'd had erected in Alabama's Judicial Building. In light of the allegations of his earlier un-Christian behavior, that monument, as well as his creation of the Foundation for Moral Law, might be seen as a hypocrite's over-compensation. (There is no Commandment explicitly prohibiting sex with children, but there should be.)

Moore appeals to the conservative right by making Christian nationalism a hallmark of his campaign—which Christian nationalism needs to be understood for what it proposes: to elevate the Christian God over the U.S. Constitution, a *radical* departure from one of America's founding principles, separation of church and state. At the recent 2017 Values Voter Summit, Moore declared, "Our foundation has been shaken to the core because we have forgotten the source of our morality"—this, from an alleged sexual predator. The admitted sexual predator, Donald Trump, also spoke.

The Values Voter Summit, founded in 2006 near the end of the George W. Bush administration, is the marquee event of the Family Research Council, which was founded in 1983. It still boggles the liberal mind that entities calling themselves the *Family* Research Council and the *Values* Voters Summit (italics mine), who together claim to be leading defenders of "faith, family and freedom" in America, could embrace such corruption as represented by Trump and Moore.

This is not to discount the corruption liberals are capable of, as I've often written about before. But Values Voters might be surprised at how many liberals are as agonized as they about the moral tone in America today. We're agonizing now at the high participation rate of liberals in the current sexual harassment scandal, just as we agonized over former president Bill Clinton's sexual misconduct. On abortion, the right's Holy Grail, many of us liberals believe there should be restrictions. As to our alleged paganism, many liberals, myself included, are believers who left the church in big part *because of* religion's politicization and ensuing hypocrisy.

As to the election on Dec. 12: The people of Alabama will decide. Moore's campaign has released a list of 50 pastors who support him no matter what. Another set of 59 pastors has released a letter declaring Moore "not fit for office"; other pastors are speaking out, deeply troubled by Moore. Weighing in finally, President Trump says, "We don't need another liberal in there, a Democrat"—again liberal-hatred. The Democrat is Doug Jones, a former U.S. Attorney who, 35 years after the crime, convicted two Klansmen for the murder of four African-American girls in a Birmingham church in 1963. Initially silent on the Moore allegations, Jones is now citing them in TV ads. With Moore's poll numbers falling, this race is a toss-up. The battle, political and moral, is on.

With fully half of all Alabama residents calling themselves evangelical, election day will be a kind of Judgment Day, requiring quiet time in Gethsemane to ponder. To be pondered there: how far political expediency has diverged from Biblical precepts of moral character; how expediency leads to hypocrisy—and has led to an alleged sexual predator on the ballot; how this vote impacts not only Alabama but the nation's soul.

One last thing to ponder: With the sexual harassment scandal currently churning nationwide, a moral reckoning—a reawakening?—seems at long last to be taking place in the larger culture. A troubled America seems to be repairing some of its troubles—repair work which History tells us nations rarely do. Meaning: One wants to land, not only on the right side of the Bible, but also on the right side of History.

—*HuffPost*, November 27, 2017

Democrats Need a New Message: How About "Economic Justice for All"?

IT'S HIGH TIME—WE'RE more than a year from President Donald Trump's earthquake election, we're less than a year from the 2018 midterms—that the Democrats come up with a new and compelling message. "Organize, organize, organize"—signing up more voters to vote, the chant from the Democratic National Committee chair, Tom Perez—is only a procedural step (and a request for money). A battle cry, it is not.

Now that we know the sum and substance of the Republicans' tax reform bill, the House and Senate versions—basically, it is a massive and permanent tax cut for the wealthy and for corporations, a small and *temporary* tax cut for the middle class and the poor, which small and temporary cuts expire in 2027, all this boondoggle adding 1.5 *trillion* dollars to the national debt—we have our battle cry.

To counter the Republicans' colossally unjust and one-sided plans—on taxes and just about everything else—Democrats should stress justice and the common good. Our new battle cry practically writes itself: "Economic justice for all."

How unjust and one-sided is the proposed tax reform bill? Among liberal observers, Nobel economist Paul Krugman declares flatly the public is "being scammed, bigly." Jonathan Chait, commentator at *New York* magazine, calls the plan a "cash grab." Jared Bernstein, senior fellow at the Center on Budget and Policy Priorities, writes, "If your income derives from your stock portfolio or your rich parent, this plan loves you. Otherwise, tough luck." John Cassidy of *The New Yorker* calls it "a travesty" and an act illuminating the "broader atrophy of the American system of governance." *The New York Times* states flatly the bill, if enacted, will "reshape major areas of American life." All done, by the way, with scant debate and no hearings—none.

Even some Republicans, the principled kind, inveigh against this bill becoming law. Steve Schmidt, Republican consultant and frequent talking head, puts it bluntly: "Every single Gen-X'er should be outraged as we watch a bunch of septuagenarians and octogenarians load another $1.5 trillion in debt on the backs of our preteen and teenage kids. The beggaring of the country for special-interest donations is immoral."

Republicans, the unprincipled kind behind this bill, defend it thus: Those tax cuts to the wealthy and corporations will create jobs—after all, the bill *is* titled "The Tax Cuts and Jobs Act." As for those temporary cuts to the middle class and the poor expiring in 2027: Hopefully they'll be extended by future Congresses. But hope is not a strategy and nothing like law. Meantime, in the coming midterms Republicans can tout the tax cuts they just handed a hurting public—which Democrats will have to point out again and again are temporary. And when the federal deficit explodes, as it must with such massive loss of revenue, Republicans can go into cutting mode—on "the welfare state." Neat.

This nefarious plan is spelled out by another rare principled Republican, Bruce Bartlett, a domestic policy adviser to Pres. Ronald Reagan, in a must-read op-ed for *The Washington Post*. As Bartlett writes, the whole point of this Republican tax "reform" is to set up an all-out effort to "starve the beast"—government—and attack "the welfare state."

Longtime Congress-watchers Norman Ornstein and Thomas Mann, in another must-read op-ed, for *The New York Times*, writing of "possibly the worst tax bill in American history," said: "Republican leaders have been blunt about their motivation: to deliver on their promises to wealthy donors, and down the road, to use the leverage of huge deficits to cut and privatize Medicare and Social Security."

In fact, right on schedule, Trump and Congressional Republicans have already announced their next target: reform of (read: cuts to) "the welfare state"—Social Security, Medicare, Medicaid. And expect another attack on Obamacare—to repeal, forget replace. As it is, the GOP Senate bill revokes the individual mandate, the mechanism making Obamacare work—or not. If this revocation remains and the law is passed, 13 million Americans could lose their health insurance.

Dear Democrats: The lines and allegiances are clear. This script writes itself—from the heart. "My fellow Americans: Republicans say 'welfare state,' we Democrats say 'social safety net.' They say Main Street but mean Wall Street and their rich donors, we say Main Street and we mean Main Street and you hard-working citizens struggling to make ends meet with paychecks that never grow. And remember how Republicans used to scream, so righteously, about Democratic spending adding to the deficit and debt? Not any more. Do you hear any Republican of conscience lamenting the $1.5 trillion they loaded onto your children and grandchildren over the next decade so some rich guy can buy a second yacht? Economic justice for all!"

And Democrats could go on: about income inequality now gone completely out of whack, about needing to give turbo-capitalism a human face, about Republicans scrapping principles and selling out to the huckster Trump, who outright lies when he says as a businessman he will not benefit at all from the new tax bill. And, Democrats: Get passionate, get Sherrod Brown passionate, as when the Democratic senator tangled with Republican senator Orrin Hatch over the bill.

"Economic justice for all": Every word of this battle cry works. Breaking it down:

"Economic": Focusing on the economic takes us away from the minefield of identity politics, which is where much Democratic attention is now directed, and *back to pocketbook concerns—which is where elections historically are won.* Trump's evil genius advisor Stephen Bannon has openly declared, "If the left is focused on race and identity and we go with economic nationalism, we can crush the Democrats"—and he's right. But instead of resurrecting candidate Bill Clinton's slogan "It's the economy, stupid," we should take it one resonant step further, to "economic justice."

"Justice": For Americans, isn't it always—ultimately—about justice? A fair shake?

"For all": Sooner or later sensible Republicans (Trump's true-believer base aside) will realize Trump is a *faux*-populist, that he pitched populist as a candidate but once in office he pivoted to the categorical opposite, his plutocratic peers. With our new slogan, Democrats can capture those Republicans, sooner rather than later, in time for next year's midterms. They can also recapture Obama voters who went Trump.

Importantly, a refocus of "economic justice for all" would bring Democrats back to their constituent origins—to the middle and working classes—which honorable origins have been forsaken since the Clinton era swerved toward the plutocracy. This refocus would also reconnect Democrats with their proud legislative history—to Franklin Roosevelt's rescue of a suffering nation in the Great Depression with his New Deal policies including the Works Progress Administration and Social Security; to Harry Truman's Fair Deal; to Lyndon Johnson's Great Society and his enactment of Medicare and Medicaid; to Barack Obama's achieving the longtime Democratic dream of universal health insurance—a legislative history, by the way, of providing economic justice for all.

Getting to economic justice again, however, will require a reset of the balance of power between moneyed interests and the citizen. To get us there, recall Franklin Roosevelt, who confronted the central problem: We "know now that Government by organized money is just as dangerous as Government by organized mob." And let us recall FDR's courage as he took on those moneyed interests: "Never before in all our history have these forces been so united against one candidate as they stand today. They are unanimous in their hate for me—and I welcome their hatred."

For his vision and courage, FDR reaped more than 60% of the popular vote in the 1936 presidential election, a historic landslide. In his

Second Inaugural Address, in 1937, FDR targeted the ethical reckoning yet to occur on Wall Street: "We have always known that heedless self-interest was bad morals; we know now that it is bad economics."

If Democrats do like FDR, they could retake the House and perhaps the Senate in 2018—and the White House in 2020. Whatever happens to the Republican tax reform bill (it's likely to pass, but Trump, useful idiot that he is, could interfere): We know where Republican hearts lie—and they're with the fat cat, not with the little guy. And if Democrats can't make electoral hay of this crucial distinction, one must ask why they are in politics. Politics in a democracy is about doing right by the little guy. The rich take care of themselves, always.

Upon FDR's death, the famous story goes, a man was seen weeping uncontrollably at the news. Asked why he was weeping, did he know the President, the man said: "No, but he knew me." FDR knew the little guy and got him economic justice in a troubled 20th century. In the 21st century Democrats are charged with the same mission. So, Democrats: Channel FDR and start chanting—"Economic justice for all."

—*HuffPost*, December 7, 2017

Plays for Our Times: *The Humans*, by Stephen Karam

Second in an ongoing series, Plays for Our Times

THE AMERICAN DREAM—THE dream that succeeding generations will do better than their parents, financially and in accomplishment—is historically unique to this country and, from cradle to grave, makes strivers of us all. But what happens—as is happening now in 21st-century America—when not only the children stumble, but the parents do, too?

In Stephen Karam's absorbing play, *The Humans*, this fraught trajectory is traced in the shifting fortunes of the Blake family—the parents are working-class from Scranton, PA, their two daughters are barely hanging on in New York City as middle-class professionals. The event bringing the family together: Thanksgiving dinner at younger daughter Brigid's Chinatown apartment. As if a family's fraught trajectory were not tinder enough, Thanksgiving always provides a playwright with a dramatic firecracker of a setting.

But this play is less firecracker than quietly thought-provoking, casting light—and pity—on striving Americans today. The characters are recognizable—as us. *The Humans* won the 2016 Tony for Best Play and was a finalist for the Pulitzer Prize in drama. (Note: The following contains multiple spoilers.)

As the play opens, the parents, Erik and Deirdre, have made their way with difficulty into Brigid's apartment, needing to navigate the wheelchair of Erik's mother, Momo. Cracks are made by the parents about Brigid's "alley" apartment; Brigid defends it as "interior courtyard." Daughter notes that they, her parents, might have helped with money, to which Dad responds, reaching way back in time, "Well, I know someone who refused to go to a *state* school."

This feels like a stereotypical generational drama shaping up, but the notes of financial trouble afflicting all family members, the play's principal theme, are sounded early, resonantly, and, rare for modern drama, in stoic fashion. As daughter Aimee the attorney says, explaining the Blakes to Brigid's new boyfriend Rich, "Our family believes in stoic sadness." In the production I saw, that line got a laugh. Sadness too is a note we may hear more of as the 21st century batters the American dream—and, to deal with that battering, stoicism may be this play's most valuable take-away.

The financial and attendant challenges are big: Aimee has just learned she is not on the partner track at her law firm, which means an invitation to leave. Adding to her pain, her girlfriend has left her and she has ulcerative colitis. Brigid, a composer, is not getting the encouragement an artist needs; a letter of faint recommendation, which she reads to the family without excuse-making, spells curtains. With massive student debt to pay off, Brigid works nights as a bartender. Deirdre, the mother, is the stable center. She's been with the same company 40 years, since she graduated from high school, working now as office manager, but making a salary one-fifth that of two guys in their twenties with "special degrees." In her tending after others and her philosophical strength, Deirdre is the office manager of the family, too.

Erik, the father, is in the direst straits: He just lost his job as head of maintenance at a Catholic high school. Not only has he lost his salary *and* his pension, necessitating the sale of the family's beloved lake property and his taking a job at Walmart in a town some distance from Scranton (so kids from his old school won't discover him). On top of financial precariousness, Erik is now burdened with shame: He cheated on Deirdre with a teacher from the school, violating the school's morality code as well as his own.

This revelation, to his daughters and coming late, throws light on all Erik's lines previous and deepens the play. For example, on the (existential) cost of living: "I thought I'd be settled by my age, you know, but man, it never ends...mortgage, car payments, internet, dishwasher just gave out.... Don'tcha think it should cost less to be alive?" On his life expectations: "End of the day, everything that *anyone's* got...one day it *goes*...whatever gifts God's given us, in the end, no matter who you are...everything you have *goes*." His toast at dinner is a plea in advance for forgiveness: "I'm thankful for having your unconditional love and support. Hope there's nothing any of us could ever do to...change that... what we've got right here, 'cause this is what matters...this family." Even the verse he's given to sing from an Irish ditty resonates: "But if blackness falls upon my lot; / If I should fall and you should not / Pray that all my fears be soon forgot, / May peace and joy be with you all."

Deirdre's lines, in retrospect, also resonate more. She feels poverty can be a gift, in what it teaches you, which is a good attitude to have, given her husband's loss of job and pension. She feels it's a gift—"It's a blessing, you know"—to have grandmother Momo live with them, but how, with straitened finances, will they care for Momo as her dementia advances? Deirdre urges marriage on Brigid and Rich—"Marriage can help you weather a storm"; if only Aimee and her girlfriend had married. As for the new storm in her own marriage: You sense she will weather it, but the shock reverberates in her offhand comments about the world's craziness ("What next?"). Even before this shock, and as stable as she is, Deirdre had existential anxiety: Her daughters laugh over her email quoting a *Scientific American* article declaring that, at the subatomic level, "Nothing is solid."

In increasingly chaotic times, both parents find solace in their Catholic faith, while their daughters don't. Erik jokes that young people find their faith in juice-cleansing and yoga. When Rich alludes to earlier depression, Erik cites religion as a "natural anti-depressant," though when Rich says he's "rebooted" his life, Erik wonders why anyone would want a second round. Deirdre gifts Brigid with a statue of the Virgin Mary: "Just keep it for my sake, okay?" There is no parallel faith in politics, though; in fact, political action to improve their station does not figure at all in this family's life—which, at a time when America's democracy is faltering, is telling.

The play ends with Erik's panic attack, which occurs after he's made confession to his daughters and is alone in the apartment. Gasping, he automatically reverts to his faith, calling out to Father Flynn. Then, in an evocation of his recurring nightmare that he has shared with Rich—of a faceless woman gesturing him toward a tunnel—he takes the lantern he gave Brigid (for the next hurricane) and exits toward the hallway, lit to resemble…a tunnel.

All these dramatic strokes and insights come in no organized fashion; the play is nonlinear and plotless, but then, Thanksgiving dinners are not generally plotted (though in the Trump era they may be more so, given the high conflict between liberal and conservative). I must confess that, upon reading the script when it was first published in 2015, I was underwhelmed: The action seemed discontinuous in the extreme, with characters directing lines past each other from the set's two levels, or focusing overmuch on arranging this, that, or getting food to table. And I do love soliloquys, which this play has no time for, only short lines overlapping.

But production can illuminate, especially a masterful production like the one currently up at Seattle Repertory Theatre. Continuity from first script to the further-developed one now on view is no doubt enhanced by having the same director at the helm, the highly-regarded Joe Mantello, who directed the 2015 New York premiere (Seattle is the first city in a national tour). Mantello mines the richness inherent in Karam's script by skillfully underscoring each character's moments of anxiety—financial, emotional, existential. And he knits the characters together, with their anxieties and their embattled love, into a believable family that is both unique and archetypal. Leading a strong cast are veteran stage and screen actors Richard Thomas and Pamela Reed; each cast member individualizes their role in memorable ways. I am glad I gave the play another look, thanks to a *Seattle Times* review. The more fraught America we live in since Trump's election also brought me back to the play.

Still, I could do without Karam's touches of horror and mystery, which seem unduly portentous: the loud thuds on the ceiling, the lightbulbs suddenly blinking out, and, especially during Erik's panic attack, the pots and pans in the kitchen suddenly falling off the counter. The playwright asserts his play is a "family thriller." But: A panic attack is sufficient unto itself. Also, as Deirdre says, "There's enough going on in the real world to give me the creeps," so why the sound effects?

Dramaturgy aside, Mantello delivers on Karam's astringent vision of our darker times, raising questions about the viability of the American dream. Karam gives us no song-and-dance optimism that we can recover that dream. He means to be as honest as possible, to (according to program notes) "avoid propaganda or a tidy resolution."

Again, what I appreciate are Karam's stoic characters, who will still dream, though in less high-flown ways than our national myth has heretofore required. Unlike the neurotic characters and dysfunctional families we too often get, these characters are normal, responsible, caring, resilient; this family is actually functional. And, unlike so many kvetching fictional families, this one is grateful for what they have: They say grace before dinner, then say it again. Karam's loose-weave structure, better than a tightly-woven plot, allows us to view these stoics in the round, as it were, and imagine how they—and we ourselves—would respond to the testing coming from all sides.

At the end of Seattle Rep's moving production, as Erik hesitantly approaches the tunnel/hallway with lantern, I was struck by a thought: of the insubstantiality of the human being and human life. But like a Giacometti statue, so thin as almost not to be, the humans in *The Humans* still stand, still act, still are. And therein lies Hope.

—*HuffPost*, December 11, 2017

Alabama Votes for Sanity and Decency—and Inspires the Country

DID ANYBODY EVER expect that Alabama—a historic bastion of slavery, segregation, and hardline conservatism in the Old South—might point the way to a New Day in Trumpian America? (Short answer: No, never.)

But in the recent special election, when Alabama narrowly elected Doug Jones, the U.S. prosecutor who convicted two Ku Klux Klansmen for a heinous racial crime, and rejected former state judge Roy Moore, espouser of hardest-line conservatism and alleged molester of young girls, Alabama did more than elect its first Democrat in 25 years to the U.S. Senate. Alabama, by its own free will and its vote, began to square itself with its dark history and took a step toward the light.

Well done, Alabama. You engineered your own reckoning and, doing so, struck a blow for sanity and decency, at a time when sanity and decency are under assault by our very own President. The whole world was watching, as Birmingham's mayor noted, wondering if the U.S. would further self-destruct in anger and chaos.

To be sure, the vote was breathtakingly close: Jones got around 50% of the vote, while Moore got around 48%, with write-ins comprising the balance. Which means nearly half the state voted for an alleged child molester simply because he had an "R" after his name, Democrats being equated with evil.

But it also means that, in addition to a groundswell of African-Americans, suburban women, and young people voting for Jones, a sufficient number of conservative Alabamans took themselves into Gethsemane for serious pondering (half of all state residents self-identify as evangelical) and decided to do right by their state and their country and forsake Moore, either by writing in another Republican name or staying home, thus helping the Democrat. As one evangelical quoted in *The New York Times* said of Moore, "He uses his faith as a cop-out."

No matter how close, though, in a democracy all that's needed to win is a simple majority. As Donald Trump himself tweeted, noting write-ins were a factor, "A win is a win." (As of this posting, Moore has not conceded. Final count is to be certified between Dec. 27 and Jan. 3.)

For Alabama, this election, narrow as it is, means deep things. For one, as some observers note, with this vote Alabama comes out from behind the long shadow of its former segregationist governor George Wallace—again, just barely, but again, trending in the right direction. For another, this election is tacit acknowledgment of past racial crimes: After all, Doug Jones is the very face of a major civil rights victory—he convicted two former Klansmen for the bombing murder of four little African-American girls in Birmingham's Sixteenth Street Baptist Church, enabling Justice finally to be served 35 years after the crime. And, throughout the South, tensions over Confederate statues and flag, post-Charleston and Charlottesville, have reopened arguments over the Civil War—was it over slavery or states' rights?

Jones referred to this dark history, of Alabama and the South, in his victory speech, characterizing this history indirectly and metaphorically as a "crossroads":

> "Alabama has been at a crossroads. We have been at a crossroads in the past. And unfortunately we have usually taken the wrong fork. Tonight, ladies and gentlemen, you took the right road."

Contrast this courageous display with Moore's campaign of racial resentment and what *Washington Post* columnist Eugene Robinson called "Christian grievance"—the lament over the loss of white privilege couched in the language of the Bible.

Fittingly, it was African-Americans—whose ancestors suffered so terribly during slavery, with the reverberations continuing—who put Jones over the top. African-American women were key to getting their neighborhoods mobilized. A major get-out-the-black-vote effort was mounted by black leaders, including former President Barack Obama, Senator Cory Booker, former Massachusetts governor Deval Patrick, and basketball legend and native Alabaman Charles Barkley. Citing Moore as a white separatist, Barkley got real in his appeal: "I love Alabama, but at some point we got to draw a line in the sand and show we're not a bunch of damn idiots."

Moore aside, the big losers in this election were Donald Trump and his strategist and wingman Stephen Bannon. Another win for sanity and decency. Both these nihilists endorsed Moore and campaigned for him (Trump across the state line in Florida). Alabama is this team's second defeat in two months, following Virginia in November, which the *Post* called "a historic Republican wipeout." Together, says the *Post*'s Robinson, these defeats show Trumpism to be "a paper tiger."

Of course the big question is: Can Jones get re-elected in 2020, when presumably the Republicans will field a more suitable candidate than Moore, in a state that remains one of the reddest in the nation? Or—is this a crazy thought?—might Moore run again, campaigning for the seat that was "stolen" from him in '17? (Run, Roy, run!) No doubt there'll be a strong conservative backlash to Jones' election; much depends on sanity prevailing. And much depends on how the schism between the Republican establishment and Trumpism plays out: Trumpism brings out extremists.

And, may I respectfully add, much depends on a Reformation among evangelicals: While some abided by their conscience and forsook Moore, still a big majority of Alabama's white evangelicals—varying from 80% to 81%—voted for the man accused of racial and religious bigotry, misogyny, and assaults on teenage girls. Some evangelical leaders are speaking of "tarnish."

For now, though, after a year of Trump's insanity and indecency, we can enjoy some measure of the inverse again: In his victory speech Jones repeated his campaign theme—"This entire race has been about dignity and respect...about common courtesy and decency." For now, after a year of Trump's attacks on our democratic institutions, to the point where expert democracy-watchers raise alarms about its even working, voters not only turned out but exceeded expectations, with the African-American community especially energized. For now, after a year of Democrats anxious over the party's lack of direction *vis-à-vis* Trumpism, Democrats, with a strong assist from the Indivisible organization, showed clarity and muscle, backing a stellar candidate and running a classic positive campaign—a model to be followed.

And, for now, when History's darker forces seem arrayed against us, the people of one state with a particularly dark past undertook to right themselves with that past and, to a small but critical degree, achieved it—redemptive, history-defying action that inspires us all. As *The Washington Post* editorialized, "It is beyond heartening."

As Doug Jones, new U.S. Senator, tweeted in victory: "Thank you ALABAMA!!"

—*HuffPost*, December 18, 2017

Films for Our Times: *Darkest Hour*

First in a series, Films for Our Times

WHAT DOES THE *great popular art form of the modern age—film—have to say to our tumultuous times, the early 21stcentury? With the weakening of the post-World War II international order—institutional bulwarks have failed to protect the individual against the ravages of a globalized economy and unending armed conflict; democracy's spread has been checked by ineffective leadership, resurgent populism and nationalism, and the threat of authoritarianism—our times as a consequence are marked by extreme polarization, loss of identity, disillusion, anger. And, sadly, culture—drama, books, TV, also film—does not offer many tools to counter the political chaos. In both politics and culture, the rational gives way to the irrational, the civil gives way to the angry.*

In the belief that culture, even more than politics, could juice the recovery of our faltering democracy, this series will examine films, from the vault as well as more recent efforts, that reflect our age's tumultuous political and social forces and, importantly, point the way upward. While much modern film focuses on the personal to the exclusion of a larger context, or focuses on the dystopian and the nihilistic, still there are gems: Films with protagonists—heroes rather than anti-heroes—keenly aware of that larger context, and the peril threatening it, and who contend. The best of these protagonists can organize others to follow them, to make a New Day.

* * *

Darkest Hour

As a model of resistance standing up to and battling tyranny, Winston Churchill during World War II looms as the example *par excellence*. As Prime Minister of a beleaguered England imperiled early on with invasion by Hitler's forces closing in on British forces—the entire British army of 300,000—who are stranded on the beaches of Dunkirk across the English Channel in France, Churchill must decide: Should he sue for peace and negotiate with the Nazi dictator and his Axis ally Mussolini, as the former P.M. Neville Chamberlain and Lord Halifax, with King George at their flank, insist? Or should he, at the risk of losing the home island itself and rendering its long and storied history as dust, resist? The stakes could not be higher: Much of Europe has already fallen, France has just done so, America would not enter the war for another year-and-a-half—England is utterly alone.

Happily not only for England but the world, Churchill resisted—with canny military strategy, deft political maneuvering, a profound belief in the English people and their character, and stirring oratory. This decision-making, and this crucially decisive time period—May 1940—are the focus of *Darkest Hour*, the magnificent film directed by Englishman Joe Wright (*Atonement, Pride and Prejudice*) and starring Gary Oldman as the P.M. in a legacy-securing performance.

In history's darkest hours, character tells. Churchill knew he was not his party's first choice as P.M. As he tells his wife Clementine, "This job is not a gift, it's revenge." Churchill was blamed, rightly, for his disastrous handling of the Gallipoli landing and its catastrophic loss of life in World War I. But he was also a historian and a politician who'd been inveighing through the previous decade, rightly, against the fascist Hitler and his plans for world domination. Once in power Churchill wasted no time on settling political scores, but formed a coalition government and set about trying to dissuade Chamberlain and Halifax.

Churchill's lowest point, as the film movingly shows, comes when Chamberlain and Halifax, still with the King on their side, force Churchill to send word through emissaries that England would consider suing for peace. Both Chamberlain, who today is sneeringly equated with "appeasement," and Halifax are given their due here: They truly fear England's annihilation, a fear eminently valid. (Plans were made to evacuate the King and family to Canada.) For Churchill, though, proud and defiant as he is, even the thought of surrender sickens and brings him near collapse. Compounding his despair is his own doubt about his record as a leader.

The tide turns, for Churchill, when the King comes round and supports his position. Also, Churchill has set in motion the evacuation of the British forces on Dunkirk, daringly instrumented through the mobilization of an armada of private vessels, a maneuver requiring, however, the sacrifice of the British garrison at Calais, whose commanding officer is ordered to draw the German fire his way "until the destruction of your command." This daring, and this sacrifice, pay off and enable England, and Churchill, to fight another day.

Then there is the oratory that still thrills—three historic speeches Churchill composed in three weeks, the first two when the hour was darkest: his debut speech to Parliament as P.M., in which he pledges the nation's "blood, toil, sweat and tears," and his first radio address to an anxious nation. In his third speech, delivered to Parliament upon the success at Dunkirk, Churchill, restored to full resistance mode, famously vows "victory at all costs"—"We shall fight on the beaches, we shall fight on the landing grounds, we shall fight in the fields and in the streets, we shall fight in the hills, we shall never surrender"—and ignites, finally, unanimous applause. The film's last line comes from Halifax, responding to the question, What just happened? Screenwriter Anthony McCarten inserts here another famous line, from American journalist Edward R. Murrow who broadcast the war from London: Winston, he says, had just "mobilized the English language and sent it into battle." I wouldn't be surprised if the screenwriter pegged that as the film's last line and wrote his way toward it, trusting, rightly, that a verbal climax has its own compelling force. (Churchill was awarded the Nobel prize for literature in 1953 "for his mastery of historical and biographical description as well as for brilliant oratory in defending exalted human values.")

The scene in the film giving some reviewers pause—the scene set in the London subway—does depart from the historical record and thus may seem "bogus." The film conjectures that Churchill, at his nadir suing Hitler for peace, recovers his resolve to fight on when he seeks out a set of passengers in a subway car, explains the dire situation facing the nation, asks their counsel—and gets it, stirringly ("Never surrender!") from every man, woman, and child present, in a manner that reinforces the national myth of the English people as stalwart and daring.

This scene, which does go over the top gloriously, works for me because I see it as imaginary: It happened in Winston's mind. Note there's almost no sound on this subway, no screeching wheels or jouncing bodies. Finding little encouragement aboveground, this small-d democrat goes underground to seek out the *demos* and, from them, takes both guidance and sustenance. All right, this Churchill reading out to his cabinet the names of these stalwarts in the subway, which he noted down in a matchbook, was perhaps *de trop*. But for those of us—and we are legion across the globe—who worry about democracy's fragility and how better to translate We the People into policy, the scene works. Besides, if we buy Shakespeare's King Henry V walking disguised among his men to gauge their resolve before what would unfold the next day as the Battle of Agincourt, the better to spur them on with his "band of brothers" speech, then can't we buy this subway scene?

As a model of resistance, *Darkest Hour* comes to us at the perfect time. While America is not in its very darkest hour—we are not threatened with foreign conquest—nevertheless we are in a dark hour indeed, a weird and dangerous one unlike any other in our history, threatened from within by a characterless force who cluelessly (or perhaps not so cluelessly) admires a nation, Russia, that explicitly seeks to undermine our democracy. The film offers countless compare-and-contrast tests for the American viewer: Churchill's sagacity, courage, and magnanimity versus Trump's stupidity, his dangerous knavery, his lying and vulgarity, his infantile me-me-me-ism, and (this just in) Trump's racism that sinks to a new and vile low. "As a portrait of leadership at its most brilliant, thoughtful and morally courageous," writes *The Washington Post*, "*Darkest Hour* is the movie we need right now." As for Trump's tweets versus Churchill's oratory, it is to guffaw, if not to cry.

Further, this film's portrait of Churchill the resister—make that Resister—offers a strong rebuke to those commentators who lately have decried the anti-Trump resistance movement here as nothing more than empty negativism. As vividly acted by Oldman, in resistance—principled resistance—one finds the room and reason to argue, maneuver, experiment, come up with a daring plan to rescue your entire army from annihilation. While the resister knows profound dejection when his principled fight stalls, he also knows highest exhilaration when principle pays off. (The real Churchill also had a wicked wit, which this film scants, but then wicked wit would be out of place in a nation's darkest hour.) Director Joe Wright admires our resistance movement: "As I travel around America I am really impressed and optimistic at the level of resistance happening in the U.S. at the moment.... People are very vocal and that's really positive." About Churchill, he "got a lot of things wrong in his career, and in his personal life, but one thing he got right was he resisted the tide of fascism, bigotry and hate. And that seems to be speaking to America now, and Britain, too."

The filmmaking is masterful—very clear on the history while revealing equally clearly the individual responses to looming catastrophe—and successfully reaches for the mythic, with snatches of Cicero and an aerial view of a battlefield in France morphing into the eye, reddened, of a classic marble statue. Much of the film is set in the War Cabinet Rooms, the underground warren of spaces where military strategy was fought over and set. All the central performances are strong: Ronald Pickup as Chamberlain, Stephen Dillane as Halifax, Ben Mendelsohn as King George. Kristin Scott Thomas brings humanity and wit to the role of Clementine; her scenes with Winston reflect a deeply loving and knowing marriage. Acting as proxy for young people to enter into the story is Churchill's young typist Miss Layton, well-played by Lily James.

And, finally, Gary Oldman's astonishing Churchill. How good to see that the former bad-boy actor—Oldman shot to stardom in 1986 playing punk rocker Sid Vicious in *Sid and Nancy*—grew up, as he acknowledges he had to, to play and indeed inhabit the most leonine of

British lions, Winston Churchill. The rebel morphed into the Resister. See *Darkest Hour*: In our own dark hour, it illuminates and inspires.

—*HuffPost*, January 11, 2018

Donald Trump, Ugliest American Ever?

WITH COMPLETE CONFIDENCE that Donald Trump's recent outrage—calling Haiti and nations in Africa "s***hole countries"—will soon be matched by another, and having suffered a bellyful of outrageousness for a full year of his presidency, by now we can safely nominate our hot mess of a president as the definitive definition of the once-upon-a-time-to-be-avoided-at-all-costs epithet, "the ugly American."

In fact, as there's no close contender, real or fictional, let's be done with it: Donald J. Trump is Ugliest American Ever.

Not an insult about one's looks, which is how the ignorant Trump might take it, the "ugly American" epithet connotes a condescending attitude on the part of the most powerful nation on earth, the United States of America, toward the rest of the world, notably the "underdeveloped" part. It attaches to those Americans interacting directly with the nationals of other countries—diplomats, international business people, and tourists, perhaps most often the latter: Recall the movies and TV shows featuring the obnoxious American tourist who demands service *pronto*?

Trump's "s***hole" insult takes the prize for condescension, oozing with a white supremacist's disdain for non-white peoples, also a turbo-capitalist's disdain for the poor. Quite rightly, the world's reaction has been blistering. If conscientious Americans hoped, post-Trump, to

[257]

repair the damage done by Trump to America's stature in the world, this abhorrent racist slur may prove fatal to repair. Rule №1 in international relations: Thou shalt show respect for your human counterpart.

Not to forget, the week before, Trump boasted about his nuclear button being bigger than the North Korean leader's, "and my Button works!"—a bad parody of the "ugly American" leader as power-mad and knocking recklessly about the world's biggest arsenal. Ugliest American, deadliest American.

But enough with the exhibits, since, as Trump is the Ugliest American Ever, they are endless. Better to go to the source itself—the novel, *The Ugly American*—and ask: How did this epithet become so enduringly popular?

In 1958, when the Cold War between America and the Soviet Union was heating up, two veterans of World War II—one a writer of popular books, William J. Lederer (he also wrote *A Nation of Sheep* and *Our Own Worst Enemy*) and the other, Eugene Burdick, a political science professor at the University of California—wrote a series of cautionary vignettes, first as nonfiction, then, at their editor's urging, as a novel. In it they depicted various American officials as they operated in southeast Asia, the area American policymakers believed must be kept from going Communist, because, per the domino theory, once one country went, they all would.

The novel opens with the American ambassador to the fictional country of Sarkhan, Louis Sears, irate because the editorial cartoon in the local newspaper depicts a short and fat American, obviously him, leading a Sarkhanese man by a tether around his neck to a Coca-Cola sign. In his ire we see the ugly condescension emerge: Sears refers to the Sarkhanese as "monkeys" who "always lie"; he does not speak the language nor interest himself in local customs. Instead he focuses on socializing and hosting American dignitaries who come to "see for themselves" the situation, biding his time until he can snag a judgeship stateside. Sears typifies "the ugly American."

By contrast, the Soviet ambassador focuses on the people: He speaks

Sarkhanese, knows local customs, engages the Sarkhanese in what they most like to do—talk philosophy—all with an objective of establishing Sarkhan and Russia as friends and allies who'd stand by each other, because "the colonial and capitalistic countries would not assist another nation unless they could profit from it."

The new American ambassador, Gilbert MacWhite, shows promise: He arrives having studied the language and, understanding he had a "fatal amount of faith in his own, unsupported judgment," he travels the region—the Philippines, Vietnam—to study firsthand how they handle the insurgent Communist threat. The keenest insight comes from the Philippine defense minister:

> *"The simple fact is...that average Americans...are the best ambassadors a country can have. They are not suspicious, they are eager to share their skills, they are generous. But something happens to most Americans when they go abroad.... Many of them...feel they must live up to their...big cars and cocktail parties. But get an unaffected American, sir, and you have an asset. And if you get one, treasure him—keep him out of the cocktail circuit, away from bureaucrats, and let him work in his own way."*

These "beautiful Americans" (my term, not the authors'), few in number, MacWhite finds. The aforementioned defense minister wins the Philippine presidency because an American liaison officer, Col. Edwin Hillandale, took his harmonica and lived among the people of a key Communist province, convincing them not all Americans were "rich and bloated snobs" and turning their vote anti-Communist. In Vietnam Major James "Tex" Wolchek persuades MacWhite and a French major to study Mao's principles of guerrilla warfare—too late in the major's case, as the French soon go down to final defeat at Dien Bien Phu, but will America learn from France's error?

Another "beautiful American," engineer and businessman Homer Atwood, and his wife (both described as physically ugly), do great good in Sarkhan by going local. Disdaining the big aid projects Americans usually construct, like dams and highways which are of little benefit to people in an agrarian society, Atwood engineers a bicycle-powered irrigation pump for the terraced rice paddies. His wife, noting the village's elderly women become bent after a lifetime of sweeping with brooms only two feet long, goes looking for a longer reed enabling the sweeper to do the job standing up (though isn't it condescending to portray the villagers as not having figured this out themselves?). Another American businessman peddles powered milk among the peasants. Finally, there is Father Finian, a Catholic priest who lives among the Sarkhanese, talking philosophy with them and hearing them out ("The white man has not always been just"), while also organizing grassroots resistance to the insurgent Communists and ultimately setting up a small nondenominational college.

MacWhite is persuaded. At novel's end, he cables Washington urging that American diplomacy be reformed in the direction of these smaller-scale, human-centered projects: "The little things we do must be moral acts and they must be done in the real interest of the peoples whose friendship we need—not just in the interest of propaganda." He also recommends all diplomats learn the language of the country of their posting, leave their big cars at home, and study Mao, Lenin, Marx, and Engels. Sadly, his request is denied as "highly impractical" and he is called stateside.

Highly critical of U.S. policy, *The Ugly American* caught a cultural moment of post-World War II questioning and became a runaway bestseller. John F. Kennedy, then a U.S. senator, ordered copies for all his Senate colleagues; as President he established the Peace Corps, reportedly as a counter to the influence of "the ugly American."

Tragically, Kennedy also set us on the path to the unwinnable Vietnam war—and one could say it was the vestigial "ugly American" traits that took us there: hubris, grandiosity, condescension toward the "gooks." The fictional American ambassador MacWhite, in his final cable to Washington urging reform, put it aptly: "To the extent our foreign policy is humane and reasonable, it will be successful. To the extent that it is imperialistic and grandiose, it will fail."

If there's any doubt that those ugly American traits still endure, Trump's "s***hole" racist insult makes the case, full stop. And, troublingly, they appear to endure in his base—they are one-third of the American electorate—who still stand by him.

In this era when America is seen to be in decline, when our own chaos (and not Communism) is our nemesis—chaos Trump too-brilliantly exploits—conscientious Americans have a momentous task. By virtue of our booming economy and booming military, America remains the world's most powerful country. But: We Americans were never tutored in the responsibilities of exercising the immense power we have, neither at the personal nor national level. To save ourselves from Trump's autocratic tendencies and reverse our decline, we conscientious Americans must not only win at the polls, but tutor our fellow Americans in the responsibilities of power.

This is the test: Can Americans quit the ugly condescension and become beautiful?

—*Medium*, February 17, 2018

Counter-Forces to the Chaos: We're Becoming Constitutionalists, Ethicists, Candidates for Office, and Other Good Things

As AWFUL AS the present historical moment is—specifically, the train wreck of the Trump administration and, generally, the post-9/11 chaos and seeming acceleration of America's decline—it is important to note that some Americans have recognized the peril we are in and, like a fire brigade in response, have stepped up to the rescue.

It's also important to note that this rescue work focuses on *foundational* repair—repair to the foundations of American democracy. These foundations were fraying before Trump came to power, but it is Trump in his day-to-day awfulness in office who's galvanized John Q. Public off his sofa and into action. In an article titled "Rallying Nation," *The Washington Post* reports on its recent poll finding that *one in five Americans* have participated in political protests since the beginning of 2016. That's a lot of protest.

While the commentariat's report cards on Trump's first year were comprehensively negative, there was little reference in them to these counter-forces emerging from the grassroots. These citizens, whom I call "the conscientious public," refuse to collapse in despair at the damage Trump the Disrupter is doing. Instead, ignoring the myriad armchair cynics, and countering Trump's base who seem to delight in "blowing the place up," these citizens are mobilizing, either individually or collectively, to fortify our democratic foundations.

Which is to say, in posing a counter-force to chaos, some of us have become:

Constitutionalists. At a time when the occupant of the White House sees himself beyond the law and treats the Attorney General as his own personal attorney, expecting him to protect the president's interests rather than those of the American people, We the People in self-defense go to our foundational document—the U.S. Constitution—the document guaranteeing our panoply of rights and outlining the proper balance of power between governor and governed.

Constant reference is made in letters to the editor and comments threads to the Constitution's various missions set out in the preamble: "We the People, in order to form a more perfect union, establish justice, insure domestic tranquility, provide for the common defense, promote the general welfare, and secure the blessings of liberty to ourselves and our posterity, do ordain and establish this Constitution for the United States of America." Especially in these deranged times, how often have we heard sighs from the public for "a more perfect union" and the imperatives to "establish justice" and "promote the general welfare"?

Likewise, there is heightened awareness of our First Amendment rights: "Congress shall make no law respecting an establishment of religion, or prohibiting the free exercise thereof; or abridging the freedom of speech, or of the press; or the right of the people peaceably to assemble, and to petition the Government for a redress of grievances." The Establishment Clause, prohibiting the establishment of a state religion, entered into public consciousness with Trump's several attempts to enact an anti-Muslim travel ban. And Trump's war on the media and his threats to ease the libel laws, the better to cow tough reporting of his autocratic tendencies, is broadly recognized as a real danger to free speech. (There needs to be a better understanding on the left of how unfettered free speech abuses this precious right.)

And, outside of a Constitutional Law class, have we ever heard so much about the Emoluments Clause, which prohibits the president from accepting gifts of any kind from foreign governments? At issue in several lawsuits is the question whether Trump can legally accept foreign payments to the Trump business organization.

Further, with every gun-related act of carnage, we are brought back to the Second Amendment and its interpretation in modern times. And, of course if impeachment proceedings are instituted against Trump, the advisability of which is questionable, everything would turn on contending interpretations of the Constitution's injunction against "treason, bribery, or other high crimes and misdemeanors."

Greater public awareness of the Constitution may seem a slim reed to point to, but it's always good to refresh one's grasp of one's founding documents and founding principles: "rule of law," "a nation of laws, not men." I know of people now walking around with a pocket-sized copy of the U.S. Constitution on their person. It beats *The Anarchist Cookbook*.

Ethicists. America lost its moral compass some time ago—was it in the '60s, '70s, '80s, '90s?—and subsequently much of America got comfortable with an "anything-goes" ethos, to our undoing. For ultimate evidence of that moral falling-off, look no further than the amoralist now in the White House.

Yet two mighty civic movements arising just in the last year— the #MeToo movement against sexual assault and the #MarchForOur Lives movement against gun violence—reflect a profound yearning to retrieve that compass once again. While both movements are about phenomena that predate Trump, his amorality no doubt acts as a spur to these grassroots uprisings. His admission on the "Access Hollywood" tape to vulgarly groping women no doubt energizes much of #MeToo.

But #MeToo is more than about physical assault; it is also about resetting the power balance between men and women, both in the workplace and in the private sphere. The women testifying against their sexual predators have shone a light on the gross, and in some cases criminal, imbalance in the power dynamics between the sexes. Reflecting our fallen times, few of these women employ moral language in making their claims, yet they are clearly arguing "This is *wrong*"—all of it: the physical assault, the power imbalance. And the public, newly conscious, is taking their point.

Likewise the #MarchForOurLives movement: Mass shootings occur so often in this gun-ridden country that one despairs there is an end to it. But the mass shooting on Valentine's Day at a high school in Parkland, Florida, leaving 17 dead and many critically injured, has led to something new and powerful: The victims themselves taking action, political action, to advocate for gun safety. And that it is young people, of all races, doing the leading spells good things for our Renaissance. Again, few of these young people employ moral language, yet again they are clearly arguing "This is *wrong*"—all of it: the carnage, the trauma. And the public, again, takes their point.

Also, of course, there is the #BlackLivesMatter movement: At a time when the white supremacist in the White House stokes racial and ethnic tensions for his own divisive ends, this movement no doubt has more to say and do to enable America to reach racial justice.

In a nation thrown off its axis in so many ways, these movements—#MeToo for greater fairness, #MarchForOurLives for gun sanity, and #BlackLivesMatter for racial justice, and, importantly, the public support they have engendered—show an America groping for its misplaced moral compass. America is trying mightily to get right again.

Candidates for office. The most tangible and perhaps most consequential counter-force to the present chaos is this: Recognizing that American democracy is under grave threat, and recognizing that a democracy is powered by the people, the *demos*, astonishing numbers of the American people are in turn becoming small-d democrats and running for elective office—at the local, state, and national levels—as the surest way to stabilize our system. The *demos* is out to save our democracy.

Indisputably, the impetus for this outburst of civic activism is Donald Trump himself—his autocratic tendencies seen in his disdain for the law and democratic norms, his constant lying, his constant attacks on truth and fact, his racism, his amorality, his scorn of statesmanship. And this catastrophe is, to the conscientious citizen, sufficient inspiration to override the well-reported fact that American political campaigns are nasty, brutish, and long. Here, you throw your hat in the ring and you know you're in for a ringer.

In what *The Washington Post* calls a "gusher," candidates as of Dec. 31, 2017 have filed to run for Congress in numbers—more than 2,100—almost twice that of 2015. Enthusiasm is especially high on the left, with some 1,133 Democrats filing to run for House seats, in what the *Post* calls a "never-before-seen gusher," as they aim to pick up the 24 seats needed to win back the majority in the November midterms.

Women are the big story this election cycle: In its most recent release, EMILY's List reports that 34,000 women (that's not a typo) have contacted the organization since Election Day 2016, expressing serious interest in running for office. These numbers relate to all levels of elective office, from local school board to Congress. As *The Economist* writes, "Women could be the undoing of Trump"—which is sweet justice, given Trump's disgusting behavior toward them. Notable also is the "record number" of women running for governor: 79, as of January—49 Democrats and 30 Republicans.

Even scientists in significant numbers are running for office, to counter the anti-science stance of Trump and his Republican cohort. According to 314 Action, as of February more than 60 scientists have announced a run for federal office, while almost 200 are running for state legislature and another 200 for local school boards.

Playing an enormous role in coalescing this outburst of electoral energy, of course, is the anti-Trump resistance movement and the Indivisible organization.

There are other good things afoot, mainly our greater sense of realism: Americans can live in their own worlds in pursuit of their personal dreams, but the peril posed by Trump has pierced through and forced us to come to grips with perilous reality. Yet we are not fatalists—not yet. We still largely retain the American belief that we can "front" Fate (a favorite verb of American transcendentalist Ralph Waldo Emerson) and prevail.

Taken together, these counter-forces—constitutional, ethical, electoral, greater realism, little fatalism as yet—reflect a powerful stabilizing reaction to the chaos President Donald Trump has unleashed and exploits.

America is in a titanic struggle with itself, one that is existential in its implications and riveting in its drama. Here's to democracy.

—*Medium*, May 7, 2018

Democrats: Stop Running Against Nancy Pelosi

A BAD TREND IS developing and it needs to stop, please.

In recent primaries, Democrats running for Congress in traditionally Republican-held districts have deemed it advantageous to run against one of their own—Nancy Pelosi, the Democrat who's now House minority leader and formerly its Speaker.

This tactic worked for Conor Lamb in Pennsylvania in April and, more recently, for Dan McCready in North Carolina. Both ran center-right campaigns, focusing on local issues rather than "nationalizing" their race—that is, pointedly not running against Donald Trump. Yet both made an exception and nationalized their race in this insidious way: Both vowed not to support Pelosi for Speaker if Democrats retake the House in November.

And featured last week in *The New York Times*, more of the same: Congressional candidate Clarke Tucker in Arkansas "signals misgivings about Nancy Pelosi" as the next House Speaker.

As an act of political cannibalism, ingratitude, misplaced allegiance, cowardice, and, yes, misogyny, this tactic needs to stop before it causes serious damage to the bright prospects for Democrats in the fall.

About the political cannibalism: It's not hard to make the case that Pelosi may have been the most successful Speaker in modern times. She was the prime force behind enactment of Pres. Barack Obama's healthcare law, wrangling the votes to get this historic bill passed; moreover she marshaled 100% of the Democratic caucus to defend the law against the Republicans' drive to repeal it last year. Pelosi also was the force behind passage of the Dodd-Frank Act in the aftermath of the '08 financial crash. This powerful progressive leader deserves defending, not subversion.

About the ingratitude: It's also not hard to make the case that, in terms of tangible service to the Democratic party, Nancy Pelosi has few peers. As its star fundraiser, Pelosi, since she entered the Democratic leadership in 2002, has as of April of this year raised $659.6 *million*—which millions of course go to campaigns of Democratic candidates like…Lamb, McCready, and Tucker.

About the misplaced allegiance: How is it possible that Republicans, incumbents and candidates alike, are increasingly embracing our incompetent clown of a president, Donald Trump, while Democrats disavow a peerless legislator and national leader like Nancy Pelosi? Republicans, always sticklers for loyalty, are one by one pledging fealty to Trump, even though Trump admires autocrats (like China's Xi Jinping and Russia's Vladimir Putin) more than democratic leaders and even though, as to party loyalty, he shows none at all, in fact has basically destroyed the modern GOP. Meanwhile Democrats, showing little loyalty themselves, turn on Pelosi. Sad.

About the cowardice: Nancy Pelosi has long been a favorite bogeyman of the Republicans, who pillory her as a hated "super-liberal," overlooking the fact that her San Francisco district is indeed a liberal stronghold and, as she's been serving it since 1987, her constituency clearly deems her a fit representative. Come on, Dems, how about showing some spine and puncturing that bogeyman? At the very least, Democratic candidates for Congress, instead of attacking Pelosi, should waive off the question about allegiance to her and treat it as "hypothetical," the standard response when a politician wants to duck a question; after all, electing a Speaker is an *internal* matter and will involve them *only* if they win their race and join the Congressional club.

About the misogyny: Hard to quantify but, if you're a woman, easy to detect. The virulent misogyny let loose at Hillary Clinton in her presidential campaign continues to exert its influence, now against the bogeyman—bogeywoman?—Pelosi. Who knows how it works: Is it a tacit, wink-wink agreement between candidate and voter that, if you vote for me, you won't have that harridan Pelosi in your life anymore?

However it works, running against Pelosi has worked thus far to the benefit of—well, what do you know!—men, and white men at that (see above). With the #MeToo movement banging the drum so loudly in this moment, the wise candidate would think twice about sounding even vaguely anti-woman.

For all these reasons, Democrats need to rethink their attacks on one of their own, Nancy Pelosi. And the commentariat might rethink the anti-Pelosi meme, too. Even the estimable Frank Bruni, the *New York Times* columnist than whom no one has a keener sense of inequity, failed to question this meme in a recent interview with candidate McCready, in a column titled "Renounce Pelosi, Ignore Donald Trump—and Win?" The question was left dangling: Yes, winning seems to require renouncing Pelosi and ignoring Trump.

Again, in tough races in traditionally Republican-controlled districts, some of which Democrats will need to pick up to retake the House, it is no doubt wise to run principally on local issues and campaign to the center-right. But if forced to nationalize the race, for heaven's sake, quit the unfriendly fire on Nancy Pelosi and quit the phony politesse of ignoring Donald Trump. Attack, attack, attack! Talk about a truly deserving target.

—*Medium*, May 21, 2018

Marching for Their Lives, the Kids Get Serious—More Serious Than the "Adults"

It's been a cheering development, and totally unexpected: In response to a crisis—in this case, the crisis of gun violence—America's young people are pointing the way to a New Day.

In the aftermath of the horrendous shooting which killed 17 of their classmates and teachers on Valentine's Day, the students of Marjory Stoneman Douglas High School in Parkland, Florida, rather than collapse or retreat, got to their feet, found their voices and each other, and came together to unite in protest against the nation's gun laws, mounting a movement—#MarchForOurLives—that has ignited nationwide.

In the best of all possible responses, the Parkland students are uniting and marching to convert their *individual* trauma into *collective* change and repair, taking the path of political action.

Importantly, despite their trauma, this student-led movement is not calling for a gun-free utopia, which would be understandable, but for common-sense restrictions on the Second Amendment. Their demands—including comprehensive background checks and bans on high-capacity magazines and assault weapons—are in the best tradition of American pragmatism and compromise. And, savvily, they are also focused on getting out the vote—for candidates who support saner gun laws.

Moreover, in their response to crisis, the #MarchForOurLives movement welcomes all races and genders to its ranks and its leadership—in salute to the American ideal (seldom achieved) of fair play and equal opportunity and in contrast to the racist and sexist trauma still being committed in the larger society, necessitating the rise of the movements #BlackLivesMatter and #MeToo.

Measured, realistic, serious, the kids of #MarchforOurLives are an ethical-moral tonic for our troubled times. Would that the "adults" were, too.

This is not to say all adults are problematic, not at all. I have long written about "the conscientious public," whose members have thrown themselves into repairing the nation's wounds laid bare after 9/11 and, since Donald Trump's election, have become constitutionalists, ethicists, and candidates for office. And there are the legions of conscientious adults lobbying for gun control on the kids' behalf, including heartbroken parents lobbying in their slain children's memory. But we are not the ones spotlighted. Rather, with the media tending to favor the bright, shiny—and crazy—object, it is the "adults" gone crazy who are granted center-stage and set the un-serious tone.

Where to start in a listing of current follies? There are the ghastly sagas, now going on for six months, of once-powerful men who abused their power and sexually abased women or young men in their workplaces. These notables were, once upon a time, some of the most honored in America (Charlie Rose, Bill Cosby, Kevin Spacey, James Levine). Their numbers include politicians (John Conyers) and officers of the law (New York's Attorney General). This week the governor of Missouri resigned over alleged threats of revenge porn against a woman with whom he'd had an affair. So many "adult" men behaving so badly has left a stench in the air.

Other "adults" now feel freer to express their inner vileness, also their lack of seriousness. Just this week, two "comedians" struck new lows, both creating media firestorms (and lame apologies): On the right Roseanne Barr tweeted a truly shocking racist comment about an advisor to former President Barack Obama, while, on the left, Samantha Bee made an equally vile comment, sexual in nature, about one of the current president's daughters. Grow up, people.

The only good thing in this cavalcade of bad behavior is that the protest coming from the conscientious public is sufficient to drive these miscreants from the scene or force their vow to reform altogether.

Of course the most egregious example of misbehaving adulthood is our president, Donald Trump, who lies and dissembles, who shows no awareness at all of a moral compass, who blames everybody but himself for failure, who has no sense of a cause larger than his ego. Who, as to sexism, is an admitted groper, and, as to racism, sees "very fine people" among the rabidly racist alt-right. Who, on the international stage, is steadily hacking away at America's good name by showing himself to be un-serious about alliances and treaties and to be the most unreliable of negotiators.

And it was an angry base who put this angry man in office. Meanwhile, the kids marching for their lives, instead of losing themselves in anger at school shootings, have harnessed that anger to get focused, get a national organization up on its feet, and get political, all to press for greater sanity. Who are the true adults here?

Sadly, American culture is not much help in portraying intelligent adulthood. The anti-hero and the dystopian reign in TV, movies, books. In theatre, leading this year's Tony awards in number of nominations are *Mean Girls* and *SpongeBob SquarePants* (Really, Tony?). How strange: At a time when kids in real life get serious about gun control, Broadway gets serious about high-school mean girls....

To be fair, the crises faced are not strictly analogous. The "adults" described above are enmeshed in cultural and political turmoil of several generations' duration and polarization, while the kids, their minds and nervous systems freshly concentrated by bullets flying at them (or calculating the odds of being shot at), bring fresh energy to their cause. Still, all things put in the balance, this is the drama now playing out on our national stage: kids gone serious and, save for the conscientious public, "adults" gone crazy, oblivious to the fact that the nation is itself marching for its life.

And for their adult response, let's stop calling them kids and call them young people.

These young people inspire. They are, at this historical moment, what serious looks like. You can see them not only finding their voice but their vocation, for a season if not for life. (Let's hope we, with their help, achieve saner gun laws in this lifetime.) The most serious of their number have announced they will take a gap year (or two) to focus on lobbying for saner gun laws, before heading to college.

Of course, the leaders of #MarchForOurLives are drawing fire from the far right and the NRA, accused of being "crisis actors" and conspiracists. Welcome to the rough-and-tumble of politics! But note how the venom has not stopped them, neither the leaders nor the members. (We have not discussed how seriously insane are the policies of the "adults" at the NRA.) This movement defies research showing that in recent decades allegiance among young people to democracy itself has waned. Here's hoping their activism reinforces their allegiance.

Finally, it remains to be seen if this movement's common-sense demands will have any impact on reaction to school shootings in areas more identifiably "gun country"; early reporting indicates a resistance or pushback.

Whatever. For now: Well done, young marchers! For your performance in Crisis Management in Real Life, you get an A-plus. You also get a place on the right side of History.

—*Medium*, June 1, 2018

Once a Champion of Human Rights, America Now Inhumanly Separates Migrant Children from Their Parents

THE COUNTRY'S FALLING-OFF—ITS ethical-moral falling-off—continues. Consider:

America, the country that spearheaded the establishment of the Universal Declaration of Human Rights within the nascent United Nations in the aftermath of World War II—which historic document, chaired by former First Lady Eleanor Roosevelt, *guarantees the dignity of every human being, whether citizen or migrant*—now, because of a new Trump administration policy of separating migrant children from their parents, America has been called out by the U.N.'s Office of Human Rights for violating said Declaration. Another ideal sacked.

But quite apart from sacked ideals, there is the awful trauma now consuming these children, some as young as one year old. And there is the awful trauma consuming their parents: A distraught father, his child forcibly taken from him last weekend, took his own life.

When did America become so cruel? Conscientious Americans are loudly protesting, while the world loudly condemns us as a nation. What is almost unbearable to imagine—the anguish and trauma inflicted on child and parent when torn from each other's arms—is now sanctioned by official U.S. policy.

This policy, announced April 6 by Attorney General Jeff Sessions, is response to Pres. Trump's campaign rhetoric to crack down on illegal immigration. In a statement aimed at those illegally crossing the Southwest border, Sessions announced a ramped-up "zero tolerance" policy, now to entail criminal prosecution. Whereas earlier illegal border crossers faced civil deportation proceedings, the new policy of criminal penalties necessitates detention, thus forcing the separation of families for months or longer. On May 7, Sessions underscored the family separation policy: "If you are smuggling a child then we will prosecute you, and that child will be separated from you as required by law." Even those seeking legal asylum are treated cruelly: Sessions just announced that those fleeing gang violence or domestic abuse do not qualify for asylum.

How many families have been separated? Hard official numbers are hard to come by. *Reuters* days ago reported 1,800 families separated in the 17 months through February, when the "lite" version of this policy was piloted. The only other official numbers provided cover a two-week period in May, when officials confirmed 658 children were separated from 638 adults. Between October and April, per *The New York Times*, separations included 100 children between the ages of four and one.

With the more draconian policy now in place, these numbers will no doubt rise. [*Update June 15: Almost 2,000 children have been separated from their parents in the April 19-May 31 period of the crackdown, according to figures obtained this date by the Associated Press from the Department of Homeland Security. These separations are not broken down by age.*]

By no means is this to say that secure borders and controlling illegal immigration are not top-priority; they most definitely are. But *must* migrant children be separated from their parents? U.S. policy *before* the new draconian policy allowed detention of families intact. Why cannot that more humane policy continue?

In response, the administration would likely point to the policy's intended objective: to serve as a disincentive to those contemplating migrating here with children. But recent reporting shows this disincentive is not working: The illegal migrant flow, while declining overall, continues because of political and gang violence in the migrants' home countries. In response to public outcry, the administration now is floating a new proposal—to detain the migrant children in tent cities on military bases. But this move is moot, as families would still be separated, not reunited.

Therefore, this appeal from the conscientious public: For the sake of these children and their parents, human beings all, let us stop the trauma, also stop desecrating our ideals, and default to the prior—humane—policy: keeping migrant families intact.

(One wonders if White America acquiesces to the separation of migrant children from parents because the beings in question are brown-skinned...? A scathing op-ed in *The Guardian* asserts that inflicting such trauma "is the whole point.")

In its condemnation of the U.S., the U.N.'s Office of the High Commissioner on Human Rights, in Geneva, exhorts the U.S. to immediately halt the practice of separating families "and stop criminalizing what should at most be an administrative offence—that of irregular entry or stay in the U.S." The practice of separating families, it says, "amounts to arbitrary and unlawful interference in family life, and is a serious violation of the rights of the child." Significantly, it goes on:

"While the rights of children are generally held in high regard in the U.S., it is the only country in the world not to have ratified the U.N. Convention on the Rights of the Child. *We encourage it to accede to the Convention and to fully respect the rights of all children.*"

In response, the U.S. ambassador to the U.N., Nikki Haley, skirted the subject entirely and attacked the U.N. itself, claiming that its "ignorantly" attacking the U.S. is proof of "hypocrisy" and alleging "reprehensible human rights records" of other countries sitting on the Human Rights Council, adding defiantly, "Neither the United Nations nor anyone else will dictate how the United States upholds its borders." But as Human Rights Watch points out, "Yes, the U.S. does have a right to protect its borders—but not by trampling the rights of vulnerable families and children."

Of course Trump blames blowback to his policy on Democrats and their "bad legislation"—a baseless claim. Democratic senator Jeff Merkley of Oregon tried to enter a detention center to observe the children's situation, but was turned away. More recently Democratic senator Dianne Feinstein, with 31 colleagues, introduced the "Keep Families

Together Act" to halt the separation of migrant families at the border. And the ACLU has filed a class-action lawsuit in federal court calling for a halt to the policy and for family reunification.

But political and legal churn aside, focus must be kept on the human—on the cruelty of the child separation policy. Are there no parents in the Trump administration repelled by the idea—now wrenching reality—of children torn from their parent's arms? This "idea" originated with Trump's chief of staff John Kelly when he was secretary of Homeland Security, but was dismissed as too extreme and immoral. Somehow whatever moral scruples there are in this administration were overcome. Meanwhile, whatever happened to the Republicans—party of "family values"?

In his tragedy *Julius Caesar*, Shakespeare lamented "Th' abuse of greatness is when it disjoins / Remorse from power." Remorse, or compassion, must be rejoined with power, in this instance and more generally—or, ultimately and tragically, America is lost.

—*Medium*, June 14, 2018

Surrendering America's Most Precious Mantle, "Leader of the Free World"

PERHAPS THE MOST precious, most honored mantle conferred on America—conferred by virtue of its own prodigious effort and the fortunes of History—has been that of "Leader of the Free World."

As the big victor of the Second World War, America emerged as the pre-eminent military and economic power. Wisely, rather than beggaring its vanquished enemies, the U.S. saw to the establishment of a historic New Day in the postwar world, one anchored in a rules-based, free-market, collective-security system.

When, then, our erstwhile wartime ally the Soviet Union transformed into a communist dictatorship, inaugurating the Cold War, international politics was dramatically reconfigured into two camps, divided explicitly over the concept of freedom: The Soviet Union represented un-freedom, the U.S., freedom. This new reality, combined with our role as guarantor of the newly-organized liberal Western order, earned America the mantle "Leader of the Free World," which mantle we have worn proudly for the intervening 70 years—although for the last half of this span we have not borne it especially responsibly (about which, more later).

Now, with our 45th president Donald J. Trump, this mantle looks to be surrendered—and traded in, by our President no less, for cheaper hardware.

If there is any doubt about Trump's pro-autocratic and anti-democratic tendencies, they were put to rest by the one-two performance in early June, with his sneering performance toward our allies at the G-7 summit in Canada, followed by his fawning performance at the Singapore summit with North Korea's dictator, Kim Jong-un.

Of Kim, whose coercive methods include having his opponents (including family) killed off and ruling through a "personality cult based on ruthless indoctrination," Trump admiringly called him "the strong head" of his country: "He speaks and his people sit up at attention," adding "I want my people to do the same." Later he said he was joking, but for the autocrat-ish Trump, it was Freudian slip. This adoration of Kim follows Trump's embrace of other autocrats around the world—Russia's Vladimir Putin, China's Xi Jinping, Turkey's Recep Tayyip Erdogan, Egypt's Abdel Fattah el-Sisi, the Philippines' Rodrigo Duterte. The title of a recent column by Thomas Friedman of *The New York Times* states it exactly: "Trump to Dictators: Have a Nice Day."

At the same time, Trump serves up insults to our allies, not to their face, of course, but by after-tweet from Air Force One—Germany's Angela Merkel, France's Emmanuel Macron, England's Theresa May—the summation of which can be encapsulated in the insult he flung at his host for the Canadian summit, Justin Trudeau: "weak." From the autocrat's point of view, to be perceived as weak is the worst.

But what's going on here is far worse than bad manners. Trump's astonishing actions—unilaterally imposing trade tariffs; unilaterally bailing out of the Paris climate accord, the Trans-Pacific Partnership, the Iran nuclear agreement, and now bailing out of the Human Rights Council of the United Nations; constantly bashing NATO—all signal a dramatic break with the rules-based, free-market, collective-security system that has kept the world in basic equilibrium since World War II.

In reaction, many in the commentariat, conservative as well as liberal, have sounded the four-bell alarm, including *The Atlantic*'s editor

Jeffrey Goldberg in a jaw-dropping post titled, in a direct quote from a senior Trump administration official, "We're America, Bitch."

And now we learn Trump's minions are actively working, in Germany, to ensure Chancellor Merkel loses her upcoming election. What a falling-off: America, who partnered with its former mortal enemy, enabling it to become Europe's economic powerhouse and one of its staunchest allies, now betrays this ally. For shame.

Equally dangerous, though less commented on, Trump's penchant for autocrats and his antipathy for small-d democrats also signals a rupture *with the American ethos of freedom itself.*

Since forever we Americans have seen ourselves as "the land of the free and the home of the brave." "Don't fence me in," "Don't tread on me"—we have marched under these banners since our foundation. Trump's flirtation with autocrats is heresy to the American ethos of the free individual—or should be. Trump's base supporters say they want America to cease being the world's policeman and focus on America first, but America getting cozy with tyrants who threaten world peace— is this really what they wanted? *Stop!*

Those to whom Trump's heresy should be most blasphemous are the congressional Republicans. In theory, they pose the best possible counter-force to one of their own, Trump the Proto-Autocrat. After all, Republicans are the party traditionally screaming about freedom, that every proposal Democrats serve up, including Obamacare, impinges on their not-to-be-messed-with freedom.

But so polarized is the political moment and so enmeshed are the Republicans in their Faustian bargain with Trump—sacrificing everything to keep power, including principles and their long habit of saluting freedom—that nary a peep has come from their quarter. Sticking it to the Dems apparently is more important than defending American freedom from perhaps the most dangerous threat to that freedom yet: the confidence man operating out of the White House. Republicans, who once mocked Democrats for "flying the white flag of surrender," have surrendered on freedom, keystone of the Republic. *Lord, forgive them, for they know not what they do.*

Fortunately, there are mighty forces mobilizing within the American public, who are fully "woke" to this president's dangerous turn toward un-freedom, who are running for elective office in unprecedented numbers to secure the badly jolted democratic project, who recognize that America is going through a grand reckoning on myriad fronts—racism, sexual assault, guns—and are out in the streets to demand a new New Day. Especially encouraging: the powerful public pushback to Trump's policy of separating migrant children from their parents—*pushback powerful enough to force Trump to reverse himself.* Well done, Immigrant Nation.

Can America ever again be Leader of the Free World? Perhaps the more proper, less self-serving question is: Can the world withstand and push back, with or without American leadership, at the forces of un-freedom pulsing in every corner? Ominous signs are everywhere: Angry populist, anti-democratic forces are trending in Europe (Germany, France, Holland, Hungary, Poland, now Italy), in Asia (India, Myanmar), in Latin America—all to the benefit of the world's aforementioned autocrats.

Americans don't often ponder international politics—which disregard is possible *only* for the Leader of the Free World, guarantor of the rules-based, free-market, collective-security system that's been our norm for decades. But more than Americans might guess, it makes an enormous difference *what kind of power* is dominant in the world—if that power demands the citizen "sit up at attention" (as the autocrat does) or views the citizen as sovereign; if it resorts to force (as the autocrat does) or to the law to settle differences; if it seeks to control, even jail, the press (as the autocrat does) or protects freedom of speech. In sum, if it guarantees un-freedom or freedom.

Thus, as it matters enormously what kind of power is dominant in the world, and as it would be calamity if the world went fully autocratic, America still presents a good case. But the mantle isn't decided by nomination. Short of conquest, it is economic and military might that determine which power dominates. On these grounds, America, with its booming economy and booming military, qualifies.

But, properly speaking, and for the world's sake, it needs to be a reformed America: less arrogant, with a less booming military, more collegial, more responsible. For in these last decades we have wielded our immense power irresponsibly—with the war in Vietnam, the invasion of Iraq in 2003 and unending war there, the descent into torture in 2004, the Wall Street-driven financial crash in 2008 that wrecked markets around the world, our "anything-goes" pop culture that pervades the globe.

Centuries ago the Greek philosopher Heraclitus wrote: "No man ever steps in the same river twice, for it's not the same river and he's not the same man." The world keeps changing, so do circumstances, so do the players. But: If America can reform itself at home by reversing the Trump-driven lurch to un-freedom, and if, by this prodigious example, we help ensure that the river Heraclitus spoke of remains free of the autocrats' pollutant, then America might once again claim the mantle most honored, Leader of the Free World.

But: The world must remain free, or the question of who's the leader doesn't matter.

—*Medium*, June 25, 2018

First Reformed: Dangerous Heresies of a Man of the Cloth

The following film review is, of necessity, chock-full of spoilers, so be advised.

THE FILM *First Reformed* is getting serious attention as a serious film from a serious filmmaker, Paul Schrader. Praised by the chief film critic in our newspaper of record, *The New York Times*, the filmmaker is also subject of a *Times* interview, in which the paper calls the film "one of the most talked-about movies of the spring."

Respectfully, I must dissent. *First Reformed* at first appears to be a serious look at contemporary ills, told from the point of view of the anguished pastor of a dying church in upstate New York who has lost his faith. But in its violent climax—the pastor suddenly turns eco-terrorist—the film commits both theological and secular heresy.

Like the proverbial lamb, I was drawn in by the *Times*' praise of the film as "an epiphany" and its mention of the film's inspiration, *Diary of a Country Priest*, the meditative classic by the eminent French filmmaker Robert Bresson. Like many who were raised in the church but have wandered away but who still believe, and like millions of other pilgrims searching for footing in these wildly tumultuous times, I am keen for works of art that show well-meaning people contending meaningfully.

So I was stunned when Schrader's cleric throws in the moral towel and straps on a suicide vest, targeting his own church. *Seriously?* The *Times* review was, curiously, silent on this violent turn, sticking to a purely aesthetic critique. Whereas the priest in the Bresson film works his sickly body to death ministering to a flock that in their pettiness is shown not worthy of the priest's sacrifice, in this film it is a suffering humanity who merits succor, while it is the cleric who sins.

We are introduced to the pastor, Ernst Toller (Ethan Hawke), as he ministers to a dwindling flock at First Reformed. His church, austere in appearance as well as teaching, has been subsumed by and serves as a kind of gift shop and tour stop to an evangelical mega-church, Abundant Life. (Toller's church, established in 1767, was a stop in the Underground Railroad.) At midlife Toller bears the scars of divorce and the death of an only son in the war in Iraq. Like Bresson's priest, Toller keeps a diary, which he narrates; early on he announces he plans to keep the diary for one year, apparently believing that the bodily pain he's experiencing means he won't live long.

Toller's turn into violence is abrupt and unconvincing, taken up after counseling a pregnant parishioner's eco-terrorist husband, who later, in anguish over bringing a child into a ruined world, commits suicide. To save the wife any bother with the police, Toller offers to hide the husband's suicide jacket and explosives—which to the veteran moviegoer is blatant signal those items will figure later in the action. Taking on the late husband's mantra about mankind's environmental devastation—"Can God forgive us?"—Toller at first takes on the man's target, a chemical plant, but then shifts his aim, unbelievably, to his own church: The chemical plant's CEO, a generous benefactor to Abundant Life, will be present in First Reformed when it celebrates, in a public reconsecration, its 250 years of existence.

Other blatant signals of Toller's imminent descent, dropped in to cue the climax: He suddenly turns on the director of the church choir, with whom he had an affair, screaming "I despise you," meanwhile commanding the eco-terrorist's wife, Mary, for whom he now has feelings, *not* to come to the reconsecration ceremony.

I confess when Toller strapped on the suicide vest, I took a hike. So powerful is the will in me to life (and not just because I am living with cancer) and so powerful is my resistance to anything death-loving, which marks much dystopian fare of today, that I had to move. But while another woman walking out with me left the theater, I lingered. I peeked in to see if Toller would rethink his homicidal plan, give in to his better angels—hear God?—but no, now he was scourging his flesh with barbed wire. I closed the door again, feeling nauseated, then caught the end: Mary came looking for him, after which, fade-out. Love is triumphant, I guess.

If this is a "serious" portrayal of humanity's struggle with wrestling our demons and quelling the red-hot anger now freely vented on all sides (and stoked by our President), then Lord help us. But then, Schrader is not breaking new ground. The Western canon of drama and film is replete with characters tragically succumbing to dark forces. What we desperately need are stories of characters *overriding* those forces, their demons. I was sorry Schrader defaulted to the Hollywood cliché of blow-it-all-up violence.

I wonder if Schrader disdains a more pacific outcome as "sentimental." As Peter Rainier, film critic of *The Christian Science Monitor*, notes: "Many of [Schrader's] signature films, as either a screenwriter or writer-director (most conspicuously *Taxi Driver*, *Raging Bull*, and *The Last Temptation of Christ*, all directed by Martin Scorsese), involve the agonies of faith and redemption, often culminating in an act of violence that is meant to be as spiritually cleansing as it is shocking." It must be said: Violence meant to be "spiritually cleansing" has got to be the worst heresy, the very definition of oxymoron.

I realize filmmakers generally reject responsibility for any violence their work may spark in audiences, but films have become an iconic medium, with enormous cultural influence. In these tinderbox times, a film giving the cultural O.K. to, say, strap on a suicide vest to "solve" a problem is *not* helpful. (The day I saw this film, a deranged gunman shot up a newspaper in Annapolis, Maryland, killing five people.)

What remains compelling is the struggle to retain faith in God, especially for a cleric. I know clerics in real life struggling with how to address moral issues, given the general amorality and the reduced status of religion in American life. The question becomes: *How to reconsecrate*?

I think of Ingmar Bergman's film *Winter Light*, not for the cleric whose lost faith has turned him cruel, but for the sexton, the bell-ringer, who shows up despite the dwindling congregation. He claims, in a short scene toward the end that, afflicted with a "broken-down body," he has endured more pain throughout his life than Christ did on the cross. Yet he goes on. And he does not speak of doing violence to others.

—*Medium*, July 2, 2018

World Cup 2018:
An Equal-Opportunity Tonic for
an Angry and Divided World

WITH THE WORLD BECOME "seasick," as *The Guardian* put it—seasick with angry nationalism, angry pushback at immigrants and refugees, and "the little guy" angry at being invisible in a globalized world—World Cup 2018 has served up a welcome and deeply refreshing tonic. How?

As the Cup culminated in the semi-finals this week, three of the four national teams involved—France, Belgium, England—display an ethnically diverse and integrated roster that, given these countries' mono-ethnic origins, is strikingly remarkable. At a time of fierce and growing anti-immigrant fervor throughout Europe, sons of migrants who bring superior talent, hustle, and a devotion to win the World Cup for their adopted country can find a place on these national teams. *Bravo*.

And, given how hard it is to score a goal in soccer, diversity of make-up is most powerfully on display when a team *finally* puts the ball in the back of the net and the players celebrate, arms around one another, jumping up and down in collective joy. It's a sight to make the eyes brim.

In sport, where teamwork counts for absolutely everything, where mutual trust and respect among players and manager must exist at the deepest level, you look at these teams, and these collective post-goal celebrations, and think: This is what our angry world could look like—if only it worked as a team.

In the case of France, 17 of the 23-man roster in this Cup are sons of first-generation immigrants, according to Afshin Molavi, senior fellow at Johns Hopkins' Foreign Policy Institute, in a *Washington Post* op-ed citing the website Multicultural Cup. The 19-year-old "phenom" Kylian Mbappe, son of a Cameroonian father and Algerian mother, has already matched the record set by Brazilian legend Pele back in 1958—scoring two goals as a teenager at the World Cup; now, with France going to the final, he could set a new record. Samuel Umtiti (parents from Cameroon) also has scored, while Paul Pogba (Guinea) and N'Golo Kante (Mali) have proved to be vital playmakers.

The head of the anti-immigrant, right-wing National Front party, Marine Le Pen, has complained of "Les Bleus," as the team is known: "When I look at Les Bleus, I don't recognize France or myself." One wonders just how she cheers on her national team. This isn't to deny Les Bleus have not had contentious times as a multicultural team, even in the recent past, but it is to say Team 2018 is the new gold standard.

Likewise, Belgium has made its multicultural point at this Cup, most thrillingly in its Group of 16 game against Japan when, after Japan scored two quick goals at the start of the second half, Belgium fought back furiously to make three goals in 30 minutes and win. Scoring those goals were Romelu Lukaku, son of Congolese migrants, and Marouane Fellaini and Nacer Chadli, sons of Moroccan parents. Proving again to be Belgium's vital playmaker is Vincent Kompany (Congo). This "golden generation" is the beneficiary of a national program launched in the early 2000s aimed at using soccer to integrate recent migrants.

England, too, has a national team multiculturally symbolic. Midfielder Dele Alli, who scored with a stunning header against Sweden, has roots in Nigeria. Stalwarts on the team are the young and powerfully skilled players with roots in Jamaica: Marcus Rashford, Danny Rose, Raheem Sterling, Kyle Walker, and Ashley Young. (One wonders how Nigel Farage, a founder of the anti-immigrant U.K. Independence Party, or UKIP, cheers on his England team.)

Meanwhile, the world beyond the Cup grows ever angrier, more divided. Germany's chancellor Angela Merkel, heretofore the great champion of assimilating migrants into the European community, is now forced by her coalition partner to compromise on that commitment, in order to keep her government in power. Here in the U.S., we have the Trump administration's "zero tolerance" policy prosecuting illegal immigrants as criminals, which entails separating migrant families, a policy applying even to those seeking legal asylum. And recall the vulgarism used by Mr. Trump, notional president of Immigrant Nation, in his reference to African nations and Haiti.

In high contrast, for a demonstration of racial and ethnic comity, keep your highlight reel of this World Cup handy.

Apart from the multicultural symbolism, this edition of the quadrennial contest in the world's most popular sport has compelled in myriad other ways—the thrills and chills of a record number of penalty-kick shoot-outs, providing almost unbearable drama; plenty of free kicks "postage-stamped" into an upper corner of the net; and regular play that was rarely regular and often dazzling.

And, in this dehumanizing time, there are this Cup's human stories. Who can forget the Iranian goalie, Alireza Beiranvand, who began life as a shepherd, ran away from a disapproving father to Teheran, lived on the street and did odd jobs until he was accepted to a soccer club— and who, in his hour in this Cup, smothered the penalty kick of living legend Cristiano Ronaldo, lying on the ball for a long thankful moment.

And surely this Cup will be noted for all its upsets, wherein a "little guy" country routs a soccer powerhouse, forcing its early exit, as happened to defending champion Germany, as well as Portugal, Argentina, and Brazil, the latter heavily touted to win this Cup. Spain, the 2010 World Cup champion, was sent home by the host of this Cup, Russia, a team that, going into this tournament, was ranked 70th in the world.

Of course if Croatia, the fourth team in the semi-finals, beats France in the final this Sunday, this Cup will be remembered as the Cup of "the little guy." And if France wins, it will make a resounding multicultural statement underscoring that, when we all play well together, we all win. Either way, in this angry and divided world, World Cup 2018 has been excellent tonic.

Hang in there, team: Only 204 weeks to go until the next Cup.

—*Medium*, July 13, 2018

Can a Narcissist Comprehend the Meaning of Treason?

SINCE THE TRUMP-PUTIN SUMMIT in Helsinki—now dubbed the "Helsinki Humiliation," at which President Donald Trump pledged allegiance to a foreign power who means us no good (Russia), while failing to defend his own nation's intelligence agencies in their unanimous findings of that foreign power's ill will toward us (interfering in the 2016 presidential election, with every sign of doing it again)—the T-word, treason, has edged into the conversation.

Former CIA director under President Barack Obama, John Brennan, characterized Trump's Helsinki performance as "nothing short of treasonous," while Republicans, though not calling it treason, still cannot defend this debacle. Sen. John McCain calls it "one of the most disgraceful performances by an American president in memory."

But whether we are properly in the realm of treason, and thus in the realm of impeachment, may be moot until another question is addressed: *Can a narcissist even "get" the meaning of treason, can he comprehend it?*

Recall during the presidential campaign and upon Trump's election, various members of the psychology profession, while hesitant to pronounce on his psychological fitness for office without personally examining him, ventured nevertheless to describe Trump as "remarkably narcissistic," as one Harvard psychologist put it. Others in the profession generally agreed: Trump presents a case of excessive self-love.

In the year-and-a-half since, we members of the public have learned what it's like to live with a narcissist—doing so without benefit of clinical training, forced to become armchair psychologists in order to "get" our president. Half of us, those on the left, find the experience unsettling in the extreme, like being trapped on a runaway rollercoaster, with Trump in his excessive self-love knocking off every last guardrail.

Norms of American democracy: What are they to the Narcissist-in-Chief? We have seen Trump blow through just about every norm heretofore attaching to the office of President. Rather than itemizing those lost norms—like severing one's business from one's service in office, like acting as a uniter rather than divider—we might better ask: What norm has Trump left untouched? Same goes for foreign policy. We have seen Trump threaten nuclear war with North Korea ("fire and fury"); insult and undercut our closest allies; blow through international accords (Trans-Pacific trade, Paris climate, Iran nuclear); and, just prior to Helsinki, again attack NATO, the military alliance that has kept the peace for 70 years.

But then, *by definition*, a narcissist in his self-love doesn't do alliances or accords, he doesn't do norms. Nor for that matter can a narcissist truly be a public servant, because he serves only himself. This gets to the internal dynamics of a narcissist—and here I am deep into armchair psychoanalyzing, but again, what else is a concerned citizen to do?

Observing Trump in operation for 18 months now, we have seen that, in his "mind," he is never ever wrong and is always brilliantly right, in all ways he is the best and the greatest and the shrewdest, and if anyone—like the press, for example—says otherwise, he brands them "the enemy." Even when shown to be wrong, as in the combined intelligence findings of Russia's election meddling, Trump may concede a smidgen, but he couches that smidgen in such qualifying language that, *presto*, he's immediately back to his erroneous, self-serving view.

So vast is the vasty deep of Trump's self-love, and so all-consuming his need for self-justification of that vast love that, for Trump, truth of necessity gets pulled and manipulated, quickly becoming rationalization and—no other word for it—lying. Moreover, in this maw of self-justification, other things are sacrificed—things dear to the conscientious public, like...conscience. And honesty and honor and duty. And ethics and morality. In Trump there is no sense of the rightness or wrongness of things; a thing is wrong if it defies His Rightness. We might spare ourselves trying to parse Trump's method leading to any one debacle—"*What* was he thinking?"—because for Trump, it's all about self-justification.

Which is how treason may come into it. In addition to levying war against the United States, the U.S. Constitution, in Article III section 3, defines treason as "adhering" to America's foreign enemies and giving them "aid and comfort." In that Helsinki press conference, Trump may not have been consciously thinking so much as engaging in full-on self-justification—of his legitimacy as president, which legitimacy may have been aided by a foreign enemy. Thus his aiding in return, seen in his denying his own intelligence agencies' findings, and his adhering to Putin, seen in his explicitly absolving Putin of blame for election-meddling. It must also be noted that undercutting one's allies is aiding and comforting the enemy.

It may be that Vladimir Putin is as narcissistic as Trump and that the aiding and comforting and adhering may by now be going both ways, along with the mutual self-justification. (Julia Ioffe notes in *The Washington Post* that the two share a "surreal" world-view.) Finally, this bit of armchair psychoanalyzing: This excessive self-love of the narcissist does not feel much like love, actually, but more like excessive anxiety and insecurity.

It's instructive here to remember the Greek myth of Narcissus, a youth so enamored of his beautiful image that ultimately, unable to find love in another, he killed himself. We might also note that it was Nemesis who egged him on in his self-love, also that the root of the word "narcissism" is *narke*, meaning stupor.

It remains to be seen if the "Helsinki Humiliation" will be pegged, retrospectively, as an early marker on the path to Trump's downfall. But whatever transpires going forward, it's useful to bear in mind the personality (we can't speak of character) of the man: As a narcissist, Trump obeys the laws of the self, not the laws of the nation.

So: If it should come to a legal showdown over Trump's businesses, or if it should come to impeachment for treason, which is a Constitutional matter, the Narcissist-in-Chief would likely respond: What law? What Constitution?

Of course, ignorance of the law, or of the Constitution, is no defense. Buckle your seatbelts, it's going to be a bumpy ride.

—*Medium*, July 23, 2018

How to Keep a Good Marriage During Bad (Trumpian) Times

IT HAPPENED ONE night (as the famous movie is titled), at dinner. My husband and I, who rarely ever argue—our views and values line up remarkably parallel, happily—had an argument. It was, for us, a doozy, "full of sound and fury," signifying—what?

Like much else in these Trump-obsessed times and this Trump-obsessed household, it was related to our new president, You-Know-Who.

It occurred shortly after the Trump administration inaugurated its "zero-tolerance" policy on illegal immigrants, which at its most inhuman entailed separating children from their parents. The headlines were heartbreaking, so were the images, the voice recording of crying children, all of it.

The evening in question, I was going on and on about the policy's heartlessness—in truth I probably got operatic about it, but appropriately so, as it's truly tragic opera, also I had just written about it. *When did we Americans become so cruel?*

Suddenly Larry, who has a super-extra-long fuse, slammed the table with his fist. What? My husband and best friend, otherwise known to me as Sweetie, slammed the table? "Enough!" he shouted. "You talk about heartless, what about the heartlessness of 5,000 homeless children right here in our own county?" (He later wrote about the problem, too.)

Stung, but not one to back down, I instantly swung into defense. So did Larry. From there the argument escalated quickly, but where it escalated to, I can't remember—this is where the sound and fury came in. It even got to the point, far out-of-bounds, where we accused each other of being insufficiently supportive of our positions, as well as of ourselves. *Whoof.*

I'll be diplomatic and say I can't remember who called a time-out, but a time-out was called and we went to the gym, for our usual after-dinner workout.

Speed-walking faster than usual, and still shaken, I turned over in my mind: *How* did that happen, that shout-fest, and so fast? Of course first I thought of better tacks I might have taken with my argument or how, like an attorney in court, I might have inserted an "Irrelevant" into Larry's. But soon enough, about the half-mile point, I realized this: We were both expressing our agony at the general heartlessness unleashed in these tumultuous Trumpian times. Our arguing signified, not nothing as Shakespeare expressed it in *Macbeth*; we were shouting on behalf of humanity.

But we were also shouting at each other, and that was the problem. Donald Trump, amoral and disruptive—and inhuman—force that he is proving to be, had invaded not only our lives, but our marriage. *Attenzione.*

When we got home from the gym, we hashed it out, to resolution (it became a late night). In our now 41-year marriage, it has been our habit to hash out any problem before calling it a day (which is one reason we have enjoyed a long marriage). Certainly, as two people engaged in public life—Larry as a lifelong public servant (32 years in the Navy, eight years as a state legislator), me as a commentator—we cannot banish Trump from our lives and still also engage. But we *can* box him into a tight and well-regulated corner.

For one thing, we agreed, with both of us so angry at the ruination Trump is causing, we need to bring the emotional temperature *way* down in our household and take a deep breath whenever our Trump-generated gorge rises, because we absolutely cannot allow The Disrupter to spin us out of our marital equilibrium. And this is a challenge, because Trump's outrages come daily, his lies accelerating.

Which led to another point we agreed on: We need to control our Trump-obsession. Full-blown obsessives lose their acuity, creativity, subtlety—all qualities we need to combat the very real perils that Trump poses to the Republic. To be fighting fit, and to maintain our marital equilibrium as well as our physical health, we need to deflate the intensity of our Trump-obsession and redirect that energy away from our nervous systems and toward our brain centers. No more shouting at each other (although shouting in Trump's general direction is still permitted).

It's at this juncture that I recall a Russian couple we knew in the mid-1990s, when we lived in Washington, D.C. I regret to say we have lost contact with Viktor and Marita, but I remember well their marital philosophy, as Marita explained to me over coffee.

During the Communist period in the former Soviet Union, when life was full of fear and terror and economic hardship, Marita and Viktor did what many other Russian couples did: They engaged in "internal migration." That is, while the outside world was Hell, in their personal lives they created Heaven and took care of their souls—with poetry, with classical music. And they protected their marriage bond, taking extra care to treat each other with the love and respect they saw nowhere in their external life. After Communism fell in 1991, Viktor landed a science research fellowship in the U.S. and here, in our freedoms, they flourished, they could relax. But even in objectively better times, they did not relax their adherence to their marital code: No matter the state of the world, you treat your beloved as beloved.

With objectively worse times now visited on America, fomented by our nefarious president, this marital code—indeed it's a code bearing on the conduct of all kinds of personal relationships—promises sustenance and value in otherwise barren times.

"Code of conduct": Even the idea elevates. *Salud.*

—*Medium*, August 4, 2018

The Republicans and Donald Trump: A Faustian Bargain (Annotated)

ONCE UPON A time, Republicans presented themselves as the party of principle—as avatars of fiscal as well as personal responsibility, small but sound government, law and order, and, in the international community, reliable leadership of the free world.

But, no more. In the GOP's deepening alliance with our faker of a president Donald Trump, principle clearly is no longer operative—and the need to hold on to power is.

Eighteen months in, proofs of Republican betrayal abound. Most egregiously: After decades of haranguing Democrats for their spend-y ways, Trump explodes the debt and deficit with his $2 trillion tax cut to corporations and the rich, and Republicans are fine with it. Likewise, the former national security scourges are hanging back from forcing Trump to deal with documented Russian interference in our elections.

Compounding this betrayal, Republicans also once presented themselves as avatars of Christian morality, but what would Jesus think of His flock embracing a man who's a sinner in *so* many ways—racist, misogynist, xenophobe, liar, marital buccaneer? (Staunchest members of the flock, Evangelicals, rationalize their pro-Trump support by pointing to his pro-life stance and appointment of two more conservatives to the Supreme Court.)

In their comprehensive betrayal of both political principle and Christian morality, then, the GOP can now be said to be the party of the unprincipled and amoral Donald Trump. (For how, see "Frontline" documentary, "Trump's Takeover.") This also can be said: In sacrificing principle and morality for power, Republicans have made a Faustian bargain with the Devil, a notion voiced by various commentators, both conservative and liberal.

Of course, it may be that, as Democratic Congressman Raul Grijalva writes in *The Guardian*, Republicans made their Faustian bargain because, *al fondo*, they are "more interested in their help-the-rich agenda than the future of our democracy" and, thus, they are O.K. both with dismantling the social safety net that the new $2 trillion deficit justifies, as well as with Trump's "daily racism [and] constant demeaning of other people." In which case, the GOP's moral bind is even knottier—by many orders of magnitude. (And, of course, there is the primal Faustian bargain that the Founding Fathers made with the Southern states, allowing the evil institution of slavery to continue.)

As a concept, "Faustian bargain" is pretty universally understood: It means selling your soul—the best of who you are, that which you cannot do without and still be—for whatever worldly objective it is that you desire: money, power, career. People "get" that if you pay with your soul, you have paid far too much.

Curious about the source, and hoping poetry would appeal to Republicans to reform altogether, I went to Johann Wolfgang von Goethe's epic poem, *Faust* (all 486 pages of it), and Christopher Marlowe's play, *Dr. Faustus*. Like many, I knew what Faustian bargain meant, but had not read the original. I confess I was disappointed (and thus took a pass on Thomas Mann's novel, *Dr. Faustus*).

First, surprisingly, Faust puts up no moral struggle at all—none—in ceding his soul to the Devil in his quest to "have all secrets at my fingertips." Goethe's Faust even says, "With me, best leave morality alone!" In Marlowe, when the Devil asks, "And tell me, Faustus, shall I have thy soul?" Faustus a few lines later responds, "Ay, I give it thee." As bargaining goes, and certainly as moral struggle goes, it's all way too easy.

Which, come to the point, describes the remarkable ease with which Congressional Republicans, except for a few rebels like Sen. Jeff Flake, have sealed the (moral) deal with Trump.

Marlowe's Faustus, aiming explicitly to become "the great Emperor of the world," even dictates the bargain's terms, instructing the Devil what to tell Lucifer, his lord:

*"Say he surrenders up to him his soul.
So he will spare him four and twenty years,
Letting him live in all voluptuousness;
Having thee ever to attend on me;
To give me whatsoever I shall ask,
To tell me whatsoever I demand,
To slay mine enemies, and aid my friends,
And always be obedient to my will."*

Another surprise: Faust is a lecher. Marlowe's Faustus admits, "I am wanton and lascivious." When the Devil procures a slattern, Faustus sneers, "A plague on her for a hot whore!" Goethe's Faust acts even more despicably: When Mephistopheles procures the innocent Margaret for Faust ("I'll sing a few moralizing bars, / All the better to seduce her"), Faust goes on to kill her brother, yet somehow it's Margaret, now pregnant with Faust's child, who goes to prison, not he! (As the Devil says, "With the police, I'm well in: / But not so much so with the courts.") Does Faust feel remorse for his criminal act? Not at all; he's off to conjure Helen of Troy, history's most beautiful woman. The Goethe is full of misogynistic reference—"whore," "hag," "witch-bitch." (Good to know #MeToo lurks ahead on History's timeline.) Still, Margaret gets recompense: When Faust dies, soul unsaved, she steps in: "Allow me to teach him."

Yet, while neither Goethe nor Marlowe present Faust as a moral character or the bargain he struck with the Devil as a moral struggle, leaving us instead with lots of bad behavior, both works are instructive on human nature and the way of the world generally. And when things fall apart and war ensues, when all morality and ethics are gone, they are especially adept at describing a world that is, in a word, Hell on earth. Rather like our world today.

Of human nature, Goethe reflects on the human being's natural self-protectiveness: "Let them go and break their heads, / Make the mess they often do: / So long as we're safe in our beds." And human fantasy: "O, throw the dice quick, / And let me be rich! / I'll be the winner! / It's all arranged badly, / And if I had money, / I'd be a thinker." And the human tendency to aggrandizement: "[E]ach, incapable of ruling / His inner self, would gladly rule his neighbor's will." And, in times of terror like now, this human tendency: "None of us are injured though, / But we all are frightened so."

Surprisingly, the Devil offers good insights, but then, he's seen and culled all. "Use your time well: it slips away so fast." And: "How men torment themselves is all I see." And: "We grow old but who grows wiser?" And this: "Where's the moderation you should have learnt?" Goethe's Faust, when he still has his soul, speaks wisely, as the scholar he is:

"Men usually scorn the things, I've found,
That, by them, can't be understood,
Grumbling at beauty, and the good,
That to them seem wearisome."

But as the world in the Faust legend goes to ruin, with the poets vividly describing the attendant destruction and suffering, they only indirectly throw light on the policy and character that could yield peace or a better day. The poets are far bigger on damnation than on ruin-avoidance. So, Republicans: Listen up to the damning annotation.

In a word: When "partisan hatred" reigns—"scattering error instead of truth"—and, at the same time, when moral discipline weakens and "sense fails," then a would-be tyrant is empowered and "ruin comes on running feet." As Goethe's Mephistopheles exults, menacingly: "The signs are tumult, force, and what nonsense brings!"

Beware, for one, when words lose their meaning—as today, when news and fact, and truth itself, are characterized by Trump as "fake." As Goethe's Mephistopheles says:

"Where sense fails it's only necessary
To supply a word, and change the tense,
With words fine arguments can be weighted,
With words whole Systems can be created,
With words, the mind does its conceiving,
No word suffers a jot from thieving."

Mephistopheles goes on:

"*My friend, the art's both old and new,*
It's like this in every age, with two
And one, and one and two,
Scattering error instead of truth.
Men prattle, and teach it undisturbed:
Who wants to be counted with the fools?
Men always believe, when they hear words,
There must be thought behind them, too."

Beware, for another, partisan hatred. Faust says of partisan zeal's exigencies: "The law is great, but necessity's greater." And when necessity is in the saddle, Mephistopheles exults: "*That's it! They no longer feel constrained....*"

"*They quickly renew eternal strife.*
Locked in hereditary bile,
They prove themselves unreconciled:
Far and wide the noise is rife.
In the end, by all the Devils, yes!
Partisan hatred's still the best,
Till final ruin ends the tale:
Here rise the sounds of utter panic,
And others bitter and Satanic,
Terrify, along the vale."

Beware, too, ceding rights. "We've given away our rights, and hence, / No rights are left for us, not one.... / Now, who'll help his neighbor? / Each man just help himself." And beware "imperious yearning": "He followed his need, and Ilium was gone."

Moral weakening is limned by Goethe in the tale of Icarus, who flew too near the sun, melting his wax wings and causing his fall. As the Chorus intones:

> "Yet, irresistibly, you ran free,
> In nets of indiscipline: you
> Divorced yourself violently,
> From custom, and from rule."

Rule-breaking leads to chaos, evil. Alluding to the Devil's cloven feet, the Chorus goes on: "Nothing's spared! The cloven feet now / Trample on all decency!" (Goethe gibes the modern age in its willful amorality: "in modernity, / Where fools now boast about their sinful stories." He advises, "Keep living Sacredness to hand.") Among the human race, the Devil himself deems "the most shameful" to be the religious hypocrites:

> "[T]heir prayers are a worse disgrace,
> These dandies come, the hypocrites:
> They've snatched a heap of souls away,
> Use our weapons too to do it:
> They're Devils in disguise, I'd say."

Marlowe, in regard to moral weakening, unleashes the Seven Deadly Sins—Pride, Covetousness, Wrath, Envy, Gluttony, Sloth, Lechery—about which the eager-to-sin Faust says, "O, this feeds my soul!" Note especially Wrath's destabilizing effect on society, as in our own angry age: "I leapt out of a lion's mouth…and ever since I have run up and down the world…wounding myself when I had nobody to fight withal."

Once underway, momentum toward war, whether civil war or foreign, is well-nigh unstoppable, as Goethe's worldly Chancellor to the Holy Roman Emperor describes:

> "What help can human wit deliver,
> Or kindly heart, or willing hand, if fever
> Rages wildly through the state, and evil
> Itself is broodingly preparing evil?"

The Chancellor goes on:

"*Look about, from this height's extreme,*
Across the realm: it seems like some bad dream,
Where one deformity acts on another,
Where lawlessness by law is furthered,
And an age of crime is discovered."

The Chancellor concludes:

"*So all the world will slash and chop,*
Destroying just what suit themselves:
How then can that true sense develop
That shows the morally acceptable?"

Those wielding the power to rebalance the chaos, at least theoretically, instead quake or hesitate. Mephistopheles scorns the pusillanimous:

"*No one dare to criticize the situation,*
Each could, and would improve his station.
Even the smallest wished to be great enough.
But for the best it proved a step too much."

Once war comes, the byword becomes: Defend yourself. As the Emperor of the Holy Roman Empire himself notes:

"*From selfishness they learn self-preservation,*
Not honor, affection, gratitude, dedication.
No one thinks that when time brings the reckoning,
The neighbor's house ignites theirs while it is burning."

While this Emperor is benevolent, beware the would-be emperor who is not. As if speaking of Trump the Vicious Incompetent, Goethe writes: "O Power, Power, will you never, / Sense *and* Omnipotence treasure?" Elsewhere he says, *ala* Trump: "To crush the innocent one... / Is the tyrant's way to free himself of an embarrassment."

What is the counter-force? Once ruin comes running, neither Goethe nor Marlowe offer much hope. Goethe does nod to the good people: Despite ruin, "[T]he good will chance it all again. / An ounce of thanks will still please them deeply, / Outweighing tons of ingratitude completely." And, too, the good reap a "dual prize": "You show compassion, and it brings you pleasure." But this hardly reestablishes equilibrium or, crucially, "the morally acceptable." For that lofty goal, none other than Mephistopheles says, "We demand a higher art" (to which this writer says, "Amen!"). Too late, Faust understands, "We must grasp things in the highest sense." Of no help at all, especially in a crisis, are "the doubters and their acid wit."

Clearly, the solution is: Avoid the slide into Chaos in the first place or, once into it, reverse *however you can*. In Trump's America, the power to reverse the slide lies with the Republicans, who control both houses of Congress and nominally could check the proto-tyrant. Of course, in the coming midterms Democrats absolutely must retake power, galvanizing to recapture the House, if not the Senate, too.

Yet—this just in—*Politico* reports new "thinking" among Congressional Republicans, to wit: that even if Democrats retake the House in November, and even if they seek Trump's impeachment, why, that would "both rally [Trump's] base and make the president sympathetic to moderates." This "lose-to-win" gambit, which requires the Senate remain GOP-controlled, has "surfaced spontaneously among a diverse set of conservatives" and "dovetails with the growing conviction...that the president could use congressional gridlock under a Democratic House majority as a...battering ram, offering it up as the picture of Washington intransigence as he vies for reelection." And if a demonized Nancy Pelosi is reelected by Democrats as Speaker, so this "thinking" goes: Game over!

One can almost hear Mephistopheles snort with laughter and paw the ground.

To recur to Faust and to Mephistopheles' taunt that "No one dare to criticize the situation," this appeal to today's Republicans, who once upon a time were principled: Will no one dare criticize—this nefarious "plan," this proto-tyrant Donald Trump? Strength being found in numbers, will no one among Republicans dare organize an anti-Trump insurgency? Or will this all be "a step too much"?

The dire fate haunting the Faust legend need not necessarily apply to America, because, even as unhappy and disoriented as we are now, we are not fatalists, we still believe we can make our own fate. So, Republicans: Throw off the Faustian bargain—for your own soul as well as the nation's.

Finally, Republicans: If an appeal to the soul means little to you, and to the far-gone corrupt it would mean nothing, then bear in mind another verdict. As the English philosopher Francis Bacon said, "The inescapable property of Time is ever more and more to reveal the Truth." The power-hungry may not care about moral questions, but they do care, desperately, about winding up on the right side of History. Think, then, about History's final estimation of collaborators and co-conspirators throughout the annals of Time.

—*Medium*, August 18, 2018

Classic Foreign Films of Human Drama: Rx for Our Fraught Times

AFTER ENDURING OVER a year-and-a-half under the "leadership" of the anti-democratic and amoral Donald Trump, many Americans barely recognize their own country. We gape at the sight of swastikas flying on American soil, we see "compassionate conservatives" scapegoating "the other," we see truth and the law under severe assault, we mourn America surrendering the mantle of "Leader of the Free World."

By no means is America vanquished, of course. The Resistance resists, protesting all the above. Record numbers are running for elective office, regenerative movements are on the march (#MeToo, #MarchFor OurLives, #BlackLivesMatter), people are "woke" like never before. On many fronts, we are working toward a reckoning.

In this mighty struggle, contemporary culture does not help much, with its penchant for the dystopian, the pathological, the wild and crazy. In low times, why indulge in low fare? More nourishing than anti-heroes "acting out" are protagonists pursuing higher purpose, humanity at its richest—seeking freedom, justice, honor, dignity, doing the right thing, and, no small matter, being serious.

In films of the classic period—the 1930s through the 1960s—both in America and abroad, characters seeking this "upper air" seemed more abundant. Which is why, in the following listing of ten classic foreign films of human drama, major *auteurs* like Fellini, Antonioni, Visconti, Bunuel, Bergman, Kurosawa, Fassbinder, Godard, even Truffaut, go missing: They do not nourish the human heart or steel the spine. This list does. (Films of the great Italian humanists Roberto Rossellini, *Open City*, and Vittorio de Sica, *The Bicycle Thief* and *The Children Are Watching*, were reviewed earlier.) All these films (but one) are in black-and-white, which enhances the drama. There are spoilers, but that should not detract from your viewing pleasure.

A Man Escaped (France, 1956)

At a time when autocrats are being normalized and the oxymoron "illiberal democracy" is become reality, this film—of a man single-mindedly bent on escaping a Nazi prison to regain his freedom (pictured at top)—is tonic. Even though we know from the title he escapes, the drama lies in seeing how Fontaine does it, how he overcomes despair, quells fear. As he picks away at his door with a flattened spoon, he must suss out who among his fellow prisoners could give him away, who will help. Whispered communication in the communal washroom becomes theological: When a priest-prisoner assures him God will save them, Fontaine says, "He'll save us if we give Him the chance." Just as he is ready to make his break, he is assigned a cellmate: Does he enlist this man in the escape or does he kill him? It's exhilarating to see Fontaine opt for humanity and lead the two of them to freedom.

Based on the true story of French Resistance fighter Andre Devigny, director Robert Bresson, who himself was a P.O.W., relates the tale *sans ornements*—the same few spaces (mainly Fontaine's cell), the same strains of Mozart's Great Mass in C Minor, and non-professional actors, although his lead, Francois Leterrier, went on become a director himself. (His cellmate is a Matt Damon look-alike). This powerful film resonates in our moment: Acts of kindness are miracles, humanity is ultimately embraced, and, importantly, we see Fontaine grieve for his prison neighbor who was executed—a man he never met face-to-face, only exchanged messages with, tapped on the wall dividing them. Mind that metaphor, Americans.

The Grand Illusion (France, 1937)

The power of cooperation across barriers of class and ethnicity, portrayed in the story of another great escape—this time in World War I—makes this film apt now. Captain Le Boeldieu, an aristocrat (Pierre Fresnay), and lieutenants Rosenthal, a Jewish scion (Marcel Dalio), and Marechal, of the working class (French icon Jean Gabin), are captured and transported to an officers' P.O.W. camp in Germany. There, the camp commandant, von Rauffenstein (Erich von Stroheim), affects an alliance with Le Boeldieu over the prospect that, when this war is over, so is their aristocratic kind.

The question becomes: Might Le Boeldieu, out of some aristocratic code of honor, reveal that his fellow Frenchmen are building a tunnel to escape? Not at all; he sacrifices himself, taking von Rauffenstein's bullet, allowing Rosenthal and Marechal to escape. (When the German learns the escapees' identity, the *pfennig* finally drops.)

Once free but deep behind enemy lines, Rosenthal, wounded, becomes a perilous drag. Having endured so much together, it's truly shocking when Marechal turns on his comrade, calling him "dirty Jew." The rest of the film, masterfully directed by Jean Renoir, is about reconciliation (and making it into Switzerland). The point here: While the film cites various things as "illusion"—the end of the war, a wife's faithfulness—there is no illusion about the need for cooperation for survival.

However, the 1% sacrificing for the 99% remains fiction.

The Battle of Algiers (Italy, 1966)

Westerners seem still not to understand the Arab world. This film, about the efforts of the National Liberation Front (FLN) to throw off French colonial rule in Algeria, movingly portrays Arab humanity, while casting a critical eye on French tactics—and Western blindness.

After a period of increasing unrest in the Casbah, the formidable veteran of both World War II and Indochina, Lt. Col. Philippe Matthieu (Jean Martin), is sent to re-establish control. It is Matthieu's tragedy, and the West's, to see the FLN strictly as a foe to be strategically outmaneuvered. He succeeds—at first: The film begins with the last remaining FLN member at large, Ali La Pointe (Brahim Haggiag, pictured), cornered, along with a little boy who's acted as courier. The film unfolds in flashback, and we see tragedy develop and play out—both sides resorting to terrorist measures—culminating in the death of Ali and the boy. And yet, two years later, as the film tells us in an end-note, when the whole population rose up and demanded it, Algeria achieved its independence.

While America is not a colonial power, it has been an occupying power. To the extent we perceive the Arab world strategically and not as human beings seeking freedom and dignity, we will fail. The film, directed by Italian director Gillo Pontecorvo, shows the ugly face of colonialism/occupation in indelible scenes of torture, epithets of "dirty Arab." O, humanity....

(Note: Saadi Yacef, FLN leader who wrote the book on which this film is based and acted in it, later served in Algeria's Council of the Nation as a senator.)

The Apu Trilogy (India, 1955-59)

The humanity of the invisible poor is at the beating heart of this coming-of-age saga of a young Bengali boy named Apu. This trilogy, by Indian director Satyajit Ray, brilliantly portrays, amidst grinding poverty, the questing of the individual soul. In Part One, *Pather Panchali*, the young Apu discovers the world through three strong women—his mother, sister, and aunt. In Part Two, *Aparajito*, the family suffers both devastating loss—the death of the father, a dreamer—but also the promise held out by education, as young Apu proves an apt pupil. In Part Three, *Apur Sansar* (my favorite), Apu, now in his twenties, married, and aspiring to become a writer, suffers a double blow—the deaths of his mother, from whom he had grown apart, and his wife, whom he adored. After great struggle, he does the soul-work enabling him to carry on.

At the outset of filming, neither the director, the photographer, or the actors (except the one playing the aunt) had ever participated in filmmaking before. (Music is by Ravi Shankar.) When Part One, *Pather Panchali*, won the Best Human Document award at the Cannes film festival, Ray, funding generated, was inspired to create the rest of Apu's story. Today, with severe political dysfunction and ever-greater income disparity, the poor loom lower than ever. This trilogy reminds us of the humanity of the masses.

Tokyo Story (Japan, 1953)

Family relations are the focus of this film set in postwar Japan, directed by Japanese master Yasujiro Ozu. Father (Chishu Ryu) and mother (Chieko Higashiyama) journey from their small village to the big city,

Tokyo, to visit their grown children. But the children, a son who's a doctor and a daughter who's a hairdresser, are too busy to see to them. Another son, a railroad functionary, sees them briefly enroute. Left alone, the parents trudge around Tokyo, at one point wandering into an industrial zone. At a loss of what to do, the children pool their resources and send their parents to a resort, but they return early. It is the daughter-in-law Noriko (Setsuko Hara), widow of their son who was killed in the war, who emerges as the figure with true family feeling, taking time off from her job to serve as guide and, importantly, enjoying their company.

After the mother dies—she shows signs of illness on the trip—the children finally show some family feeling, attending to the rituals for the dead. But, very soon, they revert to their selfish ways, putting dibs on Mother's things, leaving for a baseball game. Once again it is the daughter-in-law who shows most tenderness, leading to a moving climax between her and her father-in-law. Acting on an observation he and his late wife made—that Noriko still venerates their late son, with a shrine to him in her apartment—the father acts to bury his son ("Forget him") and enable Noriko to remarry. The deed needed to be done—Noriko masks her sorrow with kindness—and he executes it lovingly. In sum, this is a film about a family member doing right by a beloved—something rare in contemporary cinema. Critic A.O. Scott of *The New York Times* calls it "perfect."

Late Spring (Japan, 1949)

Like *Tokyo Story* and made by the same director, Yasujiro Ozu, *Late Spring* also shows a family member doing right by a beloved. Featuring the same wonderful leads as in *Tokyo Story*, this time as father and daughter, it is the story of a widowed father, a professor,  and his 27-year-old daughter, again named Noriko. Lovely and lively, Noriko truly prefers her father's company over anybody else, and the father truly enjoys her attentions. It is Noriko's aunt who intercedes with her brother—Noriko should marry—and she has candidates. In parallel, the father concocts a story about wanting himself to remarry. Noriko is stung. The scene at a Noh performance where the father nods to his prospective bride, and the figurative daggers thrown by Noriko in the same direction, is a gem. Earlier, with a divorced colleague of her father, Noriko castigates him for remarrying a younger woman.

Finally, Noriko does meet with one of her aunt's candidates and finds him O.K.; she agrees to marriage. But in a final outing to Kyoto with her father, she makes a last plea to keep things as they are. He gently refuses, saying it's "the order of human life and history" to leave the family and marry. On her wedding day, in traditional garb, Noriko kneels to her father, thanking him for his love and care over the years, and he kneels to her. In a bar later, the father laughingly confesses to Noriko's girlfriend and confidante his ruse: "Biggest lie I ever told in my life." He returns to a quiet house, a lonely future. But he did right by his daughter. The order of human life and history.

The Browning Version (England, 1951)

Modernity does not much esteem the classics, like Greek and Latin. Certainly this is the feeling of Andrew Crocker-Harris, who's taught these subjects at a boys' school, to little enlightenment, for decades. At the open, Crocker-Harris (Michael Redgrave in a skilled recessive performance) has been let go, fired, without pension. With their pending departure, his wife Millie (Jean Kent) is in a state over how to carry on her affair with the school's science teacher, Hunter (Nigel Patrick). It has all been a failure, as Crocker-Harris confesses to his successor Gilbert: He didn't have "the knack of making myself liked," thus he failed to convey the beauty of the classics; at first his epigrams dazzled the boys, but soon he grew tiresome, not even tolerated as a joke, gaining instead

a reputation for discipline, "the Himmler of the lower fifth."

There's one boy, though, Taplow (Brian Smith): While he pities "the Crock," he also gets it about the classics. In a beautiful scene, Crocker-Harris opens up to the boy how, when he was his age, he became so excited by *The Agamemnon*, by Aeschylus, that he composed his own translation—in verse; it was, he thought, "very beautiful." But, he didn't finish the manuscript. At Taplow's urging—after palming the manuscript, he reads it and deems it superior to renowned poet Robert Browning's version ("Yours is more modern, Sir")—Crocker-Harris might now finish his epic. Earlier, in a wicked scene, at a fraught moment between Millie and lover Hunter, Taplow outlines to Hunter, a man of science not familiar with the classics, *The Agamemnon*: Woman kills her husband, she has a lover—"Bloody good plot, Sir!" In our Brass Age, this richly human film, directed by Anthony Asquith and written by playwright Terence Rattigan, translates well.

The Winslow Boy (England, 1948)

Based on a true story from the early 20th century, this film is about a 12-year-old boy, Ronnie Winslow, who, as a cadet at the Royal Naval College, is expelled for allegedly stealing a postal order worth a small sum. His family believes in his innocence and, after a rough grill-

ing of the boy that nearly puts the family off, so does his lawyer (Robert Donat)—"The boy is plainly innocent." The first hurdle to clearing the family name is the law: Until this precedent-setting case, citizens could not sue the King. The lawyer, the famous Sir Robert Morton, forces a debate in Parliament and wins, gaining the historic "right to petition." Then to trial, where he also succeeds.

More than court drama, this film is about the sacrifices the family and lawyer make to establish the boy's innocence. His father Arthur (Cedric Hardwicke) sacrifices his health and, newly retired as a banker, the family's not-large savings, causing a strain with his wife. Sister Catherine (Margaret Leighton) loses her fiancé, whose father is shocked at the Winslows' disloyalty to King. And Sir Robert: A snob in manner, he is a demon not only for justice, but, better, for right: "Let right be done." He sacrifices appointment as Lord Chief Justice. Not all is sacrifice, though: The struggle brings Sir Robert and Catherine together (their last exchange is golden). This film is another collaboration of Anthony Asquith and Terence Rattigan, so good on human drama. And good for our law-bending time is the banner motto, "Let right be done."

I Know Where I'm Going! (England, 1945)

With a title that shouts emphatic intent, complete with exclamation point, you know the hero is in for comeuppance. In this film featuring (refreshingly) a heroine, introduced as headstrong child, teen, then adult, Joan Webster announces to her father that she's engaged to the

head of the company she works for, Consolidated Chemical Industries, and is heading to the Hebrides, off the coast of Scotland, to marry him. Father protests that her fiancé is as old as he is, but, no matter, she's off.

In her quest, though, Joan meets nothing but obstacles—bad weather, missed connections, and a young Naval officer home on leave from the war (World War II), Torquil MacNeil. Torquil is immediately taken with Joan, but Joan doubles down on her quest—and nearly gets them killed when she insists a young seaman take her over to the island in a gale (Torquil jumps into the boat at the last minute). Back on land, Joan gets a tongue-lashing from the young girl who loves the seaman, thus beginning her humanization, also new sight: She recognizes Torquil as true love. Played with real feeling by Wendy Hiller and Roger Livesey, this film, directed by Michael Powell and Emeric Pressberger, speaks to our turbulent times: You may be knocked off your stated course, but you just may find something better instead.

Vanya On 42nd Street (France, 1994)

Technically, this film might be considered American—it's in English, set in New York, with an American cast—but the director Louis Malle is French and the material is Russian, Anton Chekhov's play, Uncle Vanya. The only film in color in this listing, it is included mainly for Sonya's benediction at the end—a benediction sorely needed by all characters, and perhaps us, too.

Vanya (Wallace Shawn), an educated man, toils as overseer of a large estate for its owner, a professor he hates for his pedantry. Astrov (Larry Pine) is an overworked doctor, who also tends his forests; a proto-environmentalist, he's trying to counter society's ravaging of the land. Yelena (Julianne Moore), married to the professor, is beautiful, but idle and bored. And there's Sonya (Brooke Smith, pictured), her uncle Vanya's niece, and the glue that keeps the estate and household going. But, like all the principal characters, Sonya is unhappy: She loves Astrov, who doesn't even know she exists. Meanwhile Astrov and Vanya are both in love with the beautiful Yelena, who doesn't really know what she wants.

This film, set in a once-grand theatre, opens with the cast arriving, then seamlessly carries us into the play (staging is by theatre director Andre Gregory). A tale of failed ambition and unrequited love, this eminently human story speaks for all time. As does Sonya's benediction—"All we can do is live": that our part in this life is to do our work and do our duty, with the assurance that, in the beyond, "We shall rest." We Americans still somehow believe that, even in dark times, we can do better than rest, we can be happy in this life. Let's take Sonya's benediction, for good measure, and run with it.

—*Medium*, September 18, 2018

Is America Having a Breakdown or a Reckoning?
7 Arguments for Reckoning

COMING UP ON the two-year mark of Donald Trump's audacious attempt at turning America into an autocracy—strongman rule, stoked by white supremacist demagoguery and disdain for the law and democratic norms—at this milepost it's the thing to take the national temperature. This time we might ask: How are we doing in this strange new world of established liberal democracies turning illiberal?

The commentariat has intensified its examination. *The Atlantic* devotes its October issue to the question "Is Democracy Dying?" with articles ranging from "Building an Autocracy" to "The Threat of Tribalism" to "A House Still Divided" to "Warning from Europe: The Worst is Yet to Come." A two-year span being a decent runway for book authors, books on democracy's fragility are coming out pell-mell, with the title of historian Robert Kagan's new book being illustrative—*The Jungle Grows Back*.

While I don't disagree with any of the dire diagnosis offered by the commentariat, I wonder if something is missing from the ensuing dire prognosis, which predicts, in brief, imminent national breakdown. In other words, as the Italians say, *E vero, ma non troppo*—It's true, but not too true. I wonder if signs of resilience and strength and creativity in the body politic are being overlooked, scanted. America is in deep trouble, yes, but not necessarily doomed.

For I would argue that, amidst all the wild churn in Trump's America and the fear that things are flying apart, there is also, in many spheres and many profound ways, a grand process of reckoning going on. By reckoning, I mean not just coping or finding ballast; I mean addressing elemental and long-besetting problems head-on, coming to grips with and coming to terms with, at long last—"fronting" them, to use early American thinker Ralph Waldo Emerson's term. And, importantly, much of this reckoning is being forced from below—from the people—not from above. All this reckoning bodes well for a New Day in America, as discussed along the way.

So, in the breakdown-vs.-reckoning debate, seven arguments for reckoning:

One: RECORD ELECTORAL PARTICIPATION

Both in voting and, even more impressively, running for elective office, participation rates are off the charts, especially among Democrats. A recent Brookings Institution study cites Trump as the direct incentive for greater Democratic enthusiasm about voting: 67%, "the largest share in recent history," versus 42% at this point in 2010 and, in 2014, just 36%. And record numbers of concerned citizens are running for office—especially women: First they marched, protesting Trump's misogyny, now they are running in unprecedented numbers for offices national, state, and local, in what *Time* calls "a grassroots movement that could change America."

Further, civic start-ups like Indivisible and Swing Left that mobilize voters and candidates have taken deep root all across America.

How is this a reckoning? Given that democracy is government by and for the *demos*—the people—these participation rates show that the American people, the ultimate stakeholders, are mobilized both to defend our embattled democracy and repair the damage done by Trump and the Republicans. The *demos* is on the case.

Two: REGENERATIVE CIVIC MOVEMENTS

Born out of festering crises, major civic movements have emerged that are more than protest movements, they are regenerative—grappling with historic problems and, finally, pressing for repair. #BlackLivesMatter, born in the aftermath of yet another killing of a young black man (Trayvon Martin), is forcing a reckoning of our abiding racism, reaching back to America's Original Sin, slavery. #MeToo, born of women's revulsion at a critical mass of reported injury by powerful men—alleged sexual assault, trauma, damaged careers—is forcing a reckoning of many accused. #MarchForOurLives, galvanized by young people in the aftermath of yet another mass shooting, is forcing a reckoning on America's gun violence. Young people are also galvanizing around climate change.

How a reckoning? Another win for the *demos*: Finally, America, galvanizing at the grassroots and across ethnicities, is reckoning with long-besetting problems. With better equity between whites and blacks, women and men, and sanity on guns, we will be a better America. Without using moral language, these movements are declaring, powerfully, that racism, sexism, gun violence are *wrong*. Which leads to:

Three: MORAL REAWAKENING

In the post-World War II period, America relaxed its moral standards. Wishing to be less judgmental than their Greatest Generation parents, the boomers disdained moral language and judgment, which made for lots of personal freedom but also, with the unleashing of pornography, profanity, the anti-hero, and an "anything-goes" ethos, a degraded culture. It's no surprise, then, that ultimately this "Breaking Bad" culture got its amoral president. At the same time, traditional moral bastions like the church, notably the Catholic church with its massive sexual abuse of children, lost sway. But: This doesn't mean moral questions go away; they *must* be addressed—or else: Great nations fall because of moral abuse (corruption, decadence). The civic movements cited above, again without using moral language, are treating racism, sexism, and gun violence as *moral* issues, as *wrong*. Same with the massive public outcry over Trump's policy of separating migrant children from their families: It's *wrong*.

How a reckoning? Unlike a theocracy, a democracy must itself address the rightness and wrongness of things, lest we abuse and destroy our freedoms. This capacity is crucial for a superpower like America. Belatedly, after decades of foreswearing moral judgment, Americans now see the need for it in our civic affairs; it remains to be seen how we wield it in the world, especially the handling of power.

Four: INSTITUTIONAL STRENGTH

Granted, institutional strength is the weakest argument for reckoning (and could as easily be cited as breakdown). And yet, and yet: On the legislative side, while the Congress is rightfully reviled as near-dysfunctional, still, as noted above, witness the record numbers running for seats there. In the coming midterms Democrats, who unlike Republicans actually believe in government, are likely to retake the House. Also cheering: the enhanced role of states and cities, who on various fronts—immigration, climate change—have stepped up where the federal government has folded. As for the executive: If Trump achieves little else, he's shown the presidency still retains huge sway at home and in the world. And the judiciary: The courts—and, vitally, and despite Trump's disdain for it, the law—still function (see: the ongoing investigation by special counsel Robert Mueller, conviction of Trump fixer Paul Manafort, guilty plea of Trump lawyer Michael Cohen, charging of white supremacists in the Charlottesville showdown).

How a reckoning? Instead of collapse, our institutional infrastructure continues to meet its minimum basic requirement, as bulwark. Ongoing test: the Senate confirmation process of Supreme Court nominee Brett Kavanaugh, where #MeToo meets male privilege, a revolutionary spectacle the whole nation is raptly tracking. Another test: Congress has yet to reckon with Russia's meddling in our elections.

Five: ROBUST ECONOMY

Fortunately, this is the gift that keeps on producing: an economy that the Federal Reserve chair calls "almost too good to be true"—record low unemployment, wages finally inching up, stock market that won't quit, little sign of inflation. The American economy remains a behemoth—a testament to corporate strength, entrepreneurial success, Americans' hard work. And so far Trump's tariff wars have not impacted American trade. Yet serious imbalances remain: the ever-widening income gap, Trump's $1.5 trillion tax cut to the rich (with another cut promised), the growing role of money in politics. And those "hard-working Americans"?: Too many work two jobs just to survive. The growing gig economy provides workers few benefits and no job security. Given that globalization is here to stay, better responses than Trump's demonization of immigrants must be found to enable American workers to compete.

Here, a reckoning needs to happen: Fortunately, the economy is so robust that these serious imbalances could be recalibrated. It requires the will—a moral reckoning—to launch. It didn't happen after the 2008 crash (as I wrote in my 2009 commentary, "Recovery Without a Reckoning"); will it now? And note: The lack of reckoning in '09 could still hurt us: If Republicans in their deregulating zeal allow Wall Street to revert to its wildly risky ways, and if Wall Street crashes the world economy again, as it did in '08, the world will not forgive us, nor should it. The world will reckon with America. Where is our Wall Street visionary?

Six: A GOLDEN AGE FOR NEWS MEDIA

Autocrats always attempt to shut down the media, so as to exercise power without scrutiny. Since Trump cannot legally shut us down, he devalues us, denigrates us as "fake" and "the enemy of the American people." But: Recognizing the reputational stakes in play—"existential threat" truly applies here—American media by and large has not only buckled up, it has upped its game. Day-to-day reporting and analysis of Trump's hodgepodge policymaking and financial chicanery must be exceedingly challenging—Trump can contradict himself within minutes—but the media has produced. Especially noteworthy, and necessary: investigative reporting, with its in-depth look, often taking months of reporting, examining everything from Russian election meddling, to alleged collusion between the Trump campaign and Russia, to documenting the sexual misconduct driving #MeToo, and more. Standouts are *The New York Times, The Washington Post, ProPublica,* and PBS' *NewsHour* and *Frontline.*

How a reckoning? Thomas Jefferson got it wrong when he said, if pressed whether he'd have a government without newspapers or newspapers without a government, he'd take the latter. We need both, of course. In a democracy, the model of self-governance, the *demos* must be informed. Under existential threat, American media is proving itself the best ally American democracy has (while Trump is the real enemy). And, under existential threat, some of the *demos* have come to love truth even more.

Seven: COMPARED TO THE ROMAN EMPIRE....

Contrast is often made between America in its present chaos and the Roman Empire, the decline and fall of. Awareness of this peril for America has penetrated throughout the public; the *demos* is worried, anxious. As history's longest-running democracy, we are still writing our script, working our way through crisis. But can ancient Rome, while never a democracy, instruct? Two takeaways from Cambridge classics scholar Mary Beard's new book—*SPQR: A History of Ancient Rome*—offer insight:

One, a moral note: Once Rome had conquered its neighbors and lost an enemy, the seeds of collapse were planted. As the poet Virgil wrote, without significant external threat, "the path of virtue was abandoned for that of corruption." Today's analogy: America, after vanquishing its nemesis the Soviet Union and winning the Cold War, felt unconstrained to accelerate its "anything-goes" ethos. But: Morally speaking, not everything should go, as we are belatedly recognizing.

Two, a civic note: Early on, when Rome was a Republic, the *plebeians,* the citizens (males only), demanded recognition of their free status, their right to vote, and their right to representation: One of the two governing consuls, they insisted, must be plebeian. After all, as Beard writes, "Why fight in Rome's wars...when all the profits of their service lined patrician pockets?" This state of affairs—"one of the most radical and coherent manifestos of popular power and liberty" in the ancient world—endured until Rome became an empire, when increasingly powerful emperors ruled for life, civil wars became constant, violence became an accepted political tool. It was not a good sign when Emperor Augustus turned voting halls into gladiatorial spaces. In this devolution, the plebs could not maintain their rights.

American plebs will see the analogy. Happily, we are in a far stronger position than our Roman counterparts. Reckoning is in our own hands: Vote! Run for office! Hold that line! And beware the autocrat in our midst.

—*Medium,* October 4, 2018

Defending Democracy, Democrats Go High, Republicans Go Ever Lower

OUR FALTERING DEMOCRACY got a much-needed boost—finally.

If the recent midterm elections make anything clear, it's this: The Democrats are about reforming American democracy, while Donald Trump and the Republicans are about *deforming* it further.

And if the media paid less attention to Trump's tweets and other assorted outrages, people could get properly excited at the former and properly concerned at the latter.

In recapturing the House of Representatives and doing it resoundingly—winning 40 seats when 23 were needed—Democrats can now do what spineless Republicans did not these last two years: Democrats can serve as a badly-needed brake on the proto-autocrat in the White House and his audacious onslaught on American democracy.

"Democracy reform"—strengthening our democratic institutions—is the stated top priority of House Democrats when they retake power January 3 and make good on their campaign theme of "For the People." Nancy Pelosi, probable Speaker, in an op-ed in *The Washington Post* co-authored with Rep. John Sarbanes, speaks of the election as a "vote to rescue our broken democracy"—with a "bold reform package to restore the promise of our democracy—a government of, by and for the people."

House Resolution 1, that is, H.R. 1—symbolically numbered to highlight the priority that Democrats place on its anti-corruption, pro-reform measures—focuses on three main areas: campaign finance, voting rights, and ethics—key components of a sound democratic system.

The campaign finance reform part aims at undoing *Citizens United*, the Supreme Court's misguided and deeply unpopular ruling which gives corporations a blank check to influence elections. (Repeat: It aims at undoing *Citizens United*—cue the excitement.) H.R. 1 would amplify the power of small-value donations: Every dollar donated would be matched, perhaps 6 to 1, by public funds if candidates submitted to the small-donor program. Says *The Washington Post* editorial board, this would be "the biggest push to fight money in politics since the early 2000s, finally adapting the nation's rules to the reality ushered in by... *Citizens United*.... The origins of the dark money sloshing around the political system would have to be disclosed."

The voting rights part would seek to undo the Supreme Court's equally misguided ruling gutting the Voting Rights Act of 1965, which ruling placed undue restrictions on minority communities. (Cue more excitement.) H.R. 1 would seek automatic voter registration (unless individuals opt out) and take away redistricting power—gerrymandering—from state legislatures and give it to independent commissions. The *Post* editorial urges bolstering election security "well before the 2020 election": "Congress has wide authority over how states conduct federal elections. It can require much more than it now does."

As to the ethics part of H.R. 1, this administration presents such a target-rich environment, where to start? Must items: Future presidents will be required to disclose their income tax returns, members of Congress cannot use taxpayer money to settle sexual harassment cases. Importantly, the Office of Government Ethics will be revived. And various Congressional committees can launch investigations—into Trump's finances, foreign payments to Trump's D.C. hotel, separating migrant children from parents, Russian election meddling, etc. Crucially, the Mueller investigation will be protected. Senate majority leader Mitch McConnell calls all this new attention "presidential harassment," but in truth House Democrats will be exercising their oversight of the executive as required by the Constitution.

Republicans of course will note that this House bill (and related bills) will go nowhere in a GOP-controlled Senate. But the point is: Democracy reform wins with just about every voting group and forcing Republicans to vote against it, again and again—well, being anti-democracy reform will not be a good look in the 2020 presidential campaign. As *Vox* says, democracy reform is both "good policy and smart politics." (Wisely, there is little talk among Congressional Democrats of impeachment.)

In addition to rescuing democracy, Democrats vow to stop GOP assaults on Medicare, Medicaid, and the Affordable Care Act (specifically, protecting people with pre-existing conditions and bringing down prescription drug prices). Democrats also vow to rebuild the nation's infrastructure, meaning: good-paying jobs.

Also enhancing American democracy: the greater diversity that Democrats bring to this Congress—a record number of women, our first Muslim-American women, our first Native American women. The "people's house" now looks more like the people.

Meanwhile, in other news that should be much bigger than it is: Republicans are engaging in astonishing anti-democratic maneuvers in the states since losing big on Election Day.

Namely: In Wisconsin the legislature, which will remain Republican-controlled in the coming session, has passed lame-duck legislation stripping powers from both the incoming Democratic governor, Tony Evers, and the Democratic attorney general. Scott Walker, the two-term Republican who lost to Evers, signed the legislation Dec. 14. The left-leaning American Constitution Society decries the move as a "state political coup."

In Michigan, the Republican-controlled legislature is attempting to do the same—strip powers—from its incoming Democratic governor, Gretchen Whitmer, and Democratic attorney general, though at this writing it has not succeeded—yet. In both Wisconsin and Michigan, the public turned out in massive protests at the capitol. In Wisconsin, the Governor-elect vows to fight back in the courts.

Shakespeare had a word for this maneuver: usurpation of power. What would George Washington say, who as our first president exemplified the peaceful transfer of power? (Myself, I would say: Beware of weasels during lame-duck sessions.)

Media attention to these anti-democratic maneuvers has been minimal. As *Media Matters* rightly points out, even the venerated *New York Times* missed their significance with its original headline, "Wisconsin Republicans 'Stand Like Bedrock' in Face of Democratic Wins." The *Guardian* headline gets it better: "This Is Not Democracy."

And what about the ongoing snafu in North Carolina, with the GOP's alleged mishandling of absentee ballots…?

Credit Senate Republicans for growing some vertebrae in the spine for joining Democrats in unanimously opposing Trump on the Saudi war in Yemen. Let's see Republicans now address their party's drift toward autocracy.

American democracy is under siege from within. In response, Democrats are going high, with democracy reform, while Republicans, a party *in extremis*, continue to deform it. Courage, Democrats: America is not in breakdown, but in a reckoning. Carry on.

—*Medium*, December 1, 2018

Inaction on the Ghastly Jamal Khashoggi Killing Gives Autocrats What They Crave: Impunity

IF HUMAN RIGHTS SEEM A nebulous and nice-to-have ideal, then the murder and dismemberment of the Saudi journalist Jamal Khashoggi by Saudi government operatives while on foreign soil—and the ensuing firestorm in the international media—has helped the world understand how crucial the rights of the individual human being are in the face of state power bent to malevolent purposes.

On October 2, Mr. Khashoggi—a Saudi national living in the U.S. and writing opinion columns for *The Washington Post* critical of the current Saudi government—disappeared in the Saudi consulate in Istanbul, Turkey, where he had gone to pick up documents finalizing his divorce that would enable him to marry his Turkish fiancée.

Perhaps it's this mundane errand on a to-do list—a human being just going about his normal business, as is his natural human right—reinforced by the endless loop of camera footage showing Mr. Khashoggi crossing the sidewalk to enter the consulate—and to meet his death—that has seized the world's attention and resonated.

And yet: Over 100 days later, little action has been taken by the world's institutions against Saudi Arabia for this outrage inflicted on an innocent human being.

At a time when autocrats around the world are increasing in number and power and audacity, when erstwhile democracies are turning illiberal under strongman rule, it is deeply unnerving to witness this elemental weapon in an autocrat's arsenal—impunity—be moved into place.

Unless forestalled, soon autocrats can literally get away with (state) murder.

Sadly, the United States of America, once upon a time the Leader of the Free World and chief promoter of human rights on the international stage, has gone missing at this crucial juncture. President Donald Trump, a moral midget, takes a transactional view, insisting U.S. arms deals not be sacrificed for a killing allegedly ordered by his autocratic Saudi peer, Mohammed bin Salman (MBS)—"Maybe he did and maybe he didn't!" Of course, Mr. Trump exhibits certain autocratic tendencies himself, referring to "my generals" and demanding loyalty, not independence, from "my" Attorney General. Meanwhile, "his" intelligence apparatus confirms MBS ordered the killing.

Also unedifying to witness: Another autocrat, Turkey's Recep Tayyip Erdogan, metering out details of Mr. Khashoggi's grisly killing, details acquired from his own omnipresent intelligence apparatus, and sharing them with the world, not for any humane purpose—Erdogan regularly jails his political critics and dissident journalists—but for geopolitical leverage in the region.

Human rights were declared sacred in the aftermath of World War II—a historic response to a half-century of bloody warfare and to millennia of ill treatment of the masses by their rulers. Established shortly after the United Nations itself was established, the Universal Declaration of Human Rights (spearheaded by Eleanor Roosevelt) affirms in its preamble *"the dignity and worth of the human person"* and, centrally, the right to freedom of speech and belief. Various articles enumerate various human rights: to "life, liberty and security of person"; to "freedom of opinion and expression"; not to be tortured or held in slavery or subject to arbitrary arrest; to equal protection before the law; presumption of innocence until proven guilty; freedom of movement within any state—all rights belonging to Mr. Khashoggi that were violently violated, including the right to marry and found a family. Other articles enumerate the right to an education, to work, to "social security."

The ideal forum for action on the Khashoggi case would be the United Nations itself, of course. Asked about the need for an international inquiry, the head of the U.N.'s High Commission on Human Rights, Michelle Bachelet (former president of Chile), stated: "I do believe it is really needed in terms of ensuring what really happened and who are the [people] responsible for that awful killing." Would that there were more determination expressed to launch said inquiry. This was early December; meanwhile, the world waits. Others call for the U.N. Security Council to set up a special international tribunal. As *The Guardian* argues, justice for this barbaric act "means, inevitably, a trial."

Human rights organizations are in the forefront demanding a full accounting on the Khashoggi case, including, in the U.S., Human Rights Watch (see its report, "Reversing Autocrats' Attacks on Rights") and Human Rights First. It is a shock to see, in these organizations' country reports, the United States cited for human rights violations along with the likes of Russia and China. Human Rights First castigates U.S. Secretary of State Mike Pompeo's recent "New Beginning" speech as a "return to unconditional support for repression."

As to freedom of speech and opinion, the killing of Mr. Khashoggi has stirred deep unease in his fellow journalists around the world, especially those living outside their country. Autocrats, brooking no criticism, label dissident journalists as "the enemy of the people." Recognizing this newly dangerous global environment, *Time* magazine named journalists, including notably Mr. Khashoggi, as "Person of the Year" for 2018, calling them "guardians of the truth." The U.N. has characterized the political incitement to violence against journalists as "toxic": Incredibly, between 2006 and 2017, one journalist was killed every four days somewhere in the world. The U.N. urges member states to take firm steps to reverse and resist "the appalling trend of impunity."

Impunity—the freedom of autocrats to engage in state-sponsored murder and other mayhem to silence their critics—would be catastrophic for human rights, writ both large and small. Jamal Khashoggi, dissident journalist and patriot, was on a mundane errand when he disappeared forever. If he could, he would protest every abrogation of his human rights manifested in his own murder, just as he'd long been doing. His final column for *The Washington Post*, published posthumously, was titled "What the Arab World Needs Most is Free Expression."

—*Medium*, January 21, 2019

Books for Our Times:
The Jungle Grows Back: America and Our Imperiled World, by Robert Kagan

First in a series for Medium, Books for Our Times

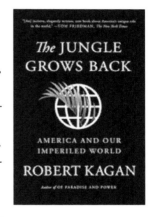

A QUICK THOUGHT EXPERIMENT: Picture a jungle. This is how we might imagine five thousand years of human history—a time of war, tyranny, and poverty. Now picture, within that jungle, a garden. This is how we might imagine the seventy years of post–World War II history—a bubble in time in which a liberal world order has dominated. Today, with that liberal world order weakening, the jungle threatens to grow back and extinguish the garden.

This is the thematic metaphor driving Robert Kagan in his latest book, *The Jungle Grows Back: America and Our Imperiled World*. His metaphor works in all ways: It aptly underscores the historical abnormality and precious value of a liberal world order—an order in which democracy reigns, contrasted to strongman rule and abuse. The metaphor also underscores the peril posed to that order, not only by the recrudescence of strongman rule around the world, but by the retreat of the garden's guarantor—America—which Kagan deems the truly indispensable nation.

For those Americans anxious about today's bigger picture—who understand that it makes a world of difference *what kind of power* is dominant in the world—this cogent 163-page book is a useful argument. Kagan, a conservative at the liberal think tank, the Brookings Institution, in this book and in regular columns for *The Washington Post*, views Donald Trump and other anti-democratic rulers as both peril and symptom of late-breaking problems in the garden.

Kagan opens the book expounding on the liberal world order's anomaly and value:

> *"The American-led liberal world order was never a natural phenomenon. It was not the culmination of evolutionary processes across the millennia or the inevitable fulfillment of universal human desires. The past seven-plus decades of relatively free trade, growing respect for individual rights, and relatively peaceful cooperation among nations—the core elements of the liberal order—have been a great historical aberration. Until 1945 the story of humankind going back thousands of years was a long tale of war, tyranny, and poverty. Moments of peace were fleeting, democracy so rare as to seem almost accidental, and prosperity the luxury of the powerful few. Our own era has not lacked its horrors, its genocides, its oppressions, its barbarisms. Yet by historical standards, including the standards of the recent past, it has been a relative paradise."*

Briskly, Kagan then describes the bubble most of his readers live in, wherein we take this liberal world order for granted: "We see all its flaws and wish it could be better, but it doesn't occur to us that the more likely alternative to it would be much, much worse." He gives historical context: "As children of the Enlightenment, we believe the expansion of knowledge and material progress goes hand in hand with improvements in human behavior and moral progress. From Montesquieu and Kant we learned that commerce tames the souls of men and nations, reducing conflict and increasing harmony and cooperation." There's more on the Enlightenment's advances, an iteration Kagan leavens with the indisputable observation that, as to human behavior, there has been, alas, "no lasting improvement." Elsewhere he comments on "the overall incompetence endemic to all human activity." In other words, it's the ideological framework, stupid, that has saved us.

The guarantor of this anomalous framework—America—is itself anomalous among nations. Speaking of the postwar establishment of this liberal world order, and threading his way through some international relations-speak (this reviewer majored in IR)—"It has been the product of a unique set of circumstances contingent on a particular set of historical outcomes, including on the battlefield"—Kagan sets the scene for the leading player, the American superpower:

> "[The liberal world order] has been, above all, the by-product of a new configuration of power in the international system, the rise to preeminence of a new player on the international scene with a unique and advantageous geography, a large and productive population, unprecedented economic and military power, and, as it happened, a national ideology based on the liberal principles of the Enlightenment."

Kagan goes on: "The present world order has favored liberalism, democracy, and capitalism not only because they are right and better... but because the most powerful nation in the world since 1945 has been a liberal democratic capitalist nation." In this, Kagan rightly connects the "right and better," the moral *raison d'etre*, with the imperative that it must be backed with sufficient power, both military and economic.

With this scene-setting, Kagan then poses the peril—"The jungle is growing back"—namely, the "authoritarianism surviving if not thriving" around the globe, including notably in Russia (Vladimir Putin) and China (all-powerful leader Xi Jinping now qualifies as "emperor," says Kagan). Would-be dictators elsewhere boast of their illiberalism. Adaptation is the autocrat's forte: "Where once we believed economic success must eventually require political liberalization, we now see autocracies successfully practicing a state capitalism compatible with regressive government."

Shockingly, sadly, the United States is now included in this litany of bad actors. As Kagan writes, "a Counter-Enlightenment of surprising potency stirs in Moscow, Budapest, Beijing, Tehran, and Cairo, in parts of Western Europe, and even in the nation that saved liberalism seventy-five years ago." This radical shift, of course, was signaled with the 2016 election of the anti-democratic Donald J. Trump.

Importantly, Kagan shows that this radical shift was prepared for by the American public itself, in its growing skepticism to America serving as the world's policeman. It's this radical loss of faith in the liberal world order that Kagan most regrets—"a profound skepticism about the liberal order's durability and even its desirability." Looking back at recent history, he writes:

> "An increasing number on both the left and the right have come to regard the struggle to uphold the order as either hopeless or mistaken. Self-described 'realists' insist that Americans must learn to accept the world as it is, not as we would wish it to be. Decrying the 'failures and follies' of the past quarter century—the wars in Iraq and Afghanistan, the interventions of the 1990s, the expansion of NATO, which they regard as a mistake, and the broader effort to support democracy in allegedly inhospitable places— they call for a new policy of 'restraint.' American policies in support of a liberal world order have not only overtaxed and exhausted Americans, they argue, but have done no good for them or for others."

Going on, Kagan notes it was President Barack Obama who argued it was "time to focus on nation building here at home" when he announced a draw-down of troops in Afghanistan. In fact, the 2016 election was "the fourth presidential contest since the race between George W. Bush and Al Gore in 2000 in which the candidate promising to pursue a narrower definition of American interests and to reduce American involvement overseas" prevailed over candidates who stood for a more expansive foreign policy.

Thus the table was set for America's retrenchment—and for Donald Trump, who persuaded persuadable voters "that the liberal order was a bad deal and it was time to put 'America first.'" Kagan cites broad agreement: "In 2016, 57 percent of Americans polled believed the U.S. should 'mind its own business' and let the rest of the world manage its own problems, up from just 30 percent a decade and a half earlier." Kagan can sympathize, saying it is a mistake to call this view "isolationist":

> "What most critics and skeptics...want is for the United States to act more like a normal nation. And it is true that for more than seven decades the United States has not been acting like a 'normal' country. No nation in history has ever been more deeply involved in the affairs of the world nor accepted more responsibility for the state of humankind than the United States since the Second World War. Very few nations in history have ever felt any responsibility for anything but themselves. The vast majority of nations do not think twice about looking after their own narrow interests 'first.' Americans have been abnormal in this respect—abnormal in their willingness to shoulder great moral and material burdens in order to preserve this abnormal liberal order."

And yet, and yet, with America's retreat, Kagan shudders at the prospect of the jungle growing back, with its spheres of interest historically producing endless war and tyranny. He looks about and laments, "There is no call to action to reverse the trends."

With this book Kagan has issued that call to action, hoping to reverse the current "excessive pessimism"; he calls his own views pessimistic but not fatalistic. Skeptics and "realists" who doubt the value of the liberal world order would benefit from Kagan's primer. This review reflects only the book's first chapter, where Kagan lays out his argument in full. The rest of the book develops all the points cited: the jungle and its warring spheres of interest; WWI; the "derangement" of the international economy in the 1920s and '30s; WWII and the establishment of the postwar liberal order, with a chapter on the "steep price" to Americans for that order; the Cold War and America's missteps since "winning" it.

Finally, two notes Kagan makes may point the way forward in this dark time. Both relate to the work of the architects of the post-World War II liberal order—Franklin Roosevelt, Dean Acheson, George Marshall, George

Kennan, Harry Truman.

One: These architects, Kagan notes, were likewise realists, who, having survived two horrific world wars, held a dim view of history and human nature. Notwithstanding the establishment of the United Nations and the spirit of cooperation it promoted, these architects continued to view the world as an international jungle, wherein, Kagan writes, "such security as was possible...could be preserved only by meeting power with greater power." In fact during the war, in 1943, FDR stated that if America did not "pull the fangs of the predatory animals of this world," they would "multiply and grow in strength" and would "be at our throats again once more in a short generation." It is a view—the international sphere as raw power politics—that Americans do not often consider. Not that the jungle cares.

Two: Kennan's theory of containment, which ultimately proved successful, not only called for containing our erstwhile wartime ally, the Soviet Union, from acting on its expansionist tendencies in the postwar era. It also called for protecting and strengthening the liberal order itself. Even if our nemesis were contained, Kennan argued, everything still depends on the "health and vigor of our own society." To cope with "the responsibilities of a World Power" (those capitals are Kennan's), he believed America needed to demonstrate a "spiritual vitality capable of holding its own among the major ideological currents of the time." Kagan writes:

> *"Americans should be grateful for the challenge, Kennan believed, for it required 'pulling themselves together and accepting the responsibilities of moral and political leadership that history plainly intended them to bear.' It is a measure of how America has changed that such sentiments, if uttered today, would be greeted by snorts of derision by the realists of our time, by utopian determinists, and by those on the right and left who reject the very idea of responsibility and moral leadership."*

This reviewer, a liberal who protests current liberalism's irresponsibility and licentiousness, could not agree more.

My fellow Americans: Mind the jungle.

—*Medium*, February 28, 2019

Plays for Our Times:
A Doll's House, Part 2,
by Lucas Hnath

First in a series for Medium, Plays for Our Times
For series introduction in HuffPost, please see p. 187.

RETHINKING A CLASSIC work of art is like rethinking your own DNA: It's not easily done, because you and said work of art are so at one. And if said work of art is a "classic"—with a vintage of at least 100 years or reaching back to ancient times—its durability is its argument. Depending on your psychic need, the truth embedded in said classic—be it drama, novel, poem—not only speaks to you in the abstract. It may change your life forever: shape your psyche, drive your actions, guide you in a crisis.

Certainly that is how the dramas of the great Norwegian playwright Henrik Ibsen (1828–1908) have affected me. Ibsen, who was revered by his fellow artists, was brilliant at showing human beings contending with the forces of their social and historical context—-with the intensely human dramas he depicted speaking as powerfully to our disjointed times as to his own. In his time, his dramas scandalized his hidebound society.

Most especially, Ibsen's plays *An Enemy of the People* (which premiered in 1883) and *A Doll's House* (which premiered in 1879) both entered my DNA when I read them in high school, with Dr. Stockmann of *Enemy* and Nora Helmer of *Doll's House* resonating at signal junctures throughout my life. Principally Dr. Stockmann, who tries to protect public safety by raising the alarm that the waters of his famous spa town have become contaminated, only to meet universal resistance and be forced into exile, learning in the process that "The majority is never right" and, in a parallel to our Trumpian era, truth-telling makes one "an enemy of the people."

Nora of *A Doll's House* resonated with me in the crisis of my first marriage. Like Nora, driven to rage and out the door forever by the infantilizing treatment from her husband—an act that George Bernard Shaw called "the door slam heard round the world"—I did the same. As I headed out the door forever, I can't say I thought, "This one's for you, Nora," but she (and my survival instinct) did point the way—*out*.

Yet, for me and no doubt for other playgoers, there has always been a big "Yes, but" to Nora's convention-defying action: In going out the door forever, Nora also leaves behind forever her three small children—a daughter and two sons—whom she abandons to the care of her emotionally ill-equipped husband Torvald. (I did not have children, so the comparison ends.) In Nora's quest for personal freedom—a quest still devoutly sought by women a century-and-a-half later—she abandons any responsibility to the very children she brought into existence and whom, or so it seemed until the door-slamming, she lovingly nurtured.

This conflict—personal freedom versus responsibility to others—appears to be what drew playwright Lucas Hnath to write his sequel, *A Doll's House, Part 2*. Every serious playwright knows Ibsen's original classic and has speculated about what happened to Nora: Hnath has said he thinks that, after her famous exit, she did "absolutely great." In his play he re-examines Nora's quest for personal freedom, but he is equally if not more interested in examining what happened to the people she left behind: What was the impact of Nora's abandonment of them?

That this is Hnath's objective is clear from his structure: The play takes place 15 years after Nora left, with its five scenes each focused on a key character, examining the impact of Nora's act on each, including, in Scenes 1 and 5, on Nora herself. Scene 2 focuses on Torvald; Scene 3 on the housekeeper Anne Marie; Scene 4 on daughter Emmy; and Scene 5 on Nora and Torvald. (That it's a male playwright questioning Nora's responsibility to others does not strike me as illegitimate. As a woman and a feminist—my first marriage made me one—I had the same question.)

Good drama, as this one is, examines what Herman Melville, another classic artist, called "the springs and motives" of character. In the masterful production now up at Seattle Repertory Theatre—ably directed by artistic director Braden Abraham and aided by a spare and elegant set and a cast who uniformly work to "keep it real"—these springs and motives of character are rendered crystal-clear throughout.

Interestingly, it is this crystal-clear delineation of motive that, for me, ultimately reduces Nora to a lesser light than she heretofore commanded as a classic heroine.

The disillusionment begins with the first scene, which opens with a knock at the famous door: It is Nora, come back to ask Torvald for the divorce he never filed for and for which only he can file (Norwegian society at the time afforded women few legal rights). The well-dressed figure she presents to Anne Marie, the housekeeper, is formidably successful: She has supported herself, very well, as a writer—she writes about women and "against marriage"; her novel about her marriage to Torvald made her name (or rather her pseudonym) in the publishing world. But, she is rather full of herself ("Surprised to see me?"). More concerning, she stipulates she does *not* want to see her children, nor does she ask much after their welfare.

Torvald, arriving home from his bank job, initially does not recognize Nora in her finery. Though he insists he is not "broken," clearly he remains broken by Nora's abandonment and, no, he's not inclined to give her a divorce. Anne Marie, in Scene 3, in salty language, unloads on Nora what she deserves: She, Anne Marie, raised the children Nora abandoned, and in doing so she, Anne Marie, abandoned her own child, not to forget she also raised Nora; thus the first words out of Nora's mouth on coming back should be, per Anne Marie, "Thank you." Blowing past this effort at a rebalancing, Nora urges her to push Torvald on the divorce. As incentive, the now-wealthy Nora promises the housekeeper her own house.

But it is the scene with her daughter Emmy that Nora seems most diminished as a human being. Emmy, her demeanor preternaturally assured, claims she has been *much* better off without her mother in her life. As Emmy goes on and on with her well-formulated argument, one expects her to break out singing "I don't care, I don't care." But anyone, most especially a mother, should be able to see her daughter's preternatural poise masks profound hurt and loss. Alas, Nora does not really see it. Emmy waxes lyrical about marriage (she's engaged to a man working at her father's bank): Rejecting her mother's life as a "nomad," she welcomes marriage, she wants to be embraced, known, trusted. (Little reference is made in the play to Nora's two sons. Who knows, with their mother abandoning them as children, they may be out now looking for love in all the wrong places.)

The final scene and its surprises will not be discussed here, but suffice it to say Torvald grows, as a human being who can express his feelings, and Nora continues to diminish in humanity, as one so captured by her own feelings she sees little else, notably her responsibility to her children. At one point I wanted to say to the self-justifying Nora, "Stop, Nora, just stop." And as Nora is now a writer, one wonders: What is a writer without her humanity, her sense of moral responsibility?

As such, *A Doll's House, Part 2* speaks directly to our times, when responsibility, especially to children, too often has been sacrificed on the altar of personal freedom, by people who take care only of themselves. Children are precious, we so often aver, yet in fact our precious children are continuously short-changed by society—see: our inaction on child molestation, gun violence, climate change, cost of college, etc.

All players in the Seattle Rep production are memorably strong in their roles—Pamela Reed as Nora, Michael Winters as Torvald, Khanh Doan as Emmy, Laura Kenny as Anne Marie. Laurie Metcalf won the 2017 Tony award for lead actress playing Nora in the Broadway production. *A Doll's House, Part 2* was nominated for Tony best play and was the most-produced play in U.S. theatres in 2018. Serious as this play sounds, it contains humor throughout, which sparkles all the more because of the seriousness.

This play will remain memorable for me because it lifted the curtain about the ultimate Nora. I am hoping the playwright will consider writing Part 3, wherein Nora may redeem herself and mature. The classic works of art, including Ibsen's plays, rarely went in for redemption, but we Americans still yearn for it.

—*Medium*, March 25, 2019

Book:
Honorable Exit: How a Few Brave Americans Risked All to Save Our Vietnamese Allies at the End of the War, by Thurston Clarke

THE VIETNAM WAR is, for many Americans, the war "they have spent decades trying to forget"—a war whose purpose and execution were misrepresented by presidents and generals; a war that angered the home front and brought cross-generational protest into the streets; a war that, in its theater of operations, ended as a lost cause.

By its title, *Honorable Exit* implies that, while the war itself was less than honorable, some measure of honor was recovered in the actions of well-meaning Americans who, in the frantic days before South Vietnam fell to the communist North in April 1975, risked their lives and defied their superiors to save 130,000 South Vietnamese—wartime colleagues and their families—from execution or concentration camps.

The author, Thurston Clarke, calls these rescuers "American Schindlers," after Oskar Schindler, rescuer of Jews in World War II made famous by the Thomas Keneally novel and Steven Spielberg film, *Schindler's List*. Clarke's subtitle—*How a Few Brave Americans Risked All to Save Our Vietnamese Allies at the End of the War*—understates the number, however: There are dozens of rescuers portrayed. But Clarke is something of a Schindler himself and clearly could not bring himself to leave off his own list any rescuer. *Caveat lector*: In addition to the author's two-page list of principal characters, the reader will need a spreadsheet and patience.

As an example of the author's method, his prologue features the iconic photo of America's first lost war—of a helicopter atop a building (misidentified as the American embassy), with a man in a white shirt leaning down to assist to freedom a mass of people on the stairway. Clarke not only tells us how the photographer got the photo, but the identities of the man in the white shirt, the helicopter pilots, and, impressively, the first five rescuees on the stairway—*and* what happened to them.

While Clarke's focus is on the rescuers, he does not stint the Vietnamese rescuees, and we get thumbnail sketches of translators, drivers, fixers, comrades-in-arms. Of necessity, given the wide scope of the tale, and the chaos of evacuation, the rescuers get only thumbnail sketches, too. Many seem to have been spiritual wanderers who, in the sorrow of the war's end, found their life's purpose in a final honorable action.

Clarke introduces the rescuers and their mission thus:

> *"Many believed that their country's political and military leaders had mismanaged the war, that Americans had a moral duty to evacuate their South Vietnamese allies, that a nation built by immigrants had room for more, and that they were saving Vietnamese from years of imprisonment...or a bloodbath.... And so they cobbled together underground railroads of safe houses, black flights, disguises, and fake flag vehicles, and smuggled friends, co-workers, and strangers past the police checkpoints at Tan Son Nhut airport in ambulances, metal shipping crates, and refrigerator trucks with airholes drilled in their floors. They impersonated chauffeurs, generals, and hospital patients, and they embossed documents with counterfeit consular stamps and signed affidavits stating that they would be financially responsible for the Vietnamese adults whom they claimed to have 'adopted.'"*

Most rescue operations required insubordination of direct orders. Perhaps the biggest obstacle was the American ambassador, Graham Martin, who resisted drawing up an evacuation plan, so as not to create "panic" in the South Vietnamese population or its army, our ally. At book's end the author concedes some moral ground to Martin's impossible task. (To remind us of scope, the U.S. diplomatic mission in South Vietnam, Clarke notes, was the largest in the world at that time.)

The rescuers included mid-rank members of the U.S. Foreign Service, various bureaucrats, businessmen, soldiers, missionaries, contractors, reporters, and spies, all turning organizational expertise to humanitarian purpose and instinctual smarts. Lists of evacuees were drawn up. Flat-topped roofs were scouted in Saigon, to serve as helipads. Convoys of jeeps and vans were thrown together. Bribes were paid. Orders to abort a flight were not received, due to convenient "radio failure." In sum, regulations were sacked, along with, the rescuers knew, their careers.

Certain details linger, such as when Americans, contacted by South Vietnamese friends on flimsy pretext, realize their help to escape was being sought. Especially moving are the Americans who, approached by parents to adopt their children, decide to do so on the spot. Once the storm breaks, the great escape unfolds on myriad fronts—by convoy, sedan, bus, helicopter, plane, barge, ship. On top of the tragedy of defeat, there is more tragedy, as when a plane in what became "Operation Babylift" crashed upon takeoff, killing the wife and son of one of the American rescuers (his daughter was found, alive, in the ruins). And there are the individual tragedies, as when a family member, for whatever reason, is denied exit at the last.

This touches on the moral dilemma, that of "playing God," that all of the rescuers faced in deciding who among their South Vietnamese charges would be evacuated—life-or-death decisions that, given their gravity and given the rescuers' moral core, stayed with them forever.

An example: After one rescuer had denied a wealthy Saigon surgeon access to a flight, despite the surgeon's bribing (he felt it was "the kind of corruption that had ruined South Vietnam"), the American "felt awful." "To ease his conscience, he approached a forlorn-looking young couple who were sitting alone under a tree. She said her boyfriend was a law student and they saw no future for themselves in a Communist country." Moved, he directed them to the flight. He would never forget them, either the young couple or the surgeon. Twenty years later, he received a phone call from the woman, reporting that she and her boyfriend had married, had children, and now lived in Seattle, where he practiced law: "'I just wanted to tell you that we took advantage of that opportunity you gave us.'" Tellingly, for this rescuer, as the author reveals at the end of the book, it is the faces of the Vietnamese he was forced to leave behind that remain clearer in his mind's eye than those he rescued.

At a time when, led by a president lacking all honor, America is becoming an international pariah, this book about Americans conducting an honorable exit to a national tragedy is, in a word, tonic.

—*Medium*, April 4, 2019

Impeaching Trump Would Be Right in Principle, But Disastrous Politically

"NO COLLUSION. No obstruction. And now—get this!—no impeachment! I tell ya, those Democrats are such losers."

This is the nightmare script Donald Trump would use in his 2020 re-election campaign for president—*if* the Democrats move to impeach him, as increasing numbers of Congressional Democrats and voices in the media are increasingly pressing. How so?

Because: If the Democrats move to impeach Trump and they lose— *and they most certainly would lose, since the Republican-controlled Senate would never ever ratify House-generated articles of impeachment from the Democrats*—then Trump, when he takes his lounge act out on the campaign trail, could effectively claim total victory ("I won the trifecta!"): no collusion with the Russians, no obstruction of justice, and—ta-da—no case proved for impeachment.

And, winning the trifecta, Trump goes on to win re-election.

If you feel, as I do, that absolutely *the* most important thing for America at this perilous moment in her history is to deny Donald Trump a second term—after all, this moment is so perilous precisely *because of* D.J. Trump—then the above script is not a winner. We are talking strategy and politics here, not principle.

Of late Trump seems actually to be asking for impeachment, as House Speaker Nancy Pelosi has astutely figured out. Why would he do so, one wonders? Because Trump may want the total and complete exoneration from the (Republican-controlled) Senate—thus fireproofing his presidency—that he did not quite get from Special Counsel Robert Mueller's report. Mueller left open the question of Trump's obstruction of justice, stating, "While this report does not conclude that the

President committed a crime, it also does not exonerate him."

Notice Trump made hash of Mueller's dangling conclusion on obstruction of justice, by taking the exoneration he got regarding collusion with the Russians and applying it to justice-obstruction as well, claiming "total and complete exoneration" on the entire Mueller investigation. Donald the Slick doesn't do nuance or logic, he does brat-in-the-sandbox one-upsmanship.

And he will do it again if Democrats move to impeach—and lose— which they will. Again, the nightmare script: *"No collusion, no obstruction, and now, no impeachment! I tell ya, those Democrats are such losers."*

Certainly, *in principle*, there is no president in the entire annals of America history who deserves impeachment more than Donald J. Trump—on all kinds of grounds. And those who hold that failure to impeach would be a dereliction of Constitutional duty have a point. Impeachment being a political and not a legal process, the grounds for impeachment would be a matter of take-your-pick: his disdain for rule of law and separation of powers; his corruption (manipulating the office of Attorney General); his cozying up to autocrats and trashing allies; his racism, misogyny, xenophobia; his grifter ways and boorishness. And, so perilous to a democracy, there is Trump's incessant lying: *The Washington Post* documents over 10,000 lies since his inauguration. For myself, every fiber strains for impeachment.

But, again: The problem is the Republican-controlled Senate—the reality check to principle.

All the above-cited grounds—uncontrovertibly principled, relating to the rightness and wrongness of things and Constitutional duty—have not moved heretofore self-proclaimed principled Republicans one jot or one tittle to brake this comprehensively unprincipled president. Republicans enjoy citing Democrats for "Trump Derangement Syndrome," but it is Republicans who have deranged their principles to make a Faustian bargain with Trump, to retain power; they would *never* impeach. (One audacious GOP Congressman, Michigan's Justin Amash, did call for impeachment, but so totally is the GOP now Trump's party that Amash's audacity has activated a primary challenger.)

In sum, as Republicans are not turning on Trump, Democrats must themselves turn Trump out of the White House—not by impeachment, a political maneuver, but at the ballot box, where democracy's stakeholders, the voting populace, can weigh in (decisively and maximally, it is to be hoped). Besides, Trump's base, granite-solid, would perceive impeachment as a political coup and never accept it.

Best that House Democrats stick with Speaker Pelosi's strategy: Continue with due oversight and the investigations—the Mueller report provides helpful guidance—while looking to the courts to provide what *Post* columnist Karen Tumulty calls "air cover as six different House committees seek documents and testimony from a stonewalling administration." (Which process is reasonably quick: Last week the courts accommodated Democrats in two such cases.) "So far," Tumulty writes, Pelosi's "strategy of keeping one foot on the congressional oversight accelerator while tapping the brakes on impeachment is winning."

Of course, Trump's preposterous refusal to cooperate with Congress unless it stops investigating him may box him into a Constitutional corner, upping the impeachment ante even more. And there is always the possibility some blockbuster revelation pushes the public to cry, "Impeach!"

In that case, Pelosi could, and should, move to impeach. As John Cassidy of *The New Yorker* writes, "Should public opinion move firmly in favor of impeachment, Pelosi would almost certainly move with it. Her objection is based on politics rather than principle." Meanwhile, per Pelosi's strategy, "let the existing inquiries play out, while aggressively challenging the Administration's stonewalling in the courts and amping up the messaging about Trump being engaged in a cover-up."

Fellow Dems, heed Speaker Pelosi: Put down the "Impeach Now" signs and focus on registering masses of new voters for 2020. Impeachment is but a battle, a political one. We must win the war—for our democracy—by ousting this proto-autocrat at the ballot box. There is principle in that, too.

—*Medium*, May 28, 2019

D-Day at 75: Rededicating Ourselves to the Mission

ON THE EVE of D-Day, long in the planning as the biggest amphibious invasion in history, General Dwight D. Eisenhower sent a message to the troops. It began:

"Soldiers, Sailors, and Airmen of the Allied Expeditionary Force: You are about to embark on the Great Crusade, toward which we have striven these many months. The eyes of the world are upon you. The hopes and prayers of liberty-loving people everywhere march with you. In company with our brave Allies and brothers-in-arms on other Fronts, you will bring about the destruction of the German war machine, the elimination of Nazi tyranny over the oppressed peoples of Europe, and security for ourselves in a free world."

It is our great blessing, as liberty-loving people, that this Great Crusade succeeded. June 6, 1944 marked the beginning of the end for the German war machine and Nazi tyranny, all vanquished by the Allies working in concert and united in high purpose.

While the men who did the fighting may not have termed their purpose as so high-flown—their expressed purpose was to get through the war and get back to their loved ones—they nevertheless risked all, they literally laid their lives on the line, and by the end of the war, 407,316 American men in uniform had made the ultimate sacrifice.

In the postwar years, the Allies secured their hard-won victory with alliances (defense and trade) and an international system dedicated to keeping the peace through mutual cooperation. Here at home, Eisenhower, the war hero, was elected President; the commander-in-chief in the field became Commander-in-Chief of the nation. For a quarter of a century not only a generation boomed, so did the country.

But now, three-quarters of a century after the Holy Grail—liberty—was secured, where are we?

The simplest response to that question is: We are lost, America of late has lost its way. We have been flailing, wildly and fearfully, since 9/11. Poll after poll shows big majorities of Americans feeling the country is "off track." What a falling-off there has been from the once-upon-a-time high purpose. Somehow, in the years following D-Day, our highest point, the hero gave way to the anti-hero, wars of no particular purpose—certainly none of high purpose—ensued, the culture degraded....

How came we to be so lost? My conjecture: We have abused our liberty, we have not handled properly the great inheritance handed down to us by the victors of World War II. Yes, the "Greatest Generation" had their shortcomings, but, when put to the supreme test, they came together and did right. In our post-9/11 delirium, we have neither come together nor done right. Doing right, exercising our liberty appropriately, requires using one's moral compass. But we set that compass aside decades ago: Liberals did not think a compass was needed, conservatives deployed it hypocritically.

Of late, however, there are encouraging signs of Renaissance, of America trying to get right again.

Out of moral revulsion at the amoral occupant now in the White House, record numbers of citizens are voting and are running for office; last November's midterm elections were a resounding rebalancing. And consider the huge field of Democratic candidates vying to oust this amoral president: It takes a scorecard to track this embarrassment of riches. And what else are the powerful social forces of #MeToo, #March ForOurLives, and #BlackLivesMatter but the populace trying mightily to get right regarding, respectively, sexual assault, gun violence, and racial injustice—all abuses of liberty?

As we are discovering, we *do* need our moral compass. Liberty without a compass leads to abuse.

At this hinge moment, for guidance we might look to another Commander-in-Chief—Abraham Lincoln—and his Gettysburg Address, specifically where he spoke of rededication to the cause. Most every American schoolchild studies this speech.

Looking back to the American Revolution ("Fourscore and seven years ago")—just as today we look back at D-Day (threescore and fifteen)—Lincoln began by honoring "our fathers" who "brought forth on this continent, a new nation, conceived in liberty." Turning to his own time (1863), he continued: "We are engaged in a great civil war, testing whether that nation, or any nation so conceived and dedicated, can long endure." Then came Lincoln's words that speak to us now, exhorting our rededication to the "unfinished work": "It is...for us to be here dedicated to the great task remaining before us—that from these honored dead we take increased devotion to the cause for which they gave the last full measure of devotion."

It is for us, the living, honoring the cause of those who perished on D-Day and the greater war, to rededicate ourselves with "increased devotion" to our "unfinished work": tutoring ourselves in the proper handling of our precious liberty.

—*Medium*, June 6, 2019

Model for the New Man, Right Here in River City

IT HAS BEEN clear for some time that, as a group, men are in flux about their place in the world, a world of dizzying change.

With women, their consciousness raised, now asserting their rights, including the right to seek power in the public sphere and to share power in the domestic sphere, men can no longer expect always to be in charge, always to be the voice of authority—as has been men's "natural" right for eons of human history.

If and when we achieve equity between the sexes, it will truly be a New Day. But so far over these last decades, progress has been sketchy. Expecting men to voluntarily surrender their "natural" entitlement and share the end-all-and-be-all of power and status: It has been a big ask, going to the essence of personhood as well as manhood.

Kudos to the men who have adapted to this new social context and who treat women as co-equal human beings, colleagues at work, partners in life. Whether they modeled themselves after an admired figure they knew or, more impressively, determined for themselves that they would extend the principle of fair play to all women: These men don't need their consciousness raised, they are their own enlightened model.

But for some (insecure) men, it's been too big an ask—to share power and status with women—and the asking accounts for tragically high rates of domestic violence and sexual assault. The rise of #MeToo has revealed shocking instances of men in high places abusing their power with women, interpreting their authority to mean all is permitted, even criminal behavior. Apart from this violent misogyny, angry young men are the public face of gun violence—they invariably are the perpetrators of our too-frequent shooting massacres—and of the white supremacy movement, whose members decry white America giving way to a more diverse populace.

In the past, the President of the United States often served as a model of male behavior—there was George Washington, father of his country, and honest Abe Lincoln. But the current one, who in addition to lacking all character is a misogynist, cannot fill that role.

Fortunately, we have a new model, right here in River City, specifically Gig Harbor, Washington: Recently in a public setting, a remarkable young man, a graduating high school senior, reacting spontaneously and from his heart, created a new mold.

It happened at the awards banquet for a program called Students of Distinction. Established in 2003, this program showcases seniors from three local high schools, nominated to compete in seven categories: academic achievement; science and technology; career and technical; music, art, and drama; athletics; community service; and overcoming adversity. Pre-banquet, all students have been subjected to 20-minute interviews by panels of local citizens (I serve on the academic achievement panel), with the students who distinguish themselves in these interviews announced at the banquet.

The overcoming adversity category is often the most moving, with students these days grappling with economic hardship, family collapse, serious health conditions. This year's group included a young woman from Africa, a refugee from the Democratic Republic of Congo, whose chief adversity was "escaping the political instability, corruption, and civil war of her native country" (as her program bio noted), then, arriving in the U.S. just two years ago, learning English well enough to achieve a commendable 3.58 GPA.

This young woman acquitted herself well in the earlier interview, because ultimately she was announced the Student of Distinction in her category. But at the banquet, when her category was called to the stage to be asked, individually, some softball getting-to-know-you questions, when her turn came, she looked out at the audience, opened her mouth, and froze. It may have been the size of the audience (200-some people), or the fact that her acquisition of English is so recent—whatever it was, like an actor who's forgotten his lines, she "went up" and went silent.

Fifteen seconds went by, thirty, a full minute. The room squirmed, the emcee didn't know what to do.

Suddenly, from the side of the room, a young man, a contestant in another category, rose up, wended his way through the tables, and, standing in front of the stage, improvised on the spot. Identifying himself not by name but as the young woman's "friend"—they went to the same high school—he went on to say: "If you got to know her, she is really, really interesting" and "If you got to know her, she is really, really nice." That's it, that was his basic message. Which he repeated, this time, his emotions getting to him, through tears.

As the hall fell into stunned silence, he returned to his table and sat down.

Talk about rising to the occasion, and then some. I can't imagine anyone in that room not thrilling to the humanitarian rescue they just witnessed. At our table, when we got our breath back, there were tears in our eyes as well, men's included.

Afterwards I made my way over to the young man. "Young man," I said, "that was pretty remarkable what you did." His response? "I had to." He still seemed a bit overcome, a bit wide-eyed, coming back to earth. (I am not naming names here, so as to spare the young woman eternal embarrassment on the world wide web.)

Though more than a month has passed, I can't stop thinking about that young hero. Especially at a time of so much bad male behavior and so many bad actors (and not a few *faux*-heroes), this young man's action is tonic and is, I submit, a model for young men going forward. As more and more women compete for power and status (the young woman in this tale hopes to become a lawyer and advocate for other refugees), ideally they would be treated by their male peers with the respect and friendship this young man exhibited. Key, I think, was that he saw her, not as female, but as a friend. And, being friends, he *had* to come to her aid.

Also, a political note: In light of the insulting and shocking vulgarism the current occupant of the White House used in reference to the African continent, this young man, who is white, shows, by extending his hand to his African friend, a new way for Americans to be in the world. Out with the ugly American, in with the beautiful one.

Another note: The program category this young man was placed in was athletics. By his magnanimous action, he overturned the stereotype of the jock with the big head and small heart. I later learned he comes from a family known for its athleticism.

In the end, as it happened, unlike the young woman, this young man was not named the Student of Distinction in his category. But, indubitably and beyond category, he distinguished himself as the model of the New Man, pointing the way to a New Day.

Buona fortuna, young man.

—*Medium*, June 28, 2019

"Let's Take Back Our Democracy—And Improve It While We're At It": Democrats' Winning Strategy in 2020

WATERSHED MOMENTS CAN produce an "Aha" of recognition. Now that Donald Trump has made his latent racism disgustingly overt, with his attacks on four freshman Congresswomen of color, accusing them of "hating America" and "seeking its destruction" and taunting them to "go back" to the countries they came from, and with Trump supporters chanting "Send her back, send her back" days later at his rally—if this isn't watershed, what is?—Democrats consequently are recognizing this:

The 2020 presidential campaign is now far bigger than healthcare or immigration or income inequality or climate change. This is certainly not to say these issues are not vitally important, because they are. But it is to say there's an overarching battle to be fought, which is:

In the 2020 campaign, Democrats need to save American democracy itself.

We need to take back our democracy from this comprehensively anti-democratic and dangerous "president" (the air-quotes are used to denote a fraud). To save our democracy, Trump and anti-democratic Trumpism *must* be defeated, resoundingly.

At issue now—as it has been historically but we have never fully settled it—is the core question: *Who is American and who can exercise the full rights of citizenship in this American democracy?* By going full racist now—and count on it: Trump's 2020 campaign for re-election will feature explicit racist appeals—Trump is making the case that only white Americans signify and count. His target: the four minority Congresswomen—Alexandria Ocasio-Cortez (NY), Ayanna Pressley (MA), Rashida Tlaib (MI), and Ilhan Omar (MN), who dub themselves "the Squad."

Equally at issue: Our democratic institutions, which have been severely damaged by this man who claims he wants to "make America great again." If he is re-elected, the damage will accelerate us to banana republic status. This institutional destruction should be borne in mind as Trump dominates and inflames the news cycle with his racist ranting. As *The New Yorker*'s astute Susan Glasser notes, "Trump's attack on the Americanness of his critics has distracted from his assault on the American system of government itself." We must remember: Both Americanness and American democracy are at stake in 2020.

Consider the institutional damage Trump has inflicted. Rule of law: He appointed a toadying Attorney General who's more personal lawyer than the people's counsel. Separation of powers: He aggrandizes the executive over the legislative. Sanctity of the vote: He refuses to secure our election system from Russian meddling, because doing so would delegitimize his presidency. As for running the government, "acting" heads now "run" things, meaning: Government is effectively closed (though regulation-cutting continues apace). And consider our reputational damage: America once was the international champion of human rights and Leader of the Free World, but Trump embraces dictators who quash rights and curtail freedoms. America once touted itself as Immigrant Nation, but Trump builds walls and cages. And consider Trump's assault on our rights, notably free speech as practiced by the press, the Fourth Estate, whom he attacks as "the enemy of the American people."

And, crucially: Consider Trump's new assault on America's ideals— notably our ideal of equality, specifically racial equality.

"All men are created equal": So begins our foundational document, the Declaration of Independence. But we all know our tortured history: "All men" initially meant only white men of property. And we all know the struggle of other constituent groups—women and minorities—to fight their way to full citizenship. But we also know we have not achieved true equality, not yet. Too many white Americans consider minorities to be lesser, not "real" Americans, echoing the 3/5 formula of our slavery past.

Let us declare, finally, for 2020, that *all* Americans are equal and are real Americans. Doing so, as we take back our democracy, we will improve it—delivering finally on our ideals.

(Trump now says the four minority Congresswomen should refrain from criticizing America. News flash, Mr. Trump: All four are American citizens—three born here, one naturalized—and, as such, they are entitled to criticize their government, most especially yours.)

Significantly, it was with racism, our ancient wound, that Trump calculated going explicit would fly with his supporters—"Many people agree with me." He knows his people: An Ipsos poll taken after his tweet-storm last Sunday but before the "Send her back" chanting shows his approval rating among Republicans *actually rising* five (5) points over the week before. This sorry reality is fruition of the GOP opting decades ago to play the race-card, which conservative author Tim Alberta charts in a new book, *American Carnage*. While some Republicans are expressing disgust with Trump's breakout into explicit racism, many others aren't. History will be harsh with the latter: Recall the photos of white Americans taunting Negro children as they integrated public schools in the 1950s and '60s. Not a pretty picture.

Significantly also, it was racism (Trump's) that united the Democrats—finally. After weeks of internecine warfare between the Squad and House Speaker Nancy Pelosi, arguing over who is purer on combatting racism, when Trump released his racist tweet-storm, Pelosi immediately came to the Squad's defense, adding that, clearly, what Trump wants is "to make America white again." On the House floor, introducing a resolution condemning Trump's tweets, Pelosi was censured, temporarily, by Republicans objecting to her citing the tweets as "racist." The resolution passed with unanimous Democratic support and four brave Republicans. (Note: This resolution powerfully echoes our foundational history and was written by freshman Congressman Tom Malinowski, former human rights advocate and immigrant from Poland.)

Going forward, if we are to save our democracy, it is imperative that Democrats remain united and not be played by the master manipulator. Trump will paint all Democrats as "extremist" and "socialist" and "America-hating," as he's labeled the Squad. I sincerely hope the Squad comprehends the gravity of this political moment. While free speech is, yes, an inalienable right, it must be exercised responsibly, which, frankly, the Squad has not always done. Memo to Squad: Pushing a racial litmus test on fellow Democrats, as you did with Pelosi, is absurd. Most Democrats, I'd venture, self-select into the party *precisely because* Democrats are truly the party of the big tent.

To conclude: Mission 2020—saving our democracy and improving it by establishing, finally, that *all* Americans are equal—is enormous and daunting. But, then, hinge historical moments are like that: huge and daunting, but presenting the opportunity to pivot, to seize the day and shift to higher gear, to front the threat Trump poses. As I have been arguing of late, what seems like breakdown can be wrested into a reckoning.

The question becomes then: *Which of the Democratic presidential candidates will step up as the visionary and the strategist that this hinge moment demands?*

And is it possible that, sensing this new and more perilous context, someone new and more visionary and strategic will step up…?

For months now, to Democrats' dismay, the announced candidates have wandered the campaign trail without piercing through with a grand vision, wrangling instead over policy—on healthcare, immigration, income inequality, climate change, etc. These issues will of course remain the main agenda items at campaign events, because they are the issues nearest the voters and the voters will press for them, ardently.

But, again, 2020 is not simply the Healthcare Election or the Immigration Election. It is bigger: It is the Election to Save and Improve Our Democracy. At some point, we need to hear from the candidates about this larger quest. This is not an either-or question, but both-and: We can address *both* the policy issues *and* The Biggest Issue of All. (And to those who counsel lying low: Fellow Democrats, we cannot *not* address Trump's explicit racism: The world is watching and so are our children.)

The next Democratic debates, on July 30 and 31, would be a good time to launch this broader quest.

The great take-away line from the movie *Jaws*—"You're gonna need a bigger boat"—applies now. Given the size and lethality of the shark in our midst, we need a bigger boat, a bigger presidential campaign. The question of supreme importance is: Who will build that bigger boat and captain it?

—*Medium*, July 21, 2019

My Fellow White Americans: Are We About Blood Identity— or America's Ideals?

ENOUGH! YET ANOTHER WHITE SUPREMACIST carries out yet another bloody massacre—this time targeting Hispanics—in El Paso, Texas, leaving 22 dead.

To stanch this deadly trend, a trend fueled by our president's racist and hate-filled rhetoric, it is past time for the white supremacist's diametric opposite—the white American of conscience—to step up and act. I offer this resolution:

Whereas: Donald Trump denigrates human beings whose skin is not white, calling them criminals, animals, and aliens and likening them to an infestation and invasion;

Whereas: Such denigration works insidiously to dehumanize non-white human beings, rendering them as lesser and not human and not American, thus justifying their subordination, deportation, murder;

Whereas: This dehumanization of non-white human beings is preeminently the agenda of the white supremacist, whose agenda Trump has championed, first with dog whistles and now with explicit racist appeals;

Whereas: White supremacists, decrying infestation and invasion, have carried out massacres in Charleston (in the former administration, killing blacks) and, in the Trump era, in Pittsburgh (killing Jews) and now El Paso (killing Hispanics);

And whereas: White supremacists, post-9/11, express virulent hatred of Muslims;

Be it therefore resolved: White Americans of conscience must *unite in solidarity with all of our non-white fellow Americans*, for the express purpose of establishing—at long last—that America is *not* about blood lines or blood identity. *At our essence, America is about our foundational ideals of equality and justice for all citizens.*

Having created America, white Americans have dominated its affairs throughout our history—a reality that white supremacists interpret as Divine Right.

Fearing the loss of that dominant power bequeathed by their forebears, and fearing their own replacement, white supremacists make a fetish of blood lines and blood identity, pointing with pride to their white European origins and the glories of a white Western civilization. As to America's extraordinary expansion and growth, the white supremacist rationalizes the crime of exterminating the native American population and taking their lands as justified—"Conquered, not stolen." And they rationalize the crime of slavery—America's Original Sin, wherein white Americans engaged in a thriving African slave trade and prospered mightily from the shackled labor of men, women, and children—justifying this heinous subjugation on the grounds of Africans' alleged inferiority. Similar "thinking" undergirds the hatred of Hispanics, Asians, others. To maintain white supremacy, violence is sanctioned.

The late, great Toni Morrison, the first African-American woman to be awarded the Nobel prize in literature, took the measure of this American history when she said such a civilization is "bereft." As she declared so acutely: *"If you can only be tall because someone is on their knees, then you have a serious problem."*

Donald Trump and other white supremacists need people who don't look like them to be on their knees. They are, in a word, bereft.

Conscientious white Americans, on the other hand, do not want any of our fellow Americans on their knees. We want everyone to stand—and stand tall. As for blood lines or blood identity: They are of sociological interest to the individual, but they are not—repeat: not—mandatory for full participation in America's democracy. It is our foundational ideals, notably those of equality and justice for all—endlessly espoused, never fully secured—as well as our shared humanity that should guide us at this perilous moment.

And best we act in solidarity with our non-white fellow Americans—black, Hispanic, Muslim-American, Asian-American, Jew. Solidarity marches in cities and towns, and solidarity events online, could project a powerful counter-force to the white supremacist's hateful ideology, now mainstreamed, filling the media space and spreading dread. Civic and social organizations coming together to form coalitions under the equality-and-justice-at-long-last banner could serve as a force multiplier of individual effort. Social media campaigns dedicated to the cause could begin to mitigate the bilious hate driving so much "discussion" in the social media sphere.

This campaign to inject conscience into the battleground that now passes for the American commons will not be easy. And, indeed, making the argument for ideals over blood lines may cause problems with certain blood relatives. (It did for me: During the Obama administration, after I had written admiringly of Mr. Obama, I heard from a distant relative—"Don't you understand we need to get that black man out of OUR White House?" So much for Christian teaching....) Reaching full equality will mean more competition for white Americans, which I believe is a big fear for the white supremacist, but more competition will redound to America's benefit.

Again: Best if we conscientious white Americans make our argument *in solidarity* with our non-white fellow Americans. And if we finally achieve that New Day, if we make of the present breakdown a grand reckoning—for full equality and justice for all—we will become the opposite of bereft. We will become, finally, truly great.

—*Medium*, August 12, 2019

A Moderate and a Progressive Mix It Up—and Find Consensus

THE FOLLOWING EMAIL exchange took place recently between me, a moderate, and Rob Crawford, a progressive. Rob is a retired humanities professor with the University of Washington/Tacoma and served as state chair of the National Religious Campaign Against Torture (NRCAT). It was over the issue of torture—when the George W. Bush administration began engaging in torture in Iraq in 2004—that Rob and I became acquainted. This exchange commenced after my recent commentary, "'Let's Take Back Our Democracy—and Improve It While We're At It': Democrats' Winning Strategy in 2020." It opens with Rob protesting my failure to defend "the Squad"—Democratic freshman Congresswomen Alexandria Ocasio-Cortez (NY), Ayanna Pressley (MA), Rashida Tlaib (MI), and Ilhan Omar (MN). I have done minimal editing; Rob approves both editing and posting.

22 July 2019

Dear Carla,

Excellent post. I was entirely with you until you called on the Squad to be more responsible. Name one thing you think is not responsible. As for challenging the Democratic centrist leadership, if not now, when? For the leadership to run scared of these voices is to court disaster, in my humble opinion. They should welcome the vigorous debate among Dems, not be intimidated by the slur of anti-Semitism, and stand up for the diversity of views—and most importantly four Congresswomen of color. That said, I personally do not know, and I don't see how anyone can know, what will be most effective against Trump in 2020. I live in trepidation of his re-election.

Rob

22 July

Dear Rob,

Well, if I had you with me that deep into the commentary—almost to the end!—I'm happy.

About the Squad and what I thought was irresponsible on their part: Yes, the anti-Semitic tropes employed by Omar and AOC calling the border detention facilities "concentration camps" and Tlaib using the f-bomb to call for Trump's impeachment—volatile terms that yielded nothing and by which now the Republicans can smear ALL Dems as "extremist." And AOC's chief of staff calling Pelosi et al. racists—wayyyy out of bounds. N.B., please: Pelosi came to the Squad's defense asap when Trump dumped his racist "Go back to where they came from" rant. Would the Squad do the same for Pelosi? (I wonder.)

A savvy politician knows the power of his/her rhetoric and, equally important, knows how one's rhetoric can be used against one, and I am not sure the youngsters of the Squad know that yet. That's why I said I "sincerely" hoped they comprehend the political gravity of this moment (this is beyond free speech). Because: Given the booming economy, and Trump's showy actions on immigration (not coherent but showy), and two more conservative justices to the Supreme Court, and then, to boot, given the gift of labeling your Dem opponent "extreme" and "socialist" and "out of the mainstream," thanks to being tagged with the Squad—Done: Trump is re-elected, easily.

You have "trepidation" re 2020? I'll see that and raise you: I have dread, profound.

I am, yes, more moderate than progressive. If our nominee is a progressive, the R's can say all Dems want "free stuff for illegals"— and, again, it's Trump in a landslide. I feel I could "afford" to be a progressive IF Trump and Trumpism were defeated. I fully agree we *need the economic restructuring that Elizabeth Warren and Bernie Sanders preach, but politically we need to regain power first, with a moderate, then pivot. Unless there is an FDR progressive on the horizon who has Trump's props....*

You say, "I don't see how anyone can know what will be most effective against Trump in 2020": Well, we'd better start figuring it out, Mr. Smith needs to get going to Washington, pronto. In my own behalf, I think there is something in my idea that saving our democracy should be part of the call to arms.

Thanks for writing, Rob. And thanks for the (otherwise) "Excellent post." I hope you are writing, too. These scary times need illumination—Trump is mining our darkest corners—and we need all humanities persons on deck.

Carla

24 July

Dear Carla,

Thank you for such a detailed and careful response. Much appreciated.

Re the Squad, Omar has been not only viciously attacked by Trump for her so-called anti-American, anti-Israel, and anti-Semitic position, but also attacked by too many Democrats, many fearful themselves of being labeled anti-Israel and therefore anti-Semitic, or "left," etc. Democrat centrists (and pardon, Carla, if that includes you) have a choice: run scared, cave to the right (not only on this, but other issues as well, especially immigration), become fearful of making Trump's racism a key issue for 2020, fearful of impeachment, fearful of alienating the fantasized swing suburban voter, fearful....

Or stand up for a Democratic party that can accommodate and even welcome a Left (which in the scheme of modern history and even U.S. history is not really that far left). There is a needed and

*long overdue debate that is now more open about the shift of the
party to the center (and on various foreign policy/military issues
even to the right; and in the past, re crime, busing, etc.). In my
opinion, the Squad is a useful scapegoat for the centrist to stigmatize
that full and much broader challenge from the Left in the party.
Warren, after all, is running second to Joe Biden.*

*Trump attacks the Dems through race-baiting and identity politics
that mixes white nationalist themes (refugees, asylum, undocumented
immigrants, and Muslims) with a classic Cold War attack on "socialism,"
"radicalism," "the far left," "they hate America," etc. I appreciated
the Dems reacted in unity against that* [with the House resolution
condemning Trump's tweets against the Squad as racist], *although
I would have preferred a censure. Yet, they need to be consistent
in defending these views as not only constitutionally protected but
well within the boundaries of legitimate debate. As you say, the core
struggle we find ourselves in is one of saving our democracy, as well as
transforming it to a more just democracy. So let's have full democracy in
the Democratic Party. Both sides need to be heard.*

*This debate should include a range of issues, including matters of
institutionalized racism and sexism, human rights violations in
detention camps for migrants, including what to call them—and
why a name like "concentration camp" makes sense to many
and why it offends others. (Personally, I lean on the side of
"concentration camp," a term and an institution that preceded and
followed the German use of it in the Holocaust. The case has been
well argued by others.)*

*As for fascism, I personally steer away from it, although at cost of
intense arguments with people close to me. I'm a historian, so I'm
careful here. Nonetheless, I increasingly agree that many of Trump's
tactics and the far-right movement behind him are fascist-like in
several respects. So the analogy, for me, is worthwhile—keeping in
mind that an analogy is both similarities and differences.*

Other matters you raise need ongoing discussion and discernment, e.g., whether the Dems should put aside the progressive positions until after Trump is defeated—including on immigration. A morally courageous and at the same time a "practical" Dem position on immigration will not be easy. I am not one to defer being open about progressive positions until after.... That does not prevent me from believing in certain political matters, advocating for a "common front," e.g., like Bernie, in the 2016 primary; get behind the winner (even if....); no third-party runs.

These are indeed scary times. I deeply appreciate your being in the fight. Personally, I have become deeply involved in migration/ immigration matters, as reflected in a recent op-ed I published.

Warm regards,

Rob

25 July

Dear Rob,

Thanks for all this thoughtful response to a subject we clearly are both intensely engaged with—the survival of American democracy.

Your various points about what the Democratic party should be ideally and what it should be doing to get there, promoting "positive change": I worry that we are now in such a "hot" political moment— let's call it a maelstrom—that such considerations are wasted motion, as against the overpowering forces of the maelstrom. You know me (our shared protest of torture): I am the first to make the moral argument, but in a maelstrom? (I keep thinking of Melville's description of the Pequod, destroyed by Moby-Dick: like "chips in the vortex.") That's why I suggest, respectfully, that such engineering wait until we have secured the fort. And that's why I tried, in my commentary, to "go big" and appeal to Dems to enlarge the presidential campaign.

The "overpowering forces" I refer to, of course, are the Republicans and their perennial ability to agree on a message and unify—even around a corrupt and even dangerous leader—and never break rank. Note how they vilified Robert Mueller in their questions at his hearing—and he's a registered Republican—but his whole investigation came to be seen by the R's as an existential threat to their Anointed Leader, corrupt and even dangerous as he is. It is stunning: The R's cannot see the peril we are all in. Chips in the vortex....

Meanwhile, the Dems wander the wilderness. Rob, I so wish a positive message could get through, but I am not sure even the early Barack Obama could (maybe Michelle Obama could—now there's a thought!). Elizabeth Warren, bless her, keeps coming up with plans—a strategy that could pierce through to Independents still open to persuasion (though did you see the recent poll showing the I's actually moving to Trump since his racist tweet-storm?). Someone who I do think has sufficient muscle with the working and middle classes, is sharp on his feet, and could articulate the mission to save our democracy is Senator Sherrod Brown. No, I would not be "fearful" about "making Trump's racism a key issue in 2020": That would be a powerful way to go, but the Squad has implied centrist Dems are insufficiently anti-racist. As to moderates being overly "fearful," I prefer the word "prudent."

Good on you for your op-ed and, better yet, good action. Which brings me to another point: How goodness and decency have always, since Time Immemorial, had a hard time prevailing. I think again of Melville—Captain Ahab gloating he has checkmated first mate Starbuck and his "soft humanity." But, we persist—yes!

Best regards,

Carla

3 August, after the second set of Democratic debates

Hi, Carla,

Quick reply as I am rushing to get ready for a backpack tomorrow.

I have mixed feelings about the recent debates. The sharpening of teeth and snarling toward each other cannot help Dems. Debate format is about something else than good and needed discussion about real policy choices. Quick preferences: I did like how both Sanders and Warren performed. Biden is looking more than insipid. Kamala Harris not impressive. I did like Cory Booker.

We might disagree on decriminalization of the border, but I thought that the few who argued for it did well in explaining why it is so important. I think a distinction can be made between decriminalization and the charge of open borders (e.g., "order at the border"). If we are going to fight for democracy, it must include human rights. What Trump is doing involves massive violations of human rights, citing an arguable rise in crime. There is deep humanitarian sentiment in this country that can be aroused against Trump's cruel, inhuman policies.

I actually liked what David Brooks wrote (a rare appreciation for me) recently—lauding Marianne Williamson's identification of dark forces and the need to name them as evil and the need for Dems to be much more out-front united in talking about the threat to democracy—back to your op-ed.

Thankfully, I will not have to read news for the coming week. I hope we don't go to war with Iran. My friend who follows this closely believes there is a 90% chance we are headed for war. A columnist recently described the Middle East and global players as an August 1914-like force-field.

Warm regards,

Rob

3 August

Dear Rob,

Before you head out into deepest Nature, I think I spy...consensus.

I love what you said—"There is deep humanitarian sentiment in this country that can be aroused against Trump's cruel, inhuman policies": Yes! That humanitarian campaign, aspirational in tone, anti-racist and pro-equal justice for all in thrust, could, one), unite all Dems while appealing to Independents and heartsick Republicans, and, two), send Trump to the dustbin of History. Apart from saving Dems from more "snarling" about healthcare (no small thing), such a campaign would help repair our democracy and achieve, finally, our ideals and restore our best selves, from whom we are so terribly alienated now.

But: So far, we have not heard that higher, humanitarian call, have we? I would argue that either a moderate or a progressive could campaign under that banner. The question of all questions becomes: Who will sound that humanitarian call?

Enjoy the Great Outdoors, Rob. I will be minding the fort.

Yours in the struggle,

Carla

—Medium, August 15, 2019

Capitalists Rethink Capitalism—Maybe

WHEN THE BUSINESS ROUNDTABLE announced its revised statement of a corporation's purpose recently, it got big media play. And why not: When 181 heads of America's very biggest businesses—including Amazon, Apple, General Motors, and Walmart—gather together and, as a body, state that they have been practicing capitalism all wrong, this is news that *is* new.

For 50 years now, corporations have adhered to the orthodoxy that maximizing profit for the investing shareholder is their sole *raison d'etre*. Economist Milton Friedman, father of this orthodoxy, declared in 1970 that "the social responsibility of business is to increase its profits"—in other words, any negative impact of corporate activity on society was to be discounted. Conservatives took to this theory like catnip.

But now, in a major U-turn for American capitalism, the other components in the equation—the employee, the customer, the supplier, the community, and the environment—are to be deemed equal in value to the shareholder in the operation of a corporation. So vows the Business Roundtable's "Commitment" statement.

The part about the employee got special emphasis in the media. While continuing to salute "America's economic model," the Roundtable acknowledges that "many Americans are struggling"—"Too often hard work is not rewarded." Thus its new commitment to "investing in our employees": "This starts with compensating them fairly and providing important benefits. It also includes supporting them through training and education that help develop new skills for a rapidly changing world."

Sounds very pretty—in fact it sounds ideal—but is it for real? While the Roundtable refers to its "modernizing" language, it's also humanizing. But, again, is it for real?

And why now? Why does this capitalist repurposing come now, when stagnant wages and severe income inequality have been a hard fact of the worker's life for decades?

No doubt the present political moment—angry, polarized, pitchforks at the ready on both right and left—accounts for American capitalists' sudden defensive shift. Describing the corporate mindset as "panic," *Washington Post* columnist David Ignatius writes that "the guardians of capitalism seem to realize that they must respond to right-wing populists and left-wing progressives alike or face a worsening political crisis that is already hobbling the country." Ignatius believes this panic could be a "turning point, opening the way for a future president to begin fixing the problems of stagnant wages and inequality that are at the core of America's disarray."

Likewise galvanizing: the "revolutionary" rhetoric of Democratic presidential candidates Elizabeth Warren and Bernie Sanders. Warren, whose poll numbers are rising and who reputedly scares Wall Street, constantly stresses the need for "deep structural change" to the economy, while Sanders speaks outright of "political revolution."

Tellingly, Warren last year unveiled "The Accountable Capitalism Act," which would, per *Vox*'s Matt Yglesias, "redistribute trillions of dollars from rich executives and shareholders to the middle class" by requiring corporations to consider equally "the interests of employees, consumers, and their communities" (sound familiar?). Prioritizing workers while "leaving business as the primary driver" (countering the "socialist" tag), Warren hoped to spur "a return to greater corporate responsibility, and bring back other aspects of the more egalitarian era of American capitalism post-World War II—more business investment, more meaningful career ladders for workers, more financial stability, and higher pay." Writes Yglesias, "As much as Warren's proposal is about ending inequality, it's also about saving capitalism."

On that point: This commentator has long wondered in print why there was not a greater awareness among business leaders of the damage done to the vessel in which the American economy sails—Capitalism—especially the damage done it *and* the world by the 2008 crash (which crash was caused in big part by business). The only way our great American experiment combining Capitalism and Democracy can work is by the responsible exercise of both. I kept calling for a George Washington visionary in the corporate sector, who brings business acumen *and* a humanitarian feel for the people, to step forth and save the vessel.

One such figure raising the alarm about capitalism itself—Larry Fink, billionaire head of the world's largest investment firm BlackRock—last year called on businesses to develop a greater social consciousness, saying in essence: "Contribute to society or lose our support." And earlier this year, Ray Dalio, billionaire founder of the hedge fund Bridgewater, issued a paper, "Why and How Capitalism Needs to Be Reformed," wherein he described how the "income/wealth/opportunity gap" poses an "existential risk for the U.S." (Another billionaire, Donald Trump, stepped forth and took the White House. Lacking in both business acumen and humanitarianism, he is giving American capitalism a bad name that will last for a long time.)

For now, we have the Business Roundtable's "Commitment" statement. More than a single individual, the heft of collective endeavor may enable the structural reform needed. Steven Pearlstein, *Washington Post* business columnist, considers the Roundtable's statement a "signal," while noting it has no legal force. (Pearlstein signals his reform ideas in his book's title —*Can American Capitalism Survive?: Why Greed Is Not Good, Opportunity Is Not Equal, and Fairness Won't Make Us Poor.*)

How has the public reacted to the Roundtable's "signal"? To take a small sample—a set of letters to *The New York Times* responding to initial reporting: One led with the "mendacity" of the C.E.O.s and ended by condemning their "ethical bankruptcy." Two cited a "cynical ploy," with one concluding: "Absent constraints by government, businesses will continue as always, putting profit before all, damn the consequences. The statement issued by the Business Roundtable is not to be taken seriously. It is just a cynical ploy to convince the gullible...that companies take the common people's needs to heart, and are conscientious stewards of the public good, so there's no need for big government to step in and rein in their excesses. Then watch their profits and personal wealth climb while the world declines." Joseph Stiglitz, Nobel-winning economist, agrees: The turnabout is too good to be true.

It remains to be seen how this "commitment" of capitalists to reform capitalism itself will fare in the coming widely-forecast recession, or how forceful it remains if the Democrats who preach reform lose the 2020 presidential election—two key "stress tests." And would these C.E.O.s consider bringing their own pay, now 254 times that of the average employee, back into the realm of the normal? Their statement is silent on this matter, while the public is not (see above). Meanwhile, capitalists might note the research showing young people's waning attachment to both capitalism and democracy....

Hope must remain tethered to reality—the historical reality of American capitalism that the great writer Edith Wharton captured in her 1913 novel *The Custom of the Country*. Citing the magnet force of money that serves as the country's "emotional center of gravity," Wharton wrote: "In the effete societies it's love, in our new one it's business. In America the real *crime passionnel* is a 'big steal'—there's more excitement in wrecking railways than homes."

At least we know the stakes: Both American Capitalism and Democracy need saving. Will we? Can we?

—*Medium*, September 3, 2019

The Hong Kong and Moscow Protests: In Authoritarian Places, a Yearning for Democracy

HISTORY HAS ITS rhythms that can produce extraordinary moments—like the present one. At a time when attachment to democracy is waning in the world's oldest and greatest democracies like the U.S. and the U.K., the yearning for it emerges in highly undemocratic places like Hong Kong and Moscow.

What a juxtaposition: While U.S. president Donald Trump continues undermining democratic norms (too many to count) and last week British prime minister Boris Johnson made the undemocratic move of suspending Parliament to block further debate on Brexit (and undemocratically expelled 21 members of his own party who opposed him), protesters in Hong Kong and Russia have bravely carried on with their months-long pro-democracy protests—at constant peril of a military crackdown ordered by their strongman rulers Xi Jinping and Vladimir Putin, respectively, who are well-known for jailing or even killing opponents.

About this paradox, *Washington Post* columnist Anne Applebaum writes: "While the news at home gets constantly worse, we are simultaneously living in an era when the ideals of democracy have never burned more brightly, especially among younger people—at least those who live in autocracies.... In two of the most authoritarian countries on the planet, unprecedented pro-democracy demonstrations are now unfolding, inspiring precisely the same generation that is bored by democracy in the West."

The Hong Kong protests have riveted the world with their zeal and numbers—some have drawn two (2) million citizens. When Hong Kong reverted from British to Chinese rule in 1997, it was with guarantees that the semi-autonomous island territory would continue enjoying freedoms that the mainland Chinese did not, in a formula termed "one country, two systems." The tensions in that formula manifested this June, when the Beijing-backed Hong Kong government drafted a bill requiring Hong Kongers charged with criminal offenses be extradited to China for trial. Appalled at the prospect of Chinese "justice," Hong Kongers of all ages hit the streets. They keep coming because they fear increasing encroachment by China.

While these protests are democratically organized—strategy is aired on-line and a consensus reached, protests surface "like water" around the city—its leaderlessness also accounts for the lapses into violence and vandalism. The world's heart stops when such lapses occur, when, for example, protesters attacked the Legislative Council or closed down the airport: These unforced errors enable China to label the protesters as "radicals" and "terrorists." (Some protesters apologized for the "inconvenience" of the airport closing and asked for "understanding and forgiveness as young people of Hong Kong continue to fight for freedom and democracy.") China also cites "foreign interference," namely the U.S. The recent protest at the U.S. consulate, with American flags flying and signs saying "President Trump, Please Liberate Hong Kong"—a protest mobilized in support of a bill wending its way in the U.S. Congress, "The Hong Kong Human Rights and Democracy Act of 2019"—only fuels that claim. (The American heart sinks at any appeals to Trump or Congress.)

When will China lower the boom? With Chinese troops now massed at the border, and given the "radical" protesters and "foreign intervention," and given the very real damage done by months of protests to Hong Kong as international banking hub and commercial center—and, crucially, given the imperative that the Chinese Communist Party remain the dominant political force—the world awaits China's crackdown.

And yet, despite the gathering peril, the Hong Kong protesters keep on protesting, with, again, numerous lapses into violence. Rejecting the recent withdrawal of the extradition bill as "too little, too late," protesters now issue broad calls for political reform, including universal suffrage and an investigation of police brutality. In a *New York Times* op-ed, two lead Hong Kong activists, Joshua Wong and Alex Chow, avow the protesters are "only defending their beloved city." Calling their resistance movement "a crisis of legitimacy for the Chinese government," they call for "the rest of the world to support our crusade for human dignity, equality and freedom." They also cite the bill wending its way through Congress. (Again, the American heart sinks.)

Meanwhile, similar protests in Moscow erupted this summer, in July.

Smaller in scale but no less passionate, and challenging no less a fearsome state in Putin's Russia, the protests nominally are not pro-democracy but anti-corruption; the protesters call themselves "the opposition." Yet their objective—to field candidates to run in a local election, rigged though Russian elections usually are—can appropriately be called pro-democracy.

As Masha Gessen, Russian-American writer for *The New Yorker* and author of many books on Russia, describes: The impetus for the protests was the "so-called election" for the Moscow legislature (city council), a "rubber-stamping body that effectively reports to the mayor but is, formally, directly elected." "This year, thirty-nine people who are not in the mayor's pocket and do not belong to one of the Kremlin-controlled political parties tried to run for seats in the legislature and were not allowed on the ballot."

Reacting to the farce of gathering constituent signatures only to have them disallowed as non-existent—"even when these people, some of them well-known in the city, insisted that they had indeed signed the candidate's petition"—in mid-July seventeen such candidates called for a constituent meeting in a central Moscow square, "a gathering that would have been protected by law if the city had actually recognized them as candidates for political office." But, as the gathering was "illegal," a police crackdown ensued, turning ensuing protests into bloody melees, in what Gessen calls "a summer of unprecedented brutality." At one point, eight "troublemaker" candidates were behind bars. Two sets of parents were stripped of their parental rights because they took their children to the protests.

The upshot? In the election, held last Sunday, the anti-Putin opposition scored impressive results, even though the disallowed opposition candidates remained barred from running. Putin's United Russia party lost 13 seats, down from 38, barely clinging to its majority of 25 seats, while candidates effectively serving as anti-Putin opposition won 20 seats.

How did this happen? Via a tactic called "Smart Vote," devised by long-time and oft-imprisoned anti-corruption activist Aleksei Navalny (who himself was disallowed from running—again). Noting that Putin's candidates usually won with just 30–35 percent of the vote, Navalny urged constituents to vote for candidates who were the most credible rivals to Putin and had the best chance to win. While not all these candidates were truly of the opposition (some were from Putin's party who ran as "independents") and while regional results were less impressive (all 16 pro-Kremlin governors were re-elected), still, the results were "fantastic," says Navalny. "We can say clearly that in Moscow this result is a triumph for Smart Voting."

"Smart Vote": Any American politico would recognize this tactic as GOTV, "Get out the vote."

Which brings us back to our own damaged democracy here. Conscientious Americans are keenly aware of the multiple injuries inflicted on our democracy by Donald Trump, aided and abetted by too many Republicans. The disenfranchising of minority voters, the widespread gerrymandering, Trump's refusal to secure our voting system from (ironically) Russian meddling. The denigration of the races and women, in a nation dedicated to equality for all. The sorrow of Immigrant Nation betraying the immigrant. An Attorney General reinterpreting justice to suit his boss (Trump).

And the sickening spectacle of the president of the United States of America, erstwhile Leader of the Free World, cozying up to the arch-nemeses of the brave protesters in Hong Kong and Moscow, Xi Jinping and Vladimir Putin....

In this context, the conscientious American can only wish democracy-seeking souls around the world all good fortune, and urge the wisdom of Martin Luther King, Jr., who preached the power of nonviolent action. At the same time, we resolve to repair the damage done to our own ship of state. Repair is underway: Voter turnout in the 2018 midterm election was the highest ever, a super-abundance of candidates is running for president in 2020 and for local offices. As I have argued before, it may seem like breakdown, but we are in a reckoning.

Perhaps the world is having its own reckoning, a recognition, to wit: *how precious it is simply to have a voice*—that is, to have a democracy, a system of government based on the *demos*, the people.

As with anything precious, once gained, it must be preserved. Courage!

Breaking news: At posting, there are reports that Russian security forces have raided and searched 200 homes and all 45 regional offices of opposition leader Aleksei Navalny's Anti-Corruption Foundation. Purported reason: to further investigate alleged criminal money-laundering at the Foundation. A Foundation spokesman calls the raids an "act of mass political repression" to stop further erosion of pro-Kremlin forces in regional elections. Said a spokeswoman: "We won't stop."

—*Medium*, September 14, 2019

Censure, Not Impeachment: Make a Moral, Not a Political Statement

WITH THE IMPEACHMENT TRAIN now leaving the station and gathering speed, it may seem futile to push for another option—censure. But making the argument early may burnish censure's appeal if the impeachment process stalls or derails—which early signs indicate it will.

Given the instigating event—Donald Trump's phone call with the new Ukraine president asking a "favor" (that Ukraine investigate the business dealings of the son of Trump's likely 2020 Democratic rival, Joe Biden), while putting U.S. military aid to Ukraine on hold—and given the partisan lines already being drawn, the high crime and misdemeanor required to impeach will be hard to prove.

While Democrats see wrongdoing and abuse of power, further imperiling our democracy—Trump demanding a *quid pro quo* for his own political gain, in exchange for nearly $400 million in military aid Ukraine badly needs in its war with Russia—Republicans see no explicit *quid pro quo*, claiming it "an absolute joke" (a voter) and a "nothing-burger" of a call (Sen. Lindsey Graham), a call based on the "hearsay" of a "partisan" whistleblower. Should the Democratic-controlled House draw up articles of impeachment, the Republican-controlled Senate will not likely change this tune, even despite new reporting of the machinations of Trump's minions—personal attorney Rudy Giuliani, Attorney General William Barr, Secretary of State Mike Pompeo—to secure Ukraine's commitment to investigate the Bidens, among Trump's other political aims.

Ahead lies the Slough of Obstruction: Administration figures said they will defy House subpoenas, meaning court delays, and now the White House says it will not cooperate in the inquiry, launching a strategy of "stall, obfuscate, attack, repeat," per the Associated Press; in response the Democrats will cite obstruction of justice. And the hearings process itself, if we get there: When *The New York Times*, after declaring impeachment "the only option," editorialized about lines of inquiry—to determine which White House and State Department staff listened in on Trump's call, and who received a readout of the call, and who were involved in the "lock down" of the record—this heart sank: Who said what to whom and when—what would any of it mean, would any of it matter?

In all this argle-bargle—procedural, judicial, partisan—*how can Truth be revealed?*

The elemental truth that Democrats want to get at is, at bottom, a moral one: that in the universe of right and wrong action, it is simply wrong—in fact it is the essence of corruption—for the super-powerful to muscle the less powerful into action serving the super-powerful. The mechanism best suited to reflect this moral point is the censure. And Trump's shout-out to China, days ago, that it too should investigate the Bidens only amplifies his moral blindness—which blindness, again, is best addressed not with the unwieldy impeachment inquiry, but with censure.

The word "censure" itself implies moral judgment or opprobrium, whereas impeachment is political. While Americans of recent generations are uneasy at being "judge-y," Trump has served up such a cornucopia of corruption, as revealed in the Ukraine case and beyond, that censure becomes really a matter of shooting fish in a barrel: Let us count the ways. House Democratic leadership has opted to focus solely on the Ukraine case in its impeachment inquiry, but the beauty of censure is that it could open out into the entire universe of Trump's corruption, his anti-democratic norm-destruction, his incessant lying.

Picture it: Congressional Censure with a Bill of 101 (or however many) Particulars.

Censure also has this advantage: It can be passed by a simple majority in the House and 60 votes in the Senate, unlike the two-thirds' vote in both bodies required to impeach. Again, in the Republican-controlled Senate, getting 67 Republican profiles in courage to impeach a president who now effectively controls their party is well nigh impossible. But appealing to a handful of Republicans in both houses to stand for the principles the GOP once stood for: That is within the realm of the possible.

Another advantage: A neat-and-relatively-simple Congressional censure would restore the oxygen that's been sucked away from both the legislative process and the presidential campaign trail by the juggernaut of media attention now fixed on impeachment. That juggernaut obscures the fact we are still talking impeachment *inquiry*, not impeachment *per se*; it also drowns out discussion of alternatives like censure or letting the 2020 elections, only 13 months away, decide Trump's fate.

Powering that media juggernaut are polls showing, week by week, rising support for impeachment. But Democrats should beware: *It is mostly Democrats who are swinging from No to Yes on impeachment, not Independents or Republicans*. According to the Brookings Institution's William Galston: "Across the surveys that report partisan breakdowns, support for impeachment now averages 78% among Democrats and 38% among Independents compared to only 13% among Republicans."

Granted, the historical record on presidential censure is scant: The only president to be censured to date has been Andrew Jackson, by the Senate in 1834, for refusing to re-charter the Bank of the United States (this censure was later expunged). But this scantiness only heightens the historic clout of just the second presidential censure in more than two centuries of national life. Again, picture it for Donald J. Trump: Congressional censure with a Bill of 101 (or however many) Particulars.

And think what Trump's censure would signal to the world: that the America the world has long respected is working mightily to recover its respectable self....

Again, with the Impeachment Train barreling down the tracks, arguing for censure may be futile. Pro-impeachment supporters argue that the array of evidence laid out by an impeachment process *could* persuade

Republican holdouts—a fantastical if. For myself, I believe no president in our history deserves impeachment more, but my abiding fear is: With the Senate refusing to convict, Trump could claim that he is exonerated of all charges, then get re-elected—truly catastrophic for America.

Better than impeachment, which will not conclude anything because it will not be passed, censure—which is moral in thrust, easily achieved, and can be broad in scope—does offer a conclusion, a transcendent one. Which is: Of this whole long and dark and ruinous nightmare Donald Trump has put America through, we could finally say, formally and for the record—it is *wrong*.

—*Medium, October 9, 2019*

Abandoning an Ally on the Battlefield: America the Treacherous?

"IF I LOSE my honor," said Shakespeare, "I lose myself."

What Shakespeare said of the individual human being applies also to the nation, a collectivity of human beings. When a nation loses its honor—its moral integrity—or, worse, as with Trumpian America, when it loses it not through defeat to an overpowering opponent but by its own heedlessness—when a nation in effect *gives away its honor*, prizing it so little—the loss feels just as grievous, perhaps even more so.

This is not to say America the Beautiful has not acted in un-beautiful ways before (see: slavery, the Iraq war, torture). But two recent instances of honor-depletion—Ukraine and Syria—occurring within just days of each other, have struck deep with conscientious Americans and leaves fresh hurt. The conscientious, by definition, are ones who prize things like honor and feel things like shame.

The Ukraine and Syria stories, dominating the news for weeks now, are quickly grasped in their shameful essence.

With Ukraine—when president Donald Trump asked "a favor" of the new Ukrainian president: that he investigate Trump's rival Joe Biden, in exchange for badly needed military aid (nearly $400 million) for Ukraine's fight with Russia—the public can see the *quid pro quo*. As House Democrats put it in their fact sheet for their impeachment inquiry, there was the "shakedown," "the pressure campaign," and "the cover up."

All of which is, in a word, corruption. Meanwhile, the White House chief of staff insists that people should "get over it," that foreign aid is leveraged this [corrupt] way all the time.

With Syria, the shame is even sharper: abandoning an ally on the battlefield to possible genocide. In a phone call with Turkey's president Recep Tayyip Erdogan and without consulting his own military, Trump acceded to Erdogan's plan to invade northern Syria and quash the "terrorist" Kurds, for the ostensible purpose of creating a buffer zone. Again, as the import impinged, the American public could see the shadow this move cast over America: that we sacrificed a stalwart ally, the Kurds, who fought alongside us—and died in far larger numbers (over 11,000) than Americans (fewer than 10)—in the battle to defeat ISIS, which battle let it be remembered was then successful.

There is a damning word for this act: treachery. Roger Cohen, columnist for *The New York Times*, reaches back to antiquity and calls it "perfidy."

Perfidy between comrades-in-arms cuts deepest. American military personnel who fought alongside the Kurds, as well as others up and down the line, have defied the formal chain of command and gone public, venting disgust at their Commander-in-Chief's abandonment of an ally. Says one soldier: "I joined the Army to prevent genocide, not to pave the way for one." The *Times* reports one officer saying of the Kurds, "They trusted us and we broke that trust. It's a stain on the American conscience," while another officer said, "I'm ashamed." *The Washington Post* quotes a senior official saying of other senior officials, including retired generals: "They are livid." As for the Kurds, officials speak of "the worst thing": "betrayal." Says Kurdish general Mazloum Kobani Abdi of the U.S.: "You are leaving us to be slaughtered."

Tellingly, Republicans in Congress, until now in lockstep with Trump, have taken note of the blot on the nation's reputation of abandoning allies on the battlefield and stepped up, *finally*, to protest: Two-thirds (129) of House Republicans joined Democrats in a House resolution condemning the Syria withdrawal, passing it 354 to 60, in what the *Times* called "the most significant bipartisan repudiation of Trump since he took office." Dishonor pierces even the thickest carapace.

Also telling: Trump did his corrupt and treacherous deeds at the bidding of corrupt and treacherous foreign strongmen. Persuading Trump to abandon the Kurds is a leader (Erdogan) who jails or kills opponents. And coming to light about Trump's Ukraine move: It was Russia's Vladimir Putin, who also jails or kills his opponents, and Hungary's president Viktor Orban, who brags of turning his country's liberal democracy "illiberal"—it was these two worthies, Putin and Orban, who filled Trump's ear about Ukraine's alleged villainy. And Trump, possessing not a trace of honor himself, bit. Putin aims to prove America is as corrupt as, well, Russia. Point: Putin.

What must be remembered in all this noise is the tragedy befalling those America shafted. Regarding Ukraine, Trump has been badmouthing the country as corrupt, which is rich, considering how corrupt Trump himself is! In fact, while it did slide into corruption through oligarchic greed in the immediate post-Cold War period, Ukraine has worked mightily to get clean in recent years; the new president won office for his anti-corruption campaign. As for the Kurds, the heart bleeds at their unending bloodshed and misery, made all the worse when we remember the U.S. has betrayed the Kurds before, most recently when President George H.W. Bush, at the end of the Gulf War, encouraged the Kurds to rise up against Saddam Hussein, then provided no cover.

Adding to the human tragedy is the tragic turn in policy: In Syria, we had a policy that worked. With a minimal footprint in-country (1,000 U.S. troops), along with U.S. air cover, intelligence, and logistics, the U.S. and the Kurds had quelled the ISIS menace and written *finis* to the caliphate. Now, untold numbers of ISIS captives have escaped—to reorganize and fight the Infidel another day. Meanwhile, Trump crows at his rallies he's bringing the troops home, but in truth he is redeploying the troops elsewhere in the Middle East. And, while he pulled out our 1,000 troops allied with the stalwart Kurds, he has sent 3,500 new troops to Saudi Arabia, whose strongman leader admits responsibility for the killing of *Post* journalist Jamal Khashoggi.

My fellow conscientious Americans: Given the company we now keep and the corruption and treachery of our own leader, we are far from America the Beautiful.

Perhaps we Americans should not be surprised that we have come to this low pass. After all, there's a certain logic to the descent: After Trump, newly elected, began trash-talking our allies and alliances and cozying up to autocrats, after we surrendered the precious mantle of Leader of the Free World, it was just a matter of time before we would see the ugly results play out. Still, for the conscientious, it is humiliating, it stings. It hurts to be given the side-eye by the world and be thought morally and ethically lesser.

Question to Trump's base: In electing Trump the Disrupter, are you O.K. with the ensuing dishonor? Yes, let us end "endless wars," but let us end them honorably—in consultation with our allies, especially allies left in the field of battle.

Americans of recent generations have not bothered unduly with honor, but, now that our national honor is in tatters, we hunger for it. Thus it is heartening to see diplomats defy State Department and White House bans and testify at the House impeachment inquiry, stating for the record that, regarding Ukraine, Trump's *quid pro quo* was "wrong." Likewise it is heartening to see military personnel break protocol and speak out of their disgust at abandoning our Kurdish ally in Syria. And it is moving to see how many Americans have taken the loss of our honor to heart.

Lost honor: We mourn it now, we want it back, but it will be hard to recover. Trade deals can be negotiated, but honor can't. Some commentators now believe the reputational damage to America is irreparable. I believe we can recover our honor, but it will take a long, long time.

As Socrates said: "Regard your good name as the richest jewel you can possibly be possessed of—for credit is like fire; when once you have kindled it you may easily preserve it, but if you once extinguish it, you will find it an arduous task to rekindle it again." Socrates' last word on the subject: "The way to gain a good reputation is to endeavor to be what you desire to appear."

—*Medium*, October 24, 2019

In Reckoning, America Recovers Its Moral Compass

GIVEN THE CACOPHONY of destruction all around—of democratic norms, of ignoble policy, of polarization grown ever more vicious, all driven by our Disrupter-in-Chief, Donald Trump—Americans could be forgiven for fearing that all is lost for the ship of state and we are going down, fast.

Compounding this fear is the knowledge that our destruction is self-inflicted, not forced by external actors or factors. Unforced, Trump surrendered our mantle of Leader of the Free World, trashed our reputation as trusted ally. Domestically, he stokes racism and xenophobia, lies incessantly while attacking the media for reporting his lies. And Republicans, once God-fearing, continue to salute this amoral leader.

Moreover, American society itself is in churn, convulsing in resistance and protest. No wonder Americans report record levels of anxiety, depression, loss of sleep. Polls show rising numbers feel America is on the wrong track—way off. And commentators tell us we can expect this churn for years to come. It is, one can hear it all around, mourning in America.

But: There are mighty counter-forces now in play, combatting the heart-breaking destruction. And what should compound our hopefulness is this: the knowledge that these counter-forces are self-driven, not forced by external actors or factors; they emanate from our institutions and American society, beset as both are. Granted, given the tilt of the ship of state, one must squint to see these counter-forces at work, but once one does, one sees how America is trying hard to get right with itself.

For instance, the House impeachment inquiry, the main event at present, seeks to restore the norms of the presidency. Like many, I was leery of the impeachment option, fearing that with a Republican-controlled Senate never convicting, Trump would claim exoneration. But the testimony of dedicated diplomats and national security officials, all corroborating the whistleblower's allegations of Trump's *quid pro quo* with Ukraine, and Democrats now opening the inquiry to the public, all reassure. Our institutions are holding. Sunlight on all the incriminating evidence is all to the good.

At the grassroots: If democracy is based on the *demos*, the people, democracy's base (as distinguished from Trump's base), is hard at work. Record numbers of candidates, including record numbers of women, are running for office at all levels, including for the presidency. Voter turnout in the 2018 midterms was an all-time high for a nonpresidential election. People are "woke": We know our democracy is in trouble and we are doing our part to fix it.

Which goes to the churn in American society: the resistance and the protesting. While the anti-Trump resistance movement *per se* is less visible (but accounts in big part for all the electoral activity), its appeal—to resist Trump in all his pathology—still applies and accounts for much of the protest.

For one: If not for the admitted sexual predator now in the White House, would the #MeToo movement have come into being? At long last, women's allegations of sexual assault and trauma are finally being heard, and their weight and horror are forcing a reckoning of the power relations between the sexes. This is all to the good.

Likewise, the #BlackLivesMatter movement has taken on new weight as Trump's race-baiting has shoved America's abiding sin, racism, center-stage. And with outright racism now made safe, the white supremacist movement has emerged from the fringes to make its case that white lives matter more. These two forces have had America wrapped around the axle of History since our inception. Now, might we have a reckoning?

On another front, #MarchForOurLives, powered into being by young people sick of massacres in their schools, is addressing another besetting problem: gun violence. Young people are also the motive force behind the new urgency on climate change. As stakeholders to the future, the young know their very existence is imperiled.

All this churn may seem, on a down day, very like across-the-board breakdown. But parsed for the immensity and durability of the problems they address—sexism and sexual violence, racism and racial violence, gun violence, climate violence—these movements, in declaring these kinds of violence wrong, not right and not to be abided anymore, can be seen as regenerative. They constitute, in a word, reckoning.

Reckoning: To speak of reckoning, as it is generally understood, is to speak of a moral sorting-out—of the rightness or wrongness of a thing—and its resolution.

The thing is, moral considerations have been derided if not jeered for decades. The post-World War II generation, the boomers, prized tolerance, not being "judge-y." But tolerating all, while determinedly not judging moral merit, led to an "anything-goes" culture, which culture got turbo-charged in the 1990s when America won the Cold War: As winners we could do anything, and we did, plumbing the depths of human behavior, reinforced in pop culture and even high culture by critics who lauded the "bent," "twisted," and "transgressive." (Those of us arguing that, as victors, we had a responsibility to handle our power and gift of total freedom, well, responsibly were sidelined.) Thus it should not surprise us that, after decades of "Breaking Bad" decadence, we got a "Breaking Bad" president.

But, our "Breaking Bad" president has left half the country nauseated. All around I hear people lamenting Trump's actions as "so *not right*" and "so *wrong*"—which is quintessential moral language. Out of our suffering, again suffering we brought on ourselves, we are groping for the moral compass we laid aside long ago. America, to save itself, might be said to be backing into a moral consciousness once again.

However we recover that compass, working it again will be to the good—again, if we handle it judiciously. Understanding the moral counter-forces at work should put a new lens on the chaos. Other factors bode well: a sturdy economy, a media at the top of its game, a national character that, so far, resists fatalism. But if we are to recover, if we are to mature as a culture and turn these Dark Ages into a Renaissance, a moral consciousness is needed. In this hinge moment for America, we need our compass.

In the weeks after Trump's election in 2016, a dear friend said, presciently: "I think Donald Trump may be just the stinker to get John Q. Public off his sofa." O.K., we're off the sofa. Now, how do we work this compass?

—*Medium*, November 11, 2019

TV for Our Times:
"Our Boys" and "Press"

First in a series, TV for Our Times

WE ARE LIVING *in a "golden age of television," or so television critics repeatedly tell us. As the genesis of this golden age, the program that set the gold standard as it were, these critics invariably point to "The Sopranos," the "edgy" drama about a mob boss who "whacks" his rivals and takes his attendant anxieties to a psychiatrist, which after its premiere 20 years ago became appointment TV for millions. Since then, "edgy" has become the dominant motif, while "normal," not so much. Which is why, in these not-normal times presided over by an amoral president and his attendant sleaze, I do not watch much scripted TV, preferring instead news, documentaries, the English Premier Soccer League, and, for relief from today's anti-heroic fare, Turner Classic Movies.*

But in and among the super-abundance of TV programming today, there are singular offerings to be found that, like a strobe-light, illuminate, with superb filmmaking and quality acting, the particular force-fields that mark the early 21st century. This series will feature programs with protagonists who, if not the heroes of old, break out of the anti-heroic mold of pathology and ennui, to, at the least, endure, and at their best, contend.

Two such offerings, aired recently, follow. (Spoilers also follow, but they should not detract from the overall viewing experience.)

* * *

"Our Boys" (HBO)

This probing and moving mini-series takes on the most intractable of subjects: the Israeli-Palestinian divide, now of many decades' duration, and the gulf between the two tribes so rarely breached. Based on an actual event in 2014 that led to war in Gaza—the murder of a Palestinian boy who was targeted, hunted down, and burned to death by a group of Israeli boys, in revenge for the killing of three Israeli boys by Hamas militants—"Our Boys" focuses on the revenge act taken by the Israeli boys and on the tough self-investigation undertaken by Israel's internal security agency Shin Bet, once it confirms the unsettling evidence that "Our killers are Jews."

In every scene, we see how blinding the hatred between the sides is—and how rare it is for someone even to step into the other realm. Simon, the lead Shin Bet investigator, once it is determined that the chief suspects are boys from an ultra-Orthodox clan, infiltrates the clan and ultimately gets enough evidence to arrest. For this betrayal, he is disowned by his own ultra-Orthodox brother and, once the news of the arrests breaks, he is targeted with death threats from his own countrymen. For his own safety, ultimately Simon must leave the country.

On the Palestinian side, it is Hussein, father of the slain boy Mohammed, who breaches the gulf, when in his grief he seeks justice for his son by daring to deal with the Israeli legal system. For this betrayal, he is denounced by his community and even shunned, initially, by his surviving son and his own wife, Suha, who refuses to accompany him into enemy territory. In deeply moving scenes—the son in a meeting of the community, the wife privately—both come round to support the embattled Hussein.

Always palpably present in the Palestinian story is the reality that the Palestinians have no state of their own—a reality voiced in a heartbreaking outburst from the otherwise stoic Hussein with his Israeli lawyer. In his deeply humane portrait of Hussein as the grieving father who summons the wherewithal to deal with the enemy, actor Jony Arbid is peerless. Shlomi Elkabetz, well-known to Israeli audiences, plays the Israeli investigator with haunted reserve.

While "Our Boys" at ten episodes might have benefited from cutting, still the length gives the viewer an immersive experience in the mindset of both the Israeli and Palestinian universes, notably the message imbibed by the young—"our boys"—that it is permissible, even heroic, to kill any representative of the hated enemy. Also eye-opening is the extent to which Israel has become a surveillance state. Dialogue is in Hebrew and Arabic, with English subtitles.

This series sparked fierce protest from the Israeli public for its central focus on the Palestinian boy's death, while the instigating murder of the three Israeli boys is treated only tangentially. But an international audience will see in this series some evidence of Israeli self-critique, something not seen much during Prime Minister Benjamin Netanyahu's ultra-right tenure. (Netanyahu called for a boycott of the series, denouncing it as "anti-Semitic" and besmirching "the good name of Israel.") In this Israeli-American co-production, the show's creators Joseph Cedar (Israeli) and Tawfik Abu Wael (Palestinian), who also directed their respective casts, are to be commended for shining a light and bringing a humane sensibility into what remains still—and tragically so—No Man's Land.

"Press" (PBS, "Masterpiece Contemporary")

Very much front and center now, with the current occupant of the White House attacking the press as "the enemy of the American people," is the question: Where do we get our news? Can our news sources be trusted? In sum: What is truth, what is fact, what matters?

"Press," a six-episode BBC series, focuses on two London newspapers—one, *The Herald*, a left-leaning broadsheet where fact, confirmable fact, is king, and the other, *The Post*, a tabloid where—well, facts are fungible and political viewpoint is not as important as photos of scantily-clad young women and the latest tidbit (gotten by scurrilous means) on the sex lives of the powers-that-be. A *Post* reporter would be the one pushing a microphone at the grief-stricken to ask, "How do you feel?" (and employing scurrilous means to get onto that doorstep for the "death knock"). In lieu of fixed principles, the tabloid is of the firm belief everyone is rotten and it knows how to find the rot.

No surprise, it is the tabloid that is thriving, with an expanding newsroom in a classy building, while at the *Herald*, finances are so tight that, as the editor of its rival snarkily puts it, "You have mouse-traps in every corridor."

Of necessity, the characters representing these two opposites are introduced as hero and villain. In this corner, representing the *Herald*, is Holly Evans, a no-nonsense former reporter now editor, who snaps at colleagues and seems to suck lemons; and in the other corner, the tabloid's editor, Duncan Allen, who as the Devil (as literary critics tiresomely tell us) has all the best lines. Additionally, Holly, per the modern anti-heroic script, has to be sullied: She gets drunk and has sex with a reporter from the *Post*, whom she naively invites to become her flat-mate—which flat-mate palms her notes on a breaking story and appropriates it as his own.

This stereotype-overload dismays, but when it's put to work in episodes 4–6, the drama is ripping. True to heroic form, Holly confronts Duncan—"You stole my work"; his reply, "Your flat-mate stole your work, I published it"—says it all about tabloid ethics. In this scene, the series' best, Duncan plies Holly to come write for him—not edit but write, as special correspondent, any story she likes. This exchange elicits their opposing world-views: Holly, a half-cynic, says the world may be "crap," but "at least at the *Herald* we try to make it a bit better," to which the full cynic says (something we hear a lot these days), "And how's that going?" While Holly's paper tries to change the world by exposing its hypocrisies, his paper, Duncan says, shows the world as it is and even influences it, with "the most outrageous story-telling." In this last, Duncan, brilliantly acted by Ben Chaplin, lets flash across his face the self-hatred eating at this formerly serious journalist.

Holly does come work for the tabloid—and lasts one day—returning to her natural home, the *Herald*, to write, not edit (and once there flashes a smile for the first time). She brings with her a major lead regarding national security that Duncan had revealed to her, which sets up the rival papers for a final epic contest. In this appropriation of a lead, Holly acknowledges she is as ruthless as Duncan.

Playwright Mike Bartlett, whose recent hit play *King Charles III* imagines the current Prince Charles ascending the throne, structures this long-form drama to a breath-taking climax; he also has the humanity to allow the Devil ultimately some redemption. The diverse cast is uniformly strong, with Charlotte Riley ably playing Holly, the most challenging role in this series and indeed in our cynical world today.

With offerings like "Press" and "Our Boys," grappling with the knottiest crises of our dark and tumultuous times, TV may be in, if not a golden age—there is still a lot of brass in the system—then a gleaming silver one. Tune in and engage.

—*Medium*, November 18, 2019

Trump the Corrupt as Champion of Anti-Corruption?

DESPITE A TORRENT of detail from witnesses, the heart of the matter probed by the House impeachment inquiry has now become manifest. It is, clearly: Corruption.

Our corrupt president, Donald J. Trump, ignoring his oath to protect and defend the Constitution, abused his power as leader of the most powerful country on earth, by exacting from a less powerful country (Ukraine) a personal, non-state objective, one enabling his own re-election and retaining power: dirt on his potential Democratic rival, Joe Biden.

We see how this corruption works, thanks to testimony of career diplomats and national security officials, to the expert guidance of House Intelligence Committee chair Adam Schiff, to skillful interrogation by House Democrats.

What do we see? We see Trump's ask couched as a "favor." We see Trump's henchman (personal lawyer Rudy Giuliani) pursue this favor outside the official diplomatic channels. We see this favor solidify into a *quid pro quo*: Though Trump insists there was no *quid pro quo*, his conditioning of the release of $400 million in military aid vital to Ukraine in its hot war with Russia upon Ukraine's investigation into Biden and his son *is* the very essence of *quid pro quo*. Fact trumps vocabulary.

We also see—astonishingly, in real time—witness intimidation, when Trump tweets derogatory comments *during* the testimony of former U.S. ambassador to Ukraine Marie Yovanovitch. Asked by Chairman Schiff what she thought the effect of Trump's message might be on other witnesses, she said: "Intimidating." Appropriately, Schiff assured her the Committee takes witness intimidation seriously.

And, true to the dynamics of a smaller country finding itself on the downside of power, the Ukrainian leadership "came to understand" exactly what Trump meant as a favor, per a front-page story in *The Washington Post*.

What else is this but extortion, bribery, mafia tactics—in a word, corruption?

None of this behavior is, by any stretch, normal or permissible in a democracy. Yet the Trump White House and its Republican minions in Congress maintain that what Trump was actually aiming to do with his Ukraine ask was in furtherance of his own "anti-corruption" policy. The absurdity! Trump the Corrupt, the champion of anti-corruption? If Trump is so keen on fighting corruption, why did he fire Ambassador Yovanovitch, who made her name fighting corruption in over 30 years of diplomatic service and earned multiple awards for doing so?

The irony would be amusing if it were not so perilous. Ukraine, once infested with oligarch-driven corruption, is in its newly-elected reformist president, Volodymyr Zelensky, seeking rebirth as a democracy clean of corruption. As the career diplomats testified in the inquiry, Ukraine, in resisting Russian aggression, is key to a stable Europe. As two young Ukrainian legislators and former journalists soberly stated on *Fareed Zakaria GPS*, more than 13,000 Ukrainian troops have been lost and their nation's future is at stake.

Yet: Republicans remain blind to Trump's now-manifest corruption. We see the ideological blinders firmly in place throughout this inquiry. Braying that Democrats are trying to undo the 2016 election, Republicans cannot fix on or comprehend the import of the evidence laid before them. They deny Trump's clear *quid pro quo* with Ukraine, and if they concede it, say it still does not rise to the level of impeachment. But rather than make even this weasel argument, Republicans more often resort to character assassination of both the witnesses and their Democratic colleagues, each vying to outdo the other in viciousness.

What we are seeing is a party in thrall, a cult of personality. As historian Robert Kagan writes, Republicans in their fanatical loyalty to

Trump would enable his corruption to become "normalized"—a death knell for American democracy.

At the same time, we see other things, more encouraging things. We see in the witnesses—the "bureaucrats" vilified by Republicans from Ronald Reagan onward—people who are decent, dedicated to the public good, deeply knowledgeable in their field, and who defied a White House ban to come before the public to set in place the evidence incriminating Trump.

We see the legislative branch, in its investigative mode, despite Republican obstructionism, functioning effectively, with the incriminating evidence enabled to come forth. We see Democrats, disciplined for once, engage in probing questioning and, stirringly, come to the aid of witnesses attacked by Republicans with passionate defenses (special shout-out to Connecticut Democrat Jim Himes). In all this, we see it is Democrats, not Republicans, who are the real conservatives, fighting to conserve democratic norms, rule of law, fairness, simple decency.

We also see the impact of the impeachment inquiry on the latest Democratic presidential debate, held last night. Initial questioning bore on the inquiry, with several candidates noting the inquiry's theme: Trump's corruption. Over the course of the debate, all candidates declared that, while Trump must be defeated, more importantly, we must restore the above virtues, mortally threatened by corruption—democratic norms, rule of law, fairness, simple decency.

Grassroots Democrats (myself included) who worried that an impeachment inquiry focused solely on the Ukraine case was too narrow, that the cornucopia of Trump's malfeasance need be litigated, can now take heart that such focus suffices. For, as Walt Whitman said of the human being, corruption "contains multitudes": It bears on power, values, ethics, everything we hold most dear; as an abuse of power, corruption *is* an impeachable offense. And grassroots Democrats (myself included) who worried that even if the House votes to impeach and the Republican-controlled Senate acquits, then Trump will claim exoneration, can take heart again: This president's corruption will be prosecuted in the 2020 presidential campaign—and it will lose.

For the first time in a long time, I feel Democrats will win in 2020 and the American ideals we love and cherish will be restored. Happy Thanksgiving.

—*Medium*, November 21, 2019

Republicans Stand by a President
Who Pardons Accused War Criminals

JUST WHEN YOU thought Donald Trump had smashed through every last guardrail of American democracy, he finds new frontiers in degradation.

In pardoning accused war criminals, Trump achieves that new low, marking a dangerous precedent for our military and scarring, perhaps irreparably, our good name and moral standing in the world.

Outrage at this degradation has gotten lost in the whirlwind of impeachment—House Democrats are reportedly drawing up Articles of Impeachment as I write—but, no matter: It is important to state for the record one's protest. In a nearly three-year tenure of unparalleled egregiousness, Trump got creative in his malevolence with this contrived show of support for "our boys."

At issue: Trump gave full pardons to Maj. Mathew L. Goldsteyn, an Army Special Forces officer who faced murder charges for killing an unarmed Afghan whom he believed was a Taliban bomb-maker, and to Clint Lorance, a former Army lieutenant serving a 19-year sentence at Fort Leavenworth for killing two Afghan civilians.

Receiving the most media play is Chief Petty Officer Edward Gallagher, a Navy SEAL cited for multiple charges—shooting civilians in Iraq, killing a captive enemy fighter with a hunting knife, and threatening to kill fellow SEALs if they reported him. Gallagher was acquitted by a military jury of all charges except a minor one: bringing discredit to the armed forces by posing for a photo with the corpse of a captive he was accused of killing. When the Navy moved to demote Gallagher and remove his SEAL Trident pin, Trump came to his rescue, blocking the demotion.

Trump's defense? "We train our boys to be killing machines, then prosecute them when they kill!" A *Fox News* host commended Trump's "fidelity to the war fighter," saying "The benefit of the doubt should go to the guys pulling the trigger." Trump claims he is "standing up for three great warriors against the deep state." So much for the Geneva Conventions; Trump is now the final arbiter of military justice.

And now we learn: *Trump will campaign with these accused war criminals, using them as props in his bid for re-election in 2020!* Starting, already, last Sunday night, at a fundraiser in Florida.

About which, VoteVets.org, a political action committee founded by Iraq war veterans in 2006, writes: "If we weren't three years into this astonishingly corrupt administration, we would find this next sentence hard to believe: President Donald Trump brought accused war criminals he pardoned to a closed-door fundraiser...as his honorable guests"—the latest in a "slew of unacceptable behavior from our Commander-in-Chief that makes a mockery of our men and women serving our country."

Up is down, day is night, wrong is right to this amoral president. Now accused war criminals are "honorable" and paraded in a presidential campaign as "heroes"?

While those in uniform and retired are up in arms about the implications of Trump's pardon of war crimes for "good order and discipline" and military justice—it should be noted the illegal actions of Gallagher and Goldsteyn were reported by their own platoon members—the leadership has not acquitted itself well here. Secretary of Defense Mark Esper fired the Navy Secretary for going outside the chain of command to work with the White House to finesse the Gallagher case. Dismayingly, the Secretary of Defense himself has not disavowed his Commander-in-Chief's unpardonable pardons.

Making the military's proper case is Gen. Martin Dempsey, former Joint Chiefs of Staff chairman: "Absent evidence of innocence or injustice the wholesale pardon of U.S. service members accused of war crimes signals our troops and allies that we don't take the Law of Armed

Conflict seriously. Bad message. Bad precedent. Abdication of moral responsibility. Risk to us."

In all this, the last line of defense to prevent the further degradation of military standards and America's moral reputation lies in the political realm, with Trump's party colleagues—the Congressional Republicans. Republicans have long held themselves out as the nation's moral guardians and, as to the military, their staunchest supporters, quick to salute the troops' valor and sacrifice. How often have Republicans harangued Democrats for "leading from behind" and for flying "the white flag of surrender"?

Sadly, about Trump's pardon of accused war criminals, Republicans are themselves flying the white flag of surrender. Worse, they have not even mounted a fight of any kind, or indicated any plans to do so, either individually or as a collective, so fearful are they of Trump's wrath. To his credit, Senator Mitt Romney of Utah has stepped up to declare it "unthinkable" to pardon someone "legitimately convicted of committing war crimes." Senator Joni Ernst of Iowa has "issues" with such pardons.

I wonder: Have Republicans asked themselves, What kind of nation is it that Donald Trump envisions for us, where accused war criminals are deemed honorable...?

Biblical devotees that they claim they are, Republicans should ponder the sowing of iniquity. Surely individual Republicans, in their hearts, know full well their leader's iniquity in his embrace of accused war criminals. (And they are wrong to mock Democrats for our upset over this matter.) Yet we see no Republican pushback to Trump, no argument, no Martin Luther "Here I stand, I can do no other" stance. And the likelihood is not great, as Republicans more and more identify with Trump's cause, including his adherence to the debunked conspiracy theory that it was Ukraine, not Russia, that meddled in the 2016 election (and Russia will again in 2020).

What we are seeing are the consequences of the Republicans' Faustian bargain with Trump: They are tethered together, deeply complicit in dishonor. And to think the United States of America, victor in World

War II, convened the Nuremberg war crimes trials, setting the moral foundation for the postwar world....

House Speaker Nancy Pelosi, speaking of the impeachment inquiry, says Democrats must pursue it in a "prayerful" manner. Politicians always seek "a path" to take a specific action. I prayerfully ask Republicans to pray and to seek a path to restore America's honor. They have the power to do so; will they find the courage?

—*Medium*, December 9, 2919

Classic Screwball Comedies: Rx for Our Fraught Times

SCREWBALL COMEDY MAY be the perfect tonic for our unhappy times—with American democracy under siege from within, leadership hapless, the public hopping mad at just about everything. In fact, we might call our times screwball tragedy.

Given screwball comedy's classic elements—unlike characters meeting in unlikely circumstances, who spark to each other ("spark" being a screwball verb) but who for their reasons resist that spark, until finally, after an often antic journey together (or escapade), they give in to the power of Love—the allure is enduring. In screwball, characters are likeable, the world is tractable, humane, *fun*—imagine!

An element I especially like: The woman exercises power equal to the man, both in action and snappy dialogue, making for more dynamic engagement than traditional romance. The comedy comes out of the revelations of human nature caught in the pixilating throes of Love—"What fools these mortals be!" Words like "romp" and "charming" apply to great screwball—again, tonic. Of course, screwball can't shoo our present crises away, but the fizzy effect lingers, reminding us: Love is the prize.

Historically, the screwball comedy came into being in the Great Depression of the 1930s, when the Hollywood studios responded to that national crisis with the stated intention of giving the masses fare to enjoy.

[406]

That era also gave us beauty—the peerless dancing of Fred Astaire and Ginger Rogers—and a spunky child, Shirley Temple, who gave people hope in America's future. Would that today's filmmakers understood the eternal need for laughter and beauty and spunk in dark times.

Screwball energy being hard to maintain, some specimens, after a bang-up set-up, sag in the second act, for example *His Girl Friday, My Man Godfrey, Libeled Lady,* and *Sullivan's Travels.* The latter film, though, captures screwball's essence: portraying the human parade, "with a little sex in it." The ten films below are listed in approximately chronological order. The spoilers should not deter from the fun.

It Happened One Night (1934)

Considered the progenitor of the genre, *It Happened One Night* became a surprise hit and won Oscars for best picture, actor, actress, director (Frank Capra), and screenplay. In it, Ellie Andrews (Claudette Colbert), a socialite engaged to a wealthy twit her father cannot abide, escapes her father's strictures and yacht by diving into a Florida bay (in a lounging gown, no less), fetching up at a bus station wearing a chic traveling outfit, complete with beret (costume changes don't get explained in screwball).

By happy coincidence, Peter Warne (Clark Gable), a reporter, boards the same bus as Ellie and takes the seat next to her, after insisting she make room for him. When in the course of the bus journey northward, Peter learns who she is, his conflict becomes ethical—does he cash in on this breaking scandal?—and personal: While attracted to Ellie, he's put off by her snootiness (he calls her "Brat") and aims to teach her a thing or two. For her part, Ellie falls for Peter, while clinging to the idea of her fiancé.

Colbert and Gable (pictured at top) are scintillating together, and Walter Connolly playing her father is both funny and endearing, especially in the final scenes with Gable and then Colbert. The film is chock full of wonderful scenes, with the hitchhiking scene the classic, when Ellie famously flags down a car, using a "system all my own."

The Awful Truth (1937)

In this charming comedy, directed by Leo McCarey, a married couple, Lucy and Jerry Warriner, has to file for divorce and start seeing others before they realize "the awful truth"—they still love each other. Played by Irene Dunne and
Cary Grant, their mutual attraction is clear to the viewer, not necessarily to them. It's fun to watch the suave Grant gate-crash Lucy's date with an Oklahoma oil man (a game Ralph Bellamy), and later, sure that she's also seeing her handsome singing coach (who's French and always in a tux), he crashes her song recital; when he tries to recover himself after falling off a chair, she works a "ha-ha-ha" into her aria. (These two fight well.) It's also fun to watch lady-like Dunne spoof the risqué singing style of a showgirl Jerry saw briefly, performing it for his new interest's stuffy family. As the minutes tick toward midnight on the day their divorce is final, the comedy modulates and real feeling comes to the fore.

But until then, everything is contended, even custody of their dog. In divorce court, when the judge says he'll take the custody matter "under advisement," Jerry says, "Yes, but when will you *know?*" Out of screwball, truth about the legal system.

Bringing Up Baby (1938)

When a paleontologist meets a specimen of the human race he's never encountered before—a hare-brained socialite—hilarity ensues, as well as a sentimental education for both. The en-
counter is initiated when, on the golf course, David Huxley, played by Cary Grant, sees his ball being played by Susan Vance, acted to fine ditziness by the normally grounded Katharine Hepburn. Because this encounter pulled David away from the financier he was wooing to fund the assembling of a pre-historic behemoth, and because Susan knows

said financier, the rest of the film, and mayhem, flows from Susan "just wanting to help" David get his heart's desire. By film's end David realizes his heart's desire is...Susan? But not before they jump down the rabbit-hole together, led by Susan, who's been given custody by her brother of a leopard named Baby, a development explained perfectly by screwball "logic" and as directed by Howard Hawkes.

My favorite sequence is early, when Susan pursues David at the country club, pulls at his coat, and tears it: "Oh, you tore your coat." He then steps on her dress, and it tears. Bound together, tighter than they could know, they two-step their way out.

Holiday (1938)

When regular guy Johnny Case meets a rich girl and becomes engaged to her, the tension between high status and regular people becomes an issue, indeed the main issue in this lesser-known comedy directed by George Cukor. That tension begins to resolve when Johnny becomes acquainted, then falls truly in love, with his fiancée's less snobby, more real sister, Linda. In a wonderful scene, Linda quizzes Johnny about
his idea that, rather than joining her family's bank, he take time off from his job in finance to determine if the field really is for him—the "holiday" of the title. With Johnny played by the ubiquitous Cary Grant, this time with not every hair in place, and Linda played by Katharine Hepburn, who touchingly conveys the loneliness of the lesser-loved sister, the viewer starts pulling for these two early on. Lew Ayres plays Linda's brother Ned, whose failure in their father's eyes has made him a lush.

The tension between high status and regular guy, in any other film, would resolve in high drama, but with screwball, it is resolved more gently—making fun of the stuffed shirts, recognizing where true (human) value lies. As she leaves home to join Johnny, Linda vows to come back for her brother, and he vows to hold on.

Midnight (1939)

This little-known gem, set in Paris, features another unlike couple: an out-of-work showgirl, played by Claudette Colbert, and a hard-working taxi-driver, played by Don Ameche. Their attraction is instant and mutual, but the showgirl, Eve Peabody, is bent  on her project: to find a sugar daddy (though she would not put it that way, not exactly). Eve exits Tibor's taxi and somehow finds her way into a posh soiree, then into the back room where a card game is in progress, with Georges and Helene Flammarion, played by John Barrymore and Mary Astor, and Helene's swain Jacques (Francis Lederer). Turns out Eve is great at cards, and soon enough she is ensconced in the Flammarion household, with Jacques in attendance. When Tibor learns of this development, he drives his taxi to the Flammarion mansion and, stepping out in a tux, crashes the party and takes control. Eve resists, but, love *must* triumph.

It's all frothy stuff, but Colbert and Ameche bring real feeling to it. Watch for director Mitchell Leisen's special touch: Early on for Tibor, and midway for Eve, both characters get very still for a moment: In their eyes is registered the seriousness beneath the froth.

Idiot's Delight (1939)

This film is more cynical than most screwball: Its anti-war heart is squeezed between two world wars. Harry Van (Clark Gable), veteran of World War I, hopes to return to Broadway vaudeville, but times have changed and he bounces around until  he lands in Omaha, faking it as a mentalist. There he meets an acrobat, Irene (Norma Shearer). They spark, but part, he feeling he's a "bust," she insisting he is great (he calls her a "dreamer"). Years pass, it is 1939, and their paths cross again in Europe: He now heads an act called "Harry

Van and 'Les Blondes,'" with six showgirls; she now sports a blonde wig, a thick Russian accent, and the company of arms manufacturer Achille Weber (Edward Arnold). Stuck together in a mountain-top hotel in an unnamed country, the borders now closed, Harry insists on going on. Told war is about to break out, Harry's response is classic: "What, *another one?*" While Harry and troupe entertain with a song-and-dance number, "Puttin' on the Ritz"—not to be missed—he tries to puzzle out if this Irene is the Omaha Irene.

Giving the film its edge is firebrand Quillery (Burgess Meredith), railing against the international arms trade; in the end he is executed. A cancer researcher declares he will stop his research: "Why should I save people who don't want to be saved?" But love prevails: An air attack forces Harry and Irene to declare themselves—"I loved you all along." Turner Classic Movies shows two endings: the one for Europe ending with a hymn, the one for the U.S. with razzle-dazzle. Maybe we need the hymn now? (This film, directed by Clarence Brown, is based on Robert Sherwood's Pulitzer Prize-winning play.)

The Philadelphia Story (1940)

A favorite of many, *The Philadelphia Story* is another tale about formerly marrieds rediscovering that Fate means for them to be together. To do so, though, Main Line socialite Tracy Lord (Katha-  rine Hepburn) must evolve from snob to human being, a metamorphosis enabled by ex-husband C.K. Dexter Haven (Cary Grant), who disrupts Tracy's pending marriage to George "Man of the People" Kittredge, by his own subtle questioning, also by bringing reporter McCauley "Mike" Connor (Jimmy Stewart) and photographer Liz Imbrie (Ruth Hussey) to cover the event for "Spy" magazine, exposure that's anathema to a Main Line family. Unexpectedly—or did the Champagne help?—Connor, initially contemptuous of the wealthy, falls in love with Tracy, causing Liz, his intended, pain. Tracy's metamorphosis to human being is complete when she sees the world, and her ex-husband, with new eyes.

My favorite scene is where Connor, full of Champagne, pays a midnight visit to C.K. Dexter Haven. Hepburn, after being dubbed "box office poison," made a hit of this play on Broadway, then used it to engineer her Hollywood comeback with one of her favorite directors, George Cukor. Cheers!

The Lady Eve (1941)

Talk about opposites attracting. When a professional card sharp, played by Barbara Stanwyck, falls in love with her mark, a shy biologist who's the son of a famous brewer, played by Henry Fonda, high amusement ensues. This meeting takes place on a cruise ship, which Charles boards after a year up the Amazon and where Jean and her father (Charles Coburn) ply their nefarious trade. The scene where Jean works her magic on Charles, fingers in his hair, he who's been up the Amazon for a year, is classic.

But when Charles learns of Jean's trade, he cuts off the budding relationship. Jean plots revenge, venturing into his orbit as a member of the English peerage, "the Lady Eve." Charles is sure he's met her before, but can't quite place where, which leads to the only slapstick I have ever enjoyed (this one involving, serially, a sofa, a roast beef, and a curtain). In this film, it is Jean/Eve who changes most, becoming a feeling human being, while Charles remains befuddled.

Fonda does befuddled so well; Stanwyck is terrific in both roles. Both are brilliantly directed by Preston Sturges. Familiar character actors appear: Englishman Eric Blore, who steps in as Eve's English cousin; Eugene Pallette, who, as Charles' father, acts as Eve's emissary to his son; and William Demarest, Charles' associate, who insists Eve *is* Jean—"I tell ya, it's the same dame."

The More the Merrier (1943)

This comedy directed by George Stevens is not often cited as screwball, but the set-up certainly is: Housing is short in wartime Washington, D.C., and rooms in apartments and homes must be shared (the "more" part).
When new boarder Mr. Benjamin Dingle (Charles Coburn) takes a liking to a young man looking for a room for a few days before he heads to war (Joe Carter, played by Joel McCrea) and he takes him in—without informing the holder of the lease, Miss Connie Milligan (played by Jean Arthur)—the "merrier" part kicks in. The attraction between Connie and Joe is instant, but there is a complication: She is engaged to Charles J. Pendergast, a very important bureaucrat. More merriment ensues as Mr. Dingle promotes Joe to Connie as a "fine, high-type young man" and as Joe woos Connie as if Pendergast did not exist: His trying to make out with Connie as they walk home after a night out is priceless.

Coburn, who usually played sober-sided characters, is a hoot playing Cupid. Jean Arthur was never my favorite, but here she is perfect. So is McCrea, whose natural acting style and physique made him the prototypical American man, who here is soon going off to war. War tempers everything: When Joe and Connie finally confess their love, through a makeshift wall dividing their rooms, merriment turns deeply moving.

Dinner at Eight (1933)

Chronologically, with *Dinner at Eight* we step back in time, to the Great Depression again; and technically, this film is more comic drama than screwball, but with Jean Harlow, Marie Dressler, and the sublime Billie Burke in the cast, it has its moments. Apart from being one of my all-time favorites, I include it because of its resonance to the present economic picture: Businessman Oliver Jordan (Lionel Barrymore)

faces the bankruptcy of his shipping line, which crisis along with his heart trouble he keeps from wife Millicent (Burke), who is focused on organizing a grand dinner with English royalty as special guests. Compounding Oliver's crisis, former diva and old flame Carlotta Vance (Dressler) informs him she wishes to sell her shares in his company's stock. Harlow's Kitty, carrying on an affair with a society doctor while married to a *nouveau-riche* financier (Wallace Beery), emerges as the main protagonist—by bringing her husband and Jordan together, to save the Jordan line.

Other crises play out: The Jordans' daughter Paula (Madge Evans), engaged to young Ernest, is smitten by the has-been actor Larry Renault (John Barrymore), a futile affair Carlotta movingly sorts out. Equally moving is when Millicent learns how ill Oliver is; and when she learns they are now broke, her reaction is priceless: "Everybody's broke, Darling. We'll economize." For a comic drama, in the end all is put basically aright, apart from a suicide. Harlow's laughter, though, is pure screwball. Director is the omnipresent George Cukor.

Finally, as a bonus film:

A Midsummer Night's Dream (1935)

Harking back to early film history, and reaching even further back to William Shakespeare for story and poetic language, *A Midsummer Night's Dream*, with the throes of Love being its entire focus, may be *the* original screwball comedy. This film, directed by  William Dieterle and Max Reinhardt, is a gauzy moonbeam, with Felix Mendelssohn's sublime symphony as score. The cast features Dick Powell and Olivia de Havilland, with—brace for it—James Cagney as Bottom (who metamorphoses from human to donkey) and a young Mickey Rooney as Puck. Every major character in this romp is pixilated by love's magic—everyone, that is, but Puck. Which distance allows Puck to make the immortal observation—and the emblematic expression of screwball comedy—"Lord, what fools these mortals be!"

—*Medium*, December 20, 2019

"A Low Dishonest Decade":
The Poet Points the Way Upward

ON SEPTEMBER 1, 1939, a poet walked into a New York bar and, surveying the darkening world of his time, wrote a poem dedicated to that day. It was, of course, the day Germany invaded Poland, and sentient people knew in their bones that war was coming; in fact, it would be a world war, another one, so soon after the first.

Remarkably, that poem speaks to us now in our own darkening times. Not that a world war seems imminent, though who knows where president Donald Trump's reckless order to have Iran's top general killed by drone will lead us? In other ways, though, the poem—"September 1, 1939" by English poet W.H. Auden—resonates now, chiming with the universally poor marks given the decade that has just closed.

The end of a decade and the advent of a new one always generate commentary—and grades—from the world's commentariat, and the 2010s have, in a word, flunked. Politically and culturally, it was deemed "a decade of disillusionment" and "the end of normal." With both the erosion of democracy around the world and the rise of a new generation of dictators, it was, as the Brookings Institution states flatly, "a horrid decade for those who aspire to a more cooperative and freer world."

In fact, in America we might call the 2010s—which saw the tenure of the admirable and temperate Barack Obama, our first African-American president, give way, in a reactionary paroxysm, to the racist, lying, corrupt, amoral, endlessly angry Trump—a "low dishonest decade," just as Auden said of the 1930s. (It's a match: Trump is likewise low and dishonest.) The collapse of Obama's signature "audacity of hope" into Trump's hot mess, and the self-immolation of America as Leader of the Free World into a dangerous and heedless behemoth not to be trusted—all this ruin occurring in just four years—has shocked sentient Americans to their core.

We can relate—oh how we can relate—to that poet sitting in a bar in 1939, "uncertain and afraid," penning his nine-stanza lamentation.

Auden levels his indictment against his decade early, noting, "Waves of anger and fear / Circulate over the bright / And darkened lands of the earth, / Obsessing our private lives." (Americans will resonate to the obsessing part.) In his second stanza, he supposes someday historians will paint a clearer picture of how Germany fell so low ("Accurate scholarship can / Unearth the whole offense / From Luther until now / That has driven a culture mad"). But for now, he notes, he must bear the "rubbish" that dictators speak; he notes "the enlightenment driven away." We today feel very far from the post-World War II era of enlightenment, security, peace.

But midpoint in his poem, Auden reverts to the bar and its denizens—his fellow human beings—and turns, if not hopeful, then prayerful: "Faces along the bar / Cling to their average day: / The lights must never go out, / The music must always play."

But if Auden is prayerful about his fellow human beings, he also holds us to account. Harking seemingly to the opening of Dante's *Divine Comedy*, in which Dante midway through life loses his way and finds himself in "a forest dark," Auden writes of us moderns, that we are: "Lost in a haunted wood, / Children afraid of the night / Who have never been happy or good." It is flawed humanity, Auden is saying, that salutes and embraces a dictator (would that Republicans knew their Auden). He speaks also of "the error bred in the bone": that "each woman and each man / Craves what it cannot have, / Not universal love / But to be loved alone." Universal peace? Not a chance if we don't want it above all else.

But the poet cannot abandon all hope (unlike the commentators cited above). In his last two stanzas he declares himself—forcefully, even defiantly: "All I have is a voice / To undo the folded lie." I love that: "the folded lie," the lie normalized from on high, repeated endlessly—a state of things Americans are now awash in, with Trump banging on endlessly about "fake" news, "hoax" investigations and impeachment—so much so that Truth loses its grounding (and its proper Capital letter). Auden is emphasizing that it is the lie, and the lying—the dishonesty—that we must fight, and fight ceaselessly. He points to "the Just"—people of character who are, properly, Capitalized—and, closing, says: "May I, composed like them / Of Eros and of dust, / Beleaguered by the same / Negation and despair, / Show an affirming flame."

Along the way to the climax, Auden famously exhorts us: "We must love one another or die." Auden also famously disavowed that line, later, as sentimental, even (his poem's indictment echoing in his mind) "dishonest." But, to "show an affirming flame" here, let us retrieve that line from Auden's outtakes and dust it off for its essential truth: Because, really, we *must* love one another or die.

The poet of course should have the last word, no more exegesis. Here is the poem in full, offered as guide out of our present "haunted wood" and "low dishonest decade."

SEPTEMBER 1, 1939
W.H. Auden (1907–1973)

I sit in one of the dives
On Fifty-second Street
Uncertain and afraid
As the clever hopes expire
Of a low dishonest decade:
Waves of anger and fear
Circulate over the bright
And darkened lands of the earth,
Obsessing our private lives;
The unmentionable odor of death
Offends the September night.

Accurate scholarship can
Unearth the whole offence
From Luther until now

*That has driven a culture mad,
Find what occurred at Linz,
What huge imago made
A psychopathic god:
I and the public know
What all schoolchildren learn,
Those to whom evil is done ·
Do evil in return.*

*Exiled Thucydides knew
All that a speech can say
About Democracy,
And what dictators do,
The elderly rubbish they talk
To an apathetic grave;
Analyzed all in his book,
The enlightenment driven away,
The habit-forming pain,
Mismanagement and grief:
We must suffer them all again.*

*Into this neutral air
Where blind skyscrapers use
Their full height to proclaim
The strength of Collective Man,
Each language pours its vain
Competitive excuse:
But who can live for long
In a euphoric dream;
Out of the mirror they stare,
Imperialism's face
And the international wrong.*

Faces along the bar
Cling to their average day:
The lights must never go out,
The music must always play,
All the conventions conspire
To make this fort assume
The furniture of home;
Lest we should see where we are,
Lost in a haunted wood,
Children afraid of the night
Who have never been happy or good.

The windiest militant trash
Important Persons shout
Is not so crude as our wish:
What mad Nijinsky wrote
About Diaghilev
Is true of the normal heart;
For the error bred in the bone
Of each woman and each man
Craves what it cannot have,
Not universal love
But to be loved alone.

From the conservative dark
Into the ethical life
The dense commuters come,
Repeating their morning vow;
"I will be true to the wife,
I'll concentrate more on my work,"
And helpless governors wake
To resume their compulsory game:

Who can release them now,
Who can reach the deaf,
Who can speak for the dumb?

All I have is a voice
To undo the folded lie,
The romantic lie in the brain
Of the sensual man-in-the-street
And the lie of Authority
Whose buildings grope the sky:
There is no such thing as the State
And no one exists alone;
Hunger allows no choice
To the citizen or the police;
We must love one another or die.

Defenseless under the night
Our world in stupor lies;
Yet, dotted everywhere,
Ironic points of light
Flash out wherever the Just
Exchange their messages:
May I, composed like them
Of Eros and of dust,
Beleaguered by the same
Negation and despair,
Show an affirming flame.

—*Medium*, January 7, 2020

American Colossus, Get Thee to Rehab: Learn to Exercise Power Wisely

WITH THE RECENT one-two punch—the betrayal of the Kurds, our allies in fighting ISIS, and now the assassination of Iran's top general, Qassim Suleimani—president Donald Trump has unequivocally established America as an international bully.

Bully, *noun*: one who seeks to harm, intimidate, or coerce those perceived as *vulnerable*; one who is habitually cruel, insulting, or threatening to others who are *weaker or smaller* (my emphases). Additionally, bullies don't give a fig what others, allies included, think of their bullying. Taken together, this definition now fits the U.S. We are in a pantheon of bad actors we don't really want to be in.

This is not to say Suleimani was not a bad actor himself, and a very bad one (and Republicans who call Democrats "terrorist-loving" should be ashamed). Iran is a leading sponsor of state terror and Suleimani was its chief architect, with the blood of Americans and Iran's neighbors, including Iraq, on his hands. But to eliminate him while he was on Iraqi soil, and not consulting the Iraqis beforehand—no wonder Iraq now orders U.S. troops out. Iraq is furious at Trump for putting an ally (themselves) in the crossfire.

And earlier, the Kurds certainly deserved consulting, not the insult of betrayal. But bullies don't care about betrayal.

Of course, Trump's bullying was on view before this: His notorious phone call with Ukraine's president last July, in which he asked "a favor"—dirt on Democratic rival Joe Biden—meanwhile withholding $400 million in military aid Ukraine needed in its hot war with Russia. This is behavior of a mafia *capo*, not the President of the United States. Plus, there is Trump's nonstop nasty treatment of our NATO allies; his reference to various African countries as "s***hole"; the list is very long.

And now that list includes Trump threatening to bomb the cultural heritage sites precious to the countries he targets, starting with Iran. Saner heads apparently talked him out of this war crime he contemplated. But imagine if Iran threatened to bomb the Statue of Liberty, or raze the battlefield at Gettysburg....

And not to overlook the other planned assassinations, the thousands of drone strikes and air strikes, some killing civilians—all clandestine—that the U.S. carries out, for what purpose, it is not clear, other than that we have the bullets, drones, and bombers....

No wonder polls show the world's opinion of Trump's America is falling. It is heartbreaking for conscientious Americans to see our nation becoming an international pariah.

There will be consequences for our contempt shown the world. Americans got a whiff of those consequences when, reacting to the Suleimani assassination, Iran, vowing "harsh" revenge, fired a dozen ballistic missiles at Iraqi bases housing U.S. troops. In those hours, Americans felt the fear that poet Emily Dickinson described as "Zero at the bone." Fortunately, no U.S. troops were killed, but unfortunately, in the fog of what seemed like war, Iran mistakenly shot down a passenger jet, killing all 176 onboard.

The big consequence of acting the contemptuous bully, of course, is this: The contemptuous bully will sooner or later find himself alone—exposed, vulnerable, in mortal peril—with no allies being moved, through the bonds of solidarity and affection, to come to his aid. In a dangerous world, going it alone, and going it contemptuously, is itself dangerous.

Biden made this point in a speech shortly after the Suleimani assassination: "At precisely the moment when we should be rallying our allies to stand beside us and hold the line against threats, Donald Trump's shortsighted 'America First' dogmatism has come home to roost." Then, in words that leap out: "We are alone now. We're alone and we'll have to bear the cost of Donald Trump's folly."

With this deadly U.S.-Iran exchange, other Democratic presidential candidates are now addressing foreign policy—finally. While the debate will address various *policy* objectives—the "endless wars" that America has engaged in since 9/11—the debate should also address another angle: *How* America acts in the world, specifically how Trump in his recklessness has made America an international bully, and the threat to America that lies therein. Biden will no doubt expand on his point that America is now alone, a dangerous place to be. The other candidates should, too.

Why? Because: America will always be a Colossus. By virtue of our booming economy and booming military—ours equals the military of the next seven most powerful countries combined—America will always be a heavy-weight in the world. Add to that a pop culture that exerts a powerful allure on the world, especially the youth, and America (in pop parlance) rules.

But: America *must* learn how to handle power better—more judiciously, more humanely, more wisely. Have we ever tutored ourselves in this all-important art? Right now, what the world sees in America is an *angry* Colossus—and the sight, and the experience, is frightening. For just one example from a super-abundance: Trump threatening North Korea with "fire and fury, like the world has never seen!" Often these life-and-death threats are fired off from Trump's toy pop-gun, Twitter.

This tension—how to handle great power—has existed since the end of World War II, when America emerged as a victor. While we used a winning hand in the immediate postwar era for good, serving as architect in constructing the institutions ensuring collective security and international cooperation, becoming "Leader of the Free World"— the apotheosis of wise power—this was also when the epithet "the ugly American" came into use, denoting the American who's an overbearing know-it-all, contemptuous of other cultures, a bully.

(Related to, but going back to America's origins, before we acquired great power, is another tension: how to handle our absolute freedom. Mishandled, this freedom deforms into what author Philip Roth called "the indigenous American berserk," the apotheosis of which now sits in the White House. We have a lot of rehab to do.)

Ultimately, the question of handling great power, the power inhering in a Colossus, is a moral one: America indeed has the power to unleash "fire and fury, like the world has never seen," but should it? It is no help that we surrendered both moral language and judgment decades ago, but, tellingly, in the grand reckoning now underway on multiple fronts—on race, sexual assault, guns, climate change, *et al.*—Americans are coming to see the need for moral judgment, to determine right from wrong. It is also no help that today's pop culture prioritizes the fight club over the philosophy club, but if the mainstream matures, pop culture may, too.

International relations requires mutual respect among nations; otherwise, when one nation feels dissed, it will seek payback, needing to "save face" and "not show weakness"—the historic path to war and what we just heard from Iran as it paid back Trump's assassination of Suleimani. In this system, big powers like America bear a special onus—the onus of understanding the impact of their actions on others not big—an onus reflected in the old adage of the rock and the egg: Rock falls on egg, too bad for the egg. Egg falls on rock, still too bad for the egg.

This is a hinge moment for America: Will the American Colossus continue to bully the world—or will it grow up, get collegial again, mature? To do so, we need to understand the peril that comes with being a bully, remember that "Zero-at-the-bone" fear when Iran vowed revenge, relearn the value of cooperation and alliances, tutor ourselves in the proper use of power. And the American public, so angry at so many things, might reconsider that anger in the context of the world's misery and of history, and cool our jets.

And, of course, we must oust Donald "Big Bully" Trump from power.

If we do all this—in other words, if we mature—we could make America great again.

—*Medium*, January 13, 2020

Films for Our Times: Syria's Tragedy Reflected in *The Cave* and *For Sama*

First in a series for Medium, Films for Our Times
For series introduction in HuffPost, please see p. 251.

ANYBODY WHO THINKS human rights are superfluous, or thinks the rise of autocracy and the weakening of democracy around the world is a benign development, needs to see these two superb documentaries, both set in Syria in hospitals, where the tragedy of war plays out most urgently. While war is always terrible, civil war is more so. Experiencing these two films, this viewer's overwhelming feeling was: People, most especially children, have a basic human right not to be traumatized by their own countrymen.

Autocrats, unconstrained by ethics, bomb their own people, as has Syria's autocratic leader, Bashar al-Assad. Since 2012, soon allied with another autocrat, Russia's Vladimir Putin, Assad has bombed his fellow Syrians, even unleashed barrel bombs loaded with toxic chemicals. In both films, the rumble of warplanes overhead and the reverberations of the bombs they drop suffuse the action. Yet humanity at its best shines through.

Documentaries, the nonfiction form of the film art, are especially adept at conveying our troubled times—its horror and humanity. These two films have been nominated for the Oscar for best documentary.

The Cave (2019)

This deeply moving film, set in an underground hospital in east Damascus, is all about trying to save the lives of those wounded aboveground. The hospital appears to be set up in the subterranean basement of an existing (but ruined) hospital, thus earning the name "the Cave." But even at these depths, the Cave shakes from the bombs bursting above.

Directing the operations of the Cave is the extraordinary Dr. Amani Ballour—called Dr. Amani in the film—a 30-year-old woman, thin and impassive. The camera stays with her throughout; we see her examining new victims, deciding their treatment, ordering the staff of 100. We see that, in this chaos, her impassive demeanor is what keeps the Cave from breaking down. A pediatrician, she warms around children, calling them "dear"; the frightened children become visibly calmed in her presence. Her own parents text their fears for her safety and remind her that her plants in her room at home await her, but we see where she is firmly planted.

We see also the patriarchal bias of aboveground life seeping into the Cave, when early on the angry husband of a victim tells Dr. Amani that a woman should be home with her children. A male colleague gently defends Dr. Amani; she swats away the bias and gets back to her life-and-death work, but the bias arises again and again.

Because of the dearth of medical supplies, the surgeon, Dr. Salim Namour, must operate largely without anesthesia. To assuage the patient (and perhaps his own sorrow), he cues up his iPhone to classical music. When he's not operating, he puffs on a cigarette and calls his family. Providing a lighter note is Samaher, a young nurse pressed into service as staff cook. She good-naturedly hears out their complaints about her "bad rice"; over time, her cooking improves.

But it is the wounded and the suffering who rightfully are the central focus of the film. They are brought to the Cave in unending flows, wave after wave. When the chemical attack occurs, this viewer had to remind herself to breathe. While it appears Dr. Amani and her team save a remarkable number of victims, the ones they cannot save are, understandably, the ones that bring these stalwarts to tears. At one point, the surgeon pulls off his cap and cries, "There's so little we can do for them!" Dr. Amani finds a room and grieves.

Especially moving is a scene with Dr. Amani and a little girl whose father was killed by a car bomb. Soothing the girl's tears, she asks about the father and says that she, too, cries. Then she asks the girl if she might become a doctor someday, noting that a doctor does "important" work. The girl agrees, adding a teacher does "important" work, too. So stirring: In Chaos, projecting to the future, imparting to youth that, no matter the Chaos, one must acquit oneself with worthy work.

Its restrictive setting notwithstanding, this film is wonderfully capacious. We see ordinary people doing extraordinary things—medically, humanly. We glimpse the character of the wounded. A political note is sounded as staff takes a moment to inveigh against "the regime," then turns back to tend the damage wreaked by "that bastard Assad." There's also the mundane: Dr. Amani dreams of wearing mascara again. And, properly, a meditative note is sounded throughout; at one point Dr. Amani asks, not rhetorically: "Is God really listening?" She wonders why anyone would bring children into this tragic world.

The filmmaking is fluid and, unlike much contemporary film, does not call attention to itself with baroque editing, other effects. The viewer will cross fingers when the camera crew surfaces outside and risks sudden death. Syrian-born director Feras Fayyad has a deeply humanistic touch. His film *Last Men in Aleppo* earned Syria's first Oscar nomination. His film about a dissident poet got Fayyad arrested by Assad's security forces and tortured. Of necessity, he directed *The Cave* remotely.

As Hollywood rains honors on fare like *Joker*, the "supervillain origin story" which snagged the most Oscar noms (11)—one *must* ask: Almost 20 years after 9/11, *why* is our pop culture stuck in nihilism?—Americans hungering for real courage under fire, fire orchestrated by a real supervillain, will find sustenance in *The Cave*. At film's end, Dr. Amani's parents text her they are proud of her; indeed she is a hero, though she'd point to everyone else as heroic. Dr. Amani has been awarded the 2020 Raoul Wallenberg Prize, named for the Swedish diplomat who rescued thousands of Jews fleeing the Nazis. Finally forced to flee Syria, Dr. Amani is now a refugee in Turkey.

For Sama (2019)

More a personal statement than *The Cave*, this filmmaker's target subject is embedded in her title, *For Sama*—her little daughter. Waad al-Kateab films the tragedy of Syria's civil war from inside the whirlwind, in the city of Aleppo, and does it with child in hand. Al-Kateab, who narrates her film, calls it a "letter to Sama and to all the children of Syria."

While Dr. Amani in *The Cave* wondered why anyone would bring children into this tragic world, al-Kateab has braved it—an act transforming her from a headstrong young woman into a mother and artist with a mission: to both keep her child alive amidst the horrors of war and to show the world that war. Only when it seems they truly may all die—she, her doctor husband Hamza, and Sama—does she reconsider: "Now I wish I hadn't given birth to you." And then she becomes pregnant again.

Like *The Cave*, much of this film takes place in a hospital, with a signal difference: This hospital, which Hamza runs, is not a subterranean cave, but aboveground and dangerously exposed. Added to that, since the hospital needs Hamza 24/7, they live above the store, so to speak. The peril is viscous, the attacks, shattering. With time, while al-Kateab continues to flinch when bombs burst, she notes Sama does not, nor does she cry. She ruminates: Will Sama ever forgive her parents for choosing to stay, not flee? Her guilt compounds when, traveling to Turkey to see Hamza's sick father, they return to Aleppo—a harrowing journey—when Assad launches another offensive.

Al-Kateab ranges back and forth in time and between the personal and the political. Crucially, she was present, with camera, when the student protests against the Assad regime took shape in 2011 and when the regime's security forces cracked down, all of which led her to Hamza, one of the few doctors who was also an activist. Unlike *The Cave*, the filmmaker also ranges outside, with her camera and Sama. Especially after a bombardment, witnessing so much death, she needs to see "people alive." She grows close to a family that likewise has opted to stay. The older boy, asked what he would say to friends who have fled: "May God forgive you for leaving me here alone." Such is their commitment to their city. Thus the wrenching sorrow when, after six months of siege, they all must evacuate or die.

In the foreground at all times, as in *The Cave*, are the Syrian people, bombed by their own leader, brought to the hospital *in extremis*. The deaths of children are especially sad: two little brothers mourning a third brother, their mother racing in to bear him away, sobbing. Says a doctor, sorrowfully: "Children have nothing to do with this, nothing." There are miracles, too: A woman nine months pregnant is brought in unconscious after a bombing. A Caesarean is performed, the baby appears dead, then, after desperate measures to get a response, his eyes open. Life!

Intensity is balanced with lightness. Early on, al-Kateab teases her new husband, "By the way, ever since you said a hospital can't be bombed, we've been bombed constantly." And when that hospital is bombed to ruins, and Hamza and colleagues are prepping a new location, they playfully begin painting each other's faces, with al-Kateab laughing, "Is this why you wanted freedom?" One doctor looks straight into the camera and says: "It's beautiful to have the word freedom painted across my forehead."

Al-Kateab's question—"Is this why you wanted freedom?"—will resonate with Americans who fear we have abused beyond repair our own precious gift of freedom. Her dedication—that no matter the world's destruction, "I keep filming"—is the artistic statement of all serious artists. The film's end-note says the al-Kateabs and their two daughters now live in the U.K.

Again, in contrast to these two masterpieces, all the honors heaped on Hollywood's nihilistic *Joker* seem pathetic. How strange: to view two documentaries on the tragedy that is Syria and come away feeling an even deeper bond with humanity. Perhaps that is because, with both these works of art, the through-line is love.

—*Medium*, January 20, 2020

"Lawlessness Normalized": What Acquitting Donald Trump Means

WATCHING THE REPUBLICAN-LED U.S. Senate cave to our lawless president, Donald Trump, and assure him acquittal in his impeachment trial, was worse than watching a slow-moving train wreck. It was like watching a slow-moving suicide.

The suicide of the rule of law—a *sine qua non* of our American experiment.

After weeks of fact-finding by the House impeachment inquiry, and after days of opening arguments and questioning in the Senate trial—all focused on Trump's extortionate "favor" put to a foreign power (Ukraine): the *quid pro quo* of dirt on a re-election rival for military aid—the question became: Would the Senate defy Trump and vote to call for witnesses and documents—both of which Trump debarred in the House inquiry—in order to conduct a proper trial?

Additionally, Trump's former national security advisor John Bolton was waving his arms wildly, declaring his readiness to testify about Trump's "pressure campaign" on Ukraine—a first-hand witness who could satisfy the Republicans' dismissal of the Democrats' case as all hearsay. (Bolton's forthcoming book is titled *The Room Where It Happened*.) That Bolton refused to testify in the House, even threatening to sue, the Democrats could let pass, if he testified in the Senate.

But no, the Republicans could not allow it. With the exception of two profiles in courage—Maine's Susan Collins and Utah's Mitt Romney—the Senate voted against ensuring a proper trial, falling in party line: 51 to 49. "World's greatest deliberative body"? *Not.*

This is far more than lamentation about partisan loss; this is foreboding. Foreboding about institutional collapse, for one. With the Senate caving to our lawless president, how can the Senate cite Trump's forthcoming lawlessness (and it will come), when it just surrendered, without much of a defense, its principal check—the impeachment option? What happens now to Senate oversight, or to its investigative function, or even to its legitimacy as a branch co-equal to the executive?

But what really is foreboding is this: Our lawless president, once "acquitted" (the scare-quotes indicate *faux*-acquittal), can and will operate without *any* guardrails at all—legal, institutional, moral. We are now at the mercy of Trump's gut, his whims, his spite and his furies. We truly are in uncharted waters, without map or compass.

And giving cover was the astonishing testimony of former Harvard law professor Alan Dershowitz, who made the claim, on the floor of the very Senate he was about to desecrate, that a president who acts in what he believes is in the national interest, including in pursuit of his own re-election, cannot be impeached for it. Jaws on the left across the land dropped, though not apparently on the right. Dershowitz now claims he was misinterpreted, but the clip that has gone viral is clear in its license. Republican senators reportedly leaned into that license. Watch out now for a turbo-charged Trump.

Our peril at this turn is best captured by Adam Schiff, Democratic Congressman from California and lead manager of the House's case to the Senate. Eloquent throughout, Schiff was perhaps most eloquent in terming these uncharted waters into which we are thrust as "the normalization of lawlessness." This phraseology—this new reality—was echoed by another manager, New York Congressman Hakeem Jeffries. Both men seemed on the verge of tears. While the so-called "conservatives" were freely pitching their Constitutional rights over the side, the Democrats were desperately trying to retrieve them; they were, in fact, doing a conservative's job—that is, conserve a component part of the American idea: the rule of law.

What was so exasperating in watching the Republicans' performance: They never really contested the matter of Trump's lawlessness, but instead banged on (and on and on) about process. For example, they harangued Democrats for not subpoenaing for their House inquiry the witnesses they called for in the Senate trial—*never acknowledging that the President debarred his Administration from answering any House subpoenas or cooperating with the House inquiry*. As the old legal maxim goes: If you have the law, argue the law; if you don't have the law, bang the table (or bang on about process). But now: Can we really say we have the Law at all...?

The closest the Republicans came to acknowledging Trump's lawlessness was to call his Ukraine gambit "inappropriate," as retiring Senator Lamar Alexander put it. This tut-tut will not keep Trump from inviting other foreign interference in our elections (China, Iran; back to you, Russia) or strong-arming another foreign power for a "favor." Also "inappropriate" was Trump's defiance in answering any subpoena: Is such defiance now the norm for presidential behavior? Do Republicans not see the anarchy—lawlessness normalized—they unleashed?

Throughout the whole process, Trump's lawyers insisted the Democrats' charge of "abuse of power" was "too vague" a standard by which to impeach, forgetting that such standard was the great "lesson learned" from the case of (Republican) president Richard Nixon. As historian Timothy Naftali says, "The Republicans have embraced a theory that permits future abuses of power." If Republicans were not so bound in their Faustian bargain with this lawless president—a bond now welded in the furnace of impeachment—perhaps they could see their error, their complicity...?

As it is, as the legal scholars at *Lawfare* note, Trump's lawyers made "the authoritarian argument for acquittal." Think about that: the authoritarian argument for acquittal. We have seen the apotheosis (or have we?) of what David Leonhardt of *The New York Times* astutely pegged just six months after Trump's inauguration, in a column titled "The Lawless Presidency." Lawless = authoritarian.

Trump's lawyers also went on and on about the "bad" precedent set by this Democratic-led impeachment. But consider the horrendous precedent set by this lawless president, soon to be acquitted, on how future presidents and holders of high office exercise power.

Already historians are weighing in on the ramifications.

Contrary to Republican claims, not all Democrats called for impeachment. I argued for censure. But House speaker Nancy Pelosi was right when she said, "The times have found us": When Trump strong-armed Ukraine with his *quid pro quo*, Democrats could not let such lawlessness stand; not to have acted would have been Constitutional malpractice. (Kudos to all House managers who prosecuted the case: In addition to Schiff and Jeffries, the team included Jason Crow, Val Demings, Sylvia Garcia, Zoe Lofgren, and Jerrold Nadler.)

Is there life after suicide—can rule of law be resuscitated as a precept of American life? It can, but it will take fierce effort and it will require taking the long view. For now, we wait to hear the rationales of individual Republican senators, to be delivered on the Senate floor, explaining their decisions not to impeach. (Later they can take themselves into Gethsemane and have it out with their consciences.) And Democrats in the House can still consider censure, can still subpoena Bolton.

Going forward—the direction Americans always want to go—we all can continue to prosecute the case for the rule of law. In such quest, common ground could be achieved between Democrats and those Republicans who abhor what their party has become. (I am glad my Republican parents are not here to see the absolute degradation of the GOP.) And, certainly, restoring rule of law—and making a big issue of Trump's lawlessness—should be central in Campaign 2020.

And, something that should sober up any Republican jubilation at Trump's *faux*-acquittal: John and Jane Q. Public will continue pondering rule of law and fairness. They will wonder: How can you have a fair trial if you don't permit witnesses or documents? Isn't it a rigged trial if acquittal is a foregone conclusion? And how can Trump blow off a subpoena, but if I did it, I'd get hauled off to jail?

In November, it is imperative we elect a President who honors the law.

—*Medium*, February 3, 2020

Films for Our Times:
Parasite

Second in a series, Films for Our Times

"INCOME INEQUALITY" HAS become cliché, yet it encompasses perhaps the world's most serious social problem. Bringing cliché to life—making vivid both the lived reality at the very top and the very bottom of the income ladder, as well as the violent climax when these two realities clash—is the South Korean film, *Parasite*. It is a stunner.

Justice is not always a factor at the Oscars, but justice was served, and great art recognized, when *Parasite* swept the big awards at this year's Oscars—for best original screenplay, best foreign film, best director, and, in a first for a foreign film in the Oscar's 92-year history, best picture.

Artists understand how difficult it is to portray social and political issues in art: If ideology and ardor overwhelm the artistry, the result is agitprop, something only a propagandist can love. But with vivid characters, revealing interrelationships between those high and low, and universally-understood metaphors that he continually weaves throughout his film, director-screenwriter Bong Joon Ho avoids agitprop to bring us a tale for our times, which unspools with the power of parable.

The metaphors begin immediately. We meet first the family at the very lowest end of the income ladder—the Kims—who live in a semi-basement. In a semi-basement, with windows high up looking out to the street, the world in all its meanness comes to you; it is, literally, in your face. When their street is fumigated, they don't close the windows: Why not get themselves fumigated for free? (Personal hygiene on the cheap.) The Kims—father, mother, 20-something son and daughter—barely eke out a living assembling pizza boxes (and are bawled out for their lack of quality control).

The film's action is kicked into gear when the Kim son's friend asks him a favor: Could he take over his gig as English tutor to a wealthy family's daughter while he, the friend, goes abroad for study? When the son demurs, saying he doesn't have a degree, his friend says, "Fake it." Before the viewer can wonder about this set-up's plausibility, boom, we see the son being led through the Park's serene hilltop fortress of a home, reporting for duty. The utility of this gig is immediately grasped by the Kims and soon, by machinations benign and cruel, the whole family is employed by the Parks: the daughter as art therapy tutor to the Park's little son; Kim senior as chauffeur for Park senior, a tech exec; the mother as cook and housekeeper. Bong's economic filmmaking plows under any plausibility questions.

In the quest of their climb upward, the Kims keep from the Parks their identity as family, believing it would spell the end of their windfall. Mostly they succeed—they execute their new roles with aplomb (the Kim daughter soon sees that art therapy means addressing her charge's early childhood trauma). The only thing that could give them away is...their smell: the smell of unwashed bodies forced to live in a semi-basement.

In pursuit of his tale for our times, Bong has plenty of surprises (not revealed here, except to note—metaphor alert—there is a basement in the Park house, too). But apart from the storyline, Bong is also telegraphing that the poor, given the opportunity and training, have the talent and resourcefulness to execute most any job. And, in this film at least, he implies family solidarity is stronger among the poor than the atomized rich, where it is more provisional (though early on, before they embark on their ruse, the Kims fall into spats and pull into themselves; being confederates fosters solidarity). Bong also implies that, in the status anxiety of the Park wife and the acting-out of her son, only the rich have the leisure for neuroses; the poor don't have the band-width. The poor are stoic, of necessity.

Bong also telegraphs the poor's capacity for subtlety: When the Kim son, new in his gig as English tutor, plants the seed among the Parks for an art tutor (angling for his sister), he does so by remarking on the "metaphoric" quality of the boy's artwork. I laughed out loud: The whole movie is a metaphor. Including the senior Kim's test as chauffeur: Can he round a corner without spilling the coffee held in the hand of Park senior? And the frequent reference to the Park home's architect and his intent; the Kim family home, the semi-basement, is the work of—fill in the blank—neglect, greed, Society, History. Throughout, the viewer can engage the film on many levels.

Fascinatingly, threaded throughout are the characters' socio-political observations, especially among the Kims in their new environs. In one exchange, after the Kims have settled into their new jobs, Kim senior says, "They're rich but still nice," to which his wife shoots back, "They're nice because they're rich."

Most stunning as metaphor is a long sequence leading to the climax: When it appears their ruse is up, three of the Kims—father, son, daughter—are seen fleeing the Park's hilltop home and, as a storm gathers, descending the city—by stairs, by steep street, by tunnel walkway—all the way back down to their semi-basement. Which, when the storm's overflow comes flooding through their windows, brings the city's sewage churning into their "living" quarters. (Talk about metaphor.) In their long trek downward, I thought of Dante's inferno, though in Dante the inferno's inhabitants were brought there by their sins, while for the Kims, it is their poverty.

Violence ensues. Made explicit is the poor's demand for respect—or else. Smell, the sense you can't see, here the smell of the poor, plays a final part in the climax.

As powerful as Bong's message is about the inhumanity of income inequality, he is subtle with the characterization. Both the Kims, driven by need, and the Parks, driven by status, come across as real, not the stereotypes they (especially the Parks) could so easily be. Bong's artistry lies in his near-magical blend of subtlety and his crystal-clear portrait of income inequality's inhumanity. The cast uniformly is superb; this is ensemble acting at its best—creating individual along with a group portrait—with the actor playing Kim senior, Kang-Ho Song, especially memorable.

Who says you can't have story *and* ideas *and* socio-political issues *and* throbbing humanity in the same film? *Parasite* points the way.

Policy-makers the world over would profit from seeing this film—a film that paints so clearly the cosmology and context of class based on income; that asks, "Who's the 'parasite'?"; that foretells the violence to come if that inequality is not alleviated.

And American filmmakers might take a cue, too. Compared to *Parasite*, some best-picture nominees—Quentin Tarantino's *Once Upon a Time…in Hollywood* and Martin Scorsese's *The Irishman*—seem insular, beside the point, boys' club. (Greta Gerwig's *Little Women*, focusing on women's equality, deserved better.)

Finally, in addition to the general public, it is the wealthy who should see this film. For, to recur to the premise of income inequality as perhaps the world's greatest social problem: Rather than violent revolution, best if justice in this realm is reached by enlightened choice by the wealthy. This film provides not only a map and mirror for our times, but also a horrific forecast, should the reigning injustice not change.

—*Medium*, February 26, 2020

Memo to All Women: Best Way to Protect #MeToo Is to Think #UsToo

MEMORANDUM

To: All women

From: A former adjudicator of sexual harassment claims

Re: Fortifying #MeToo in the post-Harvey Weinstein era

WITH THE GUILTY VERDICT of one-time Hollywood mogul and seemingly full-time sexual predator Harvey Weinstein reached this week, the #MeToo movement—which had come to be seen as "gone too far" and "out of control" in the trial's run-up—now gets a big, big break. Women of the world, let us take advantage of this big, big break—this window of opportunity—and work in concert to protect this historic and invaluable movement.

How? By getting on the same page in understanding how historic and invaluable #MeToo is. And understanding that, powerful as #MeToo is as social movement and force for change, it can also be damaged, even undone—even used against women—with comparatively little effort, spun into equal and opposing power by the force-multiplier of social media, by those wishing to push women back into subservience.

In other words, we must sail our worthy ship—call it *Pequod*—and chase the Great White Whale of sexual harassment—call it Moby-Dick—exercising our navigational skills in such a way that the behemoth does not outmaneuver us, is not allowed to turn round and ram this worthy ship of ours, destroying it as Moby-Dick did in Melville's novel, leaving only "chips in the vortex." Case in point: Climate science denialism got its big, big boost when, hacking the computers of climate scientists, deniers manipulated the data to "prove" that the scientists overstated dangerous trends.

Since the Harvey Weinstein scandal broke in late 2017 in all its nauseating depredation, other famous men who wielded their power in equally nauseating ways over women have been exposed and seen their careers ruined: TV anchor Matt Lauer, talk-show host Charlie Rose, comedian Louis C.K., political guru Mark Halperin, opera singer Placido Domingo, litterateur Leon Wieseltier. Comedian Bill Cosby, whose long legal battles preceded this era, during this time finally was found guilty of his serial predations.

This reckoning of "toxic masculinity" (newly coined term) was enabled by the brave testimony of women—waves of women—who, sick of the depravity of these men, spoke out, thus giving a second wind to #MeToo, founded back in 2006 by Tarana Burke, and building it into the present juggernaut. (Note #MeToo's cyclical nature; we want #MeToo to stay on its present upside.) With Weinstein *et al.*, the public finally "got it" about sexual harassment, so long discounted or denied, as the traumatic and often career-ending and life-altering experience it is.

At that time, as the scandals of Weinstein *et al.* broke, I wrote that, at long last and after eons, a grand reckoning on the power imbalance between men and women seemed at hand. It was thrilling, this New Day, an uplifting note in our post-9/11 tumult, in low times a good sign. But I also wrote: "My one fear in all this is that a false allegation will be filed by one women or several, which could be spun to cast doubt on the validity of the entire ongoing reckoning. Memo to women: Maintain exemplary conduct and solidarity with your sisters." I worried about Moby-Dick destroying #MeToo then; I still do.

And the element of the Weinstein trial that, in my opinion, could become that Moby-Dick is the element that, as it turned out, enabled the guilty verdict itself: the acceptance that an assault victim might continue to have consensual sex after the alleged nonconsensual assault. This judge and jury in New York accepted this new marker, acknowledging that trauma works on victims in inexplicable ways. But: Will the jury of public opinion—the sea in which #MeToo sails—always buy it? This way danger lies, I believe.

I speak on these matters from historical perspective: as a former adjudicator of sexual harassment claims in the late 1970s.

As an equal opportunity officer for a major American city (San Diego), my first responsibility was to protect women and minorities as we moved them into the nontraditional areas of work (police, fire, sanitation, etc.). Without much federal or state guidance, I drafted what I believe was one of the nation's first municipal policies prohibiting sexual harassment on the job. This drafting included defining what sexual harassment is: My working definition came to be this—behavior, whether verbal or physical, that sexualizes the workspace.

My only instrument in adjudicating was a sit-down between the complainant, the object of her complaint, and their boss. Enlightenment took place when, after I laid out the case, the object of the complaint saw the light—"Oh, I get it: Women don't like porn magazines in the common area," "Oh, I get it: Women don't like to be asked what kind of sex they like." I enunciated our policy throughout the City, including at new employee orientation—"Thou shalt not harass your fellow worker"; "Thou shalt not engage in hanky-panky with a fellow worker, then charge sexual harassment when the affair is over"; "If harassed, thou shalt keep a record."

In the three years I served, I adjudicated a dozen harassment cases, a remarkably small number for a workforce of 7,000, small perhaps because I spent most of my time out in the field, monitoring. But I did worry: What is not being reported? What am I not seeing? And I wondered: How do I adjudicate egregious harassment—assault or rape—if it comes to light? My cases involved salacious talk, porn, nastiness like razor-blades in coffee cups and hair-pulling (which I adjudicated as reckless endangerment and battery, respectively; enlightenment ensued). But with an egregious charge, while referring the complainant to a lawyer, I would want a thousand-piece orchestra—a movement.

Which, hallelujah, is what we have now: #MeToo.

What we also have now is a more egregious sexual harassment—far more. Who can forget the outrageous and cruel predation—sadism even—alleged of Weinstein *et al.*? And the mass of victims: Women alleging sexual misconduct by Weinstein now number at least 90 (that is no typo: 90). Fittingly, this fiend will now face prison time. Weinstein will appeal his guilty verdict handed down in New York, but odds are he will face some prison time. N.B., in this trial Weinstein was found guilty of only two of five charges, and they are the lesser charges: rape, not sexual predation. He also faces a criminal suit in Los Angeles.

It would take a long book to describe, degree by degree, the cultural degradation that has allowed some opportunistic men to abuse their power and exact sexual degradation of women in their employ. But, this is the cultural moment we are in and we must work with the tools we have—which again, lucky us, comprise an entire arsenal: #MeToo.

Thus it is incumbent on us, women of the world, to keep our mighty weapon in as good a working order as we can, as unsullied in name and value as we can, and perceived as fair as we can make it. In other words, to the extent we can manage this juggernaut, we must manage it *responsibly*.

To do so, I resubmit the standards described above, notably: Thou shalt not engage in hanky-panky—especially with the boss and engaged in voluntarily—then charge sexual harassment when the affair is over. I would also resubmit to women my advice above: "Maintain exemplary conduct and solidarity with your sisters."

About fairness: Recall the question marks arising about #MeToo—as blunt instrument, plowing fairness under, going "too far." An example giving many pause was Al Franken, resigning his Senate seat after allegations of fondling—without "due process" (a Senate investigation). And by now we all have heard anecdotes—say, a friend's son accused of sexual assault who claims it was "just a bad date." But such anecdotes, attaining critical mass, can hurt; it's vital that our movement be seen as fair. (To recur to my EEO role: The only time I ruled against a woman complainant—a police recruit cited repeatedly for endangering her fellow cops in responding to their call for cover—I learned later from another department head how important my ruling was: "You did yourself a world of good," he said, speaking for all department heads, "because we perceived you as fair.")

Finally, about solidarity: Given the volatility of #MeToo, how one bad case can hurt the cause, I would hope any woman considering filing a complaint or lawsuit of sexual harassment, especially against a famous man which will draw major media, will pose this basic test to herself: "If I win, will it help the cause of other women?" Even more important: "If I lose, will it hurt the cause of other women?" For we are all in it together—this cause—and we are obliged to think of our sisters.

And a semantic nit: Let's get back to speaking of "the truth," instead of "my truth." Think: Bringing *my* story, speaking *the* truth.

By no means am I saying women should hold back on a valid claim of involuntary sexual assault; this lifelong feminist cheers taking action and the Weinstein guilty verdict gives hope of a fair and successful hearing in doing so. But to protect #MeToo, it is imperative that we consider the implications *on all women* of the actions we take. Because #MeToo is not just about you or me, it is about all women.

#MeToo = #UsToo.

—*Medium*, February 29, 2020

Democrats Default to Normalcy: Joe Biden's Super-Tuesday Miracle

AH, NORMALCY. IT'S been a long time since we've seen you. But: How long you staying?

After three years—it seems like a century—of Donald the Crazy, Donald the Cruel, Donald the Destroyer, it is a new feeling, but not entirely unfamiliar, this feeling of normalcy, to see Joe Biden's smiling and familiar face, "Uncle Joe," pop up on the TV screen as the winner of state after state, 10 out of 14 in play, this Super Tuesday.

As the night wore on, I had a vision of normalcy spreading across the map—from Alabama, North Carolina, Virginia, Massachusetts, Minnesota, Texas (Texas?).

And after a year of a crowded and increasingly rancorous Democratic presidential campaign—it too feels like it's been waged a century—the race was shaping up, pre-Super Tuesday, as a final showdown between two very angry men: Bernie Sanders, democratic socialist who disdains the Democratic party label and vows a "political revolution," versus Donald Trump, belching human furnace of craziness, cruelty, destruction.

That distressing prospect was captured by *The Economist*'s current cover, showing Sanders and Trump in full bellow mode and headlined: "American Nightmare: Could It Come to This?" (Uncle Sam is shown cowering.)

Contrasted with these two angry men, moderate Joe Biden is so... refreshing. *Ah, Normalcy.*

Am I equating normalcy with nice-guy equanimity, with not-shouting? Maybe. America has been hopping angry for years now—I called 2016 "the Anger Election"—but all this anger has illuminated nothing, it has forced us far from our best selves, far from any semblance of normalcy. At our best, Americans prize normalcy.

Amidst all this anger and sub-normalcy, then, is it really any wonder that, given the chance, millions of Democrats reacted—in the moment, during the 72-hour span of a remarkable realignment of the electoral stars—and opted on Super Tuesday for the candidate who epitomizes normalcy: Joe Biden, son of Scranton PA, Uncle Joe?

About that realignment of the stars: Biden, who'd performed poorly in the debates and in the voting in Iowa, New Hampshire, and Nevada, banked everything on South Carolina, with its large African-American population who esteem him as Barack Obama's Vice-President and wingman. With Congressman James Clyburn endorsing him as "a good man," Biden won a smashing victory, enough to cause rivals Pete Buttigieg and Amy Klobuchar to drop out and endorse him, all of which provided Biden that priceless political asset—momentum—to prevail three days later on Super Tuesday.

In that 72-hour span, millions of moderate Democrats, if they'd been supporting "Mayor" Pete or Klobuchar, had to rethink their vote. Reportedly, blocking both Donald Trump *and* Bernie Sanders was the deciding factor, making Joe Biden "a safe place to go." Going into that recalculation, no doubt, was the unnerving sight of Trump's "handling" of the life-and-death threat suddenly in front of mind of *everybody* on the planet—the coronavirus pandemic. When life upends the landscape, and mortal peril lurks, it is understandable a voter would opt for normalcy.

I have been critical of Biden in the past, especially his condescension to Anita Hill in the Clarence Thomas hearing which he chaired; but he has since apologized—to her. As for Biden's debate performances: It seemed he was trying too hard or not hard enough; either way, the *elan vital* was missing. I kept hoping the former Senator or former

Vice-President would show up, because *that* Joe Biden is the institutionalist who could reconstruct our government that Donald Trump has damaged so badly, and *that* Joe Biden is the statesman who could reconnect America with the world that Donald Trump has so rudely blown off. Just having back on the world stage an American who is normal, and not a narcissistic blowhard, would be a gift.

Who knows if Biden can ride his momentum—or what his campaign is calling "Joe-mentum"—all the way to the nomination? And should he get the nomination, there is Donald Trump the Arch-Bully (and his Republican confederates) lying in wait. We all know how it goes, from Time Immemorial, for the nice guy.

And who knows how long this embrace of normalcy will last? America has gone through such churn since 9/11, that we are sometimes unrecognizable to ourselves (Nazi flags in Charlottesville?). We have plumbed the depths and found out how much crazy there is in these "United" States of America. It's a good bet there's more.

I know my progressive friends will disagree with my conferring the normalcy crown on Biden. Their argument will be that Bernie's "political revolution" is the "new normal" that America needs, and some of that argument is valid, especially the part about income inequality. But Bernie has not provided us with something so normal as a road-map to his New Day; he has provided a price-tag, but not a road-map.

And temperament in a President is key, as we are reminded daily by the current barking-mad occupant of the White House. Bernie (and Trump) are tabasco-hot, while Joe Biden is oatmeal-normal. Progressives, and Trumpians, will make a big mistake if they underestimate the yearning for normalcy among a wide swath of their countrymen—Democratic moderates, Independents, swing voters, disaffected Republicans.

Because: In the instinctual preference for normalcy manifested so clearly on Super Tuesday, the body politic is signaling the kind of America we desperately want back. We want America the Normal again. Don't be surprised if oatmeal wins in November.

—*Medium*, March 5, 2020

Biden-Warren 2020?

JOE BIDEN'S STATED commitment to pick a woman as his Vice-Presidential running mate is not only a bright spot amid the spreading coronavirus pandemic. It is a hook thrown into the future. Elizabeth Warren, I propose, is the woman best able to take that hook and run with it.

Biden's announcement during Sunday's Democratic debate with Bernie Sanders became the headline take-away. And with Biden again winning big in Tuesday's primaries in Florida, Illinois, and Arizona, he now is the prohibitive favorite to be the Democratic nominee. As such, his commitment to a woman V.P. becomes real, operational. Let the naming games begin.

The names of Amy Klobuchar, Kamala Harris, and Elizabeth Warren, all U.S. senators, head many lists. Biden reportedly leans toward someone experienced in campaign politics, which of course includes these three before they were forced to bow out of the presidential race. Other names include Stacey Abrams, whom Biden calls "the woman who should have been the governor of Georgia"; U.S. senators Catherine Cortez-Masto, Jean Shaheen, and Maggie Hassan; Governor Gretchen Whitmer; and Sally Yates, acting Attorney General fired by Trump early in his term.

Of these highly qualified women, Elizabeth Warren stands out—*on the most important grounds*. They are:

ONE: Crucially, Warren has the financial-economic smarts to engineer our post-pandemic recovery.

When this pandemic ends, there will be vast financial and economic damage to redress. To reconstruct the system, perhaps from the ground up, we need, not an ideology-driven politician, but an actual expert in things financial and economic. And since this pandemic with its almost complete public lockdown will no doubt produce massive bankruptcies, both business and personal, who better to have in the №2 role than an expert on bankruptcy?

Warren made bankruptcy her specialization as an academic, coming to it first as a Republican who believed bankruptcy was the result of moral failure, then as a Democrat who understands how capitalism can destroy if not properly managed and regulated. (Biden and Warren have talked twice recently about bankruptcy.) Recall also Warren is the founding mother of the Consumer Financial Protection Bureau, which, before it was defanged by the Trump administration, clawed back $12 billion in monies lost by Main Street to Wall Street. As for Wall Street, Warren is said to scare the "talent" there—a *very* good thing. Plus, the articulate Warren makes finance and economics understandable.

The Vice-Presidency was described by John Nance Garner, Franklin Roosevelt's V.P., as "not worth a bucket of warm spit." Vice-President Warren would make the office *work*: An avowed capitalist who is also a progressive, Warren could be the architect of capitalism's New Day, give it at long last a human face, as progressives have long advocated, addressing not only bankruptcy but the yawning income inequality. Has History found its woman?

TWO: To win, Warren can unify progressive and moderate Democrats.

To get to the White House, of course, it first must be won. To do that, the moderate-progressive divide among Democrats, which remains stark, must be bridged. For the danger is that when Bernie Sanders does leave the race, some critical number of his supporters will sit out the general election, as they did in 2016. Warren is the bridge: She was the candidate who, in my opinion, grew the most in depth and humanity over the campaign and thus is the one whose departure hurt the most. As such, she could appeal in a persuasive and feeling way to Sanders supporters, themselves hurting. Ideally, she'd team up with her old friend Bernie in a joint appeal for unity.

Is this too great an ideological leap for Warren, moving from progressive to moderate? In all presidential campaigns past, tacking to the center—where most Americans are and where campaigns are won—is The Way. Warren would execute.

THREE: As V.P., Warren would be the most valiant champion of women.

Who can forget Warren taking on Michael Bloomberg in the Las Vegas Democratic debate? Incensed that a billionaire would buy his way midpoint into the campaign, but even more incensed at his record with women in the workplace as it became known, Warren put it to him—point-blank and from three feet away: "I'd like to talk about who we're running against—a billionaire who calls women 'fat broads' and 'horse-faced lesbians.' And no, I'm not talking about Donald Trump. I'm talking about Mayor Bloomberg."

As a life-long feminist, I cannot think of a more stirring defense of women in my lifetime than Warren's, which no doubt was rehearsed but also bravely delivered—to devastating effect. The next day a friend who is not an avowed feminist (but really is one) sent me an email with the subject line, "Wow, Elizabeth." And recall also Senate majority leader Mitch McConnell whining about Warren not shutting up and uttering the unforgettable line (and bumper-sticker): "Nevertheless she persisted."

Despite several generations of feminism's second wave, women in the U.S. remain underrepresented in positions of power and women's issues remain undervalued. Can anybody imagine Elizabeth Warren backing down on the issues that matter to women—*or on anything?* And fair-minded men will be with her on this (the unfair-minded men, not so much). As for women who still can't countenance their sisters as leaders (the ladies-against-women syndrome), Warren might persuade them too—"Wow, Elizabeth."

For all these reasons and more—the biggest one being that as Vice-President, she would be perfectly poised to run for President—Elizabeth

Warren, crucially on her expertise in things financial-economic and on the strength of her character, and also her Democratic *bona fides* and productive record in the Senate, makes her own case.

But will History call? Will our next President, Joe Biden, call? Whomever he calls, I will support, whole-heartedly, be it Warren, Klobuchar, Harris, Ms. X. While some women fret that, once again, a woman stands by for a call, rather than making it, I say: Take the call. Power is power, whether captured or bestowed. Take the power and run with it—hard—and save the Republic.

—*Medium*, March 18, 2020

In a Plague-Time, We Need Truth and Experts

First in a series, Notes from a Plague-Time

How is it possible that our life—not only in America but in all the world—can change in the course of just weeks? How is it possible that mere life can suddenly become a truly existential and inextricable matter of Life-and-Death? And how, as a nation, do we shake our normal dysfunction and get to the upside and save ourselves? Can we?

So many questions—and driving them all is a microscopic leviathan, the novel coronavirus, exploding into a worldwide pandemic, with the deadly respiratory illness COVID-19 as its prize. It dawns on us, on me, that we are, in the clichéd blink of an eye, thrust into an entirely new era. Not for nothing is this virus called "novel."

Like everybody else who is not an epidemiologist, I start in this new era with a blank page and a sense of dread—though epidemiologists going on TV to explain this crisis to a panicked public also, under their clinical demeanor, seem to exude dread: They know, they can see, the awfulness coming at us. Solidarity in dread.

And yet: Soon enough, it comes to me the need to grapple, to manufacture hope and courage, to achieve balance and exercise uncommon common sense, to acquit myself with dignity, honor, smarts, and, if I can manage it, wit—and not, please God, to react like Dostoevsky's Underground Man, like a "harassed mouse." In short, to get to the other side—not to Heaven, as eulogists put it, but get to the other side of this deadly scourge. To cheat Death and emerge into more Life.

I mean to fill these blank pages with notes, impressions, things learned and things discarded—in general, things useful and constructive to this new era. I come as a commentator and an artist, but principally as a human being, in solidarity with my fellow human beings. Since it is not useful, I will not indulge in polemic—except when President Donald Trump commits yet another life-threatening act—nor will I spin a literary performance. I will also—attenzione—quote from the commonplace books I have filled over a lifetime, wherein I enter wisdom and guidance from past masters. For example, when epidemic became pandemic, Dostoevsky's "harassed mouse" came instantly to mind. So did Ralph Waldo Emerson's "Nothing so astonishes as common sense and plain dealing." I mean to put Art to work, while charting Life in this new era.

As the Chinese say, "The longest journey begins with the first step." Here goes, first with a commentary—"In a Plague-Time, We Need Truth and Experts."

* * *

If ever there was the absolute need for straight talk and getting real, it is in the life-and-death coronavirus pandemic we are experiencing now.

In brief, what do we need to save ourselves? Truth and expertise.

Yet—sadly, infuriatingly, but let us hope not tragically—what we get from the Trump White House is messaging driven by Trump's re-election agenda and his absolute need to look good and *always* be right. Meaning: Trump's lying and dissembling have gone into overdrive. To watch his press briefings, with the experts he must know he needs arrayed around him, is to see lying and truth-telling in real-time combat. Too often, the lying "wins."

But sometimes, truth-telling wins. Last week, when Trump crowed at a news briefing, nearly a daily event now, that an anti-malaria drug was being repurposed for the coronavirus—*against which, as of now, there is no vaccine or treatment, thus the public dread*—the head of the Food and Drug Administration stepped forth and said, No, such drug was not forthcoming.

Earlier, at a White House meeting, after Trump announced a coronavirus vaccine was coming soon, Dr. Anthony Fauci, respected director of the National Institute of Allergy and Infectious Diseases and now the face of the Administration's cohort of experts, leaned in and said, No, such a vaccine can not be ready for another year or year-and-a-half. It was not what Trump wanted to hear, nor what the public wanted to hear, but it is fact—the truth. Dr. Fauci did the same again when Trump tried, again, with his repurposed anti-malaria drug.

But then, what can we expect from a president whose lies are an established habit and whose number *The Washington Post* now tabulates above 16,000 in the three years since his inauguration? Pre-pandemic, we had been immersed in Trumpian untruth, its own kind of contagion. The first casualty of such a habit, and the most precious loss in a leader, is trust: How can we trust a leader whose word we cannot take? Especially in a crisis? And not to forget his distaste for expertise.

But now, in this pandemic, Trump's lying could literally kill—by giving out bad information (for example, that it's O.K. to go to work if sick: not true), downplaying the lethality of the virus, questioning the death rates across the globe, absurdly playing up his own expertise in epidemiology. But enough about Trump, who we hope will be no more than a speed-bump in the quest for a solution.

The hard truth (there's that word again: truth) is that, pre-pandemic, the experts did let us down, notably the once-vaunted Centers for Disease Control and Prevention, specifically in coronavirus testing. The CDC performed well in the H1N1 and Zika outbreaks, sending test kits to all 50 states and over 100 countries. But with the novel coronavirus, its failure—faulty tests, faulty distribution—leaves the public dangerously unprotected, thus nullifying the CDC's claim of disease control and prevention. (The CDC has been suffering funding cutbacks for years.)

For without being tested, an infected person can unknowingly infect another, who in turn unknowingly infects another, etc., etc., leading to... pandemic. Which is why doctors, upon learning of the dearth in testing, are quoted saying, "We're all going to get it" and "We are at war with no ammo." (I think of my late father, a doctor admired by colleagues for his diagnostic skills, connecting the dots between no testing and mass infection and, in his quiet way, concluding the same thing.)

But now, in this crisis, surely our salvation lies with the experts and their expertise—those researchers in labs around the globe racing, Manhattan Project-style, to develop a vaccine. Those epidemiologists and other experts running the data to advocate the strategy now increasingly followed by the world's governments, i.e., to "flatten the curve" of infection and prevent a rapid peaking of cases causing entire health systems to collapse. And, crucially, those medical personnel, doctors and nurses, now on the front lines in hospitals, treating the growing numbers of the infected and sick—and, "with no ammo," risking their own lives in the process.

And the experts who were ignored before, but whose warnings came true: They merit rehearing, for there *will* be another outbreak. In 2018, the 100-year anniversary of the 1918 flu pandemic, Dr. Luciana Borio, then director for medical and biodefense at the White House's National Security Council, told a symposium that "the threat of pandemic flu is our number-one health security concern." The next day Trump's national security adviser John Bolton shut down the NSC's pandemic unit, of which Dr. Borio was a part. Dr. Beth Cameron, also a member who was fired, in a *Washington Post* op-ed outlines how that office could have coordinated current efforts.

And other experts within government (many of whom have left or been fired): They point the way. In a simulation code-named "Crimson Contagion" conducted by the Trump administration's Department of

Health and Human Services Jan.-Aug. of last year, the draft report (previously unreported until broken by *The New York Times*) lays out a scenario "now playing out in all-too-real fashion," including the outbreak's start in China, shortages of medical equipment, command confusion. Yet, this warning went unheeded. Dr. Fauci in mid-2018 told Congress he worried about a flu pandemic. Trump keeps saying nobody thought this—a pandemic—could happen. But: Experts did—a whole universe of them. (What is lacking is an expert *strategist* to pull all the expertise together—leadership a president should provide.)

And experts like the Chinese doctor, Li Wenliang—who, months ago (Dec. 30), blew the whistle on the novel virus he was seeing in his ophthalmology practice; who, for his singular public service, was threatened with arrest by the Chinese authorities; who later contracted the virus himself and, tragically, died; who, belatedly, has been exonerated by his government. Until he died, Dr. Li intended to return to "the front line": "The epidemic is still spreading, and I don't want to be a deserter." Dr. Li was 34.

Finally: Complicating our collective defense in this battle is our extreme political polarization. For as dangerous as viral contagion is, so in its way is ideological contagion.

For decades now, conservatives have, for their own complicated reasons, assaulted expertise, especially that exercised by government "bureaucrats." And a majority of Republicans continues to repeat Trump's early response to the coronavirus as the Democrats' "new hoax" and stand by him. What a shame—what a crime?—if a disbeliever were to infect a fellow countryman who is taking the experts' warnings seriously. Bret Stephens, conservative columnist at the *Times*, takes his cohort to task: "The coronavirus has exposed the falsehood of so many notions Trump's base holds about the presidency: that experts are unnecessary; that hunches are a substitute for knowledge; that competence in administration is overrated; that every criticism is a hoax.... Above all, it has devastated the conceit that having an epic narcissist in the White House is a riskless proposition at a time of extreme risk."

What will it take—Death?—to convince the disbelieving of this virus' lethality?

Back to facts: Here is how the public can protect itself and, doing so, help "flatten the curve" of infection. The guidelines are straightforward—self-isolation, or "sheltering in place," until further notice; maintaining a distance of six feet from others, or "social distancing," *if* one must go out in public; and lots and lots of hand-washing (I am laving like Lady Macbeth at this point, but without the guilt). And of course avoid the infection of bad information and conspiracy theories by consulting the World Health Organization (WHO), the National Institutes of Health (NIH), the CDC, your state or county health department.

Today's lead headline in *The New York Times* reads, "The Virus Can Be Stopped, but Only With Harsh Steps, Experts Say." The experts give us hope (and guidelines, above).

While not every truth-teller is an expert, by definition every expert is a truth-teller. It has long been said—an ancient truism—that the truth shall make you free. In a deadly pandemic, the truth—and experts and their expertise—will keep you alive.

To Life!

Other resources on the coronavirus pandemic: See the Johns Hopkins global tracker. See information posted at The New England Journal of Medicine, International Journal of Epidemiology, Harvard Medical School, and STAT. See dedicated coverage at The New York Times, The Washington Post, The Los Angeles Times, The Guardian, The Economist, The New Yorker, The Atlantic, and Politico. For ongoing TV coverage, see "The PBS NewsHour," "Amanpour and Company" (PBS), "The Rachel Maddow Show" (MSNBC), and "Fareed Zakaria GPS" (CNN).

—*Medium*, March 23, 2020

In a Plague-Time, Reaching Out to Friends While Self-Isolating

Second in an ongoing series, Notes from a Plague-Time

As MY FAVORITE American poet Emily Dickinson wrote, "My Friends are my Estate." Shortly after my husband and I began self-isolating in response to our new plague-time, I reached out to my estate—old friends, old-old friends, new friends—to see how they were doing. Are we on the same page? Are we in the same boat, and what kind of boat is it, and how seaworthy? And how is our inner weather?

On Sunday, Mar. 15, I sent this email, subject line "Checking in with Select Friends":

Dear All: Just checking in to see how you are doing in this new reality of the coronavirus pandemic. We are self-isolating. Larry feels a bit vulnerable because he got a cold about a month ago and, as his colds always are bad ones, he's still shaking it off (almost there). He's such a social animal—he's Civic Man—but he's being a good citizen and avoiding social contact, going online. Me, I don't consider my system compromised because of the cancer; am relying on the fact I rarely get colds or flu. I am still going to the gym, while Larry walks or bikes in our neighborhood.

Strange times, hmmm....? It does feel like we are in a new realm.... Lots of ellipses now....

We worry the U.S. may be in for a battering, not only the economy but deaths, as our health "system" is so woefully underprepared.

Some of you have worried about Washington state as "Ground Zero" of the outbreak. This Guardian article makes an important distinction: We are not Ground Zero but the "leading edge" of what likely will occur elsewhere.

Just emailed a friend explaining why I am not panicking. One, because living with cancer I am already living with a kind of contagion, and I have my methods for dealing with that anxiety. Two, the self-isolation: It's the natural state for a writer.

Miss the English Premier Soccer League—all games cancelled until further notice—but at least we have Turner Classic Movies. And tons of reading. And writing.

Would like to know your thoughts, your assessment of things, how you are dealing.

Buona fortuna to all of us. To Life!

C.

The response? Geysers of thoughts and feelings—far longer and more effusive, more candid than a regular email. The tone of all fifteen who responded was serious and sober, with no joking—well, except for that of childhood friend JR (I shall use initials), who began by asking, "First I need to know, do you have a more prestigious category of friends than 'Select'? Is there a 'Select Preferred' list, perhaps, or a 'Platinum Select' group?" But then, this has *always* been his way: first a bit of wit, then down to business. How reassuring to hear this old friend's voice.

About this group: All are "of an age"—in our 60s and 70s, one in her 80s—but all presenting the vigor of people far younger. All but two are retired after careers in the professions—medicine and the helping professions, law, politics, education, business, journalism. (The two of us who are writers are not retired, but are "still at it.") These friends live all over the country, while one is Finnish, living in Finland. Politically, all are of a liberal stripe, more moderate than progressive.

Remarkably, these friends' responses break out in four ways. With their permission, I set them forth here. Of course, the picture has darkened considerably in the two weeks since my email, but the priorities and vectors these friends lay out here will, I expect, hold firm and serve as their tent-pole through whatever is coming at us.

ONE: With the coronavirus pandemic, we are indeed in a new realm, a new reality.

All recognize the historic, life-altering significance of this pandemic event. There is no denial or downplaying (and there is 100% disdain for President Donald Trump on these two particular counts). As childhood friend JR wrote, "We're clearly in the midst of a huge historic event—perhaps the biggest of our lives, for those of us who didn't live through World War II." My Finnish friend, UL, calls it "the Era of Corona." Many call it "dark times," while two believe we are in—unsettling term—"dystopia."

Given this unanimous assessment, it's not surprising that all fifteen of us are self-isolating, starting at the first official recommendation to do so. This is where our Democratic affiliation shows: Polls show Democrats far more than Republicans take this pandemic seriously and act accordingly. Example: Tracking the advance of the outbreak abroad, we restocked our vital meds (cancer, diabetes) well in advance of the outbreak here. (New polls show more Republicans acknowledging the crisis.)

Understandably, those of us living in Washington state poll higher in concern because, for a while, we *were* the epicenter of the outbreak in the U.S., with the canary in the coal mine being the Life Care nursing home in Kirkland, outside Seattle, where to date 35 residents have died of COVID-19. Acting early on that news, local friend AE and her husband removed his mother out of an assisted-living facility—just in time: Two days later that facility closed itself to all family visitors.

As for the toll expected, several quoted me back to myself: "We worry the U.S. may be in for a battering, not only the economy but deaths." Tragically, the battering has begun: As of today's posting, 3.3 *million* people, losing their jobs, filed for unemployment just this past week—a U.S. record; over 122,000 Americans are confirmed having the virus; and over 2,100 Americans have died of COVID-19.

TWO: In a plague-time, top priority is family—most especially children and grandchildren—but taken to a new dimension.

This priority, if one had children (I do not), is to be expected, but these friends are learning new dimensions of this priority *and* finding the words to express it. College roommate CB wrote that, if either her son or daughter and her family got sick, "It haunts me that...I cannot go to them," for fear of spreading disease. CB is the gentlest of souls; I have never heard her express distress before. Other parents express the same fear.

This fear is even greater if their children already have health problems. Cousin LV writes, "I have been so concerned for two of my daughters who have compromised health that I really don't think as much about me." Childhood friend CM decided not to "be there" for her daughter's cancer surgery, for fear of infection; they FaceTimed instead. Her insight: Phoning is essential—to hear the voice. "Hardly ever communicate that way anymore, but emails and texts are just not the same."

And all the grandparents lament they cannot baby-sit their grandchildren, because they themselves, given their age and pre-existing conditions, are the ones "at risk." As BS writes, after she got a cold from "my darling granddaughter," now, "sadly, I can't see either of my babies."

In this crisis, these parents see their children with new pride. CW's son and wife, working from home, tend the children of doctors who staff a hospital: "Community is alive and well," she says, seeing her own community spirit transferred. JR's daughter, a deputy school superintendent, is "point person" for remote learning while her district's schools are closed: "There is no roadmap for that," he says, adding she's "undoubtedly the most stressed-out member of our family." LO's daughter volunteers as cook at a homeless shelter: "I hope she'll be O.K. I am proud of her." A doctor friend and wife wonder if their daughter, doing her medical residency, will be recruited for COVID-19 duty.

Also in this crisis, the parent-child bond for some is changing. PL writes that her daughter and one of her sons both demanded she and husband turn around and return home after learning someone at their destination had tested positive for coronavirus. She writes: "I have never heard my children to be so bearish about protecting us. Switching roles is the new reality." She adds: Each "has our best interests in mind, the elders that we are. I am overcome by the concern our generation is receiving from those younger. It makes love very tangible."

THREE: Self-isolation notwithstanding, we anguish at the pain of fellow Americans losing jobs, income, family.

PL continues eloquently: "How fortunate we are to have a perfectly fine house to hunker down in.... That's unlike the young families who are not nearly as susceptible to the disease as we are, yet are having their lives totally torn apart and traumatized in ways that we can't imagine." For some children, there will be "the nightmare of their parents without jobs and/or income. Makes me weep." JR says he feels "so badly for people who are losing income, closing their businesses."

These pillars in their community can see the pain coming at their community. CW rues cancellation of a fundraiser that normally brings in $100,000 for a women's shelter: "A real loss of revenue for those who provide services for the most vulnerable." Her response: "We need to step up and make donations."

The pain coming at America elicits harsh judgment of Trump. CW: "I am disgusted with The Orange One's lack of early response." KM: "How ironic the Orange Man, who is known to fear germs more than the average person, now has to deal with a pandemic." For LV, Trump's press briefings, with medical experts around him, are "frightening": "They are knowledgeable—he is not; they are professional—he is not; when questions are asked of him, he always makes it about him. This is not helping me or our country." CM calls Trump "inept and actually dangerous. More lives will be lost because of it, and that's just SICKENING." We all grieve the suffering to come.

FOUR: Big question—how to bear extended self-isolation, how to bear our new reality?

Here is where my friends, in brave candor, admit to some questions, some anxiety (and because of their candor, I will not identify who says what).

If the self-isolation must be extended, one friend admits: "It becomes very scary to me when they say it could be July/August before this is all clear." Another, newly widowed, admits, "I miss having a partner to talk with." She adds, "So far, mole mode is not bad, but as time goes by, hmmm...." And another, the most extrovert of this group by far, admits: "If this isolation goes on for a long time, it is me who will suffer first." Referring to her husband, "I am the more outgoing person of us two. [Husband] is always patient and calm and takes strange situations as they come. Not me." She concludes: "But there is always the phone! I will talk to my friends on the phone and that way feel I am connected with the outer world."

And about the prospect of a "new normal"—the dread of living in a virus-infested world—one friend admits to "being depressed," not seeing humanity organizing itself in defense. Perhaps knowing we *really* are all in the same boat—and we *really* need every hand on the oars—will help? Perhaps, out of our collective struggle, a new consciousness lies ahead?

In all this, I got some petting. About my claim that living with cancer fortifies, one friend also living with cancer wrote: "You're so right, C., about your reason for not panicking. Cancer, once confronted, can do that for us." But college friend PF chided me for still going to the gym: "You write that you don't consider yourself at risk. Please ask your MD about that. To be sure." So, forthwith, I stopped going to the gym (which closed anyway) and now speed-walk in the neighborhood. And from another friend, this: "Carla, you are one of the strongest people I know and I have every faith you will come through this no matter what happens." I am blessed to front this crisis with Larry, my husband and *compagno di vita* of 42 years.

Meanwhile, to cope with self-isolation, books will be read, movies watched, closets cleaned, photos finally organized. One friend is using this "quiet time" to learn Spanish; another, Italian. Three express gratitude that the Metropolitan Opera is streaming productions for free. Of course there are ways not to cope, too: College roommate SF, from whom I learned about "being a survivor," wrote that, while out marketing, when she had just wine in her cart, a man walking by said, "You have the right idea." Not!

And, of course, while self-isolating, we can use our experience and means to reach out—online—to those suffering in our communities: by supporting hospitals (masks! ventilators!), donating to food banks, doing remote teaching, making a phone call....

Going forward—hmmm, how to go forward in a pandemic, in "a time of cholera," to echo Gabriel Garcia Marquez? We will learn how, thanks in big part to good friends. I cannot think of a better way to sign off here than to quote the sign-offs that these friends—whom I am honored to know—used in their closing. Here, a selection:

"*Buona fortuna*, yes!" "Be grateful and hopeful." "Fortunately, we have each other. Hugs, er, elbow bumps." "Stay healthy, *please*." "As always, Roomie...to Life!" "I never thought I would actually experience this [dystopia] and not just watch it on TV. Take care and stay out of Corona." "I am allowing myself to feel hopeful about November...[with] Trump gone and our country saved from four more disastrous years. Stay well during these strange times." "Sure wish we had Obama in the White House. I hope Larry is over his cold and that you both stay healthy during these uncertain times." "Please be well. You both matter greatly to a lot of people."

And finally: "Stay safe and healthy—and in touch. Much love."

—*Medium*, March 29, 2020

In a Plague-Time, the Heroic (in Hospitals) and Not-Heroic (in the White House)

Third in an ongoing series, Notes from a Plague-Time

As I GET older, after a lifetime of mixing it up with the human parade, I have come to a conclusion about people, which is:
The ultimate difference between people? *Caring for others.* There are those who do—care for their fellow human beings—and there are those who don't, for whom the concept of "fellow human being" is as foreign as...a virus. So constituted, these people are driven not by humanity, of which they are bereft, but ego and vainglory.

But: Those who care for others can live-stream (as it were) the lives of others—their fear, their pain—*as if they were their own*, because: They are. They *feel* the humanity of others. And, doing so, they feel a responsibility to act—to assuage fear and pain. While such a panoramic view of humanity may drain, it also elevates and sustains.

These models of humanity are now found, in this plague-time of coronavirus, in the hospitals across the land, on the front lines treating COVID-19 patients—the doctors of all specialties, the nurses of all grades, the various technicians, the EMTs bringing in the infected. While these paragons tend to their patients' physical bodies—what Franz Kafka called "His Majesty, the body"—they also, majestically, seek to save the above-cited human vessel housing fear and pain, and hope.

But what makes these paragons heroic, beyond run-of-the-mill humanity, is this: Their caring for others brings with it mortal peril to themselves—infection from a deadly and fast-acting virus that medical science itself still does not understand, in fact is using this pandemic to study. These heroes understand their caring can kill; they themselves could die. They understand, as one anesthesiologist put it, "You're basically right next to the nuclear reactor."

Of course not all medical heroes are of paragon character; there are those driven by ego and vainglory, too. But, *by their action in this plaguetime,* they are not much in view; stories of medical heroes abound.

Where the *un-heroic* abounds is in the White House, whose occupant *risks nothing* while our medical heroes *risk all.*

Staying with the heroic, I shall focus on the above-cited anesthesiologist—Dr. Cory Deburghgraeve—who works in a large state hospital at the University of Illinois-Chicago and whose riveting as-told-to-story in *The Washington Post* immerses one in the action at COVID-19's front lines—and in heroic humanity.

As Dr. Deburghgraeve tells us, his "entire job" now—14 hours a day, six nights a week—is intubation: "When patients aren't getting enough oxygen, I place a tube down their airway so we can put them on a vent [ventilator]. It buys their body time to fight the virus." He adds matter-of-factly: "It's also probably the most dangerous procedure a doctor can do when it comes to personal exposure. I'm getting within a few inches of the patient's face. I'm leaning in toward the mouth, placing my fingers on the gums, opening up the airway. All it takes is a cough. A gag. If anything goes badly, you can have a room full of virus." He reflects: "So, there's a possibility I get sick. Maybe a probability. I don't know. I have my own underlying condition"—bad asthma as a kid—"but I try not to dwell on it."

But he can't help but dwell on it: Being "right next to the nuclear reactor" ("My mask and hood can get covered in fluid"), the doctor notes, "I go in confident and fast, because if you miss on the first try, you have to do it again, and then you're bringing out a ton more virus." His fears are held universally by his colleagues, from doctors to EMTs, especially in light of the lack of testing for this virus.

Mortal peril established, Dr. Deburghgraeve tells of two actions that strike me as instructive. One: He describes a staff meeting where it was agreed one person should do COVID intubations during the day and another at night: "...and I started thinking: I'm 33 years old. I don't have any kids at home. I don't live with older relatives. About an hour after the meeting, I emailed my supervisor. 'I'm happy to do this. It should be me.'" *"I'm happy to do this. It should be me...."*

Two: He describes doing rounds with the doctors in the I.C.U. to check on patients he's intubated; these patients are not allowed family or visitors. Then, this: "I'm not a religious person, but I do like to stand there for a minute outside the room and think about them and what they're going through. I try to think about something positive—a positive expectation." *I do like to stand there...and think about them and what they're going through...."* He adds: "I have to find a way to hold it together in order to do this job. I tear up sometimes, and if I do, it can fog up my face shield."

I go into detail here to make a contrast—between the heroic Dr. Deburghgraeve and the un-heroic Donald Trump—in order to make this point: Can *anybody* imagine Donald Trump making the moral choice—*"I'm happy to do this. It should be me"*—or, regarding anybody stricken with COVID-19 and fighting for air and for life, Trump feeling, *"I do like to...think about them and what they're going through"*? *Not!*

But this contrast is more than character. It carries life-and-death weight.

The un-heroic Trump, being deficient in humanity and thus feeling, *compounds* the peril to our medical heroes by his abject failure to provide them with the PPE—protective personal equipment: masks, shields, capes, respirators—that they have been *begging* for, almost a month now. And he continues to refuse to invoke broadly the Defense Production Act that would require American manufacturing to retool and produce this PPE. Unlike Franklin Roosevelt who reorganized American manufacturing in World War II to meet its moment, Trump cannot meet this pandemic moment with even something so simple as a mask? (Citizens are rushing to their sewing machines and turning out masks on their own.)

And when asked about masks at a press briefing, Trump's response?

"We're not a shipping clerk." *"We're not a shipping clerk..."?* Responding to Trump's "shipping clerk" crack, Dr. Sophie Greenberg writes in the *Post*, "I am not a seamstress, but this week I found myself sewing my own mask." She adds, "Normally, a mask is discarded after every patient encounter; now, we are given one mask to use for an entire week."

It brings to mind a scholar's post-Inauguration crack, that, in Trump, we find "malevolence tempered by incompetence," though this pandemic amends that to "malevolence amplified by incompetence." I think also of Shakespeare's line given to Brutus, anxious at Julius Caesar's exercise of power: "Th' abuse of greatness is when it disjoins / Remorse from power."

Of course, also at issue—along with the contrast in humanity of medical heroes and Mr. Trump—is the eternal debate between Republicans and Democrats on the role of the federal government. But if anything is learned—will it?—from the disarray this pandemic has cast America into, it is the imperative that the federal government *must* lead the 50 states in organizing the response to national disaster. (Right now 50 governors are competing with their peers for PPE.) And, imperatively, at the apex of federal power, we need a *human being* who feels for other human beings.

Who will at least provide masks to our medical heroes.

Whose numbers, admirably, grow—despite the lack of PPE. As in war, veterans are recalled—retired doctors and nurses are returning to duty—and draftees called up—medical students are being graduated early—all to join the COVID-19 front lines.

My anxiety for medical workers is personal: I come from a medical family—father a doctor, mother a nurse when they met. I got used to seeing doctors as saviors when, driving Dad on his house calls, upon entering the house of a seriously ill patient, the whole family turned to him: "Doctor! You're here!," as if to say, "Save us!" Mom could recall being sprayed by the contents of a tubercular man's lungs when he "expired"; she'd be a nut on PPE. Our proud family tradition continues (I was pre-med for all of two weeks: I couldn't hack chemistry): A nurse niece and the doctor daughter of a cousin are both serving on the COVID-19 front lines.

Crisis lifts curtains. Yes, crisis also brings chaos, which begets more chaos. But: If we look with intent, crisis lifts curtains, it clarifies. Certainly, this pandemic—the life-and-death battle being waged, the economic collapse soon to befall—clarifies, both the horror of our defective president and the crying need for skilled and humane heroes. Fortunately such heroes are in our midst, working at this moment in our hospitals at perilous risk to themselves. It is their stories, viewed from the safety of "sheltering in place," that stirs a frightened nation (and belies the Modernist anti-hero). We observe these true heroes and tell ourselves, "Remember this."

But will we remember? America since 9/11 has been lost, flailing. Preceded by the go-go '90s, 9/11—for a brief while—brought us civility, seriousness, a yearning for normalcy. But in very short order, the go-go returned, turbo-charged even, as seen in the "heroes" that soon swallowed the spotlight: Tony Soprano "whacking" his rivals dead, Walter White "breaking bad" as a chemistry teacher producing meth. Pop culture might normally be extraneous to the point, but: Out of this skewed pop culture came…Donald Trump, host of a so-called "reality" TV show called "The Apprentice," who—History's bad joke—is now apprenticing as President of the United States of America and pretending to lead the nation through a pandemic.

This pandemic, more even than 9/11, could spell curtains for America—politically, economically, culturally. The only way we can reverse America's decline is—along with embracing truth and expertise again—to exalt (and elect) authentic skill, moral character, deep humanity.

Our medical heroes working the COVID-19 front lines point the way—upward.

—*Medium*, April 8, 2020

In a Plague-Time, Redefining the "Essential" Worker

Fourth in an ongoing series, Notes from a Plague-Time

THE FOLLOWING COMES from a "safe place"—a very safe place. In response to the coronavirus pandemic, my husband and I are "self-isolating," "sheltering in place." Moreover, we are sheltering in a gated community. The virus, of course, is not stopped by gates, but right now, we are untouched here. Like everyone else, we feel the dread, but from a safe place, comparatively.

On top of that—more cushioning: We both can "work from home," another directive for survival. But working from home has been our mode for 20 years now—me, writing commentary, and Larry, Civic Man, in and out of the house for meetings on education, homelessness, Democratic politics. Now, sheltering in place, he conducts his civic life on-line and on-camera.

Operationally, then, our lifestyle remains unchanged, except: Our formerly quiet house is noisier, by a tad, with the voices of community engagement drifting up the stairs from Larry's office, sometimes so animatedly that, not wanting to get out of my recliner where I am pinned down by my laptop, I will raise my voice to say: "Dear, keep it down, O.K.?" O.K.

Have I established, in this deadly pandemic, how safe, and pleasant, our safe place is?

About the gated-community thing, I can explain: The house was underpriced; we made an offer early, hoping to avoid a bidding war; the owner accepted our offer; and, boom—we were in a gated community, not by design but default. Financially, we are safe enough: We are not big consumers but demon savers, and Larry's Navy retirement check is deposited in our bank, first of the month, like clockwork.

Have I established the guilt underlying our sense of safety?

Further about safety: There are other factors—we are both over 65 with underlying conditions (well-controlled but underlying)—that make us grateful for this safety. It is also these factors that make us dependent, not on the kindness of strangers (*ala* Blanche DuBois in *A Streetcar Named Desire*), but for their delivery systems. (Suddenly, Literature seems a privileged thing.) Our furnace went out and our roof sprang a leak, but both were repaired by service people venturing out into Virus Land to help us.

The big need for which we are now completely dependent on others is, of course, food. Operationally, we-who-shelter have quickly come to depend on food-shopping and food-delivery services, many of them pop-up since the pandemic's onset. (Larry stopped doing our weekly Costco run the first week of self-isolation.)

The disparity of our positions—safe vs. unsafe—came into focus for me several weeks ago, in an encounter that lingers in my mind. Usually it is Larry who takes receipt of deliveries coming to the house, since his office is on the first floor. Our emails to each other are signed LL (Lower Level) and UL (Upper Level). In this instance, Upper Level took her evening walk—and took receipt of a kind of revelation.

It was already quite dark, but I could make out a man coming toward me carrying a heavy load in plastic bags. Knowing we expected a grocery delivery, I asked him, "Are you looking for the Seaquist house?" He said yes, so I directed him ("On the left") and went on with my walk. Then it hit me: He was walking because he could not work the gate-code, meaning he walked some distance to get to us.

Heading back toward the house—my circuit is just our cul-de-sac—I saw the man walking out. I asked if he met my husband, meaning: We give big tips—lavish tips—to delivery people these days and did he get his?

He said no, then noted: "It's beautiful in here." I noted the "in here."

"Yes, it is," I replied, then blurted out, "It's our first house after years

and years of apartments and we got it, our first house, in our fifties."
Guilt again.

Then I said: "Really, we want to give you a tip. Come back to the house with me. My husband must have been in the kitchen and didn't hear the doorbell."

But he said: "No, I'm fine."

And, not monitoring myself, I said: "*Are* you? Fine, I mean?"

He said, "Yeah, I am," and started moving again.

And as he moved off, I said: "Bless you, Sir." I could barely get out the "Sir" for the tears.

All this transpired of course over the requisite six feet of "social distancing"—and the infinite chasm of social privilege. And in the near-dark: I could not make out his face at all, only his voice. So many metaphors, so many excuses for injustice.

I have gone on (and on) here about safety and privilege, because: I really hope never to hear again about the "bad choices" the working class makes. This is *the* pre-eminent social-distancing mantra—it has worked terrifically—that we have heard for decades from the political right, but also from the posh precincts on the left. Maybe, pre-pandemic, bad choices *were* made by the working poor. But now, in this deadly plague, whose ways not even epidemiologists can predict, whose lethality is hammered home with every newscast—the working poor have no choice at all, none: Not for them the luxury of working from home, they must risk their very lives to deliver to people-risking-very-little their steaks, their ice cream, their eye drops.

And don't forget, after Delivery Person leaves, to Windex and wipe down, while Delivery Person ventures, not out of choice (nice, that privilege!) but from iron necessity, back into Virus Land. By contrast, today I ventured out (for physical therapy for pre-pandemic hand surgery) for the first time since self-isolating four weeks ago. The injustice is yawning.

Lethality update: On yesterday's *PBS NewsHour*, "new milestones" were noted—over two *million* infected worldwide with the coronavirus;

over 125,000 dead worldwide; the number of dead in the U.S. is now over 26,000.

I cannot imagine how, on hearing those kinds of numbers, the working poor manage their nerves, their fears, their souls.

Daily we hear, from our sheltered safety, more and more stories of the risks these workers take—and the deaths they are incurring in growing numbers. "I'm scared to go to work" states it for the millions working not only as delivery people in a broad array of services, but grocery clerks, warehouse stockers, postal workers, bus drivers, firefighters, etc. *The New York Times Magazine* devoted a long cover story to these risk-takers, titled "Exposed. Afraid. Determined." Some of these risk-takers are now deemed emergency responders. And of course there are the heroic medical workers—doctors, nurses, technicians, EMTs—risking their lives for us.

And we read, from our sheltered safety, of the 17 *million* Americans losing their jobs in just the last three weeks—a U.S. record—meaning: These people will be joining the ranks of the above-mentioned risk-takers (if they were not there already). (Update: As of April 16, that number jumped to 22 million.)

All of which means: If our lives for the foreseeable future are to be lived in the Valley of the Shadow of the Coronavirus, that is to say Death, as epidemiologists warn, then these risk-taking workers will continue to take risks on behalf of all the rest of us, likewise for the foreseeable future. It behooves all of us who are sheltered and safe to remember this sacrifice.

And it behooves those who mewl about the difficulties of self-isolation to…rethink. Think on the person who risked his/her life to bring you your peach.

It also behooves a reconsideration of the question: Who is an "essential" worker? Is it the middle manager—or any worker working in the one sector of the economy (groceries) whose numbers have soared while all other sectors have tanked, but which sector now comes laden with viral danger? Is it the President of the United States of America, who cannot organize the federal response to the pandemic—or the delivery person bringing you your food, your meds? Of course, in the best of all possible worlds, all work would be deemed essential, but we do not live in that world.

As for ourselves, Larry will continue his work on-line in education, homelessness (stand by for an explosion in homelessness), Democratic politics; I will continue with what I consider my public service, commentary. We can only hope this work is essential. But, for sure, in the Age of Corona, the workers described above, working at low-low pay but high-high risk, are this era's "essential" workers.

Will we remember this, post-pandemic—who is the "essential" worker? In a radically reordered post-pandemic world—both economy and society—will these risk-takers still "count"? Or will the essentially inessential, like the financial types who create instruments out of whole paper, or that inanity known as the "influencer," take top priority once again?

In a way, we are fortunate in the timing of this pandemic. No, I wish to Heaven we were not going through this awfulness. But in this presidential election year, we can—if we handle it right—reposition America in a more humane direction. I am glad Joe Biden, the Democrats' probable presidential nominee, a moderate, declares himself open to the points advocated by Elizabeth Warren and Bernie Sanders, the progressives who left the race—Warren's call for "deep structural change," Sanders' call for a "political revolution." Because: They have seen their points validated by this pandemic—the need for universal healthcare and the need for a more humane capitalism, one that honors the "essential" workers risking their lives for the safe and sheltered.

Out of the Dark Ages came the Renaissance. Out of this pandemic comes, perhaps…the essential?

—*Medium*, April 15, 2020

In a Plague-Time, Seeking Beauty, Truth, Lightness

Fifth in an ongoing series, Notes from a Plague-Time
Note: The online iteration of this post contains all the links cited.

WITH THE HIDEOUS toll of the coronavirus pandemic rising steeply—49,605 U.S. deaths at this posting, 187,330 deaths worldwide—and while continuing to "shelter in place" and "self-isolate," this pilgrim's heart desperately wants release, wants to soar, wants beauty, truth, lightness.

To wit (yes, wit!): Like Fred Astaire and Ginger Rogers dancing to "Pick Yourself Up." At a time when experts fear that, with the plague-induced economic collapse, we are facing another Great Depression, it is cheering to note Fred and Ginger created beauty, truth, and lightness in the depths (1936) of the first depression, urging us to pick ourselves up, dust ourselves off, start all over again.

If more reason is needed to seek Art's consolations, we now have another manifestation of American crazy: The extreme right-wing out in the streets, defying "social distancing," brandishing guns, protesting government "overreach," all fanned by the tweeting demagogue in the White House ("LIBERATE MICHIGAN")—threatening the rest of us with a resurgence of infection. It all combines to make one yearn for what the Roman poet Virgil called "the upper air," where truth and beauty reign, where instead of a heaviness of the soul there is a lightness, what Italians call *leggerezza*.

Poet John Keats' immortal line—"Beauty is truth, truth beauty"— captures great Art at its heights. Here are the high places my mind goes to, not only for deep cleansing, but for release, for solace, for hope, and, crucially, for fuel: For I go to these high places not for permanent escape, but as a respite, to replenish before I re-engage with the titanic struggle besetting the world. Where I can manage it, my forthcoming examples come with metaphor, intensifying the meaning. Starting with the aria—meta-metaphor alert—"Peace, peace, my God!" Finding peace, even fleeting, I can carry on.

This post is repurposed from one I filed just after Donald Trump's election in 2016, titled "This Blogpost is NOT about Donald Trump: Seeking Beauty, Truth, Lightness." Sad to say, all the reasons I cited then for seeking Art's consolations have proved not only valid but been magnified many times over. New development since then: Streaming video—of concerts, opera, films, plays (I recently streamed Syracuse Stage's terrific production of *Amadeus*).

Allora, the consolations of Art, which—they are just a click away—I hope will console you, too.

SONG: As promised, *Pace, pace, mio Dio* ("Peace, peace, my God!"), from Verdi's *La Forza del Destino*, sung by Leontyne Price. Marvel at the sublime "Flower Duet" from Delibes' *Lakme*. For the beauty that human voices can create *en masse*, enjoy Handel's *Messiah*, especially the "Hallelujah" chorus, sung by the King's College Choir. And for their calming effect, Gregorian chants.

MUSIC: Bach, the Master, always elevates; here's a cello suite and *Toccata and Fugue*. Vivaldi's *Four Seasons* transports us back to Nature. Here are Mozart's *Clarinet Concerto*, with jazzman Benny Goodman on clarinet; my favorite Brahms, *Opus 118: Six piano pieces*; and, for a majestic note, Beethoven's *Fifth Symphony*. For those mourning the damage done to America and the world, Chopin's nocturnes and the requiems of Mozart, Brahms, and Verdi. My absolute favorite piece of chamber music is Ravel's *Piano Trio*. The French make a point of beautiful music, so here are Debussy, Poulenc, more Ravel. For ineffable beauty, Vaughan Williams' *The Lark Ascending*, Sibelius' *The Swan of Tuonela*, and Elgar's *Enigma Variations*; for a sad beauty, the tangos of Astor Piazzolla; and for *esprit*, Walton's *Crown Imperial*. Metaphor alert: For a New Day, Mendelssohn's *Reformation Symphony* and Copland's *Fanfare for the Common Man*.

And enjoy again the American songbook—Gershwin, Porter, Kern, Berlin—all sung by Ella Fitzgerald. Enjoy again the American sound of Ellington, Goodman ("Sing, Sing, Sing"), and—as tonic reminder in a pandemic—Louis Armstrong singing "What a Wonderful World."

DANCE: See Fred and Ginger dancing to the sublime "Cheek to Cheek" and "Waltz in Swing Time" and, cited above, "Pick Yourself Up." See Fred and Cyd Charisse dancing the lovely "Dancing in the Dark." See Fred and Rita Hayworth in an amazing number in *You Were Never Lovelier*. Of course the mind seeking joy goes to Gene Kelly's iconic rain-splashed number in *Singin' in the Rain* and his iconic ballet in *An American in Paris*. Here's the iconic ballet in *The Red Shoes* with Moira Shearer. Ever-revelatory is Alvin Ailey's *Revelations*, created as "blood memories" of African-American life; the Nicholas Brothers are ever-astonishing. Metaphor alert: *Prodigal Son*, with Mikhail Baryshnikov.

PAINTING: Rather than large-scale work—history paintings, Biblical parables—I am thinking more human-scale. Portraits, for example—by Da Vinci, Botticelli, Raphael, Rembrandt, Modigliani, and Holbein the Younger for his portraiture of the great humanist Erasmus, as well as other assorted worthies. Postcards of Velazquez' "Aesop" and Daumier's "Don Quixote" sit on my desk. At this fraught time, Gilbert Stuart's portraits of our founders, including Abigail Adams, resonate.

Likewise, in fraught times, simple things resonate: the sea (Courbet), the view out a window (Bonnard), Matisse's late-in-life cutouts. Just as they did in music, the French Impressionists found the beautiful, with Manet, Monet, Degas, and Cezanne exalting everyday life. I love Van Gogh's expressiveness, especially in his final work, "Wheatfield with Crows." I love Vermeer's humanity, especially as portrayed in his "Geographer," with a man bent over maps, looking up to the light. With misogyny so blatant (still), I think of the art of Mary Cassatt, Berthe Morisot, Georgia O'Keeffe, Anon. On a somber note, I think of Michelangelo's "Pieta." Finally, metaphor alert: Goya's "Colossus," Caravaggio's "Narcissus" and "Ecce Homo," and Bruegel the Elder's "Tower of Babel."

LITERATURE: The poet Virgil, cited above, I will quote in full (it is one of my life-credos): "Easy is the descent to the lower world; but to retrace your steps and to escape to the upper air—this is the task, this is the toil." Another life-credo is from Orwell: "The fact to which we have got to cling, as to a life-belt, is that it *is* possible to be a normal decent person and yet to be fully alive" (italics Orwell's). Camus has inspiring words for this plague-time, from, appropriately, his novel *The Plague*: "...to state quite simply what we learn in a time of pestilence: that there are more things to admire in men than to despise." (In women, too.)

In American letters, I think of Emerson's question in his essay "Politics": "Are our methods now so excellent that all competition is hopeless? Could not a nation of friends devise better ways?" In Henry Adams' novel *Democracy*, a historian says: "Democracy asserts the fact that the masses are now raised to higher intelligence than formerly. All our civilization aims at this mark. We want to do what we can to help it.... I grant it is an experiment, but it is the only direction society can take that is worth its taking.... I am glad to see society grapple with issues in which no one can afford to be neutral." I think of Thoreau's advice: "Simplify, simplify."

I think of Edith Wharton's description of America's Gilded Age, in *The*

House of Mirth: "A frivolous society can acquire dramatic significance only through what its frivolity destroys. Its tragic implication lies in its power of debasing people and ideals." Read Wharton's novel *The Custom of the Country*, the "custom" being the getting and spending of money—which practice Trump ensures for his super-rich cronies by firing the Inspector General who was to oversee dispersal of the $2 trillion relief package Congress just passed. But, here I descended "to the lower world"—sorry, back to "the upper air...."

Melville, in his famous opening of *Moby-Dick*, captures the need for escape we all feel now, sheltering. Now at least we have time to commit it to memory: "Call me Ishmael. Some years ago—never mind how long precisely—having little or no money in my purse, and nothing particular to interest me on shore, I thought I would sail about a little and see the watery part of the world. It is a way I have of driving off the spleen, and regulating the circulation. Whenever I find myself growing grim about the mouth; whenever it is a damp, drizzly November in my soul; whenever I find myself involuntarily pausing before coffin warehouses, and bringing up the rear of every funeral I meet; and especially whenever my hypos get such an upper hand of me, that it requires a strong moral principle to prevent me from deliberately stepping into the street, and methodically knocking people's hats off—then, I account it high time to get to sea as soon as I can." For a portrait of the White House's present occupant, see Melville's novel *The Confidence Man: His Masquerade*.

If sheltering in place—our mode of existence for the duration— leaves you feeling little scope for personal action, and feeling your "Thinking of you" email counts as nothing *vis-à-vis* the actions of the medical heroes working this plague's front lines, consolation can be found in the last lines of George Eliot's deeply humane novel, *Middlemarch*, which sum up Dorothea Brooke's life: "Her full nature...spent itself in channels which had no great name on the earth. But the effect of her being on those around her was incalculably diffusive, for the growing good of the world is partly dependent on unhistoric acts, and that things are not so ill with you and me as they might have been is half owing to the number who lived faithfully a hidden life and rest in unvisited tombs." In plague-time, it's good to think of "the growing good of the world."

In Poetry, Auden's description of the 1930s as a "low dishonest decade" applies to our moment. That said, solace is to be found in personal ties, as Matthew Arnold in "Dover Beach" writes: "Ah, love, let us be true / To one another! for the world, which seems / To lie before us like a land of dreams, / So various, so beautiful, so new, / Hath really neither joy, nor love, nor light, / Nor certitude, nor peace, nor help for pain; / And we are here as on a darkling plain / Swept with confused alarms of struggle and flight, / Where ignorant armies clash by night."

For the long view, I go to my favorite poet, Emily Dickinson: "This World is not Conclusion. / A Species stands beyond—/ Invisible, as Music—/ But positive, as Sound—/ It beckons and it baffles—/ Philosophy—don't know—/ And through a Riddle, at the last—/ Sagacity, must go —/ To guess it, puzzles scholars—/ To gain it, Men have borne / Contempt of Generations / And Crucifixion, shown—/ Faith slips—and laughs, and rallies—/ Blushes, if any see—/ Plucks at a twig of Evidence—/ And asks a Vane, the way—/ Much Gesture, from the Pulpit—/ Strong Hallelujahs roll—/ Narcotics cannot still the Tooth / That nibbles at the soul—"

In Drama, I think of the lines from Beckett's *Waiting for Godot*, near the end: "I can't go on like this." "That's what you think." (In a pandemic, those lines bear repeating.) Not often recalled are these lines from *Godot*: "We've lost our rights?" "We got rid of them." On the loss of America's reputation, I think of the dishonored John Proctor's lament before he is hanged, in Arthur Miller's *The Crucible*: "Because it is my name! Because I cannot have another in my life!... How may I live without my name? I have given you my soul; leave me my name!" For America at its very essence, revisit *Our Town*, Thornton Wilder's masterpiece (the 1940 movie stars a young William Holden, music by Aaron Copland). For characters contending with an injust society, see the *oeuvre* of Ibsen (*An*

Enemy of the People, A Doll's House, et al.). For characters who think (or try to), see contemporary playwright Tom Stoppard, notably his plays *Arcadia* and *Rosencranz and Guildenstern Are Dead*.

Shakespeare speaks to all circumstances. We might use our self-isolation to commit to memory select speeches from Shakespeare, such as: "How all occasions do inform against me, and spur my dull revenge...." Here Shakespeare presents humanity at its best, from *Hamlet*: "What a piece of work is a man, how noble in reason, how infinite in faculties, in form and moving how express and admirable, in action how like an angel, in apprehension how like a god, the beauty of the world, the paragon of animals—and yet, to me, what is this quintessence of dust?" Jump down the rabbit-hole of scholarly argumentation and examine: Did Shakespeare spray that speech with exclamation points in the original—yes or no?

Four years ago when I posted the original version of this commentary, my mother was beginning her final descent, so I was going to the 23rd Psalm for comfort. It comforts still: "The Lord is my shepherd; I shall not want. He maketh me to lie down in green pastures; He leadeth me beside the still waters. He restoreth my soul...."

Speaking of restoring the soul: some lightness, *leggerezza*:

For sheerest delight, I go most readily to the films of the 1930s and '40s, when Hollywood served up inspiriting diversion for hard times.

See Claudette Colbert drive Clark Gable crazy in *It Happened One Night*; see Katharine Hepburn drive Cary Grant crazy in *Bringing Up Baby*; see Cary Grant drive Rosalind Russell crazy in *His Girl Friday*; see Joel McCrea drive Jean Arthur crazy in *The More the Merrier*; see screwball comedy in general. Turning romantic, see Katharine Hepburn and Spencer Tracy fall in love in *Woman of the Year*; see Bette Davis and Paul Henreid put their love in context in *Now, Voyager*; see Gregory Peck and Audrey Hepburn do the same in *Roman Holiday*. See Humphrey Bogart and Ingrid Bergman rediscover their love in *Casablanca*; see Bogie and Bacall lay the metaphors on each other in *The Big Sleep*. For more recent fare, see the hilarious *Moonstruck*. See also Bette Davis deliver her famous line, "I'd like to kiss ya, but I just washed my hair"; see a drunk Jimmy Stewart drop in on Cary Grant in *The Philadelphia Story*; see William Powell go fishing in *Libeled Lady*; see Jimmy Cagney sing and dance in *Yankee Doodle Dandy*, also dance down the White House stairs. Hear Irene Dunne sing "Smoke Gets in Your Eyes." And see *Sullivan's Travels* for the importance of laughter in bad times.

Back to the present bad times...: To endure this pandemic and economic collapse—*and* gird for the repair work afterward—observe the gallantry portrayed by Greer Garson and Walter Pidgeon in *Mrs. Miniver*, set in World War II, especially the scene where, sheltering, they gallantly talk of mundane things while German bombs drop overhead. See veterans of that war come home to altered futures and manage in the magnificent movie, *The Best Years of Our Lives*. To fight the toxic bigotry unleashed by our divisive President, see Gregory Peck fight the good fight, here against anti-Semitism, in *Gentleman's Agreement*.

Further about our repair job—post-pandemic, post-economic collapse: No less than hard-nosed George Orwell thought regeneration was possible. But it would take clear thinking—"To think clearly is a necessary first step toward political regeneration"—and language that tells the truth, not the lies we are drowning in now. Reading Orwell's essay "Politics and the English Language" will restart your engine.

Perhaps the last word, as we prime for that work, might go to Wislawa Szymborska, Polish poet and Nobel laureate. Speaking of rebuilding after ruination, she wrote, wittily: "Shirtsleeves will be rolled / To shreds."

To the upper air! And to get us there: Fred and Ginger again, dancing to..."Let's Face the Music and Dance."

—*Medium*, April 23, 2020

In a Plague-Time, Can-Do Nation Is Unmasked as Can't Do

Sixth in an ongoing series, Notes from a Plague-Time

IT IS A truth universally acknowledged, that to make a recovery, one must first recognize there is a problem to recover from—and analyze it.

The "problem" here is America's worse-than-shambolic response to the coronavirus pandemic besetting the world. In truth, our response to this deadly viral catastrophe has itself been a catastrophe. Americans, stung at the spectacle, are crying out: *How can this be happening?*

We Americans have long prided ourselves as Number One for "nimble" organization and management, for "world-beating" inventiveness and creativity. We are, after all, sole proprietors of that "special juice"—a can-do attitude. Granted, this pandemic is "novel"—something new in human history. But, normally, such a challenge would have brought out our best. "Step aside, please. *We're Americans, we've got this.*"

The scales have been ripped from our eyes. America—see: the White House—cannot organize even such a simple-but-vital thing as supplying the personal protective equipment our frontline medical heroes need as they risk their lives to save others. Going on two months, it still can't get done. And now, with "testing, testing, testing" universally acknowledged as the *sine qua non* to "going forward" (where Americans always want to go), the White House outright lies about the testing going on, ducks responsibility, refuses to lead—in sum, America *can't* do.

What this unending train wreck of a crisis reveals is: America is Number One in ineptitude, incompetence, irresponsibility. Which are serious flaws in and of their own, but which, in a deadly pandemic, will compound—incalculably—the damage wreaked in *unnecessary* death (at posting, the toll in the U.S. is over 80,500), in *unnecessary* economic destruction, in *unnecessary* suffering (per *The Washington Post*, America now has a mental health crisis).

Are we seeing the demise of the American superpower, the *coup de grace* delivered by its own hand? America's decline, bruited since 9/11, certainly *feels* accelerated; have we reached the Point of No Reversal? A column-cum-obituary by *The Irish Times*' Fintan O'Toole states it: "Over more than two centuries, the United States has stirred a very wide range of feelings in the rest of the world: love and hatred, fear and hope, envy and contempt, awe and anger. But there is one emotion that has never been directed toward the U.S. until now: pity." *The Atlantic*'s George Packer declares America a "failed state." We have amended T.S. Eliot, who imagined the world ends "not with a bang, but a whimper." It ends, it seems, in a confused mess.

In truth, we Americans have been deluded about our peerless props and reputation for some time. Two major forces weakening our system—Republican know-nothingism and a general antipathy to seriousness—have brewed for decades, gaining steam in the go-go 1990s and now blending in perfect—or rather imperfect—union in our president, Donald J. Trump. See: any White House coronavirus press briefing.

Republicans, for reasons they justified at the time, have become a Know-Nothing party—anti-science, anti-fact, anti-*truth*. Their anti-government, anti-bureaucrat, anti-elite ranting, famously aimed at reducing government so it could be drowned in a bathtub, has yielded institutional catastrophe: Government now is headed by hack political appointees (while staffed by thinning ranks of professionals) who cannot, for just one of many examples, administer the relief packages Congress, in a miracle of bipartisanism, passed to aid suffering citizens and businesses.

To their credit, some Republicans—retired—have voiced regret: Former senator Bill Frist, a doctor, now avows science will point the way, proving conscience pulses in some. But: The institutional damage has been done, aided and abetted by professing Christians who cannot see the hypocrisy of standing by an amoral and dangerously demagogic President who mocks every virtue Republicans had long, and properly, espoused—like personal responsibility, a failing whose effects, as we see, are *killing*.

Political weakening was coupled with cultural weakening. Neil Postman in 1985 wrote of it in his book, *Amusing Ourselves to Death*. In the postwar era, while some youth rebelled for a cause—to right racial and sexist wrongs—others rebelled without a cause, against "the system" and "bourgeois morality." Thus grew the cultural O.K. to cut corners, shade the truth, shirk responsibility, and yuk-yuk about it. Thus could torture, conducted by U.S. troops in Iraq, fail to rouse public furor. Heroes were out, the anti-hero was in. Over time the "transgressive" shaded into criminality. Culture being as powerful as politics in shaping a people, and with the unserious dominant, it is no surprise this degraded culture finally got its President: Donald J. Trump, Number One in grift.

(This cultural weakening was mainly, yes, a liberal thing, specifically an ultra-liberal thing, with the boomers being the "super-spreaders," to use a term of the moment. I am a boomer by age and a liberal by philosophy. My boomer and liberal friends know I have protested ultra-liberalism's licentiousness and no-boundaries policies forever: "Guys, we need to get serious." And I cite Republican know-nothingism not because I am a Democrat, but because I believe in science and the Enlightenment.)

Why do these "unserious" qualities matter? Because life *is* a serious business and when crisis hits, as it has now, these traits not only are no help at all, but—again, as embodied to imperfection in Trump's incompetence and irresponsibility—they are a force multiplier. See: Trump on ingesting disinfectant to combat COVID-19, then claiming he was only being sarcastic. In response, the world is laughing at us.

Likewise, it is no help at all in this Age of Corona when our lead liberal newspaper, *The New York Times*, in its "Sunday Review" section, focuses the entire section one week on rebuilding a better nation ("The America We Need") and then, the next week, that section leads with a full-page treatment of the nude selfie as High Art. *Seriously?* One has to ask: Is this a culture worth saving? Would it even know how?

I believe we do know how. More to the point, course-correction is *already* taking place to restore America as the Can-Do Nation, engineered by the conscientious public heartsick at Trump's fiascos and determined to push upward.

See: the universal public admiration bestowed on scientific experts like Dr. Anthony Fauci and Dr. Deborah Birx, lead spokespersons for the White House coronavirus task force. That this admiration is driven by mortal fear of a deadly virus signifies all the more: We truly know now that expertise—of which America has a superabundance—and not know-nothingism will save us. And, it is a New Day for the bureaucrat, like Drs. Fauci and Birx. Welcome home.

See also: the universal public admiration bestowed on the medical heroes—the doctors, nurses, techs, EMTs—laboring valiantly, some dying themselves, as they fight a vicious virus. These authentic heroes knock flat the anti-hero—the rogue, the disrupter who moves fast and breaks things, the mock-criminal. How refreshing to embrace—once again—the real deal.

See also: the real-deal governors of New York, California, Ohio, Michigan, Virginia, my own Washington state for can-do organizing at the state level what Trump can't do at the federal. Some of these governors are Democrats, some Republicans.

See also: the general public acknowledging the pandemic as serious and supporting, by big majorities, the sheltering-in-place orders—and, all the upending considered, adapting well. Whilst sheltering, much deep thought is taking place—a good and necessary thing. Meanwhile, disputing the pandemic's seriousness are the know-nothing protesters inveighing against government overreach and threatening us all.

We see also America in its greatest peril since World War II—as a nation, as an economy, as the magnificent experiment in self-governance it represents in History. Let us view the Trump administration's catastrophic handling of this catastrophic peril as the nadir in this country's life—and let us pivot for higher ground. First order of business becomes then: to defeat in November not only Donald Trump, but Trumpism—the know-nothing, irresponsible, dishonest, arrogant, dangerous regime of these four years, that has nearly broken the America we admire and love.

Crises instruct—or they destroy. We stand instructed, sobered. We see the need for truth and, conversely, how lies kill. We see the need for character and, conversely, how the lack of it appalls. We crave honesty, decency, seriousness of purpose. As "Amazing Grace" has it, we once were wretches, blind, but now we see. Enough with breaking bad; there is, we can sense it, a powerful pent-up need in the conscientious public to break good, to break capable, to save America.

We *can* do again. Seriously.

—*Medium*, May 12, 2020

In a Plague-Time, Fat Cats Fatten and Little Guys Help Out

Seventh in an ongoing series, Notes from a Plague-Time

IT IS DISTRESSING—BUT not all that surprising—to see fat cats fatten even in a plague-time. While the rest of humanity suffers, the fat cats, the financially robust, have the means—the lawyers, the lobbyists, the bankers, the access to power—to ensure that they will not only survive the plague, but thrive on it.

The latest spectacle of opportunistic capitalism occurs with the dispersal of the $2 trillion CARES Act—the Coronavirus Aid, Relief, and Economic Security Act—that Congress in a miracle of bipartisan unanimity passed March 25. The biggest (by far) relief package in American history is intended, as its title says, for the aid, relief, and economic security of individuals and businesses hurting in this novel pandemic.

But hurt can be variously interpreted. In a recent column titled "Crumbs for the Hungry, Windfalls for the Rich," *New York Times* columnist Nicholas Kristof describes the "Zillionaire Giveaway": Tucked in the argle-bargle of the 880-page Act, on page 203, is a $135 *billion* allocation for a sector profoundly hurt by this plague: wealthy real estate developers. (Not normally cynical, I am being hyper-cynical here.) This sector of course includes President Donald Trump and his son-in-law Jared Kushner.

The beauty of the provision, per Americans for Tax Fairness (a source Kristof cites), is that it allows the entity to leverage business losses into tax savings and refunds; plus it applies to *retroactive* losses for periods predating the pandemic. Neat! And, no strings are attached: The entity does not have to keep its employees on the payroll or pay the money back, like other corporations getting bailouts or like small businesses getting Paycheck Protection payments. Double neat! This provision was inserted by Republican senator Charles Grassley, chair of the tax-writing committee.

"In other words," as Kristof writes, "a single mom juggling two jobs gets a maximum $1,200 stimulus check—and then pays taxes so that a real estate mogul can receive $1.6 million. This is dog-eat-dog capitalism for struggling workers, and socialism for the rich." Meanwhile Trump and Congressional Republicans seek to cut the food-stamp program further and totally gut the Affordable Care Act.

More socialism for the rich playing out in the news: AutoNation, a Fortune 500 company, received $95 million in bailout monies; the burger chain Shake Shack got $10 million; the restaurant chain Ruth's Chris Steak House got $20 million. All applications were finessed by the biggest banks giving their biggest customers the concierge treatment.

Good news, though: Shamed by the ensuing public furor—mainly from bona fide small businesses —all these entities will return the bailout monies, and properly so, since they have access to other loan sources. So will Harvard, the Aspen Institute, and L.A. Lakers. (N.B., Harvard did not apply for a bailout but was granted it as an educational institution.) Still, the unappetizing spectacle of fat cats fattening stays. But why did it take a public furor? Where were the institutional checks, the oversight—the Inspectors General—that one would expect when rivers of money are involved? The problem is: Trump ignores or fires the I.G.s. Trump signaled his intent when he signed the CARES Act into law: "I'll be the oversight."

But: *Fat cats can't do oversight!* Former head of the Office of Government Ethics, Walter Schaub, calls this assault on the Inspector General role and the rule of law "late-stage corruption."

And the scale of corruption? Per Americans for Tax Fairness, this $135 billion tax cut is more than the CARES outlay for hospitals and other public health services ($100 billion), dwarfs that for food and housing aid ($42 billion), and almost matches that for the state governments bearing the brunt of the pandemic ($150 billion). Since the pandemic's onset mid-March, America's billionaires have seen their wealth grow by 15%—repeat: *by 15%.* (Allowances are made for truly beneficent fat cats like Warren Buffet and Bill Gates. Gates has publicly expressed regret he did not do more to warn of a global pandemic.)

Again, fat-cat self-aggrandizement has been a factor throughout human history. But it is so distressing to see it manifest in this unprecedented struggle with a viral peril: At this posting, the death toll in the U.S. reached 100,000. With 40 million Americans losing their jobs in these last 10 weeks—that is 1 in 4 American workers, 26% of the labor force—we now brace for historic economic wreckage.

It will take a Victor Hugo of a novelist to portray the suffering souls in this wreckage, now and to come—wreckage that might have been avoided had we had as president a Franklin Delano Roosevelt, a fat cat who cared and saved the nation, rather than the uncaring and incompetent one we have.

But it is in this context of suffering and upheaval that the real news—the *new* news—of this pandemic is taking shape: that is, the citizens, *despite whatever suffering of their own,* who are helping their fellow citizens.

It is enough to make the *Times'* conservative columnist David Brooks take heart, seeing "people showing up for each other," choosing connectedness over division.

Coming early to light were the armies of citizens turning to their sewing machines and turning out surgical masks for our medical heroes working the COVID-19 front lines, after it became clear Trump would not organize a federal response to hospitals' pleas for personal protective equipment. Newspapers published patterns and instructions on how to make a mask. What the victory garden symbolized for World War II, the surgical mask may come to symbolize for this pandemic.

This home-front industriousness of mask-making you could visualize as a montage that filmmaker Frank (*Mr. Smith Goes to Washington*) Capra might insert here. You could also imagine Capra calling the characters in his montage "the little guys."

In addition to the medical heroes, there is a new kind of "little guy" hero: those who, having survived COVID-19 themselves, turn around and donate "convalescent plasma" for those still fighting the deadly disease. One such hero is Diana Berrent, who founded Survivor Corps, a grassroots clearinghouse connecting COVID-19 survivors with organizations needing their blood. Since Berrent, a photographer and mother of two living on Long Island, founded Survivor Corps in late March on Facebook, the number of donors has grown to 42,000. On *PBS NewsHour*, she said she puts the experience of donating her plasma up along with getting married and having children ("meaning no disrespect to my family"): "There are very few opportunities in a lifetime to literally save another person's life."

Other acts of magnanimity abound. But since most such acts are treated by the media—and the culture in general—as "human interest" and thus as soft and not hard world-beating news, we do not learn about them in the normal news rundown.

Instead, we hear of these good deeds as anecdote. There are anecdotes galore of people volunteering to work at the food banks in their communities (and upping their own donation rate). There are anecdotes galore of citizens checking in on their elderly neighbors, doing their grocery shopping, picking up their meds. (It warms the heart to see the young people doing these deeds.) There are anecdotes galore about various other kindnesses, from people popping by with an emergency supply of toilet paper to stocking the neighborhood free lending library.

It takes nothing away from these good deeds if they remain unheralded. Because this is how a culture can change—from the grassroots and the heartbeat outward. And American culture does need to change. For too long, the person performing a good deed or extending a kind gesture was mocked, with a specially ugly sneer, as a "do-gooder" and "moralistic"—a peculiar condescension that only a once-great culture actively degrading itself could sanction. But in this time of peril and fear, when every last one of us in the world is under viral siege and thus vulnerable, now we see that a kind gesture or good deed carries the heft of heroic action, or at the least allays suffering. Let us remember this when the "All clear" sounds to this pandemic.

Let us also get over our fascination with fat cats—their type and their behavior. Enough with the cold theatrics of the TV series "Billions," let us study the ways of the little guy. For at the heart of the fat cat—let's wrap scare-quotes around "heart," as it is only theoretical—lies cold and sociopathic solipsism, which, if given great power, lays waste, as we have seen these last four years. But at the heart of the little guy who looks out for the other little guys in the world, there is magnanimity, hope. And if the little guys came together in solidarity (while practicing social distancing, of course)....

This movie will not end well if the fat cats prevail. It's up to the little guys and their humanist ethos to write a better script. In this plague-time we see Character—both malign and beneficent—writ large. Seeing what we are seeing, suffering what we are suffering, will we learn to write a better script?

—*Medium*, May 29, 2020

White America Must Stand with Black America for Equal Justice

It is the nonchalance that strikes the conscience as obscene:
Hand on hip, with a knee on his alleged perp's neck, a white police officer, nonchalantly and unfeelingly, snuffs out the life of yet another black man.

That nonchalance bespeaks the attitude of a certain segment of White America, the segment that crows of its supremacy over all other races. To this segment, Black America and the human beings aggregated therein are—in a word—invisible, the elemental state Ralph Ellison captured in 1952 in his now-classic novel *Invisible Man*. And being invisible—no more than an organism underfoot, not even rising to the level of sentient humanity—justice is absolutely the last thing that organism, face down on the street with a knee on his neck, could expect.

But now: That same nonchalance—of the white officer, hand on hip, snuffing out the life of another black man—has jolted another segment of White America—the conscientious segment—up off the sofa, got its full attention, primed it for action. For you cannot view this ghastly crime unfolding and, if you have *any* conscience, fail to hear the call to action—for justice.

I am, of course, describing the killing of George Floyd by Officer

Derek Chauvin of the Minneapolis Police Department on Monday, May 25—Memorial Day—the images and sounds of which have reverberated around the nation and the world. Three other officers at the scene, bravehearts all, did nothing to stop the murder.

In reaction, protests have organized, in Minneapolis and more than 140 cities across the country, comprised principally of black Americans called to the streets out of righteous and justifiable anger—with a fair representation of White America also showing up. Yes, in some cities, the protesters were overwhelmed—*in number, not in cause*—by troublemakers who torched businesses and engaged in looting.

But: No matter how energetically the Demagogue-in-Chief, the current president of the United States, stokes the embers of that looted property for political advantage—"When the looting starts, the shooting starts"—the righteousness of the protesters' cause—equal justice for Black America *vis-à-vis* the police and the criminal justice system—*must* stay at the fore. First order of business, then, for conscientious white Americans is to ensure that this righteous call for equal justice remains foremost.

Back to the nonchalance of the white officer killing a black man: Juxtapose that nonchalance with the pain and desperation of Black America denied—over and over and over—the respect and dignity that White America so blithely expects for itself and gets without effort. Every time another black man is killed by the police—without repercussion for the officer(s) involved—is yet another denial of that respect and dignity and justice that black Americans yearn for.

Consider the ultimate message of so much black art and culture: the fiery nonfiction of James Baldwin; the powerful fiction of Ralph Ellison, Toni Morrison, Colson Whitehead; Ta-Nehisi Coates' eloquent demand for reparations for the sin of slavery endured by his ancestors; Michelle Alexander's brilliant and enraging book *The New Jim Crow*; Spike Lee's films; the historical films *Selma*, *12 Years a Slave*, and *Harriet*, about Harriet Tubman spiriting escaped slaves to freedom via the Underground Railroad. What do all these works, so varied and so powerful, have in common? The cry of an entire people for respect, for dignity, for justice, for their rightful credentials to participate—for *mattering*.

And not to matter, after 244 years of American history, must be for black Americans—from where this white American sits comfortably in privilege—simply insupportable, not to be borne any longer. No wonder there are protests, going on a week now.

Therefore I, a white American, do state: I do not wish to benefit any longer from a system where a white thumb can tip the scales of justice. And I most emphatically reject an America so corrupt that a white police officer can so casually kill a black man. I have been "woke" since a teen in the '60s, when I saw on TV another white "lawman," Bull Connor, order police dogs and fire-hoses turned on Negro men, women, and children in Birmingham, and I instantly understood: That is evil. Millions more white Americans no doubt are "woke" with George Floyd's killing and see the evil in it.

My fellow white Americans: This is so clear, an easy call, it needs no long night of soul-searching in Gethsemane. It is wrong in every possible way for a white officer of the law to kill a black person so casually. Watch the video again. Hear George Floyd's words, "I can't breathe." White Americans of conscience should find it hard to breathe, too. Polls show nearly four in five—78%—of all Americans, white and black, agreeing that the officer should be arrested. Joe Biden, presumptive Democratic presidential nominee, strikes the right note: "We are a nation furious at injustice."

What to do? Again, White America must join with Black America to control the narrative of equal justice. In venues personal and public—from the next family Zoom-conference to letters to the editor—restate the validity and necessity of equal justice for Black America, restate how furious we are at the injustice. Push back against Fox News' characterization of the protesters as "radicals" and *The Wall Street Journal*'s characterization of "the race-grievance industry."

We also, together, must control the message and image of peaceful protest. Donald Trump calls the protesters "terrorists" and conflates them with the looters and troublemakers. Best way to exert that control?

Plant our pacific selves in the midst of a protest. Short of that, we can plant our pacific presence in virtual town halls and other discussion venues.

In this volatile crisis, the media must refocus—*now*. Instead of pointing the camera at the fiery and dramatic, like the looted stores of an otherwise vacant Santa Monica, focus instead on the *peaceful* protests—like the massive protest peopled with blacks *and* whites in St. Paul, capitol of the state where George Floyd was killed, gathered on the first-week anniversary. Find the drama in the pacific, because Trump is pointing to the media's fiery and dramatic images as Exhibit A (and B and C and D) as he assembles his case to declare a state of emergency and invoke the Insurrection Act.

Finally: It is crucial also to focus on the good cops in the ranks of the 800,000 police officers in the U.S., whose dedication and daily bravery required to protect us are damaged by the bad cop whose heinous act swamps the news. Hear Houston's chief of police and the sheriff of Flint, Michigan, for their humane policing. See the police officers who take the knee with protesters—a heartening spectacle of solidarity.

As for the world's fury at the U.S. for its race relations: I am not sure the world has much to show for pacific examples. We can take the world's fury as the world's expectation that America, exceptional nation, can become exceptional again on this point.

All is being revealed in this season of deadly pandemic and turbulent protest. The racism long coursing through America's depths has erupted into clear view. The malefactors who mean no good for America are likewise on clear view and at work. Will conscientious White America step up, into clear view, and stand with Black America to demand equal justice for all? Nothing less than American democracy is at stake.

But more: If we achieve—finally—our foundational ideal of equal justice for all, it is a New Day in America, a Renaissance.

—*Medium*, June 3, 2020

With Racial and Sexual Reckoning, a Moral Awakening in America?

IT'S HAPPENING—AT LAST: Moral awakening in America. But can it be sustained?

Amidst the extreme disruption of these last several years—the ancient Greeks would properly call it Chaos—and amidst the dread of the deadly coronavirus pandemic, it may be hard to parse. But there is meaning coursing through the powerful currents buffeting America at present, and it is meaning that is moral—that is, having to do with the rightness and wrongness of things.

Two constituent blocs—Black Americans and women—are standing up and declaring that the historical and established ways of treating them are wrong, wrong, wrong, and—pardon the cliché but it is universal *lingua franca*—like the enraged anchorman Howard Beale in the film *Network*, they are saying: "We're mad as hell and we're not taking it anymore."

Getting from wrongness to rightness—getting from disrespect to respect, getting from dismissal and contempt and withstanding deadly force to *mattering*, mattering as a human being with a Soul—has been, for both Black Americans and women, a moral quest, a righteous one, one lasting centuries.

And now it appears, if yet still dimly, that the struggle may yield that which has been so dearly sought: justice and equality. The questers are within reach of their Holy Grail. And it took the hammer of a mass movement—two of them, in happy fact, cresting together—to bring this New Day.

Make no mistake, this New Day *is* new. This is not a moral re-awakening, a restoring of lost status or honor. Black lives and women's lives have never mattered as much as white men's lives, neither in America nor in the world. No, this is new; this is a moral *awakening*. Moreover this moral awakening is being achieved without moral argument or language; America lost her moral compass decades ago. (How else could we elect as president the amoral Donald Trump?) Yet: It is out of a profound moral *need*—the need for justice earnestly sought but long denied—that we have clawed our way, from the ground up and not from on high, to a moral sensibility.

As for racial justice, sadly it took the death of yet another Black man—George Floyd—at the hands of a white police officer to awaken White America to the everyday violence that our Black fellow citizens have abided since slavery. The horror of Mr. Floyd's killing, and the nonchalance of its commission by a white officer of the law, has galvanized White America into the streets. The ensuing massive protests have been full of white faces—old, middle-aged, young. Young white Americans are especially prominent: They go to school with a diversity of classmates—and they are showing up for them.

#BlackLivesMatter was there to meet the moment, to take its rightful place heading the George Floyd protests. Organized in 2013 in the wake of the killing of another innocent Black man, Trayvon Martin, and protesting other subsequent police killings of Black men, #BlackLives Matter has triggered counter-forces—All Lives Matter and Blue Lives Matter (in support of the police). But the grisliness of George Floyd's killing makes #BLM's point: Black lives, especially Black men's lives, historically have not signified.

And America now takes #BLM's point: Polls show an enormous rise—by 30 points!—both in the public acknowledgment that Black men suffer unduly at the hands of the police and approval of #BLM. Even Republican pollsters are stunned at the new statistical reality. In a show of respect, Associated Press now capitalizes that which has long been lower-case: Black. Black intellectuals like Jelani Cobb (*The New Yorker*) and Ta-Nehisi Coates (*The Atlantic*) express guarded hopefulness that this post-George Floyd moment will lead to lasting change in Black stature. James Baldwin, almost sixty years ago, said: "To be a Negro in this country and to be relatively conscious is to be in a state of rage...almost all the time." Ultimately and always, it is about respect.

Particularly sweet is the vindication of Colin Kaepernick, the Black football player who in 2016 took a knee during the national anthem to protest police brutality against his brothers. For this brave act he was let go and treated as *persona non grata* both by club owners and the President of the United States. Now National Football League commissioner Roger Goodell apologizes for Kaepernick's shunning—action which, per *The Wall Street Journal*, he took in memory of his late father, Senator Charles Goodell, a Republican who lost his seat after marching with Coretta Scott King, widow of Martin Luther King, Jr. At the English Premier Soccer League's reopening, all players, whites included, wore "Black Lives Matter" on their jerseys and took a knee—a stirring sight. May the coalition-building continue.

What's the policy impact? The U.S. House has passed a big police reform bill, but the Republican-controlled Senate still can't bring itself to outlaw chokeholds or suspend qualified immunity for bad-apple police officers. For their part, police departments could shift from the warrior to guardian model. No doubt white supremacists will force their way back into the debate, threatening violence—their only argument. But: American *culture* is altering in *the* most important way—morally. Thanks in big part to #BLM, the culture is embracing a new truth: Black lives do matter.

Likewise, the #MeToo movement has powered a new reality for women. No longer can women in the workplace be subjected—with impunity for the perpetrator—to demeaning behavior or, in too many cases, violent sexual assault, causing emotional trauma and wrecked careers. Founded in 2006 by Tarana Burke, the movement exploded into new life in 2017, with the nauseating revelations of film producer Harvey Weinstein's sexual abuse and assault of dozens of women. Women by the droves chimed in "Me, too"—and brought down a cavalcade of famous men: Charlie Rose, Matt Lauer, Mark Halperin, Garrison Keillor. Thus #MeToo became a cultural *force*. (I could have used that force 40 years ago when, as an equal opportunity officer, I adjudicated sexual harassment cases one by one.)

As happens with juggernauts, counter-forces arise (#HimToo) and misuse occurs, as when a woman makes a false allegation. And by now so many allegations, both valid and invalid, have been made, each triggering a media firestorm if the man charged is famous, that a certain weariness with the movement has set in with the public.

But public weariness cannot invalidate the moral point: that sexual abuse and assault are wrong, wrong, wrong, not to be borne any longer, and are no longer a prerogative of male power. The test that this moral point remains powerful, the public weariness notwithstanding, is seen most markedly in the political arena: A valid allegation of abuse can threaten a political campaign like little else, even scuttle it. (The allegation against presumptive Democratic presidential nominee Joe Biden appears, at this posting, to lack substance.)

"The arc of the moral universe is long, but it bends toward justice." Martin Luther King, Jr. cited this truth in relation to racial justice; it relates also to sexual justice. Long a blight on human relations, racial and sexual injustice and abuse have stunted untold numbers of lives, caused untold depths of suffering. But, hard as it may be to perceive amidst the present Chaos, the arc of the moral universe *is* indeed bending.

It did not help that, in America, the moral universe has long gone missing, ignored, even derided. It would take a book to chart both the hypocrisy of the right in claiming the moral high ground despite its blasphemies (i.e., its embrace of the amoral Donald Trump) and, to be fair in this accounting, the scorn and mockery expressed in quarters on the left of anything "moralistic." In effect, the moral universe was abandoned by right and left.

But: Even if abandoned, the moral universe still exists. The ultimate test of this reality comes, as it has now, when profoundest moral *need*— the need for justice—pierces through both the crime (the killing of Blacks) and the decadence (the abuse of women) and declares itself paramount and sacred: that Black lives and women's lives matter and will be accorded equal justice. By these breakthroughs—let us call them victories—we bid the moral universe back into the public sphere.

There will be fierce reaction—from white supremacists continuing to deny Black humanity, from troglodytic males continuing to deny women theirs. And there are other powerful counter-forces: a pandemic that threatens to get worse and go on indefinitely, an economy that threatens to collapse into another Great Depression, and a presidential election that our president threatens to undermine—all guaranteed to bring out the worst in us and not the best, all working against a generalized moral awakening in America.

But none of it—none of it—negates the moral point achieved, the history achieved: justice for Black Americans and women. Amidst America's breakdown, this central achievement is a step in America's grand reckoning.

Now, to protect and defend this most precious prize....

—*Medium*, June 23, 2020

In a Plague-Time, Doubly Plagued by Our Mask-Defying Independence

Eighth in an ongoing series, Notes from a Plague-Time

"ONLY A GOOD thing can be abused," goes the old French proverb. A great and good thing—the fierce independence that drove American revolutionaries to break with the English king 244 years ago and powered us onto the world stage as Exceptional Nation—is being abused, badly, and distorted into a life-*threatening* mutation of its original motive force.

With so many Americans refusing to don face masks in this perilous coronavirus pandemic, and with the infection rate in the U.S. breaking world records for (at this posting) the 29th day in a row—reaching now more than *57,000 new cases confirmed per day*—America is now Exceptional Nation in the worst possible way. We are "winning" a race we don't even want to be in, much less win.

Yet a critical mass of Americans, citing their constitutional right to individual freedom—"I'm an American, I can do what I want to"—refuses to play by this virus' rules: Mask up when in public, wash and sanitize your hands, and socially distance.

As states reopen their economies and as too many Americans, after sheltering in place for three months, party hearty—meaning: mask-free—this staggering infection rate threatens to reach what Dr. Anthony Fauci, respected voice of the White House Coronavirus Task Force, fears could be 100,000 new cases per day, as he testified recently to Congress. Meanwhile, the rest of the world is bringing the virus under control; the European Union now bars Americans from traveling to the Continent, precisely because the U.S. is now the world's viral "hot spot," with 133,000 deaths to date.

To be sure, a virulent pre-existing condition—political polarization—complicates this selfish interpretation of individual freedom. Liberals might be expected to be the abusers, being liberal, but it is the conservative bent of mind—anti-government, anti-science, anti-intellectual, pseudo-religious—that is proving the ultimate abuser of individual freedom, thus threatening to destroy the nation and all of us with it.

Oddly, for all their independence, conservatives sound alike, reflecting the ideo-speak of long-time Republican strategist Alex Castellanos in castigating Democrats: "Christians wear crosses, Muslims wear a hijab, and members of the Church of Secular Science bow to the Gods of Data by wearing a mask as their symbol, demonstrating that they are the elite: smarter, more rational, and morally superior to everyone else." Fox News babbles about "the medical deep state." The Denier-in-Chief, Donald Trump, denies not only the utility of masks, but even the virus itself.

In response to this madness, Joe Biden, presumptive Democratic presidential nominee, has stated a position not often heard on the campaign trail: "I believe in the Enlightenment, Newtonian physics, and the Age of Reason." It is science (a vaccine) and reason (the antithesis of Donald Trump) that will save us, if anything can.

One would think that, in a life-and-death crisis, the Life Force would kick in for recalcitrant conservatives and show the way....

Perhaps only Death can penetrate the anti-mask mindset. Take for sad example Thomas Macias, 51-year-old California truck driver, who after sheltering-in-place for months went to a party without a mask—and contracted COVID-19. Before dying he posted to Facebook: "This is no joke. If you have to go out wear a mask and practice social distancing." Don't be an "idiot like me," he wrote, adding: "Because of my stupidity I put my mom and sisters and my family's health in jeopardy."

In addition to Mr. Macias' dying counsel to wear a mask, it is his social note—"Because of my stupidity I put my mom and sisters and my family's health in jeopardy"—that I emphasize here: the citizenly and moral consideration of the larger family, your fellow Americans.

To counter the viral wildfire tearing through the country, some states are finally mandating the wearing of masks in public and, acknowledging they reopened their economies too soon, before the virus was quelled, are slowing their reopening or even shutting down again. All of which will wreak havoc with the reopening of schools just two months away—not to mention the continued viability of America as an economy and a nation. All those months of citizens sacrificing and sheltering-in-place? Wasted.

Question to the party-goers: Was the party worth it, really?

I could expound here on the need for the party-goers and the recalcitrant conservatives to grow up, or the need for American democracy to mature beyond the exclusionary (and death-dealing) pursuit of individual freedom and expand the horizon to the commonweal. I could go into the psychology of not wearing a mask or try humor to bring the resisters around.

But, no: Instead of a treatise, a public-service announcement is called for. To cite the headline of a recent *New York Times* editorial:

"Seriously, Just Wear Your Mask."

—*Medium*, July 7, 2020

Trump's Storm-Troopers:
An Ominous Signal for November

IT'S HARD TO assess threat amidst chaos, to parse the signal from the noise. But this threat, amidst a pandemic and economic collapse, is real and particularly ominous:

Donald Trump's threat to send federal forces to various American cities —as he already has in "quelling" the #BlackLivesMatter protests in Washington, D.C. and Portland, Oregon—can mean only one thing: Our "president" is willing to use force against his fellow Americans to intimidate and suppress the vote in November. Or to "secure" an alleged "rigged" voting system. He is also signaling his belligerence to vacate office, should the vote go against him.

That the cities Trump targets for federal occupation are all Democratic strongholds run by Democratic mayors, who allegedly can't or won't control the "anarchists" or their urban violence—Chicago is next, with New York, Philadelphia, Detroit, Seattle, Oakland to follow—is further proof of his electoral strategy: His polls plummeting with his disastrous handling of the pandemic, Trump resorts to force.

While much is made of these federal forces—some with no identifying insignia other than "Police," with questions about their agency of origin and reference to Vladimir Putin's "little green men" who invaded Crimea—and while now we hear from protesters themselves about being beaten and bundled into unmarked vehicles—all deeply upsetting— we must fix on the dangerous implication: *This is martial force without accountability.* Moreover, not only is Trump priming storm-troopers to use force to stay in power, he has the zealots in place to carry out his orders. Chad Wolf, acting head of the Department of Homeland Security, defiantly declares: "I don't need invitations" from the states or mayors "to do our job. We're going to do that, whether they like us there or not."

To those questioning the term "storm-trooper": If one definition is "a soldier trained especially for carrying out a sudden assault," these cadres meet that definition. Of course, in the public mind "storm-trooper" evokes Hitler's Nazi militia. I use it in reference to extra-legal violence deployed by the state against its own people. That this "state" is the United States of America is, yes, stunning, but we must get over it.

(With so much press given the unmarked aspect, there's the possibility these "little green men" include far-right extremists who don police-like costumes and wreak their own havoc on protesters they tag as "antifa.")

Branding the #BLM protesters as "anarchists," "domestic terrorists," and "agitators," Trump can logically turn to his storm-troopers to quell the "rioting" and "violence." It's a classic move out of the autocrat's playbook: malign and dehumanize your opposition, so as to forcibly put it down. Which is why Democrats *must* retake control of this narrative: Yes, some violence—perpetrated, understand, by unknown "protesters"—has occurred of late, but by and large the #BLM protests have been peaceful. This historic protest, embodying our cherished rights to free assembly and free speech, is moving the nation closer to our foundational ideal, never achieved—equality.

How to quell the storm-troopers? In the D.C. protest, when the "little green men" first appeared in Lafayette Square across from the White House, media attention focused more on Trump's hijacking of both religion (flashing a Bible outside a church) and of the uniformed military for his photo op, with less attention given the violence to protesters. As D.C. is not a state, the mayor could not order the federal forces out. But in Portland's protest, both the mayor and governor have vehemently protested the federal presence. Said the mayor, calling out Trump's "personal army": "As we were starting to see things de-escalate, their actions...have actually ratcheted up the tension in our streets." Senator Jeff Merkley of Oregon says, "This isn't just an Oregon crisis. It's an American crisis. We need to stop Trump before this spreads."

Legal action is being taken. Oregon's attorney general has filed suit against the federal government, including DHS, Customs and Border Protection, U.S. Marshals Service, Federal Protection Service. The suit names "John Does 1–10" as defendants, because of the lack of individual identification, "even so much as the agency that employs them." The American Civil Liberties Union has filed multiple lawsuits across the country in response to "unconstitutional law enforcement attacks" on protesters, as well as on journalists and legal observers. Says the ACLU: "Make no mistake: Trump's...secret forces will terrorize communities and create chaos. This is not law and order. This is an assault on the people of this country."

A letter from more than a dozen targeted mayors to U.S. Attorney General William Barr and DHS' Wolf decries federal force against protesters as "an abuse of power." The mayors write: "The majority of the protests have been peaceful and aimed at improving our communities. Where this is not the case, it still does not justify the use of federal forces." They add: "These are tactics we expect from authoritarian regimes—not our democracy."

But letters and legal action seem incommensurate to the need. Especially when the ultimate legal arbiter is the aforementioned Barr, the "people's tribune" who's shown himself ever-malleable to Trump's legal needs. Barr, long devoted to enhancing executive authority, no doubt could find legal justification for Trump's extra-legal use of force. (Barr organized the federal assault on the protesters in Lafayette Square.)

And Congressional action? Following the Lafayette Square melee, the House approved D.C. statehood, which if the Republican-controlled Senate approves (it won't) would give D.C. full authority over its law enforcement. Reconvening this week after a long Fourth of July break, Congress is focusing on the next big coronavirus relief bill. But House Democratic leaders are "alarmed" at the Portland melee, with Speaker Nancy Pelosi citing Trump's "storm troopers." Yesterday more than a dozen Senate Democrats wrote to A.G. Barr (oh good!), demanding a legal rationale for deploying federal forces. Congress, holding the power of the purse, could reduce DHS funding. No doubt hearings will be held, an Inspector General investigation pursued....

How about this: Enact a law declaring, "Federal law enforcement will protect protesters with the same dedication as they protect federal buildings and the homeland."

Theoretically, the best deterrent to Trump's open war on peaceful protesters is his fellow Republicans. But, while some are breaking with him over his handling of the pandemic, none has mustered the moral backbone (of which the GOP claims a lock) to confront Trump over excessive law enforcement. Their Faustian bargain holds.

Meanwhile, the conservative *Wall Street Journal* editorializes about "anarchists" and federal property, slighting the protest's purpose. It writes, absurdly: "We understand Mr. Trump's desire to restore order, but he's also saving Democrats from themselves." It goes on: "State and local Democrats will blame federal intervention for any and all disorder, deflecting attention from their own failures.... Progressives run Portland, Chicago, New York and other cities now experiencing a surge of violence. If they want to indulge the mayhem, then let them live with the consequences." Welcome, storm-troopers.

What can grassroots Democrats and concerned Republicans and Independents do?

For one thing, we can demonstrate political maturity by discarding the "Defund the police" mantra. Progressives will take offense, but at this volatile time this mantra is kerosene to Trump's newly-vitalized "law and order" campaign theme. Already Trump's campaign is up with an online ad tagging presumptive Democratic nominee Joe Biden with the defunding label, saying "You won't be safe in Joe Biden's America." As Tom Friedman of *The New York Times* writes: "Stop calling for 'defunding the police' and then saying that 'defunding' doesn't mean disbanding. If it doesn't mean that then say what it means: 'reform,'" adding, "Defunding the police, calling police officers 'pigs,' taking over whole neighborhoods with barricades—these are terrible messages, not to mention strategies, easily exploitable by Trump." The late civil rights icon, Congressman John Lewis, saw defunding as injurious to the cause.

For another thing, continue to protest, if you choose. Peacefully, of course.

And, new idea: In every city, *ala* "the Wall of Moms" in Portland, let walls of Moms, and Dads, form up and, as they have successfully done in Portland, neutralize the federal storm-troopers. The People controlling the narrative!

Also: Let us register so many new voters for November that turnout will be so massive and the rejection of Trump so resounding that his storm-troopers will be rendered moot.

Finally, consciousness is key, being clear about our reality, for this is not "political theatre." In 1935 Sinclair Lewis wrote his novel *It Can't Happen Here*, about how the fascism engulfing Europe could replay in the U.S. In this time of social crisis, compounded by a deadly pandemic and economic collapse, we now know "it" *could* happen in America, too. In Donald Trump, we have a proto-autocratic leader who fans the flames of nationalism and racism, lies without end, has no morals or ethics, wants only the ego-satisfaction of winning re-election—and now, in pursuit of that goal, he commands federal law enforcement to move against the American people.

News flash: Trump is now "surging" federal officers into Chicago and Albuquerque....

Beware. Take care. And form up.

—*Medium*, July 23, 2020

What Joe Biden Should Promise #BlackLivesMatter Protesters —Now—As They Face Trump's Storm-Troopers

"DECLARE VICTORY, VACATE the street protests—and render Trump's storm-troopers moot. Redirect the battle to the campaign trail. When elected, I will work with you to reform America." What if Joe Biden, presumptive Democratic presidential nominee, sent this message to the #BlackLivesMatter leadership? It might read as follows:

My friends in the #BlackLivesMatter movement, to all of Black America: You have won your struggle. You have won it! #BlackLivesMatter has made its point, a righteous one: Black lives *do* matter now, in this summer of 2020, in a way that, historically, they have not mattered before. You have established a new truth: Black lives *do* matter. Amen.

Ever since the horrific killing of George Floyd under the knee of a white police officer in Minneapolis, the #BlackLivesMatter movement has argued its case in the streets, with protests that have been massive—the largest protests in all of American history—and that have been, for the most part, peaceful. Those few "protesters" causing violence did not get the #BLM memo about *peaceful* protest.

At long last, White America has heard you. Viewing George Floyd's killing, White America, in that awful moment, came to know *something* of what you have long known about America's "systemic racism"—and what it saw is sickening, shameful. White America now believes you and, importantly, White America has joined you in protest. To be sure, not all of White America believes. But a mighty swath does—and wants to advance to a New Day in which Black and White America, as

Rev. Dr. Martin Luther King, Jr. dreamed, can sit down at "the table of brotherhood"—together.

Which is why, as the presumptive Democratic presidential nominee, I, Joe Biden, ask you, #BlackLivesMatter, to consider the following—at this perilous juncture when the current (and soon-to-be-former) president, Donald Trump, has deployed federal storm-troopers into the streets of America's cities to "quell" your protest:

Declare victory, vacate the street protests—and render Trump's storm-troopers moot. Remove yourselves as the target—before the storm-troopers find their target and, crucially, before Donald Trump hijacks your cause in the name of "law and order" and exploits it to win re-election.

Why? Why would you relinquish that which you have struggled so hard to achieve?

One: Because, again, you have already made your point. And, two: Because Donald Trump, unholy racist that he is, wants your cause—your righteous cause—*to end in the streets. In blood. Your blood.*

What other message can we read from Trump's dispatch of federal law enforcement into the streets, many wearing no identifying insignia, who kidnap #BLM protesters and shove them into unmarked vehicles? *In the United States of America that we all love?* These are the goon squads of a would-be dictator. Trump is literally trying to weaponize your cause—turn your righteous cause of Black lives mattering into a "mortal danger" threatening "the American way of life" that must be put down by force.

This is the nightmare scenario now unfolding: You now stand to lose the ground you have gained, under the onslaught of Trump's storm-troopers, in the service of his campaign to "take America back"—back to the days of unchallenged white privilege, racial discrimination, basically to the culture of slavery. This is *not* the way your dream, your victory, should end. No, it should not end in the streets, in your blood.

Rather: Your victory should end in that New Day—of the equality and respect and dignity you have argued for so stirringly in the streets, of the equality and respect and dignity denied Black America for centuries.

To that better end, then, I hereby make this promise: When I am elected President of the United States, I will work with Black America to deliver—at long last—on policies and programs that will hoist Black America onto equal footing with the rest of America. That is my solemn pledge. Better healthcare: Black America with its inferior healthcare is dying in this pandemic at far higher rates than the rest of America. Better housing. Better schools for a better education. Equal access to "the room where it happens"—to leadership and decision-making. Better life and freer living, without racism's toxic stress and trauma. And, crucially, better policing and better criminal justice.

Now, this is the point in the movie where someone in the Movement asks: "Why is Whitey making this pledge? Is this a trick?"

Why am I making this pledge? Because this white American is sickened and ashamed, not only at the racism so vividly exposed in George Floyd's death. This white American is sickened and ashamed at the specimen of White America now inhabiting the White House, who is in effect ruling by the anti-everything precepts of white power. If this specimen of White America is re-elected, American democracy is well and truly destroyed. Trump's chances of re-election, dim now, would be enhanced hugely, and possibly successfully, if he can make his "law and order" case in the streets—by "quelling" the "thugs" and "anarchists" and "domestic terrorists" that he now labels you.

But if you declare victory and vacate the street protests, you deprive Trump of his pseudo-adversary. Again, you have already won—won White America's respect and belief. Staying in the streets only gets you more exclamation points—again, at the risk of losing it all to the ensuing whirlwind if Trump's war on #BLM succeeds. Besides, the street is not the only venue for protest; there is the campaign realm.

Now, I am cognizant of the power #BLM wields at this moment: "Why," you no doubt ask, "would we surrender that power by ceding the streets?" As Frederick Douglass said, "Power concedes nothing without a demand." But surely you know the "demand" exerted by Trump's storm-troops is, in physical terms, incomparably superior to unarmed protesters; the result would be strife, perhaps civil war, politicized and ugly. Why sacrifice your new moral capital—polls show a historic rise in #BLM's approval among all Americans—for blood in the streets, when you can convert that capital into both the moral reckoning America needs *and* the policies and programs Black America needs, to be achieved in the Biden administration? For now, throw your moral capital into the campaign realm—into voter registration, voter security, select candidates. Redirect the battle into creating the premises for a New Day.

Of course at this point you may say, "This is another politician desperately scrounging for votes." Let me just say, I am not desperate: My polls are great, too; my campaign is polling well ahead of Donald Trump and is pulling away by the day. When I said, "When I am elected President of the United States," that prospect also becomes more real by the day. I make my pledge from a position of strength.

There is also a moral aspect to my pledge: As a white American struck to the heart by George Floyd's killing and moved deeply by Black America's plea for respect and dignity, now that White America has heard that plea, and knowing that, at present, White America has the power to bestow it, White America cannot in good conscience now withhold it—the respect and dignity—that Black America demands. It would be my deepest honor that, in the Biden administration, Black America is—at last—made whole.

I know your lion heart may still resist my message—to vacate the streets. And how many times has White America betrayed Black America in the past? But I hope you feel how a wide swath of White America is now with you, as am I. I hope you join me, in trust, to vacate the streets and go forward in coalition.

(By the way, vacating the streets would expose the provocateurs doing violence—and those provocateurs include Donald Trump.)

History is replete with the stories of power-mongers who wreak havoc on their peoples to stay in power. Donald Trump epitomizes the old adage, "Power corrupts and absolute power corrupts absolutely." On top of Trump's absolute corruption—which corruption now includes resorting to armed force against the American people—we also have the upheaval of a deadly pandemic and economic collapse. In short: Our world, our America, has exploded, with all of America's component parts flying about us. It is our task, our historic task, to guide those component parts safely back to ground again. And it is our opportunity, our historic opportunity, to reconfigure those component parts and build back better. Coming to terms with America's Original Sin—slavery and its legacy of racism—will redeem *all of us*.

This is not the campaign I expected, nor did anyone. I have never seen America so broken, so hurting, in such peril. But: This is not the end of America's story. I have always said: Never underestimate America. History is also replete with the tragedy of absolute power destroying those who resist. To avert tragedy—always the American way—we must be strategic in parrying this monstrous president.

Dear #BLM: Vacate the streets, redirect the battle to the campaign realm, and seize the initiative with me to build a New Day in America. Thank you.

—*Medium*, July 26, 2020

John Lewis: Good Trouble: Stirring Documentary of a Hero for Our Times

"*I LOST ALL sense of fear. When you lose your sense of fear, you are free.*"
This was the recognition that came to John Lewis, the late civil rights icon and Congressman, when he had his skull broken by Alabama state police at the Edmund Pettis Bridge on Bloody Sunday, March 7, 1965. At the point of death, beaten by officers of the law who would deny him his right to vote—and, elementally, his right to dignity—Lewis lost all fear.

It is a message—getting free of fear—that resonates and instructs, not only in the present political struggle, as our white supremacist president and his abettors, the Republican party, seek to disenfranchise the African-American voter and delegitimize the #BlackLivesMatter movement in this post-George Floyd moment. More, this message resonates and instructs in all times and in all struggles, including the present coronavirus pandemic. With all the world enduring the same deadly viral threat, Lewis' counsel—"Don't get lost in a sea of despair"—can buoy.

John Lewis was about more than endurance, though. He was about moving the dial—the ethical-moral dial—on social justice. "I hated the system," he said, the system of "White" and "Colored," and he fought it all his life, making the moral point over and over and over: "When you see something that's not right, that's not fair, that's not just," Lewis intoned repeatedly, "you must find a way to make trouble—good trouble, necessary trouble." In an age of the anti-hero who can't be bothered to care, John Lewis was the tonic antithesis: a hero.

Lewis gained his heroic wisdom the hard way, not from theory or observation, but with his body and soul positioned at the front lines, in unflinching dedication to the cause of *nonviolent* social change.

Historians might call it ironic that an advocate for nonviolence got beaten, violently, so often, and was arrested, jailed. Lewis said he would "take a concussion for the conscience of the country." Thurgood Marshall, the civil rights lawyer later appointed the first African-American to the U.S. Supreme Court, asked the young Lewis why he persisted in his sacrifice: Because, Lewis said, the point was to build a *movement*. Movements, to coalesce and to gain liftoff, take that kind of rock-like dedication—"adamantine" as *The Economist* put it—and John Lewis was its personification. Former president Barack Obama in his eulogy called Lewis a "Founding Father" of that better day in America, when our ideals and reality finally meet. On his Inauguration Day, Obama inscribed his photo to Lewis, "Because of you, John."

Lewis' wisdom, along with no small amount of wit, is presented stirringly in the new documentary, *John Lewis: Good Trouble*, released just weeks before Lewis died on July 17.

Director Dawn Porter is the ideal match for this heroic figure. Her film, blessedly free of special effects and zippy editing, focuses on the man and his worthy mission. The civil rights revolution of the 1960s is seen through Lewis' eyes, his memory. In aid of this focus, we see Lewis watching archival footage from the revolution—some footage he had never seen before. We see how moved he is, even stunned, at what his younger self, and all the "young people," achieved. It's an inspired technique—and inspiring, it's to be hoped, to young people searching for their life's purpose.

This technique animates History, memorably. So often History becomes abstract, distant: What could be more banal than a "sit-in"? But to see, in this film, the sit-ins that the civil rights activists staged at lunch counters in the South—the viciousness of the white attackers, the determination of the activists—is (viewer advisory) to get sick all over again at white supremacy and, at the same time, to behold what courage looks like. (The activists role-played beforehand, determined to look their attacker "in the eye.") Kudos to Porter for unearthing an abundance of rare footage, much of which I, a former civil rights activist, had never seen.

In this rich mosaic of a film, we see all the signal events of the revolution, with John Lewis at the lead, from the sit-ins to the marches to the signing, by President Lyndon Johnson, of the Voting Rights Act of 1965. Lewis' siblings relate how worried the family was for his welfare: Their parents pleaded with him, "Don't get in trouble"; once allied with the Rev. Dr. Martin Luther King, Jr., he formulated his credo to make "good trouble." We see Lewis the Congressman meeting constituents, advocates, the public. The late Congressman Elijah Cummings tells how he was often mistaken by the public for Lewis—and was glad to be mistaken for a "great man." House Speaker Nancy Pelosi calls Lewis "the conscience of the Congress."

This great man had his defeats. He was ousted ("de-elected") as head of the Student Nonviolent Coordinating Committee (SNNC, often pronounced SNIC) by Stokely Carmichael's challenge of "Black power"— another historical irony: Lewis himself was considered a "firebrand" by the movement elders, also he considered nonviolence to be a *militant* strategy. (His movement comrade, Congressman James Clyburn, confesses he is not as nonviolent as Lewis.) In his bid for Congress, Lewis ran against his close friend and comrade Julian Bond, and won, altering their friendship forever.

Of course, the biggest defeat occurred in 2013, when the Supreme Court gutted the Voting Rights Act, ruling that, with racism a thing of the past (Mr. Obama was in the White House), historically problematic states no longer had to meet federal "pre-clearances" in conducting their elections. And with proto-autocratic Donald Trump in the White House, Lewis fears waking up some morning "and American democracy is gone." Lewis believed democracy is not a state, but an *act*, that must be protected, with its protectors deepened.

The film has many delightful moments of humanity having fun; I loved the reunion of movement activists breaking out, *a capella*, in the song they made up while sitting in jail. We see Lewis recalling a teacher who told him, "Read, son, read." The mosaic is made even richer by the presence of many white people of conscience, seen from the civil rights era onward—a promising note at this moment when White and Black America are working at the final settlement of our legacy of racism.

(Porter screened the film for Lewis once she learned of his diagnosis of pancreatic cancer; he pronounced the film "so powerful, so powerful.")

What now? John Lewis would tell us we know what we must do. In the historical context of Lewis' life and the film, Act One was the march for justice, with victory attained in the Voting Rights Act of 1965. Act Two was the reversal, in a reactionary time, when the Supreme Court gutted the Act. What will Act Three be? In ancient Greece, where Drama originated, both Greece and great drama ended in tragedy. Can America avert tragedy? We can if we make "good trouble": "Mask up, please." "Black lives *do* matter." And, in honor of the man who secured voting rights for all, we must revitalize the Voting Rights Act, we must endeavor to save American democracy—and we must exercise the franchise this November: "Vote, people!"

—*Medium*, August 4, 2020

In a Plague-Time, Classic Films of Character and Courage

Ninth in an ongoing series, Notes from a Plague-Time

ANXIETY STALKS THE land. With the coronavirus pandemic now claiming over 163,000 American lives and wreaking horrendous economic damage, combined with a racial reckoning forced by the killing of a Black man (George Floyd) by a white police officer, fully one-third of all Americans now report some level of mental distress.

While this mental distress is understandable, we must manage it—somehow. Everyone has his/her methods of coping. For me, one method is ranging back over the classic movies of the 1930s through the '60s. In them we see the lineaments of the American experience and, more broadly, the human experience—both of which are now under severe strain.

More than mere entertainment, the following films have been selected for their specific utility in the present perilous moment. They show characters who must find the courage to front and prevail over the various existential challenges before them. In all these films, the necessity to find more courage creates in these central characters new depths of character. They come out altered, refined, better than who they were going in. As Anonymous said, "Courage is fear that has said its prayers." As such, these films reflect a seriousness of purpose not always seen in films from the 1970s onward, when attitude, pathology, confusion dominate. Being classic, "of an age," these films will evoke memories of institutional and moral strength that seems to be slipping away. But watching these dramas of character and courage can also spark the will to bear up and, possibly, prevail again. Spoilers abound (sorry).

Twelve O'clock High (1949)

Fear—not only of death in combat, but fear of not acquitting oneself in one's own eyes as well as of others—is the theme pulsing through every scene in this powerful World War II film. In a pandemic, we fear agonizing viral death, not combat, but the fear of not acquitting oneself still applies, whether we acknowledge it or not.

Twelve O'Clock High, directed by Henry King, centers on the only Americans fighting in Europe in 1942, the vanguard of the American bomber corps, based in England, who conducted "daylight precision bombing" of targets in France and Germany. Not only was this dangerous mission conducted in daylight, but at very low altitudes, for the precision. (Disbelief at orders to fly at 9,000 feet rather than the customary 19,000 feet opens the film.) The casualty rate is high, the replacement rate is low, and the hard-luck 918th Group is not pulling its weight. It needs a new command.

Enter General Frank Savage, played by Gregory Peck (pictured at top). Peck, a favorite of mine who always brought a deep humanism to his roles, here plays a cast-iron commander whose first words are: "Yes, 9,000 feet. The Wailing Wall is around the corner." The conflict then, apart from the one in the air, is about approaches to command: The outgoing commander Davenport (Gary Merrill) was close to his men, "over-identifying" with them, thus allegedly he could not exact the "maximum effort" needed from them for their life-and-death missions. Savage believes pride in a job well done trumps self-pity. In his first address to the group, he states: "Fear is normal, but forget it"; he even counsels, "Consider yourself dead." Soon, though, Savage comes to admire the men he flies with (he's no desk general), and in coming to care for the men, he becomes vulnerable to fear—and becomes human: We see in ourselves such vulnerability to fear. It makes for a searing climax to the film.

Most moving for me is the scene in which Savage visits in hospital an officer he had chewed out earlier as a coward, named Gately, son and grandson of "fine officers" (Hugh Marlowe). Now more human, Savage still can't say "Job well done" to the officer who's now earned it (flying three successful missions with a fractured spine), but in an indirect way Savage bestows a benediction. War veterans tell me this film is the best they know on command. It is also good on commanding fear.

Gentleman's Agreement (1947)

With Black Lives Matter newly demanding an end to racism, this film about fighting another scourge, anti-Semitism, is instructive, both for illuminating the scourge's systemic reach and the character needed to fight it. (Anti-Semitism is also rebounding now, with far-right nationalists seeking scapegoats.)

In this film, directed by Elia Kazan, which won the Oscar for Best Picture, magazine writer Phil Green (Gregory Peck again) decides that for his series on anti-Semitism he'll pass himself off as Jewish. The revelations begin immediately: His secretary (June Havoc) reveals she too is Jewish, but applied for the job at their liberal magazine with a non-Jewish name. Phil's Jewish childhood friend Dave (John Garfield), still in uniform and looking for housing for his family so he can accept a big company promotion, spends his days looking without success (this is postwar New York City). And Phil's new love Kathy (he's a widower with a young son Tommy) reveals herself to be what he's found most disappointing in his project: the "nice people" who'd never yell "Dirty Jew" or tell Jewish jokes, yet allow others to because they don't speak up.

He's horrified when she assures his son, "You're no more Jewish than I am," giving Tommy "that early taste of superiority," that he's "the most wonderful of creatures—a white Christian American."

Thus, when "nice" white people are at last speaking up for their Black fellow Americans (and more need to do so), Kathy's conflict becomes key. Played by ever-gracious Dorothy McGuire, Kathy must acquire a new lens on her privileged life, new character—and in a riveting scene with Garfield, she does (pictured above). Other notes resonate: For one, when Phil confronts the manager of a "restricted" inn where they planned to honeymoon. Beforehand, he calls out such establishments as "more than nasty little snobs, they're traitors to everything this country stands for and on, and you have to fight them." Phil's mother (Anne Revere) reads back to him his own copy when he quits the project, about the Founding Fathers, who knew that "the tree is known by its fruit, and that injustice corrupts the tree." (We're reexamining now the Founding Fathers' corruption of slave-holding.) Finally: In reply to Tommy (a young Dean Stockwell) who asks about the Atlas figure at Rockefeller Center, Phil says Atlas "carried the world on his shoulders," to which Tommy says, "Grandma says that's what you do." Courage!

In the Heat of the Night (1967)

In this post-George Floyd moment, when White America is coming to understand the disparity in racial justice for Black America, it is a good time to revisit a film dramatizing those two Americas—*In the Heat of the Night*, directed by Norman Jewison. Interestingly, it involves law enforcement. Virgil Tibbs, a Black man, is a homicide expert from Philadelphia, PA, who, passing through  a backwoods town in the South, solves a homicide through his forensic skill. Things start inauspiciously, though: Passing through, Virgil is taken in as the prime suspect (the big reveal that the Black man is himself a police officer is wickedly drawn out). In the course of the investigation, he comes into direct conflict with Chief Gillespie over who is the killer. But, acting together, they ultimately get their man. Then Virgil leaves town.

That is the over-story; the real drama is the power dynamic between Virgil, played by the peerless Sidney Poitier, and the Chief, played by Rod Steiger with a menace leavened by hints of humanity. Ostensibly two characters of equal power—both are men of the law—the Chief constantly pulls rank, playing the white card. We see Virgil coolly keep his dignity, not giving an inch. It is fascinating to watch the two, by coming to each other's aid during their investigation, attain a bond. The famous slapping scene, in which Virgil slaps back a white suspect who's slapped him for the effrontery of questioning him, is key: The Chief sides with his partner.

Also on view is an ugly white supremacy, enacted by supporting characters and other police officers, that, sadly, reflects the now-overt racism of Trump's America. We see how race-hatred blinds the white characters; conversely, we see how, on top of forensic skill, Virgil solves the case because he "gets" human nature. Yet Virgil can never relax, not even at the Chief's house after a long day: When they share that neither has been married, and when Virgil says he's no more lonely than the Chief, the Chief is incensed: "No pity!" Not from a Black man! We pity them, and the Chief, for the chasm reopening. Virgil is cool, though, but we see the cost.

In Which We Serve (1942)

For its portrait of national cohesion at a time of maximum emergency (war)—and as tonic to those Americans distressed at the resounding lack of unity in our time of emergency—*In Which We Serve* will serve movingly. Created during World War
II in Britain, it is a comprehensive look at war and its impact on both the fighting men and their families on the home front. In commemoration of a destroyer sunk by the Germans, playwright Noel Coward, coming

off the West End success of his frothy comedy *Blithe Spirit*, wrote, scored, produced, co-directed (with David Lean), and starred in this film about the fictional destroyer, *HMS Torrin*.

Opening with narrator Leslie Howard—"This is the story of a ship"— the film is also the story of a nation, made the more vivid because the *Torrin* is sunk early on and the story—of the survivors clinging to a raft, told in flashback—is powered by their most heartfelt memories: of wives and family, service, country. The action begins with the *Torrin* being rushed into commission. We see couples asking: Will there be war? In a stiffening-the-upper-lip exchange, Captain E.V. Kinross (Coward) tells wife Alix (the wonderful Celia Johnson), "No good worrying about it til it comes, and not much good then, really," adding, "Don't be sad," to which she replies: "I'm not sad, really. I'm just gathering myself together." Such rich vignettes—of the Kinrosses, of Chief Petty Officer Walter Hardy (Bernard Miles) and wife Kath and mother-in-law, and Ordinary Seaman "Shorty" Blake (John Mills) and new wife Freda—reflect what *New York Times* film critic Bosley Crowther called "a full and complete expression of national fortitude." The film was enormously popular in England (though not with the Royal Admiralty, which dubbed it *In Which We Sink*). Enjoy the cohesion.

Ann Vickers (1933)

Serious women still do not get serious treatment in film. But Sinclair Lewis took them seriously (perhaps because he was married to journalist Dorothy Thompson, who early on saw World War II coming). Lewis' novel *Ann Vickers*, about a woman courageously navigating her way through  life by her own ethical light, was turned into a compelling film, directed by King Vidor. Played by Irene Dunne, a favorite of mine because she made womanly dignity appealing, Ann starts as a social worker in a settlement house, then turns executive running a women's prison, where she runs into opposition from the warden for her humane reforms, is framed and fired—and writes a best-selling memoir of the experience. This feat enables her to enact her reforms heading another women's prison. But the heart of the film is not her c.v., it is her relationships, not only with men and how they treat a "woman of affairs," but also with other women and, importantly, with herself: We see, on her intelligent face, a woman learning of life.

An early lesson comes from a beguiling but inconstant Army captain (Bruce Cabot), who leaves her with child. To close friend Malvina (Edna May Oliver), a doctor, she confesses she's learned a truth "every woman must learn" (Malvina quips, "Which one?"): How we deceive ourselves reading into another all we want to see. She loses the child, telling Malvina she'd already planned her daughter's education: character, integrity, career. She then falls deeply in love with a judge (the excellent Walter Huston): Their portrayal of mature love ranks among cinema's most moving. The judge, however, has unsavory acquaintances and is himself sent to prison for receiving bribes, prompting Ann to take a grievous misstep: asking an old flame now also a judge to pardon her lover. This viewer sided with him when he said, angrily, the old ethical Ann would never have asked such favor. How she sorts things out underscores the film's theme: women and their standards. Which during World War I, the suffragist crusade, and Prohibition were as vital to keep as ever. (Memo to Hollywood: Give Malvina her own movie.)

The Citadel (1938)

In honor of the over 900 American medical workers who have died in this pandemic, heroically trying to save lives, this film is instructive in going into the emotional life of one such dedicated doctor. Newly minted Dr. Andrew Manson (Robert  Donat, who'd famously play Mr. Chips the following year) arrives to serve in a small Welsh coal-mining town, only to be greeted with an outbreak of typhus. Echoing our pandemic, he meets resistance: The schoolmistress is reluctant to shut school, the villagers destroy his lab (where he correctly diagnosed the coal-miners' coughing as tuberculosis). But before he quits in disgust, he falls in league with the town's alcoholic surgeon Dr. Philip Denny (Ralph Richardson) and together, soused, they blow up the town's typhus-laden sewer; and he marries the schoolmistress Chris (Rosalind Russell). They head for London, where Denny knew Andrew wants to go.

In London Andrew becomes a society doctor, thanks to running into a medical school pal (Rex Harrison) who introduces him to his "goldmine" of a practice: consulting fees, attending surgeries (just attending, not performing), tending high society's trifling ailments. Chris grows unhappy, telling Andrew, "Your work isn't making money, it's bettering humanity, and you know it." But he is done with penury. Through a tragic turn (too integral to the drama to reveal) and a dark night of the soul, Andrew's original dedication to medicine and humanity is reborn. He articulates it defending himself before the medical board, citing the Hippocratic Oath: "Into whatsoever house I shall enter I will work for the benefit of the sick, holding aloof from all wrong and corruption." This film, directed by King Vidor, is based on the novel by A.J. Cronin, himself a doctor who once served in Welsh coal-mining towns. His best-selling novel is credited with laying the foundation in the U.K. for the National Health Service a decade later. The medical "system" here might benefit...?

A Face In the Crowd (1957)

This film directed by Elia Kazan tells an unpleasant American story: how a "good ol' country boy" from Riddle, Arkansas, who can sing and tell stories— Larry "Lonesome" Rhodes, known as

Dusty—becomes a media sensation with his "Cracker Barrel" TV show, in the course of which he comes to lust for power, to be "the influence" behind the President of the United States, to be "Secretary of National Morale." Beneath that grandiose-but-possible ambition, however, lies his growing

disdain for the "hicks" who made him popular: the people. Comprehensively unprincipled—Andy Griffith does comprehensively unprincipled to a fare-thee-well—Dusty knows no checks or balances, so somebody must stop him. Who will it be?

One thinks it will be the woman who discovered him—roving reporter Marcia Jeffries (Patricia Neal) with her "A Face in the Crowd" radio show. The attraction between them intrigues: She is brainy and "respectable," he is (again) "ol' country boy." It is Marcia who, early on, observes his power to sway people and queries him on it. To Marcia he confesses, "I know I sound like I ate the Western Hemisphere for breakfast, but down here in the boiler-room...." But she becomes so besotted with him she loses her principles (thus dramatic interest) and cannot act.

It is the show's writer, Mel Miller (Walter Matthau), who calls out Dusty as "dangerous" and finds the courage to act. Clarifying his vision: Mel loves Marcia. When she says he sounds "vicious" for a "mild man," Mel says: "All mild men are vicious. They hate themselves for being mild and they hate the windbag extroverts whose violence has a strange attraction for nice girls—who should know better." He quits, writes a book, *Demagogue in Denim* ("Never had such fun in my life!"), tells Marcia he's signed a contract to publish. Together, they confront Dusty. Viewers will see the parallel to our comprehensively unprincipled reality-star President, also take a cue in November (I hope) from the "hicks" who, turning on Dusty, vow: "We'll fix him."

A Town Like Alice (1956)

Characters of high character do not feature much in film today. Filmmakers today, to make a character "more human," tend to define humanity down. Which is why it is a pleasure to meet Jean Paget, a young Englishwoman working as a secretary in British Malaya, when World War II is underway (1942). When evacuation is ordered—the Japanese are

near—instead of heading for Shanghai, Jean, conscientiously and fatefully, answers a last phone call: It is her boss' wife, frantic her husband hasn't appeared. Delay results in all being captured and separated—the men to prison camp, the woman and children being marched, and marched, and marched, endlessly. Terrible suffering ensues. When the wife dies, Jean takes on her children, including a baby. She sells her shoes for the baby's milk. Soon all are barefoot, marching in the jungle heat, with half their number dying.

Such extreme hardship brings out character (or lack of it). Pretty and blond, Jean is propositioned by a Japanese officer: It's an out, but she refuses (another woman gets in his car). Kindnesses—sharing water, soothing the dying—shine out, countering the cruelty. Romance would seem impossible in this Hell, but Jean meets Joe Harman, an Australian soldier who's also a Japanese prisoner. Their paths crossing in tandem, they hold whispered rendezvous; their exchanges are elemental, like: Where you from? (Joe is from Alice Springs, Jean from Southampton.) Love happens. But then: Joe steals the Japanese commander's chickens—for Jean's starving group—then takes the blame when they are discovered feasting. The last Jean sees of Joe, he is being crucified by the Japanese. Not for the world would I reveal the ending.

Played by the fine English actress Virginia McKenna, Jean is a quiet hero. Joe is played by Peter Finch in his pre-leonine Howard Beale days. The film, directed by Jack Lee, is based on "true fact" from a novel by Nevil Shute (*On the Beach*). At a time of extreme partisan hatred in America, these lines echo: After Joe's crucifixion, Jean, shattered, finally lets fly her hatred of the Japanese. Then she realizes: "You can't really hate people, can you." To which an older woman says, "It's a wonderful thing to learn, isn't it?"

The Grapes of Wrath (1940)

When I planned this commentary, I knew it had to end with these last two films: tales of economic hardship and loss—of which we are seeing only the beginning from this

pandemic's fallout. Perhaps the pre-eminent novel on the subject is John Steinbeck's *The Grapes of Wrath*.

In the film directed by John Ford, the iconic Joad family—Ma (Jane Darwell) and Pa (Russell Simpson) and their son Tom (Henry Fonda, masterfully contained)—suffer travails wreaked by economic forces that are both relentless (the Okies' ramshackle homes are bulldozed flat) and invisible (their land is owned by a company that's owned by the bank that reports to auditors "back East"). In other words, to the question, Who is responsible for all this destruction, or "Who can I shoot?": No-one. We cross our fingers as their groaning truck, carrying 12, makes its way from the Oklahoma Dust Bowl to California, "Land of Milk and Honey"—which soon curdles.

With 40 million Americans now losing their jobs, the humiliations and injustices borne by the Joads resonate profoundly. Ma Joad cannot take a last look at her old home: "I never had my family stuck out on the road, never had to lose everything I had in life." Tom's credo—"I'm just tryin' to get along without shovin' anybody"—is soon bulldozed by unrelenting setbacks: from bait-and-switch promises on wages for fieldwork to scorn heaped on Okies as dumb and dirty. Tom rightly becomes enraged: "If there was a law working with me, but it ain't the law. They're trying to work away on our spirit, make us transients, make us crawl, workin' on our decency." And law enforcement? "These are our own people," he says disgustedly of the law in league with the growers. Symbolically, loss of faith is expressed early on by Preacher (John Carradine), who says he's "lost the spirit." Famously, Ma Joad has the last word, an encouraging one, about "We the People." When Pa observes, "We've sure taken a beating," Ma says: "That's what makes us tough." Amen.

It's a Wonderful Life (1946)

In all cinema, I do not know of a better representation of the abject terror of someone facing bankruptcy and losing everything—a prospect so many face now—than Jimmy Stewart's

indelible performance in *It's a Wonderful Life*, directed by Frank Captra. So distraught at possibly losing his business—Bailey Bros. Building and Loan, started by his father—and going to prison for it, and feeling he's worth more dead than alive, George Bailey contemplates suicide, so at least his wife Mary (Donna Reed) and their four children can collect on his life insurance. He is saved from self-annihilation by his guardian angel Clarence (Henry Travers), who restores him to himself by showing how humanity, and his town of Bedford Falls, would be so much worse off if he, George, had not been born. Thanks to Mary who enlists the help of all those George helped in acquiring a home or to get by, the humanity of Bedford Falls comes through for George in the end.

Such an old chestnut, yet at this time of upheaval, it is good to spend time in familiar precincts, with a film most Americans know. In many ways we are today living in Pottersville, the alternate version of Bedford Falls if George Bailey hadn't done daily combat with mean "Old Man" Potter (Lionel Barrymore), who owns everything and extracts every cent. (We have a Potter in the White House now.) Also, in this cynical age, some will scoff at the idea of a guardian angel. If so, disregard the angel and focus on his mission: to remind us of the irreplaceable human being. This viewing I was especially moved seeing that, if irreplaceable George had not been alive to save little brother Harry after he fell into an icy pond, irreplaceable Harry would not become a Navy pilot who saved a U.S. troopship from enemy planes in World War II.

The character and courage of the George Baileys of this world *are* irreplaceable. Despite early disappointments—not traveling, not going to college, not becoming an architect—George goes on, sacrificing for someone else to go on. Not without anger, though: We see how angry and hurt he is with his sacrifice. We also see how, in the end, his sacrifice is rewarded. It really is a wonderful life.

At this time of utmost crisis, this country needs all the George, and Georgia, Baileys it can recruit—people of character and courage. Take in these films, be fortified, and return to the fight to save America.

—*Medium*, August 11, 2020

How to Foil Trump's Mail-Tampering? Vote Early!

IN A STUNNINGLY anti-democratic attempt to rig the 2020 presidential election, which polls show he is losing badly, president Donald Trump now goes after the U.S. Postal Service, the primary delivery-system for mail-in ballots. In a deadly pandemic, mail-in ballots rather than in-person voting is much the safer way to cast one's vote. Presumably, the public welfare is top-of-mind for any American President.

But with polls showing him losing by double digits to Democrat Joe Biden, Trump must double-down on his anti-democratic methods, fie on the public welfare. The man who rails about rigged elections is now reaching deep into the voting system and doing the rigging himself. Not for Trump to make his argument on the merits; he must play with the mechanics and semantics and resort to outright and blatant chicanery.

What is this but the move of a proto-autocrat?

How does a proto-autocrat rig an election? First, bad-mouth the validity of mail-in voting as rife with fraud (ballot-stuffing, dead people voting, etc.), which Trump has been doing for months now—to some effect: Experts worry about declining voter confidence in the voting system. Next: Have installed as your Postmaster General a political crony and campaign "megadonor" who, immediately upon installation, announces major "cost-cutting" measures across the USPS—sorting machines deactivated, corner mailboxes removed, no overtime.

The fact that these major cuts happen *just before a major presidential election*—when, with historic voter participation expected, sorting machines and corner mailboxes and overtime would be crucial—is, per a proto-autocrat, immaterial.

Voters not equipped with a criminal mind or a narcissistic personality-that-must-win-at-*any*-cost are left, understandably, stunned at these blatant moves. This is robbery conducted in broad daylight, with the spotlights on and cameras rolling.

What's a voter to do? Let's skip further analyses or polemics and go to our own mechanics. Three (3) things we can do are:

1. *Vote early.*
2. *Vote early.*
3. *Vote early.*

In this presidential election whose very viability is threatened by the President himself—the USPS itself now warns delivery could be hampered in as many as 46 states—experts advise the voter to cast his/her ballot *as early as possible*. Voting and mailing early will better ensure your ballot is received by the USPS, delivered to the proper county election office, and counted. The hashtag #VoteByOct22 is trending on Twitter to encourage early voting.

Depending on the state where you live, you either already vote by mail-in ballot (as we do here in Washington state) or you vote in person at a polling station. It's the latter mode that, in a pandemic, is riskier, thus you need an absentee ballot, which you get by requesting it from your local election office—again, *early*. Side-step the USPS entirely and drop your completed ballot in a government drop-box.

And if you are not yet registered to vote, register *now*.

(By the way, Mr. Trump: Mail-in voting here in Washington state works fine.)

Again, *early* action is key. The USPS's problem is not funding, notwithstanding the headlines of Democrats fighting for additional USPS funding in the next pandemic relief package. The USPS' challenge is the *handling* of the mail—the sorting, routing, delivery. Thus early mailing aids in its work-flow. (Christmas is more challenging for the USPS.)

As to readers objecting to my use of "proto-autocrat" for Trump: A national leader who sends storm-troopers into American cities to quell legal protesters, kidnap them, and bundle them into unmarked vehicles; a leader who won't agree to abide by the election results; and who now is trying to hobble the USPS, is clearly a leader trying to extend his tenure, become president for life—in other words, he is an autocrat in the making.

Public outcry over this latest outrage of Trump's—and it is strenuous—will continue; it bodes to be a messy election. Conservatives will continue their silence—and it is a damning silence. Once upon a time conservatives were about *conserving* our democratic institutions, and in protecting election sanctity, they have a singular opportunity to take a stand against Trump's mail-tampering, defiantly. But, barring a miracle....

It remains to us, We the People, to rescue the Republic—through the vote.

News flash: Speaker Nancy Pelosi is calling the U.S. House back next weekend from summer recess to take action on the USPS. And at least six state Attorneys General are forming a coalition to take legal action to protect the Postal Service. Good to see some institutional rescue effort.

This election, a referendum on this wretched and proto-autocratic president, really is the most important in our lifetime. The electoral obstacles Trump is throwing up—what surprise has he in store for October?—will require more from John Q. Public than the usual exercise of pulling a lever on Election Day.

The conscientious voter must take action *before* Election Day— *way* before. The conscientious voter is the one who votes early.

The online iteration of this post contains extensive voter resources.

—*Medium*, August 17, 2020

94 Million Eligible Voters Did Not Vote in 2016. Democrats: Get Out THAT Vote!

WHEN PRESIDENT DONALD TRUMP reportedly urged his supporters to vote twice, once by mail-in ballot and once in-person, the "clarifications" followed: No, he was not encouraging voting twice—which is illegal—just "testing the system": Voters should vote by mail, then go to their polling station to verify their ballot was tabulated.

But: Clarifying nuance may be lost on Trump's more ardent supporters. Double-voting is now a real possibility. Trump clearly is trying to fog up the election so he can declare it invalid.

And just as clearly, the Democrats' mission crystalizes: We must win by *massive* and *irrefutable* margins. And we can.

How? There are reserves to be tapped—94 million of them, to be exact.

In the 2016 presidential election, 94 million eligible voters did not vote. Nothing about that sentence is a typo, neither the 94 nor the million nor the eligible. Fully 40% of eligible voters chose to stay home, despite the hoopla of the first woman nominee running for President (Hillary Clinton).

While such level of voter non-participation is an indictment of American democracy, it is also a tool—and Democrats need to use it, *now*.

Of course, eligible—of age—does not mean actually registered to vote. Here's where our work lies: We need to register as many of those 94 million as we can, and ideally to vote Democrat (blue).

Here is the toolbox: Eligible voters can find their state and *register online*—at USA.GOV and Vote.org. (The latter claims registering takes two minutes.)

Haste is of the essence: Election Day, Nov. 3, is exactly 60 days off. Each state has various requirements and deadlines for registration.

Voter discretion advised, though: Many—most?—of the 94 million eligible-but-not-registered, it can be surmised, are what political scientists call "disaffected." Either they don't believe their vote counts or they are "low-information," whatever. But, put bluntly: Disaffected is Donald Trump's siren song, his meat-and-potatoes. And put delicately: Democrats must discern the likelihood that a particular disaffected person in their sights might respond to that siren song and swing Republican (red). Why recruit troops for Trump? Again, voter discretion is advised—yours.

In your recruitment pitch, encourage newly registered voters to vote up and down the ballot (and up-and-down blue). There is always a sizeable "under-vote" in every election, in which voters vote, say, for President but not for other offices. We want a blue tsunami this year— not only for the White House but the U.S. Senate, the U.S. House, and the state legislatures—so fully completed ballots are crucial.

Also crucial: Vote early! The hashtag #VoteByOct22 is trending.

It's pointless to reexamine all the ways this President has undermined our voting system, with his incessant harping on a "rigged" result—alleging mail-ballot fraud, trying to disarm the U.S. Postal Service, trying to delay the election date, refusing to counter Russia's interference, etc. And it's pointless to ponder Trump's evil genius.

The point now is: Trump is actively rigging the system himself. Thus it is imperative that Democrats produce a blue tsunami, up and down the ballot—a tsunami so massive and irrefutable that no recount is triggered, no legal action is necessary, no Republican can quibble.

If every registered Democratic voter registered another new Democratic voter, we could get to massive and irrefutable: Per Gallup, 31% of the electorate is Democrat, versus 26% Republican and 41% Independent. Democrats, get cracking and recruiting.

While 94 million eligible nonvoters is, yes, an indictment of American democracy, converting a critical number of those 94 million into registered Democratic voters could save it.

News flash: In Texas, Democrats announce target of registering one million—1,000,000—new voters for November. If historically red Texas were to turn blue....

Go to it, Dems!

—*Medium*, September 3, 2020

With Categorical Denunciation of Violence, Biden Can Now Prosecute the Case Against Trump

THE ABSURDITY OF OUR lawless president campaigning as a "law-and-order" candidate notwithstanding, Donald Trump is doing exactly that absurd thing: claiming he is Mr. Law-and-Order while insisting his opponent, Joe Biden, is dangerous for America in every conceivable way.

This down-is-up transformation crystalized at the Republican national convention. Going in, Trump was seen as vulnerable for comprehensive mismanagement to a gross degree—of the pandemic, the collapsing economy, the racial unrest following George Floyd's killing by a white police officer. But at the convention, reality was flipped: Speaker after speaker painted a picture of a virus vanquished, an economy booming, and—truly jaw-dropping—Donald Trump as savior of a nation whose cities are aflame with racial protest, while, it follows, Joe Biden is Evil Incarnate. Trump's unctuous wingman, Vice-President Mike Pence, intoned unctuously, "You won't be safe in Joe Biden's America." In his speech, Trump delivered Part II of his "American carnage" inaugural. Four nights of flat-out lying, sung by the Anvil Chorus, did the trick: The Republicans were united—welded—to the law-and-order theme. (If you think this is hyperbole, watch any 15-minute clip of the convention; I watched it all, though bailed during Trump's peroration, due to splitting headache.)

In the aftermath, Democrats, still swooning over their own love-fest of a convention the week previous, spent too much time guffawing at the Mad Hatter aspect of the Republican convention ("How can they believe all those lies?")—while Trump barreled back onto the campaign trail trumpeting the GOP-approved Democrats-are-O.K.-with-violence/

scare-America theme. Meanwhile, this household was jumping up and down: Dems, this is dangerous, stop guffawing, control the narrative.

Finally, last week, Joe Biden in a forceful speech in Pittsburgh laid down a categorical denunciation of the violence associated with ongoing racial protest. While most #BlackLivesMatter protest continues to be peaceful, where they have been turned violent—either by far-right provocateurs, federal law enforcement agents, or frustrated #BLM protesters themselves—the public finds it difficult to parse #BLM from the violence; thus #BLM's approval ratings, having reached historic highs post-George Floyd, are now slipping.

Biden's exact words denouncing the violence, featured in a new ad taken from the speech, are worth citing in full:

> *"I want to make it absolutely clear: Rioting is not protesting. Looting is not protesting. It's lawlessness—plain and simple. And those who do it should be prosecuted. Fires are burning and we have a President who fans the flames. He can't stop the violence, because for years he's fomented it. But his failure to call on his own supporters to stop acting as an armed militia in this country shows how weak he is. Violence will not bring change, it will only bring destruction. It is wrong in every way. If I were President, my language would be less divisive. I'd be looking to lower the temperature in this country, not raise it. Donald Trump is determined to instill fear in America, because Donald Trump adds fuel to every fire. This is not who we are. I believe we should be guided by the words of Pope John Paul II, words drawn from the Scripture: 'Be not afraid.' I'm Joe Biden and I approve this message."*

In sum: While holding protest as lawful, Biden denounces looting and rioting as lawlessness. He points to the true source of the mayhem—Donald Trump himself, who's long fomented violence, and his armed militias—before denouncing violence again: "Violence will not bring change; it will only bring destruction. It is wrong in every way."

Mr. Biden should repeat it at every campaign event until Election Day. Denouncing violence, Biden can pivot to offense and attack Trump himself as Lawlessness Incarnate. Let us count the ways: Trump's businesses profiting from his tenure in office; his muscling Ukraine to investigate his likely opponent, one Joe Biden, which led to the House voting to impeach; etc. In proactively raising "Ukrainegate," Biden could acknowledge son Hunter's role and vow anew that, if elected, no family member would be involved in state business—a step enroute to returning America to a *rules-based* polity. On that point, a group of former GOP appointees to the Justice Department warn that if this lawless president is re-elected, he will be "unleashed" and autocracy is possible: "I don't know what's going to stop him."

Meanwhile, #BLM protesters, digging in against far-right provocateurs and federal agents, might recommit to Martin Luther King, Jr.'s policy of nonviolence. King understood that, in any confrontation, nonviolence always enjoys the upper (moral) hand. (I advocated #BLM declare victory at the height of its public approval and pivot to the campaign trail, to put in place an administration dedicated to racial equality and criminal justice reform.)

With violence denounced, Biden can also return to prosecuting his campaign as a referendum on Trump himself and his historically unparalleled extravaganza of incompetence and malfeasance. In no way is this campaign about Democrats being O.K. with violence. If anybody is O.K. with violence, it is the proto-autocratic Trump.

As to the referendum on Trump, number one issue of course is the pandemic. Biden's recent statement on the damage wreaked to date—"The hard truth is this pandemic didn't need to be this bad"—begins to retarget Trump for his lethal mishandling of the crisis. Biden vows a science-focused approach. Veteran journalist Bob Woodward's bombshell scoop that Trump early on knew the coronavirus was deadly, not something to be shrugged off, gives Biden another bullet-point—and justification for asking: How many of the 191,000 Americans deaths to date were unnecessary? We will also hear more from him on post-pandemic economic recovery.

Biden's passionate response to allegations that Trump referred to military dead as "suckers" and "losers," while painful for him, pierced through when he defended his late son Beau's service undertaken post-9/11. It would be good for the country to return to the norm of public service as worthy with someone who truly "gets" it.

I hope people will cut Biden some slack in his endeavor: Making the case for civility and normalcy has always been difficult, with points automatically given the Devil for audacity. (With Trump normalizing so much behavior heretofore unacceptable or amoral, Trump equates to the Devil.) In *Moby-Dick*, Father Mapple in his sermon underscores the tougher quest: "In this world, shipmates, sin that pays its way can travel freely, and without a passport; whereas Virtue, if a pauper, is stopped at all frontiers."

With Labor Day now in our rear-view mirror, the campaign until Election Day will be a scorcher. But at least with Biden's categorical denunciation of violence, he can shift from the back foot and take the fight to the proper foe—Donald Trump. Go, Joe!

—*Medium*, September 10, 2020

This Pandemic Could Be Over By Now—
IF Our President Believed in Government

Tenth in an ongoing series, Notes from a Plague-Time

AS WE MOURN THE deaths of nearly 200,000 Americans lost to COVID-19;

As we mourn the deaths of nearly 1,000 medical personnel sacrificing their lives as they endeavored to save those of us felled by the coronavirus;

As we mourn the lonely deaths of the nearly 80,000 elderly who died in nursing facilities, with their families shut out from expressing their last loving goodbyes;

As we watch parents grapple with the on-off signals whether schooling this new school year would be in-person or virtual; and as we see the extreme pressure put on the parents as they endeavor to continue their own work, thus earn an income; and as we hear of a "lost year" in their children's education;

As we watch the young people, who, trying to launch as America's bright tomorrow, were knocked back by the 2008 financial crash and, now, are knocked back again by a virus, leaving them with reduced lifetime income, reduced dreams, some with lost lives;

As we see the homeless population mushroom, with more people living in their car, if they have one, or if not, bedding down under bridges, wherever;

As we lament the closing of our favorite local businesses—restaurants and coffeeshops, pubs, bookstores, theatres, retail outlets, you-name-it; and as we see local factories, some of them longtime family operations, struggle with sudden loss of demand and close;

As we imagine the toll on mental health that all the above pain and suffering and loss has on the individual and on the family, on their well-being and on their souls;

As, pulling back and surveying the national scene, we gape in astonishment at banner headlines announcing 30,000,000, then 40,000,000 Americans losing their jobs—a record worse than the previous national nadir of the Great Depression; and as we gape at graphs showing economic activity not just sloping off, but—hair-raising sight—like a stone, dropping straight down;

And as, if we cast a glance at the world beyond, we see the world gaping back at us in astonishment as the former "can-do" nation gives proof after proof it can't do at all;

And, finally, as we look to Washington, the nation's capital, where, as guaranteed by the Constitution's provision to "promote the general welfare," we should be able to look for guidance and, if need be, salvation, but where we see only Chaos;

We can connect all the above dots and conclude this: that the aforementioned litany of catastrophe—all the pain, all the suffering, *all the loss*, so much of it permanent—can be laid at the feet of our head of government, who—worst joke ever!—*does not actually believe in government*; who does not believe in its capacity and indeed responsibility to "promote the general welfare"; whose response to a basic task required of a head of government in a pandemic—for one, organizing the distribution of personal protective equipment (PPE) to our valiant medical heroes—is to say of the federal government he heads, "We're not a shipping clerk." He likes the thrill of power, not its responsibility.

Also complicit is this nominal head of government's party, who blindly backs up his criminal inaction and now is beyond all reasoning, though in truth this party and its adherents are only delivering on decades of antigovernment rhetoric and vilification of government bureaucrats.

For the indisputable conclusion follows: Had we had a head of government who actually believed in government, who organized and coordinated the central response to the novel coronavirus, *this pandemic, six months underway, could be over by now.*

Think about that: *This pandemic could be over by now.*

And, like other advanced industrialized countries whose governments followed the science and acted accordingly, taking decisive and comprehensive action in aid of their peoples, America could be fully back to business and we could get out and about. Instead we have ruination upon ruination to ponder, sift through, clean up.

How to turn all our pain and suffering and loss, so much of it going unmemorialized in our sulfurous political atmosphere—how to turn it to account, so that it has not been endured in vain? How to resist becoming fatalists—an abrogation of the can-do American character, now severely in jeopardy—and save American democracy?

For one thing, in the coming election, up and down the ballot, we can vote for the party—the Democrats—that *actually believes in government and in its capacity to do good*. If we learn nothing else from this pandemic, it is that a coordinated, whole-of-government response is needed in a national crisis, where every government official, from the federal level to the local, rather than shirk their responsibility, steps up to the plate. The absurdity of each constituent part of the polity reinventing the wheel and, moreover, doing battle with other constituent parts for, say, PPE (to recur to the previous test) is, literally, killing.

For another thing: As we ponder and sift through and clean up the ruination, along with rolling up our sleeves, we should repeat to ourselves what Democratic presidential nominee Joe Biden declared recently: "This pandemic didn't have to be this bad." There are many other lessons to absorb, but this one, truly existential—our survival—is one.

Abraham Lincoln defined government's role thus: "The legitimate object of government, is to do for a community of people, whatever they need to have done, but can not do, at all, or can not, so well do, for themselves in their separate, and individual capacities."

A pandemic is a crisis that no one individual, no matter how fiercely self-reliant they may be, can beat back alone. The next pandemic—and epidemiologists now warn there will be more—must be met with a coordinated and comprehensive response from the people's proper protector: their government.

—*Medium*, September 16, 2020

"The Moral Obligation to Be Intelligent"—Now More Than Ever

MESSAGE TO ALL Democratic troops:
Of course it is always a good thing to be intelligent. But it is the case that we do not live in intelligent times. Instead we live in choleric times, when stupidity and anger and "out there" statements capture the spotlight, go viral, drive the news cycle. Nor are we governed by a leader who abides by Enlightenment ideals of reason and proof or plays by the rules; likewise his party.

But with a presidential election coming up in just 43 days, truly the most important in our lifetime, being and acting intelligent—being smart and savvy and real, along with the attendant qualities of moral purpose, honesty, daring, forthrightness, perseverance—is vital to unseating the most dangerous threat yet to our modern American democracy, Donald J. Trump. This president has dismantled so many institutional norms, stretched the law to breaking point, spurned our allies to embrace autocrats, that America finds herself in sight of autocracy itself—strongman rule—with near-total acquiescence from his own party.

No surprise, then, this proto-autocrat is running as the "law-and-order" candidate. Not able to point to a stellar performance in handling the deadly coronavirus pandemic, and bungling the reopening of the economy, Trump must default to hardball tactics and try to claim the mantle of the nation's savior and protector—*from the violence he himself eagerly foments.*

In this nefarious aim, Trump is aided by his Attorney General (and that possessive is intentional: William Barr is fully in the tank with Trump), who—astoundingly—now threatens to cite the sedition statute against "rioters" who create violence and destruction amid the ongoing protests for racial justice. In the main, these #BlackLivesMatter protests have been peaceful—93% of them, per a recent study. But that outstanding 7% represents, for Trump and Barr, an opportunity to exploit: to smear the law-abiding super-majority with the criminal offense of trying to overthrow the U.S. government (never mind that Trump and Barr in their heedlessness are doing just that).

Intelligent people see the danger: "Protester"—in the hands of the meanly motivated—can be conflated with "rioter" and "looter." Thus it is imperative that, if you continue to protest—and bless you if you do, as racial justice is a righteous cause—the protest must not only remain peaceful, but if anyone among your number turns violent, take pictures to document the act, get immediately to a microphone, and *disavow the violent outlier(s) categorically.* At this volatile juncture, this is Democrats' Achilles' heel—being cast as O.K. with violence—and Trump and his ever-malleable arbiter of justice are ever-ready to strike at that heel. We cannot let that happen.

Likewise, being cast as O.K. with violence against police is another cudgel Trump and Barr use against Democrats. Barr cited the "police-free" zone established in Seattle's Capitol Hill during recent #BLM protests as his specific trigger to invoke the sedition statute. In Los Angeles, when two sheriff's deputies were shot in their patrol car, as noted in a *Wall Street Journal* editorial, "protesters who blocked the entrance to the hospital where the two are being treated…chanted 'We hope they die.'" *Note the conflation of protesters with violent actors in our leading conservative paper.* This editorial, titled "We Hope They Die," goes on: "Democratic mayor Eric Garcettti called the chants and protests at the hospital 'unacceptable' and 'abhorrent.' But he and other Democrats need to do more to condemn and ostracize these protesters. Democrats may fear the wrath of Black Lives Matter, but the backlash elsewhere in America will be far greater if pleasure at cop killing becomes common on the left." A *Journal* columnist cites "insane" protesters for getting in the police's face to shout obscenities ("Democratic Madness").

And: Retire the message "Defund the police," because communities where police presence has been reduced are seeing more crime, and those hurt communities are invariably of color. "Reform the police" says it better. Any message that mixes signals is not smart, not intelligent.

Other minefields to beware: Saying or doing anything that can, in the opposition's hands, be used against us. Think—be intelligent—before you tweet, retweet, TikTok, etc. Game out the worst-case scenario, should your message be twisted and beamed back at you—and at all Democrats. When passions run hot, the impulse to say and do hot things is overpowering. But: Overpower that impulse. Hillary Clinton's "deplorable" comment at this same juncture in the 2016 race did her campaign mortal harm, ceding, absurdly, the moral high ground to the amoral Trump. As they said in World War II, "Loose lips sink ships." Mind the lips, think of the ship.

Some will call this censorship, an infringement on free speech; let's call it responsible speech. Others will dismiss this appeal altogether, find its recommendations blatantly obvious. But in battle, it is always good for all troops to sign off on mission review. (Think of General Dwight D. Eisenhower addressing the troops as they prepared to launch D-Day in 1944.) Republicans appear to treat this 2020 presidential race as merely a *political* contest; Democrats understand we are in an *existential* battle for the survival of American democracy. We *must* win.

Troops will also be mindful of the military policy of IFF: Identification friend or foe. Not every member of the opposition remains with the opposition. Republicans of conscience have broken with their party and announced they will vote for the Democratic presidential nominee, Joe Biden. Those new friends include former Republican presidential nominee and now senator Mitt Romney, former Ohio governor John Kasich, former New Jersey governor Christine Todd Whitman. Continuing to act with intelligence may peel off more disillusioned Republicans.

And kudos to Democrats for, by and large, not returning like for like to Trump's constant stream of epithets and denigration—"Sleepy Joe," "nasty woman," "loser"—though that nasty loser *so* richly deserves it. We are testing whether the proposition of staying high while he goes low is the winning way.

In sum, our guidance is this: "the moral obligation to be intelligent," a credo popularized by literary critic Lionel Trilling in a 1963 book of that title. Taken in reverse order, each element of this credo carries weight: "to be intelligent"—the thrust of this entire appeal; the "obligation"—more than provisional, bearing on duty; with the obligation being "moral"—bearing on the rightness and wrongness of things.

And with the late-breaking, heart-breaking news of Ruth Bader Ginsburg's death: Not only must Democrats do everything procedurally possible to ensure a liberal replaces her on the Supreme Court. But, truly: In all modern public life, who better exemplified than "the Notorious RBG"—she was its perfect union —"the moral obligation to be intelligent"?

Back to battle stations. Be intelligent. Good luck.

—*Medium*, September 21, 2020

In a Plague-Time, Rereading
Albert Camus' *The Plague*

Eleventh in an ongoing series, Notes from a Plague-Time

I.

WHEN I WAS *a child, I spake as a child, I understood as a child, I thought as a child....* What I was 13 or 14, a smart girl but in no way wise, I read Albert Camus' canonic novel *The Plague*. It was not a regular class assignment; I read it on my own. No doubt I came to *The Plague* because I saw a kind of plague in my own household—my parents were estranged, I was their go-between. To compensate for the tension, I hoovered books, all kinds, including those best understood as an adult.

Thus my early under-interpretation: My main take-away from this parable of plague, apart from rats being the plague's carrier, was that the central character, a medical doctor, despite tending plague-ridden patients all the way through and despite extreme exhaustion, somehow never gets sick himself. How could this be? My father was a doctor and I asked him. It was then I learned about "immunities."

Yet I sensed in Camus the moral strength that I sought for myself in those early years; I was looking for courage, the elixir. Of course as an adult I have learned one must manufacture one's moral courage oneself. But at the time I kept on reading Camus—actually, I read *about* Camus rather than more Camus (I read *The Stranger* in college and "got" it).

And what I read about Camus was thrilling. As I understood him, he insisted that, most especially when a moral question was at stake, one *must* act, not just quiver in fear, and one must act no matter how "absurd" the circumstances. Thus I found the courage, as my parents' go-between, to say to my mother, "Be nicer to Dad," *and* weather her glare. I absorbed from Camus that life itself was absurd, full of impossible complexity, demands, tests, and that, despite the unending absurdity, one must never act in "bad faith." I "got" that precept clearly: One knows the corners that cannot be cut, the lines that cannot be crossed. When I learned he had served in the French Resistance, during the absurdity of Occupied France, I fell in love with Camus—moral philosopher, writer *engagé*, and, now I learn, Nazi fighter! Camus was my first philosopher and one always remembers one's first philosopher. I did not yet understand the colonial dimension (absurdity?) of Camus' life—born in the French colony of Algeria but living, and engaging, much of his adult life in France itself, the *metropole*—but I would later.

I would also understand, much later—while living through a plague myself—Camus' canonic novel. *But when I became an adult, I put away childish things....*

II.

When our plague set in six months ago, reading lists for the inquiring and fearful minds "sheltering in place" appeared everywhere, with Camus' novel on nearly every one, along with Daniel Defoe's *A Journal of the Plague Year* and Giovanni Boccaccio's *The Decameron*. I ordered them all, but then decided to set them aside, for later, when (I hoped) the fear would reduce and I would be more informed on our plague's carrier—the coronavirus—and could track the fallout, make sense of it, thus be more able to take in Camus' ultimate meaning.

For I also had learned that, in casting the plague as his metaphor, Camus meant to portray not only a biological event, but a political one as well. Working on the novel during World War II, then seeing it published in 1947, shortly after war's end, Camus meant to show the insidious spread of a malignancy like fascism in a host body particularly receptive. With the novel's opening line—"The unusual events described in this chronicle occurred in 194- in Oran"—the time-frame set is the war, though the war does not play a role; malignancy does. Opinion is mixed on Camus' success with the political parable. But observing the fallout of our plague—both biological and political—I commend Camus as boon companion on this trek.

Even more valuable, and what escaped my teenaged comprehension: Camus is brilliant in limning the internal weather of his characters and then externalizing it as dialogue among them, as he charts their passage, during a plague deadlier than ours—death comes in 48 hours—to moral responsibility and action (or not). In showing humanity in mortal crisis—the story-line is simple: A plague sets in, people endure or die, the plague goes away—this ultimately is a deeply philosophical novel.

Camus set his story not in a fictional city but a real one, a commercial port on the coast of Algeria. He did not much like Oran, precisely because of its one-note commercial quality; he far preferred his beloved Algiers for its variety. But Oran suited Camus' metaphoric purpose: He could portray Oran as monolithic, with its residents' actions and reactions readily rendered. "Our citizens," he writes, "work hard, but solely with the object of getting rich. Their chief interest is in commerce, and their chief aim in life is, as they call it, 'doing business'"—materialism Camus the humanist sends up as "completely modern." Also "modern" are Oran's "relaxed morals," love as a thing "consumed," inattention to God. Such superficiality would not likely withstand fascism's appeal; in the novel the plague's lessons are forgotten by Oran's townspeople as soon as the "All clear" is sounded.

As to the biological event: The first truth to strike one new to experiencing plague is to understand that, as Camus puts it, "This calamity was everybody's business." But this understanding of inexorability, even of plague's existence, comes slowly. Even the doctor, Bernard Rieux, does not discern at first the significance of the dead rat he steps on when we first meet him. When the evidence becomes clear—mysterious deaths mounting—and he convenes the municipal Health Committee, his do-something is countered by Dr. Richard's wait-and-see. At the mention of "plague," the Prefect "hurriedly glanced toward the door to make sure it had prevented this outrageous remark from being overheard in the corridor." But this power-that-be listens to science: He announces an epidemic and has the city's gates shut. The doctor knows the score, though: With not enough serum and the bacillus mutating, "The only hope was that the outbreak would die a natural death."

Another truth conferred by plague: people's feeling of "exile"—"that sensation of a void within," being stuck in one's "prison-house": "At such moments the collapse of their courage, willpower, and endurance was so abrupt that they felt they could never drag themselves out of the pit of despond into which they had fallen." Exile is made sharper if married couples and lovers are caught separated: "Always a moment came when we had to face the fact that no trains were coming in." (Doctor Rieux' wife is away at a sanatorium.) Generally, during this plague-time, Oran's citizens "drifted through life rather than lived": "They forced themselves never to think about the problematic day of escape, to cease looking to the future, and always to keep, so to speak, their eyes fixed on the ground at their feet." As Camus famously writes, "Thus each of us had to be content to live only for the day, alone under the vast indifference of the sky." The townspeople themselves maintain "a saving indifference, which one was tempted to take for composure. Their despair saved them from panic."

III.

As the plague continues, composure gives way; on certain minds plague has "an incendiary effect"—heavy drinking, madness, suicide. Soon, "the whole town was running a temperature." Their worst imaginings make goners of some while, strangely, saving others. In this febrile state, Doctor Rieux realizes, soon the whole town will be a "madhouse." This is when the internal drama is engaged: As the doctor recognizes, "It's an absurd situation, but we're all involved in it, and we've got to accept it as it is." When he is reproached for "abstraction," not having the heart to sign a certificate enabling a husband to rejoin his wife in Paris, he thinks: "When abstraction sets to killing you, you've got to get busy with it."

The doctor's saving sense of duty is his counter to the plague; his therapy is work—all played out in a sublime chapter with him at the window, just after acknowledging the plague's existence. He thinks: "Everybody knows that pestilences have a way of recurring in the world; yet somehow we find it hard to believe in ones that crash down on our heads from a blue sky." He thinks: "No one will ever be free so long as there are pestilences." He recalls reading that "some thirty or so great plagues known to history had accounted for nearly a hundred million deaths." Then he pulls himself up, sharply: These "extravagant forebodings dwindled in the light of reason.... It was only a matter of lucidly recognizing what had to be recognized; of dispelling extraneous shadows and doing what needed to be done." Opening the window, he hears a machine-saw and thinks: "There lay certitude; there, in the daily round. All the rest hung on mere threads and trivial contingencies; you couldn't waste your time on it. The thing was to do your job as it should be done." This character-sketch-cum-credo reminds us why we love novels. Later, as the plague grows, he has a revelation: "Finally, he realized that he was afraid!" Back to work.

Other key characters come into focus through their own similar thinking. Upon introduction, these characters strike one as archetypal—the Traveler, the Journalist, the Bureaucrat, the Priest—but they gain individuality and depth in their struggle; fear, as Camus writes, enables "serious reflection," the anteroom to action. Jean Tarrou, the traveler, reveals himself in an exchange with the hotel manager: When the latter reports a chambermaid has come down with a "queer kind of fever," Tarrou says it was all the same to him, to which the manager says, "You're like me, you're a fatalist," to which Tarrou clarifies: "I said nothing of the kind and—what's more—am not a fatalist." It is *not* all the same to Tarrou. Raymond Rambert, the journalist and the one begging the doctor for permission to return to his wife in Paris, confronts him angrily: What do we live for—love or duty? Bent on escape, Rambert noses around for a smuggler. Joseph Grand, the bureaucrat, is a lowly clerk in the Municipal Office who, evenings, works on the manuscript— of what: a novel?—that will bring back his wife who left him (he hasn't gotten past the first sentence). This man "of no significance" Camus hails for his quiet humanity and decency.

Earlier, Rambert and the doctor have a revealing exchange about truth. When Rambert asks if he can interview Rieux about the living conditions of the town's Arab population, Rieux asks if he will print "an unqualified condemnation of the present state of things." When Rambert equivocates, he declines. The doctor, Camus writes, was "a man who was sick and tired of the world he lived in—though he had much liking for his fellow men—and had resolved, for his part, to have no truck with injustice and compromises with the truth."

Of course in a plague, debate about God arises—Does He exist? If He exists, how could He allow this pestilence, all this death? Father Paneloux, the Jesuit priest, is a moralist of the punishing kind. In his first sermon—well-attended by the secular townspeople ("It can't do any harm")—disgusted at their "moral laxity," he lashes into them, thundering: "Calamity has come to you, my brethren, and, my brethren, you deserved it." Later, after standing vigil for a child dying of plague, he atones. In a second sermon, he confesses his earlier words "lacked in charity"; he urges the congregation (smaller this time) to "try to do what good lay in our power." Earlier, though, after the child had died despite Doctor Rieux' efforts, they argue. Paneloux urges him to "love what we cannot understand"; Rieux fires back, "Until my dying day I shall refuse to love a scheme of things in which children are put to torture." Father tries to allay: "You too are working for man's salvation," to which the doctor replies: "Salvation's much too big a word for me." In parting, the doctor, a gentler moralist, says: "What does it matter? What I hate is death and disease. And whether you wish it or not, we're allies.... God Himself can't part us now."

It is Tarrou, the traveler and non-fatalist, who comes up with an action plan to fight the plague: to organize volunteer sanitary squads to assist the overworked medical workers, by carting away bodies, cleaning up infected areas, etc. "Officialdom," he argues to Rieux, "can never cope with something really catastrophic." When Rieux tells him officialdom is thinking of using prisoners for that purpose," Tarrou replies, "I'd rather free men were employed."

Thence to the novel's moral heart: Tarrou asks what the doctor thought of Father Paneloux' sermon; Rieux says he does not believe in collective punishment. They agree, though, that plague has its good side: "It opens men's eyes and forces them to take thought" (Tarrou) and "It helps men to rise above themselves" (Rieux). "All the same," says Rieux, "when you see the misery it brings, you'd need to be a madman, or a coward, or stone blind, to give in tamely to the plague." Tarrou then asks: "Do you believe in God?" No, Rieux says, "I'm fumbling in the dark." Then why, Tarrou presses him, "do you yourself show such devotion, considering you don't believe in God? I suspect your answer may help me." Rieux says he's fighting against creation as he found it; he became a doctor because "it was particularly difficult for a workman's son, like myself." Tarrou notes that, "since the order of the world is shaped by death," then "your victories will never be lasting," to which Rieux replies, "Yes, I know that. But it's no reason for giving up the struggle." "No reason, I agree," says Tarrou, "only, I now can picture what this plague must mean for you." "Yes. A never-ending defeat." Tarrou asks, "Who taught you all this, Doctor?" "Suffering." As they wrap up, Rieux says: "Out with it, Tarrou! What on earth prompted you to take a hand in this?" "My code of morals, perhaps," says Tarrou. "Your code of morals? What code?" Says Tarrou, "Comprehension." If this kind of writing is your *tasse de thé*, this passage rivets. Riveted, I could connect

Tarrou's need to enact his moral code to something he expressed earlier, that "The only thing I'm interested in is acquiring peace of mind." Peace of mind is acquired in moral action.

Meanwhile, Joseph Grand the bureaucrat becomes "a sort of general secretary to the sanitary squads," running the statistics. (In the margin I wrote, "Reader feeling much better now that sanitary squads are at work!") And when Rambert, the journalist who's trying to escape has a change of heart.... I shall reveal no more, and this is only the first half of the novel. (Per the late Tony Judt, the characters Rieux, Tarrou, and Rambert all reflect some aspect of Camus himself.)

IV.

One should beware of instrumentalizing a canonic work, lest its elegance be damaged. But six months into our own plague, this reader cannot refrain from comparing and contrasting *The Plague* to our American experience of plague. As in our pandemic, in the novel the medical authorities speak of "flattening the curve" of infection, although the doctor who exulted "The graph's good today"—Dr. Richard of "wait-and-see"—was soon carried off by the plague. Sadly, in our plague at this point, over 200,000 Americans have been carried off.

By now we know the feeling of exile in our prison-houses; by now some of us have discovered the salvation of work to fend off fear (Camus refers to work's "doping" effect). As for a population's capacity to withstand plague, Americans will note how Camus' introduction of Oran as materialistic ("doing business") and modern ("moral laxity") chimes with our own qualities. But straight-line compare-and-contrast soon breaks down, because, compared to a monolithic Oran, America is far more multifarious and dynamic; our tale cannot be told in the unitary voice of "our citizens." Add to this, unlike the novel's Prefect who listens to science in handling the plague, our imperfect Prefect in the White House denies science, fobs off responsibility, lies about his "successes," causing unnecessary suffering and death; bungles reopening the economy, causing unnecessary ruination; and in thrall to his proto-autocratic ego, knocks off more democratic guardrails, just when we need them most, and now even threatens violence to stay in office.

Thus, on top of plague, Americans are dealing with economic collapse, racial reckoning, *and* salvaging our very democracy. And none too intelligently, sadly: The battle of "ideas" between our Prefect's fevered base and anyone outside that base is so polarized and inflamed as to be self-destructive and, well, stupid. About which Dr. Rieux says, "Stupidity has a knack of getting its way; as we should see if we were not always so much wrapped up in ourselves." Or wrapped up in the "bad faith" of conspiracy theory (Camus writes of superstition's "mental pabulum"). The worst of bad faith is seeing our imperfect Prefect's base *and* party falling for his oceanic and dangerous lying, a plague in and of itself.

Our tragedy lies here: that our extreme polarization is preventing us from seeing a truth that Tarrou, advocating for decency, voices: "All I maintain is that on this earth there are pestilences and there are victims, *and it's up to us, so far as possible, not to join forces with the pestilences*" (italics mine). Have we joined with the pestilence? Much in our politics and culture, and current presidential campaign, indicates yes.

All this said: When in the novel the citizens of Oran allow themselves to think ahead, beyond plague ("the illusion" of a future), they merely want a return to normalcy. And when the plague begins to ebb, there is sporadic talk of turning their suffering to account with "a new order of things"—which talk however is soon forgotten in celebrating their return to the old life. Like Oran's citizens, Americans have "gone to school with suffering"; will we make of our suffering a new order of things? Will we vote for it? That hope is there. America once manufactured its hope. Camus writes, "Once the faintest stirring of hope became possible, the dominion of the plague was ended." We need every conscientious volunteer we can muster fighting our political plague. Combatting racism, white supremacy, untruth, our Prefect's moves to dismantle American democracy are major acts of "good faith."

V.

Discussion of a masterpiece must end with the masterpiece. For its portrait of humanity mustering in crisis, *The Plague* joins my pantheon of humanist novels that include *Moby-Dick* (a favorite of Camus) and *Middlemarch*. For this and other novels, and his powerful essays and journalism, Camus was awarded the Nobel prize for literature in 1957. His untimely death in 1960, in an auto accident, robbed the world of a signal moral voice.

There are criticisms to be made of *The Plague*, notably the lack of Arab characters, despite its Arab setting. But Camus' defenders note that, with his political parable, his target was Vichy France, the regime that collaborated with Nazi Germany. His point was to show the ease with which that infection took place. Camus finished the novel in the early post-war years, when French forgetting was already underway.

For my part, I missed the presence of any woman taking the fight to the plague. The women who do figure in the novel do so self-effacingly, as men's backstop. Inwardly I crafted a *communiqué*: Monsieur Camus, there are some women who formulate their moral credo and fight for it every day, valiantly. In some women, there beats a lion's heart.

A last criticism: Sometimes Camus shows himself too much the tragedian, notably in his portrait of the ineluctability of the plague and its universal impact on humans. (Or perhaps this is my vestigial American resistance to the tragic scheme of things.) For example, he intones that, under the plague's dominion, "The town was peopled with sleepwalkers," who "lost every trace of a critical spirit." From my shelter, I see the critical spirit alive and thinking; I also see a new seriousness among my fellow Americans, which again Camus writes is enabled by fear. He also pronounces, in the plague's crush, the death of love and friendship. But I do not find that so, instead discovering new depths in old friendships, new depths in my marriage. Camus belies his own pronouncement with the rich, and new, friendship between the doctor and Tarrou. At the plague's worst, there is a lovely moment when, breaking from their taxing work, they take an hour "for friendship's sake" and go for a swim.

But: Camus' sense of tragedy is not so total as to deny to the human being all agency, all room for maneuver. One can always act, he insists, and one must. And in the most important measure—the moral, bearing on the rightness and wrongness of things—action begins with taking responsibility, no matter the countervailing pressure, be it foreign occupation, plague, chaos, or the moral vacuum of modern life. For Camus, tragedy lies in moral collapse. (Judt made the distinction that "Camus was a *moraliste* but he was no moralizer." His genius lay in his finesse.)

Such action need not be dramatic, as when I as a girl admonished my mother to be nicer to Dad; it was right to do, but led to our decades-long estrangement. (I later led the way to our jointly turning tragedy into peace.) Moral action also inheres in simple decency—the kind word or gesture, thinking of others. Camus is emphatic on the power of decency during plague. As the doctor, who might be thought heroic, tells Rambert: "There's one thing I must tell you: there is no question of heroism in all this. It's a matter of common decency. That's an idea which may make some people smile, but the only means of fighting a plague is—common decency."

If we despair the absence of conscientious actors in this struggle, Camus assures us there is ample supply. He salutes those who, "refusing to bow down to pestilence, strive their utmost to be healers." Of the volunteer sanitary squads that Tarrou organized, while "sooner or later contagion did its work," still, "when all is said and done, the really amazing thing is that, so long as the epidemic lasted, there was never any lack of men for these duties"; volunteers "never failed to appear when summoned." And further assurance: "to state quite simply what we learn in time of pestilence: that there are more things to admire in men than to despise." (Women, too, Monsieur Camus, women, too.) This last truth, from "my" philosopher, has served as a credo over my lifetime. I had to wait until the last page to find it again.

Famously, the novel's last paragraph warns of plagues to come. While Oran's citizens celebrate victory over the pestilence and, starting to forget, resume their old way of life, Camus writes that "the plague bacillus never dies or disappears for good." Epidemiologists now tell us the same; we must mind the biological event basically forever going forward. Honoring Camus' original intent with his novel, we must also continue minding the malignancy of political plague. Finally, there is the existential plague of death. Death is "everybody's business."

Camus would have us remember this: Plague of any kind—whether biological, political, existential—presents both "bane and enlightenment." It's our *choice*.

—*Medium*, September 29, 2020

Trump Becoming COVID Patient #1 Restores the Pandemic as Campaign Issue #1

THE EXCEPTION PROVES the rule: With president Donald Trump, who has denied the seriousness of the coronavirus pandemic since its onset, now contracting COVID-19 and hospitalized for treatment, the pandemic is restored—properly so—as Issue #1 in this presidential campaign.

Despite his strenuous efforts to make the campaign about "law and order" or the alleged weaknesses of Democratic nominee Joe Biden, the felling of the President himself to the virus, along with numerous other Republicans—may they all recover as newly enlightened people— underscores, as *nothing* else could, the dominion of this vicious virus.

Until the virus is vanquished, America will flail and founder. The same can't be said of any other issue. Thus, it is Issue #1.

This reprioritizing is all to the good and just in time, because: I fear that, with the media spotlight so fixed on Trump's every desperate and distracting gambit to get re-elected—the most desperate and distracting being last week's abominable "presidential" debate—the less our attention is fixed on the pandemic's insidious corrosion of America's economic landscape. This corrosion, going on seven months, may be irreparable.

Damage such as: The millions of human lives upended by a hemorrhaging economy—over 40 million people lost their jobs in the pandemic's first three months—with another relief package coming from Congress still iffy. The word "upend" is used a lot these days, but are we really focusing on the upending? Many workers are now permanently unemployed, as their status goes from temporary layoff to permanently cut. Imagine the sorrow and suffering, and now panic, of those human beings, our fellow Americans.

Damage such as: Businesses, local and national, going under. Small businesses numbering 1.4 million went under in the three months ending in June, representing 13% of the 30.7 million small businesses operating nationwide. Storied brand names, too, have gone under: Brooks Brothers, the clothier to Abraham Lincoln in his presidency; J.C. Penney; Lord & Taylor; Hertz.

Damage such as: Cities and towns upended. To read of the devastation of the downtowns of our iconic cities—New York and Washington, D.C.—is chilling, out of a dystopian novel: the vacant storefronts, restaurants and hotels near-empty, the arts establishments closed, all with dismal prospects for a full comeback anytime soon, if ever.

In the ten-ring circus that is Donald Trump, are we tracking this corrosion? Apart from the human suffering, such corrosion, per experts, threatens the very viability of American capitalism itself.

Biden and the Democrats should focus laser-like on Trump's abysmal handling of this deadly pandemic—and how, if elected, they would quell it. That a Trump campaign adviser still claims Biden wears a mask as a "prop"—*even as his boss languished in the hospital with COVID-19*—is laughable if it weren't so dangerous. In that abominable "presidential" debate, Trump again mocked Biden for his mask-wearing; the irony is too subtle for Trump to comprehend he was felled by that "Democratic hoax." In that mess of a debate, Biden did manage to nail it: Referring to Trump's response to the horrendous rates of infection and death, "It is what it is," said Biden: "It is what it is because you are who you are. That's why it is. The President has no plan."

Also: That Trump's Rose Garden announcement of Amy Coney Barrett for the Supreme Court turned out to fell so many other Republican figures—senators Mike Lee and Thom Tillis, the Republican National Committee chairwoman—might just be coincidental. But it also, given the mask-free hugging and schmoozing and the logic of the coronavirus, might be, you know, logical. Experts peg that event as a "super-spreader."

Other Republicans testing positive include former New Jersey governor Chris Christie and senator Ron Johnson. Yet even after contracting

COVID-19, Johnson made a crack about "unjustified hysteria" regarding the pandemic. Such irresponsibility in a representative of a looming "hot spot" (Wisconsin) is tragic. So much for Republican enlightenment.

Biden, on the enlightened path, can stress what he said weeks ago: "This pandemic didn't have to be this bad." He can stress again that "I believe in the Enlightenment, Newtonian physics, and the age of reason." He can stress again what he managed to state in that brawl of a "presidential" debate: "You can't fix the economy until you have fixed the COVID crisis." Most importantly Biden can stress that, as a Democrat who believes both in government's capacity to do good and in a President's responsibility to organize the federal response to a crisis, *this pandemic could have been over by now—OVER.*

Writing in the 18th century about industrialized nations, famed Scottish economist and thinker Adam Smith speculated that "there is a great deal of ruin" in such nation. But: As there is with everything under the sun, there is an end even to ruin—to the point where, buried by the rubble, the phoenix cannot rise again.

In the 28 days left in this campaign, let us focus on the pandemic's ruin—and stopping it.

—Medium, October 6, 2020

No, America Is Not "Irredeemably Evil." Democrats: Show Our Love of Country.

DEMOCRATS HAVE LONG gotten a bad rap—and a bad rep—from Republicans. Somehow, the conventional knowledge now goes, Republicans are the flag-waving patriots and Democrats "hate" America.

This bad rap was brought home vividly for me in late 2009. I had just given a talk on my commentary titled "Recovery Without a Reckoning," about Wall Street's recovery from the 2008 financial crash—the crash it caused but from which it appeared to learn little, going back to its old risky ways.

Afterwards, a man came up to me and introduced himself as a Republican. He said he gathered from the publicity for the event that I was a Democrat, but he came anyway because of the word "Reckoning" in my talk's title: He remained a free-marketer but he agreed with my argument that Wall Street needed to factor in Main Street far more than it had in the past and, going forward, post-crash. And, yes, there was a moral aspect at issue, thus the reckoning: Wall Street's continuing heedlessness of Main Street was wrong. I said I loved this country too much to see its beautiful principles abused.

This was when he—Mike—made the point that has stayed with me: "I wish I heard other Democrats say they loved this country," he said. "I never hear that." He went on: Democrats seem only to criticize America, run her down (I remember he said "her"), and they never express love of country. In the warmth of our exchange, I suddenly could see how Mike, a conscientious Republican, perceived "the other side." We ended with a handshake and thanks.

I have continued thinking of what Mike said, because I think he has a point.

But the bad rap has continued and, in the extreme polarization now besetting us, it drives—inflames—rhetoric. Sadly, it suffuses the editorial pages of our lead conservative paper, *The Wall Street Journal*, which, in addition to our alleged America-hating, propagates other categorical (and wrong) thinking: that Democrats "blame America first," that as "elites" we sneer at regular Americans, that we want a "radical," "socialist" revolution in this country.

In the *Journal*, the word "irredeemable" became attached to our alleged America-hating in the wake of the killing of George Floyd, a Black man, by a white police officer. Where Democrats see that heinous act as the clearest possible evidence of white supremacy and systemic racism—the white man kept his knee on the Black man's neck for an eternity, clearly unconcerned about accountability—the *Journal* sees America-hatred. One columnist decries Democrats' aim to "overturn a pervasive, irredeemably racist American social structure," another decries Democrats lecturing on "the nation's irredeemable sinfulness." The words "irredeemable," and "racial grievance industry," have become tics.

And the *Journal*'s Peggy Noonan wrote this about the Democratic national convention: "[A]part from the 'We The People' gauziness, there was a nonstop hum of grievance at the convention. To show their ferocious sincerity in the struggle against America's injustices, most of the speakers thought they had to beat the crap out of the country—over and over. Its sins: racism, sexism, bigotry, violence, xenophobia, being unwelcoming to immigrants. The charges, direct and indirect, never let up. Little love was expressed, little gratitude. Everyone was sort of overcoming being born here."

Stuck in categorical (and wrong) thinking, the *Journal* cannot grasp that, the more one loves something, in this case America, the more one hurts when it has gone wrong, or when the beloved object, again America, has betrayed its own principles. Democratic friends tell me the image of Mr. Floyd dying under the white man's knee is staying as vividly with them as the falling of the Twin Towers on 9/11—and that the shame of it "shoved" them into the streets to protest, which protest the *Journal* too often conflates with "riot."

But Noonan has a point, as did Mike from my earlier encounter: Democrats do not often state outright our love of country. Why is that? Perhaps it is because we Democrats tend to argue from a policy standpoint (see: Affordable Care Act) or in the abstract (see: Justice), both of which can *seem* divorced from feeling, especially the more vigorously we argue our point. Or perhaps we look at Republican hypocrisy—waving the flag while dismantling democratic norms and institutions—and decide we don't want *that*, to get into a contest of flag-waving. But: In not openly expressing love of country, we do leave ourselves open to a bad rap on our rep. So, let's declare it outright now: Democrats *do* love America—profoundly.

Unlike Donald Trump.... Pray tell, Republicans, *Wall Street Journal*: By what *conceivable* measure can Trump's actions—from his "American carnage" Inaugural to his present refusal to accept the upcoming election's result or his encouraging armed militias to "stand back and stand by"—ever be interpreted as love of country? What *higher* end, apart from his own aggrandizement, has Trump been after? (Time's up.) That Republicans and the *Journal* still—still!—rally around Trump is evidence they see the 2020 election only as a *political* contest, not the *existential* one Democrats do.

And it is because of this existential, life-or-death reason—American democracy is in peril, can we save it?—that Democrats should break an old habit and sing out our profound love of America, at each and every turn.

Like *The Washington Post*'s liberal columnist Ruth Marcus did, in a 2017 column whose title I still remember three years later: "I Have Never Loved My Country More." Writing of some Trump outrage now superseded by multitudes more, Marcus opened with "I have never respected a president less, nor loved my country more" and closed noting "the patriotism Trump has awoken, in me and so many others. Because our fundamental fight is not against Trump. It is for America."

Which prompts me to express my own love of America—happily, gratefully.

In the years after 9/11, when America stumbled into war in Iraq, I was lamenting to a friend, whose rejoinder was, "You are such an idealist," not meant as a compliment. But, thinking about it, I did take it as a compliment: Yes, I responded later, I *am* an idealist—*because America herself is built on the ideal,* and they are the most beautiful ideals in human (versus kingly) history: equality, fair play, rule of law, self-governance, second chances. But: America has never achieved these ideals, not in their totality and not for all our citizens—but if we did, if we *finally* delivered on our foundational ideals, I feel we would be golden, America would enter a Golden Age. And it is in my revulsion of Donald Trump—all right, my near-hatred of the man, engendered *precisely because of the injury he has inflicted on America the Beautiful*—that I have come to recognize how profoundly beautiful and dear and vital those ideals are. I keep thinking of the French proverb: "Only good things can be abused": Trump, and the Republicans, have taken a singularly good thing in human history and abused it nearly into the ground. But, believing in second chances—in *redeemability*—and believing it with all my heart, I believe we can turn this titanic struggle into rebirth—a Renaissance.

Wow, that felt good! Love elevates! Out of the Slough of Despond....

Join me, fellow Democrats. Express our love of country in whatever forum: Zoom town-halls and meet-ups, letters to the editor (print is forever!), all the better if in mixed political company. Who knows: In the 23 days left until *the* election of our lifetime, hearing such love may sway an undecided voter or one understandably so discouraged by all the venom that he/she swore off voting ever again. Finally: Expressing such love is tonic for our own souls—and for America the Beautiful herself.

I have never loved my country more.

—*Medium*, October 10, 2020

Books for Our Times:
Twilight of Democracy: The Seductive Lure of Authoritarianism, by Anne Applebaum

Second in an ongoing series, Books for Our Times

WE LIVE IN troubled and turbulent times: The great experiment in self-governance—democracy—appears to be faltering, the liberal world order appears in retreat, and authoritarian reign appears on the rise. To make sense of the chaos, what better voice to hear than one that is measured and real, deeply read and experienced, someone who "walks point" into the trouble and turbulence and comes back to report, in a personal and not oracular tone, "Here's what I think is going on."

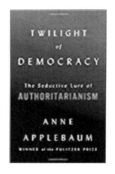

That is the voice Anne Applebaum uses in her new book, *Twilight of Democracy: The Seductive Lure of Authoritarianism*, a short book (only 189 pages) that is big on the contours of our times. While the title *Twilight of Democracy* might strike one as Wagnerian, Applebaum's treatment is provisional and, in the end, hopeful that—if we stick together and keep thinking clearly—we can make our way through the dark to a better place.

This is the voice that first drew me to Applebaum, with her columns in *The Washington Post*, where she wrote for 17 years; she shifted this year to *The Atlantic* as a contributing writer, writing at length. In fact her voice is so free of polemic yet liberal-seeming that I assumed she was center-left, as I am, and did not know, until this book, that she identifies as center-right: Married to a Polish public figure and living in Poland, to be anticommunist, as she explains it, is to be of the right, not the left. Being of the right, and also forthright, she assesses in this book her former ideological comrades as they journeyed, self-blinded, into authoritarian thinking. (She did the same recently for *The Atlantic* in a brilliant essay on Republican complicity.)

That journey, and the ensuing parting of ways, is vividly traced in her book's opening, in which she describes a party she and her husband Radek hosted at the turn of the millennium, New Year's Eve 1999. While the guests—journalists (like herself), government officials (like her husband), diplomats, hailing not only from Poland but from around the world—were nominally conservative, "at that moment in history, you might also have called most of us liberals," not only classical free-market liberals but believers in democracy—rule of law, checks and balances, the European project. Yet today, 20 years later, half of those guests, now moved far-right, "I would now cross the street to avoid....They, in turn, would not only refuse to enter my house, they would be embarrassed to admit they had ever been there." She follows up with some to learn the Why of their transformation—these meetings are tense, tape-recorders going—but finds only ideological defensiveness. In essence, this book is an inquiry into the Why: the lure of authoritarianism. The book ends with another party.

Applebaum's *tour d'horizon* of democracies tending authoritarian ranges from new ones—in addition to post-Franco Spain, there are Poland and Hungary, freed from Soviet domination, both quickly turning illiberal—to those of longer duration: France, England, Italy, and of course the U.S. (Applebaum is American-born). On the matter of duration, Applebaum sounds this sobering note: Democracy is not necessarily forever. "Given the right conditions, any society can turn against democracy. Indeed, if history is anything to go by, all of our societies eventually will."

Just as Applebaum book-ends her account with parties, she book-ends her inquiry with two reigning ideas. The first I found especially illuminating, in showing how, in a *democracy*, authoritarian rule comes not through violence but via the aid of small-d democrats. This idea was propounded in the French writer Julien Benda's 1927 book, *La Trahison des Clercs*, or *The Betrayal of the Intellectuals*, in which he observed the elites, left and right—writers, journalists, essayists—whose output supported either "class passion" (Soviet Marxism) or "national passion" (fascism), accusing them, per Applebaum, of "betraying the central task of the intellectual, the search for truth." (I get now the Why of Applebaum's dispassion.) Sarcastically, Benda called these fallen intellectuals *clercs* or clerks, minions who paved the way for Hitler and Stalin. Her own book, Applebaum writes, "is about this new generation of *clercs* and the new reality they are creating." One thinks immediately of the "alternative facts" deployed by Donald Trump's *clercs* in his quest for strongman rule.

Applebaum's other reigning idea, cited at the end, is from Italian novelist Ignazio Silone, specifically his essay written in the 1950s, "The Choice of Comrades," in which he described, per Applebaum, "why he was still engaged in politics, despite so many disappointments and defeats." Silone had been Communist, then anticommunist; he may have collaborated with the fascists before turning antifascist; he'd been "under illusions and then been disillusioned," seen the excesses of two different extremist politics. Still, says Applebaum, "he thought the struggle was worth continuing. Not because there was a nirvana to be obtained, and not because there was a perfect society to be built, but because apathy was so deadening, so mind-numbing, so soul-destroying." Echoing today's atmosphere, Silone's countrymen felt, per Applebaum, "that 'all politicians are crooks' or 'all journalists lie' or 'you can't believe anything.'" Silone understood the impact: "Political regimes come and go," he wrote, but "bad habits remain"—and the worst habit is *nihilism* (italics mine), "a disease of the spirit."

In between these ideas—the blind passion of the *clercs*, the nihilism of the *clercs* and the people—Applebaum traces how democracy can erode from within. She speculates on the psychological need—resentment, chiefly—that enables a *clerc* to argue a lie in the face of fact and how a *clerc* comes to devalue messy democracy for the simplistic illiberal one-party state—it really is, *al fondo*, all about power. Food for my thought: the nihilism of the right—"All is decadence, all is lost" or "Only God can save us"—that Applebaum sees among former ideological comrades. Quite rightly, she cites the nihilism of the left, too—its distrust of institutions, the media, even "bourgeois" democracy itself. One former comrade she takes us close to is British prime minister Boris Johnson, whom she knows from his journalism days. She tells us how she lost her own faith: when the Bush administration engaged in torture in Iraq (my brief too) and when John McCain picked Sarah Palin as his V.P. She shows us how the far-right exploits the public's dissatisfaction with democracy—its messiness, its ineffectual response in crisis, its corruption—with promises to "make [name of country] great again" (see her chapter titled "The Future of Nostalgia").

And, importantly, she zeroes in on the tango that would-be strongmen dance with *clercs* to disable democracy and achieve one-man rule, with a detailed look primarily at Hungary's Viktor Orban and also Poland's Jaroslaw Kaczynski.

In sum, Applebaum covers a lot in a short space. Like the guide I cited up front, she paints the big picture and lays out the "deets." Concluding, she says: Democracy is in twilight and that twilight can lead either to permanent darkness or to better days. She leaves us with this: "Liberal democracies always demanded things from citizens: participation, argument, effort, struggle. They always required some tolerance for cacophony and chaos, as well as some willingness to push back at the people who create cacophony and chaos." We struggle on, we push back. And someday we will party.

Further about the author: Applebaum has also written three books of history on the former Soviet Union, with one, "Gulag," winning the Pulitzer Prize.

—*Medium*, October 14, 2020

For Republicans, 2020 Election is Political. Democrats Understand It Is Existential.

IT IS CLEAR—FROM the audacity of their actions, from the near-unanimity of their ranks—that the Republicans view the 2020 presidential election solely as *political*: that is, the absolute need, *no matter the cost to institutions or norms*, to retain governing power.

Their latest audacity and its cost? Ramming another conservative onto the Supreme Court (Amy Coney Barrett), at the cost of destroying the Court's conservative-liberal balance, making it 6 to 3, and rewriting their own rules of blocking President Barack Obama's nominee Merrick Garland. Audacity upon audacity, Republicans pronounce themselves shocked, shocked that Democrats, growing ever confident of winning both White House and Senate, should even consider "packing" the Court as they themselves are doing. Republicans can read polls as well as any pol, thus knowing a blue tsunami is heading their way, this particular audacity comes off as deeply cynical, a last "win" before their banishment to the political wilderness.

But Court-packing is only the latest Republican audacity. Others include: voter suppression, *faux*-dropoff boxes for ballots, gerrymandering (and cutting short the 2020 census to favor future gerrymandering). But most egregious: standing by a President, Donald J. Trump, who not only destroys the institutions and norms integral to American democracy since our inception, but takes us into territory where we never, *ever* should be: into strongman rule, autocracy. Nearly zero is Republican pushback to Trump's embrace of the world's autocrats or to his own proto-autocratic acts: killing truth with lies, sliming the media as "the enemy of the American people," pardoning accused war criminals, condoning white supremacists, equating protesters with domestic terrorists, and ominously, signaling armed militias to "stand back and stand by" as he refuses to say he will agree—as any small-d democrat would—to abide by this election's results.

To all appearances, Republicans look at all this accrual of power, ill-gotten as it may be, and their complicity with a proto-autocrat and say: "Well-played." Yes, there have been demurrals to Trump's vandalism (senators Sasse, Romney, Murkowski, Collins), but they are few and, soon enough, they're back in lockstep. Oddly for politicians, they seem not to know how to organize an insurrection. Instead, they purr: "Well-played."

Meanwhile: Democrats look at Republican accrual of power, ill-gotten as it definitely is, and their former colleagues' complicity with a proto-autocrat and say: *"Oh. My. God."* (This, from the supposedly unchurched, vice the church-going Republican hypocrites.)

Like Hamlet, Democrats know a hawk from a handsaw: Where Republicans see legitimate plays for power, Democrats see the tarnishing of institutional guardrails, then the desecration of those guardrails knocked off altogether. For one: An Attorney General, putatively the chief arbiter of Justice and the people's tribune, changed out for a wax figure who himself molds Justice to suit his client's anti-democratic demands. For another: The U.S. military co-opted into appearing ready to take action against its own citizens assembled in peaceful protest (the George Floyd protest in Lafayette Square). The military immediately corrected that misimpression, but: Trump did not. There again, with Trump and his Republicans, "the readiness is all," to quote Hamlet again.

The desecration goes on. As the party that believes in government's capacity to do good, Democrats see Trump's abject failure to organize the federal response to the deadly coronavirus pandemic—with the death toll now nearing a *quarter of a million* American souls (220,200) and the collapse of the American economy, whose price-tag experts now peg at $16 *trillion*—as abject executive malpractice, a crime against American humanity. (Modern-day Republicans have never believed in government and, despite these ruinous numbers, still don't.)

As the party that believes in the liberal world order, with its rules-based organization and alliances, Democrats look at the damage Trump has inflicted on that order and our allies as an unconscionable and irresponsible exercise of the superpower's power. (Once upon a time, the Republicans believed in America's leadership role in the world.)

As the party of human rights, Democrats are appalled at our government's silence at foreign powers' abuse of those rights—Saudi Arabia's murder and dismemberment of dissident journalist Jamal Khashoggi and China's brutal clampdown of Hong Kong's democracy movement, the incarceration of its Muslim Uighur population in concentration camps, its surveillance state. But then, Trump can't discomfit his autocrat pals.

All this desecration on the part of Trump and Republicans of our foundational institutions and norms of American democracy—and the resacralization, as it were, of this patrimony on the Democrats' part—raises the question: Who *really* are the conservatives here? The Democrats are now liberal *and* the true conservative both.

Republicans see this desecration and conclude it is bearable, the cost of doing (political) business. But Democrats—both leadership and grassroots—see the desecration and understand the cost is *not* acceptable, *not* to be borne. Democrats see the *existential*—that is, life-and-death—stakes of this election: It is, in sum, *to rescue our democracy.*

Democrats understand we cannot have a democracy—government of, by, and for the people, the *demos*; in a word, self-government—that does not abide by Truth and Justice, that countenances violence and corruption, that blatantly abuses power for mere political gain and at the expense of, indeed destruction of, the Republic. (And Republicans arguing America is not a democracy but a republic is no defense.)

Democrats understand something else existential: With so much of American life in flux—racial unrest at injustice, women calling out discrimination, the income gap growing even starker due to the pandemic—Democrats see the opportunity to take these crises and make of them a better day. We are talking not only of rescue, but reform, Renaissance.

That is why we are seeing massive early voting going on, with long, socially-distanced lines of voters willing to wait for five, even ten hours in order to make their voice heard with their vote. That is why we see Democrats, who in this pandemic have been shown far more observant of masking and other official guidance than Republicans, abandoning their shelters and braving the aerosolized coronavirus to personally ensure their vote gets cast, sidestepping the U.S. Postal Service that Trump scurrilously tried to disable. And, excitingly, that is why this election is on track to see the biggest voter turnout in modern history: Democrats "get" the life-and-death stakes of this 2020 election.

And Democrats get that a landslide for Joe Biden is *the* best weapon against Trump's armed militias.

If the once-Exceptional Nation can turn existential peril into Renaissance, we will be exceptional again. We get there via one path and one path only: Vote.

—*Medium*, October 19, 2020

Are We Producing More History Than We Can Consume...?

AMERICAN DEMOCRACY TILTING *toward strongman rule! A deadly pandemic entering its third wave—more people dying, more jobs lost, more businesses going under, the price-tag now $16 trillion! Black Americans marching, insisting their lives matter; women insisting the same! Wildfires burning in the West, hurricanes churning in the East, both at historic rates, heralding climate change is here, with denialists still denying—*
   Hel-l-l-l-p....
   "Monkeys in treetops." That's how Franz Kafka described his racing mind: Like monkeys in treetops, leaping from limb to limb, screeching—and making no sense at all to the owner of the tree. Minds—my own and very likely yours too—have *very* good reason to race these days. While "monkeys in treetops" might be a clinical description of madness (Kafka was not diagnosed mad but he was depressive), the very good reason our minds race (I sincerely hope) is because of information-overload—emphasis: overload.
   "We live in ridiculously eventful times. Love, Carla" was how I signed off a recent email with an old friend. She worries people cannot even think anymore, events are breaking so fast. With other friends who commend me for keeping up my pace as commentator, I write back, "There's no end of material—ha! It's like trying to drink from a fire-hose." But I confess: Yours Truly can just b-a-r-e-l-y track events, much less suss out meaning.

Winston Churchill said of the Balkans, once the world's tinderbox: They "produce more history than they can consume." Production of event, of history, is one thing; consuming it—making sense of it—is the tricky part. Which of late has gotten even trickier, thanks to—beware single-factor thinking—Donald Trump, who is a tinderbox of his own nefarious kind.

It is fair to say—trying to be fair and balanced, though the man doesn't do either himself—Donald Trump *is* the single factor behind America's authoritarian drift (it still stuns me to write that: authoritarian drift?). And while he is not responsible for the pandemic, he *is* responsible for a colossally incompetent response to it, causing, it is also fair to say, unnecessary death and ruination. As for the mattering of Black lives and women's lives, Trump's explicit racism and sexism give voice to powerful reactionary forces once underground in American life and thrusts them center-stage.

And speaking of stages: How about that first "presidential" debate? Trump bullying, interrupting, acting out like a two-year-old (which is an insult to two-year-olds). I could not watch it, I could only listen, working crossword puzzles to kill time (though, as writer Raymond Chandler joked, "Time died hard"). To prevent tonight's debate from descending again to verbal bumper-cars, microphones can be muted—which speaks volumes about the abject state of our Trump-devolved politics.

All this spectacle—this history being produced—is, as the conscientious observer senses, not benign, it is not mere spectacle. There is danger here. Tinderboxes are volatile, explosive. We sense that our way of life, our magnificent American experiment in democracy, stands to be altered, and altered beyond recognition, even destroyed. No wonder Americans report records levels of insomnia. Republicans mock Democrats for "Trump Derangement Syndrome," but they should look at themselves and their once-professed ethos they have tossed aside: Who's deranged?

How to consume this history, how to make sense of it?

Of course—of course!—the *very* best way to consume this history is to put it to its *very* best possible use, thus producing a better day: That is, turn Donald Trump, and his Republican accomplices, out of office, by voting on Nov. 3. Make yourself feel even better by voting early.

But until then? And after? How do we consume the history to come, which promises to be no less turbulent, no less confusing? And what if, God forbid, Trump is re-elected? How do we consume that (apart from renewing our passports)?

For myself, as a commentator, I work hard at getting perspective on the matter at hand. What is the best route, the best lens, to gain it: Is it political, cultural, literary, psychological, philosophical, metaphorical, mythical, or, speaking of history, historical? (And speaking of two-year-olds, the infantile must factor in: An international relations major, I think often of my professor who maintained that, as conceptual framework, children fighting in a sandbox explains a lot about international relations, and I'd add domestic politics, too.) To gain perspective, my instinct is to step *way* back; recurring to my training as a playwright, I visualize myself sitting in the top row of an ancient amphitheater, watching the action onstage and asking, *What* is going on here? What are the motive, and emotive, forces at play?

And, crucially, what does it all *mean?* This is harder to do, and more fraught, because the cost of coursing down the wrong track to a wrong conclusion—the wrong conviction—is, as we all feel it these days, dangerous. Friends note there are more ellipses (....) in my emails of late; I finally realized those ellipses indicate that, while I may have named the problem, the meaning of it all is yet to be nailed. About this meaning, these friends of late are repeating themselves: "I don't know, I don't know, I don't know." Meanwhile, Republicans express no doubt at all about knowing the meaning of it all—the prize (and price) for ideological capture. For myself as commentator, once I feel sure—O.K., pretty sure—that I've nailed the meaning, I jump off the cliff and post it, praying I am not Icarus-of-the-wax-wings and have built a craft sturdy enough to fly *and* land.

Of course, the moment I land—the moment anyone venturing a

notion about the meaning of the present historical moment finally lands—the landscape is bound to alter again. That's why they call it tumult.

History may well serve up more tumult for America—especially if Donald Trump is re-elected. Even if the Biden-Harris ticket prevails (which I believe it will), there will be years and years of repair work, tumult. To the extent Americans think of History, we see ourselves as its shaper, not its plaything. Perhaps it's this aspect of this moment, when we feel overwhelmed by History's production, that confounds us most. But I hope we recognize we ourselves produced this tumultuous history—by electing a disrupter with no follow-up plan. I suspect my fellow Americans have been pondering History a lot of late.

As for those monkeys in treetops, the psychological cacophony of History's overload: Do the practical American thing and give them something to do. Like yardwork.

—*Medium*, October 22, 2020

Nothing Works—and Everything Matters Profoundly

"NOTHING WORKS AND nothing matters." This idea seems to auto-complete much that is in the atmosphere at this fraught moment. It is a kind of nihilism that has afflicted Democrats ever since the ascension of Donald Trump. "Nothing works and nothing matters."

But: Is it just my eyes that tear up when I think of our wounded country? Despite things not working on so many levels, it matters *mightily*—not just to me but, I venture, to masses more. Rather than feeling numb or truly nihilistic, masses of Americans have never cared *more* deeply or agonized *more* anxiously about the outcome of a presidential election than the one nine days away. "Nothing works—and everything matters profoundly."

The "Nothing works" idea signifies in two ways. One is the mechanical, the functional. Most notable example: the dysfunctional federal response to the pandemic, now claiming 225,000 American lives—*a quarter-million*—with this week seeing the highest daily infection rate yet—almost 83,000; worse is to come with winter. Bollix is due to an incompetent president, but also to fellow citizens refusing to mask up.

Another mechanical example: our voting "system"—pardon the scare-quotes, but we hardly have a system in the true sense. Instead, we have a fractionated network of vote-gathering that differs by state and county; in Republican-controlled states, the emphasis is on vote-*disallowing*. Add now the complication of the pandemic when mail-in ballots must be an option, an option Trump slams as fraudulent, and who has 100% faith in this "system"? If the count is close, there will be a legal fight, there may even be blood.

The other way "Nothing works" signifies is the moral and, again, it relates to Trump: how, no matter how egregious, salacious, or outright illegal an act he commits, nothing sticks to him—from the Access Hollywood tape in 2016 in which he brags of groping women and which would end the campaign of any other politician through a cornucopia of misdeeds and malfeasance too abundant to itemize. The point is: Nothing sticks to Trump, thanks to his devout base.

This is when Democrats began muttering "Nothing works," in 2016, per *Washington Post* columnist Molly Roberts: "This bleak sense that Donald Trump could not be stopped became a refrain for battered progressives when he was first elected four years ago." (I'd add it's heard among moderates, too.) Now with the 2020 election pending, and "nary a dent" to Trump's popularity after *The New York Times*' bombshell showing his tax returns revealed him "a failure and possible fraud," Roberts saw this refrain "undergoing a worrisome revival": "Today, Democrats are in danger of making the same mistake: believing that 'nothing matters,' or feeling too silly to keep on screaming 'This is bad!' when voters across the country seem to delight in everything devilish the incumbent does." Quite rightly, Roberts calls this "Nothing matters" thinking "a trap," and says: "[W]hat matters really ought to be a question of *values* that we aren't yet ready to give up on."

Indeed a crescendo of "Nothing matters" commentary engulfs us.

Recurring to the moral realm, writing how "everything happens and nothing matters," *The New Yorker*'s Susan Glasser ends with: "Through impeachment and scandal and now pandemic and recession, a more or less straight line of roughly forty per cent of Americans have supported the President, no matter what.... Previous Presidents—all of them—saw their ratings go up and down depending...on their performance in office. Not Trump. He appears to be living a politician's dream: *a Presidency free of consequence and devoid of accountability*" [my italics]. As for the mechanical, in "The Election That Could Break America," *The Atlantic*'s Barton Gellman drills down into our election "system," showing how all manner of legislative legerdemain by the GOP could skew the final count and throw the entire election into question.

By no means is this to say these writers are unduly dark; after all, they are describing objective reality. But it is to say: Dour as the picture is, it does not follow that "Nothing matters." I see the front page of *The New York Times*' "Sunday Review" section for Oct. 18, consisting solely of the words "Corruption. ANGER. Chaos. INCOMPETENCE. Lies. DECAY" [sic: capitalization]—and my caring reaches an even deeper profundity.

And—happy objective reality: Millions of other Americans feel the same, witness *the massive turnout in early voting*. As of this posting, almost 59 million voters have already voted—with about 40 million voting via mail-in ballots and another 19 million standing in line, sometimes for hours, to vote in person, and doing so while braving infection by the coronavirus. This turnout, recorded daily by the U.S. Elections Project, is, per *Vox*, "on pace to be the highest in a century."

What accounts for this outpouring? Profoundest caring. The American voter gets it: We see "Nothing works" and, rather than collapse and auto-complete to "Nothing matters," we are moved by our love for America—a beautiful idea we see in mortal danger—to declare, "Everything matters profoundly"; thus, we are voting. In this way, we say not only do we want a country that works again, like America historically worked. We want also to reckon *finally* with racial and sexual injustice, income inequality, climate change. Best way to do that is with a landslide for normalcy and sanity, the Biden-Harris ticket.

Are we writing a new script? In Western Civilization, "Nothing works" auto-completes to tragedy—ancient Greek tragedy, Shakespearean tragedy, Modernism's *Waiting for Godot*. We are going after Godot. In everyday life, saying we're going after Godot auto-completes to optimism. But with America now "going to school with suffering," optimists are a vanishing breed. Something more real is coming into being. Americans have lost their easy smile, but an earned one is coming instead. Bless our hearts!

—*Medium*, October 25, 2020

"Shut Up, Hamlet, and Drive":
Appeal for an Essential Art

I.

REMEMBER THIS MOMENT, my fellow Americans. Remember this dire moment, fraught as any we have known in our lifetime, when, nearing the 2020 presidential election, we want—no, we *yearn with all our hearts for*—the exact opposite qualities of those possessed by the current occupant of the White House, Donald J. Trump.

Remember this profound yearning of (we hope) a big majority of the American people for the higher, *essential* qualities—character, honesty, responsibility, courage, decency, dignity, intelligence, empathy, prudence, moral purpose. And remember the things we profoundly yearn for, achieved only with these qualities: the essential things that once were capitalized—Truth, Justice, Honor, Trust, Reputation, the Soul.

Consider America's ruination, the falling-off, our nadir as a democracy. Astonishingly, in just four years, Trump has reduced the world's sole superpower to a near-failed state now scorned, dismissed, even pitied. How did he do this? By acting out the musclebound brat, compelled by nothing more than egoistic want and whim. By heedlessly disrupting a rules-based international order. By his catastrophic handling of the coronavirus pandemic, scorning science and reason, going with his gut, even when he himself was stricken. By his rushed reopening of the economy, more concerned with market performance than the death and suffering he has inflicted on the American people. By refusing to say he will abide by the election's results, threatening violence to keep his power.

Again, in this dire moment, remember our yearning—for the essential qualities, essential things.

II.

In truth, however—and here is the disconnect: We have not expressed much need for these essential qualities or things for a long, long time. Instead of essential need, we have merely wanted. And we wanted the near and immediate: to scratch the itch of ego, to rebel without a cause against any rules, to go with the visceral and fie on the intellect, to amass the market's wealth and fie on humanity. In other words, *our wants have produced the President we now abhor.* Donald Trump is as much a product of our (degraded) culture as our politics. Add to that, we wanted to "walk on the wild side," whether it was the law, sex, whatever. Childishly, though, we wanted this walk to come without consequences: "Sow the wild oats and hope for crop failure." Trump checks those boxes, too. He hits what I call the omnifecta of disaster.

Perhaps the greatest damage we did ourselves was to loosen allegiance to a moral code. I speak of the post-World War II generation, the boomers, of which I am one. Unsure how to handle our inheritance of absolute freedom, with some rebelling against parents seen as hypocritical, boomers ditched the code and pursued personal dreams. Meanwhile, we were also expected to "save the world," as our parents did, though how you do that without a moral code, we did not work out. Since the sandbox, we learned from peers (the big majority ultimately) that to raise a moral point was to be "judgmental" and thus a "party-pooper." Stigmatizing was done with laughs, though; and I'd laugh back, "There

will come a day...." That day has come, it seems.
What has an "anything-goes" ethos wrought in Art? In the main—
select gems notwithstanding—not much that can console or instruct,
much less entertain us, in our nadir-cum-pandemic when we yearn for
what Virgil called "the upper air." The theme? The unspeakable made
speakable, safe. Literature has echoed with the unspeakable act Philip
Roth's anti-hero committed with a piece of liver, in his 1969 novel *Portnoy's Complaint*. A more heinously unspeakable taboo was broken with
Truman Capote's 1965 *In Cold Blood*, a deep-dive look into the killer's
heart. Later Nicholson Baker hogged the spotlight with his novel about
phone sex, *Vox*. In film, *Last Tango in Paris*, a "breakthrough," featured
an unspeakable act with butter; *Wall Street* gave the green light to greed.
In TV, "Breaking Bad" states it for "in the main," not only in TV but
for all the arts. In theater, David Mamet ruled with angry and profane
dramas; Eve Ensler broke through with *The Vagina Monologues*. (Toiling
as a playwright at the time, on 9/11 I bailed for the upper air of commentary.) In art, the portrait of humanity has become...pretty ugly ("Piss
Christ"?). All these works, representative of their genre, were hailed by
critics for being "transgressive." But: *How* can "transgressive" ever leave
us anything but depleted, ever produce anything higher, *essential*? That
was not worked out, either. Making it harder and harder to ask was the
steady backbeat of "dumb and dumber" and "wild and crazy" and porn.

Looking back, we see the falling-off, the degradation degree by degree from a Golden Age—the age of Faulkner, Hemingway, Fitzgerald,
Steinbeck, Wharton, Cather, *Their Eyes Were Watching God, All the
King's Men, Casablanca, The Best Years of Our Lives, Our Town, Death
of a Salesman*—all tarnished to the present age of brass. Yes, there have
been important moral voices in this age, preeminently Martin Luther
King, Jr. and James Baldwin; important social breakthroughs, preeminently the civil rights movement; and cultural gems—*A Raisin in the
Sun, Angels in America, The Moviegoer, Woman Warrior, Gilead, Lincoln
in the Bardo, Lincoln, Hamilton, Spotlight*. But they were islands, surrounded—in the main—by the lesser.

Some will quibble with this theory, some will argue vehemently against it, others will cite other cultural favorites (I prefer works of some moral import). But: It is hard to argue that we are not in a brass age, both politically and culturally—see again: Donald Trump. Of course it is human to want to "break bad," and I am human, but I would betray my best self to "go there," so I don't, I can't. Peddling my morality plays to theaters, I got terrific rejections, first acknowledging my script as "something of value," but, alas, "not our cup of tea." Their cup? Time after time, *The Vagina Monologues*, which a *New York Times* theater critic called "probably the most important piece of political theater in the last decade." But: Just how "important" is it now, in our nadir, in our suffering? And, in our descent, how many moral artists have we lost?

In America, the lesser—the transgressive, the wild and crazy—took over by default, in lieu of a moral sensibility. In this, America is no different from other once-great powers—Greece, Rome—ultimately weakened by their abuse of that greatness and power, by decadence. Writing in the 18th century, English poet Alexander Pope traced the problem: "In the fat Age of Pleasure, Wealth, and Ease / Sprung the rank Weed, and thriv'd with large Increase." The rank weeds have taken over.

And yet: In our suffering—over a quarter-million fellow Americans have been lost to the virus, we hear our world-beating economy crashing around us, race relations long festering demand a final reckoning—there is rising in us the yearning for a New Day. Rank weeds cannot sustain; binge-watching "Breaking Bad" will not elevate; indeed a "Breaking Bad" culture got us Trump. But where to look—not only for sustenance, but for a map? How can America avert Tragedy?

III.

For sustenance, we can look to the world's great storehouses of Civilization. Being of the West, my touchstones are Western, but I am open. I just have to think of those touchstones and I am comforted, refreshed—the music of Bach, Beethoven, Brahms, Ravel; the ineffable drawings of Holbein; the paintings of Van Gogh, Rembrandt, Vermeer, da Vinci, Raphael, Goya, El Greco, Manet, Matisse; the novels of Austen, Eliot, Dickens, Woolf, Tolstoy; the moral philosophy of Camus; the tonic essays of Orwell; the poetry of Yeats and Auden; the social dramas of Ibsen, the plays and stories of Chekhov, and of course the plays and poetry of Shakespeare. Getting me through a pandemic as he has enabled me to live with cancer is the Stoic, Marcus Aurelius: "Reject your sense of injury." (It is good to learn that Shakespeare wrote *King Lear* during a plague and, rereading Camus' *The Plague*, that the plague eventually did die out.)

But: As for a map—a precedent for how a great nation, the world's oldest experiment in democracy, can undo its ongoing death throes and work its way through insidious plague, insidious leadership, economic collapse, and reckonings of all kinds, all to save itself—is there such a map, a precedent? No, there is not, neither in History nor Art. Western Civilization, like all others in the world, tells us such a grand recovery project cannot work out, that Tragedy is the end not only of all human life—death—but all human endeavor; thus "the tears in things," as Virgil wrote. The ancient Greek dramas are all tragedies—tales of hubris, revenge, blinding anger, killing ambition, moral blindness. Likewise the tragedies of Shakespeare, for like motive: hubris, revenge, blinding anger, killing ambition, moral blindness. The Moderns tell us much the same, with anti-heroes "acting" without much belief. Even the peerless Shakespeare held politics to be corrupting (see especially: *Coriolanus*), which is no help for us wedded to a form of government whose definitive feature and motor is self-governance—of, by, and for the *demos*. And Shakespeare's greatest hero, Hamlet: Faced with the question of how to avenge the murder of his father the king by his uncle and how to restore order, he ruminated and ruminated.

Conscientious Americans will note a theme here: *Can* we press through to a New Day? To the end, Don Quixote tilted at windmills; must we? In Camus' *The Plague*, as the plague lifted, there was talk of creating "a new order of things," but, returning to their old life, people forgot about it; must we? The ancients say we must, so does Shakespeare. America may indeed be doomed, Tragedy may indeed be our Fate, but still, the American heart cannot countenance it....

Dammit: This American heart says No! After the Dark Ages, came the Renaissance. Shut up, Hamlet, and drive.

IV.

We can look to ourselves, I think. In suffering comes wisdom, insight, a vision of what could be "if only." We need to get from "if only" to "Glory hallelujah, it is." Of course that is infinitely easier said than done, but the saying is needed—and not much heard right now—and the doing *is* possible. While the Can-Do Nation has been revealed, with Trump's calamitous handling of the pandemic, as can't-do, to our universal humiliation, this need not write The End to the American story; we *can* do, still—and in fact *are*. That The End is even a possibility, and that we realize The End is a possibility, reflects a sobering of the American spirit—a good thing in and of itself.

In sum: We need to become heroes again. We need to take our sobered American spirit and *act*.

We have, swirling around us, a "sea of troubles," a superabundance of them. How to proceed in this maelstrom of crises? All-out and nonstop. Some of our crises—racial reckoning, sexual reckoning. income inequality—stem from problems long with us that, History's timing being unaccountable, are all now at a culmination point, demanding settlement. Other crises—a proto-autocratic President threatening violence to go full autocrat, a deadly pandemic—are, like the coronavirus, novel, but they are likewise a culmination of less-visible weaknesses in our system that we must repair. With the latter: Our disgust at our proto-autocratic President reminds us how precious our democracy is and how invaluable our tools to keep it—the vote (we must turn out a massive turnout), the protest (we must keep all protest nonviolent). And our disgust at our anti-science President's handling of the pandemic can convert, like a scientific experiment, to restoration of the actual Renaissance's ideals of science, reason, proof—advance.

Heroes need a moral compass—and our long-boiling crises of racial and sexual reckoning are manifesting an army of such heroes working such compass. Racial reckoning is being pressed by courageous souls, Black and white, acting on the searing evidence of far too many Black Americans killed by white police officers. Let us salute those heroes who, refusing to suffer any longer in their minds "the slings and arrows of outrageous fortune," are taking action against that particular "sea of troubles"—white supremacy—"and" (let us fervently hope) *"by opposing end them."* Making the moral argument against white supremacy's illegitimate and killing and self-destructive dominion will take heroes galore; Black Americans have long made the argument, now more white Americans must. Likewise, sexual reckoning: The searing evidence of the criminal behavior of some powerful males against women in their employ leaves no doubt about its moral depravity. Let us salute the women who take action against another "sea of troubles"—toxic masculinity—and wrestle their trauma to wage their case. These two vividly moral cases—talk about right and wrong!—are being litigated in the public square without, for the most part, specifically moral language, yet they are powerfully persuasive as is. In this, America could be said to be *backing* into a moral consciousness once again—it's the American way—bringing us to that upper air we need for the good fight.

The hero's Holy Grail? If we front all these crises and battle them to settlement—it will take longer than this election cycle, it will take years of repair—we can build back an America that is fairer, smarter, deeper, better. Americans are not natural philosophers, but most of us understand America as an *idea*, moreover as the *ideal* of that idea—equality, fair play, rule of law, second chances, fill in your own small-d democratic blank. But: In reality America has never achieved these ideals, not really, not for everybody. Our present crises show how violently out of whack from them we are. If we slay our various dragons—all self-created or self-exacerbated—America will get to a Renaissance. In our heroic and historic endeavor, we have historic props, and then some. The great American poet Emily Dickinson argued with God, reclusively but bravely. Ralph Waldo Emerson, great Transcendental essayist, argued with himself about basic things, although we might argue with Emerson about his severe individualism: In this pandemic, mask-defying individualists are killing the rest of us. Walt Whitman argued that the human being contains "multitudes" and, thus, contains contradictions: If we contradict ourselves in this moment—disabling the prevailing anti-heroic culture to build back better—so be it. To address the turbo-capitalism that produces income inequality now reaching obscene levels, we need legions of Edith Whartons, a writer who bravely analyzed her own upper class and rendered its tragedies not as satire but as serious fiction (*The House of Mirth*). Above all, this endeavor of rescuing American democracy will require "soft humanity" to muscle up: Herman Melville, in *Moby-Dick*, characterized First Mate Starbuck as soft, unable even to imagine organizing a mutiny against the mad Captain Ahab. We need to imagine, to organize. (Republicans: This includes you. See also: Goethe's *Faust*.)

V.

Why is this important? Even today, the very idea of capital-A Art makes Americans' teeth itch, so why this talk of Art? Because: It is *vital*—life-and-death vital—the stories we tell ourselves and the stories our artists tell us. And, of course, Art *will* have the last word. From earliest human history, Art in the form of pictographs on the walls of caves and tombs told humanity's story. In my mind's eye I see an ancient amphitheater where, onstage, the American story is playing out. What will be Art's last word about America as idea and ideal, about us as actors?

If we keep going with the "anything-goes" ethos—the once-unspeakable rendered safe and now normalized, the wild and crazy made even wilder and crazier, the dumb and dumber going for dumbest, the pornographic and profane polluting even more—we will run ourselves deep into the ground, become a socio-cultural hot mess; we will be wreckage. And signposts tell us that ethos still dominates. Memoirs of addiction and alcoholism, neuroses and excess, continue to tumble forth. The arts pages of our newspaper of record, *The New York Times*, carrying on while the arts establishment has shut down because of the virus, reflect a surprisingly scanty vault with which to nourish us. Likewise *Slate*, which ran the headlines, "The only show nihilistic enough for America" and "The second-dirtiest song to reach №1." Burlesque versions of *Alice in Wonderland* and *The Nutcracker* are on offer. Recently I watched a streamed reading of Moliere's *Tartuffe* in which Tartuffe (wait for it) mooned the viewer—unfunny anytime, but in a pandemic-cum-existential-crisis, *yech*. Such "artists" seem not to understand—at all—the existential crisis America is in. But with their tight-tight narcissistic focus, how can they possibly see the bigger picture, the dark clouds gathered? Recently *The New Yorker* usefully asked, "Has Self-Awareness Gone Too Far in Fiction?" I believe it has, and not only in fiction. Narcissism's root is *narke*—stupor. That stupor was cast on Narcissus by...Nemesis.

In sum: We need a new Art, an Art of the *essential*—to reflect the heroes now at work, to reflect America's reawakening in this dire moment to qualities and things that are higher, *essential*.

But: We have been at this moment of reawakening before, and not that long ago. In the shock of September 11, 2001, when foreign terrorists struck at the American homeland in horrific and historic fashion, supposedly "everything changed," supposedly a New Day was heralded. Irony supposedly died, Mozart's Requiem was heard everywhere, we were nicer to each other, we even got philosophical. But within months, the "anything-goes" ethos was back, even edgier than before. Thus we failed—we did not even recognize—the moral test of Abu Ghraib, when America descended to torture, in Iraq in 2004. Where were the designated humanists—the artists—protesting the abject human depredation of torture? To quote myself at the time: "That many artists peddle edgy anti-human product may explain their silence: One can't create kink *and* protest it." The public, too, missed the cue and made a massive bestseller of an erotic novel featuring torture, playing at it—*Fifty Shades of Grey*. Fifty shades of shame.

Will the present reawakening—fueled by a superabundance of a "sea of troubles"—be different?

To get to a New Day, Hamlet is not the hero we need. It hurts to write these words, because I have loved *Hamlet* all my life and embraced the Danish prince as the great pre-modern hero, the one who defines self-consciousness; I have felt at one with him as he thought and thought about *everything*. I still thrill to his soliloquys, the most beautiful in all Literature, that capture so precisely Life's richness, its unfolding—"What a piece of work is man," "How all occasions do inform against me, and spur my dull revenge," and, of course, "To be or not to be." And yet: Hamlet makes a bloody hash of things; he does not act wisely, neither for the greater good or even for himself, his prime objective. Instead of killing Claudius, Hamlet might have organized his overthrow, planned for an enlightened reign. He so mistreats Ophelia that she kills herself (toxic masculinity?). He fakes madness. And, crucially, he does not give much thought to the people his house rules. For all his nuanced and thrilling thinking, his ultimate action is a colossal misfire. Carnage everywhere.

I realize I am treading deep into blasphemy in questioning the utility of Hamlet as hero. And I realize I am treading deep, deep into The Absurd in suggesting that, in Western culture, we are playing by the wrong playbook, the playbook of Tragedy. But: Is it not the case that, in this moment fraught as any in our history, with American democracy in peril of dying, we not only yearn for the exact opposite qualities and things exemplified by the current occupant of the White House, but we want, with all our hearts, to save the burning house of American democracy, to rescue it from annihilation? To mix metaphors (so I contradict myself): We need to rebuild and repurpose this mammoth aircraft *while it is in flight*, which should take care of any mundane requirement for excitement and entertainment, as will the understanding we are poised on a hinge point in our history, hinge points being inherently dramatic. Yes, this heroic rescue operation defies the rules of Tragedy, all Civilization, but then, defiant determination is also the American way, as is reinvention. This is not a nationalist argument ("USA! USA!"), but is, again, idealist, as most Americans are: The ideal and the idea of America are too beautiful to let die—and they *will* die if we don't rescue them.

This historic rescue operation is already underway—heroes are already waging reckonings, the conscientious public has already reached catharsis. Catharsis conventionally is seen as purgation of emotion, but it is deeper: It is the moment at the climax when a character recognizes, finally, what he/she did not recognize before. Long ago, before I bailed from theater, in response to a director who reminded me that, in theatre, "We give the audience what it wants," I said we had to do better: to give the audience what it needed but did not know it needed. Now the audience—the conscientious American public—*knows*. We know, from deep-down, what we *need*. It took four years of a madman's chaos and depredation to teach us, but now we know: We *need* the essential qualities of character, honesty, responsibility, courage, decency, dignity, intelligence, empathy, prudence, moral purpose, and we *need* the things that properly are capitalized: Truth, Justice, Honor, Trust, Reputation, the Soul. In the "anything-goes" ethos, these elements were mocked, dismissed (prudence, anyone?). Exit: "Anything-goes." Enter: The Essential.

How brilliant, how original, how nation-saving, if we put our catharsis—the knowledge of our ultimate need for the essential—to a saving use, rather than succumb to classic Tragedy's tragic ending. To do so we need an Art, and artists, telling us stories diametrically opposed, not only to classic Tragedy, but to the Modern or Post-modern ethos. For one thing, redefining humanity upward, where our yearning yearns, not downward to pathology or dysfunction. Enough with "breaking bad"; it is, literally, a dead end. For another, we need an Art that recognizes once again the hero, recognizes the heroes now battling away; enough with the anti-hero. These heroes battle on behalf of the common good, beyond ego or individual exploit. And this new essential Art must recognize these heroic ranks can include women and all people of color, not just the white male variant. We need an essential Art that looks at the age-old conventions and archetypes and story-lines that have led us to the very brink of Tragedy. For one, the fascination with the trickster, Melville's *Confidence-Man*, whose apotheosis is Donald Trump. (Melville's subtitle is *His Masquerade*.) In this essential Art we need critics to get over their fascination with the "transgressive," the "bent" and "twisted"; who understand with Melville's Father Mapple in *Moby-Dick* that: "In this world, shipmates, sin that pays its way can travel freely, and without a passport; whereas Virtue, if a pauper, is stopped at all frontiers." Can critics give Virtue a break? Can they start taxing vice? Applauding vice merely pushes at an open door which "soft humanity" itself can't help pushing. And can critics retire the tiresome convention, regnant since John Milton's *Paradise Lost*, that the Devil has all the good lines? This Devil in the White House is *boring*—dangerous but boring. Raising the moral point, *the* ultimate point, and pursuing it, is the infinitely harder task, the harder toil. Clearly, we must learn how.

If we can pull off this Renaissance—and we can do this, Americans are not fatalists, not yet, not even in this supremely fraught moment—we will have matured as a nation, as a culture. And once we have matured, we will have a new challenge: How better to handle our power, individually and as a nation, which power again we have abused to our present downfall, which power we have never tutored ourselves how to handle; but that is for another day, another appeal. And if a matured America can pull off this Renaissance, we will have expanded Art beyond the age-old categories of Tragedy and Comedy—to what? We can work that out later.

For now, my fellow Americans, what will it be: Wreckage—or Renaissance?

—*Medium*, October 27, 2020

Build Back Better with Biden—for a Fairer, Smarter, Greener, Deeper America

"BUILD BACK BETTER" is the 2020 campaign theme for rebuilding the economy, put forth by Democratic presidential nominee Joe Biden. But building back better—or building *forward* better, if you wish—is a good and feasible theme in general, as Americans approach Election Day and think beyond it, to the monumental repair job necessary in a post-Donald Trump future.

The following message, then, is for any independent or undecided voter out there—can there possibly be any left at this frenzied point?—to urge a vote for the Biden-Harris ticket. This is also to outline the repair job in store and how, with seemingly every element of American life flying up in the air, a vote for the Biden-Harris ticket is a vote for the sane and humane reassembling of American life.

A FAIRER AMERICA. Notably, with his selection of U.S. Sen. Kamala Harris, a woman of Black and Indian descent who served as California's Attorney General, Biden commits himself to a reckoning on race relations—*the* problem bedeviling this nation since the benighted days of slavery, America's Original Sin. With the hideous killing of George Floyd, a Black man, by a white police officer, which hideousness caught on tape stunned the world; with the most massive protests in American history arising in reaction, of Black and white Americans marching together; and with Biden declaring, "We are a nation furious at injustice"—we are a nation primed to reckon. A Biden-Harris administration, especially if it wins with big numbers and has a big mandate, will be in position to move the keystone into place and make our foundational claim to full equality, finally, a reality.

What this means: It means White America will face more competition—in the workplace, in society; it means surrendering the entitlement and privilege we have exercised for so long. It means unlocking the talents and gifts of all Americans of color—in the workplace, in society; it means their fuller experience of life, liberty, the Soul. All of which means America herself will benefit—from a newly energized populace and spirit.

A SMARTER AMERICA. No, I am not claiming an edge in I.Q. for Democrats over Republicans. What I mean by "smarter" breaks out in four ways. One: By promoting a fairer America as described above, and benefiting from the unleashed intelligence and talents of all Americans, we will simply operate smarter. Two: Science and reason, not know-nothingism and fear, will be Biden's north star in corralling the pandemic, which corralling, he rightly believes, is imperative to fixing the economy. Three: With Democrats' belief in government's capacity to do good, democracy's institutional delivery-system will recover functionality. And, four: Freed from Republicans' blinding cant and ideology, we can recover things elemental to a functioning nation, things like… sanity, balance, hope, wit and wisdom, normalcy.

What this means: With these motive elements at the fore, America can compete better in the post-pandemic world, a world likely to be so altered that only the most nimble and original can compete, much less lead. Enough with attack and destroy, back to research and development, once America's forte. Enough with polarized kludge, on to better argument. Polarization of course will continue, it may even get worse, but Democrats at the helm will help.

A GREENER AMERICA. Biden's comprehensive climate plans—"The Biden Plan for a Clean Energy Revolution and Environmental Justice" and "The Biden Plan to Build a Modern, Sustainable Infrastructure and an Equitable Clean Energy Future"—ring even to the untutored ear (like mine) all the right notes for going forward in the 21st century. Biden pledges America to "lead the world" in shifting to planet-saving clean energy. He pledges environmental justice against polluters harming low-income communities and communities of color. His pledge to build a modern, sustainable infrastructure = jobs galore (specifically, union jobs). And this special pledge: "Fulfill our obligation to workers and communities who powered our industrial revolution and subsequent decades of economic growth"; meaning, no worker left behind. This $2 trillion investment plan will be paid for in part by rolling back the $1.5 trillion Trump tax incentives enriching corporations.

What this means: Pledging to be a "transitional" president, Biden will set America's train on the optimal track to the future, ensuring security *and* livelihoods for our children and grandchildren. And despite the tax to them (and polluting the world with their greed), corporations and Wall Street are warming to Biden's plans, per *The Wall Street Journal*, while *Politico* terms the Street "giddy." Wall Street sees profit, if not also patriotic duty.

A DEEPER AMERICA. With over a quarter-million American lives lost to the coronavirus, with our world-beating economy crashing and taking down businesses large and small and millions of jobs, and with climate change in the form of harsher wildfires, floods, and hurricanes making denial impossible, Americans, to quote Albert Camus in *The Plague*, are "going to school with suffering." While this hard reality has given rise to record levels of mental illness (depression, anxiety, insomnia), there is also on the rise something less quantifiable but of signal significance: a new seriousness and sobriety, a philosophical cast of mind not seen in America in these last "wild and crazy" decades. You see this new depth in our nominee Joe Biden, grown in the course of this campaign.

What this means: Philosophical maturation—of Biden at age 77, of America at age 244—bodes well for the long-view mentality needed for the post-Trump repair job ahead, from the revitalization of institutions and norms almost lost to the reanimation of lives rebirthed. It also bodes well for America's re-entry into the world—not as the arrogant bully Trump was, but as a colleague who recognizes the value of allies and alliances; who as a chastened super-power—who no doubt will remain a super-power—will handle power more wisely; who, as such, can hope to regain the world's trust. And it bodes well for learning the home lesson of our recent history: to never, ever allow strongman rule again.

Meanwhile, consider the Republican string of disasters just in the 21st century (and pardon the forthcoming strongly partisan note): There was George W. Bush, the Iraq war, our shameful descent to torture, the 2008 financial crash, the omnifecta of disaster known as Donald J. Trump, his calamitous handling of the pandemic, another crash. And in the preceding century there was of course Richard Nixon, whose Watergate scandal birthed the public's distrust in government. This dying party, the GOP, can ponder these things whilst deep in the political wilderness—and perhaps rebirth itself. (By the way: Why do polls still show greater faith in the GOP to handle the economy, when Republicans have crashed it twice just this century and Democrats have twice cleaned it up—with, as Fate would have it, Mr. Biden to lead the recovery both times?)

Build back better—for an America that's fairer, smarter, greener, deeper. Not a utopian plan, but a salvage operation, working with the resources at hand and with the genius of the American people. Thank you, Mr. Biden, not only for this map for repair, but for running a non-ideological *unity* campaign, vital to repairing something else—America's Soul.

Go, Biden-Harris! Go, Democratic House! And go, fingers crossed, Democratic Senate! Out of the Dark Ages, into the Renaissance.

—*Medium*, October 31, 2020

In a Plague-Time, Running for Elective Office: Personal Insights

Twelfth in an ongoing series, Notes from a Plague-Time

FIRST, THE GOOD news: The unexpected bonus of running for office in a plague-time? When you "dial for dollars," to ask for a donation, more often than not you *will* reach the person you're calling, because: "Sheltering in place," people are at home and they are answering their phones.

I start with this good news, because there will be more elections and, as epidemiologists tell us, there will be more pandemics. Keeping American democracy going through whatever comes at us in future is vital—and knowing there are actual benefits to running for office may enable you to raise your own hand, throw your own hat in the ring.

I report all this from close observation: My husband is running for County Executive. A Democrat, he is running against an incumbent, a Republican. The following is meant not as a testimonial to the virtues of my husband or Democrats, but as a candidate's guide to the circumstances of conducting a campaign during a pandemic. And I post this on Election Day, so as not to electioneer beforehand (and also while my husband and I can still hope for victory). Still, if you live in Pierce County, WA, and object to electioneering, stop reading now. (Washington state is 100% mail-in balloting, with the majority of ballots reported already mailed.)

Larry discovered this bonus connectivity with the voter immediately. Not only do people answer their phones in a pandemic, they are ready to talk, often at length, both about their issues as well as their insights gained from the pandemic. With the County Exec being in charge of pandemic management at the local level, these voter insights are invaluable (ex., need for coronavirus testing, parents' difficulties with homeschooling, etc.). As to connectivity, Larry has a basis of comparison, having served four terms in our state legislature, pre-pandemic, when he campaigned in person: He feels he has gleaned as much as if not more from his pandemic phoning than standing on people's doorsteps. As for dialing for dollars: One might expect that spigot to shut off entirely in a pandemic, but the dollars have kept flowing—an indicator of implicit faith in the economy recovering.

Of course, there are challenges to campaigning in a pandemic. The major one: getting your message out and reaching the voter, when the traditional in-person methods—meet-the-candidate events in people's homes, town halls, community conversations, debates—are no longer possible. However, I have been impressed how much of traditional in-person campaigning can migrate to online—and translate well, thanks to Zoom technology. Town halls, for one: Larry has convened town halls of up to 50–75 people logging on. As I pass his office, I can see a gallery of faces filling his computer screen. Again the connectivity remains: Judging by the sound of voices, these town halls are as lively as they were pre-pandemic. Same for debates: Close-ups on the candidates' faces bring the viewer closer.

Still, outreach is *the* challenge in a pandemic, and the bigger your electoral map, the more challenging it is. Our county is eight (8) times the size of the legislative district Larry represented; there are huge swaths of the county he knows he's not touched at all. Much depends, then, on the tech-savviness of your campaign team. Larry's team, young and tireless, is extremely so. (Being of retirement age, he says you haven't lived until you've been directed by your 20-year-old campaign manager in a TikTok video.) Texting turns out most cost-effective, as it is comparatively inexpensive *and* allows for voter feedback. Voters do feed back.

It is in a pandemic that the reality of a "news desert" becomes manifest: In too many areas in America, local newspapers have run dry of financing and shut down, leaving coverage of local campaigns scanty if not nonexistent. To his disappointment, Larry's many detailed position papers elicited little to no response from the press—*because the press is not much there anymore*. Even a matter as important as his discovery (thanks to a whistle-blower) of a local dam polluting the water went nowhere(!). This reality of news deserts should cause all conscientious Americans to ask: *What dogs are not barking?*

News deserts notwithstanding, some venues remain, and it helps to get editorial board endorsements. Larry did not get the endorsement of our major remaining news venue, in Tacoma, *The News Tribune*, which endorsed the incumbent. Our Democratic politician friends believe it was because the board, endorsing so many Democrats in our politically split county, felt the need to endorse at least one Republican, but who knows? In another sign of the times: Larry's young and tech-savvy campaign team, who get their news from digital sources, assures him endorsements from *newspapers* don't mean much anymore. Our main hope: Larry got 44% in the primary, ensuring continuing donations and other endorsements (unions, politicians, citizens, other County Execs). Historic Democratic turnout today would help.

Finally, I end with two other bonuses to running for elective office in a pandemic, which come under the general heading of ballast.

One: *the sheer nerve-saving benefit of keeping busy—staying engaged—during a time of fear and deadly danger.* Thus I chose, as throughout my "Plague-Time" series, the image of Doctor Plague, above, and not of my husband (still I await the wag saying, "That doesn't look like Larry at all"): Doctor Plague reminds that this pandemic is deadly (the U.S.

is entering its third surge), novel (the virus is mutating)—and likely to remain with us well into 2021. In this context, then, being engaged in something beyond fear and nerves is downright salvific. Our opportunity arose when Larry, over dinner, mentioned a Tacoma City Councilmember, "acting on behalf of" others, proposed that he, Larry, run. I, knowing full well the campaign experience (the late dinners), but also sensing salvation, instead of saying "Absolutely not," I said, "That's interesting, let's talk about it." Larry is at it, campaigning from early morn til late at night; I am at it, reading, writing commentary. As I tell friends, we are "crazy-busy," but we are contented.

Two, and related: *the necessity to live in the Realm of the Possible, to put out a positive message.* Even in the hyper-nasty politics of the Trump era, voters ultimately (we should hope) still respond to the constructive—solutions, not insults; analysis, not ideology; and especially in what seems unending calamity, a vision of a New Day. This positivity works both externally *and* internally: This household has no time (well, almost none) for lamentation or high dudgeon; instead, we brainstorm the issues together, then put out, to the public, messaging that accentuates the positive. This positivity is not Pollyanna, but Emerson: "fronting" the dire times—pandemic, hyper-nasty politics, possibly The End of American Democracy. Yes, we are tired, but not too; more, we feel grateful and full of purpose. It is why the pulse in this household during these dire times has remained steady-state. And while I have the occasional sleepless night, the Candidate sleeps deep.

So: When you get the call sounding you out about running for elective office, even in a plague-time—most especially in a plague-time, I'd say—vote Yes. You have *no* idea—and I mean that in *the* best possible way. As Teddy Roosevelt knew, there really is no place like being "in the arena."

—*Medium*, November 3, 2020

The American People Save American Democracy—Just Barely

AMERICAN DEMOCRACY, as much as any candidate, was on the ticket this 2020 presidential election. And the American people—bless them!—saved it. But just barely.

While Joe Biden will be our next President (thank God!), and Donald Trump will not (thank God!), the inescapable fact is: *Trumpism won big and is here to stay.* That is to say: *Anti-democracy.* And no countervailing "blue wave" rose up on Election Day to reckon with all of Trumpism's malignities.

So, we rejoice, after four long days of electoral counting. But our rejoicing is tempered.

After four long, harrowing years of a President (Donald Trump) who knocked off every guardrail of American Democracy, with the approach of Election Day and the chance to make *major course-correcting* change, any democracy-loving American had to hope post-election headlines would declare, with exclamation point: "American Democracy Saved by the American People!"

But the inescapable point instead is: Trumpism—law-manipulating, institution-abusing, norm-busting, ally-insulting, dictator-embracing anti-democracy—won big. How big? Nearly half—*nearly half*—of the American electorate voted for four more years of it: more Trumpism. Specifically: 70,356,821 at this moment—or *47.7% of the total vote.* We are a profoundly divided nation, alien to each other, near-ungovernable.

No doubt those voting for Trump favored him for more *personal* reasons—his scorning of "elites," his non-politician "telling it like it is," his handling of the economy pre-pandemic, his bad luck with a pandemic ("not his fault"), some projecting him as savior. But beyond the personal, there is stone-cold Reality: Four more years of anti-democratic Trumpism, wielded from the White House, was...unthinkable. Former Trump administration officials expressed fear that, if re-elected, Trump would be "unleashed" from all law, any remaining institutional constraints. Meaning: The proto-autocrat could go full autocrat—and destroy American Democracy. Because with Trump re-elected and unfettered, what was to stop him? What counter-force?

Happily—though to be sure, it is modulated happiness, it's more like relief—it is the *other* half of the American people who proved to be the "what" that stopped the proto-autocrat, to be that counter-force.

But—*and this is the fact tempering our rejoicing: These saviors—the true saviors here—constitute just barely a majority of the current electorate. And they—we—just barely saved our beloved democracy.* All hail to us—or rather, semi-hail.

It remains to be seen at this early juncture—watching the happy crowds celebrating Biden's victory, I see a sign in Biden's lettering saying "Bye Don!"—it remains to be seen how Trump's supporters react. Will there be violence, will there be blood? Such threats—infamously reinforced with Trump's signal to his armed militias "Stand back and stand by" in the first debate—remain real. Thank God, with Joe Biden, no more presidential sanctioning of armed militias! *This* thought brings home the horrors we have endured (and brings the tears): *With no more presidential sanctioning of armed militias, American Democracy is saved.*

No doubt Trump will keep screaming "Fraud" and keep seeking recourse with the law—which law, by the way, Trump otherwise disdained. Still: *Restoration of Rule of Law is another sign American Democracy is saved.* (*News flash:* Statement from President Donald J. Trump— "Beginning Monday, our campaign will start prosecuting our case in court to ensure election laws are fully upheld and the rightful winner is seated.") And between now and the 10 weeks until Inauguration Day, national security experts worry Trump may exercise "emergency authorities." Will he? Of course he will, but what?

Happily, the American people will now stand a better chance against the coronavirus with a President who believes in science and in government's capacity to do good. (*News flash*: President-elect Biden is to announce Monday a task force on the virus, signaling corralling it is Priority №1.)

Amidst our celebrations—again, modified fireworks—Democrats have lots to think about, now and during the coming Biden presidency: *Why the HUGE, nearly victorious vote for Trumpism?* How to bring back to the fold all those millions of working-class Trumpists who once were Democrats? Realigning the party to its working-class roots and away from the moneyed interests of the Clinton era is key. Also: Given that Trumpists were O.K. with Trump's racism, and given there will be no grand reckoning absent a blue wave, how to make the case that racial inclusiveness redounds to the interests of both White America and America herself?

But those are political questions, to be tackled later. For now, let us mini-celebrate. Tributes and thanks to the following for giving their all, never mind a narrow victory:

The voters of the just barely majority. As of this moment, they number 74,523,535 or just 50.5% of the popular vote—*so, so close*. While so, so close, this number nevertheless signifies the biggest popular vote for an American President in our history. Let us also remember: Many of these voters braved the aerosolized coronavirus, standing in long lines for hours.

The state and local officials who conducted a smooth-running count—another sign of a saved American Democracy. It was inspiring to see governors, mayors, secretaries of state step up and deliver, often with voices choked with feeling.

The ballot counters. These volunteers—they are not permanent government employees but paid volunteers—did their tabulating under intensest pressure. The eyes of the world, billions of them, were trained on their backs, their masked faces.

The poll workers, many of them young people who stepped in to take the place of older workers more susceptible to the virus. Well done, youth of America.

The media. Except for Fox News and other conservative outlets, the media has evolved to a point where Trump's lies are being called out as lies. This lies-outing/truth-calling is crucial, not only til Inauguration Day, but going forward. *Only with truth can American Democracy continue saving itself.*

A note in passing: With American Democracy saved, just barely, it behooves the American education system to underscore once again *civics education* in schools, from preschool through college. Moreover, after this brush with strongman rule, forced on us by the proto-autocrat Trump, this civics education must include compare-and-contrast with the autocratic rule that is, in fact, trending throughout the world. I note Zeynep Tufekci's point, that America awaits a *more competent* authoritarian. I think of Yascha Mounk's long-running research showing big numbers of young people being O.K. with autocrats for their supposed efficiency; these young people need to understand the costs—just as we, the bare majority, have learned the costs.

Finally, if anyone disputes the initial-caps—American Democracy, Rule of Law: Again, our form of government, so weakened and so damaged, not only by Trump but abused over the years, felt indeed nearly lost to us. But: This Election Day, the American People have saved American Democracy, just barely. And it feels all the dearer for being such a near thing. The Ship of State, though damaged, yet sails. Halle-half-a-lujah.

—*Medium*, November 7, 2020

End-Essay:
Can America Save Itself from Decline?

"If destruction be our lot, we must ourselves be its author and finisher.
As a nation of freemen, we must live through all time, or die by suicide."

ABRAHAM LINCOLN ENUNCIATED this profound truth when he was a young man of 28, a state legislator with stirrings of national ambition. In his Lyceum Address, he laid out his evolving understanding of the nature of American Democracy, then just 50 years old—a system of government created by our ancestors "to display before an admiring world" the "truth of a proposition," hitherto deemed "problematical," namely, *"the capability of a people to govern themselves."* What moved Lincoln in 1838 to make his Address was the "mobocratic" spirit he saw abroad in the land—"the growing disposition to substitute the wild and furious passions, in lieu of the sober judgment of courts; and the worse than savage mobs, for the executive ministers of justice," a reference to mobs meting out "justice" to negroes, whites perceived in league with negros, and abolitionists. The implications of this mob "justice" were clear to Lincoln, thus he titled his speech "The Perpetuation of Our Political Institutions." As President of the United States 23 years later, Lincoln immediately became embroiled in this country's bloodiest blood-letting, the Civil War, from which he emerged victorious—and savior of those institutions.

Now, over a century-and-a-half later, while the circumstances are different, the source of peril remains as Lincoln diagnosed: *ourselves.* "If destruction be our lot, we must ourselves be its author and finisher." Now, as then, there is no foreign enemy that can "step the Ocean" to quell us; only we can do that. And, from the unsettling evidence of late—laid out in this volume—America seems intent on doing precisely that: quelling ourselves and our wondrous institutions. What I am saying is: We do seem to be doing what Lincoln most feared—committing suicide—in slow motion, although during Donald Trump's tenure, the pace accelerated.

In these two volumes, this national suicide is mapped in three ways. *Political suicide*—the increasing dysfunction of political institutions; the increasing polarization of the people, one from another and from leadership, now taken to the point of enmity—which I traced (in Vol. I) to Ronald Reagan ("Government is not the solution, government is the problem") and Republican House speaker Newt Gingrich's flame-throwing politics and rhetoric. Which flame-throwing Donald Trump (in Vol. II) then took to the nuclear level, both domestically—igniting his base with racist and white supremacist messaging, declaring war on the media ("fake news") and on fact—and abroad—unilaterally abrogating treaties (Paris climate accord, Iran nuclear deal) and trashing the alliances (NATO) founded by the postwar generation that's provided a general peace since World War II. *Economic and financial suicide*—which earlier I charted from the 2008 financial crash going forward, with Wall Street and business continuing to resist reform that would better ensure the security of Main Street. Which security Donald Trump then "ensured" with tax cuts for the wealthy and a trade war with China. *Cultural and moral suicide*— which may be best reflected by the wildly popular TV series "Breaking Bad," in which a high-school chemistry teacher, learning he has terminal cancer, turns to producing meth to provide for his family "after." Which amorality Donald Trump then took to shameful lengths—pardoning accused war criminals, cozying up to strongman rulers with horrific human rights records, "breaking bad" in unimaginable ways, e.g., declaring any election he did not win to be a fraud.

This is no way to run a democracy, to govern ourselves.

To be sure, there were bright spots in this parade. Recounting early 21st-century America only as a season of suicide masks those bright spots—the brightest perhaps being the election in 2008 of our first

African-American president, Barack Obama, an event that would have moved, and stunned, the Great Emancipator, Abraham Lincoln. (A foreign friend who'd just taken American citizenship said of Obama's election, "I have never seen my fellow Americans *so* happy.")

Yet: So volatile and contentious is the atmosphere among the American people that what would seem a historical bright spot (like Obama's election), rather than illuminate our path to a Renaissance, instead ignited fierce and lethal fires of reaction—which reactionary fires Donald Trump stoked into a raging wildfire, from his incendiary announcement to run for president to his contested departure from the White House. That this fierce reactionary fire is fueled principally by racial hatred—America has yet to come to terms with its Original Sin, slavery—is no accident and would not surprise Lincoln, nor Obama; the white supremacist Donald Trump knows well his arsenal. Plenty other flammable elements feed that reactionary fire: growing income inequality, a jobs landscape altered dramatically by globalization, and more.

The point here is: Despite the occasional bright spot, the *overall* trend-line for America is downward—national decline—with the malignancy coming from within, not from without; that is, by suicide. The polarization taken to the point of enmity means we can't even talk about it.

Add to this picture the complication—strange to call such a grave event a "complication," but in terms of America's trend-line, it is: The coronavirus pandemic, declared in March 2020 by the World Health Organization and continuing as I write in November, which has forced not only America but the entire world into lockdown. Perhaps not surprisingly, given the many internal forces at war with each other—political, cultural, ethical-moral—America has acquitted itself poorly in managing the virus. With President Trump shirking any responsibility to organize the federal response, the once-upon-a-time Can-Do Nation is unmasked (as I wrote) as Can't-Do.

Thus our present low point. The question becomes again: Can America save itself from decline?

Again, it may be Abraham Lincoln who points the way to "the upper air"—with his characterization of Americans as "freemen." "*As a nation of freemen, we must live through all time, or die by suicide.*" Key word—and key trap—is "free." It has been my long-standing theory of the case, borne out (sadly) by the contents of these volumes and other works, that we Americans, bestowed with the precious gift of absolute freedom, have not always handled our freedom well, that too often, especially the postwar generations, have wasted it or abused it, not properly valuing its preciousness. (See again: "Breaking Bad.") Add to this waste and abuse of freedom, there is the power factor: America has been the world's super-power for 75 years, since vanquishing Nazism in World War II. America wields *enormous* power in the world—politically, economically, militarily, culturally, especially our pop culture. But can it be said that we—America *and* Americans—have wielded our super-power wisely, responsibly? The answer has to be No. And, given the knock-on effect for the world, as well as History's stern judgment of how we acquit ourselves, it *matters* if the world's super-power behaves unwisely, irresponsibly.

And: Who represents the very worst—*the apotheosis*—of an America gone amok in its abuse of freedom and power? Yes: Donald John Trump.

Trump was the poster-child (I use the term "child" advisedly) of "I want what I want—*and I want it NOW!*" Assembled in one man-child were all the worst traits of a very bad child on his very worst day, exercising his "freedom" not by building up but "freely" tearing down—wild, impulsive, vengeful, nasty, not very smart though claiming to be smartest, crude, amoral, and so, so, so angry. Bottomlessly angry; Trump was the Marianas Trench of Anger. And that such a man-child so comprehensively bad should be invested with the most powerful office of the most powerful nation on earth.... Such man-child must become the bully. Which Trump instantly morphed into, literally shoving aside other world leaders at an early summit meeting to take the center spot for the group photo, and going on to do much worse, as cited earlier, trashing allies and alliances, including betraying allies on the battlefield (the Kurds). How often, as Trump heedlessly wreaked havoc in the world, did I think of Shakespeare's words, which Brutus said of Julius Caesar: "Th' abuse of greatness is when it disjoins / Remorse from power."

But: America did not just get unlucky with this President. No, Trump came *out of* the American character—the darker side, where freedom and power are exercised primitively, without thought of others, without conscience. He was the *pre-eminent* Ugly American, the epithet given the overbearing American already identified in the early post-World War II years. That nearly half of the electorate in 2020 voted to re-elect this...person of no qualities...is stunning. Thus it is ill-advised to refer to Trump in the past tense; he, and Trumpism, will continue to threaten American Democracy *and* bollix the massive repair job we must mount to undo the ruination he wreaked, the trauma he inflicted.

Going forward—where Americans always want to go—we can go forward *only* if we front all the ruination *and* understand the Why of it, not just "move on" or "put it behind us" without unpacking it, as we Americans are wont to do. In a way, simply reverse-engineering Trump's qualities (or lack thereof) will take us a goodly way. Emphasizing *responsibility*, versus Trump's irresponsibility, which itself comes out of our postwar culture's "anything-goes" ethos. Emphasizing *reason*, versus Trump's un-reason and seeming insanity, which itself comes from our postwar culture's everything-is-relative-there-is-no-truth ethos. Emphasizing *organization*, versus Trump's utter lack of it, which itself comes out of our postwar culture's go-with-your-gut ethos. Only with these sober qualities, and others, can we repair our governmental institutions, the economy, the public commons, also quell the pandemic.

Along with this massive repair job is a repair job of another kind: the Grand Reckoning on racism and sexism that also—no accounting for History's timing—crests in this moment and demands, finally, resolution. (The capital letters signify the momentousness.) The killing of George Floyd, an African-American man, asphyxiated by a white police officer, whose agonizing death echoed around the world and whose banner is carried forward by the #BlackLivesMatter movement; and the violent sexual assault of women, as testified by myriads of women, often against men of stature, whose hideousness also echoed around the world and whose banner is carried forward by the #MeToo movement: In these two struggles—moral in nature, bearing on the rightness and wrongness of things—lie the ultimate tests of the American character. As Lincoln said as President, commemorating the dead at Gettysburg, "It is altogether fitting and proper that we should do this"—that we quell these scourges long afflicting the nation and, doing so, free up vast, vast new sources of energy, redounding to America's benefit.

There is also the challenge of restoring ourselves in the world, after Trump's trashing our allies, working his sword-arm as Commander-in-Chief of the world's mightiest military, crowing about the size of his nuclear button. Trump surrendered our most precious mantle, Leader of the Free World, and something equally precious: our reputation. To get both back, America needs to show itself, once again, trustworthy. Humility and even an apology are in order. And we must tutor ourselves how to handle our immense power. As I titled a commentary long ago, "Distinguishing Between Can and Should: What a Great Power Should Be Able to Do." Can we deliver? It's cheering to see the world welcome the ascension of Joe Biden to the White House.

All this repair work—with ourselves, with the world—will take a kind of American not dominant for generations: a mature American, grown-up, serious and sober. This more mature American—this Beautiful American—has come into view again during this deadly pandemic: Suffering confers, as poet Emily Dickinson wrote, "a formal feeling." And earlier, a conscientious America stepped forth, protesting the Iraq war and torture. Combined, this America bodes well for maturity. Maturity requires a willingness to front matters of moral weight—racism, sexism, tutoring ourselves in handling power. America has been "breaking bad" for decades; again, to reverse-engineer Donald Trump, can we "break good"? Even to utter such intention, in the ethos of recent decades, is to invite jeers. Lest one think serious and sober mean grim: Let yuk-yuk give way to the earned smile and wit. In maturity lies...Renaissance.

(Retroactive apologies to the Reader: I am keenly aware certain catch-phrases—"'anything-goes' ethos," "'Breaking Bad' culture"—appear repeatedly in my commentary. My defense? "Simply, Your Honor: The evidence *is* the evidence and I cite it to make my case." As a moral artist, I believe culture, especially its moral component, even more than politics, shapes a people and their fate. I seek cultural catch-phrases that signify, also cite touchstones that have shaped me: Emerson, Melville, Dickinson, Camus, Shakespeare. Again, apologies for repetition of the evidence.)

The stakes could not be higher—saving American Democracy, reversing America's decline. Throughout History, great powers rise and fall—Greece, Rome, Egypt, Persia, Spain, France, Great Britain. Once decline is in train, great powers, historically, have not risen again. Must this be America's fate? Americans tend not to believe in fate: Even suffering Donald Trump and the pandemic, we are not fatalists, not yet. (Of course, Fate may have other plans for us.) It may be our pragmatism that saves us: "Well, that didn't work, let's try this"—"that" being the disruption of Donald Trump, "this" being maturity: the responsible use of freedom, seriousness of purpose, rededication to democracy, i.e., self-governance. This requires understanding that Trump is not just disruptive, he is *anti*-democratic: He still yearns to be King of America, and nearly half the electorate still backs him in his anti-democratic aim. America is the world's oldest democracy; we need to show this beautiful ideal has muscle, staying power. Ours is not a nationalistic quest; it is saving an ideal. *If we solve for the problem of our democracy, we also solve for our decline.*

The work before us is immense. We quake at the prospect of the mountain before us, but we also quiver in excitement and anticipation of the climb. As the characters in Samuel Beckett's play *Waiting for Godot* say: "I can't go on like this." "That's what you think." We go on. Abraham Lincoln is watching us—and he has our back.

CARLA SEAQUIST
November-December 2020
Gig Harbor, Washington

IMAGES: SELECT LISTING

Most of the images in this volume—of public figures, books, films, other iconography—are stock images, available via Google Image.

The following select images—of vintage political illustrations, art-works, etc.—include:

P. 181: "The Brains," by Thomas Nast, *Harper's Weekly*, October 21, 1871.

P. 306: Illustration of Faust and Mephistopheles by Harry Clarke for edition of Goethe's *Faust* published by Hartsdale House, New York, 1925.

P. 372: "The Magnet," by Joseph Keppler, Jr., *Puck Magazine*, June 1911.

P. 421: "Colossus," by Francisco de Goya, created 1808-1812.

P. 450: "Plague Doctor," by Anon., circa 1656, during bubonic plague, Rome.

P. 486: "The Bosses of the Senate," by Joseph Keppler, *Puck Magazine*, January, 1889.

P. 572: "The Scream," by Edvard Munch, created 1893,

P. 579: Laurence Olivier as Hamlet, from the film production, 1948.

MORE ABOUT THE AUTHOR

CARLA SEAQUIST IS a commentator, author, and playwright. Since 9/11 she has focused on commentary, writing on politics, culture, and ethical-moral issues, first for *The Christian Science Monitor* (2002-2009), then *HuffPost* (2009-2018), and now *Medium*. Her earlier book of commentary, *Manufacturing Hope: Post-9/11 Notes on Politics, Culture, Torture, and the American Character*, was published in 2009. She is also the author of *Two Plays of Life and Death*, which include *Who Cares?: The Washington-Sarajevo Talks* and *Kate and Kafka*. Ahead is a long-planned play, *Prodigal*. She has completed a memoir, about her relationship with her mother, titled *The Main Event: A Mother and Daughter Turn Tragedy into Peace*.

Ms. Seaquist's early career in civil rights began with organizing the women's caucus of the Brookings Institution in Washington, D.C., and culminated with the post of Equal Opportunity Officer for the City of San Diego, for which she received N.O.W.'s Susan B. Anthony award for "courage and hard work on behalf of women and minorities." She was also appointed to the California Governor's Task Force on Civil Rights. Ms. Seaquist majored in international relations in college (School of International Service, American University) and graduate school (School of Advanced International Studies, Johns Hopkins University). Long a resident of Washington, D.C., she now lives in the "other" Washington (Gig Harbor), where she served on the board of Humanities Washington. Her husband Larry, a former Navy captain, served four terms as a State Representative (Democrat), chairing the House committee on higher education his last two terms. He is at work on a book titled *Doing Democracy in America*.

www.carlaseaquist.com